WINSTON
CHURCHILL

The
SECOND
WORLD
WAR

IV

WINSTON
CHURCHILL

The
SECOND
WORLD
WAR

WINSTON
CHURCHILL

The
SECOND
WORLD
WAR

ALSO BY DAVID REYNOLDS

*The Creation of the Anglo-American Alliance,
1937–41: A Study in Competitive Cooperation*

*An Ocean Apart: The Relationship Between Britain
and America in the Twentieth Century*
(with David Dimbleby)

*Britannia Overruled: British Policy and World Power
in the Twentieth Century*

The Origins of the Cold War in Europe (editor)

*Allies at War: The Soviet, American, and
British Experience, 1939–1945*
(coedited with Warren F. Kimball
and A. O. Chubarian)

*Rich Relations: The American Occupation
of Britain, 1942–1945*

One World Divisible: A Global History Since 1945

*From Munich to Pearl Harbor: Roosevelt's America
and the Origins of the Second World War*

IN COMMAND
of HISTORY

Churchill
Fighting and
Writing the
Second World
War

Random House | New York

IN COMMAND
of HISTORY

DAVID REYNOLDS

Published in the United States by Random House,
an imprint of The Random House Publishing Group,
a division of Random House, Inc., New York.

RANDOM HOUSE and colophon are registered trademarks
of Random House, Inc.

LIBRARY OF CONGRESS CATALOGING-IN-PUBLICATION DATA

Reynolds, David.
In command of history : Churchill fighting and writing
the Second World War / by David Reynolds.
p. cm.
Includes bibliographical references and index.
ISBN 0-679-45743-7
1. Churchill, Winston, Sir, 1874–1965. Second World War.   2. World
War, 1939–1945—Historiography.
3. World War, 1939–1945—Personal narratives, British—
History and criticism.   I. Title.

D743.42.R48   2005
940.53'092—dc22   2004051087

Printed in the United States of America on acid-free paper

www.atrandom.com

2 4 6 8 9 7 5 3 1

FIRST U.S. EDITION

Endpaper illustration courtesy of Roger Katz/Hatchards;
photography by Caroline Forbes

Book design by Barbara M. Bachman

For Margaret

Looking back it seems incredible that one could have got through all these six volumes and I suppose nearly two million words.

—*Winston Churchill, 12 May 1954*

I am often asked: "How much of his books did he really write himself?" It's almost as superficial a question as asking a Master Chef: "Did you cook the whole banquet with your own hands?"

—*Denis Kelly, one of Churchill's research assistants, 1985*

Let's always remember that the Churchill Memoirs are the biggest literary and historical project that *LIFE*, or for that matter any other publication, has ever undertaken.

—*Andrew Heiskell, publisher of* Life, *April 1947*

Words are the only things that last for ever.

—*Winston Churchill, May 1938*

ACKNOWLEDGMENTS

IN THE LAST TWO DECADES I have published three broad books about
the twentieth century from various vantage points, but I have also kept coming back to the British and American experience of the Second World
War—exploring it first as diplomatic history, then as military and social history,
and now combining those genres with biography and intellectual history.

The seed for this project was planted back in the 1970s, when, while writing
about Anglo-American relations before Pearl Harbor, I became aware of how
much our understanding of that topic had been shaped by Churchill's memoirs.
The late Henry Pelling suggested that I should write a book about his books—an
idea encouraged on many subsequent occasions by David Cannadine. But the
project did not become feasible until Churchill's postwar literary papers were
opened to scholars in 1995. Their location just fifteen minutes from home was
particularly convenient. Although I have traveled to many other archives in
Britain, and some in America and Australia, my main base has been the Churchill Archives Centre at Churchill College, and I am immensely grateful to its
director, Allen Packwood, for his help and advice. He and his young and energetic staff make this a model archive in which to work—my warm thanks to them
all and to Piers Brendon, Allen's predecessor.

Sir Winston's daughter Lady Soames DBE has generously taken an interest
in this project, sparing time for several conversations. I have benefited greatly
from her prizewinning life of her mother—a remarkable mixture of empathy and
detachment—and also from the candid and moving biography by Winston Churchill of his father, Randolph, Sir Winston's son. Sir William Deakin, by then the
only survivor of Churchill's impressive "Syndicate" of research assistants, welcomed

me most warmly to his home in southern France, where I was able to pose questions, bounce ideas off him, and examine some of his papers. He died in January 2005. I am also grateful to Lady Onslow (Jo Sturdee) for talking with me about her time as Churchill's postwar personal secretary; to Hugh Lunghi, one of Churchill's wartime interpreters, for insights into conference diplomacy; and to the present Lord Moran for helpful conversation about his father. Like all students of Churchill I am indebted to Sir Martin Gilbert, whose official biography and companion volumes of documents I have used constantly during my work. My gratitude also to Mary Ray and David Ray Kaehler for the loan of an American edition of the six volumes and to Professor Antoine Capet for kindly giving me three volumes of the French edition.

In the course of my work I have given a number of seminar and conference papers. For the opportunity to do so, I am grateful to the following: International Churchill Society Annual Conference, 2003, Bermuda (David Boler); Library of Congress/Churchill Centre, Washington, D.C. (Irene Chambers, Daniel Myers, and Jim Muller); Rutgers University, New Brunswick, New Jersey (Lloyd Gardner and Warren F. Kimball); University of Kansas at Lawrence (Theodore A. Wilson); Westminster College, Fulton, Missouri (Jerry D. Morelock and John R. Hensley); Menzies Centre for Australian Studies, London (Carl Bridge); Australian National University, Canberra, and Deakin University, Geelong, Victoria (David Lowe); Institute of Historical Research, London (David Cannadine and Roland Quinault); "Actualités des Sciences Humaines" colloquium, Trinity College, Cambridge (Claude Imbert and Jean Khalfa); Centre d'Études en Litteraires et Civilisation de la Langue Anglaise, Université de Rouen (Antoine Capet).

Several friends have generously taken time from their own books to read parts of my manuscript. My warm thanks to David Cannadine, Peter Clarke, Warren F. Kimball, and Zara Steiner for their comments and encouragement. Alan Brinkley kindly shared ideas and information about Henry Luce. It is a pleasure, once again, to work with Robert D. Loomis at Random House and Stuart Proffitt at Penguin. Bob is a model editor, offering encouragement and constructive criticism in just the right measures. Stuart, who came to the book late, has picked it up with his customary energy and insight. Clare Parkinson and Timothy Mennel, the two copy editors, saved me from many mistakes. Throughout the long haul I have once again benefited immensely from the support and shrewdness of my agent, Peter Robinson. It has also been exciting and enjoyable to work with Russell Barnes and Blakeway Productions on the related film for BBC Television.

A full list of archives and collections that I have consulted may be found in the Guide to Sources. In each case I am greatly obliged to the staff for their advice and friendliness, but I should like to mention particularly Patricia Methven, Alan Kucia, and the archivists at the Liddell Hart Centre for Military Archives at King's College, London; Christine Penney and the staff of Special Collections at Birmingham University Library; Jim Palma of LBS Ltd., Worthing; Elizabeth Martin and her staff at the library of Nuffield College, Oxford; and the Department of Special Collections and Western Manuscripts at the Bodleian Library in Oxford. As a veteran of the old days of the Public Record Office annex in Portugal Street, I can say with feeling that it is a pleasure to work in the current National Archives in Kew. In the United States I am especially grateful to Bill Hooper and Pamela Wilson at the Time Inc. Archive in New York; to Leslie A. Morris and her staff at the Houghton Library, Harvard University, particularly Susan Halpert; and to Jerry D. Morelock and John R. Hensley for their hospitality at the Winston Churchill Memorial at Westminster College, Fulton, Missouri.

Extracts from the Churchill papers and from published works by Sir Winston are reproduced by permission of Curtis Brown Group Ltd., London, on behalf of the Estate of Sir Winston Churchill, copyright © Winston S. Churchill. For permission to quote from other documents I am grateful to Lady Avon; Lord Bridges; Lord Moran; the Trustees of the Liddell Hart Centre for Military Archives at King's College, London; Houghton Library at Harvard University; Time Inc.; and the University of Birmingham Information Services, Special Collections.

As usual, my deepest obligations are to my family—to my parents, who, during my Kentish childhood, kindled an early interest in Churchill and nearby Chartwell; to my son, Jim, for indulging his father's strange distractions; and, above all, to my architect wife, Margaret, who provides the structural foundations for everything.

CONTENTS

INTRODUCTION

A NOTHER BOOK ON CHURCHILL? Can there be anything new to say? The answer is, emphatically, yes. Churchill waged the Second World War twice over: as Prime Minister steering his country from disaster in 1940 to victory in 1945, and again as the conflict's principal historian, with six volumes of memoirs published over the subsequent decade. The saga of his premiership is celebrated, the story of his war memoirs virtually unknown, yet Churchill the historian has shaped our image of Churchill the leader. As he liked to say when locked in wartime controversy, "I shall leave it to history, but remember that I shall be one of the historians."

No other war leader performed such a double act. By May 1945, Hitler, Mussolini, and Roosevelt were all dead. Stalin lived another eight years but kept his silence. De Gaulle published three volumes of memoirs but not until a decade after the war's end, and an English translation was slow to appear. Churchill, by contrast, was quick off the mark, wrote on an epic scale, and reached a global audience. *The Second World War* appeared between 1948 and 1954 and totaled nearly two million words. The book was published in fifteen different countries and eleven languages, while extracts appeared in some fifty newspapers and magazines in forty countries. These extracts were on a generous scale: *The New York Times,* for instance, devoted thirty full-page installments to all except one volume, reproducing more than one third of the text.[1] People who never opened the books picked up many of Churchill's themes from these serial versions and their headlines.

So Churchill made history as statesman and as historian. And he had performed a similar feat twenty years before. For most of World War I he stood at the apex of the British government—at the Admiralty or the Ministry of Munitions— and between 1923 and 1931 he published six volumes about that war and its aftermath, under the title *The World Crisis*. The First World War and Churchill's account of it influenced the way he waged the Second and how he wrote about it.

For Churchill was above all a man of words, who made his living through books and journalism. In the 1920s and 1930s, this was a precarious existence, particularly for someone of such sybaritic tastes, and in 1937–1938 he even put Chartwell, his beloved country house in Kent, on the market. *The Second World War*, however, made Churchill's fortune and also secured his place in history. The intricate book and newspaper package crafted in 1946–1947 was worth $2.23 million—the biggest American nonfiction deal to that time. Translating that into today's values is an imprecise business (see "A Note on Money"), but at the very least we are talking about $18 million dollars—maybe $50 million— and, thanks to Churchill's canny lawyers, most of it came tax free. As for the volumes themselves, much of their authority derived from the mass of wartime documents that Churchill included, courtesy of a unique deal he had extracted from the British Cabinet Office. At the time Churchill wrote, no ordinary mortal could expect to inspect, let alone reprint, wartime documents until the twenty-first century. *The Second World War* also owed its power to Churchill's words-manship—to purple passages like the evocation of his mood on becoming Prime Minister in May 1940 ("I felt as if I were walking with destiny, and that all my life had been but a preparation for this hour and for this trial") or his reaction to the news of Pearl Harbor ("Being saturated and satiated with emotion and sensation, I went to bed and slept the sleep of the saved and the thankful"). Even now, writers follow the phases and phrases by which he structured events: The Gathering Storm, Their Finest Hour, The Grand Alliance, The Hinge of Fate, Closing the Ring, Triumph and Tragedy. J. H. Plumb's judgment in 1969 holds true today: we still "move down the broad avenues which he drove through war's confusion and complexity."[2]

Churchill was a politician as well as a historian. He was able to write *The Second World War* only because he lost the election of July 1945. Otherwise, the burdens of office would have been too much for his time and health as he entered his seventies. Of course, most political memoirs are written in retirement, mellow or bitter, but these are unusual in being the memoirs of a past *and* future Prime Minister. Wounded by the rejection of the people, Churchill was determined to get back to 10 Downing Street, and to do so by national election rather than party coup, as in 1940. *The Second World War* was therefore composed with one eye on his political future—in the sense both of watching the clock and also of minding his words. In the event, Churchill lost the election of February 1950 and had to wait until October 1951. If he had returned to Downing Street in 1950, his publishers had contingency plans to have the last volumes completed by another hand.

Churchill was also a man of war. He started adult life as a cavalry officer and, although quickly vaulting into journalism and then politics, he returned to the front for a time in 1916 and never lost his fascination for things military. This set him apart from other twentieth-century Prime Ministers, indeed from all his predecessors since the Duke of Wellington. But the Iron Duke had commanded at the highest level and with supreme success, whereas Churchill never rose above the rank of battalion commander in a quiet sector of the trenches. Deep down, he yearned to be a great general, and his supreme hero was Napoleon — another little man in a big hurry. At the Admiralty in 1914–1915, Churchill had tried to run operations on sea and land, and the disaster at Gallipoli haunted him for decades. As Prime Minister from 1940 to 1945 he finally had the power to wage war as grand strategist and, thanks to modern communications, as battle-field tactician in a way no British leader has done before or since. *The Second World War* shows Churchill in command.

Millions of words have been written about Churchill. There is, however, surprisingly little about Churchill the writer, even though that was how he earned his living and spent much of his time.[3] And no one has studied *The Second World War* in depth, despite the fact that it not only shaped our understanding of that conflict but also sheds a revealing light on Churchill's three most important personae: historian, politician, and soldier. This, then, is

. . . *a book about a book*: how the memoirs were researched and written. Churchill's drafts and working papers are now open to researchers — nearly four hundred files, including one for virtually every chapter. From these, it is possible to see what Churchill wanted to say and chose not to, how he edited the wartime documents to sharpen his case or soften its impact. These files also record the work of a remarkable set of research assistants (known as the Syndicate), including the future head of an Oxford college (Sir William Deakin), the wartime military secretary to the Cabinet (Lord Ismay), and a former Vice-Chief of the Imperial General Staff (Sir Henry Pownall). Churchill also availed himself of numerous readers, notably Secretary to the Cabinet Norman Brook, who not only commented on the text but also wrote parts of it.

. . . *a book about the other books* with which he competed to make history. Churchill enjoyed a relatively clear field when writing about appeasement in the 1930s. On the Battle of Britain, he slotted into an already-existing national myth.

On other issues such as the Second Front, he was firmly on the defensive, forced to combat a range of American memoirs already critical of his conduct—such as those by Elliott Roosevelt (the late President's son) and General Dwight D. Eisenhower. In the decade 1945–1955 the public history of World War II had still not yet set firm; from this battle of the books emerged interpretations that have endured to the present day. In recent years, historians have become fascinated with the theme of war and memory, but largely as cultural and social history.[4] Yet the influence of political memoirs on public memory has been profound, and Churchill's story shows clearly why this relationship deserves closer attention.[5]

. . . *a book about the war itself.* Making sense of the histories takes us back to the events themselves. To evaluate Churchill's interpretations and those of his rivals, we must take account of subsequent research. Anachronism, of course, is a danger—there is much that writers in the 1940s could not have known or said— so in analyzing *The Second World War* I therefore try to address three questions:

- What did Churchill know at the time and attempt to conceal?
  A striking example is the Ultra secret and the work of the code
  breakers at Bletchley Park.
- What might he have said if he and his researchers had dug deeper or
  thought laterally? For instance, there was not one but two battles of
  Alamein—leaving us with a very different view of "Monty."
- What do we know now? For example, the Red Army, which scarcely
  figures in his memoirs, largely won the land war in Europe.

. . . *a book about the Cold War:* As he narrated the past, Churchill was preoccupied by current affairs. Volume 1 (about the 1930s) appeared at the height of the Berlin blockade and preached the lessons of appeasement. Volume 6 (on dealing with the Russians in 1944–1945) advocated negotiation from strength, at a time when Prime Minister Churchill was seeking détente in the Cold War. His account of the politics of the atomic bomb was distorted by his desire to revive the transatlantic nuclear alliance. And he modified his treatment of wartime leaders—Truman and Eisenhower, Tito and de Gaulle—to avoid offending men who still mattered in current diplomacy.

. . . *a glimpse into Churchill's mind:* the memoirs were not just an exercise in self-defense and self-promotion; at times they became an attempt at self-knowledge. Churchill was certainly not writing a classic autobiography in the style of Jean-Jacques Rousseau or John Stuart Mill, but the wartime documents forced some real heart searching about his wartime career. He was shaken by his underestimation of the tank in 1939–1940, chastened at his complacency about the effect of airpower on seapower in 1940–1941, and privately not as sure as he claimed in print that the Allies could have beaten the Russians to Berlin in 1945. The documents also prodded him to resurrect events half forgotten. Despite a prodigious memory, he sometimes got things completely wrong. His conflation of several visits to Roosevelt's home on the Hudson River resulted in a serious distortion in his account of the development of the atomic bomb. The excavation of memory also resulted in the unearthing of guilt. One can see this clearly in his drafts about the Greek campaign of 1941 and the Dieppe raid of 1942; one can sense it in the way he slides over Katyn in 1943 and Auschwitz in 1944.

Finally, this is *a book about a neglected phase of Churchill's life,* what we might call the Second Wilderness Years, from 1945 to 1951.[6] It is the story of how he pulled himself back from humiliating defeat in 1945, using all his skills as a writer and politician to make his fortune, secure his reputation, and win a second term in Downing Street. To do so meant running the equivalent of an academic research group while also acting as Leader of the Opposition and a globe-trotting statesman. All this from a man in his seventies, long past the statutory age of retirement.

ALTHOUGH CALLED IN shorthand "Churchill's war memoirs," the six volumes constitute a complex literary text that must be understood against the circumstances of its creation.[7] The volumes combine wartime documents and postwar reflection; they incorporate the work of Churchill and of his assistants; they reflect the deadlines imposed by his publishers and by his own political agenda; they involve self-analysis as well as self-justification. The six volumes also represent the labor of eight years, during one of the most active and diverse decades of Churchill's formidably energetic life. Each volume had a character of its own, reflecting the pressures and priorities of the moment. That is why I examine each one separately, giving a pair of dates (such as *Their Finest Hour,* 1940, 1946–1949) to indicate what it was about and when it was written. Since I am analyzing two pasts—what happened during the war and what Churchill wrote about it afterward—I have used the present tense for the text of the book ("Churchill tells his readers") and the past tense for wartime events. Within each volume, I have followed the same format, beginning with a chapter on how it was composed and ending with one on its reception. These sandwich two or three chapters looking at the contents of the volume and its interpretation of wartime events. To understand the significance of Churchill's argument, I have situated it against what else was being said about the war at the time (particularly in rival memoirs) and what we now know from subsequent scholarship. I offer my summing-up of the whole work at the end of chapter 31 (pages 500 to 508). This, then, is a book about personal biography and public memory, which offers novel insights into the greatest war in human history and a new perspective on Britain's most famous war leader.

TO CONTEMPORARIES AND TO POSTERITY, it seemed inevitable that Churchill would write *The Second World War*. What he had done for the Great War he would do for its even greater successor on an even grander canvas. Yet Churchill did not jump straight into his memoirs in the autumn of 1945. There were many unresolved questions to answer. Would all his earnings disappear in tax? Could he combine politics and writing? Was his reputation secure, or did it need literary gilding? I therefore begin this book by showing how Churchill wrestled with these questions. Above all, there was the legacy of July 1945. At the time, it seemed like the end; a lesser man would have succumbed completely. But Churchill had risen from the ashes before—after Gallipoli and again during the 1930s. In his Second Wilderness Years he transcended defeat so completely that, for the last decade of his life, his political stature and wartime reputation were almost above criticism. Only with his death in January 1965 could the process of historical revision begin in earnest. That is why my book begins with an epilogue and ends with a prologue. For a while, Churchill almost turned time on its head: such was his command of history.

IN COMMAND
of HISTORY

EPILOGUE | *July 1945*

ON 5 JULY 1945, the British people went to the polls. It was a strange affair. The last general election had been held a decade before—Hitler put paid to the one due in 1940—so nobody under the age of thirty had ever voted for a government. And nearly three million eligible voters were over-seas, serving in the armed forces in occupied Europe or in Asia, where the war still raged. To accommodate their votes, the result would not be declared until 26 July.[1]

Winston Churchill spent most of those three weeks abroad. On 7 July he flew to Bordeaux and was then driven south to Hendaye, near the Spanish border. At the Château de Bordaberry, placed at his disposal by a Canadian admirer, Chur-chill enjoyed a week's vacation with his wife, Clementine, his youngest daughter, Mary, and a small staff. It was, in fact, his first genuine break since becoming Prime Minister in May 1940. He ignored the official papers in his "red boxes," to which he was normally addicted, and spent a good deal of time in the ocean, floating "like a benevolent hippo," in the words of his private secretary Jock Colville.[2] He also picked up his paints again, having worked on only one canvas during the whole war—at Marrakech in January 1943.

At meals, Churchill ruminated about the war. On 9 May 1940, a revolt in the Conservative party had forced Neville Chamberlain from the premiership and catapulted Churchill into the office he had sought all his life. Five years later, on 8 May 1945, from a balcony in Whitehall, he addressed ecstatic crowds celebrat-ing the German surrender.

"This is your victory," he told them.

"No," they shouted back, "it is yours."[3]

That half decade had been the most dramatic and momentous phase of Churchill's long life—"five years of continuous excitement," he called them. Already, certain war stories had taken firm places in his repertoire. One, told repeatedly, was the high point of the Battle of Britain, on 15 September 1940, which he had followed from Fighter Command's nerve center in west London. Another was his order in July 1940 to attack and neutralize the French fleet in North African ports—"a terrible decision, like taking the life of one's child to save the State." Asked whether the humiliating surrender of Tobruk in 1942 was the worst moment of the war, he replied emphatically: "Oh, no, it was painful, like a boil, but it was not a cancer." For him, the two critical moments of the war, "when everything was at stake," were the Battle of Britain and the Battle of the Atlantic.[4]

In July 1945, Churchill was seventy years old. He could easily have retired from public life and written his memoirs: the week at Bordaberry showed that the war years were vivid in his mind and patterns had already taken shape. Yet Churchill also looked ahead to his imminent meeting with Josef Stalin and Harry Truman at Potsdam, near Berlin. Beyond that, after Japan's defeat, loomed the great peace conference, a better version of Paris in 1919, when the new world order would be decided. But all that turned on remaining Prime Minister: "I shall be only half a man until the result of the election poll," he declared. Conservative Central Office stuck to its forecast of a majority of one hundred seats in the Commons. When Churchill flew to Berlin on 15 July, he was confident that he had a political future.

Potsdam was the old imperial seat of the Prussian monarchy. Yet Churchill, for all his sense of history, was surprisingly disengaged. He trotted round Sans Souci in a quarter of an hour, his mind on either the conference or the election. Nor was he excited by Berlin, merely observing that "if *they* had won the war, *we* would have been the bunker."[5] By contrast, his companions were profoundly moved by the ruins of the Thousand-Year Reich that had so nearly vanquished the British empire—the upturned marble-topped desk and litter of Iron Crosses in Hitler's office, the Berliners on the Reichstag steps bartering clothes and boots for food from Russian soldiers. Sir Alexander Cadogan of the Foreign Office found the city "a staggering sight" and doubted it could ever be rebuilt; to Lord Moran, Churchill's doctor, the "evisceration" of Berlin reminded him of the first time he watched a surgeon open a belly and the intestines gushed out. But Churchill remained detached. Asked for his impressions, he could say only, "Poor Devils." Instead, his thoughts kept returning to "this bloody election," which, he said, "hovers over me like a vulture of uncertainty."[6]

The first week of the conference went reasonably well. Churchill was reassured, as at every wartime meeting, by personal contact with Stalin (who predicted a Conservative majority of eighty). He was delighted by his first encounters with Truman, who seemed resolute and supportive, unlike the dying Roosevelt at Yalta in February. When Churchill flew home to Britain at lunchtime on the twenty-fifth, he planned to be back at the negotiating table within forty-eight hours. To King George VI that evening, he predicted a majority of between thirty and eighty. So confident was Lord Moran that he left half his luggage in Potsdam.

Thursday, 26 July 1945, was a total nightmare for the Churchill family. The eleven o'clock BBC radio news indicated that Labour was heading for a massive victory. Churchill's son, Randolph, and his son-in-law, Duncan Sandys, were among the Members of Parliament who lost their seats. The family lunched in "Stygian gloom," almost choking on their food, his daughter Mary wrote in her diary. Clementine Churchill, superbly patrician throughout that day, told her husband, "It may well be a blessing in disguise."

He grunted, "At the moment it seems quite effectively disguised."[7]

At seven in the evening, he was driven to Buckingham Palace and tendered his resignation. A few minutes later, the Labour leader, Clement Attlee, arrived to kiss hands on his appointment as the King's new first minister. Attlee was no less surprised than Churchill, having at his most optimistic hoped that the Tories could be held to a majority of forty seats.[8] Instead, Labour enjoyed a majority of 146 over all the other parties. Only twice had the Tories suffered a worse electoral disaster: after the Great Reform Bill of 1832 and in the Liberal landslide of 1906. The twenty-sixth of July 1945 was not merely a defeat but a humiliation.

Winston and Clementine had literally nowhere to go. For most of the war they had lived in "the Annexe"—part of a government office block facing St. James' Park, which was more modern and bombproof than 10 Downing Street. Now they had to move out. Their country house, Chartwell in Kent, was in disrepair, having been mothballed for the war, and they had sold their London apartment in Morpeth Mansions near Victoria Station in 1939. For some months, Clementine had been eyeing 28 Hyde Park Gate, in Kensington near the Albert Hall, but no deal had yet been concluded. So they moved into a suite in Claridge's Hotel, until their daughter Diana Sandys generously lent her family's London apartment. On Friday, 27 July, Churchill held a last, somber Cabinet meeting at 10 Downing Street. Afterward, he spoke lugubriously with Anthony Eden, his wartime Foreign Secretary. "Thirty years of my life have been passed in this room. I shall never sit in it again. You will, but I shall not."[9] His map room was empty, the private secretaries' office deserted, and there were no "red boxes."

Having spent five years at the heart of government, Churchill found himself abruptly cut off from the arteries of power. It was almost literally mortifying.

That weekend, the Churchills went out to Chequers, the Prime Minister's official country house in Buckinghamshire, where Winston had spent some of the most dramatic moments of the war. The surface routine was just the same: card games, croquet on the lawn, a movie after dinner. In the past, when the films ended, Churchill could have expected a new box rushed down from London. He would have geared up for several hours of nocturnal dictation, dispatching orders across the world. Now there was nothing, and the family watched in dismay as black despair descended. Even his favorite Gilbert and Sullivan records had no effect. Only a mixture of march music and, finally, *The Wizard of Oz* got Churchill woozily to bed. On Sunday, there was a farewell dinner, well lubricated with champagne. At the end, everyone signed the Chequers visitors' book. Winston added his name last. Underneath he wrote a single word: "Finis."

CHAPTER 1

TO WRITE OR NOT TO WRITE?

H AD CHURCHILL WON the election of 1945, he would probably not have written his memoirs—certainly not in the form they did take. A further spell in office for such an exhausted man, assuming he survived, would have sapped his energy and dulled his appetite for any major writing project. But while electoral defeat made possible literary triumphs, Churchill did not retire from politics and statecraft. Such was the scale of his defeat in 1945 that he burned for political vindication, and the story of *The Second World War* is inextricably bound up with his zeal to keep on making history. Nor, despite expectations, did he embark straightaway on the war memoirs. He was to take the plunge only when the conditions were right, and they took time to establish. It was not until the spring of 1946 that Churchill resolved the conundrum: to write or not to write.

BETWEEN 1923 AND 1931, Churchill had published six bulky and remunerative volumes on the First World War, entitled *The World Crisis*, which A. J. Balfour, the former Prime Minister, described as "Winston's brilliant Autobiography, disguised as a history of the universe." It seemed certain that another set of memoirs would follow the conflict of 1939–1945, and he made many comments during the war to this effect. One was recorded by his private secretary Jock Colville—a diarist with Boswellian aspirations—as Churchill mused expansively over brandy at Chequers in December 1940. He said that after the war he had no wish to wage a party struggle against the Labour leaders who were now serving so well in the coalition. "He would retire to Chartwell and write a book on the war, which he had already mapped out in his mind chapter by chapter. This was the moment for him; he was determined not to prolong his career into the period of reconstruction."[1]

In November 1941, Churchill had a dinner conversation with William Berry, Lord Camrose—a close friend and also owner of the *Daily Telegraph* and *Morning Post*. According to Camrose, Churchill said that his intention was to retire immediately after England had "turned the corner," by which Camrose understood him to mean once victory had been achieved. He added that he was determined not to repeat the "ghastly error" made by David Lloyd George after his war premiership of 1916–1918, carrying on in office till humiliatingly pulled down in 1922. "While he did not say so," Camrose noted, "I am sure he also had in mind that he would make provision for his family. To do this he would have to be able to write."[2]

Publishers had long been salivating about a new set of Churchill war memoirs. As early as 28 September 1939, Thornton Butterworth, who published *The World Crisis*, reminded Churchill that "although we are only in the early days of the war, there must come a time when authors will be able to lay down their arms and take up their pens once more." Butterworth hoped that Churchill would then write the history of the second "World Crisis" and entrust it to the publishers of the first *World Crisis*. He received only a curt acknowledgment from Churchill's secretary at the Admiralty. The following summer, Prime Minister Churchill was more interested by a proposal from Lord Southwood of Odhams Press for a £40,000 deal for four volumes. But with the Battle of Britain about to break, he scribbled on 2 August 1940, "I do not feel able to give this consideration yet." The following spring, the literary agency Curtis Brown, who had represented him for some years, constructed a bigger package involving Odhams and American publishers such as Houghton Mifflin, amounting to £75,000. From this point onward, such proposals received a standard reply from Kathleen Hill, Churchill's personal secretary, stating that he would make no decision about his war memoirs while in office.[3]

After the 1945 election, however, the offers started flooding in. King Features, one of the world's leading newspaper syndicates, reminded him of their interest via a telegram sent at 6:36 P.M. on 26 July, before Churchill had even gone to the Palace to resign. That night, Emery Reves, who had handled foreign rights for many of Churchill's prewar articles, sent urgent telegrams from New York assuring Churchill that he could arrange the best possible terms for the memoirs and articles: "Could come [to] London for negotiations anytime." Curtis Brown sent equally importunate letters pressing their services. But Churchill was not to be tempted. The standard reply from Hill stated that Churchill was "not undertaking any literary work at the present time."[4]

There were several reasons for Churchill's coyness. Having lost job, home, and reason for living in a matter of hours, he needed time to recover. In August 1945, the accumulated exhaustion of five years took hold. Also important was his tax status. On legal advice, Churchill had officially ceased to exercise his "professional vocation" as an author on 3 September 1939—the day he became First Lord of the Admiralty. Although his wartime speeches were published in six volumes between 1941 and 1946, all the editorial work was done by a journalist. Churchill was able to claim that he had not resumed his profession as an author. Thanks to this tax loophole, the substantial income earned by the war speeches was not subject to income tax at the punitive wartime rates. Any return to writing, even a single article, could jeopardize that favorable status, both in the present and retrospectively.

In secret, Churchill had already half promised any war memoirs to the London publishers Cassell and Company. On 24 November 1944, Churchill wrote to Sir Newman Flower, the head of Cassell's—who in the 1930s had published his four volumes on the first Duke of Marlborough—stating that "I shall be very pleased to give your firm a first refusal, at the lowest price I am prepared to accept, of publishing rights in serial and book form . . . in any work I may write on the present War after it is over." This was hardly a firm commitment. Churchill made clear, "I undertake no obligation to write anything," and, even if he did, "the lowest price I am prepared to accept" gave him plenty of room to refuse an unattractive offer.[5]

In the weeks after the election, Churchill's intentions about the war memoirs remained unclear. According to Sir Edward Bridges, the Cabinet Secretary, on 28 July, Churchill "said he was not sure whether he would write his memoirs of the present war." He "thought he would do so but the work would not be completed for four or five years." On 7 August, Lord Camrose noted: "At the moment, he has decided that he will not publish his account of the war direction in his lifetime." And on 31 August, Churchill told Charles Eade, the editor of his war speeches, that he had received an offer of £250,000 ($1 million) from America for the memoirs and was confident he could write them in a year. But his present idea was that they should not be sold and published until some ten years after his death. Laughing, he said that he would quite like to have £250,000, but "in fact, I should get only 250,000 sixpences." Given current rates of income tax and surtax, Churchill faced the prospect of paying nineteen shillings and six pence in every pound (97.5 percent) of his literary earnings to the government. He told Eade, in a quip he had been using for half a century, "I agree with Dr. Johnson that only a block-head writes except for money."[6]

Churchill's mood that summer was often very bleak. He complained to his doctor of depression and insomnia: "I go to bed at twelve o'clock. There is nothing to sit up for." He would wake at four, his mind full of "futile speculations," unless he took another sleeping tablet. "It would have been better to have been killed in an aeroplane, or to have died like Roosevelt," he said. Nor was family life much consolation. At the end of August, Mary Churchill received a poignant letter from her mother, written among the dustcovers and mildew of Chartwell: "I cannot explain how it is but in our misery we seem, instead of clinging to each other, to be always having scenes. I'm sure it's all my fault, but I'm finding life more than I can bear. He is so unhappy & that makes him very difficult." Winston was totally undomesticated. He had little understanding of the difficulties of daily life outside the official cocoon, complaining about the lack of meat, staff, and so on. For her part, Clementine was highly strung and needed frequent rests from her husband's emotional and practical demands. In a few days, she told Mary, "we shan't have a car. We are being lent one now. We are learning how rough & stony the World is."[7]

The only ray of light was that Churchill spent most of September on vacation in Italy, staying in villas placed at his disposal by Field-Marshal Sir Harold Alexander and General Dwight D. Eisenhower. On 5 September he wrote to his wife, "I feel a great sense of relief which grows steadily, others having to face the hideous problems of the aftermath." Alluding to her comment on Black Thursday, he now struck a more positive note: "It may all indeed be 'a blessing in disguise.'"[8]

At Lake Como, between painting fifteen pictures, he regaled his companions with recollections of 1940 and 1941, such as the "magic carpet" of Dunkirk and his first wartime meeting with Roosevelt, off Newfoundland. These had been brought to mind by his blue-bound minutes and telegrams from the war, which he had read avidly throughout the flight from England. He seemed scarcely to take his eyes off the pages, except when rekindling his cigar. "They are mine," he told Moran. "I can publish them." But that did not mean he would. On 2 September, he said that he wasn't in the mood for writing and, echoing his remarks to Charles Eade, added that "I shan't write while the Government takes all you earn. Dr. Johnson said that only a fool wrote when he wasn't paid for writing." He took the same line with the International News Service, whose European manager, J. Kingsbury Smith, pursued Churchill throughout his vacation, begging for even five minutes face-to-face. "I never thought it would be so difficult to catch up with a gentleman to whom I was authorized to offer one million dollars," he said. Smith finally cornered Churchill in the lobby of the Hotel de Paris in Monte Carlo on 1 October, only to be told it was hardly worth being an author if nineteen and sixpence in the pound went to the government.[9]

BACK IN ENGLAND, Churchill found the domestic situation much improved. Thanks to Clementine, the family's new home at 28 Hyde Park Gate was ready, and the renovation of Chartwell was under way. Opportunities were also opening up to make money. *Life* magazine, the great American picture weekly, was one of his suitors for the war memoirs, and it proposed a feature article about Churchill's paintings. *Life*'s photographers paid several long visits to Chartwell, capturing Churchill, the house, and his studio, and their labors provided the magazine's cover story on 7 January 1946, an eight-page article with color reproductions of eighteen paintings, mostly from his 1945 trips to France and Italy. Apart from posing and proofreading, Churchill did nothing on behalf of the article, thereby preserving his tax status. In return, $20,000 (£5,000) was deposited in his bank account in November.[10]

Another money-spinning opportunity emerged in October 1945, again without prejudice to Churchill's tax position. On 17 October, Clement Attlee told Churchill that the Labour Cabinet had decided to lift the ban on disclosing the proceedings of the secret sessions held by the Commons during wartime. In most cases, secrecy had been imposed to avoid giving the Luftwaffe notice of the dates and times of future sittings, but Churchill had delivered five major secret speeches during the war and immediately approached *Life*, which offered $50,000 to publish them—only "a pig in a poke," remarked *Life*'s owner, Henry Luce, "to keep a position in the meat market." They would be "worth the space plus the money if, in some sense, Churchill becomes 'our author.'" On 20 December, Churchill saw Charles Eade to discuss editing the speeches as another book published by Cassell's. He told Eade that the last volume of his war speeches had brought in £3,500 and reckoned that the secret session speeches should make more, perhaps £5,000.[11]

Life had intended to use three of the speeches, but in the end printed only two (at no reduction in fee), for fear of saturating the market for Churchilliana. It published the speech of 23 April 1942, offering a *tour d'horizon* of the global war, in its issue of 28 January 1946, followed on 4 February by the address of 10 December 1942 about France and the North African landings. Churchill had submitted the texts for official approval, and Sir Edward Bridges, the Cabinet

Secretary, asked him to omit three unflattering pages about Charles de Gaulle, currently President of France, from the second speech.[12] It was, however, the April 1942 speech, from which Bridges had requested no cuts, that caused a major fuss.

The British and Australian press seized on Churchill's (brief) references to the surrender of Singapore in February 1942. Particularly inflammatory were his comments that "the 100,000 defenders of Singapore surrendered to 30,000 Japanese after five or six days of confused but not very severe fighting" and that "it does not seem that there was very much bloodshed." In Australia and Britain there were calls for an official inquiry into the debacle in the Far East in 1941–1942, but the British government had no desire to open this can of worms. A public postmortem into the Malayan campaign could set a dangerous precedent, Attlee told Ben Chifley, the Australian Prime Minister, on 31 January. If Singapore, then why not "other disasters such as Tobruk, Crete and Hong Kong"? The "strong feelings aroused might well be inimical to Commonwealth solidarity."[13] Chifley entirely agreed and followed Attlee's public line: what mattered was to learn lessons rather than apportion blame. This could best be done by publishing the final dispatches of the commanders involved, which Whitehall was doing with deliberate slowness, and by commissioning official histories of the campaigns. To the relief of Attlee and Chifley, the furor in both countries soon died down.[14]

There were other problems, however. Aware that he could be criticized for the lucrative deal, Churchill had arranged with *Life* to give the texts gratis to all British newspapers for simultaneous publication. But *Life's* issue of 28 January 1946 hit the newsstands a few days before the cover date, and reports of the speech appeared in the British press on the twenty-fifth, long before editors had received the text. Anti-Tory papers seized on the issue. An editorial in the *Daily Mirror* claimed that "some of the most dramatic stories of the war" were reaching the British people "by kind permission of an American newspaper." This would be "regarded by many citizens as an affront to Great Britain." The matter was taken up in the Commons by Labour left-wingers, one of whom, Adam McKinlay, called it "grossly offensive" that "documents of State" should be "sold to the highest bidder" and "used in newspaper articles for private gain by former Ministers." McKinlay demanded legislation to recover 50 percent of earnings made by former ministers that "derived from publication of books or newspaper articles based on official documents collected during their term of office."[15]

Churchill was in America when the row blew up. In public, he kept his mouth shut—replying "no comment" when asked about the Australian reaction—but he phoned Eade daily in late January to ascertain reaction in London. The storm blew over when the full texts were published. The *News Chronicle*, swallowing its initial reservations, said the April 1942 speech revealed Churchill "at his fullest power as a war leader." But when the book edition appeared, Churchill made sure that a copy was sent at his expense to all sitting MPs and those who had lost their seats in 1945—nearly one thousand in all.[16] The fuss about Churchill's secret speeches underlined the fact that making history was a sensitive business, especially when making money from it as well.

PRIVATELY, CHURCHILL'S PHYSICIAN, Lord Moran, likened the election defeat in July 1945 to a major operation. The vacation in Italy had helped heal the wound, but a scar remained, and it kept getting inflamed as party colleagues probed the reasons for their rout at the polls. Some blame could be laid at his door, such as the wartime neglect of party organization and postwar planning, not to mention his notorious charge that a Labour government would need "some form of Gestapo, no doubt very humanely directed in the first instance" to implement its socialist program. Of course, it was plausible to argue in retrospect that, given the national swing to the left, the Tories were bound to be defeated and that Churchill's stature prevented an even greater disaster. When all is said and done, however, Churchill knew that he had presided over one of the worst defeats in Conservative history. Far narrower defeats in 1910, 1923, and 1929 had all produced severe leadership crises.[17]

There were times when Churchill seemed ready to retire, as his wife fervently hoped. "The difficulties of leading the Opposition are very great," he told the Duke of Windsor on 15 December, "and I increasingly wonder whether the game is worth the candle." The murmurings from the Tory hierarchy were discreet but clear: "Winston needed a rest. He ought to get on with his book; it was his duty; no one could write the history of the war as he could." His lack of engagement in parliamentary business that autumn was widely resented. What averted outright revolt was appreciation of his wartime achievement. On 4 December 1945, R. A. Butler noted a general consensus that Churchill could not be pushed: "Either he goes early if he wants to or we just see things through." The hope was that he would see sense and go quietly. "In my view, Winston's day is over," Lord Cranborne told Anthony Eden, the heir apparent, in January. "We owe him a debt of gratitude such as this country has seldom owed to anyone. But he now belongs to the past, and even he is bound to find this out. It is really a time for patience, however galling that may be." Many Tories hoped that Churchill's winter vacation in America would facilitate a graceful exit.[18]

———

BY JANUARY 1946, the underlying issues relating to Churchill's war memoirs were therefore clear. Most thorny was the tax position. There was also the question of ownership and copyright. He had confidently told Moran in Italy that his war telegrams and minutes were his property and he could publish them. But, as Churchill well knew, any publication depended on approval by the Cabinet Office, which claimed that these papers were Crown copyright. And Churchill's place in history was at issue. The publicity aroused by his secret-session speeches showed that there was intense interest in anything he said or wrote about the war—as long as the material was carefully handled. Yet the humiliation of July 1945 had left him with a yearning for political as well as historical vindication. Could he combine politics and writing?

To understand how Churchill finally got started on his war memoirs in the spring of 1946, we must address these three issues more closely. To do so takes us back through the era of appeasement and the war—illuminating an unfamiliar side of his "finest hour," the story of Churchill as author—and on to his American trip of early 1946, when he found his voice again. The battles over contracts, papers, and reputation form the subjects of the next three chapters, because it was only when these were resolved that Churchill could fight the Second World War anew, this time with the pen not the sword.

CHAPTER 2

CONTRACTS | *Churchill Against the Publishers*

C HURCHILL'S CAREER as a Member of Parliament ran virtually unbroken from 1900 to 1964—almost two thirds of the twentieth century. But although Churchill's life was politics, he lived by writing. Yet his literary activity has attracted too little attention from biographers and historians. Four youthful accounts of his military experiences in India and Africa launched him as an author. In 1906, he published his first substantial work of history: a two-volume biography of his father, Lord Randolph. While in office almost continuously from 1908 to 1922, he kept up a flow of newspaper articles, earning considerable sums. The first two volumes of *The World Crisis* appeared during 1923, and the advances helped Churchill renovate Chartwell—a rundown manor house near Westerham, in northwest Kent, which became his pride and joy. Despite returning to the Cabinet as Chancellor of the Exchequer in 1924, he carried on with *The World Crisis*, completing it in 1931 as a six-book epic, taking the story up to the end of the Lloyd George coalition in 1922.

Churchill's earnings as an author helped fund his political career and his self-indulgent lifestyle. "My tastes are simple," he once declared. "I like only the best."[1] His bills for food, cigars, and drink were substantial; he ran a London apartment and an expensive country house, and all his domestic needs were provided by servants. In the twenties, he just about made ends meet, but in 1929 the Tories lost their parliamentary majority, and Churchill his £5,000 salary as Chancellor. Financial disaster followed on the heels of political defeat as Churchill's American investments collapsed in the Wall Street crash. By the spring of 1937,

Churchill was even ready to sell Chartwell if he could get "a good price"—say, £25,000.[2]

Today, the popular image of Churchill in the 1930s centers on his pugnacious campaign against appeasement. Yet most of his working hours in that decade were occupied by a frantic output of articles and books. As soon as he lost office in 1929, he embarked on a study of his martial ancestor John Churchill, first Duke of Marlborough, in whose palace, Blenheim, named for his greatest triumph over the French in 1704, Winston had been born. *Marlborough, His Life and Times* was to be in two volumes, but like *The World Crisis* it soon got out of hand. Not until the fourth volume, published in September 1938, could Winston let his hero rest in peace. Needless to say, his publishers were very aggrieved, while Churchill moaned that what had begun as a labor of love ended up like a ten-ton weight on his head.[3]

The problem was that Churchill kept being diverted into new projects in order to secure more advances and pay his bills.[4] In 1931–1932, there was a one-volume edition of *The World Crisis* and a selection of essays entitled *Thoughts and Adventures*. Following the success of six "Great Stories of the World Retold," the *News of the World* commissioned another half-dozen articles. In the autumn of 1932, with only half the first volume of *Marlborough* written, Churchill was touting another big book, *The History of the English-Speaking Peoples*, which was taken up by Newman Flower, the chairman of Cassell and Company. In December, Churchill and Flower agreed on an advance of £20,000, to be paid in installments until completion in 1939.[5] Like Harrap's, Cassell's staple was dictionaries. It required considerable daring to make such a huge commitment to a notoriously willful author in the depths of the Depression. Even so, no one could have imagined that it would be a quarter century until the *English-Speaking Peoples* appeared—or how the firm would be compensated for the delay.

As the 1930s wore on, Churchill continued his prodigious but erratic literary course, with more profitable diversions such as a film script on the life of King George V for Alexander Korda and a sparkling little volume of his newspaper articles entitled *Great Contemporaries*. In June 1938, in need of cash when his American investments again slumped, he signed a contract with George Harrap for another big book, this time about Europe since the Russian revolution. Harrap's offered an advance of £1,500, and Churchill got £500 more for the newpaper rights.[6] That same month, Harrap's brought out *Arms and the Covenant*, a collection of Churchill's most powerful speeches on defense and foreign policy from the last decade, then a year later Thornton Butterworth published a parallel collection of his newspaper articles, *Step by Step, 1936–1939*. These two books made money (though not as much as Churchill hoped) and bolstered his reviving political reputation as a farsighted prophet. But, as usual, by mortgaging his future to pay for the present, he was delaying repayment of past literary debts.

In 1934, he had commissioned a senior Oxford historian, Keith Feiling (who had been his son, Randolph's, tutor at Christ Church), to start the groundwork for the *English-Speaking Peoples*. But it was not until the spring of 1938, with Marlborough finally about to meet his maker, that Churchill could get his mind around the new project. His principal assistant was now Bill Deakin, a young Oxford historian recommended by Feiling, who had helped with the last volume of *Marlborough*. The *English-Speaking Peoples* was not complete when Germany invaded Poland and Churchill returned to the Admiralty. He spent long hours on it that autumn and delivered a 500,000-word manuscript in the middle of December 1939. But Cassell's was not ready to pay the remainder of the advance because the text ended abruptly in 1865, rather than running up to 1914. Churchill, now deep in planning the campaign in Norway, proposed a 10,000-word epilogue to cover the remaining half century, but Desmond Flower, the chairman's son, wanted a proper set of chapters covering the development of the British empire, the growth of democracy in Britain and America, and Anglo-American relations up to the Great War. Churchill promised to deliver the additional chapters by 30 June 1940, and another young Oxford historian, Alan Bullock, was set to work boning up on Australia and the empire.[7] But at the end of April 1940, with the Norwegian campaign in chaos and new responsibilities for defense policy, Churchill confessed defeat. Bullock was told that an arrangement had been made with the publishers to finish the book after the war, and Churchill therefore did not need any further assistance at present.[8]

ONE MIGHT ASSUME that this ended Churchill's life as an author for the duration of the war. Far from it! Managed through intermediaries, to preserve the tax purdah he had entered at the beginning of the war, Churchill's literary career not merely continued in 1940–1945 but soared to quite dizzy heights.

To compensate Cassell's, he let them publish his speeches since 1938. The contract, signed in November 1940, included a statement approved by his tax lawyers: "It is understood that Mr Churchill cannot and will not undertake any work whatsoever in connection with this publication, all references being exclusively to the compiler." As with *Arms and the Covenant*, this was officially Randolph, whose name appeared on the title page, but much of the work was done by Desmond Flower and Kathleen Hill. Although Cassell's wanted to call the book *Their Finest Hour*, Churchill refused, eventually adopting Randolph's suggestion

Into Battle. (As was the case for many of his works, the American publisher, Putnam, chose a different title: *Blood, Sweat, and Tears*.) The speeches sold well, especially in the United States, where they were a Book-of-the-Month Club selection in May 1941, and by June 1942, Churchill had received accumulated royalties of over £12,000.[9] *Into Battle* ended in November 1940. Five more volumes of war speeches followed, one per year between 1942 and 1946, and then the secret-session speeches. The compiler of all these was Charles Eade, editor of the *Sunday Dispatch*, again with the author looking over his shoulder.

Churchill could also recycle old writings. Emulating major authors such as George Bernard Shaw, he decided it would be more profitable to assume the cost of publishing his own books, employing a firm of publishers for printing and sales on a cost-plus-commission basis. In the summer of 1941, he bought back the copyright to several of his earlier works from Macmillan and Company, which had acquired them when Thornton Butterworth was forced into liquidation. Churchill concluded this buy-back contract on 3 August 1941, just before leaving for his Atlantic conference with Roosevelt. He paid Macmillan's £1,500 and promised that the firm would be his "sole agents" on all new works.[10] Macmillan's started reprinting books such as *Great Contemporaries*, but sales did not match Churchill's expectations. In April 1943, with Churchill facing another cash crisis, he decided to sell the copyright back to Macmillan's. The deal was concluded in June, and Churchill received a much-needed £7,000—a sign of how much his stock had risen in the intervening two years.[11] As usual, he was treating literary contracts like a futures market—signing, selling, and bartering them in the endless search for ready cash.

Then, suddenly, Churchill hit the really big money. In July 1943, Brendan Bracken, his business factotum, extracted an offer of £20,000 from Alexander Korda and MGM for the film rights to *Marlborough*. After playing off Korda against Filippo Del Giudice and J. Arthur Rank of Two Cities Films, Mrs. Hill secured a top figure of £50,000 from Two Cities. Churchill was in Canada and America in September, conferring with Roosevelt, but contracts were exchanged on 6 October 1943 and a first tranche of £30,000 deposited in his bank account. It was made clear that, because of his tax position, Churchill must in no way be connected with the script. As astutely noted in the *Daily Herald* on 16 November under the headline CHURCHILL'S BIG FEE, "the money has been paid for the use of the Premier's name for publicity purposes" because "any scenario writer of skill" could do the job from the book itself and other biographies. This was the only significant leak, however, and the remaining £20,000 was quietly paid in July 1944.[12]

The film deal began the transformation of Churchill's financial and literary fortunes. Using this money, Churchill decided in September 1943 to buy back from Macmillan's the copyright he had sold them just three months before! The publishers duly obliged, and Churchill set aside £7,000 of his newfound wealth for the purpose. In January 1944, Alexander Korda offered £50,000 for the film rights to *The History of the English-Speaking Peoples*, which had still not been published. This was more complicated than *Marlborough*, since those rights had been granted to Cassell's along with the book. But, pressing their advantage, Newman Flower and his son said they would be happy to surrender the film rights in return for first refusal on Churchill's anticipated war memoirs. In October 1943, Churchill had grumbled to Charles Eade about the size of the Cassell's advance and the small print run for the 1942 volume of his war speeches. "I don't think they paid me enough," he muttered. But now he was willing to accept their terms, on the understanding that he was not committed to write a word, in order to secure the £50,000 from Korda.[13]

However, Macmillan's still had the sole right to publish his new books—a point Mrs. Hill had overlooked. Daniel Macmillan made it clear that his reprints of Churchill's earlier works were intended to prepare the ground for the war memoirs. This brought the buyback of copyright to an abrupt halt in April 1944. At this moment, with much of his mind preoccupied by the impending D-Day landings, Churchill was also locked in an unpleasant struggle with Harrap's, which had contracted in 1938 for the book on Europe since the Russian revolution. Churchill's lawyers stressed that the deal with Korda and Cassell's over the *English-Speaking Peoples* depended on purchasing his freedom from Macmillan's and Harrap's.

On 27 April 1944, Churchill concluded the buyback of copyright; then on 10 August he sent Daniel Macmillan formal notice to terminate the agreement in six months, as he was entitled to do under its terms. He explained that "it is incumbent upon me to put my affairs on a solid basis when I am free to do so. Please do not think that I am giving the notice because of other commitments, as this is not the case." The last sentence was strictly correct—no new commitments had been signed—but Churchill was, of course, preparing the way to do so.[14]

George Harrap was more difficult to buy off. He did not want the money, only whatever new book Churchill now planned; both sides agreed to go to legal arbitration. In preparation, Churchill jotted down reasons why it was now impossible to write a history of Europe since the Bolshevik revolution. "I suppose I have not read a dozen books during the last five years." Writing on such sensitive matters "would adversely affect the interests and friendships of this country." The proposed book had "become abhorrent"; his interests had shifted to the "tremendous events" of the last five years. And the public would expect his next book to be "an account of this present struggle," not the Russian revolution and Mussolini's rise to power. Twice, Harrap's offered a new contract on more attractive terms, but Churchill was adamant, asserting that the company's behavior had been so improper that "I do not want to have any further dealings of any kind with them." On 7 September 1944, George Harrap capitulated, explaining that "it is distasteful to us, whether we are in the right or not, to litigate the matter with a man to whom every one of us is so much indebted." This message was communicated to Churchill at the second Quebec conference. At the end of October, Harrap's formally renounced the contract, whereupon Churchill refunded the £1,500 advance with interest, and each side paid its own legal costs.[15]

Released by Macmillan's and Harrap's, Churchill was finally able to sign with Cassell's and Korda. On 24 November, Churchill sent two parallel letters to Sir Newman Flower. The first indicated that in return for Cassell's giving up the film rights to the *English-Speaking Peoples*, Churchill would give the company first refusal on "any work I may write on the present War after it is over." His lawyers, however, made sure that he explicitly preserved his freedom as to an acceptable price and also on whether or not he chose to write anything. The second letter was a note of the understanding they had reached on *The History of the English-Speaking Peoples*. The publishers conceded what they would not accept in 1939–1940, namely, a 10,000-word epilogue instead of several substantive chapters to round off the story to 1914. In return, however, they expected to publish the book six months after Churchill left office as premier. After further legal niceties, the Korda deal was signed, and Churchill received a check for £50,000 on 6 April 1945, just a month before the war in Europe ended.[16]

The conduct of these negotiations is revealing. On Churchill's side, the bargaining was hard, often ruthless, but the Prime Minister kept clear of the rough-and-tumble, leaving that to Bracken, Hill, and his lawyers. What helped him win the day was his now formidable status. Macmillan's was obliging in part because Daniel's brother and codirector, Harold, was a Tory MP and one of Churchill's ministers. Harrap's conceded because a legal row against the country's war hero was not merely pointless but unseemly. The *Daily Herald* again caught the gist of the story. While stating Churchill had made no decision about his war memoirs, despite "many record offers," it claimed that what stood in his way had been a book contract signed when Churchill was "merely M.P. for Epping, discredited by his own Party and a lone wolf." Now this obstacle had been voluntarily removed by a publisher who "did not want to embarrass a statesman to whom the nation owes so much."[17]

These deals were therefore signs of Churchill's burgeoning stature. Savior of the nation in 1940, he was now also the architect of victory. Whether or not Del Giudice and Korda seriously intended to make these films—both were ardent admirers of Churchill, and Desmond Flower believed that Korda's offer was simply a way to express his appreciation—these payments, for doing nothing, showed how Churchill's stock had risen.[18] Their combined total was at least £100,000. This was a bull market at a totally different level from the sums he could have commanded a few years before.

WHAT, THEN, WAS CHURCHILL'S position on the war memoirs in August 1945? Contractually, he had to offer the book to Cassell's, but he was not obliged to write anything or to accept Cassell's offer. And how were terms to be negotiated? The literary agency Curtis Brown was desperate to act for Churchill again, even offering in September 1944 to reduce its normal 10 percent commission to 2.5 percent or less. But the agency was given the brush-off by Mrs. Hill ("if Mr. Churchill has need of your services at any time he will not hesitate to ask you for them"), and when, despite this, the firm renewed its contacts in August 1945, Churchill's reaction was fierce: "Tell Mrs Hill she must be very careful not to get me involved with these people."[19] Churchill was now convinced that agents, whatever their commissions, took too much and earned him too little. But it was no longer appropriate for him to handle negotiations personally. Not only were they too intricate and he too old, but to enter into the sordid cut and thrust of hard bargaining would demean his Olympian reputation, which was now a priceless asset. During the war, he had used Brendan Bracken as his "honorary man of business," abetted by his senior secretary, Kathleen Hill.[20] But Mrs. Hill retired at the end of 1945, and Bracken, despite his business acumen, was not a sufficiently substantial figure. And so Churchill turned to Lord Camrose.

William Ewert Berry, born in South Wales in 1879, had shown a genius for journalism from an early age. After a few false starts, he and his younger brother, Gomer, carved out a niche for themselves in London, turning around the *Sunday Times*. In the twenties, they branched out in all directions, acquiring the Allied Newspapers chain of provincial papers, the Amalgamated Press printing empire, and even Cassell's, before selling it to Newman Flower. William's biggest coup was to purchase the *Daily Telegraph* in 1927. Starting with a mere 84,000 readers, his hands-on editing and lavish features pushed circulation over the half-million mark by 1937 and up to 900,000 in April 1940. The two brothers (ennobled during the war as Lords Camrose and Kemsley) divided their empire in 1937, with William retaining the Amalgamated Press and the *Daily Telegraph*.

For most of the interwar years, he was not particularly close to Churchill. But in 1938–1939, increasingly concerned about national defense, Camrose commissioned Churchill to write fortnightly articles for the *Daily Telegraph* and then championed him for Cabinet office in the summer of 1939. Camrose never got the Cabinet post he coveted when Churchill became premier, unlike Churchill's other press baron, Max Beaverbrook. But Beaverbrook was an unscrupulous buccaneer, whom Churchill used as what Attlee called "a kind of stimulant or drug." Camrose, though ruthless, was known as a man of integrity and shrewd judgment. Tall, imposing, and laconic, he struck Desmond Flower as "a cross between an elder statesman and Buddha," though with "a twinkle in his eyes." During the war, Churchill and Camrose lunched regularly and usually sat together at the Other Club, a fortnightly dining club that Churchill had cofounded before the Great War.[21]

At one of these dinners, Churchill informally promised Camrose the newspaper rights in Britain and the British empire to any war memoirs. In January 1945, the press lord told his son Seymour that the *Daily Telegraph* had been offered "*first* refusal, though it's problematic that they will ever get written."[22] Churchill kept him informed of his negotiations with Cassell's and Korda in 1944 and showed him the juiciest American offers for the memoirs that came in during 1945. It was also Camrose who came to the rescue when, still strapped for ready cash, Churchill again considered putting Chartwell on the market after his election defeat. Instead, Camrose arranged for the house to be bought privately by a group of friends and admirers and leased back to Churchill for a nominal rent during his lifetime, and then given to the National Trust (a private charity that maintained property and land of outstanding historic interest or natural beauty). The press lord contributed £15,000, and sixteen others gave £5,000 each. On 29 December 1945, Churchill told Camrose, "I feel how inadequate my thanks have been to you for all your kindness." When the deeds were signed, he intended to express his appreciation to all the donors, "but to none more than you, my dear Bill, who have never wavered or varied in your faithful friendship during all these long, baffling and finally tumultuous years."[23]

Yet there were still literary debts to pay off, notably to Cassell's for *The History of the English-Speaking Peoples*. Under his November 1944 arrangement, the firm was supposed to publish the book six months after he left the premiership: in the event, January 1946. On return from sunny Italy in October 1945, Churchill gloomily got down to work. "I am making slow progress," he told Camrose on 17 October.[24] He managed to persuade Cassell's that the epilogue should end not in 1914 but 1874: anything later, he argued, would "overlap the historical and biographical works which the author has already written."[25] Much to Churchill's relief, Cassell's also said that it could not publish before the end of 1946 because of continued paper rationing. On the other hand, Churchill was no longer happy with what he had rushed to finish during the Phony War. In March 1945, he had engaged the Cambridge historian Denis Brogan to review the whole text for a fee of £1,000. In the autumn, Churchill reread the manuscript in the light of Brogan's comments and then threw himself into wholesale revision of the eighteenth century.[26]

Since Churchill had already paid tax on the full advance from Cassell's, the Inland Revenue had agreed that completing the book would not prejudice his status.[27] On the other hand, this status still seemed to block any new work, particularly his memoirs. Charles Eade came up with an ingenious suggestion. How about *Winston Churchill's Own Story of the War (as told in a series of conversations with Charles Eade)*? Or with "anyone else you prefer," he graciously added. Since Churchill would only talk, rather than write, that could satisfy the Inland Revenue.[28] This idea did not go down well at Chartwell. More promising was a suggestion from several American newspapers: to sell them his papers and then be paid to "edit" them for publication. This would avoid income tax since the papers would be deemed capital assets. Here was "an interesting situation in America," Churchill told Camrose on 15 October, "if it were possible for us to take advantage of it."[29]

After talking with his solicitor, Anthony Moir of Fladgate and Company in Pall Mall, they consulted Leslie Graham-Dixon, a leading tax barrister, who delivered a preliminary opinion on 8 January 1946, the day before Churchill left for the United States. In principle, Graham-Dixon agreed that Churchill's war papers, created after he officially retired from his profession as an author on 3 September 1939, could be deemed capital assets. But he warned that anything Churchill did to prepare these literary assets for sale or publication might be cited by the Inland Revenue as evidence of Churchill's "emergence from a most profitable purdah." Even a single broadcast or article could be taken to show that he had resumed his profession as an author, thereby prejudicing the sale of the war papers as capital assets. Graham-Dixon's advice was clear: stay in literary purdah and resist the allure of quick cash. While Churchill was in America, Graham-Dixon promised he would be "constantly" applying his mind to this question.[30]

CHAPTER 3

PAPERS | *Churchill Against the Bureaucrats*

C HURCHILL'S BREEZY ASSURANCE about his papers in September 1945—"They are mine. I can publish them"[1]—covered another legal tangle, in this case bureaucratic rather than financial. For more than a decade the Cabinet Office had labored, with considerable success, to prevent retiring government ministers from removing official papers and writing revealing memoirs. Security was an important motivation, but so was a desire to prevent repetition of the acrimonious battle of the memoirs that refought the war of 1914–1918. During the interwar years and World War II, Churchill was deeply engaged in this bureaucratic struggle, as well as his struggle over contracts. So we need to delve into another corner of his neglected literary history to understand why *The Second World War* rested on quite unique access to official documents.

DURING CHURCHILL'S EARLIEST years in office, there was no record of Cabinet proceedings apart from a personal letter penned by the Prime Minister to the monarch. Ministers often acted on hazy and disputed recollections of what had been agreed. But when David Lloyd George became premier in December 1916, he established an inner War Cabinet and a Cabinet Secretariat under Maurice Hankey, a former colonel in the marines. Hankey owed his position initially to Lloyd George's patronage but held it for more than twenty years because of his remarkable industry and bureaucratic skill. It was he who composed the first-ever Cabinet minutes (an agreed summary of discussions and decisions) on 9 December 1916.

When the War Cabinet was disbanded in 1919, Hankey tried to forestall a hemorrhage of official papers. He drafted a set of instructions stating that "Cabinet Minutes and Papers are not the personal property of members, and on the Minister leaving office it is the duty of the Secretary to recover from him, or, in the event of his death, from his executors, all Cabinet papers issued to him from the Cabinet Office." But the first meeting of the new Cabinet, on 4 November 1919, struck out this paragraph. Its members felt that secrecy was adequately safeguarded "by the rule that no-one is entitled to make public use of Cabinet documents without the permission of the King." They also added the provision that Cabinet ministers should have access at any time to the Cabinet records for the period in which they had been in office. Although there is no direct evidence, it is likely that the rules were rewritten to satisfy Lloyd George and Churchill— both of whom were in the vanguard of ministers planning war memoirs. Lloyd George had a researcher working in the War Cabinet records while he was still Prime Minister in 1919–1922.[2]

In August 1922, the press announced a contract between Curtis Brown (on behalf of Lloyd George) and Sir William Berry (the future Lord Camrose) for a book and serialization package worth £90,000. It was dubbed "the biggest deal in the history of publishing." Berry acquired the serial and book rights for Lloyd George's memoirs in Britain and the empire. He also represented the American publishers Funk and Wagnall's, who wanted to publish the memoirs in the United States and Canada after having them serialized in *The New York Times* and the *Chicago Tribune*. This complex deal, and Berry's role as its linchpin, is a precedent for the selling of the Churchill memoirs in 1946, but at the time it was soon dead in the water. Such was the public outcry at Lloyd George's profiteering that before the end of the month it was announced that he would give all the £90,000 to charities connected with war relief: "He feels unable to take any personal advantage for himself out of the story of the struggle and suffering of the nation." Two months later, the governing coalition collapsed, and Lloyd George was free to get on with his memoirs. But with no income to gain, he turned to lucrative newspaper columns, extricated himself from the contracts, and returned the advances. Between 1933 and 1938, he did publish six volumes on the war and two on the peace, but the yield, though good, proved considerably less than its earlier promise because he was now one of yesterday's men. The lessons of this cannot have been lost on Churchill and Camrose after World War II.[3]

Despite Lloyd George's silence, the decade after 1918 saw a rash of polemical memoirs by generals and politicians, many of them using official documents to embarrassing effect. Having lost custody of Cabinet papers, Hankey tried to clarify the procedures for their use in print. Two controversies involving Churchill's *World Crisis* established crucial precedents.

In August 1921, Lord Esher published a short book entitled *The Tragedy of Lord Kitchener*. In it, he attacked Churchill for leaving his post as First Lord of the Admiralty in October 1914 to take personal command of the besieged port of Antwerp—implying that he had done so impetuously and without authority—and Churchill wanted to publish evidence in refutation. On 30 January 1922, the Cabinet—of which he was a member, though on this occasion he sat in anxious silence—agreed that ministers thus attacked should be allowed to vindicate their actions by publishing relevant documents, provided this "did not affect current public interests or breach the fiduciary relations of individuals." This "Vindicator Clause" became an established part of Cabinet Office case law, and Churchill used it to good effect against Esher in the first volume of *The World Crisis*. Such was the controversy surrounding much of Churchill's time at the Admiralty that the clause appeared to give him almost carte blanche in quotation from official documents.[4]

This provoked a backlash, however. When volume 1 was serialized in February 1923, Labour MPs put down several parliamentary questions asking whether Churchill had official permission to quote so freely from Admiralty telegrams. There were more questions in April, after the book appeared, about whether quotation from and facsimiles of these telegrams jeopardized British naval codes. Churchill, now out of office, was incensed to read the response of the Prime Minister, Andrew Bonar Law, which implied that Churchill had breached the oath of secrecy taken by all Privy Councillors. He was also alarmed at reports of a special Cabinet committee to establish guidelines for the use of official documents in memoirs and other publications.[5]

The Cabinet committee never met, and the row blew over, but Churchill had learned a lesson. In 1926, as he finalized volume 3 while Chancellor of the Exchequer, Churchill sent potentially sensitive chapters to interested departments, such as the Foreign Office and the Admiralty. He also sent the whole text to the Prime Minister, Stanley Baldwin, suggesting that, rather than troubling himself with the text, Baldwin should leave it to Hankey to advise on whether reasons of public interest precluded publication of any document.[6] On 8 December 1926, Hankey sent a lengthy response, making many editorial suggestions but stating that, apart from a few points such as references to code breaking, he "did not notice anything to which exception could be taken on public grounds."[7] The next day, Churchill requested explicit official approval to avoid a recurrence of the 1923 row. Baldwin, he said, had already read the book, "without any feeling of disquiet," but the Prime Minister should be in a position, if questions were raised, to tell the Commons that Churchill had sought and obtained the necessary approval.

> I expect I am the first person who has published anything, who has sought such permission. In my opinion, it ought to be a rule that sanction should be sought before publication. On the other hand, such sanction should not be unreasonably refused in view of the immense amount that has been published by all sorts of persons in the highest stations.

Hankey suggested that it would be tactful for Churchill, as a Privy Councillor, also to ask permission from the King. But on the crucial point he was reassuringly explicit: "If the Prime Minister consults me *re* the publication of documents, I shall tell him I cannot see any objection."[8]

These exchanges in December 1926 set enduring precedents. Hankey scrutinized each of the remaining volumes of Churchill's war memoirs on behalf of the Prime Minister. He persuaded a reluctant Lloyd George to follow the same procedure for his memoirs in the 1930s.[9] In this rather casual way, the Cabinet Secretary became the official censor of political memoirs — a role of considerable importance in our story. And the letter of 9 December embodied Churchill's basic attitude to official documents for the rest of his life. On the one hand, he expected to keep the papers from his periods in office; on the other hand, he was ready to submit anything he wished to publish to the government of the day. He believed those two principles struck a proper balance between private interest and public duty.

SENIOR CIVIL SERVANTS, however, still wanted much tighter control over official documents. On 6 March 1934, Edgar Lansbury published a biography of his father, George — a Cabinet minister in the Labour government of 1929–1931 — that included lengthy quotations from two Cabinet memoranda, for which no permission had been sought. Seizing on the case, the Cabinet Office had Lansbury prosecuted for a breach of the Official Secrets Act.[10] On 21 March, the day after Lansbury's conviction, the Cabinet approved new guidelines drawn up by Sir Rupert Howorth, Deputy Secretary to the Cabinet, and based on the Hankey draft rejected in 1919. These required future ministers to return all Cabinet minutes and papers on vacating office and gave the Cabinet Secretary the task of ensuring that they complied. In addition, he was asked to write to all ex–Cabinet ministers (or, if deceased, to their executors) requesting return of any papers that they still held. In recompense, former ministers were to be told that they could have access to all Cabinet minutes and papers issued to them during their period in office, on the understanding that these must be consulted in the Cabinet Office.[11]

On 17 October 1934, the Cabinet also codified the principles under which biographers could have access to Cabinet documents. This followed representations by Lady Milner, whose late husband, a wartime minister, had been attacked in Lloyd George's war memoirs. It was agreed that access to papers held by the Cabinet Office should not be given to ordinary historians and biographers who simply wanted to produce a better book. (At this time, the archives of government departments were open only up to 1885.) But where "Cabinet or other similar Secret documents had already been published with authority" they could also be shown to anyone who had "a good title to vindicate the memory of a deceased person" and who claimed that his memory had been damaged by the publication. Prime Ministerial approval was still required, as was permission to publish anything from those documents, but this was a significant enlargement of the Vindicator Clause. It also barred access to these documents for normal historical researchers.[12]

Howorth told a colleague that under these new rules it would be "very difficult for Ministers in future to write Memoirs in the same indiscrete [sic] and wrongful fashion as has been customary since 1918." In September 1934, he had sent a circular to seventy-one former Cabinet ministers and sixteen executors setting out the decision and inviting return of all papers. Most recipients cooperated, and by one year later only nine ex-ministers held out. However, these included the two great memoir writers of the wartime generation: Churchill and Lloyd George.[13] In a lengthy correspondence in 1934 and 1935, Churchill told the Cabinet Office that he had "invariably obtained the prior sanction of the Government of the day" before printing any documents in his possession. He also asserted that the original typescripts of memoranda submitted to the Cabinet were "my property," as were memoranda dictated or printed for the Cabinet but never circulated. He also claimed ownership of copies of "private letters which I have written to colleagues on matters of secrecy."[14] On 19 April 1936, Hankey dined at Chartwell, and Churchill agreed to hand back his set of Cabinet minutes for the Baldwin government of 1924–1929. They were duly collected by a junior member of the Cabinet Secretariat, Lawrence Burgis, though he had to borrow a suitcase from Churchill to do so, such was their bulk. Hankey noted: "I am hoping to recover a great part, if not all, of the Cabinet papers in due course."[15]

His hopes were vain, however. In 1936, Churchill was moving back into official circles via the government's secret committee on air defense, for which Hankey was the main conduit of documentation. Churchill therefore probably deemed it prudent to make a cooperative gesture at little cost, having no plans to write a book on his years as Chancellor. But he still retained a mass of Cabinet papers, particularly for 1919–1922, and on these he remained defiant.[16] In April 1940, with Churchill at the Admiralty, a junior member of the Cabinet Office toyed with the idea that "we might have another go at Mr. Churchill, now that he has an official private secretary (or rather four or five)." But, having looked at the bulky file, he added, "my heart fails me." Howorth agreed. On 22 April (near the height of the Norway crisis), he noted that "no useful purpose could or would be served by reopening this controversy at this juncture."[17]

By this time, Churchill was already preparing the ground for a possible set of memoirs on the current war. On becoming First Lord in September 1939, he instructed his staff to arrange at the end of each month for the printing of all his "minutes" (here meaning his official directives). This practice continued in enlarged form after he moved to 10 Downing Street. The prints were explicitly headed the Prime Minister's "Personal Minutes"—doubtless to preempt Cabinet Office claims that such papers were government property. He was equally careful to refer to his wartime messages to Roosevelt, Stalin, and other leaders (similarly printed in monthly installments) as "My Personal Telegrams." These collations served as a ready reference for war work, but they would also be a convenient source for any future memoirs.

Labeling his papers "personal" did not, however, give Churchill the right to remove them when his tenure in office ended. In the spring of 1945, with the coalition about to break up, Sir Edward Bridges, Hankey's successor as Cabinet Secretary, wanted to reiterate the 1934 policy, while Churchill naturally wanted to revive the more liberal 1919 rules. Bridges considered this to be legally untenable, but Norman Brook, his deputy, considered it "most unlikely that the Prime Minister will abandon, in deference to legal argument, the distinction which he seeks to draw between Cabinet documents which a Minister wrote himself, and other Cabinet documents."[18]

Reluctantly, Bridges concocted a revised version, WP 320, which was approved and circulated under Churchill's name on 23 May. Less than a week later, the coalition collapsed. WP 320 was recirculated when Churchill's caretaker government resigned in July 1945. This "Note by the Prime Minister," entitled "War Cabinet Documents," included three provisions that would prove absolutely central to Churchill's war memoirs:

- "Ministers leaving office may take with them copies of War Cabinet memoranda and other documents of State which they wrote themselves."
- "Ministers of Cabinet rank may at any time have access in the Cabinet offices to documents issued to them while they were in office."
- "[S]uch documents may not be quoted or published without the permission of the Government of the day."

Ministers who did remove documents they wrote included Hugh Dalton in May and Leo Amery, Anthony Eden, and Churchill himself in July. All were later to produce bulky and lucrative war memoirs, which would have been impossible without the calculated liberality of the first two provisions of WP 320. In August 1945, Churchill told Charles Eade that he had sixty-eight monthly volumes of minutes and directives and so envisaged "no difficulty in writing the history of the war."[19]

BUT CUSTODY AND access were not the whole story for would-be memoirists. Much would turn on how generous "the Government of the day" was in granting permission to publish. In practice, as we have seen, interpretation of that third provision depended largely on the Cabinet Secretary. If Lord Camrose is the key figure in the negotiation of Churchill's contracts, Sir Edward Bridges is the man who matters in the saga of his papers. He described himself in 1942 as "in some sense the guardian of the secrecy of confidential Papers and communications of past years" and was convinced that "if permissions are freely granted, it is awfully hard to know where to stop."[20] During World War II, Bridges was particularly concerned to prevent a repeat of the battle of the books that had, in his view, soiled the aftermath of the Great War. Some of the cases he dealt with laid down precedents. And the attitude taken by Churchill, as Prime Minister, varied subtly, reflecting his personal view of the writers and also the way in which each case might impinge on his own authorial interests.

Admiral Lord Chatfield had been First Sea Lord (the principal naval officer at the Admiralty) from 1933 to 1938 and then Minister for the Coordination of Defence in 1939–1940. In June 1941, he submitted the manuscript of his memoirs to the Cabinet Office. Bridges read it and advised Churchill that part 3, dealing with "the Naval and Political story of our lack of preparation for war" from 1933, should not be published without drastic alteration, because it would "give rise to controversy and weaken our war effort" and because it revealed what had happened in meetings of the Cabinet or its Committee of Imperial Defence.

Churchill had no time for Chatfield, describing him as "a sailor who prolonged his official life after he had left the Navy by building up credit with the advocates of appeasement." But, although endorsing Bridges's proposal, he added an important rider: "After the war a far greater latitude in the disclosure of official information can be given. There are only a few things which should never be mentioned." Doubtless the Ultra secret lay behind Churchill's second sentence, while anticipation of his own war memoirs probably prompted the first. In the Cabinet meeting of 24 November 1941, Churchill presented the Chatfield case entirely in terms of the undesirable "controversy and ill-feeling" that would be generated in wartime, while noting that "it might well be possible to adopt a less rigorous attitude" after the war. The Cabinet agreed, and Bridges transmitted this judgment to Chatfield.[21]

In May 1942, another minister of the appeasement era was ready to go into print: Lord Londonderry, who had served as Secretary of State for Air from 1931 to 1935—the critical years of British rearmament. Bridges considered his text "of third-rate quality and of no importance whatsoever, except as regards its author," but publication in its present form "would certainly get us into trouble with Lord Chatfield and other more serious writers who have been discouraged from writing about immediately pre-war events." But Churchill took a generous view of this case, even though he and Londonderry had argued vehemently in the 1930s over appeasement. (The fact that Londonderry was his second cousin may not have been irrelevant.) "I really think pre-1935 is ancient history," Churchill told Bridges. For the period after that date, Londonderry should be told what quotations from official documents should be excluded "in the public interest." Yet, Churchill added, the "principle that permission must be obtained is also modified by the maxim 'permission should not be unreasonably withheld.'" He also noted that "the precedents in favour of fairly free publication *after* the war is over are very numerous," citing among others "my own voluminous writings." Little wonder that a Cabinet official, going through the file later, tabbed this document "Riposte from Churchill the author!"[22]

Given his personal and professional interests, Churchill presented Londonderry's case equivocally to the Cabinet and shifted responsibility by asking for a second opinion from one of its members, Sir Stafford Cripps. The Cabinet accepted the compromise that Bridges pressed on Cripps—namely, that "permission should be withheld for the publication of those passages in the book for which the consent of the Government was required."[23] In communicating the decision to Londonderry, Bridges stretched those words to say that consent could not be given to publication "save after drastic deletions and amendments."

Bridges's strategy from then on was to procrastinate for as long as possible. The Cabinet Office drew up a lengthy list of possibly questionable passages and encouraged the relevant departments to object. Although Londonderry was incensed at the treatment he had received—claiming with justice that the Official Secrets Act and the Privy Councillor's Oath had been "stretched to their utmost limit" to censor his book—he blamed ministers rather than civil servants. When *Wings of Destiny* finally appeared in March 1943, he sent Bridges one of the six free copies provided by his publisher, casting blame on the War Cabinet but thanking Bridges for his help: "without knowing the full story I am quite sure you did all you could for me."[24]

Bridges was particularly keen to silence civil servants who wanted to sell their stories. The big fish (in Bridges's view a real shark) was none other than his predecessor as Cabinet Secretary, Maurice Hankey. Like Chatfield, Hankey had evolved from an official into a minister, and then, in 1941–1942, into a severe critic of Churchill's leadership style. Enforced retirement enabled him to complete his insider account of the Great War entitled *The Supreme Command*, based on a detailed diary he had kept as Cabinet Secretary. In accordance with the rules he had helped concoct in the 1920s and 1930s, Hankey submitted volume 1 of his manuscript for the Cabinet Secretary's approval in September 1943. As usual, Bridges played for time, and it was not until March 1944 that he discussed the matter with Hankey, suggesting that the memoirs in their present form would damage the confidential relationship between ministers and officials. Hankey spent much of 1944 on revisions to accommodate these concerns, and he submitted the whole work that autumn. By then he had secured a publisher—none other than Cassell's, which was just about to secure first refusal on Churchill's future memoirs.[25]

With Bridges obdurate, Hankey wrote directly to Churchill, arguing that his book was about events at least a quarter century old and that much of the decision making had already been revealed in memoirs and biographies. He also reminded Churchill, "I myself had some misgivings about publication of 'The World Crisis' and other memoirs just after the war, but on reflection I came to the conclusion that this consideration was outweighed by their contribution to history. Experience has shown that I was right." Bridges submitted a response, emphasizing the effect of publication on trust between minister and officials, not least his own position, and Churchill sided firmly with him. The three papers from Hankey, Bridges, and Churchill were submitted to the War Cabinet. Because of their sensitivity, they were placed in double boxes (so civil servants could not see them) and were not listed as an item on the Cabinet agenda for

29 January 1945. The drama of the evening was heightened by Bridges himself. Asking (almost uniquely) for permission to speak, he assured the Cabinet with deep emotion that he did not keep a diary and would never do so. According to the brief record of the meeting, "there was unanimous approval that Lord Hankey should not be allowed to publish his diary" (*not* what Hankey had requested), and Bridges was asked to convey the War Cabinet's decision. Given the delicacy of the matter, Bridges was at pains to secure Churchill's endorsement of the letter, while the Prime Minister was equally keen to ensure that it went out over the Cabinet Secretary's signature.[26]

Hankey considered Bridges's case to be "incredibly weak," pinning his argument on Churchill's *World Crisis*. In the chapter about launching the Gallipoli campaign, he claimed to have found twenty-five references to official minutes and documents in the account of just one month. What was the difference between that, he asked, and quoting from a diary? Hankey also cited the preface to volume 2 in which Churchill said it was "absurd to argue that the facts should not be fully published, or that obligations of secrecy are violated by their disclosure in good faith." There was already, said Churchill in 1923, "a whole library" on the Dardanelles campaign, and he had a right to tell his side of the story. After V-E Day, Hankey asked for a meeting with Churchill, only to be told that he was far too busy with the election. The matter was then left to Clement Attlee.[27]

Although more relaxed about ministerial memoirs, Churchill shared Bridges's abhorrence of revelations by civil servants. But what about biographies? Were those about Prime Ministers a special case? In 1944 and 1945, Bridges and Churchill were faced with applications from the authorized biographers of the two previous incumbents, Neville Chamberlain (1937–1940) and Stanley Baldwin (1935–1937). Once again, Cabinet Secretary and Prime Minister sought to apply the 1934 decisions in distinctive and often rival ways. These cases are of added interest because effective biographies of Baldwin or Chamberlain, published right after the war, would have cramped Churchill's style in the first volume of his own memoirs.

Chamberlain lost the premiership in May 1940 and died in November, already stigmatized as one of the "Guilty Men" who had brought Britain to the brink of disaster. His widow, Anne, keen to retrieve his reputation, started seeking a biographer within weeks of Neville's death. She considered several eminent historians, including E. H. Carr, G. M. Young, and Arthur Bryant, before settling in August 1941 on the Oxford don Keith Feiling, who was sympathetic to Munich and had written a history of the Tory party. Feiling was initially hopeful about access to official papers, noting, "Bridges and others are friends."[28] He inquired in

1941, only to be fobbed off, but he returned to the charge in September 1944 when research on Chamberlain's letters and diaries was complete and much of the book was in galleys. Under the 1934 rules, Feiling had good claim to see Cabinet papers as the vindicator of a dead politician's reputation, but he did not know this. Bridges, not mentioning the Vindicator Clause, told him that his request "would be difficult to grant," and Feiling did not push the point. The lack of Cabinet papers impoverished the book and still distressed Anne Chamberlain years later.[29]

Nonuse of government documents did not, however, spare Feiling from official censorship when he sent Bridges the galleys in October 1944. The Cabinet Secretary wanted to delay publication until two to three years after the end of the war. Churchill, asked for permission to quote some of his correspondence with Chamberlain, avoided close involvement. As with Londonderry, there were personal reasons: Feiling had been the Oxford tutor of his son, Randolph, and had also done considerable work for him on *Marlborough* and *The History of the English-Speaking Peoples*. But Churchill did tell Feiling, in a letter dictated while in Moscow in October 1944 that, although happy to permit the quotations, he felt "the end of next year is very early for the publication of a book of this kind." This gave Bridges some license for his stand.[30]

As with the Londonderry case, Bridges's strategy was to turn editing into a weapon of delay. Having taken five months to review the manuscript, the Cabinet Office identified more than one hundred "objectionable" points. The list was "deliberately drawn as widely as possible," noted Sir Gilbert Laithwaite, the undersecretary to whom Bridges had entrusted the task. Even phrases in Chamberlain's diary such as "Chairman of the Cabinet Committee" were queried. (It was not until Margaret Thatcher's premiership that the government officially acknowledged the existence of Cabinet committees.) Bridges also used his other standard delaying tactic: encouraging Whitehall departments to add their own objections. In particular, he invited the Foreign Office to condemn quotations of Chamberlain's abrasive diary comments about foreign governments as "contrary to the public interest." Sir Alexander Cadogan of the Foreign Office did not think Chamberlain's 1938 strictures on Americans and Russians would cause much surprise or harm, but correspondence with him served Bridges's procrastinatory aim. Feiling's sanitized biography finally appeared in December 1946.[31] There was a further parallel with the Londonderry case. "I do not think Bridges is the obstacle," Feiling told Anne Chamberlain, "but probably scruples in some F.O. people." Once again, the official censor had deftly covered his tracks—keeping secrets secretly.[32]

At this time the Cabinet Office also received an application from G. M. Young concerning his biography of Stanley Baldwin. Young and Feiling had both helped Churchill with his books in the 1930s, but otherwise the two cases were very different. Unlike Chamberlain, Baldwin was still alive; unlike Feiling, he had enlisted the support of Churchill. On 7 July 1945, after a direct request from the former Prime Minister, Churchill sent Bridges a firm instruction:

> I see no objection to Mr. G. M. Young having access to papers for the period when Lord Baldwin was Prime Minister, it being understood that quotations should not be made which either (a) affect military or diplomatic interests, or (b) reveal definite conversations in Cabinet. Wide latitude should be given to Mr. Young for the period concerned on behalf of Lord Baldwin and, as long as I am in office, either Mr. Young or Lord Baldwin should correspond with me on any doubtful points.[33]

Bridges did not conceal his irritation but noted, "I should imagine that a workable arrangement can be made which is consistent with the Prime Minister's intentions and also with the procedure laid down." When Bridges and Laithwaite saw Young in August 1945, they said they were "anxious not to give Mr. Feiling the impression that different standards were being adopted" in the two cases. Bridges's private self-defense was that "Feiling had not asked to see Cabinet records or papers." This was true only in the strict sense that he did not ask formally in writing.[34]

Why was Churchill so solicitous of Baldwin? In private, he could be quite vituperative, commenting in the summer of 1947, "I wish Stanley Baldwin no ill, but it would have been much better if he had never lived." Even in 1961, he still took the view that "Baldwin had been a poor leader. Chamberlain had been better than Baldwin, in fact quite good."[35] But in July 1945, Churchill's personal opinion of Baldwin was secondary to other considerations. The war in Europe was over, and he had signed his agreements with Korda and Cassell's. A set of war memoirs was, at the very least, a distinct possibility. In that case, it would surely be useful to Churchill to have established a precedent for a historian to act as proxy for an ex–Prime Minister, examining official records on his behalf. As with *The World Crisis*, Churchill intended to be his own historian but not his own researcher. The precedent he set as premier helped smooth his work as author.

WHAT, THEN, was Churchill's position in the paper chase when suddenly evicted from 10 Downing Street in 1945? Because of the new rules, there was no longer any question, as in 1922 or 1929, of walking off with complete sets of Cabinet conclusions. But, as permitted under the provisions of his own note, WP 320, he took a mass of "personal" minutes and telegrams, mostly in the form of the monthly prints produced during the war.[36] Initially dumped in the library at Chartwell, they eventually became part of the "Chartwell" papers at Churchill College, Cambridge. What Churchill called his "working files"—more than six hundred bulky folders accumulated by the Prime Minister's office and later known to researchers in the National Archives as the "Premier" files—were left in the basement of the Cabinet Office. Under WP 320, Churchill had right of access to these and, thanks to his 7 July minute about Baldwin's biography, he had set the precedent for his researchers to see them as well. Thus, Churchill had a substantial amount of papers to hand, but almost all of them were his own writings. The answers he received and the records of Cabinet debates were accessible but not in his possession, and this decisively shaped the kind of book he could write.

Custody of papers was one side of the coin, but quotation from them was a separate issue on which the case law had been accumulating during the war. Churchill espoused secrecy in wartime but much greater openness after hostilities ceased. He took a tough line on books by civil servants but was more indulgent about those by or about ministers, especially Prime Ministers. And, as the Chamberlain and Baldwin cases show, he regarded the living and the dead as separate categories. All this ensured a privileged position for himself, should he choose to write anything after the war. But WP 320 reiterated the principle that any work using official documents should be submitted to the government before publication. Churchill had won the battle of the papers, but the battle of the books had not yet begun.

CHAPTER 4

REPUTATION | *Churchill Against Mortality*

O N 12 NOVEMBER 1940, Churchill delivered perhaps the most moving speech of his long career. Rarely recalled in comparison with his pugnacious war oratory, it was a tribute in the Commons to Neville Chamberlain, who had died three days before, after a grisly battle with cancer. Rarely had a man's reputation been so dramatically transformed: lauded as peacemaker by delirious crowds on his return from Munich in September 1938, Chamberlain was now reviled as an architect of appeasement. Churchill reminded a packed, hushed House of the vicissitudes of fame.

> It is not given to human beings, happily for them, for otherwise life would be intolerable, to foresee or to predict to any large extent the unfolding course of events. In one phase men seem to have been right, in another they seem to have been wrong. Then again, a few years later, when the perspective of time has lengthened, all stands in a different setting. There is a new proportion. There is another scale of values. History with its flickering lamp stumbles along the trail of the past, trying to reconstruct its scenes, to revive its echoes, and kindle with pale gleams the passions of former days.[1]

CHURCHILL SPOKE FROM THE HEART, for his own reputation had bobbed up and down on the tides of fortune. A good statement of how he was seen in the interwar years may be found in volume 3 of Lloyd George's memoirs, published in 1934. Lloyd George devoted more than five pages to "one of the most remarkable and puzzling enigmas" of the era. His peg was the "insensate fury" of the Tories when he tried to include Churchill in his 1916 coalition. To the question "Is he more dangerous when he is FOR you than when he is AGAINST you?" Andrew Bonar Law, the Tory leader, had replied: "I would rather have him against us every time." Having defected from the Tories in 1904, Churchill compounded his treachery by attacking his old party "with a vigour and witty scorn which rankled." This, asserted Lloyd George, was why the Tories were so determined in 1915 to make him the prime scapegoat for Gallipoli. But the objections went deeper still. Critics acknowledged Churchill's "dazzling talents," his energy, his courage, and his industry. "His mind was a powerful machine," but within it lay "some tragic flaw in the metal . . . some obscure defect which prevented it from always running true." When the mechanism did go wrong, such was its power that it went disastrously off the rails, together with all those who were coupled to him. Churchill was a man of "genius," said Lloyd George. Such vision and imagination were very rare and "in an emergency" should be "utilised to the full," albeit under "a vigilant eye." But Churchill's future would depend on whether he could establish "a reputation for prudence without losing audacity."[2]

Lloyd George's appraisal was by no means unusual. Both Baldwin and Chamberlain kept Churchill out of office in the 1930s for similar reasons. In May 1936, Baldwin joked privately that, at birth, a host of fairies showered upon Churchill's cradle a multitude of gifts—"imagination, eloquence, industry," and so on. Then one fairy said that no person had a right to so many gifts and gave him such a shake that he was denied "judgement and wisdom." In July 1939, Chamberlain cited Churchill's "ability" and his "notorious" lack of judgment. He recalled the Baldwin Cabinet of 1924–1929 when "Winston's ideas and memoranda tended to monopolise the time of the whole Ministry," causing major rows, and the way Churchill flitted from one idea to another every week.[3]

But, one might respond, all this was before 1940. Surely Churchill's "finest hour" drew a veil over what came before? Yes and no. The successive defeats of 1941 and 1942 saw sustained if muffled criticism about "midnight follies" and "cigar-stump diplomacy." In the months from D-Day to V-E Day, Churchill was again on a high, but then came Black Thursday, 26 July. "I won the race—and now they have warned me off the turf," he told his staff that evening.[4] It was hard not to take such a crushing defeat as a personal indictment, and Churchill was driven anew to ponder the vicissitudes of reputation.

In early 1946, his doctor, Lord Moran, mused on Churchill's state of mind: "It seemed to him that all his actions had been called in question. His record in the war was submitted to the nation, and it had not given its approval. He confessed to me that the size of the Labour majority made him rather ashamed." For five years, Churchill told Moran, he had "enjoyed the trust and affection of the whole country." Then, in a night, that confidence had been withdrawn. "Why had they deserted him in the hour of victory?" Had he, perhaps, been "a little too confident about the verdict of history?"[5] The verdict of history was the subject of one of Churchill's favorite aphorisms. "History will say," declared Churchill in an exchange with Baldwin in the Commons in the 1930s, "that the Right Honourable Gentleman was wrong in this matter." Pause. Broad grin. "I know it will, because I shall write that history." He adopted a similar line to Stalin in January 1944, after a vigorous exchange of telegrams about whether Britain could have secured a separate peace in 1940. "I agree that we had better leave the past to history," he wrote in a draft reply, "but remember if I live long enough I may be one of the historians."[6] Churchill's sense of the fickleness of fame—expressed in his tribute to Chamberlain and revived by the events of July 1945—impelled him to be his own historian.

Yet the election defeat of 1945 also pushed him to stay in politics. Being Britain's war leader was not enough: "I wanted—I wanted to do the Peace too," he murmured to one of his secretaries in August 1945.[7] Even deeper, one may surmise, was a search for vindication. Churchill had never been elected Prime Minister, having been catapulted to the top by a sudden Commons revolt in May 1940, and when he submitted himself to the electorate in July 1945 he was rudely rebuffed. A sense of unfinished business made him reluctant to abandon his political career.

Thus, the search for vindication drove him in two potentially incompatible directions: to write his war memoirs and to continue as Leader of the Opposition. It did so, moreover, at a time when he was conscious of failing powers. Five exhausting years in office, followed by a shattering defeat, left him often low and despondent in the autumn of 1945. He had always been obsessed with the brevity of life—his father had died at forty-five—and this had been a powerful reason for acting like a young man in a hurry. By 1945, he had reached his three score years and ten. How much longer could he expect? Was it possible to play a dual role as historian and politician, as he had in his prime in the 1920s? In Churchill's philosophy there was no afterlife, just "black velvet"—eternal sleep.[8] Immortality existed only in the mind of posterity. So reputation was the last battle, and the most important, of life's unending war. When Churchill left for America on 9 January 1946, he had still not decided how to wage it, but he had closed off no options, as historian or as politician. His time in the United States helped make up his mind on both counts.

—

IN BRITAIN, inside accounts of the war were being carefully controlled. Bridges and the Cabinet Office ensured that documents were restricted and memoirs vetted; Attlee had firmly rejected postmortems into wartime disasters such as Singapore. The situation was very different in America, however, where a congressional investigation into Pearl Harbor was already under way. In Washington, there was no Privy Councillors Oath, no Official Secrets Act, no career civil service managing the machinery of government. Outsiders came and went as department heads and senior bureaucrats, with minimal sense of collective responsibility, and the freedom of the press, enshrined in the First Amendment to the Constitution, made it very difficult to prosecute on grounds of libel or official secrecy. Thus, it was from America that the most serious attacks on Churchill's reputation would come. This became clear when Harry Butcher published *My Three Years with Eisenhower*.

Butcher was a former CBS executive who had served as Eisenhower's aide and PR man throughout his time in North Africa and Europe. His diary was a personal record of events and meetings, interleaved with key documents, including messages from Churchill. For publication, Butcher cut it to about two thirds of the original one million words, but it was still full of gossip and controversy. The book revealed the bitter Anglo-American strategic arguments about invading northern France in 1942 and southern France in 1944. In August 1944, for instance, Butcher depicted Churchill with tears rolling down his cheeks as he complained of American "bullying" and even threatened that he might have to go to the King and "lay down the mantle of my high office." The tone was certainly not reverential. After Eisenhower dined with Churchill in August 1942, he told his staff stories of the Prime Minister slurping his soup, nose in plate, "to the accompaniment of loud gurglings," and of how he unself-consciously called for a change of socks in the middle of the evening. At one point, according to Butcher, Churchill walked to an open door, rubbed his shoulder blades vigorously against the frame, and said, "Guess I picked 'em up in Egypt."[9]

Butcher claimed that "General Ike" asked him to keep the diary. But as Butcher rushed into a book contract as soon as he was back stateside in the summer of 1945, Eisenhower tried to distance himself from the project. The general was already being hailed as a future President, and any book about him was hot property. On 18 December 1945, just as serialization commenced in *The Saturday Evening Post*, Ike wrote an anxious letter assuring Churchill that "publication of all of this stuff is as much of an astonishment to me as it can be to anyone else." He hoped that his "host of warm friends" in Britain would "not for a single instant believe that I could be party to anything that would in any sense disturb the valued personal and official friendships I made in Great Britain." By the time Churchill arrived in America, serialization was well advanced. Having "skimmed over" the articles, he told Eisenhower on 26 January 1946, "I must say I think you have been ill-used by your confidential aide. The articles are, in my opinion, altogether below the level upon which such matters should be treated. Great events and personalities are all made small when passed through the medium of this small mind."[10]

Churchill was clearly irked by *My Three Years with Eisenhower*. Serialization occupied ten weekly issues of *The Saturday Evening Post* and therefore spanned most of his visit to America. There was further press comment when the book itself appeared in April. The reviewer in the *Chicago Tribune*, true to the paper's anti-British tone, featured the transatlantic strategic arguments and quoted Eisenhower's remark in July 1942 that there were "only two professions in the world in which the amateur excels the professional. One, military strategy and, two, prostitution." Quentin Reynolds, the former London war correspondent, said that Butcher wasn't antagonistic to Churchill: "he just saw him as he was, which was not quite as the world saw him." *The Milwaukee Journal* led with Churchill's comment on 31 May 1943 that a diary simply reflected a writer's changes of opinion and made him look indecisive or foolish when published. "For his part, the Prime Minister said, he would much prefer to wait until the war is over and then write impressions, so that, if necessary he could correct or bury his mistakes." The reviewer added that this "would not be any news" to readers of Churchill's memoirs of World War I, in which he "never made a mistake." But Butcher's diary was going to make it difficult for Churchill to be "so facile in glossing over his World War II proposals."[11]

Butcher's Churchill was rather entertaining but, in another memoir published in April 1946, he emerged as a much more sinister figure. Ralph Ingersoll, publisher of *Time* magazine in the late 1930s, had served from 1943 to 1945 as an Allied staff officer for D-Day and northwest Europe, including a spell at Montgomery's headquarters. *Top Secret* was a searing indictment of those campaigns, especially what he saw as British perversion of Allied strategy for its own imperial ends. Much of his venom was reserved for Montgomery—"a boor" and "a very bad general"—but Churchill was the butt of repeated attacks for trying to divert the Allies into the Balkans: "the magnet" of British strategy. Ingersoll quoted Harry Hopkins as saying that George C. Marshall was "the only general in the world whom Churchill is afraid of" because Marshall was immune to Churchillian oratory. He also opined that Eisenhower was chosen as Supreme Commander because the British expected him to be "neither bold nor decisive, and to be neither a leader nor a general." Despite British machinations, Ingersoll argued, the Americans had managed to win the war their own way. But he warned his countrymen to adopt a much more self-interested attitude in the future, otherwise the British would drag them into another struggle for the Balkans, this time against Russia. He dismissed as "dangerous nonsense" claims that the Russians had "aggressive ambitions" and warned that an Anglo-Soviet conflict could escalate into "World War III."[12]

Ingersoll helped establish the persistent image of the sincere but naïve Americans, intent on the quickest possible military victory, and the devious British, "using every means at their disposal" to get their way. The claim that Churchill had a consistent, ruthless Mediterranean strategy, focused on the Balkans, was a charge that preoccupied him when writing his war memoirs. Equally important from the perspective of British officials was Ingersoll's cavalier attitude toward confidentiality. His acknowledgments began with the sentence "I never could unscramble my sources of information for this book." To "the best of my knowledge," he added, "what I used in this book does not violate the security of information permanently 'classified.'" None of the generals under whom he served had been "burdened with seeing the manuscript before publication." Here was a classic example of what Jock Colville called the Americans' "well-known disregard of official secrets."[13]

By the spring of 1946, therefore, Churchill could be under no illusions about what might happen if he left his reputation to "history" without being one of the historians. In a letter to Attlee in May 1946, he referred explicitly to the books by Butcher and Ingersoll: they were "very offensive and disparaging to this country and to my own personal conduct of the war" and contained much that was "quite untrue and in some cases malicious." By the time this letter was written, Churchill had already decided to write his memoirs. But one other factor helped make up his mind. In Britain, he had been sobered and silenced by electoral defeat; in America, he found his voice again as a politician and statesman.[14]

THE PRIME REASON for his American trip was vacation. Still not recovered from the strains of the premiership and the shock of the election, Churchill gladly accepted the chance to stay at the Miami home of a Canadian admirer, Frank Clarke. The prospect of sun, painting, and lavish hospitality was delightful. A vacation in Florida, justified on medical grounds, would also put some distance between himself and Tory critics. He told Moran: "There are a lot of flies buzzing around this old decaying carcass. I want something to keep them away." And Churchill yearned for more than winter sun. Whereas in Britain he was "a controversial figure," in America "they will take things from me. . . . It may be that Congress will ask me to address them. I'd like that."[15]

The seed for a big speech had been sown in the autumn. On 3 October, Dr. Franc L. McCluer, the President of Westminster College in Fulton, Missouri, invited Churchill to give the annual Green Foundation lectures, usually a series of three or four addresses. Westminster was a small Presbyterian college in the rural Midwest. Normally, such a letter would have received a polite refusal from Churchill's secretaries, but on the bottom was a postscript: "This is a wonderful school in my home state. Hope you can do it. I'll introduce you. Best regards— Harry S. Truman." McCluer had secured Truman's involvement via the President's military aide, General Harry H. Vaughan, a Westminster alumnus. It was the presidential postscript that made all the difference to Churchill. He told Truman that a full lecture series was out of the question, but "if you, as you suggest in your postscript, would like me to visit your home State and would introduce me, I should feel it my duty—and it would also be a great pleasure—to deliver an Address to the Westminster University [sic] on the world situation, under your aegis. This might possibly be advantageous from several points of view." He added that it was the only public-speaking engagement he had in mind; "the explanation for it would be my respect for you and your wishes."[16]

In due course, Churchill arranged several other lectures, but Fulton was always given special significance. "Under your auspices anything I say will command some attention," he wrote Truman on 29 January, "and there is an opportunity for doing something good to this bewildered, baffled and breathless world." The combination of Churchill and Truman at Fulton ensured that on 5 March 1946 this tiny college town (population 8,000, average student class of 350) was overrun by the international media, and Churchill's words were broadcast across America and the world. Afterward, Churchill told McCluer he hoped he had "started some thinking that would make history." On the train back to Washington, he said to Frank Clarke that Fulton had been "the most important speech" of his career.[17]

Churchill's message may be summed up in four sound bites.[18] The best known is the phrase "iron curtain." This term dates back at least to the First World War, but it was revived by Nazi propagandists in the dying days of the Third Reich and reported in the British press. Churchill used it privately on several occasions in May 1945 (see below, chapter 30) and publicly in the Commons in August 1945: "it is not impossible that tragedy on a prodigious scale is unfolding itself behind the iron curtain which at the moment divides Europe in twain."[19] But it was not until Fulton that the phrase hit the headlines: "From Stettin in the

Baltic to Trieste in the Adriatic, an iron curtain has descended across the Continent." East of that line, in "the Soviet sphere," Communist parties were "seeking everywhere to obtain totalitarian control," and, except in Czechoslovakia, "there is no true democracy."

Churchill also warned his audience that problems with the Soviet Union would not be removed "by a policy of appeasement." In retrospect, the so-called lessons of appeasement are a familiar feature of post-1945 diplomatic rhetoric in the West, from Korea to Vietnam, from Suez to Iraq. But Fulton was probably the first time that Churchill or any notable British public figure had used the term "appeasement" so deliberately in public about the Soviet Union.[20] It complemented his tendency in the speech to equate communism and fascism, for instance as he warned of a third world war if his advice was not heeded: "Last time I saw it all coming and cried aloud to my own fellow-countrymen and to the world, but no one paid any attention." And so, he said, "one by one we were all sucked into the awful whirlpool. We surely must not let that happen again."

Churchill's third theme was the need for "the fraternal association of the English-speaking peoples" based on "a special relationship between the British Commonwealth and Empire and the United States." He wanted to continue wartime arrangements such as close military consultation and shared bases. In time, Churchill even envisaged common citizenship. These ideas were not novel. At Harvard in September 1943, he had spoken about such a "fraternal association," and he also delivered a long speech on this theme to the Commons in November 1945.[21] But, as with the phrase "iron curtain," it took the remarkable circumstances of Fulton to bring the "special relationship" to the attention of America and the world. From there, it passed into the lexicon of international politics.

Churchill's thesis about Anglo-American relations was the most contentious part of his speech. In the first few days, it provoked strenuous criticism from liberals such as Eleanor Roosevelt on the grounds that Churchill was calling for a transatlantic military alliance that would break up the United Nations. This helped distract attention from Churchill's fourth main sound bite. Although Fulton is now generally known as "the iron-curtain speech," that was not Churchill's title, which was "The Sinews of Peace."

What did Churchill mean by this variant on the old adage that money is the sinews of war? Essentially he was saying that Anglo-American unity constituted the precondition of peace. He dismissed talk of inevitable military conflict, asserting of the Russians that "there is nothing they admire more than strength, and nothing for which they have less respect than weakness, especially military weakness." When he talked of a margin of strength going beyond the balance of power, he was moving toward a concept of containment. But he did not use such a word, because it would have been too static: Churchill wanted to transcend the deadlock, not entrench it. He urged negotiation from a position of strength— provided by the "special relationship"—as the only way to prevent another war. What was needed was "a good understanding on all points with Russia" under the authority of the United Nations and backed by "the whole strength of the English-speaking world." This, said Churchill, in a sentence added on the train en route to Fulton, was "the solution which I respectfully offer to you in this Address to which I have given the title 'The Sinews of Peace.'"

Of the four sound bites, the one about the special relationship was "the crux of what I have travelled here to say." Three weeks before, he had visited Washington to discuss the speech with President Truman and Secretary of State James Byrnes. Afterward, he told Attlee that the speech would be "in the same direction as the one I made at Harvard two years ago, namely fraternal association in the build-up and maintenance of U.N.O., and inter-mingling of necessary arrangements for mutual safety in case of danger, in full loyalty to the Charter. I tried this on both the President and Byrnes, who seemed to like it very well." The most pressing international issue for Britain at the time was not the Cold War but whether the U.S. Congress would approve a massive postwar loan to save the country from bankruptcy. Byrnes flew down to Florida specially for a meeting with Churchill about this. Churchill was also conscious that Britain had now been cut out of the atomic-bomb partnership and that the Combined Chiefs of Staff were withering away.[22]

The structure of Churchill's address confirms that its prime focus was the special relationship. He spoke first of "the two great dangers which menace the homes of the people, War and Tyranny." He argued that war could not be prevented or the UN made to work effectively without a special relationship. Only then did he introduce the "iron curtain" theme, to justify his contention that "time may be short" and that the "fraternal association" should be formed soon. The alternative was to learn these lessons yet again "for a third time in a school of war." Rather than proposing an Anglo-American axis to wage the Cold War, Churchill was invoking the threat of World War III to justify a special relationship.

Why, then, has the Fulton speech been understood as the clarion call to Cold War? Churchill himself was partly to blame. For a man so attuned to words, he was surprisingly indecisive about titles. His speech was originally billed as being simply about world affairs. By mid-February 1946, President McCluer was getting anxious. Churchill replied that he had still not made up his mind but that the speech would probably be called "World Peace." Only the day before Churchill spoke was the title changed to "The Sinews of Peace." Many of the advance texts for the press did not use this title, and that affected the balance of some reporting.[23]

Context mattered even more than content. By the time Churchill spoke, the Soviets and Americans were facing off at the UN about the Red Army's failure to withdraw, as agreed, from northern Iran. His comments on Russia were therefore likely to hit the headlines, particularly when packaged in such a compelling phrase. What's more, Moscow unleashed a massive counterattack on Churchill. A three-column front-page editorial in the party newspaper, *Pravda*, on 11 March was followed the next day by a lengthy article in the government paper, *Izvestia*. On 13 March, most remarkably, *Pravda* printed a question-and-answer session with Stalin himself about Churchill's speech. The drama of the moment is conveyed by some of *The New York Times*'s banner headlines on Thursday, 14 March:

STALIN SAYS CHURCHILL STIRS WAR AND FLOUTS ANGLO-RUSSIAN PACT;

SOVIET TANKS APPROACH TEHERAN

SEES RACE THEORY

Russian Leader Likens Churchill to Hitler for Plea to U.S.

SAYS SOVIETS CAN WIN WAR

The full text of the interview, printed on page 4 of *The New York Times*, amplified these points. Stalin castigated the Fulton speech as "a call to war with the Soviet Union." Churchill was arguing that the English-speaking peoples, "being the only valuable nations, should rule over the remaining nations of the world." This was a "racial theory" based on language — "one is reminded remarkably of Hitler and his friends." Historian William Taubman has speculated that Stalin's apparently emotional denunciation of Churchill was carefully calculated: "By exaggerating Churchill's warnings, by treating them as a fully-fledged 'call to war,' he would alarm the Western masses while mobilizing the Soviet people." Whatever the motives, Stalin's response as much as Churchill's words ensured that the Fulton speech went down as one of the opening salvos in the Cold War.[24]

What's more, the delicacy of the Iran crisis and the vehement Soviet reaction prompted the British and American governments to dissociate themselves from the Fulton speech. On 11 March, two Labour MPs put down a Commons motion asking Attlee to repudiate Churchill's tone and content. This was signed by more than one hundred others, including a future Prime Minister, James Callaghan. Attlee declined to comment, stating that Churchill had spoken "in an individual capacity" in a foreign country. What Churchill said was, however, broadly in line with official policy, and Attlee, given the gist of Churchill's argument in advance, had told him, "I am sure your Fulton speech will do good."[25]

The Truman administration had been consulted much more closely. Not only did Churchill discuss the speech with the President for ninety minutes on 10 February, he also solicited comment on the almost final text from Admiral William D. Leahy, the White House Chief of Staff. "I can find no fault in his proposed address to the people of America," Leahy wrote in his diary. Truman read a copy during their train journey from Washington to Fulton. According to Churchill, the President "told me he thought it was admirable and would do nothing but good, though it would make a stir. He seemed equally pleased during and after." Given all this consultation, historian Fraser Harbutt has argued that the Truman administration used the Fulton speech as the centerpiece of its new campaign to shift public opinion behind a posture of confrontation toward the Soviet Union. It was the anti-Soviet thrust of Churchill's remarks more than their Anglo-American theme that attracted the budding Cold Warriors in Washington. But given the intensity of comment in both the United States and the Soviet Union, the Truman administration, like the Attlee government, found it prudent to distance itself from Churchill.[26]

As Fulton moved rapidly from notoriety to celebrity—a visionary warning rather than a reckless polemic—Churchill gained sole credit for a speech that British and American leaders had been happy to facilitate. Stalin's vituperation did not upset Churchill—on the contrary. Words deleted at the last minute from his speech in New York on 15 March betray his satisfaction:

> It is extraordinary that the head of a mighty, victorious government should descend from his august seat of power to enter into personal controversy with a man who has no official position of any kind and had been particularly careful to say that he spoke without the authority of any government. I shall not let the implied compliment turn my head. Nor am I dismayed by harsh words, even from the most powerful of dictators. Indeed I had years of it from Hitler and managed to get along all right.[27]

The Fulton speech also ruffled feathers among his Tory colleagues, who had not been consulted in advance. Anthony Eden, his professional heir apparent and the party's foreign-affairs spokesman, was severely embarrassed. Not only was he still taking a more conciliatory line in public toward the Soviet Union, but he had, that very day in the Commons, denied the claim by a Labour MP that his party leader was about to make "a sensational speech in America" putting Russia "on the spot." Eden responded: "I certainly have not heard anything of the kind from my right hon. Friend and, may I add, I do not believe it for one single moment." Lord Salisbury, the Tory elder statesman, feared that Fulton could wreck Britain's bipartisan policy of firmness toward Russia by persuading Labour left-wingers that it was really "the policy of the Right." Salisbury believed that the speech strengthened the case for Churchill retiring from the Tory leadership: that way "he could say what he liked, without associating the party with it." Eden also entertained hopes that Churchill would "now be less anxious to lead" and would "want to pursue an anti-Russian crusade, independent of us."[28]

Churchill's long absence from Westminster and his dramatic unilateral speech brought Tory doubts about his leadership to the surface. On 15 March, *The Evening News* carried an article headlined CHURCHILL WILL 'HAND OVER' SOON. Clearly inspired by party critics, this piece claimed that Tory MPs expected him to call a meeting of the Shadow Cabinet "before too long" and announce his desire to retire. It was known, the paper added, that he wanted more time to write his war memoirs. But there was no consensus on an alternative leader: Eden, Harold Macmillan, and R. A. Butler all had their backers. According to *The Star*'s political correspondent, "this rivalry for the succession is a reason Mr. Churchill can use for his remaining at the top." And Churchill firmly quashed such speculation in a statement from New York: "I have no intention whatsoever of ceasing to lead the Conservative Party until I am satisfied that they can see their way clear ahead and make better arrangements."[29]

Churchill sailed home from New York on 20 March 1946. Vacation had turned into resurrection. At the end of January, his secret-session speeches had been published, arousing controversy but also reminding the English-speaking world of his stature as a war leader. At the beginning of March, he had hit the headlines even more emphatically as a prophet of Cold War, using language that evoked his thirties battle against appeasement. The President of the United States had sat beside him as he spoke; the leader of the Soviet Union had blasted him for what he said. This was heady stuff. Buoyed by his new celebrity status, Churchill had also hardened his mind against political retirement.

During a low in the 1945 election campaign, Churchill had told his doctor sadly, "I have no message for them now." After the defeat, President Truman could only wish him "the happiest possible existence from now to the last call." But by the spring of 1946 Churchill had found a new voice—indeed, a new life. Rejected as a national leader, he was once more a world statesman.[30]

CHAPTER 5

TAKING THE PLUNGE

T HE QUEEN MARY DOCKED at Southampton on 26 March 1946. Such was the media interest that Churchill held an impromptu press conference in the ship's gymnasium. Asked about his war memoirs, he said he was not writing them at the moment, adding: "I think on the whole it is more likely that I shall not publish anything while I am alive." When the reporters looked surprised, he smiled and said: "But you must not take that as a final decision."

Pressed further, he denied receiving any offers from American publishers, whereupon his wife nudged him and said, "Yes, you have had one or two."

Churchill grunted, "Before I left." It was unclear whether he meant before leaving America in March or Britain the previous December.[1]

Despite his disclaimers, Churchill was ready to take the plunge. On contracts, papers, and reputation, he could now see the way ahead. Over the next few months, he made the critical decisions that paved the way for *The Second World War*.

CHURCHILL'S NEW MOOD was immediately apparent. On 29 March, he lunched with Bill Deakin, his prewar research assistant, now back at Oxford after a distinguished Balkan war. Churchill "said he was going to write his war memoirs," Deakin later recalled; "would I deal with the political and military side?" He agreed to start at the end of the year. On the evening of 2 April, Churchill saw Anthony Moir, his solicitor, who had been investigating the tax problem. The next day, he met with Desmond Flower of Cassell's, who had first refusal on the war memoirs, and on the fourth General Hastings Ismay, still Military Secretary to the Cabinet, as he had been during Churchill's premiership. Among the topics they discussed was additional research assistance for the memoirs.[2]

Action, therefore, on all fronts—but the most pressing matter was the tax aspect. Having evaluated various schemes, the barrister Leslie Graham-Dixon advised Churchill to give his papers to a special trust, which should be created before Churchill resumed professional activity as an author to avoid the papers losing their status as capital assets. The trustees could then sell the papers to a publisher, without liability for tax. The publisher in turn would engage Churchill to write a book. This contract would be liable for income tax, but the fee paid would be deliberately small, in contrast with the sale of the papers by the trust. Provided this strict sequence was observed, Graham-Dixon believed the papers could be sold without incurring tax.[3]

On 11 April 1946, Churchill sent Moir a memorandum indicating the papers at Chartwell that should constitute the trust. He divided them into four parts, of which the second comprised records of "the Second Great War" from "about 1934" until July 1945. Why Churchill drew a line "about 1934" is not clear. He may have envisaged this as the starting point for his memoirs, or he may have recalled the Cabinet Office circular of September 1934, which heralded the new, tougher policy about official papers. What should be noted—though nobody did at the time—is that Churchill made no reference to the 1940–1945 papers of the Prime Minister's office, which had been moved for safekeeping to the basement of the Cabinet Office. Only in 1952 did Anthony Moir learn of their existence, but it was then too late to include what became known as the "Premier" files within the trust, and they were deposited in the Public Record Office. This, as we shall see, had considerable significance for Churchill's memoirs and for future historians.[4]

The Literary Trust was established on 31 July 1946. To it, Churchill assigned all the papers listed and "all his interest therein." The trustees were Clementine Churchill, Brendan Bracken, and another close friend of Churchill, the Oxford scientist Lord Cherwell. They could dispose of the papers and give the income at their discretion to Churchill's children and spouses, though not to Winston or Clementine. But until 1 August 1951, all or part of the income could be accumulated, because the trust would be liable for estate tax if Churchill died during its first five years. Clause 11 prohibited the trustees from making public any documents relating to the British government or its ministries since 1900 without the permission of the Prime Minister of the day. This embodied Churchill's express wishes and was the basis of the case he had been arguing for years with the Cabinet Office: these are "my papers," but you can approve publication. The settlement also left him with important veto powers, for instance over the sale or publication of any papers and the appointment of new trustees. In a separate memorandum dated 31 July, he expressed a clear preference that either Randolph or the latter's son, Winston, should write an official biography (as he had for his own father) and that the papers should remain at Chartwell before ultimately being deeded to the National Trust.[5]

Churchill therefore retained considerable authority over "his" papers, but the Literary Trust was sufficient for its purpose—namely, to separate ownership of the documents from authorship of the book. Once legally "paperless," Churchill moved quickly to the next stage of Graham-Dixon's strict sequence. On 4 August, only four days later, he wrote to Lord Camrose reminding him of Cassell's right of first refusal. Cassell's was willing to relinquish that right to Camrose (on the understanding that they would remain the British book publishers), and Churchill indicated that this was what he now desired.[6] Camrose, in effect, became Churchill's unpaid literary agent (on the understanding that the *Daily Telegraph* would have the British serial rights), entrusted with the task of selling the remaining rights to the highest bidder, as he had done for Lloyd George in 1922. Camrose now prepared for an autumn visit to New York to conduct a literary auction.

MEANWHILE, CHURCHILL had resumed his political duties, but on his terms. As soon as he returned from America, he asked Eden to take over the tedious daily business of leading the Opposition in the House of Commons, while Churchill remained the Leader of the Party. He would concentrate on campaigning against the communist threat and, as in the early 1930s, against abandoning India. Churchill said he intended to carry on leading the party "for a year or two." Eden tried to insist there was no room for a "Deputy Leader of the Opposition in the House"—the leader had to be present on a daily basis—but eventually agreed to substitute when necessary for Churchill in the Commons and as chairman of party committees. As an Eden biographer has observed, Churchill's exchanges with Eden "showed how completely he still dominated their relationship."[7]

Tory MPs continued to grumble in private: Churchill prevented the party from developing fresh policies; he seemed mainly concerned to score debating points off the government in "crotchety" exchanges; he might go overboard (as in the early 1920s) about "the bolshevik bogey."[8] But R. A. Butler noted at the end of the Parliamentary session in August 1946, "It is with politics as with the wolf pack, the strongest wolf will retain his lead if his fangs are still firmly bedded in his jaw. It has become clear after endless armchair exchanges that Churchill is fitter than for many years and is prepared to fight." Others also caught the new mood. "A short time ago I was ready to retire and die gracefully," Churchill told Moran on 27 June. "Now I'm going to stay and have them out"—referring to the Labour government. "I'll tear their bleeding entrails out of them." Bracken told Beaverbrook in October: "Winston is in very good fettle and is determined to continue to lead the Tory Party until he becomes Prime Minister on earth or Minister of Defence in Heaven."⁹

During 1946, therefore, Churchill consolidated his political position, while ensuring (thanks to Eden's tractability) that politics would not impede writing. He also boosted his stature as an international statesman. Fulton had echoed around the world, and while most politicians would be grateful for one such address in a lifetime Churchill produced a second in the same year when he spoke at the University of Zurich on 19 September 1946 about "The Tragedy of Europe." Instead of "ruin" and "enslavement" by warring nationalisms, he proposed "a kind of United States of Europe," for which the first step "must be a partnership between France and Germany." Churchill made clear that Britain should be a "sponsor," not a direct participant, and he did not offer a detailed blueprint. What attracted international attention, as at Fulton, were the slogans: "United States of Europe" and "Council of Europe." The Zurich speech, said *The Times* next day, showed once again that Churchill was "not afraid to startle the world with new and even, as many must find them, outrageous propositions." Churchill became a patron of the burgeoning European movement.¹⁰

The battle for reputation was never ending, however. While Churchill was carving out a new future, others were chipping away at his past. In October 1946, Elliott Roosevelt, one of the President's sons, brought out a sensational memoir about the war, serialized in *Look*. His criticisms of Churchill paralleled those of Ralph Ingersoll earlier in the year but with a headline-catching twist: purportedly "verbatim" quotations from Franklin about Winston, from the Atlantic conference in August 1941, for instance: "A real old Tory, of the old school" with his "eighteenth-century methods" of running the empire. Or this, supposedly from Roosevelt at Teheran in 1943: "If there's one American general that Winston can't abide, it's General Marshall. And needless to say, it's because Marshall's right." In his own voice, Elliott Roosevelt denounced Churchill for fighting "an unceasing battle to avoid a cross-channel invasion into Europe" in 1942–1943 and for trying in 1944–1945 to "shift the weight of the offensive so as to protect British Empire interests in the Balkans and central Europe against his Soviet ally." At Fulton, Churchill's "savage onslaught against the Soviets" launched "a trial balloon for outright war against his former ally." Throughout the book, Elliott presented himself as his father's mouthpiece and as keeper of the flame for the wartime United Nations, the unity of which the President had sought to perpetuate into the peace. The title, significantly, was *As He Saw It*.[11]

The book owed a lot to an unidentified collaborator who tarted up Elliott's draft in the worst journalistic fashion, transforming indirect speech into verbatim quotes. The finished product was deplored by the Roosevelt family: Franklin Jr. told Lord Beaverbrook that Mrs. Roosevelt had not seen the final "hotted up" version when she wrote a laudatory introduction and asked that the family's regrets be passed to Churchill.[12] A close associate of Roosevelt, Supreme Court Justice Felix Frankfurter, stressed "the complete unreliability of this account of the Roosevelt-Churchill relations."[13] All this was in private, however. "Elliott Roosevelt has been writing a foolish book; he attacks me," Churchill told Moran during an August conversation in the studio at Chartwell. He mentioned Elliott's charge about delaying D-Day by two years. "I don't care what he says. He's not much of a fellow." Churchill's gaze was fixed on the canvas; he sounded almost absentminded as he worked away with his brush.[14] But the lofty tone was contrived. Such criticism needled Churchill; he also knew that more was to come.

Harry Hopkins, Roosevelt's *real* wartime confidant, had planned one book on the war and another "on Roosevelt as I knew him" but not a word was written by the time he died in January 1946. His widow turned to Robert E. Sherwood, a bestselling playwright and author and also a wartime White House speechwriter. Hopkins had served as go-between for Roosevelt and Churchill, and his papers contained masses of material from and about the Prime Minister. In June 1946, Sherwood spent the summer in England conducting an extensive series of interviews. Beaverbrook, Ismay, and Eden were all obliging, and eventually Churchill consented to respond to a list of thirty-two lengthy questions. His typed answers, phrased in the third person as "Mr. Churchill's impression," were mostly brief. Some questions, such as one concerning Anglo-American relations over the atomic-bomb project, provoked a "No Comment." Occasionally Churchill was forthright—a cross-Channel attack "could not have been achieved on a great scale before 1944"—but most of his replies were guarded, and he asked Sherwood "to let me see what use you think it necessary to make of them in your book about Harry." Churchill could have been left in no doubt that a much more substantial insider account than Elliott Roosevelt's was on the way, with himself at its center.[15]

Sherwood was persuasive and persistent, but what really opened doors for him was a letter of endorsement from Truman, which Sherwood copied and enclosed with his requests for assistance. In this, the President expressed "peculiar satisfaction" that Sherwood was writing a book about "that valiant servant of the public," Harry Hopkins. "If I can be of any assistance please do not hesitate to call upon me. I hope also that you will receive the fullest cooperation of all whom you approach in the performance of this great trust." In January 1948, Sherwood told the President's secretary that Truman's "most generous letter" in 1946 had been "of incalculable value" in helping him obtain information for *Roosevelt and Hopkins*.[16] Not least, one may surmise, at Chartwell, only a few months after Fulton. Otherwise Sherwood would probably have received the same brush-off as the young historian Forrest Pogue, who was working on the official U.S. military history of the campaign in Europe in 1944–1945. Despite introductions from Ismay and Eisenhower, Pogue's questionnaire in January 1947 went unanswered. Churchill told Ike, "It would be difficult for me to answer the questions Dr. Pogue has put without writing at least one volume." And Churchill intended to publish that volume himself.[17]

SHERWOOD AND POGUE posed a challenge because they could read sensitive American papers and many documents from the Prime Minister himself. On the British side, meanwhile, Churchill could still not be sure how generous his own government would be about the use of official papers, because Bridges had now secured Attlee's support in his campaign to tighten the rules.

In the spring of 1946, Admiral Lord Chatfield applied to publish the rest of his memoirs, covering the period 1933–1940. This prompted the Cabinet Office to draw up new guidelines on ministerial memoirs. At the same time, Lord Vansittart wanted to publish some of the papers about the German threat that he had written in the 1930s when Permanent Under-Secretary at the Foreign Office. Fearful that this would open the floodgates, Attlee asked Bridges for another set of guidelines on the use of official documents in memoirs by civil servants. Vansittart had actually obtained outline approval for his project from Eden, then Foreign Secretary, back in 1941, and he was invoking the 1934 Vindicator Clause to defend himself against accusations of extreme Germanophobia.[18] But Attlee insisted so strongly that "Civil Servants, unlike Ministers, have no personal need to justify their actions to the public since they are not publicly responsible for them" to Parliament that Vansittart was told that a mistake had been made by Eden.[19] He was left fuming about what he saw as a blatant double standard: one law for officials and another for politicians such as Churchill.[20]

The new guidelines were approved by the Cabinet in May and July and summarized in a Commons statement on 1 August. The guidelines on ministerial memoirs (CP 188) elaborated two general principles: that ministers should be treated differently from civil servants and that, since defense matters had been especially censored during wartime, there should be "a correspondingly greater measure of relaxation" in peacetime. It would, however, be necessary to keep secret on grounds of "public interest" information that would be "injurious to us in our relations with other nations, including information which would be of value to a potential enemy," or "destructive of the confidential relationships" between individual ministers and between ministers and their advisers. One further point was that extensive quotation from official documents "should only be allowed in very exceptional cases; and then only when the document is in some sense personal to the writer."[21]

Churchill naturally took an interest in these matters. He invited Bridges to lunch on 21 May 1946 and read out extracts from his correspondence with Lloyd George in 1934 and 1935, when they colluded against returning Cabinet documents. It was an oblique but clear reminder that, if he wanted, Churchill could be very difficult; Bridges advised Attlee to secure Churchill's support of the new rules. In a carefully worded reply, dated 29 May, Churchill expressed "general agreement" with the principles of CP 188 but suggested that a former Prime Minister "should be accorded exceptional consideration"—as he had extended to Baldwin. He also noted that "an unusually large proportion" of his own work had been done in writing and argued that he must consider his position "in relation to American revelations," such as the "very offensive" attacks on him in the books by Butcher and Ingersoll.[22]

By the autumn of 1946, the Literary Trust had been established, and Camrose was preparing to auction the American rights. Churchill now needed a clear commitment from the government about the use of his papers. Taking Ismay's advice, he sent Bridges a "personal" letter on 23 September. "I am pressed from many quarters," Churchill wrote disingenuously, "to give my account of the British war story and, without at present making any definite plans, I have been getting my papers in order and considering the project." He reiterated that he would be quoting almost entirely from documents he had composed and that he would agree to "a final revision of the text in detail" by the government before publication. Churchill said he would like to know, "without necessarily accepting the view as final, whether *in principle* there would be any objection" to his publishing three types of material:

1. Papers he had written for the Cabinet as First Lord of the Admiralty, Prime Minister, or Minister of Defence.
2. Texts or extracts from his "immense series" of minutes.
3. Material from his "personal" telegrams to Roosevelt and other heads of government. Quotation from the replies would, he acknowledged, require appropriate permission, but, if that was problematic, these documents could easily be summarized.

"I feel I have a right, if I so decide," Churchill wrote, "to tell my tale and I am convinced it would be to the advantage of our country to have it told, as perhaps I alone can tell it."[23]

Bridges took Churchill's letter to the inaugural meeting of his interdepartmental Committee on the Use of Official Information in Private Publications. He presented the case in a most favorable light, pointing out that Churchill was

in fact offering to co-operate with the Government in making sure that nothing contrary to the public interest was published in his book. This was of great importance. It was an advance on the attitude taken by certain former Ministers after the first world war, and would be most useful in persuading other writers to follow Mr. Churchill's example.

The committee was receptive to Churchill's arguments, but Bridges felt that since this was the first test (and probably the biggest) of the new principles agreed in May, the matter should go to the Cabinet. He prepared a Cabinet paper for Attlee's signature, showing how Churchill's letter conformed to the principles in CP 188. He told the Prime Minister, "The memorandum has been drafted as a statement of facts and arguments tilted rather gently in favour of acceptance of Mr. Churchill's proposal? Is this what you would wish?" Attlee did not object.[24]

Churchill's letter and Attlee's covering memo went to the Cabinet on 10 October 1946. The only dissent came from the Foreign Office, alarmed by press reports that Churchill's first volume might appear in 1947, with others in quick succession. Ernest Bevin, the Foreign Secretary, was still trying to avoid a total breach with Russia, and he told Attlee that publication of such documents at the present time would be "a grave embarrassment" to the government. "Nothing ought to be written until peace has been finally settled." But Bevin was not at the Cabinet meeting on 10 October to argue his case. Churchill was given formal permission to include memoranda, minutes, and telegrams of the sort that he had

mentioned, on the understanding that before publication "the text would be submitted for final revision on behalf of His Majesty's Government, in the light of
the situation existing at the time." That same day, Bridges sent Churchill the
news in a letter of remarkable deference:

> As you will see, it is 100% acceptance; with no provisoes [sic], other than
> those which you yourself suggested.
>
> You know, I hope, that I and my colleagues in the Cabinet Office will
> always be ready to give you any help we can over these questions of docu-
> ments and so forth. It will be our endeavour to be as helpful to you as you
> have been to us. We are most grateful to you.[25]

Bridges proved helpful about far more than documents. Churchill intended
to be his own historian but not his own researcher, and in April 1946 Ismay had
suggested the names of Norman Gibbs of Oxford and Edward Rich of Cambridge, both of whom had been working in the Cabinet Office's Historical Section. Gibbs was thirty-six and Rich forty-two; they may not have been the kind of
"young men" that Churchill had in mind. So in August, Ismay suggested that
Churchill approach Bridges. By the end of September, after inquiries at Oxford,
Bridges suggested some possible names, even offering to "see any people who
seem to be prima facie suitable and form an opinion of them" if Churchill
wished. On 14 October, four days after his fulsome letter about the official
papers, the Cabinet Secretary brought two young men to Churchill's room at the
Commons for half-hour interviews. They were Alastair Buchan, son of the
famous novelist, and James Joll—both age twenty-seven. In due course, they
became distinguished scholars of international affairs and might easily have cut
their teeth on Churchill's war memoirs. Although that did not happen because
Churchill found a far more senior assistant, what matters here is the Cabinet Secretary's readiness, far beyond official obligation, to expedite Churchill's war
memoirs.[26]

Why was Bridges so helpful? In part, he was making virtue out of necessity. In
1945, Churchill had removed his papers; in 1946, he was starting to write his
memoirs. His promise that the Cabinet Office could see the manuscript in
advance was an invaluable quid pro quo, and Bridges doubtless hoped to hold
him to it by being helpful. But Bridges's tone and actions suggest he considered
the memoirs not merely inevitable but desirable. The Cabinet Secretary was the
driving force behind the ambitious program of official histories of the war, established in 1941. These were academic volumes, but Bridges also wanted some-

thing more popular, even propagandistic, and in 1943 and 1944 he explored the idea of an overview history of Britain's war effort in two or three volumes, to appear within a couple of years after victory. The Cabinet's Advisory Committee on Official Histories feared that, long before the detailed volumes appeared, "other Histories would be published," and these "might convey a misleading impression which would not be removed by the publication of an official History some years later." Much depended on finding the right author, but the great and the good of the English historical profession said no, including G. M. Trevelyan. So Bridges dropped that idea in June 1944 in favor of a series of short, accessible overviews of aspects of the war by well-known authors, also to appear as soon as possible. Names being touted included Arthur Bryant on the navy and E. M. Forster on the war in Western Europe. But again the proposed authors were not available, and the idea lapsed.[27]

If not Trevelyan or Bryant, why not Churchill? There is no direct evidence, but it is likely that Bridges saw the war memoirs as a surrogate for an overview official history. After all, who was better qualified to write it? Churchill was a renowned popular historian and also the dynamo of Britain's war effort. The tide of "other Histories" was already swelling across the Atlantic. Sherwood's proposed book, of which Bridges was well aware, was another reminder that many Americans would soon be telling their own stories, often, as Ismay said, featuring secret material "likely to have a good sale—or cause a bad smell." The ideal antidote would be a guaranteed bestseller from Britain's wartime Prime Minister, approved by His Majesty's Government. When volume 1 appeared in 1948, Bridges told Churchill "how delighted are all of us, who have worked for you in the war, that you have found time to write this great work that we used to dream of."[28]

Churchill's war memoirs as Britain's official history? Without such an inference, it is hard to explain the remarkable conduct of the Cabinet Office. In private, officials admitted that Churchill was being given "exceptional facilities" and that his book "had always been regarded in a category by itself." The Attlee Cabinet was asked to approve Churchill's right to publish his papers, minutes, and telegrams but was not told that he and his assistants were being given virtually open access to wartime files. Normally, research took place in the Cabinet Office itself or the archives of the relevant department. But by April 1947 there was a note on file stating that "when Colonel Deakin states that Mr. Churchill wishes to see any particular paper himself, we shall have to allow the paper in question to leave the office." (Papers leaving the office were invariably attached to a cover note requesting speedy return, but many are still to be found in the Churchill papers.) In the summer of 1947, Churchill's new naval research assistant, Gordon Allen, asked the Admiralty for the same facilities as those accorded to authors of the official histories. "As you are no doubt aware," he added, "Mr. Winston Churchill is now engaged in the preparation of his 'War Memoirs' and his book will be sponsored by the Cabinet." That, of course, was wrong, but Allen's error was understandable and revealing: for "Cabinet" read "Cabinet Office," and one is not far from the truth. As Norman Brook, Bridges's successor as Cabinet Secretary, noted in August 1947: "Our general doctrine is that Mr. Churchill, and those who are helping him with his book, should be given all possible facilities and assistance." Without that doctrine, as we shall see, *The Second World War* would have been a very different book.[29]

ON 16 OCTOBER 1946, six days after Churchill received Cabinet permission to quote from his papers, Lord Camrose left for New York on the *Queen Elizabeth* to negotiate the American publishing deal. But he was not going alone. On board was another agent of Churchill's, Dr. Emery Reves.

Reves was a forty-two-year-old Hungarian Jew who ran his own international press syndicate. Driven out of Berlin in 1933, he operated from Paris until 1940 and then settled in New York. From 1937 to 1939, Reves's syndication helped Churchill keep afloat financially and remade his reputation, spreading his views across Europe, Latin America, and especially the United States. After the war, Reves reestablished his European operations, commuting frequently to Paris, and by sheer persistence forced his way back into Churchill's circle, offering fertile suggestions about how to market the memoirs. Their personal relationship warmed during 1946. Churchill felt a debt of gratitude to Reves for his help in the 1930s and, according to Reves, had promised tearfully in Miami in January 1946 to reward him with a share in the war memoirs.[30]

Despite letters and meetings, Reves had nothing firm to go on until 3:00 P.M. on the afternoon of 15 October 1946, when he received a phone call at the Ritz in Paris. The main source for what happened over the next few weeks is Reves himself, in recollections dictated twenty years later off the top of his head.[31] Although seriously misleading in places, they can be checked against documents on both sides of the Atlantic. Together, Reves and the archives reveal a remarkable story.

The phone call came from Churchill, with an impossible summons. Camrose was leaving for New York at lunchtime the next day. "I want you to go with him. Will you come over to London and have dinner with me tonight—I want to talk to you." Reves was incredulous. The *Queen Elizabeth* was on her maiden postwar voyage after reconversion from a troopship, and every cabin had been sold for months. Churchill said he would contact Cunard—"they used to be very nice to me." Twenty minutes later, he phoned back. "You have a stateroom with a bath, so can you be here for dinner?" Even in the days of Eurostar and budget airlines that would have been a tall order. In 1946, there were few flights between London and Paris, and Reves had already ascertained that all were booked. Eventually, he found a private plane at Le Bourget, but the pilot had engine trouble and could not take off. The next morning, Reves secured a seat on a regular Air France flight, but it was an hour late leaving, and he despaired of getting from Croydon airport to Southampton in time for the ship's departure at 1:00 P.M. There was now no time to speak with Churchill, but a chauffeured car stood waiting at Croydon and got him to Southampton Docks by half past one. The police whisked him on board as the last passenger. Exhausted but elated, Reves made contact with Camrose—only to discover that the press lord had no idea that he was coming and little enthusiasm for his company. Hastily, Reves cabled Churchill. The cryptic reply expressed confidence that Reves would do an excellent job but enjoined strict confidentiality and warned "you must realise that you do not actually represent me."

What was going on? There is no hard evidence, but probably Churchill had cold feet at the last moment about Camrose—not about his old friend's integrity but probably his capacity to conduct these negotiations single-handed. As Reves observed in 1966, Camrose "was more experienced in buying copyright than selling it" and knew little of the New York publishing scene or its personalities. Aside from whether Churchill wanted Reves to share in the deal, he had probably decided that the literary agent could be a useful adviser to the press baron. But when Reves started sniping at Camrose behind his back, he was told: "Pray be guided by C. in everything."[32] During the voyage, the two men hammered out a modus vivendi. Camrose would talk to the newspapers, and Reves would contact magazines and book publishers, but Camrose was determined to keep all formal negotiations in his own hands. In Manhattan, they met most evenings to compare notes, but relations remained strained. Camrose had already satisfied his own commercial interests by securing serial rights in Britain and the empire for the *Daily Telegraph*. He was in New York to get the best deal for Churchill. Reves, by contrast, wore two hats: Churchill's unofficial agent and bidder for his own cut of the memoirs.

On 15 November, Camrose sent Churchill a progress report. After "a tiresome and most vexatious three weeks," he had now seen all the people that mattered, being careful not to show eagerness or attract attention. So far, "not a word of my doings has appeared in the papers." Camrose had words of praise for Reves, calling him "a clever salesman with an abundance of ideas and many useful con-tacts. I have used him a great deal and am very glad he came over. Where he is to figure in the ultimate picture I do not, at the moment, know but we can discuss this on my return." Although Churchill's memoirs were regarded as "the out-standing work for years to come," there was some fear among the newspapers that Sherwood's book on Hopkins would scoop the highlights of the war, particularly on relations with Roosevelt. Camrose also advised that the memoirs "would ulti-mately realise more money on a royalty basis but this would cover a long period and in any case I have always understood you to say that you wanted an outright sale." On that assumption, he had asked all interested parties for their bids by Fri-day, 22 November.[33]

On the face of it, a syndicate was likely to offer the best deal. Marshall Field, the Chicago media tycoon, Helen Ogden Reid of the New York *Herald Tribune*, and the book publishers Simon and Schuster made a package offer of $1.1 million for American serial and book rights and for world serial rights outside Camrose's domain. The press lord was ready to accept, but Reves was doubly affronted. Not only did he believe that Churchill was being sold too cheaply, but the deal would exclude him completely. Summoning up all his credit with Henry and Clare Luce, he urged them to make a better offer. Henry, just back from China, came up with $1.4 million for the American serial and book rights. This left Reves with a chance to secure the remaining world serial rights, but he still wanted a share of the American book deal as well. He asked Camrose to sell Luce only the serial rights and begged for time to find a book publisher who would cut him in. He then approached Houghton Mifflin in Boston, to whom he had already sold books on the basis of no commission and a cut of the royalties— his preference for big-money deals. In a frantic two-hundred-mile dash, Reves took the train from New York on 26 November and lunched with Henry A. Laughlin, the company's president. Surprised but delighted, Laughlin made an immediate offer of $250,000 for the book rights—$50,000 for each of the five pro-posed volumes.[34]

Helen Reid and her associates wanted to keep bidding, but Reves persuaded Camrose to bring the auction to a close.[35] Prompted by Churchill, Camrose probably felt Reves deserved a share of the profits, and he was, in any case, desperate to leave New York, having been there for more than five weeks. On 28 November, the press baron sent Churchill a terse but triumphant telegram: "Please inform [Chartwell] Trust have closed with Henry [Luce] for 1150. Book goes to Houghton Mifflin for 250. Total 1400." After selling Canadian serial rights to the Montreal *Standard* for a further $110,000, Camrose left New York aboard the *Queen Elizabeth* on the twenty-ninth, "delighted at the prospect," though he had to hide in his cabin from the persistent Reid. Also on board was Emery Reves. "Could you repeat miracles [by] asking your friend Cunard [to] cable New York to give me cabin," he had telegraphed Churchill with customary chutzpah.[36] In a final twist to the tangled story, Luce then accepted an offer from *The New York Times* (outbid at an earlier stage), which felt it could not endure the loss of face if Churchill's memoirs appeared under another masthead. The newspaper agreed to pay $400,000 of Luce's $1,150,000 bill in return for the right to serialize the memoirs simultaneously.[37] Since it was a daily newspaper and *Life* an illustrated weekly, there seemed little danger of overlap. But this deal shocked Houghton Mifflin, who feared that the double serialization would decimate its sales. Relations between book and serial publishers were initially very tense.

In January 1947, Camrose exchanged letters with the trust and Churchill to acquire the papers from the former and to commission the latter to write the books. He had now put together the other major partners in the deal, including Cassell's for the British book rights (£40,000) and Keith Murdoch's Australian newspapers (£75,000). His total purchase price was £555,000 (over $2.23 million). After deducting £5,000 in stamp duty, the trust would receive £375,000 for the papers and Churchill (as author) £175,000, payable in five installments. American taxes would, however, reduce these sums to £322,500 and £122,500; Churchill's receipts (but not the trust's) would also be subject to British taxation. Depending on how one calculates inflation, the deal would have been worth anything from $18 million to $50 million today (see "A Note on Money," page 538).[38]

Tying up the details on the American side took months of further negotiation. Separate contracts had to be signed between the *Daily Telegraph* on the one hand and, on the other, Houghton Mifflin, Reves's newspaper agency, and the combine of Time Inc. and *The New York Times*. The three American publishers had to settle their own turf wars, for instance, on how much of the book could be serialized. Houghton Mifflin needed a royalty arrangement with Emery Reves; *Life* and *The New York Times* had to agree on how to handle serialization. Houghton Mifflin also battled with Cassell's about third-country rights—the former eventually taking South America, the latter continental Europe. The lawyers for *Life* and *The New York Times*, wanting everything spelled out in small print, descended on London en masse in April 1947. They pressed Churchill for a direct contract, rather than one negotiated via Camrose, but that did not suit Churchill's legal needs. They demanded that Camrose indemnify them for libel, but he refused, having no such indemnity from Churchill. It took ten days of legal haggling with Camrose and one *Telegraph* lawyer battling it out against two large American teams. At one point, Camrose had them down to his country house but provided only a rather frugal lunch. "I don't want them to think we're too rich," he told his son quietly.[39]

The logjams eventually broke. On 2 May, Reves concluded his deal with Camrose for the foreign-language serial rights. "I almost felt like signing a marriage licence," the confirmed bachelor remarked. On 14 May, Laughlin heard that Camrose had initialed the draft contract with Houghton Mifflin. "I shall drink your health this evening in Krug 1929," he cabled Reves, "for this is really something to celebrate . . . the most successful publishing venture of all time." Reves told Laughlin that the offers for the foreign book rights convinced him that "we have acquired the American rights under most favourable conditions." The French offer was 80 percent of the American price, the Dutch 40 percent, whereas he reckoned that American book rights were worth "at least ten times" those in either country. Even Cassell's, he told Laughlin, was "paying almost as much as you do for a market which is less than half yours."[40] The main reason, of course, was that Churchill was selling his memoirs outright, at much less than he might have secured long-term from royalties. But he wanted money up front and was more than content with what Camrose had achieved.

The serial publishers were also delighted. "Let's always remember," Andrew Heiskell of *Life* told his staff, "that the Churchill Memoirs are the biggest literary and historical project that LIFE, or for that matter any other publication, has ever undertaken."[41] In May 1947, the deal was announced to the world, without exact figures. The American press guessed $1 million for a projected one million words, which suited headline writers nicely: "Churchill's Memoirs Bring Dollar a Word." This eclipsed previous nonfiction coups, such as $300,000 in 1930 for the memoirs of General John J. Pershing, U.S. commander in France in 1917–1918. *Time* magazine, part of the Luce empire, called it "the plumpest literary plum of World War II." *The New York Times* splashed the story over two columns on its front page on 15 May, under a picture of Churchill "working on his memoirs in his study in England." The next column featured a report of his speech in London the previous day to launch the United Europe campaign. Churchill the historian and Churchill the statesman—that continuing double act had helped sell the memoirs. It would also shape the way they were written.[42]

I.

THE GATHERING STORM

1919–1940

1946–1948

SETTING A COURSE

W HEN THE CONTRACTS were signed in 1946, Churchill had only a hazy conception of his memoirs. Their scale, shape, and content were still to be determined. He also had to forge a team of research assistants, establish working relations with his publishers, and get his text approved by the Cabinet Office. Summoning *The Gathering Storm* into existence was no easy task, but it set Churchill's course for *The Second World War* as a whole.

CHURCHILL'S AGREEMENT with his publishers spoke of five volumes. An outline dated 1 January 1947 indicates his early thinking.[1]

VOLUME I

    BOOK I   Between the Wars, 1919–39

    BOOK II   Twilight War September 1939 to May 1940

    BOOK III   Total War (May 10–December 31, 1940)

VOLUME II 1941

    BOOK I   Alone

    BOOK II   Russia Invaded

    BOOK III   Pearl Harbour

VOLUME III 1942
> BOOK I **Japan Strikes**
> BOOK II **Alamein and Stalingrad**
> BOOK III **'Torch'**

VOLUME IV 1943 AND 1944 • Preponderances
> BOOK I **Africa Freed**
> BOOK II **Italy Defeated**
> BOOK III **Teheran**

VOLUME V 1944–1945 • Victory
> BOOK I **Anzio**
> BOOK II **D-Day & Rome**
> BOOK III **Yalta**
> BOOK IV **Potsdam**

This scheme bears little relation to the final work, which ran to six volumes, each comprising two books (see the Appendix, "Churchill's Six Volumes"). What Churchill envisaged in January 1947 as books 1 and 2 of volume 1 became the eventual *Gathering Storm,* while an enlarged version of book 3 was published as *Their Finest Hour.* This was a consequence of the scale on which he was writing: *The Gathering Storm* ran to 784 pages in the American edition (June 1948) and 640 in the small-type British version (published the following October). During 1947, Churchill came to recognize that volume 1 would have to end at May 1940.[2] The inflation of these opening volumes clearly had implications for the memoirs as a whole. In March 1948, Churchill warned his advisers, "it may be that an extra volume will be required."[3]

Why did the project expand so much? As Churchill got down to work, he became fascinated by the 1930s, exploring what happened and imagining what might have happened. In the autumn of 1946, he envisaged only five chapters up to the outbreak of war in September 1939. The total grew to eleven in January 1947, seventeen by July, and twenty-four in October, before he settled on the eventual twenty-one. Although at an emotional level he was most engaged by the summer of 1940—his finest hour as well as Britain's—appeasement aroused his *intellectual* interest in a way that has few parallels elsewhere in the war memoirs.[4]

There was another, more structural reason for Churchill's verbosity: documents. Far more than his previous works, *The Second World War* quotes at vast length from the minutes and telegrams he wrote at the time. Churchill turned this feature into a virtue, insisting in the preface to volume 1 that these documents afforded a unique record of war at the top as viewed at the time. But it was also easier to print contemporary evidence than to write retrospective analysis—important considerations for a man with one eye on the political clock. The first book of *The Gathering Storm* was less afflicted with documentitis—partly because of Churchill's intellectual engagement; partly because he was out of office in the 1930s and so did not generate minutes and telegrams. But there were speeches and letters aplenty from the era of appeasement, and the official papers start in earnest with Churchill's return to the Admiralty. In short, the storm of documents is beginning to gather in volume 1.

The minutes and telegrams had been printed at Churchill's behest during the war, usually in monthly volumes. Until 1950, when political pressures became acute, Churchill selected most of this material himself, going through the originals and marking those items to be "pruned" for printing as a new set of documents for the book. Often, he would do preliminary editing of the document as well. He or his assistants might later revisit the material for additional gleanings, and these "gleans" would also be set in print for possible use. The selected documents were then strung together in chronological order, often with minimal connecting narrative, and sent for printing as a very rough draft chapter. In later versions, text would be moved and themes highlighted, but the principle of documents in chronological order would rarely be violated for long. Churchill liked to say that he wrote "the way they built the Canadian Pacific Railway. First I lay the track from coast to coast, and after that I put in the stations."[5]

Documents, in the form of "prunes" and "gleans," constituted Churchill's track. His stations came in two types. Some were constructed by Churchill himself from dictated personal recollections. These might cover isolated episodes (such as Eden's resignation as Foreign Secretary in February 1938) or outline a whole book (as with his two-page essay about "how frightfully lucky" he was to be in Opposition not office in the 1930s). He did a great deal of structured reminiscing in 1946 and 1947, and this was printed on more than one hundred galley pages under the heading "History of the War." This material included some of Churchill's most rooted memories, especially meetings with Roosevelt and Stalin, and most of it was worked into eventual chapters. Churchill could dictate anywhere—even in a car—but his preferred time was at home late at night, with a secretary and a research assistant in attendance. Fortified and lubricated by a good dinner, he would pace up and down his study at Chartwell for several hours—sometimes measuring his words, sometimes speaking in such a torrent that it was hard for the secretary to follow. At times, he got so carried away that the argument went completely off the rails. However, he usually amended it in the sober light of the following morning, when the typescript was ready for his inspection over breakfast in bed. The result was usually a mass of amendments, as in the dictation about his fateful meeting with the French on 16 May 1940 (page 74). In the interwar years, Churchill's secretaries took shorthand notes and then typed them up, but during the war Kathleen Hill typed as he spoke, using a specially muffled typewriter to avoid disturbing his train of thought; this was the practice for the war memoirs.[6]

The other kind of "station" was constructed by the research assistants, who wrote drafts on political or military events. Papers from Bill Deakin, for instance, provided the base for Eden's resignation (chapter 14), the "rape of Austria" (chapter 15), and the narrative of the Czech crisis of 1938 in chapters 16 and 17. Into these drafts Churchill interleaved his own speeches and letters. His description of the conquest of Poland in September 1939 was taken almost unchanged from a memo composed by Henry Pownall. Much of this research was original and of high quality. Deakin's sources for the Czech crisis included evidence at the Nuremburg trials, Italian materials such as the Mussolini-Hitler correspondence, recent French memoirs, and Keith Feiling's biography of Chamberlain. For the Polish war, Pownall exploited his privileged access to the Cabinet Office's Historical Section to study a U.S. War Department analysis of the German campaign, a captured German report, "The Luftwaffe in Poland," and a top-secret 1946 paper by the British Joint Intelligence Committee (JIC) on German dispositions—sources that would not be available to normal historians for another twenty-five years, even fifty in the case of the JIC records. Although Churchill in the preface to each volume stressed that he was offering only his personal view of the war—a "contribution to history" rather than history itself, "for that belongs to another generation"—the work of his research assistants gave his volumes historical depth and originality that were absent from most memoirs.[7]

Documents, dictation, and drafts—these "three Ds" were Churchill's staple ingredients. Yet blending them together was not easy, and the chapters went through many revisions. In the process, Churchill usually condensed the documents (or relegated some to appendixes), expanded his own dictated narrative, and fashioned the research drafts into his own words. A good example of the latter process is the opening of chapter 4, entitled "Adolf Hitler," about the temporarily blinded corporal nursing his bitterness as Imperial Germany fell apart in the autumn of 1918. This started life as a 2,100-word draft by Deakin on "The Rise of Hitler" (see page 72). Churchill stayed close to the original on matters of fact; even some of the more colorful phrases are Deakin's, such as Hitler's "fervent and mystic admiration" for Germany. But Churchill often tightened the prose. Thus, the sentence about Hitler remaining in hospital "during the ensuing months in which defeat and revolution swept through Germany" became "while . . . defeat and revolution swept over Germany." He added sharper nouns and adjectives from his own distinctive vocabulary—in the reference to Hitler's "deep though concealed resentment" the word "deep" was changed to "harsh," and "he had dreamed of becoming a great artist" became "he had nursed youthful dreams of becoming a great artist." As an orator, Churchill also had a keen sense of the dramatic. Whereas Deakin introduced the name Adolf Hitler after the first sentence, Churchill does not reveal it until the end of the paragraph. The suspense, of course, is artificial—we immediately guess the identity of the blinded corporal—but withholding the name in this way serves to highlight the banality of Hitler's past and the similarities of his experience with that of millions of ordinary Germans.[8]

To some chapters he devoted close and repeated attention, but others were nodded through with little amendment, leaving excessive narrative from the drafts or a surfeit of documents. Revision was done from galley proofs, for he insisted on seeing how his text would look in print. The rough version of the chapter—a mess of printed documents, typed dictation, and drafts, covered with handwritten scrawl—went off by courier to his printers, the Chiswick Press. Their galleys, usually printed within twenty-four hours in multiple copies, were sent to the assistants and often to former colleagues for comment, then cut and pasted with typescript and manuscript additions, before going back to the printers. Most chapters of *The Second World War* went through six to twelve versions before being dispatched to the publishers. That was not the end: Churchill had no compunction about amending his text in page proof and even when the pages were ready to be bound. These working methods were not entirely novel—the nineteenth-century French novelist Honoré de Balzac had driven printers to distraction by constant revision—but Churchill was in a league of his own. In June 1947, nearly a year before publication, he had already settled an initial printer's bill of £1,444 (more than $5,800).[9] But he was able to afford the expense thanks to the massive payments from his publishers.

Churchill's working practices as a historian had been honed during the 1930s, on *Marlborough* and the *English-Speaking Peoples*, but for *The Second World War* he was working on an altogether grander scale. The mass of documents was far greater, his assistants more numerous, and the sums of money involved much larger. There were also many more calls on his time, as Leader of the Opposition and an international statesman. He was operating less as an author and more as what scientists today would recognize as head of a research

The Rise of Hitler. 2100.

In October, 1918, a German ~~private~~ corporal ~~was~~ employed by an attack / a British attack temporarily blinded by chlorine gas in ~~the fighting~~ near Commines, ~~and~~ He was taken to hospital in ~~North Germany~~ Pomerania, where he remained ~~during the ensuing months in which~~ while defeat and revolution swept ~~through~~ over Germany. ~~His name was Adolf Hitler, a common soldier~~ He was of Austrian birth ~~who~~ and, for four years, had ~~undergone the experience of war~~ some with a Bavarian regiment ~~in the trenches~~ on the Western Front. There were no distinguishing characteristics which could mark him apart from his fellows except perhaps a certain dreaming simpleness of mind, and a ~~deep~~ harsh though concealed resentment at his own personal failure to establish himself in the world. The son of an obscure Austrian customs official, he had dreamed of becoming a great artist, but having failed to gain entry to the Academy of Art at Vienna, he had lived as a starvling in that capital and later in Munich, a casual labourer, hungry and without roots. Like many Germans from beyond the borders of the Reich, he had an almost morbid sense of racial loyalty and it was his fervent and mystic admiration for the German race which

Churchill's research assistants produced draft narratives on key topics. This is from Bill Deakin's 2,100-word essay on the rise of Hitler—the annotations are mostly by Churchill—which may be compared with what was finally printed as the opening of chapter 4 of The Gathering Storm.

4

Adolf Hitler

The Blinded Corporal — The Obscure Fuehrer — The Munich Putsch, 1923 — "Mein Kampf" — Hitler's Problems — Hitler and the Reichswehr — The Schleicher Intrigue — The Impact of the Economic Blizzard — Chancellor Bruening — A Constitutional Monarchy! — Equality of Armaments — Schleicher Intervenes — The Fall of Bruening.

IN OCTOBER, 1918, a German corporal had been temporarily blinded by chlorine gas in a British attack near Comines. While he lay in hospital in Pomerania, defeat and revolution swept over Germany. The son of an obscure Austrian customs official, he had nursed youthful dreams of becoming a great artist. Having failed to gain entry to the Academy of Art in Vienna, he had lived in poverty in that capital and later in Munich. Sometimes as a house-painter, often as a casual labourer, he suffered physical privations and bred a harsh though concealed resentment that the world had denied him success. These misfortunes did not lead him into Communist ranks. By an honourable inversion he cherished all the more an abnormal sense of racial loyalty and a fervent and mystic admiration for Germany and the German people. He sprang eagerly to arms at the outbreak of the war, and served for four years with a Bavarian regiment on the Western Front. Such were the early fortunes of Adolf Hitler.

As he lay sightless and helpless in hospital during the winter of 1918, his own personal failure seemed merged in the disaster of the whole German people. The shock of defeat, the collapse

52

THIS DOCUMENT IS THE PROPERTY OF HIS BRITANNIC MAJESTY'S GOVERNMENT

MOST SECRET.

TO BE KEPT UNDER LOCK AND KEY.

It is requested that special care may be taken to
ensure the secrecy of this document.

THE PRIME MINISTER'S PERSONAL MINUTES

MAY 1940

SIR EDWARD BRIDGES.

Prepare at once an outline for a revision of the existing system of dealing with economic problems and placing it under the Lord President. I had in mind that trade, transport, shipping, M.E.W., food, agriculture, would all come into a general group, over which he would exercise a large measure of executive control. How would this fit in with the present Home Affairs Committee? Let me have this to-night or to-morrow early. About two sheets of paper would be sufficient.

(Intld.)   W. S. C.
17.5.40.

LORD PRESIDENT.

I should be very grateful if you would deal with this question, as well as with the general question of further evacuation of children, and make a recommendation to the Cabinet.

2. I am very much obliged to you for undertaking to examine to-night the consequences of the withdrawal of the French Government from Paris or fall of that city, as well as of the problems which would arise if it were necessary to withdraw the B.E.F. from France, either along its communications or by the Belgian and Channel ports. It is quite understood that in the first instance this report could be no more than an enumeration of the main considerations which arise, and which could thereafter be remitted to the Staffs. I am myself seeing the military authorities at 6·30.

(Intld.)   W. S. C.
17.5.40.

SECRETARY OF STATE FOR WAR.

Are you proposing to arm the men of the balloon barrages? I understand they have no weapons. Surely they should be included among your parashots?

(Intld.)   W. S. C.
17.5.40.

Churchill had his wartime telegrams and minutes printed every month during the war with an eye to future literary use, taking care to label them "personal." Here is the first page of his minutes as Prime Minister.

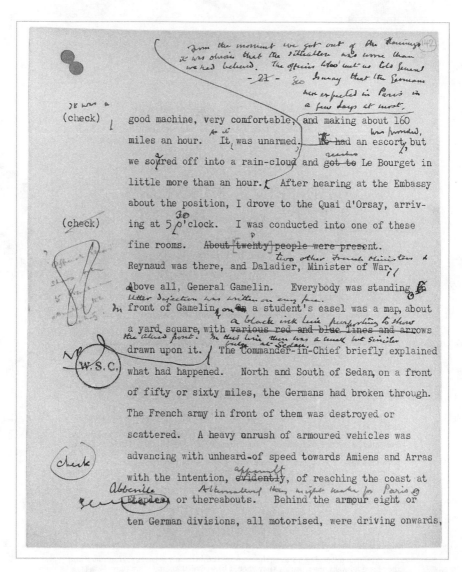

Churchill's dictation about his visit to Paris on 16 May 1940—one of the most vivid moments of Their Finest Hour. *Apart from a marginal query from Ismay noting the official French record of the meeting, the other annotations are Churchill's, including the stark, mood-setting sentence "Utter dejection was written on every face."*

group. As such, he relied heavily on others to help him shape his complex materials into an accurate and compelling historical narrative. Four groups of people played their parts: his inner circle of assistants; friends and colleagues who commented on parts of the manuscript; his publishers and paymasters; and the civil servants who gave his volumes an official vetting.

BILL DEAKIN WAS Churchill's most trusted assistant, their close personal relationship forged in the 1930s. Not only was Deakin an academic historian—his wartime career in the Balkans sparked a professional interest in Mussolini and Hitler—he could also tune his words to Churchill's ear. Deakin's papers, though scholarly, were the least arid of all those produced by the Syndicate. It was not long before he was writing them for immediate use in the text, using the pronoun "I" as if authored by Churchill himself. But Deakin was no longer the struggling research student and junior don who had "deviled" for Churchill in the 1930s. He returned from the war to substantial teaching and administrative responsibilities at Wadham College, Oxford, and told Churchill when first approached in April 1946 that he could not offer any real help until December. Even then, his visits to Chartwell were less frequent or lengthy than in the 1930s—usually odd weekends or snatches of the university vacation.

Initially, Churchill had envisaged Deakin directing a number of "young men" from Oxford. But he changed his mind after being put in touch with General Sir Henry Pownall, a retired senior officer, age fifty-eight.[10] Churchill paid Pownall £1,000 a year—the same sum he had offered to Alastair Buchan and James Joll, though that was for full-time work. But he got a good deal more for his money. Pownall's personal experience at the top had come during some of the decisive phases to be covered in the war memoirs: prewar rearmament, the fall of France, the dark days of 1941, and the surrender of Singapore. Although not a trained historian, Pownall was a capable staff officer who had written many strategic studies and, equally important, knew how to read between their lines. He was on the Advisory Committee for the Official Military Histories, which gave him ready access to papers and staff at the Cabinet Office's Historical Section, and he was privy to the Ultra secret, having been given wartime clearance to read and disseminate the wartime decrypts of intercepted German signals. Another bonus was that he was more available than Deakin, being retired and living not far from Chartwell, at Wittersham in Kent.

Pownall started work in November 1946. At first, he concentrated on the campaign in France in 1940, where he had been a senior staff officer at the headquarters of the British Expeditionary Force. In the spring of 1947, he worked on the comparative statistics for British, French, and German airpower in the 1930s, spending time not only in the Cabinet Office's Historical Section but also in Paris. "What you are sending me is exactly what I want," Churchill wrote on 17 January 1947; by the summer, it was "My dear Henry" rather than "My dear Pownall."[11] On the other hand, Pownall remained essentially a staff officer. His essays were brisk, efficient analyses but lacked the color and imagination provided by Deakin. He got frustrated by Churchill's erratic working habits (as he had when Vice-Chief of the Imperial General Staff in 1941) and often blew off steam about them in private. Asked in May 1948 to dig out some documents from the Cabinet Office, he remarked, "I think W.S.C. ought to be provided with *copies*. You know what happens to papers chez lui!"[12] For Churchill's purposes, Pownall was more available than Deakin but less creative.

Pownall had been brought in by his old army friend Hastings Ismay. Churchill had unbounded faith in "Pug," as Ismay was generally known because of his doglike face and fidelity. Having acted as Military Secretary to the Cabinet throughout Churchill's premiership, Ismay stayed on to serve Clement Attlee. From April 1946, when Churchill first asked for help, Ismay started feeding him official documents as well as recollections of unrecorded incidents. "Please remind me of things as they occur to you," Churchill responded appreciatively in October. "It is a great help to have one's memory jogged."[13] Ismay proved particularly useful about Churchill's foreign trips, to France in 1940 and to America later in the war. One of his greatest virtues was temperament. He had the patience and congeniality that Alanbrooke, Churchill's principal wartime military adviser, famously lacked, and despite the strain of acting as wartime broker between Churchill and the Chiefs of Staff, Ismay only once came close to resignation. Likewise, working on the memoirs, he was more subtle and courtierlike than Pownall when trying to change Churchill's mind. Yet Ismay's input to volume 1 was irregular. He provided useful help in 1946 and seemed in a position to do more after his retirement as Military Secretary that November. But from March to December 1947 he was in India, assisting Lord Mountbatten in managing Indian independence. Although copies of the proofs were dispatched to him (via diplomatic bag!) and he sent back comments, this long absence from Britain greatly diminished his contribution to *The Gathering Storm*.

For the war at sea, Churchill used Commodore Gordon Allen, a retired naval officer who had served at Jutland in 1916 and became Senior Naval Officer at Combined Operations Headquarters by the end of the Second World War. He started work at the beginning of July 1947. Like Pownall, Allen was paid £1,000 a year plus expenses, though in this case for full-time work.[14] His home in Cobham near Weybridge in Surrey was also well placed for visiting Chartwell and for journeys into London to consult records at the Admiralty. He worked intensively on volume 1 for the rest of 1947, researching topics such as the defenses of the great fleet anchorage at Scapa Flow, and also helped Churchill refine his narrative of the evacuation from Norway and other existing drafts. Allen was diligent and keen—constantly pressing Churchill to say more about naval operations—but he was a reserved man who lacked the sociability of Deakin, Ismay, or even Pownall and was somewhat in awe of Churchill. Their relations remained formal and rather aloof—in the later stages of the memoirs Churchill preferred to deal with him on paper rather than in person. That said, Allen's presence ensured that the war at sea bulked large in all Churchill's volumes, not just for his time at the Admiralty. By contrast, Churchill did not recruit an airman until volume 5, and this had significant implications for the content and balance of *The Second World War*.

Deakin, Pownall, Ismay, and Allen were the four senior members of what became known as the Syndicate. The other recruit in 1947 was Denis Kelly, a struggling young barrister, age thirty-one. Kelly had studied history at Oxford before being called to the bar in 1942. After army service in India and Burma (where he won the Military Cross), he returned home to find the Inns of Court overflowing with returned barristers. He was taken in by a friend of his father's and given some income-tax cases, but this was not enough to make ends meet. He therefore responded with alacrity in May 1947 when Leslie Graham-Dixon, the legal brain behind the Literary Trust who had chambers in the same building, asked if he would like to catalog Churchill's papers for a fee of one hundred guineas per month plus expenses. This had become a matter of some urgency since the trust could not be formally constituted until a proper inventory had been made.[15]

On 17 May, Kelly made the first of innumerable trips from his London home down to Chartwell—commuter train to Sevenoaks, branch line to Westerham, taxi along the winding country lanes to the great man's house. "Your task, my boy, is to make Cosmos out of Chaos," Churchill told him, and that took Kelly four months. Some of the documents had been properly kept: a casket of Marlborough letters and the bound volumes of Lord Randolph's papers had pride of place in the library. But the two muniment rooms in the basement were truly chaotic. Government red boxes, loose files, crates of press cuttings, and some seventy black tin boxes, of the sort used by Victorian solicitors, were jumbled amid souvenirs and gifts—including an American submachine gun and a samurai sword passed on by Mountbatten. Kelly found Churchill's school notebooks and recent bank statements mixed up with correspondence from Roosevelt and Stalin and proof upon proof of his earlier books.

The muniment rooms were near the oil furnace, which roared away most of the year since Churchill hated a cold house. And Chartwell's electrical wiring was distinctly primitive and prone to shorting out. Churchill reluctantly agreed to install fire-resistant steel cabinets in October 1947. The papers were also insured and the most important documents photographed, the films being lodged in the vault of Churchill's London bankers, Lloyd's of Pall Mall. The bank also acted as temporary home for dozens of the deed boxes while all this work was being carried out. The manager waived any fee, saying that "the privilege of being entrusted with records of such immense historical importance" was sufficient.[16]

Kelly was also alarmed at the damage wrought by Churchill's previous writing. Files had been extracted from their boxes, pruned for the choicest fruit, and then returned in ravaged state, not always to the correct place. On receipt of the latest proof, old material was relegated to a debris box, into which successive revises were piled in disarray. Already *The Second World War* was creating a similar "trail of ruin," as researchers rummaged indiscriminately in the files and key documents were literally cut and pasted into the text. If this continued, Kelly warned, the archives would "relapse into the chaos from which they were about to be rescued." These papers were the crown jewels of the book deal—in legal and financial terms a greater asset than Churchill's authorship—so the trustees took heed. Once Kelly's work as emergency cataloger came to an end, the trust retained him for £240 per year as archivist, and he tried with mixed success to prevent a renewed descent into chaos.[17]

Because Kelly was at Chartwell much more than were Deakin and the others, he was gradually drawn into the memoirs themselves. On 7 December 1947, Churchill asked him for comments, "positive or negative," on volume 1. Although Kelly began circumspectly—"I sincerely hope that you will not find my comment so free as to be unseemly"—he soon became more forthright, urging Churchill to clarify "the dramatic thread" of the narrative and heighten the personal aspects of the story.[18] Available, willing, and junior, Kelly fell into the role of the dogsbody Churchill needed to check facts, tie up loose ends, and generally get the text into publishable form—some of the jobs Deakin had done in the 1930s. But Kelly was not a trained historian, and he also lacked Deakin's blend of energy, intellect, and charm. Tall, gawky, and bespectacled, "dear Denis" was regarded as rather "wet" by Churchill's family and female secretaries, and there was considerable competition to *not* sit next to him at dinner—indeed, Clementine soon tried to avoid having him come for meals, as Churchill's diary makes clear: "Mr Kelly to sleep" but "Mr Deakin to dine and sleep." Nor, despite his admonitory memos, was he a paragon of organization, often phoning apologetically from London to say he had missed the train. Denis Kelly rendered Churchill loyal and often valuable service, but his limitations, particularly in the central coordinating role thrust upon him, are also part of the story of the war memoirs.

BEYOND THIS INNER circle comprising Deakin, Pownall, Ismay, Allen, and Kelly were others who also contributed to the memoirs. The diplomat Sir Oliver Harvey loaned the diary he kept when he had been Eden's private secretary; this offered intimate glimpses into the political crisis surrounding Eden's resignation. Sir Stafford Cripps, by then Labour's Chancellor of the Exchequer, provided extracts from his diary about the opposition to Chamberlain and appeasement in 1939. (Although he asked Churchill to destroy the extracts after use, they are next to Cripps's letter in Churchill's files.) And, from a completely different social milieu, Pownall secured an account of the sinking of the destroyer *Acasta*, which had helped cover the evacuation from Norway, written by its sole survivor. Leading Seaman Carter, tracked down to his home in Portsmouth, was paid £25 for his story of the courage of the *Acasta*'s captain and crew against impossible odds. Printed with acknowledgment, it fills a whole page of Churchill's final chapter on the Norway campaign.[19]

Churchill made particular use of his contacts in Westminster and Whitehall. Viscount Portal, wartime Chief of the Air Staff, read the material on radar and aerial mines. This was particularly valuable in the absence of an airman on Churchill's team. Extended comments from two top diplomats—Lord Vansittart and Sir Orme Sargent—helped him in redrafting key chapters in December 1947. Churchill's longtime scientific adviser, Lord Cherwell, contributed and critiqued material on air rearmament and radar and also read a whole set of proofs. Sir Edward Marsh—Churchill's former private secretary and himself an author of note who had helped on earlier books—went through the drafts for style and punctuation, renewing a long-running battle between them about commas. "They should only come in when it is absolutely necessary," Churchill told him in August 1947, "to make b[loody] f[ool]s understand."[20] Clementine Churchill also plowed loyally through the text, often fixing on minor obscurities, but some of her comments were acute. For instance: "All the accounts of Naval Actions seem to be written by a sailor for sailors & not for the General Public by a master of narrative." (Fortunately, Commodore Allen does not seem to have read this note.)[21]

The most unlikely of these consultants was Isaiah Berlin, the Oxford philosopher, to whom Churchill had taken a shine when the latter was writing informed and gossipy analyses of Washington politics from the wartime British Embassy. In January 1944, Churchill asked Eden to name the author of these weekly reports, and was informed that they came from "Mr. Berlin, of Baltic Jewish extraction." Clementine told her husband that Mr. Berlin was in town and asked if Winston would spare a moment to thank him for his war work. To her surprise, the Prime Minister suggested a lunch and, over the table, cross-examined his guest about the American scene. Mr. Berlin proved disconcertingly vague about the state of U.S. war production and the prospects of a Roosevelt fourth term. Asked by Churchill what was the most important thing he had written, he replied, "White Christmas." Churchill's private secretary, Jock Colville, divined the confusion and explained it later to an amused Prime Minister. The "Irving-Winston-Isaiah" story went around Whitehall and thence to *Time* magazine. Not only did it enhance Isaiah Berlin's cachet, it also unlocked a door that Deakin reopened in late 1947. He persuaded Churchill to send the 1930s chapters to Berlin, who received a generous honorarium of two hundred guineas for his comments.[22]

Contributions of a different sort came from Churchill's publishers. Desmond Flower of Cassell's did a formidable technical job on *The Second World War*, but he offered little critical input (age forty in 1947, he was only four years older than Churchill's son, Randolph). Lord Camrose was also sparing with literary criticism, though on the business side Churchill continued to rely heavily upon him. From New York, both Henry Luce and Arthur Hays Sulzberger, respectively owners of *Life* magazine and *The New York Times*, commented on drafts of volume 1, but thereafter their input was limited. Among Churchill's publishers, three men stand out: Henry Laughlin of Houghton Mifflin, Daniel Longwell of *Life* magazine, and the ubiquitous Emery Reves. Each tried to shape the war memoirs to fit his own commercial agenda, in the process making a distinct critical contribution.

Reves and *Life* had been wooing Churchill for years, but Laughlin was cut into the deal late in 1946 and did not meet Churchill until the following summer, when he came to London to sign the contract with Camrose. The next day, 6 July, he wrote a reverential letter on blue Claridge's notepaper, telling Churchill "how greatly pleased and honoured" his firm was to be publishing the memoirs and expressing the hope that its work would be up to his expectations in every way. The same tone was evident in October when Laughlin's senior editor, Paul Brooks, expressed impatience that Churchill had divided his volumes into books but then sometimes confused the two terms: "Mr Churchill has got himself all balled up in his books and his volumes." Laughlin wrote a scathing rebuke of such "contemptuous criticism of one of the world's clearest thinkers."[23]

Although Laughlin never lost his respect for Churchill, he had soon begun to treat him like a normal author. In September, he expressed unhappiness about the early working title for the volume, "The Downward Path," which might seem "somewhat discouraging" to the reader. Could Churchill think of a phrase conveying the enthusiasm when he took over the premiership?[24] In February 1948, he urged that the overall title should be "Memoirs of the Second World War," because the book provided not just "the facts of the war" but a sense of how it was lived at the top: this was what made it "intensely exciting reading." Churchill was initially taken with the idea, but Reves and Flower argued that the word "memoirs" conveyed "something frightening to the general public."[25] Laughlin retreated gracefully, but he had clearly found his voice. And because he spent every summer at a family property in Ireland and made shorter trips to Europe at other times during the year, he was able to deal regularly with Churchill face-to-face.

Daniel Longwell, chairman of *Life's* board of editors from 1946 to 1953, had used the paintings and the secret speeches as bait to hook Churchill. That cost $70,000. For the memoirs, *Life* was paying three quarters of a million dollars, and in August 1947 Longwell traveled to London, anxious to see what they were getting for such a massive investment. He was allowed to read the current galleys of volumes 1 and 2 in his hotel. The material was still very rough, but Longwell was interested in content not form. He estimated that with proper illustrations these two volumes would be serialized in twelve issues of the magazine, covering perhaps 178 pages. He told Churchill that this was roughly equivalent to the editorial content of three and a half issues of *Life* and that each weekly issue was a $2 million operation. Even by *Life's* standards, Churchill was big business.[26]

At the end of August, Longwell returned the galleys, marked to show passages of "great interest" and those of "wavering interest." After checking with Camrose, he delicately noted that presumably many documents would be condensed in later revisions.[27] Longwell told his colleagues there was "nothing revelatory or particularly newsworthy" in volume 1. He considered volume 2 "a much more completed" entity, which really got going with the fall of France. Longwell felt overall that "we don't have a great work here now," but it already had "high moments" worthy of the author of *The World Crisis* or *Marlborough*. Much would depend on Churchill's ability and willingness to finish it off: "The state of taste next year, the fortunes of England, the shifts of history, all may affect our luck, but these were part of our purchase." *Life* and the other American publishers were betting not just on Churchill's literary skill but also on his health and political commitments, as well as on the public appetite for war memoirs and the evolution of the Cold War. Theirs was truly a gamble on history.[28]

For most of 1947, Emery Reves flitted around the world to construct a remarkable network of deals. On 2 December, he sent a note of the contracts to date: serialization by thirty-one newspapers in twenty-five countries, mostly in Europe and Latin America, including mass-circulation papers such as *Le Figaro* in France and *La Prensa* in Argentina. Reves had also lined up translations of the books into eleven languages, including French (Librairie Plon), Spanish (José Janes), and Italian (Arnoldo Mondadori). In occupied Germany and Japan, all publishing arrangements had to be made via the Allied military authorities, who offered derisory sums, so Reves advised Churchill to wait until business conditions there became more normal. In the meantime, he signed a contract for a German-language translation with the Swiss publisher Alfred Scherz.[29]

In Eastern Europe, Reves found great interest, "but of course they dare not sign a contract." He suggested approaching the Russian government directly about publishing the memoirs in Moscow. The answer would probably be negative, but if they did agree it would have considerable effect in the Soviet bloc and might earn some rubles, "in case you would like to make another trip to Yalta." (Such joshing asides were a sign of their warming personal relationship.) "Certainly ask the Bear if you wish," Churchill replied, "but don't bring me into it." A Russian edition did not begin appearing until 1954, after Stalin's death, and progressed only as far as volume 3. A full translation had to wait for the demise of the Soviet Union in the 1990s.[30]

BY JULY 1947, Churchill had a presentable draft of volume 1. This was what Longwell read in August and Reves had been hawking. *Life* wanted to start serialization in mid-January, and just before leaving London on 26 September Longwell received a telegram from his publisher, Andrew Heiskell: "I hope and pray that before your departure you can pin author down on scheduled delivery date." Longwell forwarded the telegram to Chartwell. "They certainly won't pin him down," Churchill noted. Anxious to speed progress, *Life* sent books that Churchill needed, even advance proofs of upcoming American war memoirs. After Walter Graebner of his London office reported "fountain pen trouble," Longwell rushed over several of them "with all our best wishes." And when Churchill's poodle, Rufus, to whom he was devoted, was run over by a bus during the Tory party conference in Brighton in October 1947, Graebner paid $158 for a replacement from the same kennels. "Rufie II" stayed with Churchill until his death, age fifteen. But he never became completely house-trained, as guests walking the halls of Chartwell sometimes discovered to their cost.[31]

In early October 1947, Churchill had a new set of galleys run off. To ensure that his publishers did not jump the gun, these were firmly labeled "Provisional Semi-Final." By the end of the month, he had progressed to "Provisional Final."

It became clear to *Life* that more inducement was required than pens or poodles. Graebner told Churchill that they were "ready and anxious" to finance a working holiday for him and his research staff.[32] Foreign vacations were almost impossible for the British in that austere postwar era, because of the draconian exchange controls, and Churchill could not have made any trip if his New York publishers had not footed the bill. Back in the 1930s, he had fallen in love with the Mamounia Hotel in Marrakech, and *Life* was now happy to renew his acquaintance. He flew there via Paris in a private plane on 10 December and did not return to England until 19 January 1948.

The Mamounia was one of the world's grand hotels. Churchill's criteria were demanding, but even he found the food and drink "beyond criticism" (though this was not true for the temperature of his bathwater). He required chauffeured cars and extra rooms for offices and a painting studio, and he took with him his daughter Sarah, Bill Deakin, and two secretaries. Lord Cherwell came for a few days at the end of December, and Mrs. Deakin was invited for Christmas—"as this will enable me to keep Bill till at least the New Year," Winston told Clementine.[33] She herself came out in the New Year with Lord Moran, after Winston developed a bronchial cold and Sarah became agitated. To fund all this, *Life* opened a local account in Churchill's name, on which he or his secretaries could draw. The total bill came to $13,600. That did not include the plane, which was provided by an Australian admirer, the mining tycoon W. S. Robinson.[34]

Churchill regarded this as a working vacation, with equal emphasis on each word. He worked on the book in the morning, usually in bed, and painted all afternoon. He slept at 6:00 P.M., then dined and played cards with Sarah before another session on the book until the early hours. Progress could be measured by the "bags" sent to and fro—forty-seven from London, twenty back home. Some of their contents were ordinary mail or personal items—more paints or cigars—but most were revised chapters sent to the Chiswick Press for reprinting and the new sets of proofs that the printers dispatched in return. "Arrived home safely after a delightful holiday in which book has made progress otherwise impossible," Churchill cabled Longwell on 21 January 1948. In 1975, Bill Deakin's recollection was rather different: "He didn't do much work. He wanted company. He painted most of the time." But *Life* chose to regard it as money well spent—in fact, Henry Luce had intended to act as host until hospitalized for surgery.[35] This trip set the pattern for lavish working holidays in exotic locales, sometimes more than once a year.

Under the sun and the palms of Marrakech, Churchill and Deakin "bulldozed" volume 1 into shape—this became in-house jargon for the last big push.

The revised proofs generated from there in January 1948 were labeled "Almost Final." At Marrakech, Churchill also addressed several larger, structural questions about the volume.

One was the mass of documents, which continued to disquiet all his publishers. On 22 December, Emery Reves told Churchill that the "Provisional Final" version of book 1 was "overwhelming" but urged him to paraphrase most of the documents or relegate them to the appendixes. Reves's critique, repeated on 5 January, upset Churchill so much that his daughter Sarah urged him to "listen to a very few" and then "write this book from the heart of yourself." That, of course, was what Reves was really saying, but Churchill took umbrage and sent back huffy cables about there being "no question of altering the whole character of the work in [the] manner you suggest." It was a reminder that, even more than most authors, he was acutely sensitive about his work—eager for comment yet defensive about any criticism, however constructive. But he did heed these and similar comments when revising. On 14 January, Reves cabled that the first five "Almost Final" chapters were "absolutely perfect." Denis Kelly agreed they were "incomparably better."[36]

Much of this debate turned on Churchill's coverage of the 1920s. The "Provisional Final" draft included two chapters about British politics and diplomacy from 1922 to 1931. Isaiah Berlin judged them "too episodic and insubstantial" and felt the book only got into its stride with the rise of Hitler. He suggested they be cut or drastically shortened. Arthur Sulzberger favored condensation but not elimination, "since they present far too poignant a lesson for present day study." Longwell agreed that the chapters were "a little lengthy" but did not want to encourage more tinkering. As someone who would simply gut the text for serialization he had always intended to move briskly up to Hitler and the 1930s. Emery Reves had much more interest in the book itself and wanted the "excellent" chapters 2 and 3 to stay unabridged—"domestic picture essential for understanding coming events," he wrote. Henry Laughlin agreed, stressing that American readers knew little of 1920s Britain. In London, however, it was all familiar stuff, so Desmond Flower sided with Berlin and urged severe cuts. What Flower wanted were more vignettes of contemporary statesmen, not just Stanley Baldwin and Ramsay MacDonald but also their continental counterparts—"for me personalities make history, not vice versa."[37]

This debate illustrated again the diverse interests of Churchill's publishers. Their discordant clamor also underlined Sarah's advice about Churchill needing to listen to his own voice: rarely when composing later volumes did Churchill solicit comment in such a broad and open-ended way. Eventually he decided to squeeze the two chapters into one, further condensing his already brief account of the 1920s. The contrast in coverage of his years in office and in opposition proved a significant feature of book 1 of *The Gathering Storm*.

Marrakech also focused attention on titles—a matter over which Churchill continued to dither. He toyed with "The Downward Path" and "Towards Catastrophe," but, as Laughlin had argued through the autumn, both struck too negative a note. Another idea was "The Loaded Pause" (used for the chapter on Spain in 1936–1937). This conveyed Churchill's idea of a single thirty-year war from 1914 to 1945 but sounded cryptic and flat. By the new year, the issue had become urgent, because Houghton Mifflin's salesmen were about to descend on the bookshops and needed to know what they were selling. On 7 January, Reves suggested "Gathering Clouds," "The Gathering Storm," or "The Brooding Storm," tactfully noting, "But you probably have better." On 31 January, Churchill's secretary Jo Sturdee put before him a sheet of paper and requested a decision "very soon." On it she had typed "Towards Catastrophe" and "The Gathering Storm." Churchill put a line through the first. He added in blue pencil:

'From War to War' instead of 'Between the Wars' Bk I
'Twilight War' Bk 2

A decision at last. It was the first of several painful extractions.[38]

By contrast, what Churchill called the "moral of the work" had been in his mind for years. In January 1941, he had told Harry Hopkins that after the Great War he had been asked to propose the inscription for a French war memorial. He suggested:

> In War: Fury
> In Defeat: Defiance
> In Victory: Magnanimity
> In Peace: Good Will

His suggestion had been rejected, so Churchill—jackdawlike as ever with a glittering phrase—carried it over into the memoirs. The only change, made in late 1947, was to substitute "Resolution" for "Fury" in the first line. This moral was printed at the front of each volume of *The Second World War*.[39]

SYNDICATE, CONSULTANTS, AND publishers all helped shape *The Gathering Storm*. But another powerful interest group had a stake in Churchill's memoirs: His Majesty's Government. The heart of Churchill's bargain with Sir Edward Bridges was that he could keep his papers, but Whitehall must approve what he published. Bridges had steered this arrangement through the Cabinet in 1946 but was then replaced as Cabinet Secretary by his deputy, Norman Brook, who served from 1947 to 1962. It was Brook who vetted all six volumes of the war memoirs.

Bridges and Brook were both skilled managers, adept at stitching up bureaucratic compromises and lubricating the gears of government. Brook also shared Bridges's conviction that Britain's war record should be displayed to the world. He supported the program of official histories and the special access given to Churchill—like Bridges, treating the former premier as in effect *the* official historian. Yet there were important differences between the two Cabinet Secretaries. Bridges was the son of a poet laureate and a product of Eton; his successor was a grammar-school boy from Wolverhampton. But as Brook rose via Oxford to the top of the civil service, he developed his own social style. A fastidious dresser, he would never have been caught, as his predecessor once was, with holes in his socks. He also had a charm and sociability lacking in Bridges, who was shy and austere, whereas Brook had immense presence: big frame and incisive words, yet a quiet voice and a companionable manner. Bridges earned Churchill's respect and gratitude for loyal wartime service, but Brook won Churchill's trust and affection. On the memoirs he would become almost an additional member of the Syndicate.[40]

Churchill sent Brook a copy of the "Provisional Final" text on 10 December 1947. His covering letter struck a preemptive note. In book 1, "I do not think there is anything in it which is detrimental to the public interest"; as for book 2, the only official documents quoted were those written by himself.[41] Warned by Deakin that Churchill was off to Marrakech to bulldoze the book, the Cabinet Secretary read the manuscript in a week and then asked Bridges to examine it over a weekend, stressing the need to get their views to Marrakech by Christmas. Their joint comments went off on Christmas Eve. On 6 January 1948, Churchill's secretaries started sending Brook the "Almost Final" version, revised before his comments had been received. Many passages had been cut or amended; much new material had been added. Brook had therefore to read all the chapters again, referring some contentious passages to the relevant department. The "Final" version required similar, if more cursory, examination.

It is worth underlining what such editorial work entailed. The Cabinet Office was the junction box of Whitehall, and demands on Brook's time and energy in the winter of 1947–1948 were unremitting. Britain's economy was in crisis—a sluggish recovery compounding the yawning dollar gap. Negotiations over the Marshall Plan and a new Western European defense pact jostled on the Cabinet agenda with the intractable conflict in Palestine and the Cold War confrontation over Germany. Yet Brook not only found time to vet very rapidly three versions of *The Gathering Storm* but also acted as informal proofreader. On 3 April 1948, for instance, after dispatching his official comments on the "Final" proofs, he sent Deakin ten foolscap pages of unofficial suggestions to improve the text, as well as four and a half pages detailing typographical errors. A lot of the work was done by his staff, but such care shows how much Brook (like Bridges) had invested in Churchill's quasi-official history. Both wanted to make it good, rather than merely harmless. Moreover, Brook's patient solicitude (Churchill even phoned with a query on Easter Sunday while the Cabinet Secretary was on vacation in Suffolk) created a bank of goodwill on which Brook could draw when requesting amendments.[42] The back channel established with Bill Deakin (a Fellow of Wadham, Brook's Oxford college) also proved useful. By talking with Deakin and sending him copies of the proposed amendments, Brook helped ensure that official concerns were hammered home. In all these respects, *The Gathering Storm* set precedents for later volumes.

Brook's main anxiety about volume 1 was the extent to which Churchill, while out of office in the 1930s, obtained secret information from officials and serving officers, such as Ralph Wigram of the Foreign Office and Desmond Morton on intelligence matters. This was an important feature of Churchill's draft: it reinforced his claim to have been acting in the public interest against a government whose appalling blindness forced patriotic officials to break normal rules. Brook and Bridges agreed that circumstances in the 1930s were "wholly exceptional" but feared that such revelations might damage future relations in Whitehall, if ministers became less willing to trust their officials and civil servants decided that the Churchill precedent justified leaks to MPs. The Labour party was inherently suspicious of the loyalty of Whitehall, and it is significant that Brook did not breathe a word of his concern to Clement Attlee, sorting out matters with Churchill discreetly.[43]

Brook's other anxiety also concerned confidentiality. In his draft second chapter, Churchill made reference to his 1945 instruction that "the fullest facilities should be accorded" to Stanley Baldwin's official biographer (G. M. Young) in consulting government records. As we saw (chapter 3), Bridges deplored this liberality, which stood in marked contrast to his own obstruction of Keith Feiling, Chamberlain's official biographer, and Brook was keenly aware that the two cases had been handled very differently. Without mentioning the Feiling case, Brook warned Churchill that this passage might be cited as a precedent by other authorized biographers and said he would be "very greatly obliged" if Churchill omitted all reference to this "quite exceptional procedure."[44]

On 20 January 1948, Bridges drew Brook's attention to another sensitive issue. In book 2, Churchill quoted papers he had written as a member of the War Cabinet. Should he not acknowledge Crown copyright in such documents? And, if so, did that imply that the government could claim some share of his earnings? This point had been raised by the Labour MP Adam McKinlay in February 1946 after Churchill had published his secret-session speeches. Brook consulted Sir Norman Scorgie, Controller of the Stationery Office, who conceded that there might be grounds for a new rule that if an ex-minister made "a fat profit out of writing about his official work, then he should hand over part of the swag to the state." But, Scorgie went on, there was nothing in current practice to justify that position. Although reassured, Brook was careful to lay the issue before Attlee, who in turn put it to the Cabinet. The Prime Minister said he could see no grounds for suggesting that Churchill should pay royalties to the state on his memoirs, and none of his Cabinet colleagues disagreed. Whether they considered Churchill a special case or a useful precedent is not recorded.[45]

On 27 January, Brook dined with Churchill and had a long talk about the book. Churchill agreed to remove all reference to the special facilities offered to Young, but on the issue of leaks in the 1930s from officials he was stickier. "After discussion we agreed to do a deal on this point," Brook recorded. Churchill would delete most of the sensitive references while retaining a tribute to Desmond Morton, whose help could be represented as a special act by an old friend.[46] The following day, Brook, authorized by Attlee, wrote Churchill to say that the government had no objection to his quoting from Cabinet papers he had written in 1939 and 1940, providing the preface stated that he had obtained "permission to reproduce the text of certain official documents of which the Crown Copyright is legally vested in the Controller of His Majesty's Stationery Office." Churchill agreed, printing Brook's formula on the acknowledgments page of *The Gathering Storm* and of each subsequent volume.[47]

Although Attlee generally followed Brook's advice about the war memoirs, he did raise one important issue on his own. In discussing the Norway campaign, Churchill wished to print extracts from a Cabinet paper by the Chiefs of Staff, attacking his plans. Attlee objected: "I think we should stick to papers written by Mr. Churchill." The Cabinet Secretary urged Attlee to avoid "an absolute rule" on this: "Mr. Churchill quotes so many of his own documents that there is some danger of his creating the impression that no-one but he ever took an initiative."[48]

Although Attlee agreed not to impose a total ban, he was "most apprehensive" about setting a dangerous precedent. Officials criticized by Churchill in his memoirs might demand the right to vindicate their conduct by reference to contemporary documents. Publication of some of these papers would be "most embarrassing"—Attlee cited those about the fall of Singapore, mindful perhaps of the fuss in early 1946 over Churchill's secret-session speech.[49]

The Prime Minister's opinion, all the more powerful since he rarely took an independent line on the memoirs, set a pattern for volumes to come. Churchill always intended that he would highlight his side of the story, but Attlee's ruling ensured that relatively few replies were printed to Churchill's minutes, particularly in the form of official Cabinet papers. As Brook warned, this enhanced the impression that Churchill won the war almost single-handed.

BULLDOZED AT MARRAKECH and vetted by Brook, volume 1 was now close to completion. In the process Churchill had created a set of durable working practices. His inner circle of researchers and writers was in place, and he had established distinctive working relations with each member. He had set up a unique system for research, writing, and revision, at vast but sustainable expense. He forged contacts with his publishers on both sides of the Atlantic, not least the agreeable practice of free vacations in exotic places so that he could finalize the text. He also reached a remarkable working arrangement with the Cabinet Office whereby he and his advisers enjoyed wide-ranging access to secret documents in return for official vetting of the manuscript and unofficial use of the Cabinet Secretary as an additional proofreader. And the scale on which he wrote the first volume had follow-on effects for the whole project, pushing it inexorably to six volumes rather than five. In these and many other ways, the composition of *The Gathering Storm* from 1946 to 1948 set Churchill's course for the whole *Second World War*.

When Churchill wrote the label "Final" on the revised proofs he sent to the printer on 30 January 1948, it was a significant concession. Serialization was set to begin in mid-April, and the publishers were near panic. But "Final" did not mean finished. Underneath, Churchill added, "Subject to Full Freedom of Proof Correction." He continued to tinker with this "Master Copy" for weeks, sending a stream of "overtake" corrections. For Houghton Mifflin and Cassell's, who required an exact text, the whole thing became a nightmare; even the serializers were severely stretched. How they published *The Gathering Storm* and how the world received it are the themes of chapter 9. But first we need to look at what Churchill said.

CHAPTER 7

THE UNNECESSARY ROAD TO MUNICH

IN THE PREFACE to *The Gathering Storm*, Churchill introduces his war memoirs as a continuation of *The World Crisis*, constituting together "an account of another Thirty Years' War." He also asserts that "there never was a war more easy to stop" than the one that broke out in 1939, recalling that when President Roosevelt asked what the conflict should be called, he had immediately replied, "The Unnecessary War." This motif of avoidability enables Churchill to present his story as a "human tragedy" and to "lay the lessons of the past before the future"—playing with alternative scenarios in an extended piece of what would now be called counterfactual history. The overall theme of volume 1 was "how the English-speaking peoples through their unwisdom, carelessness and good nature allowed the wicked to rearm," and his account has shaped our image of "the appeasers" ever since.[1]

CHURCHILL'S CRITIQUE of appeasement was not the first in the field. Three Beaverbrook journalists, including Michael Foot, had already pilloried Britain's leaders of the 1930s so successfully that their post-Dunkirk polemic, *Guilty Men*, sold 200,000 copies in its first six months.[2] Two other books published in 1948— *Munich, Prologue to Tragedy* by John Wheeler-Bennett and *Diplomatic Prelude* by Lewis Namier—took a similar line to *The Gathering Storm* and also utilized many of the same printed sources. Their case was strengthened by the fact that none of Britain's three Prime Ministers of the 1930s published his own version of events. Ramsay MacDonald (1929–1935) had died in 1937, exhausted and vilified, while Neville Chamberlain (1937–1940) lasted only six months after the end of his premiership. Stanley Baldwin (1935–1937) did survive, and at the end of the war he took steps to rehabilitate his reputation by commissioning G. M. Young to write an authorized biography. Under Churchill's permissive ruling about access to official papers (chapter 3), Young even had his own room in the Cabinet Office by September 1945.[3] But he made slow progress, and his anodyne biography did not appear until 1952.

At the top of the next rank of politicians, Anthony Eden was seriously planning his own memoirs in 1946. That autumn, the literary agency Curtis Brown negotiated a contract with Faber and Faber for two volumes on his tenure as Foreign Secretary (1935–1938 and 1941–1945). The Cabinet Office reluctantly agreed that Eden came into the "exceptional" category hitherto restricted to Baldwin and Churchill,[4] and his research assistant was also granted a room in the Cabinet Office in order to inspect documents on Eden's behalf. It is fascinating to imagine the impact if Eden *had* published his account of the 1930s in 1948. It would have stolen some of Churchill's thunder and might even have offered an alternative view, since Eden, though making his name as an antiappeaser, would also have had to defend his own stance while in office. But nothing of the sort occurred. Instead of Churchill's Syndicate, Eden had only a single part-time research assistant—Harry Hinsley, the young wartime star of Bletchley Park—and he was soon submerged by lecturing and administration at Cambridge. Eden himself was overwhelmed at Westminster, since he was acting as de facto Leader of the Opposition while Churchill got on with his memoirs. In the 1950s, Eden returned to the Foreign Office, then became Prime Minister until toppled by the self-inflicted Suez disaster. His first volume of memoirs naturally concentrated on defending his premiership. *Facing the Dictators* did not appear until 1962, and *The Reckoning*, on Eden's war years at the Foreign Office, was published only in 1965. By then, Eden was merely dotting the "i"s and crossing the "t"s of an authorized version instead of stamping his mark on a blank page of history. Ironically, it was Churchill who published the first inside account of Eden's resignation as Foreign Secretary in 1938.

The only possible competitor to Churchill was Chamberlain's official biographer, Keith Feiling, who had finished a draft by 1944. But Sir Edward Bridges kept him out of the Cabinet documents and took months to nitpick his way through the text. When Feiling's neutered biography appeared in December 1946, some reviewers offered praise. "I am convinced," wrote Lord Templewood (Chamberlain's old colleague Sam Hoare) in a dig at *Guilty Men*, that history's judgment on Chamberlain "will be very different from the partisan verdict of a people's court in 1940." But Richard Law, the Tory politician, considered it a "serious weakness" that the biography did not use official papers, as in private did Lord Dunglass (the future prime minister Alec Douglas Home), who had been Chamberlain's parliamentary private secretary. Family and friends were generally disappointed with the book. Given the tide of events since Munich, no biographer would have had an easy task, but Feiling had been sunk by Bridges.[5]

Perhaps the best statement of contemporary wisdom was a review in *The Times* in December 1946 by Thomas Jones, Deputy Secretary to the Cabinet in the 1920s. He called Feiling's book "a provisional but authoritative biography" of "a peace Prime Minister of the second rank, called to guide the ship of State in a gathering storm and then, as the darkness thickened, to make way for the greatest of our war pilots." Already the verdict of history was being prepared and also its language. Feiling used "The Twilight War" as a chapter title, and Churchill explicitly borrowed it for book 2. The phrase "the Gathering Storm" was featured in the *Times* headline for Jones's review, perhaps lodging it in the back of Reves's mind. In more ways than one, Feiling's *Chamberlain* paved the way for Churchill's memoirs.[6]

CHURCHILL HAD USED the phrase "the Unnecessary War" in private in October 1940 and publicly in a major speech in Brussels in November 1945, so the basic theme was not new.[7] But his belief that the conflict was the result of a failure of political leadership sharpened in 1946 and 1947, amid the deepening Cold War. At Fulton in March 1946 he insisted that there "never was a war in all history easier to prevent by timely action," adding, "I saw it all coming and cried aloud to my own fellow-countrymen and to the world, but no one paid any attention. . . . One by one we were all sucked into the awful whirlpool. We surely must not let that happen again."[8] On 22 November 1947, he told Henry Luce that he intended to bring out in book 1 that

in those years there happened exactly what is happening today, namely no coherent or persistent policy, even in fundamental matters, among the good peoples, but deadly planning among the bad. The good peoples, as now, drifted hither and thither, to and fro, according to the changing winds of public opinion and the desire of public men of medium stature to gain majorities and office at party elections.[9]

In his opening chapter, Churchill denounces "the follies of the victors" between 1919 and 1929: the Versailles Treaty left Germany embittered but largely intact, while the breakup of the Habsburg empire led to "the Balkanisa-tion of South-Eastern Europe." He also highlights the Bolshevik victory in the Russian Civil War, which shook "the foundations of European civilisation" and left a fateful legacy: "As Fascism sprang from Communism, so Nazism developed from Fascism."[10] But Churchill does not dwell on the 1920s because Germany was still disarmed. Until 1934, "the power of the conquerors remained unchal-lenged in Europe and indeed throughout the world." Had the disarmament clauses of the Versailles Treaty been enforced, this "would have guarded indefi-nitely, without violence or bloodshed, the peace and safety of mankind."[11] By locating the crucial turning point in the 1930s, Churchill absolves the Tory gov-ernment of 1924–1929, in which he was Chancellor. This, he says in chapter 2, was a period of "very considerable recovery" at home and real "distinction" in for-eign affairs. In 1929, "the state of Europe was tranquil, as it had not been for twenty years, and was not to be for at least another twenty."[12]

Thereafter the rot set in. Prime Minister from 1929 to 1935 was Labour's Ramsay MacDonald, but in the book he is a shadowy figure, "brooding supinely" and in "increasing decrepitude" after 1931 over a nominally national govern-ment dominated by the Tories.[13] The truly culpable figures are MacDonald's suc-cessors, Baldwin and Chamberlain—also the Tory leaders who kept Churchill out of office during the 1930s. The best Churchill can say for Baldwin is that he was "the greatest Party manager the Conservatives ever had"; we are told that he "took no active share in foreign policy" apart from his "well-known desire for peace and a quiet life."[14] Although Churchill did not write the famous index entry on Baldwin ("confesses putting party before country"), that summed up his opinion. Whereas Baldwin wanted to be left in peace; Chamberlain wanted to make peace—in dealing with Hitler, Churchill argues, this was folly of the high-est order.[15] Together, they facilitated Hitler's resistible rise and an unneces-sary war.

There is, however, a tension in Churchill's account. He insists it was during the period from 1931 to 1935 that "the entire situation on the Continent was reversed." He says that "once Hitler's Germany had been allowed to rearm with-out active interference by the Allies and former associated Powers, a second World War was almost certain"—"inevitable," according to an early draft.[16] Yet 1931 to 1935 was the MacDonald era. One device Churchill uses to resolve this latent contradiction is to represent Baldwin as "virtual Prime Minister" during that period, but his main way is to highlight a series of missed opportunities *after* 1935. Churchill had always been intrigued by the what-ifs of history, and in 1931 he contributed an essay about Robert E. Lee's victory at Gettysburg to a collection called *If It Had Happened Otherwise*. In *The Gathering Storm*, he develops a whole series of counterfactuals.[17]

For instance, at the beginning of chapter 11 he depicts "a new atmosphere in England" in early 1936. The breakdown of collective security and a general backlash against Mussolini's assault on Abyssinia had, he says, forged a cross-party consensus that was "now prepared to contemplate war against Fascist or Nazi tyranny." Yet the government stuck to its "policy of moderation, half-measures, and keeping things quiet," taking no action against Hitler's reoccupation of the Rhineland in March. In an early draft of chapter 13, Churchill had admitted, "Nothing could have stopped Hitler after the seizure of the Rhineland except a very serious war." The published text, however, reads: "Many say that nothing except war could have stopped Hitler after we had submitted to the seizure of the Rhineland. This may indeed be the verdict of future generations. Much, however, could have been done to make us better prepared and thus lessen our hazards. And who shall say what could not have happened?"[18]

A second putative turning point occurs with the abdication crisis. In October 1947, Churchill decided to expand his account of Edward VIII's abdication from one sentence to two pages and to set it alongside Baldwin's admission to the Commons on 12 November 1936 that, had he gone to the country on a rearmament platform, the outcome would have been certain defeat. This, says Churchill, "carried naked truth about his motives into indecency. That a Prime Minister should avow that he had not done his duty with regard to national safety because he was afraid of losing the election was an incident without parallel in our Parliamentary history." The impression produced on the House was "so painful that it might well have been fatal" to Baldwin but for the sudden crisis over the King and Mrs. Simpson. Baldwin's shrewd judgment of public opinion and Churchill's unpopular pleas that the King be given time to overcome his infatuation turned the tables. Churchill says that the forces he had gathered on defense, on the verge of a breakthrough, were now "estranged or dissolved"; "I was so smitten in public opinion that it was the almost universal view that my political life was ended."[19]

Baldwin did retrieve himself over the abdication crisis, but historian Paul Addison is surely right that Churchill exaggerated its effect on foreign policy. The main reason why Churchill's "Arms and the Covenant" campaign faltered after December 1936 was the relaxation of Anglo-German tension that lasted until the Austrian Anschluss in March 1938.[20] But Churchill's interpretation of this episode became widely accepted, together with his edited and misleading account of what Baldwin told the Commons on 12 November 1936. Baldwin claimed that it would have been impossible to be elected on a rearmament plat-form in 1933 and 1934, in the pacifist aftermath of the East Fulham by-election, but that, as the public mood changed, he was able to do so successfully in 1935. Instead Churchill offers a bowdlerized version of Baldwin's words, using the ver-sion already printed in his collection of speeches, *Arms and the Covenant* (1938). By various omissions (three of them unacknowledged), including Baldwin's key sentence, "I am speaking of 1933 and 1934," Churchill implies that the Prime Minister had chickened out in the election of 1935. Once again, Churchill shifts blame to the period *after* MacDonald retired.[21]

Underpinning Churchill's account of 1936–1938 is his optimistic estimate of potential German resistance to Hitler, particularly during the Munich crisis. Churchill was confident that if Britain and France had taken a tough line on Czechoslovakia, the German generals would have mounted a coup against Hitler. He took seriously their assertions at the Nuremberg trials and also under interrogation, as relayed by Ismay from British military sources in Germany, par-ticularly testimony from General Franz Halder, then army Chief of Staff. But readers of Churchill's draft were not persuaded. Sir Orme Sargent, though a lead-ing Foreign Office critic of the Munich agreement at the time, warned against "overrating the possibility of an army revolt in September 1938. . . . [T]he gener-als were repeatedly planning revolts; but at the last moment they drew back, either because the situation was too favourable for Germany, or because it was so unfavourable that they could not as patriots play into the hands of the enemy." From Churchill's research team, Bill Deakin advised him not to "put too much store" on Halder's account, and Pownall could find no corroboration in White-hall archives.[22]

Churchill therefore softened his tone. The phrase "We now know for certain what was happening on the other side" became "We may now look behind the brazen front which Hitler presented to the British and French Governments." Echoing Sargent, he added the qualification that "the generals were repeatedly planning revolts, and as often drew back at the last moment for one reason or another" and also admitted: "It was to the interest of the parties concerned after they were prisoners of the Allies to dwell on their efforts for peace." But he retained a lengthy version of the generals' story, noting that it "has been accepted as genuine by various authorities who have examined it. If it should eventually be accepted as historical truth, it will be another example of the very small acci-dents upon which the fortunes of mankind turn." He sums up "The Tragedy of Munich" as follows: "Hitler's judgment had been once more decisively vindicated. The German General Staff was utterly abashed. . . . Thus did Hitler become the undisputed master of Germany, and the path was clear for the great design."[23]

Churchill's account of the Czech crisis shows his capacity to incorporate specific criticism, often almost verbatim, without blunting his essential thrust. It also exemplifies his principles of interpretation: contingency not determinism, individuals rather than impersonal forces, and the ostensible deference paid to the verdict of "history" while seducing future historians. Of course, Churchill's counterfactuals cannot be verified, but it is a tribute to both his vision and his craftsmanship that many of his turning points are ones that scholars still ponder, particularly the Rhineland and Munich.[24]

IN THE EARLY 1930S, Churchill repeatedly urged that it was folly for the victors to disarm and to allow Germany to rearm while German grievances had not been resolved. His whistle-blowing about the Luftwaffe after 1933 helped galvanize the government into action on air defense, and his lurid prophecies about Hitler's intentions were amply vindicated by unfolding events. In *The Gathering Storm*, chapters such as "The Locust Years" and "Air Parity Lost" document Churchill's public warnings, informed by secret intelligence about German rearmament. But his account distorts, too: air rearmament did not constitute the totality of defense policy, nor was the Nazi threat the only challenge for British diplomacy.

Take, for instance, Churchill's survey in chapter 9 of the origins of radar. As one of the earliest such accounts to appear, it attracted considerable attention and leaves the strong impression that little would have been done on the issue but for Churchill's own intervention, primed by Professor Frederick Lindemann, his old friend and scientific adviser from Oxford. "The Prof" was a vegetarian, a teetotaler, and a nonsmoker, but, forgiving such vices, Churchill valued his forceful advocacy and lucid presentations of science to laymen. The duo undoubtedly stirred things up in 1934 and 1935, but movement was already afoot within Whitehall. Churchill was invited to join a Cabinet subcommittee on air defense in June 1935, and he agreed provided the Prof was included on the Air Ministry's technical committee under Sir Henry Tizard. Like Churchill in politics, the Prof was something of an outsider from the science establishment in the 1930s, and he and Tizard had become bitter enemies. *The Gathering Storm* notes that Lindemann was forced off the Air Ministry committee in 1937 but attributes this to professional jealousies and also resentment that Lindemann had the ear (and the voice) of Churchill. Churchill fails to explain the substance of the dispute—not surprising, because Lindemann was pushing ideas that, if implemented, "would have brought chaos" to the radar-research program and "greatly disrupted" its integration into a larger system of air defense.[25]

Although Lindemann supported radar, he pressed for other experiments, particularly with aerial mines. Dropped by aircraft or fired from the ground, these were supposed to float down on parachutes and create a "curtain" into which enemy bombers would fly. As Churchill admits in an early draft chapter, he took up this idea of an "aerial mine-curtain" together with another about using "the fastest single-engine planes with adequate wireless to track the enemy bomber formations from a superior height." But in the revised version, he simply says, "I had two ideas to contribute, some explanation of which will be found in the Appendix." No such appendix exists—probably another example of the rush to finalize the text—but the omission was fortunate.[26] Readers are left with the misleading impression that Churchill was an early and total supporter of radar. It was only in June 1939, after his visit to the secret radar-research stations on the Suffolk coast, that he became a full convert. He refers to the visit at length in his text, without making clear its decisive importance.[27]

Churchill and Lindemann were wise to warn against relying on only one technology: had the Germans early on developed the "windows" technique (scattering metal strips to confuse detectors) then radar might have been disastrously neutralized in 1940. Moreover, radio detection was an untried idea in 1935, and Churchill doubted that Britain would have enough time to develop and deploy it. "I thought the war would come much quicker than it did," he wrote revealingly in an early draft, defending his alternative ideas.[28] But although it was therefore right to experiment, aerial mines never proved technically feasible, whereas radar was successfully implemented. This was not simply because of a single "wizard" technology. "Radio Detection and Ranging" (radar, for short) depended on rapid communication of data to centralized control rooms and swift deployment of fast fighters to intercept the enemy bombers. On neither of these matters did Churchill have any significant input. As with his ideas about the tank in World War I, Churchill's interest in technology was on the level of individual gadgets rather than integrated systems. Yet, and this is equally important, he was a quick learner. Once shown the prototype air-defense system as a whole in June 1939, he seized on it with informed enthusiasm. As *The Gathering Storm* rightly says, when Churchill became Prime Minister in 1940, he had "the advantage of a layman's insight into the problems of air warfare resulting from four long years of study and thought based upon the fullest official and technical information."[29]

The radar row is a good illustration of a general point: Churchill's vision in the 1930s, though farsighted, was not as clear as his memoirs suggest. Nor was he a lone voice crying in the wilderness, but one of several actors—in office, official-dom, the military, and Parliament—engaged in a complex battle to shift govern-ment policy on air defense. What mattered when assessing the Luftwaffe threat was not the crude total of planes but serviceable frontline strength—in other words, the number of combat aircraft for which the Germans had fuel, spare parts, and trained pilots to keep airborne in wartime. On these criteria, it would seem that Churchill exaggerated German potential, for instance predicting in September 1935 a total of 2,000 frontline aircraft by October 1936 and possibly 3,000 per year after that. In fact, the total was barely 4,000 even in September 1939. Moreover, German air rearmament for most of the 1930s had been directed toward a war against Poland and France. Only in 1938 was Britain desig-nated a likely enemy, and the Luftwaffe never really developed either the capac-ity or the doctrine for strategic bombing. But, in thirties Britain, discussion of the German air threat was conducted in alarmist rather than analytical terms. Chur-chill admits as much in *The Gathering Storm*: "I strove my utmost to galvanise the Government into vehemence and extraordinary preparation, even at the cost of world alarm. In these endeavours no doubt I painted the picture even darker than it was."[30]

In the 1930s, Churchill and his Whitehall sources were partly victims of Nazi disinformation, but they also entertained exaggerated fears about bombing itself. During the whole of the Second World War, 147,000 people were killed or maimed in the United Kingdom as a result of aerial bombardment.[31] But when Churchill addressed the Commons on 28 November 1934, he predicted that over seven to ten days of intensive bombing, between 30,000 and 40,000 Lon-doners would be killed or maimed and that, "under the pressure of continuous air attack," at least three or four million people would flee the metropolis for the surrounding countryside. In July 1936, he was even more hyperbolic as part of a delegation of senior MPs to see Baldwin: his estimates for bomb tonnage and casualty rates implied figures of 5,000 dead and 150,000 wounded from a single all-out raid on London. The first set of predictions does not appear in the extracts from his speech of 28 November 1934 printed in *The Gathering Storm*; the sec-ond is buried in an appendix.[32]

It is now clear that these exaggerations of the Luftwaffe and of the potency of bombing had a double-edged effect on the government: stimulating air rearma-ment but also inducing diplomatic paralysis. Until Britain had built up a bomber force sufficient to deter German attack, it seemed suicidal to risk war by con-fronting Hitler. This was the fundamental axiom of Chamberlain and the Chiefs of Staff during the Czech crisis of September 1938.[33] Only the deployment of radar and of the Hurricane and Spitfire fighters in 1939 gave confidence in home defense. Moreover, this preoccupation with the air diverted attention from the other two services, particularly the army—a consequence deplored at the time by none other than Henry Pownall, then an army bureaucrat.[34] A British Expeditionary Force for France and Belgium was low on Churchill's list of priorities. When he spoke of a "Grand Alliance" with France, he meant "the Union of the British Fleet and the French Army, together with their combined Air Forces."[35] In contrast with his passion for air rearmament, Churchill was slow to support peacetime conscription, unlike many critics of appeasement. He signed only two of the five Commons motions about national service introduced between July 1938 and April 1939, claiming in a newspaper article in May 1938 that "if our Fleet and our Air Force are adequate, there is no need for conscription in time of peace."[36]

As Donald Cameron Watt has observed, Churchill's rearmament campaign "never focused on the issues that might have made an impact on German military opinion."[37] Air rearmament had a bias toward isolationism—the defense of the United Kingdom—whereas greater resources for the army would have signaled an intention to project British power across the Channel. In all this, of course, Churchill was broadly at one with Chamberlain, most politicians, and public opinion, still haunted by the Somme and Passchendaele. That is why in May 1940 only 10 British divisions were to be found alongside 104 French, 22 Belgian, and 8 Dutch. As the military pundit Basil Liddell Hart wrote of the Western Front of 1914–1918, "It was heroic, but was it necessary? It was magnificent, but was it war?"[38] Churchill agreed that, even if Britain had to fight, a repeat of Flanders Fields would indeed be an unnecessary war. What he does *not* say about rearmament in *The Gathering Storm*, therefore, points us to his doubts about mass invasion of the Continent in later volumes of memoirs. And his refrain of the early 1930s, "Thank God for the French Army" reminds us that he, like most policymakers, never imagined the collapse of the Western Front in 1940.[39]

On diplomacy, as on defense, Churchill's retrospective concentration on Germany (informed by the events of 1940) distorts the events of the 1930s and, at times, his own part in them.

Since the archives were opened in the 1970s, it has become clear that British policymakers discerned a potential three-front threat in the 1930s. The menace of German airpower at home was combined with Japan's challenge to British interests in Asia and with Italy's threat to Egypt and the Suez Canal. Japan was, in fact, the initial concern after its invasion of Manchuria in 1931, and this provided the spur to British rearmament. Although the revival of German power took precedence after Hitler became Führer, in 1936 and 1937 it was the combination of Mussolini's empire building in Abyssinia and the Spanish Civil War that preoccupied ministers. Not until 1938, with the Anschluss and the Czech crisis, did Germany return to center stage. Even then, policymakers could not forget that from July 1937 Japanese and Chinese forces were locked in a major war across eastern China.

In *The Gathering Storm*, however, Churchill's eyes are fixed on Berlin. Just occasionally he glances east. "Surely there was fighting in 1931 between Japan and China?" he asked Deakin in a revealingly vague note on 30 June 1947. A couple of pages on the Manchurian crisis were duly added to chapter 5, but after that there is virtually nothing about events in Asia. The gap was noticed by Denis Kelly very late in the day, on 8 January 1948, and a brief reference to Japan's signature of the 1936 Anti-Comintern Pact was hastily inserted in chapter 12. Deakin suggested on 31 January that the Japanese story should be dealt with as "an introduction to their entry into war" in 1941. Churchill agreed, and the matter was relegated to volume 3. Yet Asia's virtual absence from *The Gathering Storm* skews Churchill's account of issues on which he is particularly critical—such as the Anglo-German naval agreement of 1934 and Chamberlain's campaign of Italian appeasement in 1937 and 1938. Wise or not, both were reactions to the menace of Japanese seapower.[40]

Although there are more references to the Mediterranean in *The Gathering Storm*, these do not bulk large. As with Japan, this mirrors Churchill's priorities in the 1930s. Warning the Commons during the Abyssinian crisis in October 1935, he pointed to German rearmament: "*There* is the dominant factor; *there* is the factor which dwarfs all others."[41] Contrary to many League of Nations enthusiasts, notably Eden, Churchill was not keen to make Italian aggression a moral and political issue. In Europe, Mussolini (about whom Churchill remained complimentary in public) was a potential bulwark against German expansion. Churchill supported the Stresa Agreement of April 1935, in which Britain, France, and Italy guaranteed Austria's independence. On the other hand, Churchill could see the danger if the League's council in Geneva imposed half-hearted sanctions against Mussolini, doing nothing to save Abyssinia yet also undermining cooperation against Hitler. At the height of the furor over the Hoare-Laval Pact, in which Britain and France ceded two thirds of Abyssinia to Italy, Churchill was vacationing in Spain and North Africa. "Looking back," he writes in *The Gathering Storm*, "I think I ought to have come home," speculating that he might have been able to marshal the antigovernment forces and bring down "the Baldwin régime." But his speeches and letters at the time suggest that he (as with many in the government) was genuinely undecided as to whether "Geneva or Stresa represented the best hope of containing Germany." By staying away from Westminster, he was able to remain on the fence.[42]

The Spanish Civil War receives only brief mention in chapter 12 of *The Gathering Storm*, where Churchill presents the two sides as equally barbarous: "In this quarrel I was neutral." His main point is to endorse the official policy of nonintervention, arguing that "with all the rest they had on their hands the British Government were right to keep out of Spain."[43] At the start of the Civil War, however, Churchill leaned toward Franco. A "revivified Fascist Spain in close sympathy with France and Germany is one kind of disaster" he wrote in an article in August 1936. "A Communist Spain spreading its snaky tentacles through Portugal and France is another, and many may think the worse." It would be "better for the safety of all if the Communists are crushed," he told his wife the following month, and in April 1937 he admitted to the Commons, "I will not pretend that, if I had to choose between Communism and Nazi-ism, I would choose Communism." Not until 1938–1939, with Hitler again on the march and Franco triumphant, did he state clearly that a fascist victory in Spain would be more dangerous to the British empire.[44]

On the other side of the diplomatic fence, Churchill tended to exaggerate the potential for a "Grand Alliance" against Germany—that slogan from the era of Marlborough that he used as the centerpiece of his speeches in 1938.

With regard to France, it remains debatable how far British appeasement was the reason or merely a pretext for French inertia in the 1930s. Churchill, as usual, includes qualifying passages that carefully straddle this divide. "More than once in these fluid years French Ministers in their ever-changing Governments were content to find in British pacifism an excuse for their own. Be that as it may," he adds, "they did not meet with any encouragement to resist German aggression from the British." In characteristically counterfactual mode, he leaves his readers with the impression that, over the Rhineland and elsewhere, British resolve could have tipped the balance. Yet historians now agree that there were many reasons for French inactivity—political, economic, and military. This was a country polarized between right and left, sapped by a series of feeble ministries, and wracked by a Depression that came in mid-decade, later than elsewhere in Europe, thereby undermining rearmament at the crucial moment. British isolationism was certainly a motive for French appeasement, but only one of several.[45]

On the Soviet Union, Churchill plays up signs of its readiness to intervene in the Czech crisis of 1938. Again, this issue remains controversial, but such evidence as has been gleaned from the Soviet archives suggests that Stalin had not decided what to do if the French honored their obligations, thereby bringing his own treaty with the Czechs into play, and certainly did not intend to act alone. Churchill again registers the necessary qualifications, notably on Soviet good faith, but the weight of his account is on the "astonishing" degree of "indifference," even "disdain," displayed by British and French leaders toward Moscow. For this, he adds, alluding to the Nazi-Soviet Pact, "we afterwards paid dearly."[46] In support, he highlights a public declaration by Maxim Litvinov, the Soviet Foreign Minister, and also private assurances by Ivan Maisky, Stalin's Ambassador in London, which Churchill passed on to the Foreign Office. (At an earlier stage, Churchill had a whole draft chapter entitled "The Maisky Incident.") Churchill also writes of the "intimate and solid friendship" between Moscow and Prague, arguing that Stalin felt "a very strong desire to help" the Czechs on account of "a personal debt" he felt to President Eduard Beneš because the latter had forwarded intelligence of German contacts with the Soviet military, which had triggered Stalin's purges in 1937. This assertion, fusing a talk he had with Beneš in 1944 and Russian-émigré gossip passed on by Isaiah Berlin, was toned down after pressure from a skeptical Deakin. But it served to enhance what Churchill called "the salient fact for the purposes of this account"; namely, "the close association of Russia and Czechoslovakia, and of Stalin and Beneš."[47]

Unlike in later volumes of the memoirs, the United States does not bulk large in *The Gathering Storm*. But one of Churchill's most trenchant criticisms of Chamberlain is over President Roosevelt's offer in January 1938 to convene an international conference to explore a general peace settlement. This cut across Chamberlain's plans for separate bilateral talks with Hitler and Mussolini, so the Prime Minister asked FDR to delay. A few days later, pressed by Eden, he invited the President to go ahead, but Roosevelt did not act. It is unlikely that the President had anything substantial in mind when he made his offer, but Churchill asserts: "We must regard its rejection—for such it was—as the last frail chance to save the world from tyranny otherwise than by war." That Chamberlain, he continues in mounting incredulity, "should have possessed the self-sufficiency to wave away the proffered hand stretched out across the Atlantic leaves one, even at this date, breathless with amazement." Here, transparently, the Cold War background to *The Gathering Storm* shines through. After Lend-Lease and the Marshall Plan, it was hard to recall the suspicion in 1930s Britain about American isolationism. Chamberlain's 1937 aphorism—that it was "always best and safest to count on nothing from the Americans except words"—expressed conventional wisdom in Whitehall. In a way Churchill did not intend, he was right to say of

British handling of the Roosevelt initiative, "One cannot to-day even reconstruct the state of mind which would render such gestures possible."[48]

TOGETHER WITH his counterfactuals, Churchill's simplification of the international scene in the 1930s—merging several conflicting storm clouds into one—is central to his critique of British appeasement. But the thrust of Churchill's indictment is also sharpened by what he *doesn't* say about politics at home, both in the 1920s (when he was in office) and in the 1930s (when he was not).

Although book 1 of *The Gathering Storm* runs nominally from 1919 to 1939, it skates very rapidly over the 1920s, especially after Churchill condensed two chapters into one after the debate at Marrakech. In consequence, Churchill omitted some interesting material—for instance, a long and defensive passage about what he had called in September 1945 "the biggest blunder" of his life: his approval as Chancellor in 1925 of Britain's return to the gold standard. Probably reacting to John Maynard Keynes's famous polemic, the draft argues that his decision had been right but the exchange rate had been too high. Why Churchill cut this passage is not clear, but it may have been in deference to Norman Brook, who suggested in December 1947 that it would be better to stick to the thirty-years-war theme and exclude material that made the book seem like a political memoir. (The evils of the return to gold were still an obsession for many of Brook's Labour masters.)[49]

Churchill also skates over his actions as Chancellor in other ways. Convinced in the 1920s of the need to combat the domestic appeal of Bolshevism—for instance, by extending pensions and cutting unemployment—he tried to reduce other government spending, of which the navy was a prime recipient. Thus, the apostle of a big navy in 1911–1914 became the Admiralty's fiercest critic in the mid-1920s, arguing that it now had more than enough. Both periods saw a major arms race, but in the first case Germany was the challenger, in the second Japan. Churchill was at pains to dismiss any serious threat. "A war with Japan!" he exclaimed to Baldwin in December 1924. "I do not believe there is the slightest chance of it in our lifetime."[50] Each year as Chancellor he hammered away at the naval estimates, particularly the budgets for cruisers, submarines, and the base at Singapore.

To formalize the position, Churchill designed the rolling Ten-Year Rule. Back in August 1919 the Cabinet had instructed the military services to operate on the assumption of no great war during the next decade. With that period nearing its end, in July 1928 Churchill persuaded the Cabinet that the rule should be continued subject to annual review, and it was not formally abandoned until

March 1932, after Japan's conquest of Manchuria. In drafts for *The Gathering Storm,* Churchill recalls that in the 1930s, when urging rapid rearmament, he was reproached for perpetuating the Ten-Year Rule. "It was said that this lulled the fighting departments into a false sense of security, that Research was neglected, and only short-term views prevailed." In one draft he admitted, "there may be some substance in this." But he went on to argue that each policy was right in its own time: the big difference was Hitler from 1933. This was a valid point, and it is the one he advances in the page-long discussion of the Ten-Year Rule eventually printed at the end of chapter 3. On the other hand, Churchill's musings in draft and his failure in the text to mention his battles with the Admiralty suggest that this was sensitive ground. Significantly, he changed the title of chapter 3, which deals with Europe in the later 1920s, to "Lurking Dangers." Its original title, "Germany Arms," might have undercut his central claim that the crucial mistakes were made *after* he left the Treasury.[51]

Labour's victory in May 1929 drove Churchill out of office, and he did not return in the Tory-dominated national government of 1931. The 1930s are now conventionally dubbed Churchill's "wilderness years." He used that phrase on the last page of *The Gathering Storm,* referring to the end of "eleven years in the political wilderness," but it was popularized by Martin Gilbert's book *Winston Churchill: The Wilderness Years* and the related TV series shown on both sides of the Atlantic in 1981–1982. Historian Alastair Parker has, however, questioned the appropriateness of this phrase, arguing that in the 1930s Churchill tempered his criticism of the government's foreign policy because of his persistent hopes of returning to office.[52] Little of this emerges in *The Gathering Storm.*

Churchill's campaign against the government's India policy in the early 1930s seems, in retrospect, a quixotic flourish by an incorrigible diehard. But it is now clear that much of the Tory party was unhappy about the proposed devolution of power and that in early 1931 and again in mid-1934 the government was in serious danger over its India bill. Churchill was genuinely outraged by the issue, but he also saw in it a chance to evict Baldwin and join a reconstituted national government led by Austen Chamberlain, the Tory elder statesman. Yet although the India bill dominated British politics from 1933 to 1935, filling 4,000 pages of parliamentary transcript with more than fifteen million words, it is hardly mentioned in *The Gathering Storm.* To do so would have distracted from Churchill's focus on Germany and betrayed his political motives.[53]

A new chapter opened in the summer of 1935, with the India bill passed and Baldwin now Prime Minister. Churchill expected that the autumn election would produce a smaller majority for the national government, more solicitude by Baldwin to the Tory right, and in consequence a Cabinet post for himself, ide-ally the Admiralty. He alludes to these hopes in *The Gathering Storm* but repre-sents his exclusion from office after the election as providential: "[N]ow one can see how lucky I was. Over me beat the invisible wings." He takes the same line when relating how Baldwin passed him over for the new post of Minister for the Coordination of Defence in March 1936. Again admitting disappointment, Churchill adds: "This was not the first time—or indeed the last—that I have received a blessing in what was at the time a very effective disguise."[54]

At the time, however, Churchill was desperate for office. On 8 March, the day after Hitler occupied the Rhineland, he called on Neville Chamberlain, then Chancellor of the Exchequer. According to Chamberlain's diary, Churchill said he was in "a very difficult position" because Baldwin did not propose to announce the name of the new minister until after the Commons debate on the Rhineland. He said he wanted to make a "telling speech" on foreign policy if excluded from the post—which Chamberlain understood to mean a "fierce attack" on Baldwin—but "not if there were any chance of its being offered him." Chamberlain refused to give any hint, and on 10 March Churchill pulled his punches in the Commons, making little reference to the Rhineland while offer-ing a broad and, to use Chamberlain's word, "constructive" survey of the defense scene. His reward was the appointment of Sir Thomas Inskip on 14 March.[55]

At that point, Churchill realized he had no chance of office as long as Bald-win remained premier, and this freed him to be more outspoken. A little-known sign of the new mood is his plan, immediately after Inskip's appointment, to write a polemical book, *The Foreign Policy of the Baldwin-MacDonald Regime*. Chur-chill moved fast: on 19 March 1936, George Harrap was ready to draw up a con-tract. By the end of the month, however, Churchill had changed his mind, perhaps because a deal for fortnightly articles in *The Evening Standard* would earn more money and attract greater attention. The book was never written, but Churchill returned to his outline of fourteen chapters when working on *The Gathering Storm*. "Consider incorporating in revise of Book I," he wrote on the top page. Certainly there are parallels between the two. In both, Churchill damns Baldwin for his deference to public opinion and the "inaccuracy" of his statement on German air strength. In the 1936 outline, one can find distinctive phrases used in *The Gathering Storm*, such as "The Economic Blizzard" and Baldwin "the great Party manager" with his "desire for a quiet life." Yet there are subtle differences between 1936 and 1948, not least in Churchill's treatment of Anthony Eden.[56]

Eden became Foreign Secretary in December 1935 and retained the post after Neville Chamberlain assumed the premiership in May 1937. With Baldwin gone, Churchill's political hopes revived, and this again affected his handling of foreign policy. Rearmament was now quickening, Hitler was relatively quiet, and Churchill persuaded himself that the government was moving toward his policy, "Arms and the Covenant." Then came Eden's resignation as Foreign Secretary in February 1938, mainly over whether to hold talks with Italy but also over Chamberlain's handling of Roosevelt's initiative. In *The Gathering Storm*, Churchill devotes a whole chapter to Eden's exit, treating it as a major turning point. This begins with a stark statement of policy differences between Chamberlain and Eden and ends with the purplest passage of *The Gathering Storm*, as Churchill recalls receiving the news of Eden's resignation on the evening of 20 February 1938. Throughout the war, he tells his readers, he never had any trouble sleeping, even in the darkest days of 1940. But that night, "sleep deserted me. From midnight till dawn I lay in my bed consumed with emotions of sorrow and fear," thinking of this "one strong, young figure standing up against long, dismal drawling tides of drift and surrender." Now, says Churchill, he was gone. "I watched the daylight slowly creep in through the windows, and saw before me in mental gaze the vision of Death."[57]

The stark introduction and vivid conclusion were introduced in later drafts to make the resignation more dramatic. This is not, perhaps, surprising. Eden was Churchill's closest lieutenant for most of the 1940s, first as his wartime Foreign Secretary and then as Deputy Leader of the Opposition. In fact, he helped shape the account of 1935–1938 given in *The Gathering Storm*. Sent the relevant chapters for comment, Eden pressed Churchill to highlight his differences with Chamberlain in 1938 and also to tone down criticism of the government over Italian sanctions and the Rhineland crisis in 1935–1936.[58]

In the 1930s, however, Churchill was skeptical about Eden. In his March 1936 book outline he attacked him for pressing ahead with League of Nations sanctions against Italy "when the hour for a new German plunge had arrived" (the Rhineland).[59] As for the crisis of 1938, Churchill told Eden in private on several occasions that he "should have chosen a bigger issue for resignation." In 1943, according to Lord Halifax, Churchill said that Eden "had staged it badly and hadn't made any effort to work with all the powerful factors (such as Winston!) who would have co-operated." The sleepless-night story is not unique to *The Gathering Storm*—Churchill told it at least twice in private in 1945 and 1946—but the reason he gave for his sleeplessness was different from that in the doom-laden account in his memoirs. "I was too excited," he told Moran at Yalta. "It was a grand thing to do, but I never felt it was done in the right way. More could have been made of it."[60] In fact, Churchill was often scathing about Eden in private. "I think you will see what a lightweight Eden is," he told his wife in January 1936, after Eden was appointed Foreign Secretary, and in February 1940 Churchill went so far as to say "he would rather have Chamberlain than Eden as Prime Minister by eight to one."[61]

In the light of recent research, the whole Churchill-Eden-Chamberlain triangle in 1938 looks very different from that in Churchill's memoirs. In February, Churchill viewed Eden's resignation from the Foreign Office as a shock but not a mortal blow to his hopes of working with Chamberlain. Although abstaining in the Opposition's vote of censure, he was the fourth Tory MP to sign a statement expressing continued support for Chamberlain and his policy, and in the summer he still believed that a satisfactory agreement could be reached concerning the Sudetenland.[62] It was only after Munich that Churchill's opposition to Chamberlain became unqualified. Again he abstained in the Commons, but this time only after being dissuaded from actually voting against his own party leader. By contrast, Eden was almost persuaded by the premier's final speech in the Munich debate to vote with the government rather than abstain and, hopeful of returning to office, made conciliatory noises in private to Number 10. Churchill did nothing of the sort on this occasion, unlike February, and dramatized his abstention by sitting in the Commons chamber while the votes were counted. His ringing denunciation of Munich as "a total and unmitigated defeat" contrasted with Eden's more tempered criticisms.[63] While Eden continued to pull his punches during 1938 and 1939, Churchill eclipsed him as the most trenchant critic of appeasement. The government U-turn in March 1939, with its guarantees to Eastern Europe, was seen as vindication of Churchill not Eden, and by July several newspapers were campaigning hard for his return to office—"led by the *Daily Telegraph*," Churchill added to his draft, after a suggestion from Lord Camrose.[64] In September 1939, a top job for Churchill was essential if Chamberlain was to seem serious about the war. He was given the Admiralty and a seat in the new War Cabinet. Eden, although a former Foreign Secretary, could be fobbed off with a non-Cabinet portfolio at the Dominions Office.

Throughout the 1930s, therefore, Churchill had agitated for office, out of thwarted ambition and also out of the conviction, amply justified after 1939, that he could make a difference. His problems were tactical. Was open criticism or quiet persuasion the best route back? At what point should he burn his bridges and mount direct attacks? Under both Baldwin and Chamberlain, the prophetic voice was often muted, but in the memoirs it sounds out clear and strong. At times, book 1 of *The Gathering Storm* is almost history with the politics left out.

———

AFTER THE GUARANTEE of Poland's independence and territorial integrity, Churchill felt much closer to Chamberlain: a line had now been drawn. However, as Churchill notes in his memoirs, this was a decision "taken at the worst possible moment and on the least satisfactory ground." Czechoslovakia was the most advanced industrial state in Eastern Europe, with the best army, but Britain had refused to guarantee it, and Poland "with hyena appetite" had joined in its destruction. Moreover, the Polish guarantee compromised any chance of British agreement with Stalin, whose troops could fight Germany only by crossing Polish soil, which the Poles had no intention of allowing, having fought a brutal war with Russia in 1921–1922. Churchill has no doubt in his chapter on "The Soviet Enigma" that the British government should have made the search for a Soviet alliance its priority, leaving the implications for Poland till later: "The alliance of Britain, France and Russia would have struck deep alarm into the heart of Germany in 1939, and no one can prove that war might not even then have been averted." This counterfactual is open to question in the light of what we know now: Hitler was determined to gobble up Poland, and after Munich he was sure British leaders—those "worms"—would not resist him. But these passages remind us that war came under circumstances that Churchill did not choose. How to square Britain's commitments to Poland and its alliance with Russia would prove one of the greatest diplomatic headaches of his wartime premiership.[65]

The most significant counterfactual in book 1 of *The Gathering Storm* is Churchill's repeated claim that Britain would have been wiser to fight Hitler in September 1938 over Czechoslovakia than a year later over Poland. At the end of the chapter "Munich Winter," devoting three pages to this issue, he acknowledges the core of the retrospective case for appeasement—namely, that the extra year allowed Britain to modernize the RAF and deploy the essential radar system. During the drafting, he wrote an essay on how the Battle of Britain might have gone if waged a year earlier and was forced to concede that, given the "very narrow margin" of victory in 1940, "it might have been lost if fought in 1939." So in the final version, shifting ground, he insists that there was "no possibility of a decisive Air Battle of Britain" until Hitler had occupied France and the Low Countries, thereby obtaining bases within striking distance of southeast England, and that the German Army was not capable of defeating France in 1938 or 1939: "The vast tank production with which they broke the French Front did not come into existence till 1940." He concludes, therefore, that "the year's breathing-space said to be 'gained' by Munich left Britain and France in a much worse position compared to Hitler's Germany than they had been at the Munich crisis."[66] Churchill's argument is problematic—for instance, French tank production also increased dramatically in 1939 and 1940—and, as we shall see, German victory in 1940 resulted from tactical surprise more than material superiority. But many historians would now agree with Churchill's verdict: September 1938 was the time for confrontation, not negotiation.[67]

Book 1 of *The Gathering Storm* is weakened by too many counterfactuals, by fixation on German airpower, by Churchill's exaggeration of potential allies and by neglect of his political ambition. It is the book of a man excluded from office for a whole decade but for whom, in retrospect, that ostracism proved providential. As Vansittart reminded him, commenting on the drafts, those in power in the 1930s had to balance the threats from Hitler and Mussolini, could not ignore Japan or rely on the French, and at every stage had to fight the Treasury for money to rearm.[68] Out of government, Churchill did not have to make hard choices between relative evils. (He did in 1924–1929 but skips neatly over that period in his memoirs.) In the 1930s and even more in *The Gathering Storm*, he could focus on a few great causes—chosen on their merits but also for political advantage. India and the abdication nearly destroyed him, but Hitler remade his political career, and in 1938–1939 his now outspoken criticism of appeasement was vindicated by events. At this point, his "contribution to history" merges with history itself. Here the deeds and the book become one, and both have withstood the judgments of posterity.

CHAPTER 8

TWILIGHT FOR CHAMBERLAIN,
NEW DAWN FOR CHURCHILL

T HE TWILIGHT WAR" — book 2 of *The Gathering Storm* — deals with
Churchill's second period at the Admiralty, 3 September 1939 to 10 May
1940, in "the room I had quitted in pain and sorrow almost exactly a
quarter of a century before."[1] As in the Great War, he intervened in strategy and
operations far beyond the normal brief of a First Lord of the Admiralty, which was
to protect the budget and political interests of the Royal Navy. Once again, he
tried to open up the flanks of a static continental war — this time in Scandinavia
rather than Asia Minor — and the Norway campaign, like that in the Dardanelles,
ended in failure and recriminations. In 1940, however, the political outcome was
very different from 1915: instead of disgrace and resignation, Churchill was catapulted into 10 Downing Street. The winter of 1939–1940 was Chamberlain's twilight, but it heralded a new dawn for Churchill.

Book 2 relates this now familiar story but also much more. In it, Churchill
wrestles with the false assumptions of the Phony War — about the strength of the
French Army, the supremacy of British seapower, and the irrelevance of tactical
airpower, about the impotence of Japan, the vulnerability of Italy, and the potential of Turkey. "The Twilight War" prefigures much of Churchill's wartime strategy.

CHAMBERLAIN HAD originally envisaged a War Cabinet of ministers without
departments but changed his plan, partly because he hoped that responsibility for

a major ministry would leave Churchill little time to meddle elsewhere. Wishful thinking! Despite his own burdens, Churchill fired off a barrage of minutes about other departments, some of which were extremely blunt. "I hear constant complaints from every quarter of the lack of organisation on the Home Front," he told Sir John Anderson, the Home Secretary. "Can't we get at it?"[2]

Churchill prints this and other such minutes in the early chapters of book 2, including several he sent on all aspects of the war to the Prime Minister. "As we meet every single day at the War Cabinet this would seem unnecessary," Chamberlain told his sister on 17 September 1939, "but of course I realise that these letters are for the purposes of quotation in the Book he will write hereafter. Hitherto I haven't answered them, but the one I got yesterday was so obviously recording his foresight and embodied warnings so plainly for purposes of future allusion that I thought I must get something on the record too which would have to be quoted in the book." (It was.) Churchill's future war memoirs became an in-joke in Whitehall. In January 1940 Lord Halifax, the Foreign Secretary, forwarded to Chamberlain a long letter from Churchill about lack of action in Scandinavia with the note, "It's one more for the book!" (He was right.)[3]

During the autumn of 1939, relations between the First Lord and the Prime Minister settled down. Churchill accepted that Chamberlain was serious about the war, even if often disagreeing about how to conduct it, while Chamberlain decided that Churchill was animated by impulse rather than ambition: "Winston is in some respects such a child that he neither knows his own motives or sees where his actions are carrying him."[4] What helped cement their new relationship was the dinner the Churchills gave for the Chamberlains on 13 November in their apartment in Admiralty House. The two couples had never dined socially before; indeed, Churchill could recall no other "intimate social conversation" in two decades of political business. But that night, Chamberlain waxed eloquent about his six years in the 1890s, spent, at the behest of his father, trying to grow sisal on a barren island in the West Indies. Churchill, who knew the story only in barest outline, devotes a whole page to it in his memoirs, to show how Hitler failed to realize that, at root, he was dealing with "a hard-bitten pioneer from the outer marches of the British Empire!" Clementine pooh-poohed the anecdote when she read it in draft—"Three months annual holiday & access to a gay little town like Nassau is not a very lonely, arduous existence"—but Churchill clearly found the evening revealing and reassuring.[5]

These early chapters also introduce Churchill's greatest wartime ally. On 11 September, President Roosevelt sent Churchill a note inviting him to keep "in touch personally with anything you want me to know about." Churchill says he "responded with alacrity, using the signature of 'Naval Person,' and thus began that long and memorable correspondence—covering perhaps a thousand communications on each side, and lasting till his death more than five years later." He also notes, "I had only met him once in the previous war. It was at a dinner at Gray's Inn, and I had been struck by his magnificent presence in all his youth and strength. There had been no opportunity for anything but salutations."[6] This allusion to 1918 amused Robert Sherwood, the biographer of Harry Hopkins. "During the last war," Sherwood wrote Beaverbrook in May 1948, "Mr. Churchill repeatedly asserted that he and Roosevelt had never met before Argentia [the Atlantic meeting in August 1941] but evidently his memory has been refreshed." In *Roosevelt and Hopkins*, published later that year, Sherwood stated that in 1918 Churchill "apparently failed to take much notice" of Roosevelt and "had promptly forgotten this encounter." This "was a somewhat sore point with Roosevelt."[7]

During the Phony War, the Churchill-Roosevelt correspondence amounted to only seven messages and a phone call from Churchill, and these do not bulk large in "The Twilight War." Churchill originally intended to quote one message from the President and three from himself, but on 1 April 1948 the normally vigilant Norman Brook realized that he had not obtained the consent of the U.S. government.[8] Five days later, he learned that the Truman administration was objecting to reproduction of *any* Churchill-Roosevelt messages, claiming that this would fuel congressional demands for publication of the whole correspondence, which would reveal FDR's bias toward Britain during the period of U.S. formal neutrality. Brook protested, but—to resolve the immediate problem of *The Gathering Storm*, the newspaper serialization of which was imminent—he provided Churchill with paraphrases of the three messages sent to Roosevelt. Churchill had been unaware of Brook's slipup—"he spoke (to my relief) more in sorrow than in anger," the Cabinet Secretary noted—and expressed thanks for the "excellent" paraphrases, which he included wholesale in his text. The two pages that Norman Brook contributed to "The Action off the River Plate" began his distinguished career as the most unlikely ghostwriter of *The Second World War*.[9]

CHURCHILL'S MAIN TOPIC in "The Twilight War" is naturally the war at sea. At the Admiralty, he threw himself into the task, his formidable capacity for work fortified by an hour's sleep in the afternoon: "By this means I was able to press a day and a half's work into one." He also forged a close partnership with Admiral Sir Dudley Pound, recently appointed First Sea Lord and therefore

Churchill's senior staff officer. On 3 September 1939, they "eyed each other amicably but doubtfully," Churchill tells us—the first draft simply said "doubtfully"—but soon "our friendship and mutual confidence grew and ripened." On the face of it, theirs was an unlikely combination. Pound was aloof, grave, and a bit of a plodder. He welcomed Churchill's pugnacity and drive but feared his mercurial nature. He decided from the start to fight only on really important matters, and even then indirectly. Rather than block Churchill openly and force a row, the First Sea Lord usually commissioned a staff study and then came back with a paper showing coldly and factually why the idea was impossible. By then, Churchill's mind had often moved on to something else.[10]

The new First Lord initiated a weekly radio broadcast in which, recalled his Director of Naval Intelligence, Admiral John Godfrey, in 1965, "good news was made to seem better; bad news was toned down, delayed or sometimes suppressed." In particular, Churchill consistently exaggerated U-boat losses. In *The Gathering Storm*, he prints some of these statements with footnotes admitting that the figures did not correspond to what "we now know." According to Godfrey, the figures were estimated pretty accurately at the time by Naval Intelligence, but Churchill and Pound deliberately ignored them. When the First Lord claimed, for instance, in February 1940 that 28 U-boats had been sunk, Godfrey estimated 9. (The correct figure was 10).[11]

What Churchill recognized, of course, was that good news was vital for morale. And as Godfrey observed, "no one was more conscious than Mr. Churchill of the popularity of the bringer of good tidings." In *The Gathering Storm*, Churchill reports at length his debut speech to the Commons as First Lord on 26 September 1939. "I had a good tale to tell," not least the claim that the Royal Navy had already destroyed a quarter of operational U-boats, and the speech, he says, was "extremely well received by the House." Reaction at the time was documented by the MP Harold Nicolson. Chamberlain spoke first, "dressed in deep mourning relieved only by a white handkerchief and gold watch chain." During his lugubrious statement, wrote Nicolson, one felt the confidence of the House "dropping inch by inch." Beside the Prime Minister sat the hunched figure of Churchill, "looking like the Chinese god of plenty suffering from acute indigestion." The impact of his speech was far greater than one could divine afterward from the printed text, because he sounded every note "from resolution to sheer boyishness." Not only could one feel "the spirits of the House rising with every word," said Nicolson, but in those twenty minutes Churchill "brought himself nearer the post of Prime Minister" than ever before.[12]

For all the First Lord's boosterism, however, in 1939–1940 the war at sea did not go according to plan. That became clear to Churchill in 1947 when he stumbled on a "Memorandum on Sea-Power" that he had sent Chamberlain at the end of March 1939—one that definitely did not read well in the light of subsequent events. How Churchill presents it in *The Gathering Storm* is of interest, not only as an example of his editorial methods but also for what it reveals of his conception of naval warfare and grand strategy on the eve of war.[13]

Churchill's memo of 25 March 1939 rested on two basic assumptions. One was that "the submarine has been mastered. . . . There will be losses, but nothing to affect the scale of events." The other assumption was that "in my opinion, given with great humility (because these things are very difficult to judge), an air attack on British warships, armed and protected as they now are, will not prevent full exercise of their superior sea-power." In other words, Churchill was saying, the balance of seapower was back where it had been forty years earlier, with surface vessels ruling the waves, able to counter the threats from below and above.

Secure in these assumptions, he went on to assess the challenges posed by Britain's three potential adversaries: "Assuming Italy is hostile, which we may perhaps hope will not be the case, England's first battlefield is the Mediterranean." He was confident that British forces alone could secure "complete command of the Mediterranean, certainly within two months, possibly sooner." The damage to Italy "may be fatal to her power of continuing the war.

"On no account must anything which threatens us in the Far East divert us from this prime objective," Churchill continued. If Japan declared war, Britain must accept that "all our interests in the Yellow Sea [such as Hong Kong and Shanghai] will be temporarily effaced," but Singapore should be "easy" to hold: "A fortress of this character with cannon which can hold any fleet at arm's length only requires an adequate garrison and supplies of food and ammunition, preferably for a year; but even six months would probably do." By then, the navy would have cleaned up the Mediterranean. Churchill did not think the Japanese would even try to attack Singapore. "It is as far from Japan as Southampton is from New York," and they would have to commit an army of 60,000 men and the bulk of their fleet across vulnerable lines of communication. "They are an extremely sensible people," and one could "take it as quite certain that Japan would not run such a risk." As long as the Royal Navy was undefeated and Singapore secure, "no invasion of Australia and New Zealand is possible," Churchill concluded. The very idea was "ludicrous."

What then of Germany? Assuming Britain had secured the Mediterranean and no attack had been launched against Singapore or Australia, he wanted the

British fleet to take control of the Baltic. Here must be "the sole great offensive against Germany of British sea-power." At the last minute, however, Churchill drew back. He added in pen: "However by that time the entry [into the Baltic] would probably be fortified & Denmark in German hands. Therefore the whole idea is purely hypothetical as well as remote."

This memo of March 1939 was not entirely original. Churchill was only following conventional wisdom in the Admiralty when he asserted that the submarine and the aircraft had been mastered. On the threat from below he had to change his tune quickly in the autumn of 1939—on 14 October a U-boat attack forced the Home Fleet temporarily to evacuate its supposedly impregnable base at Scapa Flow in the Orkney Islands—but on the threat from above he remained complacent, and this was of prime importance in 1940–1941. As for grand strategy, Churchill was addressing the problem that crippled all naval planning in the 1930s: the Royal Navy could cope with two enemies but not three. Germany was obviously the prime danger, threatening the British Isles themselves, but Britain was committed to send the Mediterranean fleet to Singapore in the event of war with Japan, to reassure Australia and New Zealand. Since this paralyzed action against Italy, Churchill was at pains to deride any threat to Singapore. His ideas on knocking out Italy paralleled those advanced at the time by Admiral Sir Roger Backhouse, then First Sea Lord, who favored a preemptive air and naval attack on Mussolini. But further analysis, and the replacement of Backhouse by Dudley Pound in May 1939, prompted a change of heart. Pound argued that the strength of Italian airpower precluded any offensive action in the Mediterranean, and this suited the Foreign Office, which favored passivity against Italy to keep the fleet free for Singapore. In his views about the Baltic, Churchill was on his own. Lord Chatfield, then Minister for Coordination of Defence, told him that action there would depend on the position in the Mediterranean and Far East.[14]

Churchill's memorandum of 25 March 1939 constituted the strategic foundation of his tenure as First Lord of the Admiralty. In 1947, however, it required a lot of explaining. His first thought was to print it whole with a long preamble of extenuation. This was "no more than my personal outlook" at the time; "some of it reads oddly in the light of what happened in the second and third years of the war"; and "I frequently modified or changed my views" once in contact with "expert Naval opinion" and "the hard teaching of daily events." In successive drafts during the autumn of 1947, however, Churchill cut many of the embarrassing parts and then decided to turn the paper into a prose overview of his thinking in September 1939, without indicating its provenance. He asserts that if Mussolini had entered the war, the Mediterranean should have been Britain's "first battlefield" and that victory there ("within two months and possibly sooner") might have been "fatal" to Italy's "power of continuing the war." He admits he had "accepted too readily" prewar Admiralty assumptions that the U-boat had been mastered and that surface warships were safe from the air. On the other hand, he says, during the first year "nothing of major importance occurred" in the U-boat war, and "no British capital ship was sunk by air attack." He prints a lengthy paraphrase of his confidence about the Far East, shorn of the more hyperbolic phrases, but insists that his assertion that Australasia would be in no danger "in the first year of world war" proved entirely correct. As for the Baltic material, this disappeared from the chapter entirely, because it became a central theme of the whole of "The Twilight War."[15]

On his fourth day at the Admiralty, Churchill asked the Naval Staff to prepare "a plan for forcing a passage into the Baltic." While not oblivious to the threat from the air, he was confident it could be countered. He urged the Admiralty to strengthen several older "Royal Sovereign" battleships with watertight side compartments (bulges) against torpedoes and with armor-plated decks as defense against bombs. As Churchill liked to put it, the bulges were the "galoshes" and the decks the "umbrella" to protect the R-class vessels. This was not a novel idea: in volume 2 of *The World Crisis* (1923), Churchill had expatiated on the "bulged" battleship as "the beginning of the torpedo-proof fleet." Now he resurrected these ideas in order to seize command of the Baltic (Operation Catherine). In a minute of 12 September, printed as an appendix to *The Gathering Storm*, Churchill calls this "the supreme naval offensive open to the Royal Navy" (an echo of his 25 March memo), the success of which "would probably determine the action of the Scandinavian States."[16]

Initially, Churchill drafted a full chapter entitled "The Baltic. Catherine. New Construction," but in November 1947 this material was cut and fused with the previous chapter to form "War Cabinet Problems." In that chapter, Churchill describes more briefly his plans for the R-class battleships and says he "deeply regretted" that they never came to fruition—"one reason after another was advanced, some of them well-founded, for not putting the work in hand." (In the draft he called the idea nothing less than "a short cut to victory.") In a later chapter, "A Dark New Year," he quotes his minute to Pound on 15 January accepting "reluctantly" that Catherine would not be possible in 1940. Again, his account conceals the anger of the initial draft, for the murder of Catherine was classic Pound—a Churchillian idea embraced in principle but smothered in practice. The First Sea Lord "was all for exploration," Churchill tells us with studied precision.[17]

On Italy, meanwhile, Churchill did an about-face. In the winter of 1938–1939 he often spoke of the Mediterranean as "our decisive battle-ground at sea" from which Mussolini's navy could be driven in a matter of weeks. But after the Italians decided to stay neutral, Churchill made virtue out of necessity, presenting a paper to the Cabinet on 18 October entitled "Possible Naval Détente with Italy in the Mediterranean," which claimed that "everyone can see how necessary it is to have Italy friendly and how desirable to have her an Ally." Churchill reproduced this in full in an early draft, then relegated it to an appendix, before removing it entirely. All that remains is a throwaway line about how the disasters in Poland "made me all the more anxious to keep Italy out of the war" and also the heading "Possible Détente with Italy," which he and the Syndicate forgot to remove from the contents summary for this chapter.[18]

New friendliness toward Italy did not, however, mean that Churchill had lost interest in the Mediterranean; only that he was looking farther east. In "The Ruin of Poland," he prints extracts from a Cabinet paper he wrote on 25 September 1939, speculating on the prospects for a "south-eastern front" if Russia and the Balkan states felt threatened by Nazi moves toward the Black Sea after victory in Poland. But Churchill did not print the next sentence: "I should imagine that this movement was very near and it will entail a general war in the Balkans." He also removed, again without indicating the gaps, passages showing his keen desire to bring Turkey into the war and his readiness to send British and French troops to Constantinople—"in spite of Russian complications, this line might be explored."[19]

Why did Churchill edit out his hopes in the early weeks of the war for Italian amity and a Turkish alliance? Probably because they proved to be so much at odds with subsequent events: Mussolini joined Hitler in June 1940, while the Turks sat on the fence for the whole war. Moreover, talk of a Balkan front and of sending British troops to Constantinople sounded too much like the Dardanelles all over again. In the Great War, of course, Turkey was an enemy, not a potential ally, but the same sense of its importance pervades The World Crisis. In many ways, in fact, Churchill's thinking in 1939–1940 reflects that of a quarter-century before: bulged battleships, the significance of Turkey, his restless probing for opportunities in both the Baltic and the Mediterranean. In The Gathering Storm, as in volume 2 of The World Crisis, he also plays down his desire for action in both theaters at once, highlighting the eastern Mediterranean in the earlier memoir, and the Baltic in this. Revealing his enthusiasm for both might have suggested recklessness rather than drive.

Churchill's basic aim in 1939, as he says, was to counter the Admiralty's "defensive obsession" and seize the initiative. In *The World Crisis*, he contrasted the "negative" and "forward" schools of admirals, and his battle with Pound continued that struggle. "I could never become responsible for a naval strategy which excluded the offensive principle, and relegated us to keeping open the lines of communication and maintaining the blockade," he told the First Sea Lord in a paper of 11 December 1939 that was not used in the memoirs. In 1915, the Dardanelles plan had started as a naval operation to insert a squadron into the Black Sea and mushroomed into a major amphibious campaign. Similarly, by January 1940 Churchill was lobbying for nothing less than "a new theatre of operations in Scandinavia." This was not, he stressed, "action merely for action's sake" but to wrest the initiative from Germany, where it had lain since the start of the war.[20] As in 1915, so in 1940, Churchill's strategy was predicated on the assumption of stalemate on the Western Front.

CHURCHILL IS RENOWNED as a pioneer of the tank, partly because of his own account in *The World Crisis*, though in reality he was one of several godfathers: the armored prototypes he sponsored in 1914–1916 were more like personnel carriers than mobile artillery.[21] He is even better known for his 1930s warnings about German airpower—which, as we have seen, he somewhat distorted when recollecting them in *The Gathering Storm*. Churchill was alarmed at strategic bombing, the civilian casualties of which he greatly exaggerated, whereas he was relatively complacent about *tactical* airpower. Writing for *Collier's* magazine in January 1939, he cited the Spanish Civil War as evidence that, "so far as fighting troops are concerned, it would seem that aircraft are an additional complication rather than a decisive weapon." Spain and China showed "that an air attack on trench lines and fortified points is incomparably less effective than the bombardment of artillery." In parallel, he played down the modern potential of the tank. An article entitled "How Wars of the Future Will Be Waged," for *The News of the World* in April 1938, extolled the "glorious" contributions of tanks to the victory of 1918 but doubted that they would "play as decisive a part in the next war. . . . Nowadays, the anti-tank rifle and the anti-tank gun have made such great strides that the poor tank cannot carry a thick enough skin to stand up to them." He speculated that, if tanks were to advance, "it will very often be only as moles"—armored bulldozers cutting trenches at right angles to enemy lines.[22]

The "mole" was, in fact, Churchill's deus ex machina of the Phony War. "The Front in France" contains a brief reference to "one kind of long-term method" by which "I then thought the fire-power of the defensive could be overcome." The reader is directed to Appendix O, where one finds a note relating how Churchill, as he had for armored vehicles in 1915, turned to the Directorate of Naval Construction for prototypes. Starting with "a suggestive little machine, about three feet long" in the Admiralty basement, he staged bigger and better demonstrations for the Prime Minister and leading generals. Eventually, in February 1940, the Cabinet approved construction of 200 "narrow" and 40 "wide" Cultivators. In its final, "mammoth" version, the mole was 77 feet long and 8 feet high, weighed more than 100 tons, and could cut a trench five feet deep and seven and a half feet wide at half a mile per hour. But as Churchill admits, "a very different form of warfare was soon to descend on us like an avalanche, sweeping all before it," and in the end only a handful were produced. Churchill kept five in reserve till the end of the war, in case they were needed to breach the Siegfried Line. Such was the tale of Cultivator, he tells us: "I am responsible but impenitent."[23]

Gunpower not airpower, moles rather than tanks, the supremacy of defense over offense—these were Churchill's prophecies of land warfare in the late 1930s. He acknowledges his errors briefly in *The Gathering Storm*: "in the war of armies I was under the thrall of defensive fire-power."[24] But earlier versions were far fuller, because Churchill seems to have been genuinely shaken by what the "Provisional Final" draft of October 1947 called his "incredible neglect" of the tank in the 1930s:

> In my conscience I reproach myself for having allowed my concentration upon the Air and the Navy to have absorbed all my thought. . . . [T]his Tank business was so much in my personal sphere that I am surprised I did not push it further. Undoubtedly I rested too much under the impression, derived from long thought about the previous war, "Cannons can kills tanks". This was proved true, but not at the onfall.

There "really was no reason," he went on, why the British Expeditionary Force (BEF) in France in May 1940 should not have had two or three well-equipped armored divisions—"in which case quite a different story would have been on record." This was a remarkable self-indictment, but all that survives in print is a general paragraph lamenting the absence of "even one armoured division" in the BEF.[25]

In 1939 and 1940, however, British strategy was not to force a decision on the Western Front but to prepare for a long struggle, perhaps lasting three years, in which the empire's material resources and financial reserves would eventually prove superior. That said, Chamberlain hoped Nazi Germany might collapse from within more quickly, bringing to power a post-Hitler regime with which Britain could negotiate. This hope reflected an underlying assumption of British intelligence that the German economy was already "taut" and might break from shortage of raw materials.[26] Since Winston the Bulldog is usually portrayed as the complete antithesis of Neville the Appeaser, it is important to look more closely at how he thought at the time that the war would be won.

On 8 October 1939, Churchill urged a stronger tone to the official rejection of Hitler's latest peace proposal. But, he told Chamberlain, his revisions did "not close the door upon any genuine offer." His covering note for the Cabinet implied that peace was possible in principle with a German government that had liberated the Poles and Czechs, made suitable reparation, and showed by "acts, not words" that its "sole aim" was to "build a free, a peaceful and a prosperous Europe in which Germany, as one of its greatest nations, should play a leading and an honoured part." This would, of course, have required a massive change in policy and politics—nothing less than a German revolution—but it would have been a negotiated peace. Just how far Churchill was in 1939 from the eventual Allied slogan of unconditional surrender is suggested by the way, on Gordon Allen's advice, he cut this "Note on the German Peace Suggestions" and the accompanying correspondence from the draft of book 2.[27]

On Britain's overall strategy of playing for time in a long war, Churchill was supportive in late 1939, at times even optimistic. "I feel we may compare the position now very favourably with that of 1914," he told Pound in an appraisal written on Christmas Day. (Churchill was no believer in holidays.) "I also have the feeling (which may be corrected at any moment) that the Kaiser's Germany was a much tougher customer than Nazi Germany." The parenthesis was prudent, but the prediction is still striking. Another memo to Pound on 15 January 1940 contained the phrase "but the war may well be raging in 1941," suggesting Churchill did not rule out the possibility it might end earlier. Both memoranda are quoted in *The Gathering Storm*. On the other hand, the Cabinet minutes of 12 January (not printed) quote Churchill saying that "up to the present he had felt that time was on our side, but he was not sure that this would continue to be so." Was the RAF gradually overtaking the Luftwaffe, or was it the other way around? This was the meeting at which Churchill pressed to mine Norwegian territorial waters (the "Leads") and criticized how since September "we had let the initiative rest with Germany."[28] By now, he was keen for action, but it was still action within the overall strategic framework. Mining the Leads would imperil German imports of iron ore and tighten the raw-material bottleneck that, Whitehall believed, was Hitler's greatest weakness. And Churchill only turned, as in 1915, to the flanks because of his fundamental confidence that the Western Front was secure.

DURING THE WINTER MONTHS, when the upper Baltic was frozen, Swedish iron ore was sent overland to Narvik and thence to Germany in ships that kept within Norwegian territorial waters. This saved them from attack by the Royal Navy. The answer, Churchill claimed in the Cabinet on 19 September 1939, was to mine the Leads and drive the ships into open sea. When the Russo-Finnish War broke out on 30 November 1939, the War Office began exploring the feasibility of sending troops across Norway and Sweden to help the Finns, using Narvik as a base. Churchill eagerly supported these ideas, and prints in *The Gathering Storm* a lengthy paper of advocacy he sent to the Cabinet on 16 December. "I sympathised ardently with the Finns," he says by way of preface, and "I welcomed this new and favourable breeze" to the iron-ore project. The second claim is true, the first more questionable. On 16 November, he had told the Cabinet "it would be a mistake to stiffen the Finns against making concessions to the USSR." This followed his line that autumn that any strengthening of Russia's position in the Baltic was desirable because, despite the Nazi-Soviet Pact, Britain hoped for a Grand Alliance. In *The Gathering Storm*, however, his U-turn on Finland goes unmentioned.[29]

Churchill's plan to mine the Leads was strongly opposed by Lord Halifax and the Foreign Office, fearful of how such a breach of Norwegian neutrality would be regarded by the United States. It might also give Germany a pretext to thrust through neutral Belgium and Holland. On 12 January 1940, a majority of the War Cabinet sided with the Foreign Secretary. This, complained Churchill three days later, was symptomatic of "the tremendous array of negative arguments and forces" being put up against attempts at the offensive, warning that "victory will never be won by taking the line of least resistance."[30] It was not until the fall of the Daladier government in France on 19 March, in part because of the failure to help Finland, that the War Cabinet agreed to go ahead. Early on 8 April, the first minefields were laid around Narvik. The next morning, Hitler invaded Denmark and Norway.

The Nazi assault on Scandinavia came as an almost total surprise to the Allies. It represented a major intelligence failure, both at the level of collection (German ciphers were as yet unbroken, and photographic intelligence was in its infancy) and also in terms of analysis. (The Joint Intelligence Committee still lacked the capacity to coordinate the independent appraisals from individual departments.)[31] Chamberlain's own asides betray the general complacency: on 29 February, for instance, he assured the Cabinet that "there was nothing very formidable to be feared from German retaliation." On 5 April, the day the Cabinet finally agreed to mine the Leads, he crowed to a Tory gathering that "one thing is certain": Hitler had "missed the bus." Churchill prints this speech at length in his chapter "Before the Storm." He does not twist the knife, observing merely that "this proved an ill-judged utterance."[32]

Yet Churchill was implicated in the intelligence failure. "He personally doubted whether the Germans would land a force in Scandinavia," the Cabinet minutes record on 3 April. When signals started arriving four days later that German warships had left harbor, the Home Fleet was sent northeast rather than east, to counter a possible breakout into the North Atlantic sea-lanes. Churchill, with the Great War again in his mind, seems to have hoped for a major fleet engagement on the model of Jutland, this time conducted properly. Four cruisers and accompanying transports had been held in the Clyde, packed with troops, in case the Germans tried to occupy Narvik and other ports. On 8 April, Churchill unilaterally ordered the troops to be disembarked, so that the cruisers could put to sea at once for the apparently impending naval battle. When this was discovered in Cabinet, recalled Sir Ian Jacob years later, there was a long and embarrassed silence. In an early draft, Churchill wrote: "History will ask the question whether the British Government had any right to be surprised." In the final version, no answer is given; indeed, that question disappears. Instead, Churchill shifts the focus from Allied failings to the "surprise, ruthlessness and precision" of the German onslaught on "innocent and naked Norway." He does his best to show that the Royal Navy was made ready—"everything available was ordered out" on the assumption "that a major emergency had come"—without making clear that the emergency was envisaged as a fleet engagement not an amphibious landing.[33]

British operations in Norway were also a mess. Churchill, as he says in his memoirs, still focused mostly on Narvik, in the far north, whereas Chamberlain and Halifax wanted to concentrate British forces on the central port of Trondheim, far more significant now that this had become a battle for Norway itself. On 13 April, the Cabinet decided to do both operations, but the Chiefs of Staff then had cold feet about a frontal attack on Trondheim. After further delays, it was agreed to mount a "pincer" attack on the port via Namsos and Andalsnes. This looked fine on paper, but Namsos was 100 miles to the north and Andalsnes 150 miles southwest—in both cases separated from Trondheim by snow-covered mountains to be traversed by totally unequipped infantry.[34] Not surprisingly the troops could not break through, and had to be evacuated in early May. Although Narvik was captured at the end of the month, the Dunkirk crisis made it necessary to abandon Norway entirely. The loss of the aircraft carrier *Glorious* during the evacuation capped this sorry chronicle of disasters.

As in *The World Crisis*, so in *The Gathering Storm*; Churchill's instinct was to find scapegoats. For Trondheim, he targeted Air Vice-Marshal Philip Joubert de la Ferté, the RAF liaison officer with the Admiralty, who had agitated against a frontal attack. He "certainly exerted himself volubly to emphasise all this cold feet business," Churchill wrote in some "Rough Notes." "I did not forgive him, and a long time passed before he got his head above water again." (All mention of Joubert disappeared at Ismay's suggestion.)[35] For Narvik, the scapegoat was General "Pat" Mackesy, the ground-forces commander, who refused to mount a frontal attack, preferring to capture the flanking peninsulas first. Although the chapter on Narvik admits points in Mackesy's defense—for instance, his transports had been loaded for an unopposed landing—Churchill is adamant that the Narvik attack, "so brilliantly opened by the Navy, was paralysed by the refusal of the military commander to run what was admittedly a desperate risk."[36]

Churchill sacked Mackesy in mid-May 1940 and had not forgiven him seven years later. "My belief is that under 2,000 Germans, maybe only 1,500, held up between 15,000 and 20,000 men with all the power of the Fleet," he told Pownall on 22 November 1947. "I want to know what the German story is, because we are looking for the truth." After checking British and captured German documents, Pownall told him that 2,000 was the correct figure for the German regular troops, but that British forces were only 4,000, and the Germans had also armed 3,000 sailors from destroyers sunk by the Royal Navy. While these men were not comparable to regular troops, they did give the Germans numerical superiority. Pownall therefore suggested "some modification" to Churchill's account: "With all the facts we now have, many people will think Mackesy was right; especially as we did capture Narvik in the end by his more dilatory method." Pownall's careful redraft pitted "over four thousand of our best regular troops, including the Guards Brigade and the Marines" against the German defenders, "whose regular troops, apart from crews rescued from sunken destroyers, we estimated, rightly as we now know, at no more than half their number."[37]

Aside from venting his still simmering frustration, Churchill in his drafts reflected on deeper lessons from Norway. His "Rough Notes" on Trondheim noted how the Luftwaffe "dominated the operations" throughout the campaign, harassing Allied troops and ships at every turn. Although losses at Namsos and Andalsnes were much lower than feared, the perils and horrors of landing, or of evacuation, without the command of the air, struck deep into all British authorities, including myself, for years to come. The expression which I certainly used long afterwards, "We mustn't get Namsosed," embodied that feeling of dread for this experience, which made me take a ~~very~~ pessimistic view about the chances of getting away from Dunkirk, where I thought the whole power of the German Air Force would be laid upon us and might be decisive. It also affected ~~all~~ my thoughts about landing in France in 1942, and even in 1943. Though we had command of the air, and could wallop them, "Namsosed" came across my mind in Torch [the North African landings], and in Sicily. However, after a while we had overwhelming air command so the boot was on the other foot.

Nothing of this passage survives in *The Gathering Storm*, where Churchill contents himself with a general comment that the Germans "comprehended perfectly the use of the air arm on a great scale in all its aspects." But, having underestimated tactical airpower in 1939, his new fear of being "Namsosed" by the Luftwaffe did indeed cast a long shadow over Churchill's strategy in the dark middle of the war.[38]

In *The Gathering Storm*, Churchill is quite candid that Norway was a fiasco: the "superiority of the Germans in design, management and energy were plain." Drafts were more outspoken, speaking of "the helpless confusion, mismanagement and disaster at all points of the campaign."[39] At the strategic level, this proved to be the wrong war in the wrong place at the wrong time. Churchill points to the seven-month delay in implementing his proposal to mine the Leads, asserting in another breezy counterfactual that had he been allowed to act "with freedom and design" back in September, "a far more agreeable conclusion might have been reached in this key theatre, with favourable consequences in every direction." One could equally argue, as he does three chapters later, that it was "lucky for us that we were not able to build up a substantial army and air force round Trondheim." This might have left the Western Front even weaker than it was.[40]

Since 4 April 1940, Churchill had taken the chair at the Military Coordination Committee, where the three service ministers and the three Chiefs of Staff tried to thrash out a common position. As he says, this left him as merely "first among equals," but with his position as First Lord of the Admiralty, it made him a prime candidate for blame when Norway went wrong. Gallipoli was, of course, the specter that haunted him in 1940 and again in 1947–1948. The comment that Admiral Sir Charles Forbes "was very upset at having to bring his ships into this sort of Dardanelles" appears in "Rough Notes" on Trondheim but not in the final text. At Narvik, General Mackesy seems cast as a latter-day General Sir Frederick Stopford (the commander at Suvla Bay in August 1915), dallying on the beaches when victory was within his grasp.[41]

One can gauge the sensitivity of these chapters by the fact that Clementine Churchill scrutinized them with particular care. She said in the 1960s that Gallipoli had been the most agonizing moment of her life, fearing her husband would "die of grief." When Winston wrote in a draft of volume 2 that Gallipoli had ruined him "for the time being," she noted, "for a quarter of a century." On reading the Norway chapters, she urged her husband not to "give the names of minor generals who have been unlucky, or who have not done well" and particularly mentioned "the General who was sent to Narvik. He will write to The Times." Against Churchill's admission that he had to bear "some of the odium of the ill-starred Norway campaign," Clementine noted: "You might mention that had it not been for your years of exile & repeated warnings re the German peril Norway might have ruined you."[42] In the final text, Churchill admits that, "considering the prominent part I played in these events" and the impossibility of explaining in public the bureaucratic shambles, "it was a marvel that I survived and maintained my position in public esteem and Parliamentary confidence." His original version had been even franker: "it was a marvel—I really do not know how—I survived and maintained my position in public esteem while all the blame was thrown on poor Mr. Chamberlain."[43]

THE NORWAY DEBACLE enabled the Opposition to demand a Commons debate on the war situation, which was held on 7–8 May 1940. Although Churchill does not mention it, a target for many speakers was all the wasted attention on Narvik. "If we had held Trondheim," insisted Leo Amery, one of the leading critics, "the isolated German force at Narvik would have been bound to surrender in time."[44] (Narvik, of course, had been Churchill's obsession.) On operational grounds, Churchill probably bore as much of the blame for the mess in Norway as he had for Gallipoli. But in 1915 he was the prime scapegoat for a Tory opposition that had not forgiven his defection to the Liberals a decade before and who drove him from office with vindictive relish. In 1940, by contrast, the hatred of Labour and dissident Tories was reserved for Chamberlain, whose failure to read Hitler was compounded by his arrogance toward any critics. His taunt on 5 April that Hitler had "missed the bus" was hurled back at him during the debate; his call on 8 May for support from "my friends in the House" was treated as cynical partisanship at a time of national crisis. As the debate gathered momentum, it became a vote of confidence, and when Chamberlain's majority fell from above 200 to 81, he had little choice but to resign.

On 9 May, Churchill tells us in the final chapter of *The Gathering Storm*, Chamberlain held various consultations about a national government, including a meeting with Halifax and Churchill in the afternoon at 10 Downing Street. The next morning brought news that the Germans had invaded the Low Countries, and Chamberlain briefly toyed with the idea of staying on, but Labour leaders made clear that they would not serve under him. And so, Churchill tells us, Chamberlain summoned him and Halifax once more to Downing Street at eleven o'clock on Friday, 10 May. Chamberlain set out reasons, notably supposed Labour animosity toward Churchill, why Halifax might be a wiser choice. "Usually I talk a great deal," Churchill continues, "but on this occasion I was silent," and "a very long pause ensued. It certainly seemed longer than the two minutes which one observes in the commemorations of Armistice Day." Then Halifax alluded to his position as a peer, which meant he would not be able to speak and act where it mattered, in the House of Commons. After some minutes in this vein, says Churchill, "it was clear that the duty would fall upon me—had in fact fallen upon me."[45]

"I have had many important interviews in my public life," Churchill tells us, "and this was certainly the most important."[46] It is therefore remarkable that his account is one of the most misleading passages in *The Gathering Storm*. In fact, noted as early as 1955 in Leo Amery's memoirs, the decisive discussion took place at 4:30 on the afternoon of 9 May, not the morning of the tenth. Immediately afterward, Halifax related what had happened to Sir Alexander Cadogan, his Permanent Under-Secretary, who included it in his diary that night, and Halifax wrote up his own account the following morning. These records and their dating were later accepted by Norman Brook when he inquired into the matter after Amery's memoirs appeared[47] and are also taken as definitive by Churchill's official biographer.[48] In them, there is no reference to a long silence. This first emerged when Halifax told the story to an old friend in June 1941; even more colorful versions followed from Winston and Randolph Churchill in 1942. Challenged on the discrepancies by Halifax's biographer in 1989, Sir William Deakin claimed that in the memoirs Churchill was "hamming up" the story for its dramatic qualities, building on Feiling's biography. Deakin chivalrously added that the factual errors must have been his fault.[49]

Yet Feiling offered no account of these meetings. The passage was actually a classic piece of Churchill's dictation—about an event so personal that his Syndicate could not check.[50] As with his account of the sleepless night after Eden's resignation, his version of how he gained the premiership is probably embellished. Yet factual inaccuracy was balanced by poetic truth. In May 1940, Halifax's peerage was not an insuperable problem—as the case of Lord Home in 1963 was to show. At root, Halifax had no appetite for the job of war leader; indeed, the prospect made him feel physically sick. Even in 1945, after years as Foreign Secretary and Ambassador in Washington, he called himself a "layman" in all things military. Chamberlain's outlook was the same. "How I do hate and loathe this war," he told his sisters in October 1939. "I was never meant to be a War Minister." Churchill, in contrast, was "enjoying every moment of the war."[51] A soldier by training, a military historian by avocation, a would-be general to the marrow of his bones, Churchill was truly the man for the hour. Admittedly he had been complacent about armored warfare, tactical airpower, and the vulnerability of the French, but by background and temperament he was far more likely to cope with the shocks of 1940 than Chamberlain and Halifax. His recent record also counted in his favor. Throughout the 1930s he had agitated for office, sometimes equivocating in the process, and, free from ministerial responsibility, he had ignored inconvenient problems such as Japan. But, in consequence, he was untainted by appeasement. As he says when explaining the "marvel" of how he had survived the Norway fiasco, "for six or seven years I had predicted with truth the course of events, and had given ceaseless warnings, then unheeded but now remembered." Clementine applauded in the margin: "Very true & very good."[52]

So Churchill soars to his peroration. After seeing the King on the evening of Friday, 10 May, and starting to form a government, he went to bed at three o'clock "conscious of a profound sense of relief. At last I had the authority to give directions over the whole scene. I felt as if I were walking with destiny, and that all my past life had been but a preparation for this hour and for this trial."[53] In May 1940, Churchill at last took command of Britain's history. At the time this owed as much to good luck as good judgment. Eight years later, however, the hand of Providence was easier to discern, and Churchill's extended essay in retrospective wisdom has guided the writing of history ever since.

CHAPTER 9

PROPHET OF THE PAST
AND THE FUTURE

TODAY ONE THINKS of *The Second World War* as a set of books—black bound with gilt lettering in the case of the Cassell's edition, red with gilt on black panels for Houghton Mifflin. But many people in Britain and America derived their most vivid impressions of Churchill's memoirs from press serialization.

The newspapers published a succession of short extracts, the *Daily Telegraph* offering its readers forty-two between 16 April and 17 June 1948. These filled much of the editorial page—a big chunk of what was still, because of paper rationing, only a six-page newspaper. The extracts, selected by Herbert Ziman, one of the paper's editorial writers, were taken evenly from across the whole volume—Churchill returns to the Admiralty almost exactly halfway through, in number twenty-two. Although starkly presented, without illustration, Ziman's headlines stamped out Churchill's big themes: "A Rebuff to Roosevelt: Eden's Resignation," or "Chamberlain's Change of Heart Came Too Late"—about March 1939. *The New York Times*, with more newsprint, was less pinched in its treatment. The first installment opened down two columns of the front page and then continued across most of an inside page. This set the pattern for the first seven of the thirty installments, which ran on weekdays from 16 April to 30 May, after which Churchill was relegated to a full inside page. Unlike the *Daily Telegraph*, *The New York Times* included photographs and other illustrations.

The memoirs took a very different form in the pages of *Life*. The magazine presented *The Gathering Storm* in six weekly installments from 19 April to 31 May 1948. Although it printed Churchill's preface in full and much of chapter 1, on "The Follies of the Victors," *Life* then jumped rapidly to 1936 in the first issue, devoted the next two to the years up to the outbreak of war, and the remaining three installments to Churchill's eight months at the Admiralty. Throughout, however, the text took second place to the visuals. Daniel Longwell had always intended to do "something entirely original in serialization," and each issue was lavishly illustrated, with contemporary photographs and *Life*'s own shots of Churchill at work and at home, as well as special picture sections on such themes as the Marlborough connection and Churchill and the navy (a series of historic paintings led off by a full-page one of Admiral Nelson). After heavy lobbying, *Life* was even allowed to photograph the interior and gardens of 10 Downing Street (much to the annoyance of Camrose, who "rather fundamentally resented our bigness and bustle," in the words of Walter Graebner, *Life*'s bureau chief in London).[1] The magazine's treatment located Churchill as the climax of a grand historical epic, stretching back over the centuries, in which family and nation were entwined. With so much illustration, *Life* used less text, printing 51,000 of Churchill's 265,000 words, compared with 93,000 in *The New York Times*.[2] Churchill's didactic points were not lost, however. Installment two, for instance, on 26 April, contained a photo section with the Churchillian title "Great Contemporaries," featuring full-page formal portraits of Baldwin and Chamberlain at their most imposing. Beneath were Churchill's damning verdicts.

Churchill carefully monitored the promotion of his work, infuriating Ziman at the *Daily Telegraph* by rejiggering the selections.[3] On learning that Harold Nicolson had been commissioned by *Life* to write a portrait of Churchill to launch serialization, Churchill exclaimed, "I shall sue him in every court for any libel." In fact, Nicolson wrote an affectionate encomium—"by the force of his character and intelligence he saved his country; he saved Europe; perhaps, even, he saved the world"—but at his request, *Life* sent Churchill the typescript, with an invitation "to alter it in any way you like."[4] When Desmond Flower of Cassell's was asked by the BBC to offer a publisher's view of the memoirs—because they were "the literary event of our generation, possibly of the century, and the public will be keenly interested in how the book has been made"—Churchill wanted to see Flower's text. And in April, Emery Reves requested copies of some of Churchill's amended galleys, telling Churchill that his method of dictation, multiple proofs, and heavy revision had "never been applied by any writer," and foreign publishers wanted to use examples in their volumes or promotional material. "I really do not think there is any need for that," Churchill replied sternly.[5] When a report on his working methods appeared in *Time* (another part of the Luce publishing empire) on 10 May 1948, Churchill was incensed. This made reference to his "squad of helpers" and repeated revisions. "When volume 2 was delivered last week it was marked 'Final—Subject to Full Freedom of Proof Correction.'"[6]

Newspapers and magazines printed only extracts and could cope with last-minute amendments, but an exact text was essential for book publishers. Otherwise, it was difficult to move from galleys (long columns of text) to page proofs (in which text, maps, and tables were fitted together on final, numbered pages). Without accurate page proofs, it was impossible to produce an index or calibrate the production process—books being sewn together as a series of "signatures," usually of thirty-two folded pages. Churchill's indifference to deadlines and his passion for "overtakes" were therefore a nightmare for his book publishers. To make matters worse, Houghton Mifflin was not a free agent. In order to maximize profits, it was desperate to get the memoirs accepted by the Book-of-the-Month Club. Laughlin wanted the club to take the whole series in advance, but its editors insisted on judging each volume in turn. That meant Laughlin had to wait for an acceptable draft from Churchill, then lobby the club intensively and hope for a slot at a good time of year for sales. At the same time, he did not want to fall too far behind the serial publication, which provided a massive publicity buildup.

Much, therefore, hung on Churchill's punctuality. Despite printing the so-called final proofs on 30 January 1948, he continued tinkering with them for weeks. With serial publication set for April and the Book-of-the-Month Club promotion for July, Laughlin felt the vise closing around him and sent one of his senior editors, Paul Brooks, to London in February to wrest chapters from Churchill's grasp. His staff started keyboarding the text in mid-March, only to receive another bombshell. "Author insists on reading proof," Brooks cabled on 16 March. "Cartographer in Brighton with nervous breakdown." Swallowing hard, Laughlin rewrote the schedule and commissioned his own maps. On 8 April, Brooks sent a new "final" text. "We have emerged from the soup," he announced. Churchill had changed his mind and did not want to see any further proofs. Brooks flew home exhausted, only to be followed by a stream of overtakes, which Houghton Mifflin accommodated up to early June but then drew a line. In all this rush, the index had to be compiled in only three days. When Laughlin airmailed Churchill a first copy of the volume, he waxed eloquent on "the most worthwhile venture in our century of publishing" and his conviction that the book was "likely to last in influence for countless years to come." But his staff was shattered. Having hoped for five months to turn Churchill's text into bound volumes, they had done the job in two.[7]

In some ways, Cassell's had an easier task. It was dealing with one serial partner rather than two, was not locked into a book-club deadline, and did not operate 3,000 miles from the author. But Churchill's eventual text was 100,000 words longer than his preliminary estimate, and Cassell's could not get enough additional paper and cloth because of continued rationing. It could have printed fewer copies, but that meant lower sales, so Flower opted for smaller type. Having sent Churchill examples of the twelve-point type for approval back in January, he now backtracked and used ten-point, as well as squeezed the margins. Churchill was appalled when he saw the final page proofs, comparing them most unfavorably with Houghton Mifflin's. At least, he told Flower tartly on 14 July, Cassell's had printed at the front, "This book is produced in complete conformity with the authorised economy standards." Privately, friends joked that they would read Winston's memoirs after they had purchased a magnifying glass.[8]

Cassell's other great problem was that Churchill regarded the British edition as definitive. He therefore expected Flower to print all his corrections, including those too late for Houghton Mifflin. The publisher did its best to oblige—even removing type from the machines to make last-minute alterations—but by 2 July Flower had to call a halt because the pages were being bound.[9] Flower's flexibility enabled Churchill to amend some embarrassing passages in the American edition, but the constant changes played havoc with proofreading. Cassell's ended up printing two pages of "Errata and Corrigenda" and inserted a slip noting further emendations. The most egregious referred to page 56. There, we are told that the French Army was the "poop of the life of France." The emendation slip reads: "For 'poop' read 'prop.'" (Denis Kelly likened this typo to the notorious, though probably apocryphal, newspaper account of Queen Victoria "pissing over Clifton Suspension Bridge to the cheers of her loyal subjects.") "I was shocked at some of the mistakes," Churchill wrote Cassell's on 10 August, "especially 'poop' for 'prop,'" and he decided to include a professional proofreader on his team. Of Mr. C. C. Wood, more anon.[10]

Back in August 1947, Reves had told Churchill that most publishers attached "the greatest importance" to including at least fifty pictures, cartoons, facsimiles, and the like. But by March 1948, most had dropped the idea because the extra length of the text had dramatically inflated their costs. Houghton Mifflin, for instance, had to raise its price to six dollars, retaining the original five dollars only for prepublication orders. The general feeling, in Reves's words, was that a few token photos "would rather cheapen the book." Many European publishers brought out each volume as two separate books: this was true in France, Greece, Italy, Norway, Sweden, and for the German translation published in Switzerland.[11]

Also abandoned at the final stage was the idea of a bibliographical note. On 1 April 1948, Deakin sent Churchill a draft that was divided into printed documentary sources, such as Hitler's speeches; biographies and memoirs, including *Mein Kampf* and Feiling's life of Chamberlain; and general secondary works. In a preamble, Deakin wrote, as if from Churchill: "In the preparation of this volume, I have drawn largely on my private papers at Chartwell and upon official documents relating to my period in office, together with published records of my speeches and writings." The bibliographical note was duly printed, without the final section of general works, but on 10 April Deakin noted that it had "been scrapped by Mr. Churchill." Why is unclear. Space may have been a factor, but the note covered only one page. Perhaps mindful of Norman Brook, Churchill decided to avoid drawing attention to his privileged access to Whitehall archives. Whatever the explanation, this omission set a precedent. Although the memoirs contain some footnotes, mostly inserted by Deakin, Churchill did not provide an overall guide to his sources. This helped further to blur the line between memoir and history.[12]

What Emery Reves dubbed "the race among the publishers" was won by the Greeks on 11 June 1948, followed by Librairie Plon in Paris a week later. Houghton Mifflin came in third on 21 June. Cassell's edition did not appear until 4 October, nearly six months after serialization had begun, with Flower fuming that he would lose sales in British empire markets to the Americans.[13]

Publication of volume 1 was not, therefore, a single event. It occurred in various forms over half a year, during which international affairs were in flux. *The Gathering Storm* broke over a Europe that was in the grip of the Cold War.

ON 17 JUNE, having completed its serialization of the memoirs, Camrose's *Daily Telegraph* printed an editorial entitled "A Unique Record," about Churchill's "almost continuously topical contribution" to contemporary history. The current world scene was not very different, it said, from that depicted in his early installments: "a battered and restless Europe, prostrate and defeated enemies, divided and grudging allies." Yet, the paper continued, the lesson was not "fatalistic despair." Churchill insisted that World War II had been the Unnecessary War, "not an inevitable catastrophe bound to occur when evil men gained power abroad, but a tragedy in which the misjudgements and kindly dreams of men of good will in our own country encouraged wickedness elsewhere to seize its opportunities." In a similar vein, *The New York Times* punctuated its serialization with editorials on the lessons of the Unnecessary War for 1948. "Unmistakably, inexorably, he shows the perils of appeasement and vacillation," the paper told its readers. Given "the ominous parallelism" between both postwar eras, it was America's responsibility to see that "such catastrophes do not recur."[14]

These were indeed somber months for British and American foreign policy. The Marshall Plan was still wending its way through Congress, as Western Europe's economies failed to revive. A communist-led coup had brought Czechoslovakia firmly into the Soviet orbit, while in Italy's bitter election the left won 30 percent of the vote. The gravest problem was Germany. Unable to secure Soviet agreement for the country's recovery, Britain, America, and France decided to rebuild the western zones of occupation on their own and introduced a new currency to replace the barter economy. At the end of June, the Soviets cut off all land access to Berlin, deep inside their zone, so the British and Americans supplied the beleaguered city from the air. We now know that the Berlin Airlift was a success and Stalin had to end the blockade in May 1949. In mid-1948, however, many feared World War III.

In his speeches, Churchill played up the lessons of the past for the present. On 26 June, he addressed a rally of 100,000 Tories at Luton Hoo in Bedfordshire, warning that Berlin raised issues "as grave as those which we now know were at stake at Munich ten years ago." Despite the universal desire for peace, "we should all have learned by now that there is no safety in yielding to dictators, whether Nazi or Communist." A "firm and resolute course," he told his listeners, was "the only chance of preventing a third war." On 9 October, five days after the Cassell's edition was published, he told the Tory conference in Llandudno that only America's atomic arsenal prevented "the subjugation of Western Europe by Communist machinations backed by Russian armies." He pointed to Czechoslovakia, "where Stalin has perpetrated exactly the same act of aggression in 1948 as Hitler did when he marched into Prague" in 1939. "I hope you will give full consideration to my words," Churchill told his audience. "I have not always been wrong."[15]

These speeches were reported prominently and at length in the British and American press. Ramming home his warnings in August 1948 was *The Sinews of Peace*, the latest set of his collected speeches, edited by his son, Randolph, which covered the period October 1945 to December 1946. Its centerpiece was Fulton, from which came the book's title. "Re-reading that speech in the light of after-knowledge," Randolph wrote in his introduction, "many people may wonder what the fuss was all about. They may perhaps conclude that one of the most dangerous and thankless tasks in politics is to tell the truth and to give warning of danger in good time."[16] *The Sinews of Peace* also included Churchill's other great oration of 1946—the Zurich speech on European unity—and this idea was also in the headlines that summer. On 7 May, in The Hague, Churchill had renewed his call for a Council of Europe. Endorsing it two days later in "Lessons of the Past"—one of the editorials inspired by *The Gathering Storm*—*The New York Times* reminded its readers that it was "the hesitancy and division of the West-European nations that made most of them an easy prey for totalitarian conquest." Since America's "strange policy" of standing on the sidelines had contributed to the disaster, *The New York Times* urged implementation of the only thing that might have spelled success in 1939: namely, a "hard and fast" transatlantic alliance.[17]

The year 1948 was therefore magnificently Churchillian. The first volume of his memoirs hit the headlines at a time when its lessons seemed supremely relevant. Derided in the 1930s, only to be vindicated by events, he was now declaiming with equal forthrightness on contemporary events. The actor as chronicler, the historian as statesman—for a politician cast twice into the wilderness, it must have seemed very sweet. And, just in case there were any lingering doubts about Churchill's renaissance qualities, in April 1948 the Royal Academy of Arts elected him Honorary Academician Extraordinary. Two of his paintings were exhibited at its summer exhibition—for the first time under his own name. To round off the year, December saw publication of *Painting as a Pastime*, two articles from the 1920s now put together as a book. The first impression soon sold out, and two more were printed in 1949—in all 57,000 copies—and it proved the most popular of his postwar one-volume works.[18] Thus, in a single year, Churchill had brought out a prodigious work of history, a major collection of speeches on international affairs, and an engaging essay on art. The man who feared he had lost his voice in 1945 was now speaking to a multitude of audiences.

Churchill's resurrection nonplussed the high priests of the Tory party, for whom he was still a figurehead leader. He had left Eden to run parliamentary business, jollied along with the usual nods and winks about soon becoming Leader. He impeded R. A. Butler's research department in its efforts to modernize Tory philosophy, and when Harold Macmillan urged a more efficient Shadow Cabinet, with a management committee and secretariat, Churchill replied brusquely, "I propose to continue the present system as long as I am in charge." In December 1947, according to Harold Nicolson, Butler complained "that Winston never consults them, never agrees, and often lets them down." Yet such was his stature that a palace revolution was impossible: "We must wait and wait and see which dies first," moaned Butler, "Winston or the Conservative party."[19] The previous summer had seen a halfhearted attempt at a putsch. When the Chief Whip, James Stuart, suggested that perhaps Churchill now deserved to spend more time with his paint box, he flared up and Stuart backed off. The Tories' problem, as one backbencher put it, was that Churchill was the only real "big noise" the party possessed. Even if he took little interest in party management, he was still a huge electoral asset, as shown by the audiences and press coverage for his public speeches.[20]

Prolific author, international statesman, and political leader—this was the image of the man who published *The Gathering Storm* in 1948. One can also see it reflected in the way the book was received.

IN NORTH AMERICA, *The Gathering Storm* sold more than any other volume of his war memoirs—more than 530,000 copies by July 1951. The bulk of these (385,000) were to Book-of-the-Month Club subscribers, vindicating Henry Laughlin's determination to secure a deal. Another 26,000 were sold by Houghton Mifflin's Canadian subsidiary.[21] By the time the book appeared in June 1948, millions of Americans were already familiar with its highlights via *Life* and *The New York Times*. As Laughlin feared, this probably reduced Houghton Mifflin's sales and, as several reviewers remarked, also removed some of the glitter. But the book was still accorded a tremendous critical reception, with lead reviews in the prestigious *New York Times* and New York *Herald Tribune* weekly book supplements and treatment by big-name reviewers such as the veteran journalist Vincent Sheean and the theologian and social commentator Reinhold Niebuhr. It was also reviewed at length in big-city newspapers across the country. Thus, millions who did not read the serials or the book got a taste of Churchill.

Some American reviews were positively reverential. "It is like entering a cathedral," wrote Peter Lyne in *The Christian Science Monitor*. "The hush of greatness is all around." Marjorie Stoneman Douglas in *The Miami Herald* called it "the greatest book of the summer by one of the greatest leaders of the world who is also one of the greatest writers." At the other extreme, a few considered Churchill a voice from the past—"a man of empire" in the words of the *Chicago Tribune*. The majority agreed with *Time* that the book contained "almost no disclosures of inside information" to "drastically alter the contemporary picture of events." But that served only to enhance the book's stature—most reviewers treated it more as history than as autobiography. According to *Newsweek*, the book "puts to shame all the rest of the growing shelf of memoirs" about the war. "Few books belong in the category of great events, and this is one of them," wrote Anne O'Hare McCormick in *The New York Times*. "Few books make history in the sense that the epoch they depict will always live as they saw it. This is such a book."[22]

The interplay of past, present, and future intrigued many reviewers. McCormick spoke of its "prickling parallels to the present uneasy truce." William H. Harrison in *The Washington Star* concentrated on the Unnecessary War—"a thesis singularly apposite to the hour."[23] Some reviewers did question Churchill's black-and-white account of appeasement. According to Professor Walter P. Hall of Princeton, writing in *The Journal of Modern History*, "so absorbed was he in viewing the misdeeds of Hitler that he ignored Franco almost altogether and was not averse to a considerable appeasement of Mussolini." And the military correspondent Hanson W. Baldwin pointed out that Churchill's account of a Germany already rearmed by 1935 and eclipsing Britain and France two- or threefold in arms production by 1938 was "at sharp variance" with captured German documents, which showed the "lack of German preparedness for total war" even in 1939. But virtually no one questioned Churchill's portrait of the gullible appeasers. It is "almost impossible to confute," stated Professor Preston Slosson in *The American Historical Review*. "He does not damn Neville Chamberlain" wrote Lewis Gannett in the New York *Herald Tribune*, "he destroys him."[24]

Not all comment was laudatory. *The New York Times* printed a long letter from Joseph P. Kennedy, Roosevelt's Ambassador to London in 1938–1940 and a keen supporter of Chamberlain, asserting that Churchill's accounts of the Munich and Prague crises of 1938–1939 were "replete with serious inaccuracies." After giving some examples, Kennedy concluded that "Mr. Churchill's misquotation of documents that are public make it difficult for one to rely on his quotations from documents that are not generally available." Kennedy's charge was reported in the British press, but Bill Deakin thought it was not worth replying to this "Irish Catholic, isolationist mugwump," adding that Sir William Strang, one of the Foreign Office's specialists on Germany in 1938–1939, was said to regard Churchill's account of Munich "as the most effective in existence." In the end, Randolph Churchill entered the lists on his father's behalf with a long and detailed letter to *The New York Times*, challenging Kennedy's assertions and admitting only two trivial errors. It all proved to be a storm in a teacup.[25]

Reviewers also reflected on matters of style. *Time* found "very little of the wonderful and moving rhetoric of the Churchill speeches of the war years." The style was "generally simple, almost biblical." Sterling North, in the *Philadelphia Bulletin*, detected the influence of the Old Testament, Shakespeare, and Edward Gibbon. Several commented on the way Churchill used "artful simplicity to counter his majestic rhythms"—a favorite example being his description of a farewell lunch in March 1938 for the German Ambassador, which ends: "This was the last time I saw Herr von Ribbentrop before he was hanged." Underlying all discussion of style lay the assumption that this was entirely Churchill's work. "One of the most engaging things" about the book, declared Hamilton Basso in *The New Yorker*, was that "he wrote it himself," whereas "when we read the speeches and public papers of Roosevelt, it is hard to know *whom* we have hold of." The "tremendous personality of the author . . . glowers and shines in almost every sentence," enthused *Newsweek*. Professor Hall claimed that *The Gathering Storm* was more "indispensable" to the historian than Feiling's life of Chamberlain because "Churchill had the advantage of reading the *Ciano Diaries*." But for researching Ciano, Mussolini's son-in-law, and for much else, credit was due to Bill Deakin. No reviewer seemed to guess that the memoirs were the work of many hands, even if Churchill was their presiding genius.[26]

But some reviewers did not take Churchill entirely at his own estimation. The English author Rebecca West, writing in the *Saturday Review of Literature*, said Churchill was right in his denunciation of appeasement in the 1930s. Without him in 1940 "we would have been destroyed." But, she added, there were more volumes to come, in which Teheran, Yalta, Potsdam, and other "terrible matter" would have to be explained. This point was also made by some other reviewers. "Churchill is most critical of Chamberlain's fatal belief in personal diplomacy," noted Orville Prescott in the weekday *New York Times*. "Yet Churchill and Roosevelt later fell into the same error at Teheran and Yalta." When Churchill's memoirs reached 1945, Anne O'Hare McCormick predicted, "the historian will have a hard time justifying the statesman."[27]

The multiple refractions of past, present, and future therefore shed a light that was sometimes complex rather than clear. Perhaps the most intriguing example in *The Gathering Storm* may be found in Churchill's discussion of Poland. In the American edition, his chapter "Munich Winter" notes that "the Germans were not the only vultures upon the carcass" of Czechoslovakia because the Polish government immediately demanded the frontier district of Teschen. There follows a remarkable paragraph on how the "heroic characteristics of the Polish race must not blind us to their record of folly and ingratitude which over centuries has led them through measureless suffering." They were "glorious in revolt and ruin; squalid and shameful in triumph. The bravest of the brave, too often led by the vilest of the vile!" In short, "there were always two Polands; one struggling to proclaim the truth and the other grovelling in villainy."[28]

This astonishing vituperation appeared in the serials as well as the book—it was on the opening page of *Life's* third installment—and naturally prompted some angry letters to Churchill. "Is the Polish Nation to be grateful," asked the President of the Polish American Congress in Illinois, "for the glorious opportunity that your Government gave the folly-ridden Polish heroes to die in battle at Narvik, Tobruk, Monte Cassino and lastly the Battle of Britain—for the allied cause and the survival of your empire?" And "is the Polish Nation to be grateful to you, so free of folly, for your treacherous deal at Teheran and Yalta which destroyed its national freedom and entombed it beyond the Iron Curtain?" Polish-American outrage was echoed in anti-British newspapers like the *Chicago Tribune* and noted in the British media. The communist government in Warsaw was said to be "delighted" with Churchill's words, which it used as anti-British propaganda.[29] After representations from various quarters, Churchill sent Cassell's an overtake on 9 July 1948 cutting out the "glorious in revolt" and "two Polands" sentences and adding a passage of sympathy for Poland's "new subjugation."[30]

"I am much distressed about the Polish passage and have cut it to rags in the English edition," Churchill told Eddie Marsh on 18 July. "It was written in a feeling of anger against the behaviour of the present Polish government and the temporary subservience of the Polish people to them." This explanation rings rather hollow. He had revised the draft several times for the American edition, and Cassell's version still contains his references to "vultures upon the carcass" and Poland's historical record of "folly and ingratitude."[31] What can be inferred about his motivation? As we saw in chapter 7, Churchill would much rather have gone to war over Czechoslovakia in 1938 than Poland in 1939. He felt sympathy for the Czechs and a rapport with their leader, Beneš, that were not replicated in the Polish case, except briefly with General Wladyslaw Sikorski. In writing the offensive passage, Churchill was probably also looking to the end of the war as well as to its origins. Since Poland was Britain's ostensible casus belli in 1939, he felt, as he often said, honor-bound to achieve the best possible Polish settlement and devoted hours of his time to its negotiation. In the process, he found the Poles almost as much of a headache as the Russians. In this passage, we catch a whiff of his raw frustration. For Churchill, the Polish question was at the heart of the Unnecessary War and the unnecessary Cold War as well.

ALTHOUGH CASSELL'S published the British edition on 4 October 1948, they stopped taking booksellers' orders for the first impression at the end of June. The print run of 221,000 was double that of any nonfiction book the house could remember.[32] The sales were matched by the reviews. Churchill's memoirs "stand by themselves," wrote Harold Nicolson. "As history they are accurate and objective; as autobiographies they rank with the many great self-portraits which the English genius for intimacy has produced; as literature, they are models of composition, variety and style." Nicolson, of course, had already authored *Life*'s prepublication "Portrait of Winston Churchill"—so this was an interesting example of literary incest—but his sentiments were widely echoed. An editorial in the *Evening Standard* called the book "a vital tract for the times"; the politician Leo Amery welcomed "a great epic" written with "majestic sweep" in the style of Gibbon; while Sir Harold Butler in *The Fortnightly* was sure "the tragic muse has never devised a more poignant tale of human perversity." *The Gathering Storm* would prove "a national monument," predicted the reviewer for *The Manchester Guardian*. "The reputations of Ramsay MacDonald, Baldwin, and Chamberlain have been settled for good" by Churchill's "devastating portrait."[33]

British reviewers therefore played variations on many of the same themes as their transatlantic counterparts. Yet there was a difference. In America, Churchill seemed somewhat two-dimensional—a foreign statesman, widely admired, sometimes criticized, but not intimately known. In Britain, by contrast, he had been at the epicenter of national politics for forty years and was much more controversial. And because Churchill's memoirs were a bid to shape the past and mold the future, there were many former and current politicians who deemed it essential to mount a counterattack. Yet such was Churchill's position by 1948 that this had to be done with the stiletto rather than the bludgeon.

Take, for instance, Viscount Templewood, who reviewed the book on BBC radio and in *The Listener*. In his previous, commoner incarnation as Sam Hoare, he had been one of Chamberlain's closest Cabinet colleagues, intimately associated with appeasement. Templewood felt obliged to open with fulsome praise for a "great man" and a "great book." Only then could he suggest that this story of "appeasement and blindness versus courage and foresight" was too simple. He noted "the inescapable effect of French weakness" on British policy, cast doubt on the Roosevelt initiative of 1938, and suggested that "the events of recent years" justified Chamberlain's suspicion of Russian motives in 1939. He took issue with Churchill's "confident answer" that Germany gained more than Britain by Chamberlain's failure to fight in 1938, stressing the benefits of bringing radar and modern fighters into operation and ensuring unity both at home and in the British empire. And, on the Phony War, Templewood argued that Churchill was "equally to blame" for any failings or inertia, because "I was never member of a Cabinet in which there was more substantial agreement." Lest Churchill's talents "as a writer, an advocate and a leader may make us over-simplify the issues that he has raised," Templewood concluded, "I have thought it right to suggest some of the questions that still need fuller evidence before history gives the final verdict."[34]

Another appeaser unhappy with Churchill's interpretation was Lord Halifax. In May 1948, when the serial version appeared, he told Chamberlain's widow that Churchill's account seemed to him incorrect at many points and said he intended to tell him so when appropriate—but he did not expect to make much impact, because he reckoned "the main purpose of the book is not only to write history, but, also, to 'make a record' for W.S.C."[35] The day Cassell's volume was published, Halifax wrote directly to Churchill, criticizing his juxtaposition of Chamberlain's comment after Munich as he drove through the cheering London crowds—"all this will be over in three months"—and his declaration from the balcony of 10 Downing Street, "I believe it is peace for our time." Halifax insisted that there was no connection between the two remarks—the first simply referred to the ephemerality of public acclaim—but "the inevitable implication" of Churchill's juxtaposition was that "Neville was trying to deceive the British public." Receiving no reply, Halifax wrote his own correction, which was printed in *The Times*. This prompted a brisk private exchange between Churchill and Halifax, but the latter soon backed off. Whatever his personal feelings, Halifax did not mount a public defense of appeasement, and his own memoirs did not appear until 1957.[36]

Potentially the most damaging criticism was directed against Churchill's account of the 1920s rather than that of the 1930s. On 2 November 1948, *The Times* printed a long and detailed attack by Lord Hankey, the interwar Cabinet Secretary, on the Ten-Year Rule, for the continuance of which in 1928 Churchill had accepted responsibility in *The Gathering Storm*. Hankey argued that all through the 1920s, including Churchill's tenure at the Treasury, "the rule had been used to cut the Services to the bone." He asked whether, if Churchill had held office in the 1930s, he "would have been any more successful in overturning the consequences of his own Ten Year Rule than those whom he pillories." Ismay immediately entered the ring on Churchill's behalf, and he and Hankey fought a couple of courteous rounds in the correspondence column before the paper called a halt. *The Times* also printed a letter in support of Hankey from Lord Stanhope, Churchill's predecessor as First Lord of the Admiralty, and a reminder from Vansittart that "a respectable number of people knew that Germany was rearming" in the 1920s. Churchill himself thought of joining the debate. In mid-November, he drafted a long reply to Hankey and Stanhope, using classified material provided by his wartime aide Leslie Hollis, now at the Ministry of Defence, to argue that the problems of the navy were not his fault but that of others who came later. In the end, Churchill did not send the letter, presumably feeling it more dignified to stay aloof.[37]

Others developed the same line of criticism. Lord Chatfield's memoirs on the 1930s, finally unshackled by the Cabinet Office and published in 1947, contained a blistering attack on the "dangerous" Ten-Year Rule and its effect on the armed forces in the 1920s. "Gagged and bound hand and foot, they were handed over to the Treasury Gestapo," he wrote bitterly. "Never has there been such a successful attempt to hamstring the security of an Empire." Although Chatfield mentioned no names, Churchill was clearly his target. When the military historian Sir Basil Liddell Hart reviewed The Gathering Storm, he made damning comments about Churchill's emasculation of the fledgling Royal Flying Corps when Air Minister in 1919–1920 and his constant attack on the Tank Corps' budget as Chancellor. Liddell Hart used this as evidence for his larger critique of an emotional man whose "dynamism is too strong for his statesmanship."[38]

Sir Walford Selby, a senior Foreign Office figure in the interwar years, claimed in letters to several papers that Churchill had neglected the way Treasury control over Whitehall had paralyzed foreign policy.[39] Privately, Pownall had made the same point, applied to rearmament, while helping draft the war memoirs. "I cannot overemphasize the importance of Mr. Chamberlain's influence on financial provision made for the Services," both as Chancellor (1931–1937) and as premier (1937–1940), he told Churchill. "It was a long and painful business which deeply affected the Army's preparations" and explained the reluctance of the Chiefs of Staff to risk war in 1937–1938. But Churchill's account of appeasement focused on leaders. It was only when Whitehall's archives were opened in the 1970s that the Treasury's interwar dominance over diplomacy and defense became clear to historians.[40]

The most outspoken attacks on The Gathering Storm came from the left. In the Daily Herald, W. N. Ewer called the book "a passionate, almost pathological endeavour by a haunted man to prove that for thirty-odd years he has always been right." Ewer conceded that Churchill was usually right—his real complaint seemed to be that Churchill should leave others to say so rather than "boast and brag." Probably the nastiest review of any volume of the war memoirs was penned by Michael Foot in Tribune, under the title "Churchill's 'Mein Kampf.'" Though Churchill was "a great man," said Foot, that did not "entitle him to write bad history for the benefit of the Churchill legend." Foot landed some telling blows, for instance noting the virtual omission of Japan from volume 1, Churchill's con-

cealed equivocations about Italy, and his near indifference to broad socioeco-
nomic forces—"he pictures an almost stationary world upset by the wild ambitions of wicked men." But Foot spoiled the argument by his partisan accounts of
Spain and rearmament and by his vituperative tone, particularly the claim that
although *The Gathering Storm* was "vastly more enjoyable and instructive than
Hitler's *Mein Kampf*," in "personal conceit and arrogance there is some likeness
between the two."[41]

Appeasers and officials, disgruntled Tories, and angry left-wingers—all fired
their barbs, but none did serious damage. Thus, Churchill's first volume burnished his fame as a visionary statesman and completed the indictment of the
appeasers. It also gave the public new insights into episodes such as Eden's resignation and the development of radar and lodged phrases such as "the Gathering
Storm" and "the Locust Years" in the historical lexicon. At a deeper level, it probably even influenced our conception of the whole conflict as "the Second
World War."

In Britain, the war of 1914–1918 had been known as "the Great War," the
term "world war" or *weltkrieg* being predominantly American or German usage.
After September 1939, Whitehall statements on the current conflict simply
referred to "the War." The term "Second World War" was popularized by Roosevelt in 1941 as a way of persuading American isolationists that they could not
ignore the European struggle; Churchill sometimes adopted it, but he often
spoke of "the war against Nazism." In June 1944, the publishers Macmillan asked
for an official ruling, noting that many American publications were using the
terms "First World War" and "Second World War," and Bridges, then Cabinet
Secretary, set out some options:

'War of 1914–18' and 'War of 1939–?'
'First World War' and 'Second World War'
'Four Years' War' and 'Five (or six, or seven) Years' War'

Asked for his opinion, Churchill circled "First World War" and "Second World
War," but Bridges did not make any official statement, arguing that this matter
would be "decided by popular judgment."[42]

Asked in the Commons in October 1946, Attlee also declined to "to prescribe
an official designation for use on all occasions," though he thought that Second
World War was "likely to be generally adopted." Churchill himself equivocated.
Embarking on his war memoirs in April 1946, he used the working title "The

Second Great War," and it was not until September 1947, little more than seven months before serialization, that he committed himself to "The Second World War."[43] The issue was not decided officially until the turn of 1947–1948, when it became urgent to agree on a title for the series of British official histories of the war. The Cabinet's Committee for the Control of the Official Histories endorsed "History of the Second World War," and Attlee duly accepted it. American usage was a major reason for the committee's decision, but it was also noted that Churchill intended to use that phrase for his memoirs. Two other British surveys of the conflict published in 1948 also had the same title, but there is little doubt that Churchill's memoirs served to consecrate the title "The Second World War" in Britain.[44]

MASSIVE SALES and laudatory reviews are two measures of a book's success. Shaping the content and determining the vocabulary of historical debate are even greater achievements. On all these counts, The Gathering Storm was a triumph. But what about the bottom line? In financial terms, Churchill scored less highly than he might have, for he had sold all his rights in The Second World War back in 1947. That made sense given his need for ready cash and his fear of creeping mortality, and the deals arranged by Camrose were spectacular by the standards of all previous memoirs. But because he received a substantial payment for each volume and no share of the royalties, Churchill did not cash in on the work's massive and enduring appeal. Instead, his publishers, who had risked big money on a work they had not seen, reaped the rewards for their gamble.

Just how big a reward? The case of Cassell's is instructive. Charles Wood, a veteran proofreader whom Churchill was now using to check volume 2, did his own calculations on 29 October 1948. A sale of 200,000 copies at 25 shillings each brought in £250,000. Subtracting the booksellers' discount of one third (some £83,000) and production costs (estimated at about one sixth of the price, or a total of £36,000), Wood arrived at a net profit of £130,000. Even if one also allowed £5,000 to £10,000 for advertising, Wood told Churchill, "Cassell's would seem to have done quite well." Wood, who was not well disposed to Cassell's, had omitted distribution costs and overhead—both of which must have been considerable—but in February 1949, The Spectator's gossip column stated "on reliable authority" that Cassell's had paid a total of £50,000 for the five volumes of Churchill's memoirs and had netted "not far short of £100,000" already on volume 1, "which must be a record for publishers in this country." An embarrassed Desmond Flower assured Churchill's solicitor on 8 February that no one at Cassell's had made such a statement. He noted that the stated purchase price was incorrect—it was actually £40,000 (the equivalent of $160,000)—but he did not contest the figure for net profits. It is reasonable, therefore, to suppose that within weeks of publishing volume 1 Cassell's had already realized perhaps double the price they were committed to paying for *all five* proposed volumes of Churchill's memoirs.[45]

II.

THEIR FINEST HOUR

1940
1946–1949

CHAPTER 10

BETWEEN MEMOIR AND HISTORY

SERIALIZATION OF *Their Finest Hour* began on both sides of the Atlantic on 4 February 1949, only four months after Cassell's had published *The Gathering Storm*. The book version was published in America on 29 March and in Britain on 27 June. Of all six volumes, this one, about the period from May to December 1940, mattered most to Churchill emotionally. Its two component books, entitled "The Fall of France" and "Alone," covered the most dramatic months of the war and included some of his most vivid memories. But the volume is far more than memoir. Not only could Churchill now draw on reams of documents from his premiership, but with the Phony War over there were also dramatic military campaigns to describe in France, North Africa, and the skies over England, as well as intricate diplomacy with the United States to relate. Thanks to his assistants and their privileged access to official archives, his volume offered the fullest and most original account of the war of 1940 published to date—indeed, for many years. Yet there were things even he could not discuss, particularly one of Britain's greatest wartime triumphs: the Ultra secret.

AMONG THE RESEARCH assistants, Henry Pownall made the largest contribution to *Their Finest Hour*. He wrote the background narrative on the fall of France, drawing on official records and his own experience as Chief of Staff to the ill-fated British Expeditionary Force. A lengthy extract from a report he wrote on 28 May 1940 appears in the chapter on the retreat to Dunkirk, covering nearly two printed pages. In fact, Pownall kept a detailed diary during this period, which he used in compiling his drafts, but seems to have concealed its existence from Churchill. This was surely wise. If Churchill had read it, he would have discovered Pownall's fury at the time about Churchill's meddling in the conduct of operations. The entry on 23 May 1940, for instance, fumed at the Prime Minister's demand for an eight-division counterattack, at only one hour's notice, involving troops from three separate national armies—"The man's mad."[1] In book 2, Pownall also wrote the base accounts of the North African campaigns against the Italians.

Bill Deakin, by contrast, contributed much less to the early drafts. Apart from narrating Anglo-French diplomacy in 1940, his main tasks were background papers such as "A Note on Spain" and material for the chapter on Germany and Russia. But he did play a major role in pulling the volume into final shape in the summer of 1948. Gordon Allen was recruited only in July 1947, when much of book 1 was in rough draft. He did, however, refine it at various points—for instance, on the naval aspects of Dunkirk—and also helped significantly with two sensitive chapters about the neutralization of the French fleet at Oran in July 1940 and the abortive attack on Dakar in September. In all this, he drew extensively on Admiralty archives and on drafts for the official histories, like Pownall exploiting to the full Churchill's special status. The account of the Dunkirk evacuation, for instance, which includes a table detailing the types of ships involved, came from an internal Admiralty narrative of February 1948. Thus, Churchill was allowed to scoop the inside story long before the official history was published.[2]

Pug Ismay was in India from March to December 1947, but before leaving he contributed a good deal to early work on volume 2 and then read the drafts carefully in 1948. In May 1946, for instance, he sent Churchill recollections of the conferences with the French that they attended in May and June 1940, and these were woven into the text of book 1. At the end of November, he provided vignettes of Churchill's visits to bomb-damaged areas, which were duly incorporated in the chapter on the Blitz.[3] One of these describes a tour of Margate on the Kent coast. There, Ismay reminded him, an encounter with an anguished proprietor in the ruins of his café prompted Churchill to instruct the Treasury that all damage from enemy action should be compensated by the government. These moving passages, though elaborated in Churchill's own words, originated entirely from Ismay, even down to the mistakes. After *Their Finest Hour* was published, the disgruntled mayor of Ramsgate wrote to say that it was *his* town rather than neighboring Margate that Churchill had visited. "Margate" quietly became "Ramsgate" in the next edition.[4]

Ismay was also responsible for the tribute to Sir Edward Bridges in chapter 1. Unprompted, Churchill had already made mention of his "immeasurable" debt to Ismay as Military Secretary to the Cabinet, whereupon the latter drafted a fulsome passage on Bridges—much less a Churchill favorite than Ismay but whose cooperation over official papers made possible the war memoirs. The paragraph in chapter 1 on Bridges's efficiency, industry, and selflessness as Cabinet Secretary is substantially as written by Ismay in March 1948. Churchill added the references to his being the son of a poet laureate and to his "exceptional force, ability and personal charm." The wisdom of Ismay's advice can be inferred from Bridges's handwritten letter of thanks a year later, on receiving a presentation copy of volume 2:

> While I hope that I don't care much about what people in general think, that you should feel disposed to write of me as you have, in your great book, is something which means an enormous lot to me. And I feel it would be intolerably churlish not to write and thank you, for myself and my wife, for the quite overwhelming generosity of what you said. This is something which will encourage me for years to come, whenever I feel dispirited.

"So grateful for your letter," Churchill cabled, "which gave me the greatest pleasure."[5]

The content of volume 2 therefore owes a great deal to this inner circle of research assistants. Behind them, Denis Kelly continued to play his part as archivist and ad hoc researcher, but Churchill's estimation of his importance is indicated by Kelly's absence from the acknowledgments of volumes 1 and 2. The main addition to Churchill's literary entourage in 1948 was Charles Wood—a retired proofreader who had worked on *Marlborough* in the 1930s. Slight and small, Wood was the same age as Churchill but did not smoke or drink. His main virtue, as Kelly later recalled, was "a ruthless eye for misprints and inconsistencies." Retired in his little house in the north London suburb of Golders Green, Wood found time hanging heavy. As soon as the memoirs deal had been announced in May 1947, he started pressing his services in a series of letters, only to be politely rebuffed. But after the massive errata list for volume 1, crowned by "the poop" of France, Churchill took Deakin's advice. On 4 October 1948, Wood was invited to lunch at Chartwell and given the galleys of *Their Finest Hour*.[6]

A meticulous proofreader, Wood was pedantic and opinionated. This, as much as Churchill's habitual parsimony, probably explains the reluctance to bring him on board. Even then, Churchill issued firm instructions about reducing, not increasing, the number of commas, identifying inconsistencies without arguing their merits, and certainly not going through original documents.[7] But Wood was soon exceeding his brief in typically abrasive style. Many people, he told Churchill, found punctuation a difficult subject: "I understand it myself, but few do"—including, he made clear, Sir Edward Marsh. As for *The Gathering Storm*, Wood considered that "typographically and editorially the book is a botch, a disgrace to the printer and publishers alike" and set about revisions for the second edition with gusto. On 9 November 1948, Desmond Flower of Cassell's complained to Churchill that Wood was "altering the sense and wording of many passages" in the draft of volume 2; a few weeks later, he reported that Wood had removed 219 commas and added 217. In December, the two of them had a flaming row about whether punctuation should appear inside or outside quotation marks. Flower, of course, was defensive about volume 1, but he could not stand a proofreader lecturing a publisher. Churchill saw the problem—once calling Wood "indefatigable, interminable, intolerable"—but he was determined not to repeat the errors in *The Gathering Storm*. So "Mr. Literary Wood" (as he was known in contrast to "Mr. Accountant Wood") became a fixed if fractious member of Churchill's team.[8]

For all its members' individual skills and experience, however, the team lacked coherence. They were part-timers, and the captain was caught up in several games at once as politician and statesman as well as author. No one acted as full-time manager, and this mattered because Churchill was now working on several volumes simultaneously. On 24 February 1948, he told his advisers that he would concentrate on volume 2 for the next two weeks, then review the publishers' proofs of volume 1, before making a renewed push on volume 2 in order to have a presentable copy ready by 1 May to secure the next tranche of money from his publishers. After that, he would turn to volume 3, "the prospect of which I find refreshing."[9] Three separate volumes, in various stages of completion with multiple galleys in circulation—clearly, this required a firm hand on the tiller. Deakin had provided that in the late 1930s but, now more senior, he was deeply involved in Oxford. Pownall organized periodic team meetings and tried to extract guidance from Churchill, but he too was part-time. In May 1948, he tackled "Master" inconclusively about what he called a "Focus Miss"—a female personal assistant dedicated to coordinating the proofs and handling correspondence. Pownall was sure Kelly was not up to this task. As for Wood, he did proofreading "very well," Pownall told Ismay, and this might avoid another "balls up" over errata, but Wood did not "cut enough ice with Winston to be able to act as a permanent 'P.A.,' which is what is really needed."[10] The team soldiered on without a clear focus or a proper manager. What it achieved under the circumstances is remarkable.

BEYOND THIS INNER CIRCLE, Churchill continued to draw freely on official help—for instance, asking Leslie Rowan, John Martin, and other former private secretaries to ferret out information from the archives.[11] He recruited additional assistants for specific tasks, such as Albert Goodwin and R. V. Jones on the Blitz. Once more, Sir Edward Marsh read the volume for style and punctuation, sparring with Charles Wood over use of the comma. And Clementine Churchill again labored through the text, offering her usual mixture of minor and substantive comments. On a draft of "Alone," she told Churchill severely, "the minutes are too wholesale and there is hardly any fresh stimulating material."[12]

Such "documentitis" particularly worried Churchill's American publishers. In July 1948, detailed critiques of the 1 May draft were prepared independently by William Jay Gold, who edited the memoirs for *Life*, and Paul Brooks at Houghton Mifflin. "I never thought that we should be making editorial suggestions to Mr. Churchill," Brooks commented to Laughlin, "but these seem so obvious that I think it would be foolish not to have a try." Gold and Brooks offered similar advice. While liking Churchill's treatment of the battles of France and Britain, they found other chapters too full of minutes and lacking in what Gold called "connective tissue." This applied particularly to the war in the Mediterranean and North Africa—a theme of limited interest to American readers though not, as we shall see, to a British audience or to Churchill's overall argument. Gold felt the volume seemed "to fall off markedly in interest after the Dakar chapter."[13] Partly because of these comments, Churchill moved Deakin's draft chapter about Germany and Russia from volume 3 to strengthen the end of *Their Finest Hour* and scrapped one entitled "Behind the Fronts"—really his December 1940 minutes warmed over.

Churchill's personal involvement was intense but sporadic, dictated by financial deadlines and by the rhythms of the parliamentary calendar. Having produced a serviceable version for 1 May 1948 and duly received the publishers' payments (£69,000 to the Literary Trust and £35,000 for himself—the equivalent of $420,000), he did little on the memoirs for the next three months, which were overshadowed by the Berlin blockade and fear of war with Russia. "When Parliament shuts down he'll be at us again," Pownall rightly predicted.[14] On 11 August, Churchill summoned Ismay and Allen to Chartwell, with volume 2 now his priority. Capitalizing on his winter trip to Marrakech, Churchill contrived another working holiday funded by *Life* and *The New York Times*, this time in southern France. Estimating the cost at $8,000 or $9,000, Daniel Longwell of *Life* phoned Houghton Mifflin to suggest it contribute $1,500 of the total. But the book publishers were not keen at "this nibbling away of the profits" and, when Paul Brooks replied that they would have to consult Emery Reves, their backstage partner, Longwell said hurriedly: "Never mind, we'll bear all the expense ourselves, only, for God's sake, keep Reves out."[15] Houghton Mifflin was not troubled again about Churchill's "working vacations," which suited it fine.

On 22 August 1948, Churchill's entourage took the ferry to Calais and then traveled on a special coach in Le Train Bleu to the Riviera. In Aix-en-Provence, they established themselves in ten rooms in the Hôtel du Roy René. Christopher and Mary Soåmes stayed for ten days, Clementine Churchill for a month. After her departure, Churchill spent a week at Beaverbrook's villa on the Côte d'Azur and then a few days at the Hôtel de Paris in Monte Carlo, another favorite, before returning to England on 2 October. The total cost to his publishers was $8,844. Even more than at Marrakech, in Provence Churchill's presence caused a social sensation. Gifts of flowers, chocolates, and wine poured into the hotel—including three much appreciated cases of Pol Roger 1928. Churchill's secretaries returned several paintings and courteously declined a host of invitations to local events, thereby depriving their boss of such treats as a rugby match at Marseilles and "buffet dinner and movies" on a visiting U.S. warship.[16]

Once Bill Deakin arrived on 30 August, Churchill began a steady cycle of revisions, which circulated to and fro among his hotel in Aix, his research assistants at Hyde Park Gate, and his printers at the Chiswick Press. By the time Deakin returned to England on 19 September, they had worked through book 1 and most of book 2. Deakin told Walter Graebner of *Life* that he had not seen Churchill "so jovial and good-natured" in twelve years. The vacation had been "most pleasant and fruitful," Churchill assured Henry Luce. "Great changes, extensive additions and an enormous improvement have been made in the book as a whole."[17]

Since the text sent to the publishers on 1 May 1948 had been called "Final," this new version, distinguished with a large asterisk, became the "Starred Final." It was printed on 11 October, and 150 copies were distributed as a base for serialization and translation. This became known as the 150 version. Thereafter, Churchill was diverted by the Tory party conference, the new parliamentary session, and the celebrations over *The Gathering Storm*, published on 4 October. His limited book time was spread across several fronts. On 18 November, he told his assistants that first priority was "emergency treatment" of volume 2, now that it had been subjected to the green pen of Mr. Wood—a process that became known as "Wooding." Then he wanted to clear the revised edition of volume 1 and get volume 3 into presentable shape for the 1 May 1949 payment. Both these tasks were to be done by the end of 1948, so he could turn in the new year to selecting documents for volumes 4 and 5.[18]

At this stage, Churchill envisaged only a series of overtakes to amend the "Starred Final" version of volume 2, but after Wood, Kelly, and Deakin had gone through the chapters again, he ordered a completely new "Revised Final" version to be printed and circulated to foreign publishers. On 2 December, he told Camrose, "there are so many corrections and important changes from the original 150 version that I am sure it would be better to set it up afresh from the revised text." Steeling himself, Henry Laughlin of Houghton Mifflin accepted Churchill's instructions, but Emery Reves cabled on 5 December: "Translation everywhere greatly advanced. Book One practically completed and set." To save "a full month's work and expenses," Reves asked for a few pages indicating major amendments to the October version. Churchill sent a blunt no: "Corrections are fundamental and far-reaching and I cannot accept responsibility for inaccurate versions. . . . I must ask that the true version of the text that is now being sent to you should be strictly adhered to."[19] Compliance with these instructions did not save the publishers from a stream of overtakes in early 1949. The last set, number twenty-one, was dated 7 March. Three days later, Paul Brooks at Houghton Mifflin replied that they could not include those changes because the volume had already been printed and a bound copy was on its way to Churchill by airmail.[20]

THEIR FINEST HOUR therefore evolved in response to the input and criticisms of Churchill's assistants, friends, and publishers. But, more so than *The Gathering Storm*, it was also shaped by the emerging historiography of the war. In France, several top politicians of the period had published their memoirs by 1948. The most significant was by Paul Reynaud, Prime Minister in the last months of the Third Republic, whose *La France a sauvé l'Europe* appeared in two massive volumes in 1947. In his review of *The Gathering Storm* for *The Observer*, Reynaud deftly presented himself as a French Churchill—critic of appeasement and disarmament in the 1930s, champion of all-out war in 1939–1940. His memoirs were similarly Churchillian in scope, going right back to Versailles to offer a lengthy analysis of Hitler's rise and then, in volume 2, a detailed narrative of his brief but dramatic premiership from March to June 1940, including the fullest account to that time of the French defeat.[21]

This was an ambitious work, which attracted considerable attention in Britain including a lead review in *The Times Literary Supplement* by the eminent historian Lewis Namier, who had recently published a study of Munich. Namier felt that both the man and the memoir were seriously flawed. Allowing for the similarities with Churchill—Cassandras who became Caesars at the eleventh hour—Reynaud, "restless and uneasy . . . hardly seems equal to a crisis of the first magnitude," and anyway his country had gone down to defeat. Reynaud the author, similarly, had "failed to master his material"—twelve hundred pages could have been cut to four hundred by eliminating "masses" of irrelevance. Namier concluded that Reynaud "had a strong case and a good cause," yet his failure as a memoirist "deprived his person and record of a tragic greatness which could have been theirs." Privately, Churchill was also dismissive. Although sparring with Reynaud's memoirs at various points in his own, he had little time for what he called an "endless book."[22]

On the British side, no heavyweight politicians had entered the ring—the Eden-Hinsley combination (chapter 7) was getting nowhere—and no significant memoirs had yet appeared from the highest level of the British armed forces. The most self-promoting general, Montgomery, published two slim volumes in 1948—*El Alamein to the River Sangro* and *Normandy to the Baltic*—but these were versions of his published dispatches. Monty and his British counterparts were constrained by continued military service or by the Cabinet Office's rules about memoirs by officers and officials.

Across the Atlantic, however, where such controls were minimal, 1948 saw a spate of major memoirs about the war. Cordell Hull, Roosevelt's Secretary of State from 1933 to 1944, weighed in with eighteen hundred tedious pages that made Reynaud seem succinct. Hull praised Churchill in 1940—"no people in history had a more courageous and inspiring leader in the moment of their greatest need"—but also mentioned their clashes over empire and protectionism. According to Hull, he and Roosevelt advocated "sane and practical liberalism in our foreign affairs" against Churchill's "conservatism."[23] Here was a moderate restatement of Elliott Roosevelt's 1946 critique of Churchill the imperialist.

In his April 1948 memoirs, Henry Stimson, Roosevelt's Secretary of War, took on Churchill the strategist. Stimson insisted on the closeness of the Anglo-American alliance—yes, there had been differences, but these were "the quarrels of brothers"—and he dismissed the extreme Ralph Ingersoll line, that British opposition to the Overlord plan to invade Normandy was "mainly guided by a desire to block Soviet Russia by an invasion farther east." But Stimson had no doubt that Churchill had unremittingly opposed Overlord, mainly for fear of repeating the carnage of the Somme or Dieppe. Only at Cairo and Teheran in late 1943, he said, did the American strategy win through.[24]

November 1948 saw publication of the biggest U.S. war memoir to date, *Crusade in Europe* by Dwight D. Eisenhower. "Ike" had become the great American hero of the war, and his account of the campaigns in North Africa, Italy, France, and Germany was a bestseller, translated eventually into twenty-two languages. Disingenuously, he told Churchill he had reluctantly decided to set the record straight after "so many biased and prejudiced accounts" by "irresponsible people."[25] *Crusade in Europe* was at pains to praise "a great war leader" and "a great man," but, like Stimson's memoirs, it did raise questions about Churchill's strategy, such as his obsession with the Balkans. Ike also referred to Churchill's deep misgivings about Overlord and perpetual keenness for new operations in the Mediterranean, frankly admitting their clash over southern France in 1944.[26]

On the whole, Churchill was not displeased with *Crusade in Europe*. "I admire its tone and temper," he cabled its author, "especially on the few questions about which we disagree."[27] But both Stimson and Eisenhower had now cast doubt on his enthusiasm for Overlord. From two such famous and respected figures, these charges carried far more weight than from the likes of Ingersoll and Elliott Roosevelt. This may explain the remarkable chapter in book 1 of *Their Finest Hour*, entitled "The Apparatus of Counter-Attack."

In mid-September 1948, a month after receiving an advance copy of *Crusade in Europe*, Churchill cut down the minutes in this draft chapter about June 1940, sharpened its focus, and dictated new material connecting it to D-Day in 1944. The rewrite highlighted Churchill's instructions in 1940 for commando raids and particularly for tank-landing craft and artificial harbors—ideas, he noted, that he first advanced back in 1917. Commodore Allen tried to tone down the consequent impression that Churchill was the originator of LCTs (landing-craft tanks), and Churchill printed much of a section drafted by Allen about the general development of landing craft. But this did not substantially affect the thrust of the chapter, which Churchill rammed home at the end:

> In view of the many accounts which are extant and multiplying of my supposed aversion from any kind of large-scale opposed-landing, such as took place in Normandy in 1944, it may be convenient if I make it clear that from the very beginning I provided a great deal of the impulse and authority for creating the immense apparatus and armada for the landing of armour on beaches, without which it is now universally recognised that all such major operations would have been impossible.

Considerable sleight of hand was involved here. Landing craft had many uses in many places; supporting their construction was not the same as endorsing the Overlord plan of 1944. But Churchill had set down his marker. He gave notice that he would "unfold this theme step by step in these volumes by means of documents written by me at the time."[28]

In addition to Stimson's and Eisenhower's books, Churchill was probably also responding to Robert Sherwood's *Roosevelt and Hopkins,* which started serialization in Britain and America in June 1948 and appeared in book form in October. The Prime Minister's "aversion to a Second Front" was a theme running through the whole work: "It was certainly no fault of Churchill's that two American Expeditionary Forces went into France, north and south, in the summer of 1944." According to Sherwood, Churchill's advocacy of the "soft underbelly" approach to Europe reflected not a desire to preempt the Soviets in the Balkans but what the U.S. Joint Chiefs of Staff considered to be his "incurable" preference for "eccentric operations" rather than frontal attack. Offensive though these comments were, what made Churchill really angry was Sherwood's use of documents.[29]

In April 1948, Sherwood sent Churchill the first half of his book, taking the story up to the spring of 1942. It was full of juicy quotations from Hopkins's memos and from official documents, British as well as American. Kelly and Deakin were asked to identify sensitive passages, and their list was forwarded to the Cabinet Office. Brook's anxieties transcended Churchill's: Sherwood quoted War Cabinet documents and even Hopkins's record of King George VI's caustic observations on Eamon de Valera, the Irish premier. But he shared Churchill's concern that Sherwood was going to publish numerous extracts from Churchill's messages to Roosevelt, not least the massive letter on Britain's predicament dated 8 December 1940, which had been the trigger for the Lend-Lease program of financial aid. Brook considered it "wholly inappropriate" that this letter "should be published for the first time in a book of this kind"—further evidence of how he viewed Churchill's memoirs as virtually a British official history. On 29 April, Churchill saw Sherwood and gave him a list of the documents he wanted omitted or paraphrased: "The principle to which I must adhere is that no correspondence between me and President Roosevelt, and no textual quotation of British Government documents must be printed in this work. You are writing a life of Harry Hopkins and not a history of the War, or an account of my policy as set forth in my telegrams to the President."[30]

At this stage, the exchanges were amicable and cooperative. Sherwood accepted most of the cuts, and Churchill could see a larger utility in his project. Many of the proposed quotes showed how nonneutrally FDR was acting months before Pearl Harbor, yet the U.S. War Department had apparently raised no objection. That suited Churchill very well in his battle with the State Department to quote the Roosevelt-Churchill correspondence in his own book.

In March 1948, the State Department claimed that the Truman adminstration was under pressure from Congress to open the correspondence, as part of Republican efforts to expose Roosevelt as a warmonger in 1940–1941, and any revelations by Churchill would fuel those demands. Privately (and not for communication to Churchill) the State Department made it clear that Truman had personally said no. He was concerned about his own position in an election year and about damage to current negotiations for a transatlantic alliance—what became NATO in 1949. Brook sidestepped the problem in volume 1 (see above, chapter 8), but the correspondence was central to *Their Finest Hour,* and Churchill was furious. "It would be a most serious injury to the story and would in fact prevent it from being told in its full truth, if these telegrams were omitted," he told Brook on 12 April.[31] After further unavailing pressure from the British Embassy, Brook suggested a personal approach to Truman himself. Churchill agreed, seeing his case and Sherwood's as interlinked. "Suppose that my letter to the President does not achieve satisfactory results," he told Brook on 5 May, "it will be a very good thing if the War Department allow Sherwood to make all these disclosures. Our case will then be overwhelming."[32]

Churchill's letter to Truman, sent the same day, emphasized that he was only quoting from his own messages to Roosevelt and would summarize FDR's replies. He also made clear that nothing would appear in print before 1 January 1949. He instanced the many American books on the war that had referred to him, without any prior consultation—including the recent works by Stimson and Hull—and hoped Truman would "recognize that I too have a right to place on record a coherent and integral account of the part I played in the war, which is also an important part of the story of my country." Churchill sent his letter and the relevant galleys via Admiral William Leahy, the President's Chief of Staff. "I hope you will help me in these matters," he told Leahy, "knowing that the interest of the United States ranks with me almost equally with that of my own country."[33]

After reading the galleys, Leahy told Truman he could "find no valid reason why these messages should not be published," and that was also the view of John Hickerson in the State Department. Whereupon Truman wrote a cordial letter to

Churchill on 18 May saying that there was no objection to publication and dismissing the previous fuss as "a misunderstanding as to what you had proposed to do." Possibly there had been some confusion, but much had happened in the two months since Churchill's initial request. In April 1945, Truman had stepped into a dead man's shoes, totally unprepared, and in late 1947 he even offered privately to serve as Eisenhower's Vice President on the Democratic ticket. It was only on 8 March 1948 that Truman announced he would run for the presidency, but a Gallup Poll indicated that he would lose the election to any of the likely Republican candidates. Two of FDR's sons, Elliott and Franklin Jr., worked openly to make Eisenhower the Democratic candidate. By the end of April, however, the Ike boom had abated, and the deepening Cold War bolstered public support for the President. On 14 May, defying the State Department, Truman recognized the infant state of Israel, thereby ensuring the vital Jewish-American vote. By the time he replied to Churchill's letter on 18 May, he probably felt in a much stronger position, which any fuss about a few wartime letters would not dent. But timing was everything. The presidential race was "very bitter," he told Churchill, and he was therefore "more than happy" that the volume would not appear until 1949.[34]

Churchill was delighted at Truman's letter. "I am very glad that this is satisfactorily adjusted," he told Brook on 31 May.[35] A week later, he received the next installment of Sherwood's book, covering 1942–1943, which the author needed to clear for imminent serialization in *Collier's*. At this point, their exchanges turned sour. Now that his correspondence with FDR had been settled, Churchill had no reason to tolerate Sherwood's revelations as a possible bargaining chip. Moreover, *Roosevelt and Hopkins* was now trespassing on the heart of his own story, with an account sent by Averell Harriman to Hopkins of Churchill's visit to Stalin in August 1942. Churchill fired off a series of angry telegrams to Sherwood, finally telling him on 15 June that he was referring the text to the British government, since only it could give permission for quotation from his telegrams to Roosevelt, Hopkins, and Stalin. He also complained about other references in Hopkins's papers that were "disparaging" to himself and Randolph or "prejudicial to Anglo-American relations at the present time." He warned that the existing text would "certainly lead to much painful controversy, both official and personal."[36]

Sherwood, though shaken by this barrage, was a seasoned campaigner, with his own friends in high places. In Britain, his book was being serialized by the *Sunday Express*, owned by Churchill's crony Lord Beaverbrook. The Beaver told

Sherwood it was "utterly ridiculous" for Churchill to suggest that he should submit the text to the British government and surmised that Churchill simply wanted the freedom to "describe these events in his own way." Fortified, Sherwood wrote to George Marshall, the Secretary of State, whom he had interviewed for the book. He said he suspected that these "vituperative cables" were prompted by Churchill's sensitivity on Overlord. "As you probably know, Mr. Churchill now takes the position that he was always whole-heartedly in favor of OVERLORD, and presumably he intends to write his own record that way." Sherwood therefore interpreted the telegrams "as a threat to scare me into censoring Harry's papers to conform to his own wishes."[37]

Sherwood decided to delete all further Churchill quotations from his book, so as not to feel "compelled to submit the rest of the manuscript to him," but he maintained a courteous correspondence. Churchill, for his part, simmered down. "I do not judge the matter too seriously," he told Brook on 8 July, "especially as it makes clear that I should have full latitude in stating our case."[38] The only lasting casualty of the row was the opening to Sherwood's book. In April 1948, Brendan Bracken, a director of Sherwood's British publisher, Eyre and Spottiswoode, had been optimistic about persuading Churchill to add a foreword to *Roosevelt and Hopkins*. But on 4 August, Sherwood concluded with studied understatement that "in view of recent developments, I consider it extremely unlikely that any endorsement will be forthcoming from Mr. Churchill."[39]

THROUGHOUT CHURCHILL's battle of the books with the Americans in 1948, he received the closest possible support from Norman Brook. The Cabinet Secretary had become almost a part of Churchill's team, and on volume 2 his dual role as official censor and unofficial editor became yet more evident. During 1948, Brook and his staff read book 1 of *Their Finest Hour* no less than four times—in January, March, June, and October—commenting as before on matters of substance to Churchill and on typos and style to Bill Deakin. They also checked passages for factual accuracy, such as Churchill's list of ministerial appointments in May 1940 and his statistical tables of the British war effort, both of which appear in chapter 1. In addition, the Cabinet Secretariat acted as conduit for all Churchill's requests to foreign governments (including the Dominions) to quote from wartime cables. Churchill asked Brook to handle these permissions in January 1948, and Brook acceded—something he would surely never have done for any other private citizen. Sir Orme Sargent of the Foreign

Office warned Brook that these permissions could be sensitive. In communications with the United States,

> we should make it clear that we are doing so on behalf, and at the desire, of Mr. Churchill. I do not think that it would be wise to let it be known that H.M. Government have been given such a wide opportunity to approve or comment on the book—it is Mr. Churchill's own story and in the eyes of the world the present Government must not be held responsible for what he says in it.

There was also the question of whether to request Soviet approval to reproduce messages between Churchill and Stalin. Sargent, like Brook, thought not. It might generate "irritating correspondence," with no guarantee that the Soviets would consult the British in similar circumstances. "In the last resort, if the Soviet Government complain about any particular passage, we can quite simply say that this is Mr. Churchill's book and that it has not been written by H.M. Government."[40]

Brook acted as censor as well as broker. The Foreign Office queried Churchill's references to some diplomatic issues that were still sensitive, such as Ireland, Palestine, and Franco's Spain. Churchill usually deferred to their anxieties. The Cabinet Secretary also remained vigilant about Attlee's wish that the memoirs not quote from staff papers, lest this encourage officers to write their own justifications. As we shall see, this served to obscure significant differences between Churchill and the Chiefs of Staff in July 1940 about the nature of the invasion threat. On the other hand, Brook allowed Churchill to include in the same chapter a memo from the Chiefs of Staff reporting current troop deployments in likely invasion areas. "On a strict interpretation of Mr. Attlee's recent ruling about the publication of Chiefs of Staff documents," Brook noted, "we ought presumably to ask that this be paraphrased." But he felt that "this Chapter is already in danger of creating the impression that our military authorities did nothing until they were told to by Mr. Churchill; and the textual reproduction of this Minute is a useful corrective."[41] But Brook rarely had such an opportunity. The minutes, Churchill told his assistants, "frequently call departments and Ministers to account. It is not possible to print the replies and counter-arguments which are extant."[42] Churchill's principle, reinforced by Attlee's rule, ensured that the memoirs did give a one-sided account of wartime policymaking, in which, as Brook feared, the only dynamic figure seemed to be Churchill.

Brook's main anxieties about *Their Finest Hour* concerned security. In February 1949, he had MI5 check out the Chiswick Press, which was printing all Churchill's documents and galleys, fearful that their staff might pass on wartime secrets. Nothing suspicious was found.[43] He was also worried that verbatim quotation of wartime telegrams might allow the Russians to penetrate British codes. The risk was relatively small—Moscow would need to have kept copies of other telegrams sent on the same day in order to exploit Churchill's text—and wartime codes would not help with current messages. But Sir Stewart Menzies, the head of MI6, known as "C," feared that Churchill's example might encourage other memoirists to print telegrams that were closer to codes still in use. He wanted to paraphrase a few of the messages so that the memoirs could not be relied on as a key. Churchill was keen to talk with "C," whom he had not seen since leaving office, and the two men dined together on 9 June 1948. The next day, Brigadier Arthur Cornwall-Jones, the Cabinet Office liaison with MI6, noted that "although the Great Man was not particularly impressed" with the arguments that Menzies adduced, he accepted what was proposed. A number of telegrams were duly sanitized by the Cypher Policy Board in November 1948, usually by changing words or word order in a few places, and a note was added to the acknowledgments: "At the request of His Majesty's Government, on security grounds I have paraphrased some of the telegrams published in this volume. These changes have not altered in any way the sense or substance of the telegrams." Both the editing and the note became standard practice in subsequent volumes.[44]

The biggest intelligence issue raised by the memoirs concerned not British codes but those of the Axis. Churchill had been at the center of Britain's spectacular success in decoding German signals and using the consequent intelligence in operations. After 1945, concealing the success of the code breakers at Bletchley Park was of paramount importance. On 31 July 1945, the Joint Intelligence Committee approved a general directive to heads of the Official History programs that the existence of such intelligence "should NEVER be disclosed." Historians on their staffs who were not privy to the Ultra secret should be instructed "not to probe too deeply into the reasons for apparently unaccountable orders being issued." The underlying justifications for secrecy were twofold: first, and more obvious, not to arouse the suspicions of future enemies about British skill in signals decryption, which would encourage them to take countermeasures. Second, and more interesting, was the fear that if the Germans and Japanese became aware of the part played by special intelligence, they might claim they had not been fairly defeated—an echo of the "stab in the back" myth about the German

collapse in 1918, which Hitler had exploited so successfully. Reasons or rationalizations, these arguments justified a major program of censorship. The official
histories of the war carefully concealed all traces of Ultra, becoming what has
been called "the last deception operation of the Second World War," and would-
be memoir writers in the know were pressured to keep silence. Remarkably, it was
not until 1974 that the wartime head of Air Intelligence, Frederick Winter-
botham, with reluctant official approval, published his personal account, *The
Ultra Secret*.[45]

Here, as in so many respects, *The Second World War* set a defining precedent.
On 27 January 1948, Churchill told Brook he would find it difficult to complete
his memoirs without including some statements "implying that we were able to
break the codes and cyphers of enemy powers." He asked the Cabinet Secretary
not to lay down a general rule against such disclosures. The head of the London
Signals Intelligence Centre was aghast. Given Churchill's "unrivalled authority,"
his memoirs would be "more widely read than any other book of modern times."
Not only would his disclosures be widely noted, they would have a "snowball-
like" effect, encouraging others to break silence, and "the flood-gates would
open."[46] In April, Brook spelled this out to Churchill. Many who served at
Bletchley Park were no longer in government service and were "bound only by
their personal undertakings to say nothing about their war-time work. If, when
they read your Book, they feel that a person of your great authority has thought it
safe to refer to these matters, there is a danger that they may conclude that their
obligation to complete secrecy may be relaxed."[47]

Retreating from his earlier stance, Churchill accepted the appropriate censorship. Words such as "intercepts" or "intercepted signals" were routinely purged
by the intelligence authorities, as in the comment in "Desert Victory" that "they
brought me hour-to-hour [intercepted] signals from the battlefield."[48] Where knowledge of German intentions was admitted, it was necessary to show that this could
have been acquired from captured documents. In April 1948, Deakin spent a
"nightmare" weekend going through the Chartwell archives to try to justify Churchill's account of Hitler's meetings with Franco and Pétain in October 1940. He
felt "practically certain" that the information came from an "ordinary source" after
the war, probably the transcript of Pétain's trial, but he had not been with Churchill when the passage was added, and the transcript ran to one thousand pages.[49]

After their initial panic, the intelligence authorities were relieved that Churchill said so little about signals intercepts in volume 2. "If these are the only kinds
of references Mr. Churchill is going to make to the subject we have in mind,
there is not much cause for alarm," Cornwall-Jones told Brook in February 1948,

after reading the first galleys.[50] And Churchill made no allusion, even in drafts, to his keen interest in the work of Bletchley Park, which started to break German Air Force codes within days of his arrival at Number 10. By the autumn of 1940, he was receiving a daily buff box from "C," to which only he had the key, containing the choicest pieces of raw intelligence and a summary of principal revelations. Churchill also did his best to shake up the handling of intelligence, pressing the Chiefs of Staff for an integrated organization to override the jealous monopoly of the individual services. He never fully succeeded, but under his acgis the Joint Intelligence Committee and its staff gained much greater power. And Churchill understood the need for rapid and effective distribution of intelligence to senior commanders. Again, this took time to achieve, but from late 1942 it became an essential element in Allied victory. In the 1980s, Sir Harry Hinsley (Eden's first research assistant and subsequently the official historian of wartime British intelligence) went so far as to suggest that Allied intelligence superiority had reduced the war by three or four years.[51]

This was speculation, of course, and Hinsley later shortened his estimate to two years, but precision is not the point. Incontrovertibly, intelligence was a vital part of the war effort, and Churchill played a commanding role in that epic story. "No British statesman in modern times has had a more passionate faith in the value of secret intelligence," historian Christopher Andrew has observed. "None has been more determined to put it to good use." Churchill famously said of staff at Bletchley Park that they were "the geese who laid the golden eggs and never cackled," but it was equally important that he, too, kept quiet. In the first volume of *The World Crisis*, he had made free with information acquired from German naval intercepts. In 1927, he was a member of the Baldwin Cabinet that published Russian intercepts to justify breaking off diplomatic relations, whereupon Moscow changed its methods and the British decrypyted no more high-grade Soviet signals until 1944.[52] By the time he wrote *The Second World War*, Churchill had learned his lesson, accepting Brook's advice and allowing the intelligence services to sanitize his work. This set a decisive example in protecting the Ultra secret, but it also concealed one of his greatest contributions to Allied victory. In this crucial respect, memoir fell short of history.

CHAPTER 11

"VICTORY AT ALL COSTS"

C HURCHILL'S ACCESSION to the premiership on 10 May 1940 co-incided with the start of the German blitzkrieg in the west. Six weeks later, France sued for an armistice, leaving Britain to fight on alone against relentless air attack and the threat of imminent invasion. If this was Britain's "finest hour," as Churchill asserted on 18 June, then it was also his own. The object of volume 2 was to validate both these contentions, and in this Churchill succeeded triumphantly. Most subsequent historians agree that 1940 was the apex of his career and one of the epic moments in British history.

It is ironic, therefore, that *Their Finest Hour* often obscures the magnitude of his achievement. It presents a simplified version of 1940, at times almost a caricature. Yet in this volume, like its predecessor, there are hints of a more complex historical reality—of a man as surprised by events and as uncertain of the future as were all his colleagues, who nevertheless transcended his doubts to offer inspiring national and international leadership. Comparing the memoirs with the documents is not to debunk Churchill. On the contrary, revealing the man behind the myth serves to enhance his stature.

WITH HINDSIGHT, the fall of France seems one of the most inevitable moments of World War II. The awesome Panzers and the feeble Third Republic have become historical clichés. One must therefore stress that May 1940 was by no means inevitable and that it came as a devastating shock to British policymakers. The disintegration of the French front was "incredible news," Neville Chamberlain confided to his diary on 15 May, five days after the German attack began. "The mystery of what looks like the French failure is as great as ever," Lord Halifax, the Foreign Secretary, noted in his diary on 25 May. "The one firm rock on which everybody had been willing to build for the last two years was the French Army, and the Germans walked through it like they did through the Poles."[1]

In 1940, Churchill was as surprised as the rest of Whitehall; in 1947–1948, drafting his memoirs, he had to come to terms with his earlier misconceptions. A critical question was why the French and British forces rushed forward to the River Dyle, in eastern Belgium, the moment that country's ostrichlike neutrality was violated on 10 May. Plan D, as it was known, meant an improvised encounter battle for which the Allies were ill prepared. In chapter 2 of *Their Finest Hour*, Churchill devotes four pages to "the haunting question" of whether it would have been wiser to stay put on the French frontier, inviting the Belgian army to fall back on "these strong defences," rather than "make the hazardous and hurried forward leap to the Dyle." A corollary of Plan D was that, by throwing his armored and motorized troops into Belgium, General Maurice Gamelin, the French Commander in Chief, denuded other parts of his front, particularly around Sedan. This was protected by only two inferior divisions with no permanent fortifications, on the assumption that the Ardennes was impassable to large armies. "Looking back," writes Churchill, the Chamberlain Cabinet, "in which I served, and for whose acts and neglects I take my full share of responsibility," should have probed French strategy far more vigorously during the winter of 1939–1940. He implies that it shrank from doing so to avoid "an unpleasant and difficult argument" in which the French could always ask why the British were doing so little themselves. On 10 May, he says, the French had ninety-four divisions on the Western Front, the British nine—one fewer than the Dutch.[2]

Chapter 2 therefore opens up a major theme of Churchill's account of the Battle of France—his criticism of Belgian policy and French strategy—for which he was later fiercely attacked from across the Channel. By implying that the British accepted Plan D out of deference to the French and solicitude for the Belgians, he seriously distorts British thinking in 1939–1940. We now assume that Germany intended to deal first with the French and then turn on the British, for Churchill's sequence of "The Fall of France" and Britain "Alone" has guided historical analysis. At the time, however, British intelligence suggested a different scenario. Assuming that Hitler needed quick victory for economic reasons, it seemed possible that he would concentrate on knocking Britain out of the war by strategic bombing and, in order to do so, would focus his campaign on the

Netherlands and Belgium, to gain air bases within range of southern England. In other words, the British government was almost more concerned with the Low Countries than France, and French strategy, in turn, took account of these British fears. Although Plan D was partly aimed at securing full use of Belgium's twenty-two divisions, it was also intended to persuade the British to commit their air force to the continental land battle in order to preempt German capture of Belgian airfields. The French feared that the main RAF plan—for eventual strategic bombing of the Ruhr Valley—might provoke a German invasion of France while doing nothing to help the French Army.[3] However imprudent, Plan D was therefore a genuinely Allied strategy, attempting to balance French, Belgian, and British interests. But none of this is apparent from Churchill's account. He added his speculation about the wisdom of Plan D in January 1948 but never probed further into its rationale.[4]

So the British and French raced to the Dyle while the Wehrmacht thrust around the south of them toward the sea. In the first few days, Churchill was deeply absorbed in constructing his coalition government. It was only on 15 May that the magnitude of the crisis was driven home, as he describes in some of the most colorful pages of *Their Finest Hour*. (See the draft on page 74.) At 7:30 in the morning, he was awakened by a phone call from Paul Reynaud, the French premier. "He spoke in English, and evidently under stress: 'We have been defeated.' As I did not immediately respond he said again: 'We are beaten; we have lost the battle.'" Incredulous, Churchill said he would fly over for a conference. He and Ismay arrived the following afternoon to find the situation "incomparably worse than we had imagined." At Gamelin's briefing at the Quai d'Orsay, everyone remained standing: "Utter dejection was written on every face." For about five minutes, the French Commander in Chief explained how German tanks and motorized units had broken through the line and were advancing "with unheard-of speed" toward the Channel.

> When he stopped there was a considerable silence. I then asked: "Where is the strategic reserve?" and, breaking into French, which I used indifferently (in every sense): "*Où est la masse de manoeuvre?*" General Gamelin turned to me and, with a shake of the head and a shrug, said: "*Aucune.*"
>
> There was another long pause. Outside in the garden of the Quai d'Orsay clouds of smoke arose from large bonfires, and I saw from the window venerable officials pushing wheel-barrows of archives on to them. Already therefore the evacuation of Paris was being prepared.

Churchill admits he had not comprehended "the revolution" of armored warfare; he was equally astonished that the French had held nothing back for a counterattack. Staring at the wreaths of smoke from the bonfire of French vanities, Churchill struggled with what he calls "one of the greatest surprises I have had in my life."[5]

It is a superbly artful passage—vivid vignettes expressing fundamental truths. Reynaud's defeated phone call and Gamelin's monosyllabic shrug evoke the *faiblesse* of France. Old gentlemen push wheelbarrows while German tanks, the last word in modernist warfare, race toward the Channel. The official record of this meeting on 16 May, which Reynaud used in his 1947 memoirs, tells a rather different story. Gamelin was terse, clearly demoralized, but Reynaud and Daladier joined in an extensive discussion, which was more businesslike and less melodramatic than in Churchill's telling. But Churchill did not accept the French account. He simplified the official minutes and incorporated Ismay's recollections, personally adding the telling touches of the old men and their wheelbarrows, Gamelin's hopeless shrug, and his laconic "*Aucune.*"[6] In these few paragraphs, barely forty pages into the volume, he pens the obituary of the Third Republic. Broken in spirit and backward in technology, France contrasts starkly with the Britain Churchill will depict in the rest of *Their Finest Hour*.

For the French, the most emotive issue in May 1940 was the question of British fighter reinforcements. In the air, the RAF could make a significant contribution, but the government was determined to protect Britain against direct German attack. On 10 May, there were six RAF fighter squadrons in France; four more arrived during the next two days, and Churchill, pressed by Reynaud, secured on the sixteenth Cabinet agreement for another four. But then the head of Fighter Command, Sir Hugh Dowding, and the Chiefs of Staff dug in their heels. In chapter 2, Churchill states that Dowding told him "that with twenty-five squadrons of fighters he could defend the Island against the whole might of the German Air Force, but that with less he would be overpowered." Dowding later denied he had so confidently used the word "could," but Churchill did not amend this in subsequent editions. The Dowding story, placed significantly just before Reynaud's despairing phone call on 15 May, serves as a benchmark for all that follows. The next 150 pages relate a succession of French pleas for more fighters, but here was Britain's bottom line. On 16 June in London, Jean Monnet (then a member of the French economic mission in London) made a final appeal, still employing the "usual arguments" that France was "the decisive battle," but Churchill stood firm. He adds that General Charles de Gaulle, who accompanied Monnet, told Churchill in English, "I think you are quite right."[7]

De Gaulle is invoked here to justify Churchill's position on the RAF, but he serves more generally to embody "Fighting France" in contrast to his "defeatist" superiors, led by Marshal Philippe Pétain and General Maxime Weygand, who now sought an armistice. In chapters 9 and 10 Churchill presents de Gaulle as a brooding figure at the last Anglo-French conclaves, "impassive" and "imperturbable." At Tours on 13 June, Churchill glimpses him in a crowded passage: "I said in a low tone, in French: *'L'homme du destin'*" (corrected by Deakin from Churchill's original franglais, *"l'homme de la destinée"*). And three days later: "I preserved the impression, in contact with this very tall, phlegmatic man, 'Here is the Constable of France.'"[8] In these pregnant phrases, the latter with its Shakespearean echo, Churchill brings onto the stage his great French protagonist.

In view of their tempestuous wartime relationship and the harsh words about de Gaulle later in the memoirs, it is worth noting a cordial exchange that the two men had while Churchill was working on volume 2 on the Côte d'Azur in September 1948. Learning that de Gaulle was in the vicinity, he sent a note of greeting. This elicited a very warm handwritten reply from the general, expressing *"toute l'admiration et toute l'amitié que je porte à votre personne. Si, avant que vous ne quittiez la France, votre itinéraire passait près de Colombey-les-Deux-Eglises, nous serions, ma femme et moi, très heureux et très honorés, de vous y recevoir tout à fait dans l'intimité."* Although Churchill did not take up the invitation to visit the de Gaulles, he wrote again from England in October asking the general to confirm dates of his visits to Britain in June 1940.[9]

Sunday, 16 June 1940, was notable above all for the British offer of "an indissoluble union" with France. This was to take effect immediately, resulting in a single War Cabinet, joint organs of government, and common citizenship. Using Reynaud's memoirs, Churchill goes on to describe how the idea was rejected by "the defeatist section" of the French Cabinet, quoting with relish the French military's judgment that in three weeks England would "have her neck wrung like a chicken." At the end of this chapter, "The Bordeaux Armistice," Churchill indulges in more counterfactual speculation about the consequences of the French signing the union. Despite an immediate Nazi occupation of all France, the French government would have continued the fight from North Africa, and the British and French fleets "would have enjoyed complete mastery of the Mediterranean," laying Italy open to blockade and bombing. Churchill is at pains to show his support for the union idea during the war—to rebut contrary views attributed to him during Pétain's postwar trial. But it soon became something of an embarrassment to London, and in the summer of 1945 both Churchill and Attlee insisted publicly that the union proposal was a dead letter. To that end, in his memoirs Churchill is keen to play down its significance, stressing that it was approved by the War Cabinet "in a state of unusual emotion" and that he personally "was not the prime mover."[10]

The offer of union was indeed a half-baked and last-ditch bid to keep France in the war and gain hold of the French fleet. But it reflected a strong tide of official opinion in 1939–1940 that an institutionalized Entente Cordiale was essential to win the war and secure the peace. Mindful of the alienation of the interwar years, Sir Orme Sargent of the Foreign Office had proposed on 28 February 1940 "such a system of close and permanent co-operation between France and Great Britain—political, military and economic—as will for all international purposes make of the two countries a single unit in post-war Europe." His ideas were endorsed by Halifax and Chamberlain.[11] There were plenty of skeptics in Whitehall, of course, but Sargent's minute indicates the direction of British policy during the Phony War. The debacle of May–June 1940 therefore marked a profound parting of the ways, with lasting consequences on both sides of the Channel. It also sparked a grave political crisis in London. Just weeks into his premiership, Churchill had to wrestle with the fateful question: if France fell, could Britain win the war alone?

"FUTURE GENERATIONS may deem it noteworthy that the supreme question of whether we should fight on alone never found a place upon the War Cabinet agenda," Churchill states categorically at the start of chapter 9. As with many of his assertions, this is strictly correct yet seriously misleading. There are no items on the Cabinet minutes headed "Surrender" or "Negotiated Peace," but when Churchill wrote that he and his colleagues "were much too busy to waste time upon such unreal, academic issues," he knew that these issues had seemed all too real in late May 1940.[12] The way he conceals this debate is the most significant cover-up in *Their Finest Hour*.

The discussions centered on five meetings of the War Cabinet on 26, 27, and 28 May. Halifax, shaken by the French collapse and appalled at the prospect of saturation bombing, began to look for a negotiated settlement. The Foreign Secretary did not advocate immediate surrender, but—like Reynaud, who was in London for part of this time—he wanted to use the Italians to ascertain Hitler's likely peace terms. Halifax insisted he would fight to the end if Britain's integrity and independence were endangered—for instance, if Hitler demanded the fleet or the RAF. But should terms be secured to guarantee this independence, even if that meant sacrificing part of the empire, then "we should be foolish if we did not accept them" and thereby "save the country from an avoidable disaster."[13]

Under pressure from Halifax, Churchill conceded some ground. On 26 May, he is recorded saying that "if we could get out of this jam by giving up Malta and Gibraltar and some African colonies he would jump at it." On the twenty-seventh, he indicated that if Hitler "were prepared to make peace on the terms of the restoration of German colonies and the overlordship of Central Europe," that would be an acceptable basis for negotiation. But Churchill was sure that such scenarios were "most unlikely"—Hitler's current position allowed him to set terms that "put us completely at his mercy"—and he insisted "we should get no worse terms if we went on fighting, even if we were beaten, than were open to us now. . . . A time might come when we felt we had to put an end to the struggle, but the terms would not then be more mortal than those offered to us now."[14] The two Labour members of the War Cabinet, Clement Attlee and Arthur Greenwood, sided with the Prime Minister, and Chamberlain came round to Churchill's view, too, which left the Foreign Secretary isolated. The idea of sounding out the Italians was dropped, and the War Cabinet accepted Churchill's position that no question of peace terms could even be raised until the Battle of Britain had been won. However, the whole debate assumed an eventual negotiated peace rather than total victory. Halifax and Under-Secretary R. A. Butler were particularly emphatic on this point. As reported by the Swedish Ambassador on 17 June, they said that "common sense not bravado would dictate the British Government's policy." While this did not mean "peace at any price," no "diehards" would be allowed to stand in the way of a compromise peace "on reasonable conditions."[15]

Halifax's biographer, Andrew Roberts, has attacked as "simplistic and unhistorical" the tendency to depict this in "the black and white of the treacherous Halifax versus a heroic Churchill." On the other side, John Lukacs has dramatized a fundamental clash between the "visionary" Churchill and the "pragmatist" Halifax on which "the fate of Britain" and even "the outcome of the Second World War" largely hinged.[16] Who is right? To some extent the Cabinet discussions of 26–28 May reflected the circumstances of the moment. As late as 28 May, Churchill was telling junior ministers that "we should certainly be able to get 50,000 away" from the beaches of Dunkirk and that "if we could only get 100,000 away, that would be a magnificent performance."[17] By the time the evacuation ended on 4 June, 338,000 Allied troops had been evacuated, two thirds of them British, and this transformed Britain's prospects.

It is also clear that the Cabinet discussions were clouded by emotion. They occurred less than three weeks after the fateful meetings over the premiership. Halifax's diary for May is full of comments on Britain's new leader, praising

Churchill's "courage" and inspiration yet lamenting his impulsiveness and poor judgment: "I have seldom met anybody with stranger gaps of knowledge, or whose mind works in greater jerks." Churchill's irregular hours, rambling meetings, and tendency to speak in order to think were antithetical to how Halifax operated. During the decisive War Cabinet meeting on the afternoon of 27 May, the Foreign Secretary finally exploded. "I thought Winston talked the most frightful rot, also Greenwood," he noted in his diary, "and after bearing it for some time I said exactly what I thought of them, adding that if that was really their view, and if it came to the point, our ways must separate." Shaken by this hint of resignation, Churchill was "full of apologies and affection" afterward in the garden. But, wrote Halifax, "it does drive me to despair when he works himself up into a passion of emotion when he ought to make his brain think and reason"—hence the reference in June to "common sense not bravado."[18]

Halifax was not treacherous, but he was naïve. Although the Foreign Secretary kept talking of terms that guaranteed Britain's independence and integrity, the Prime Minister was surely right that even to broach negotiation at this stage would start the country down a slippery slope. When drafting his memoirs in 1948, Churchill had no doubt that this had been a critical moment in the war. He never intended to print much on the discussions of 26–28 May—Halifax was a close postwar colleague and Tory leader in the House of Lords—and he locates his brief references in "The Rush for Spoils" as a debate about trying to dissuade Mussolini from entering the war, rather than in his chapter about Dunkirk. But there he clearly hints at what was at stake: "One cannot easily make a bargain at the last gasp. Once we started negotiating for the friendly mediation of the Duce we should destroy our power for fighting on."[19]

In a draft, Churchill had actually exposed Halifax. His "Provisional Final" version says, "The Foreign Secretary showed himself willing to go a long way to placate ["buy off" in an earlier typescript] this new and dangerous enemy"—and noted a conversation between Halifax and the Italian Ambassador on 25 May hinting that Gibraltar, Malta, and Suez were on the table. Then he continued, in clear contrast, "I found Mr. Chamberlain and Mr. Attlee very stiff and tough."[20] It was Ismay who urged discretion. "I feel sure that Halifax would be hurt by any inference that he was not as tough *during the war* as the rest of them," he wrote on 17 September 1948. As evidence, Ismay cited an extract from Halifax's diary for 26 May (which he had been sent) to the effect that Halifax did not believe anything could be done to buy off Italy but wanted to avoid seeming "too unsympathetic to Reynaud in his distress."

Churchill was unconvinced. "General P," he wrote in the margin. "You have not perhaps read Reynaud's account. I have however."[21] Nevertheless, he cut the incriminating references to Halifax and some suggestive passages quoted from Reynaud's memoirs, asserting simply that "I found my colleagues very stiff and tough," leaving the impression that it was the French premier who did all the running toward Rome. But, as often happened in the flurry of last-minute amendments, the documents were not edited as rigorously as the text. Churchill's telegram to Reynaud on 28 May still makes reference to "the formula prepared last Sunday by Lord Halifax" suggesting that if Mussolini "would co-operate with us in securing a settlement of all European questions which would safeguard our independence and form the basis of a just and durable peace for Europe, we should be prepared to discuss his claims in the Mediterranean."[22]

The veil with which Churchill obscured the War Cabinet discussions of 26–28 May has been torn aside in recent years. But discussion has revolved almost entirely around Halifax, often caricatured as a craven appeaser, while Churchill's own bellicosity is taken for granted. On the face of it, that may seem reasonable. "You ask, What is our aim?" he famously told the Commons on 13 May in his first speech as premier. "I can answer in one word: Victory—victory at all costs, victory in spite of all terror; victory, however long and hard the road may be; for without victory there is no survival."[23] But this was before Reynaud's desperate phone call and the French collapse. As the days passed, "victory at all costs" seemed ever more utopian. On 4 June, Churchill scribbled a hasty note to Stanley Baldwin: "We are going through v[er]y hard times & I expect worse to come: but I feel quite sure that better days will come! Though whether we shall live to see them is more doubtful." And in July 1946, Ismay recalled for Robert Sherwood a talk with Churchill on 12 June 1940, after their penultimate conference with the demoralized French leaders at Briare. According to Sherwood's notes:

> When Churchill went to the airport to return to England, he said to Ismay that, it seems, 'we fight alone'. Ismay said he was glad of it, that 'we'll win the Battle of Britain'. Churchill gave him a look and remarked, 'You and I will be dead in three months time'.

The significance of this story is heightened by Ismay's reaction when Sherwood asked for permission to quote it in *Roosevelt and Hopkins:* "I would prefer that this intimate heart to heart conversation were never given to the world."[24]

Churchill's line in *Their Finest Hour* is that "I was always sure we should win." On 28 May 1940, however, he issued a general injunction to ministers and officials about the need to show confidence in "our ability and inflexible resolve to continue the war till we have broken the will of the enemy to bring all Europe under his domination." No mention here of total victory, in what was supposed to be a morale-boosting statement. This might be dismissed as reflecting the mood before the "deliverance of Dunkirk," but on 3 August he told the Foreign Office that a "firm reply" to Hitler's current peace overtures was "the only chance of extorting from Germany any offers which are not fantastic." Both these statements were printed in the war memoirs—a reminder once again that the documents need to be read as closely as the text, for the two do not always tell the same story.[25]

The statement of 3 August 1940 was reminiscent of his notes for Chamberlain on 8 October 1939, deleted from drafts of *The Gathering Storm*, about not closing the door on any genuine offer from Germany. To understand all this, we must remember that "unconditional surrender" was only promulgated as an Allied war aim in January 1943, when America and Russia had added their overwhelming might to Britain's cause. In the summer of 1940, it was inconceivable that Britain alone could enforce total victory on a Germany that now dominated continental Europe. A negotiated peace at some point with an alternative German government seemed the only credible outcome. Just how long Churchill himself privately accepted this scenario is evident from comments he made in the War Cabinet eighteen months later. So sensitive were these that they are recorded only in the Cabinet Secretary's "Confidential Annexes" and have not attracted the attention of historians. On 27 November 1941, Churchill recalled that in July, after Russia entered the war, "we had made a public statement that we would not negotiate with Hitler or with the Nazi *régime*." But he added that he "thought it would be going too far to say that we should not negotiate with a Germany controlled by the Army. It was impossible to forecast what form of Government there might be in Germany at a time when their resistance weakened and they wished to negotiate."[26]

In short, Churchill's public rhetoric is not an exact guide to his private policy in 1940. Whatever he said to raise morale, his best hope at this time was an eventual negotiated peace with a non-Nazi German government. His worst fear, despite his innate confidence, was that he would not live to see it. Thus, the stark contrast between Churchill and Halifax is mistaken on *both* sides: the Prime Minister, like the Foreign Secretary, was more complex than caricatured history allows. Churchill looked into the abyss in May and June 1940, yet he still managed to inspire his country and the world. We need to look more closely at how he managed to do so.

HIS ORATORY, of course, was indispensable. "Victory at all costs" on 13 May. "We shall fight on the beaches . . . we shall never surrender" on 4 June. And on the eighteenth his great call to "so bear ourselves that, if the British Empire and its Commonwealth last for a thousand years, men will still say, 'This was their finest hour.'" But words were not enough. Sometimes they were actually counterproductive: Halifax, for one, feared that Churchill was carried away by his own grandiloquence, and the Prime Minister had therefore to adduce credible reasons for fighting on—"common sense not bravado." Yet such reasons were not easy to find. Reflecting in September 1940 on the dark days of 1917–1918, Lloyd George considered the present crisis to be bleaker. In the Great War, it had taken four years to defeat Germany, even with major allies; this time, Britain had been evicted from the Continent and was fighting alone. To win, wrote Lloyd George, Britain would have to cross the Channel, itself no easy task, and then wage a war of attrition against Germany, with little prospect that America would send "another huge Army to Europe."[27]

Churchill's reasons—or rationalizations—for fighting on are doubly significant. He conceals them from the text of his memoirs—though, once again, one can find intimations in the documents themselves—and they help explain his strategy over the next three years of the war. His hopes of eventual success turned on two main assumptions about the underlying weakness of Germany and the imminence of American entry into the war.

British intelligence had persuaded itself (and most policymakers) that the German war economy was already overstretched and that underlying shortages of food and raw materials, especially oil, would soon have effects. In the War Cabinet debate of 26 May, Attlee stated, as if it were simple fact, that Hitler "had to win by the end of the year," if he was to win at all, and Chamberlain agreed. In their "Future Strategy" paper on 4 September, the Chiefs of Staff predicted that unless Germany could "materially improve her position," shortages of supplies "may prove disastrous" for it in 1941. From this, they drew the remarkable conclusion that Britain should aim "to pass to the general offensive in all spheres and in all theatres with the utmost possible strength in the Spring of 1942." Churchill seems to have shared these assumptions. On 26 May, he took the line that "if only we could stick things out for another three months, the position would be entirely different." He had always been struck by Germany's sudden collapse in

1918, ruminating at length in *The World Crisis* about how Bulgaria proved to be, in effect, the first domino. He alluded to this publicly in his "finest hour" speech on 18 June 1940, reminding MPs, still dismayed by the French armistice, that for most of the Great War

> the Allies experienced nothing but disaster and disappointment. . . . During that war we repeatedly asked ourselves the question: How are we going to win? and no one was able ever to answer it with much precision, until, at the end, quite suddenly, quite unexpectedly, our terrible foe collapsed before us, and we were so glutted with victory that in our folly we threw it away.[28]

Against this menacing but brittle enemy a major land war might therefore not be needed. In their 4 September paper, the Chiefs of Staff insisted that "it is not our policy to attempt to raise, and land on the continent, an army comparable in size to that of Germany"; rather, they proposed to wear down the enemy and secure "conditions when numerically inferior forces can be employed with good chance of success." At that point, Britain should "re-establish a striking force on the Continent with which we can enter Germany and impose our terms."[29]

How exactly could the enemy be worn down? In the summer of 1940, with Nazism having dominated continental Europe, Churchill admitted that the blockade, Britain's traditional weapon, had been "blunted." But in July, he created the Special Operations Executive (SOE) to help "set Europe ablaze." According to the Chiefs of Staff, SOE would further the economic degradation of the enemy by sabotaging industrial plants and communications and would enable local resistance movements to prepare "a general uprising," which, "coinciding with major operations by our forces, may finally assist to bring about his defeat."[30] Even more important was strategic bombing. "The Fighters are our salvation," Churchill wrote in a memorandum of 3 September, at the height of the Battle of Britain, "but the Bombers alone provide the means of victory." The RAF must "pulverize the entire industry and scientific structure on which the war effort and economic life of the enemy depend, while holding him at arm's length from our Island. In no other way at present visible can we hope to overcome the immense military power of Germany."[31]

How does Churchill handle these themes in *Their Finest Hour*? He prints a lengthy extract from the Chiefs of Staff's "Certain Eventuality" paper of 25 May about resisting invasion, but the section outlining how bombing, blockade, and subversion could eventually enable Britain to impose terms on Germany is not mentioned. He prints his comments about bombing on 8 July and 3 September, but the first is buried in his appendix of assorted documents and the second appears in the chapter "September Tensions" as part of a memorandum headed "The Munitions Situation."[32] Their significance for strategy is thereby obscured.

As for SOE, this is completely absent from *Their Finest Hour,* even though Churchill spent a good deal of July 1940 adjudicating a Whitehall power struggle about which department should control it. In fact, SOE is mentioned only once in Churchill's six volumes—in a 1943 minute in the appendix to *The Hinge of Fate.* Security was undoubtedly a factor: SOE documents, like those on plans for British resistance if the country was overrun, were strictly classified. But whereas Churchill had wanted to mention home resistance, there is no sign that he ever intended to discuss SOE. Historian David Stafford has called the omission "a classic example, conscious or not, of selective memory."[33] The root explanation is presumably Churchill's determination to prove his early and consistent support for a cross-Channel invasion. As noted, he was far more interested in the initials LCT than SOE, devoting much of his chapter "The Apparatus of Counter-Attack" to ideas for landing craft and artificial harbors. "Setting Europe ablaze" had proved a damp squib, and strategic bombing failed to take off. So Churchill rewrote his strategy in the light of D-Day and postwar American criticism. In doing so, he tried to deceive his readers (and perhaps himself) on an issue of central importance.

The D-Day invasion was possible only because America had become Britain's ally. Expectation of this was Churchill's second ground for hope in the summer of 1940. The Chiefs of Staff's paper of 25 May emphasized that without "full economic and financial support" from the United States *we do not think we could continue the war with any chance of success.*"[34] Churchill went even further, insisting on several occasions that a Luftwaffe blitz on Britain would inflame American opinion and provoke a declaration of war. At Chequers in August 1940, he told de Gaulle that "the bombing of Oxford, Coventry, Canterbury, will cause such a wave of indignation that they'll come into the war!" Recognizing the political constraints on President Roosevelt, Churchill increasingly predicted the November 1940 election as the turning point. On 1 November, four days before the vote, he told his private secretary that Roosevelt "would win the election by a far greater majority than was supposed" and that "America would come into the war."[35]

Churchill was right about the scale of Roosevelt's victory but wrong about its effect. This was partly because the Blitz proved less destructive than feared, and Hitler's invasion never happened. More important, Churchill tended to exaggerate the cultural unity of what he liked to call "the English-speaking peoples." The America he knew was anglophile (and anglophone); he had little awareness of the anglophobia that many European immigrants brought with them and then magnified in America. Hence his comment to French leaders on 31 May that an invasion of England would have a profound effect, "especially in those many towns in the New World which bore the same names as towns in the British Isles."[36] He also underestimated the political constraints on Roosevelt. On the other hand, it would be wrong to imply that Churchill was naïve about the United States. In private that summer, he was skeptical about American help and took a hard line when bargaining for it. Once again, his simple confidence in public is not the whole story.

How Churchill conducted the transatlantic relationship in 1940 is a theme of the next chapter. Here, the point is to stress how he played the American card as his second main justification for fighting on, though, like his belief in German weakness, little of this emerges in the memoirs. Buried in a two-page extract from a cable to Dominion Prime Ministers on 16 June are the words "I personally believe that the spectacle of the fierce struggle and carnage in our Island will draw the United States into the war." Speculating on what might have happened if 200,000 "German storm troops" had got ashore, he remarks, "I even calculated that the horrors of such a scene would in the last resort turn the scales in the United States." Otherwise, the false hopes of 1940 play no part in his narrative. Yet at the time they were essential illusions. Here are the notes for Churchill's secret speech of 20 June 1940, where he puts the German and American factors together:

> If Hitler fails to invade or destroy Britain he has lost the war.
> I do not consider only the severities of the winter in Europe.
> I look to superiority in Air power in the future.
> Transatlantic reinforcements.
> If get through next 3 months get through next 3 years

Halifax was right: in 1940, rhetoric was not enough. There had to be reasons, or rationalizations, for fighting on, and these Churchill also provided, at a time when even he sometimes shared the doubts of others. This is a neglected but no less estimable feature of his finest hour.[37]

EQUALLY STRIKING is the way this dubious political outsider established his dominance over Westminster and Whitehall during the second half of 1940. Here, too, the war memoirs are rarely transparent and sometimes decidedly opaque.

In chapter 1 of *Their Finest Hour*, Churchill frankly admits that his sudden accession to the premiership offended many Tories, mindful of his maverick behavior in the 1930s. He records their "vehement demonstration of sympathy and regard" for Chamberlain on 13 May, adding that "in the early weeks it was from the Labour benches that I was mainly greeted." He also notes the widespread demands, particularly from the left, for a purge of the "guilty men" responsible for appeasement—mentioning that Halifax, Simon, and Hoare "were the principal targets." (An early draft read "were deemed particularly obnoxious.") Churchill then recalls his aphorism "If the present tries to sit in judgment on the past it will lose the future." This argument and "the awful weight of the hour," he says, "quelled the would-be heresy hunters."[38]

In reality, political infighting continued through the summer. Churchill was a Prime Minister without a party, because Chamberlain remained Tory leader. "To a large extent I am in y[ou]r hands," Churchill wrote on 10 May, and Chamberlain remained in the War Cabinet as Lord President of the Council with de facto control of domestic policy. On 7 June, Churchill reminded the press lords of the strength of Tory feeling in the Commons—Chamberlain had received "the bigger cheer" on 13 May. (This was a common Churchill refrain for months afterward.) Although he could "trample" these men, "they would set themselves up against him," he warned, and "in such internecine strife lay the Germans' best chance of victory."[39]

On several occasions in May and June, Churchill tried to draw Lloyd George into his government, only to be stymied by the animosity between Lloyd George and Chamberlain. Churchill's wooing testifies to his desire for national unity, seeking to bring the country's last war leader and greatest living Liberal into the coalition. At a deeper level, his persistence, against all evidence of Lloyd George's failing powers, shows the hold the "Welsh Wizard" still had over his erstwhile protégé. Near the end of *Their Finest Hour*, Churchill refers to Lloyd George in 1940 as "our foremost citizen."[40] Mere fluff? Or another echo of Churchill's mood in those early months of his premiership when the previous war still seemed much more glorious than the current one, when "their" finest hour (and his) was histrionics and not yet history?

Behind this infighting lurked a belief that Churchill was a caretaker Prime Minister. Only after Chamberlain was operated on for bowel cancer in September did he note revealingly in his diary that any ideas of a postwar premiership were now gone: "I know that is out of the question." Lloyd George saw himself as a future peacemaking Prime Minister, ready to take control when the battle for survival had been won but the impossibility of total victory was clear. He told his secretary in October 1940, "I shall wait until Winston is bust."[41] Fantasies of a comeback are, of course, the last hopes of ousted politicians. But Churchill's own sense of fragility is evident in the determination with which he seized the leadership of the Tory party when terminal illness forced Chamberlain to resign in October 1940. He does not say that his wife, true to her Liberal roots, argued passionately that this would compromise his standing as a truly national leader. Instead, he makes clear his own conviction that, given Tory dominance in the Commons, he would otherwise have remained a precarious Prime Minister. The party leader—probably Halifax if Churchill had declined—would wield the real political power, leaving Churchill with "only the executive responsibility." The unspoken analogy, evident to anyone of Churchill's generation, was the fall of Lloyd George in 1922—premier of a coalition dominated by Tories, around which his own Liberal party had disintegrated. "You will yourself be much stronger with the Party machine behind you," opined Sam Hoare on 10 October. "This means there need be no repetition of the LG collapse after the last war."[42]

In October 1940, Churchill used Chamberlain's illness to effect a wider reshuffle. Though he does not mention this in *Their Finest Hour*, his real aim was to make Eden Foreign Secretary and shift Halifax to Chamberlain's old post as Lord President of the Council. But, Eden noted in his diary, Halifax did not want to move, and Churchill feared that, if pressed, he "would ask to go altogether, which Winston did not want at the moment Neville was leaving." A new opportunity occurred in December, with the sudden death of Lord Lothian, British Ambassador in Washington. Churchill says he offered the post first to Lloyd George, mentioning only at this point the previous bid to draw him into the War Cabinet. He explains that when Lloyd George declined on grounds of age, he then turned to Halifax. For a Foreign Secretary to become an Ambassador was, says Churchill, a sign of "the importance of the mission," as so much turned on Anglo-American relations. But he admits that there was "much disapprobation and even hostility" from the Labour side of the coalition on account of Halifax's prewar record. Persuaded by appeals to his sense of duty, Halifax reluctantly went west—whereupon Eden, says Churchill after a paragraph celebrating disingenuously their "close agreement" on foreign policy over the past four years, "returned to the Foreign Office like a man going home."[43]

During 1940, therefore, the caretaker Prime Minister gradually entrenched himself in Downing Street. He also established an unparalleled dominance over the Whitehall machine. Churchill's elevation to the premiership appalled most senior civil servants, convinced he was largely to blame for the Norway fiasco, with its overtones of Gallipoli. "Everyone here is in despair," noted Jock Colville of Chamberlain's private office on 10 May. "I cannot help feeling that this country may be manoeuvred into the most dangerous position it has ever been in." But Colville soon became one of Churchill's most devoted acolytes. Writing in 1968, he and Ian Jacob described the depth of official skepticism about Churchill in May 1940 and the way it was dispelled within weeks. Churchill galvanized a leisurely government machine up to wartime tempo with his stream of minutes, some of them bearing the minatory red label "ACTION THIS DAY."

The change of gears was not achieved without friction, however. On 23 June 1940, Clementine wrote her husband a letter, then tore it up, and finally steeled herself to send a new version four days later. In this, she chided Winston for what had been reported as his "rough, sarcastic and overbearing manner" to staff and his "contemptuous" attitude to other people's ideas, begging him to use his "terrific power" with "urbanity, kindness and if possible Olympic [sic] calm." This remarkable letter testifies to the strain Churchill was under in May and June—reveling in the position for which he had long yearned, desperate to prepare his country for the impending onslaught, and justifiably suspicious that many around him were lacking in loyalty or fervor.[44]

Little of this personal pressure registers in the memoirs. A rare exception is in Churchill's account of his decision not to evacuate the garrison of Calais, which protected the vital flank of the Dunkirk evacuation. Churchill sent a hortatory message to the garrison commander, Brigadier Claude Nicholson (who later died in German captivity), and then dined with Ismay and Eden. "One has to eat and drink in war," Churchill writes, "but I could not help feeling physically sick as we afterwards sat silent at the table."[45] In a draft, not eventually printed, Churchill makes another comment on those grim weeks: "it is a defect of character to be unfeeling in the midst of suffering, of which I hope I am not guilty, but it is less bad than becoming incapable of action."[46]

And Churchill loved to act. His opening chapter unabashedly admits that "the post which had now fallen to me was the one I liked best"—there was "no comparison between the positions of number one and numbers two, three and four." Tellingly, he reverts to the searing lesson of Gallipoli in 1915, when "I was ruined for a time" and "a supreme enterprise cast away, through my trying to carry out a major and cardinal operation of war from a subordinate position." The

Military Coordination Committee and other messy compromises of Chamberlain's last weeks were now cast aside as Churchill appointed himself Minister of Defence. He established no separate department but simply took over direction of the Chiefs of Staff Committee, leaving the Service Ministers to run their departments while he and the Chiefs ran the war. His powers, he says, were "undefined"; he quotes with approval Napoleon's maxim that a constitution "should be short and obscure."[47]

In chapter 1, Churchill draws attention to his official minutes. "I am a strong believer in transacting official business by *The Written Word*." He also prints his instruction to Ismay and Bridges on 19 July 1940 disclaiming any responsibility for "matters relating to national defence on which I am alleged to have given decisions unless they are recorded in writing." This is both preamble to and justification for the stream of minutes in succeeding chapters and in a lengthy appendix (seventy-eight pages in both the British and American editions, or about one seventh of the total text) that range autocratically over every aspect of the war. Those dated 1 September 1940, for instance, cover glider units, German guns at Calais, the attack on Dakar, recreation for the troops, and the defense of India. Since these documents are a feature of volumes 2 through 6—Emery Reves reckoned that, at the extreme, they constituted about 70 percent of *The Hinge of Fate*—it is worth considering why they bulk so large.[48]

An obvious reason is convenience. Churchill was always in a hurry—racing against the deadlines of electoral politics and impending mortality—so it was easier to print old papers than dictate new prose. He also seems to have believed what he says in the preface about contemporary documents being superior sources to subsequent reminiscence (conveniently ignoring the way he edited them with the benefit of hindsight). But there was probably an additional reason for Churchill's addiction to his minutes and telegrams, and this takes us to the heart of his project. He wanted to reposition the image of Churchill in 1940.

In *Their Finest Hour*, the famous speeches do not bulk large. Churchill quotes from them, but not at length and without much buildup. In part, this neglect is because Churchill gave only seven broadcast speeches between May and December 1940, the same number as during the Phony War when at the Admiralty. Furthermore, those speeches were already well known, having been spoken or rebroadcast to the United States and the world. In October 1940, Churchill allowed the record company HMV to market a gramophone disk of his big four speeches of 19 May, 18 June, 14 July, and 11 September, with profits going to charity.[49] In 1941, *Into Battle*, a collection of his speeches from 1938–1940, became a bestseller. In Britain, 60,000 copies were printed, as were another 60,000 in the United States, where it did better than any previous Churchill volume.[50]

"Churchill's speeches have themselves become major events in the war," wrote one American reviewer in June 1941. The commentator Edward R. Murrow spoke of Churchill mobilizing the English language and sending it into battle.[51] But Churchill was not content. All his life he had been known as a man of words—orator, journalist, historian—and some of those great phrases of 1940 were not freshly minted for the Battle of Britain but recoinages. The word patterns of "Never in the field of human conflict has so much been owed by so many to so few" (20 August 1940) can be found in at least five of his speeches or writings between 1899 and 1910.[52] Lord Moran recorded a revealing conversation after their flight to Italy in September 1945, when Churchill was absorbed in the prints of his wartime minutes. "People say my speeches after Dunkirk were the thing," he remarked. "That was only a part, not the chief part. They forget I made all the main military decisions." His war memoirs were intended to make this point—using the minutes to rub it in very firmly.[53]

CHURCHILL THE warlord is the main focus of *Their Finest Hour*, complementing Churchill the orator, already familiar from the wartime speeches. Together, they form our predominant image of the man of 1940, indefatigable and inspirational in Britain's darkest hour. Yet there was much more as well. Churchill was totally unprepared for Germany's blitzkrieg warfare—having trusted the defensive power of the French Army—and suddenly had to adapt to fighting on alone. At the same time, he was trying to establish his political position at Westminster and get his own way in a skeptical Whitehall. Both struggles absorbed a huge amount of time and emotional energy. Churchill recognized the bleakness of Britain's predicament—whatever his public bravado, there were moments of private doubt—and he had to adduce plausible reasons for fighting on. Much of this does not appear in the war memoirs, though it can sometimes be discerned by a careful reading. To see the whole picture makes Churchill a more impressive figure than the almost blindly pugnacious bulldog of popular stereotype.

CHAPTER 12

THE BATTLE OF BRITAIN AND
THE MEDITERRANEAN GAMBLE

W HAT GENERAL WEYGAND called the Battle of France is over. I
expect that the Battle of Britain is about to begin," Churchill told
the Commons on 18 June 1940. "Upon this battle depends the sur-
vival of Christian civilisation."[1] These stark words, quoted in chapter 11, constitute the fulcrum of *Their Finest Hour.* The most familiar chapters of book 2 deal
with the threat of invasion, the battle for air supremacy, and the Blitz on British
cities. But the last third describes the wider war developing through new conflicts
in the Balkans, German plans to attack Russia, and the covert alliance with
America. Above all, book 2 shows how, despite the invasion threat, Churchill's
government decided to divert all its spare forces to save Egypt. This resulted in
General Wavell's victory over the Italians, with which the volume ends, but also
left Britain's Asian empire naked against Japan and opened a Mediterranean theater that would preoccupy the Western Allies for the rest of the war.

"WE SHALL FIGHT on the beaches," Churchill assured the Commons on
4 June, but he told the Chiefs of Staff on 28 June that "the battle will be won or
lost, not on the beaches, but by the mobile brigades and the main reserve." Churchill prints this paper in chapter 13 of his memoirs and hints that it reflected a
strategic disagreement—"I was not entirely satisfied with the military dispositions." Yet he conceals the clash that contributed to the dismissal on 19 July of

General "Tiny" Ironside as commander of Home Forces. Ironside, obliged after Dunkirk to improvise an anti-invasion plan without tanks, trucks, and other heavy equipment, placed his faith on a "crust" of beach defenses backed by defensive "stoplines" well inland. Local field commanders, notably General Alan Brooke on the south coast, wanted to create a mobile reserve, and Churchill's minute of 28 June was an intervention in this debate. Brooke's arguments, plus an impressive performance when showing the Prime Minister his troops on 17 July, helped ensure that he succeeded Ironside two days later. Although Churchill mentions the change in command, he says nothing about the reasons behind it, and the causal chain is further obscured because he states that he paid his visit to Brooke on 19 July.[2]

Churchill admits that in July and August he and his advisers believed that East Anglia was more likely to be attacked than the south coast. But he plays down the very real fears among the military that the Germans might attempt a series of surprise landings without first achieving air supremacy. Ironside identified 9 July as the likely day. In a 1947 draft, Churchill said that "invasion excitement rose to its peak even in high quarters during the first week of July," and he quoted the Chiefs of Staff asserting, contrary to him, that invasion might come "at any moment," but this passage was cut in the autumn of 1948. In "The Invasion Problem," hints of their argument may be discerned in Churchill's minute of 10 July and Admiral Pound's reply dated 12 July. Yet the effect is much reduced because Norman Brook, sensitive to Attlee's wish to minimize quotation from the Chiefs of Staff, urged Churchill to paraphrase Pound's memorandum. The Cabinet Secretary provided a draft that Churchill adapted, prior to making even more radical cuts.[3]

These deletions are of real historical significance. The panic of early July showed how rattled the army, navy, and intelligence staff had been by their failures to anticipate the invasion of Norway and the blitzkrieg in France. Compensating for past complacency, they now lurched to the opposite extreme, claiming that lack of evidence of invasion did not mean it was not about to happen. Churchill took a more robust view, asserting that there would be no raids or landings unless and until the Luftwaffe controlled the skies. In June and early July, he and the military were arguing from instinct, not information. From mid-July, however, their vision began to improve, and in his memoirs Churchill commends "our excellent Intelligence," stressing the value of aerial photography along the enemy coast. Undoubtedly, this new source was of great importance, but signals intelligence, especially derived from cracking the German Air Force codes, was of equal value—often guiding photo overflights to appropriate places. But Churchill had agreed to preserve the Ultra secret: hence his stress on aerial photography.[4] From both these sources Whitehall gained a clear impression of the buildup of invasion barges aimed at the south coast and the concentration of the Luftwaffe for a bid to achieve air supremacy.

In his chapter on the Battle of Britain, Churchill tells his readers that 15 September was "the culminating date." This was, he says, "one of the decisive battles of the war and, like the Battle of Waterloo, it was on a Sunday." Churchill spent much of the day at the headquarters of Air Vice-Marshal Keith Park, commander of Number 11 Group, Fighter Command, at Uxbridge in west London, and his account of this visit, running to more than four pages, constitutes the centerpiece of his chapter. It also serves as a counterpoint to his meeting at the Quai d'Orsay four months earlier.[5]

Churchill had recounted this story many times—for instance, to Moran on his Italian vacation in September 1945—and he dictated a draft for the book as early as October 1946.[6] He and Clementine were taken to the bombproof operations room, deep underground, linked by phone to fighter stations and observation posts across southeast England. It was, he says, "like a small theatre," and "we took our seats in the Dress Circle." The drama unfolded before them across a huge map table, on which some twenty young men and women maneuvered disks representing the enemy formations. Behind them, ranks of bulbs on a giant blackboard showed the disposition of Park's fighter squadrons—ranging from "Standing By" at the bottom to "In Action" (red bulbs) and "Returning Home." After a while, the map table showed that a major attack was in progress, with waves of German aircraft crossing the coast. Soon, the lights on the blackboard indicated that most of Park's planes were engaged and that no squadrons were left on standby. In the hitherto businesslike atmosphere, Churchill sensed mounting anxiety.

"What other reserves have we?" he asked.

"There are none," Park replied—his grammar crumbling under the strain. Churchill looked grave. "The odds were great; our margins small; the stakes infinite." Another five minutes passed. The flashing lights showed that most of the squadrons were on the ground, but the disks on the table were now being pushed back eastward. The Germans were returning home. As Winston and Clementine climbed back to daylight, the all clear sounded. Back at Chequers, he went to bed for a delayed afternoon nap—"I must have been tired by the drama of No. 11 Group, for I did not wake till eight." Then he was told that 183 enemy planes had been shot down, for a loss of fewer than forty. That day, says Churchill, "was the crux of the Battle of Britain."

There is a striking echo here of his exchange on 16 May 1940. To Gamelin: "Where is the strategic reserve?" "*Aucune.*" To Park: "What other reserves have we?" "There are none." The verbal similarity, conscious or not, highlights the profound differences between these two symbolic moments. September 1940 is a modern war of telephone cables and electric lights—all the more dramatic because we know that at the other end of the phone men are locked in mortal combat. What a contrast with those "venerable" functionaries piling up the bonfire of the Third Republic! Electricity not wheelbarrows. Businesslike vigor rather than hopeless lethargy. Victory instead of defeat. These two beautifully contrived vignettes encapsulate Churchill's vision of the Battles of France and of Britain. Highlighted in serial editions, retold in books and articles, they have proved profoundly influential.

Churchill's account of 15 September was sparklingly new: "All this *very, very* good," noted Clementine, his sternest critic.[7] But the rest of his chapter told an already familiar story because here, unusually, the historiography of Britain's war had already taken firm shape. In March 1941, the Air Ministry had issued a publicity pamphlet entitled *The Battle of Britain*, combining a detailed narrative with extracts from pilots' reports. Priced at threepence, it was expected to sell 50,000 copies, but in the first week sales and orders already exceeded one million in Britain alone, as well as half a million for a forthcoming illustrated edition priced at sixpence. The pamphlet was also marketed widely in America and in foreign translations. In line with wartime Air Ministry policy to avoid glorifying a few air "aces," no personal names were mentioned on the British side, with the exception of Churchill. The pamphlet used as an epigraph his tribute in the Commons on 20 August 1940: "Never in the field of human conflict has so much been owed by so many to so few." It featured 15 September as "The Greatest Day" and concluded that future historians may compare the Battle of Britain "with Marathon, Trafalgar and the Marne." (For the French edition, "Trafalgar" was removed.) "More than anything else," writes historian Richard Overy, this widely read pamphlet "gave the conflict the legendary dimensions it has borne ever since."[8]

Churchill reread the pamphlet when preparing his chapter and considered it "admirable." In November 1946, he wanted to trace its author, and Ismay came up with Albert Goodwin, an Oxford history tutor who had done the basic research while serving at the Air Ministry in 1940–1941. Churchill recruited Goodwin to develop his chapter on the Battle of Britain and write a background paper on the Blitz. Thus, the original pamphlet was reinforced by its principal researcher and later through additional material from the Air Ministry Historical

Branch, which had commissioned the original project.[9] Churchill adopts the pamphlet's chronology of the phases of the conflict and its focus on 15 September. He admits that postwar records had reduced the enemy's losses that day from 183 to 56, but only a close reading of his text yields the information that more German planes (76) were lost on 15 August.[10] Churchill even accepts the way the Air Ministry had repackaged his own wartime rhetoric. When he spoke on 18 June 1940 about "the Battle of Britain," he signified the whole Nazi campaign of assault, blockade, and attempted invasion. Thanks in large part to the Air Ministry pamphlet, however, the term became applied entirely to the struggle for air supremacy in August and September 1940, and that is how it is used in *Their Finest Hour*. Similarly, when Churchill lauded "the few" on 20 August 1940, he was referring to *all* Britain's airmen. His famous sentence was followed by a brief tribute to the fighter pilots, "whose brilliant actions we see with our own eyes day after day," but then two whole paragraphs about "the shattering blows" inflicted by unseen British bombers "night after night, month after month" on the "war-making structure of the Nazi power." But in the Air Ministry pamphlet, juxtaposed between photos of Spitfires and their pilots and shorn of reference to the bomber crews, his words became indissolubly linked to Fighter Command. Churchill had already adopted this linkage in his victory broadcast on 13 May 1945, and he was happy to leave it that way in his memoirs.[11]

By following the official account of the battle, Churchill slides over many questions that were already being raised. He acknowledges that roughly two German planes were lost for every British plane rather than three as claimed at the time, but he says nothing about the balance of trained pilots — arguably more important than the number of serviceable planes. As captured German records already made clear, if Fighter Command was "the few," the Luftwaffe pilots were fewer.[12] Furthermore, the Luftwaffe's bomber force had been seriously damaged by the campaign in France, losing 30 percent of its plane strength in May and June, but this is masked by Churchill's determination to separate the Battles of France and Britain in his narrative.[13] One might respond that it was asking too much of Churchill and his researchers to make such intricate comparisons. Yet he had pushed Pownall to study air strength and troop balances in great detail when analyzing the crises of September 1938 and September 1939. And he was keen to open up his chronological compartments when discussing the German Navy, insisting that the losses inflicted on it by the British in the Norway campaign meant that it was "no factor in the supreme issue of the invasion of Britain."[14] But that, of course, was an exercise in self-vindication — to show that the Norway fiasco had lasting value. Churchill had no such incentive to probe the myths already encrusting the Battle of Britain; on the contrary, his memoirs only added new layers.

In other respects, too, *Their Finest Hour* follows the Air Ministry line. Churchill steers clear of the controversy about Sir Hugh Dowding, who was replaced as head of Fighter Command soon after the battle. But an early draft explained that he had reluctantly yielded to Air Ministry pressure on this, adding that "I was wrong not to insist on my view."[15] And although there are brief words of praise for the supporting cast, such as factory workers and antiaircraft personnel, Churchill's eyes are firmly fixed on "the few": "At the summit the stamina and valour of our fighter pilots remained unconquerable and supreme."[16] In particular, Churchill plays down the contribution of radar, which was "still in its infancy," he tells us. "It gave warning of raids approaching our coast," but the Battle of Britain "was fought mainly by eye and ear," using "observers, with field-glasses and portable telephones." Even at the time, however, it was agreed that the combination of the radar system and the single-wing fighter had proved decisive, in tandem allowing unprecedented speed of response. Churchill's stance in his memoirs owes something to the accidents of structure — having originally intended to discuss radar in his chapter "The Wizard War," this material was later moved into volume 1 — but the gap was probably also deliberate. As we saw in chapter 7, above, neither Churchill nor Lindemann, his scientific adviser who read these chapters, contributed much to radar's development in the 1930s and therefore had little incentive to extol it in *Their Finest Hour.*[17]

Churchill's two chapters on the Blitz are the usual mix of documents and text, spiced by an unusual number of personal anecdotes (mostly from Ismay). On the other hand, "The Wizard War" — about how the Air Ministry jammed or diverted the radio beams used by the Germans to guide their night bombers onto British cities — is an arresting piece of new narrative, noteworthy for the paucity of documents in it. The contrast owes something to Churchill's personal interest but more to the quality of the drafts he received. In late 1946, he drew two young academics into his circle of consultants—Albert Goodwin on the Blitz, R. V. Jones for "The Wizard War"—but they proved very different in serviceability. Oppressed by his teaching and administrative responsibilities at Oxford, Goodwin labored for eight months in 1947 to produce his "Blitz Narrative" on 1940–1941. Though an impressive piece of original research, it ran to ninety foolscap pages and was far too detailed for Churchill.[18] Parts were cannibalized for the narrative, but Goodwin's impact on the volume was minimal compared with that of Jones, who had impressed the Prime Minister as a young Air Intelligence officer in 1940. (Churchill's supporting reference had secured Jones a chair at Aberdeen after the war.)[19] The young scientist, a Lindemann protégé, had played a major part in piecing together the evidence for the German beams in 1940–1941, and his April 1946 report for the Air Ministry, "The Radio War," was the base for Churchill's chapter. Only twenty-five pages in length, it was described by Denis Kelly as "a brilliant short account."[20]

Churchill had no time to compose the kind of reflective memoir desired both by his publishers and by Clementine, who urged him in October 1948 "to give us a complete story of the Battle of Britain as though we have never heard of it" instead of relying on existing accounts.[21] He was still capable of superb set-piece narration, notably about 15 September 1940, but such passages are rare. Where he rose to reflective heights, it was often on the shoulders of others, as here with Jones. These early chapters of book 2 of *Their Finest Hour* graphically illustrate the strengths and limitations of Churchill's war memoirs.

ALTHOUGH A BELEAGUERED isle, Britain was also the heart of a great empire, and the summer of 1940 saw momentous decisions about how—indeed, whether—all of it could be defended. With Italy entering the war, the French Navy no longer an ally, and Britain threatened by invasion, Churchill says that "Admiralty first thoughts contemplated the abandonment of the Eastern Mediterranean and concentration on Gibraltar" to protect Britain's Atlantic lifelines. Churchill says he resisted such a policy but moves briskly over this fundamental clash with Admiral Pound and the Naval Staff and consigns to an appendix his order on 17 June about keeping the fleet at Alexandria even if Spain as well as Italy entered the war.[22] At the beginning of July, he approved a memo by the Chiefs of Staff affirming the government's determination to hold the Middle East, from Egypt to Iraq, and the eastern Mediterranean for as long as possible. Unmentioned by Churchill, this was a decision of "immense importance" because it effectively "reversed the pre-war order of global priorities" that had given precedence to Singapore and Australasia.[23]

In fact, the Far East is conspicuous by its absence from volume 2, as it is in volume 1. On 13 and 28 June, the British government sent messages to the Australian and New Zealand governments outlining the invasion threat and the new Mediterranean policy and warning that Britain could not address these "and send a fleet to the Far East." Although Churchill approved both messages, neither is mentioned in *Their Finest Hour*. Instead, he prints his long telegram to Australia and New Zealand on 11 August reasserting the pledge to send a fleet to the Far East if Japan invaded either country "on a large scale." Since he continued to insist that this was "very unlikely," he was able to claim that the new Mediterranean commitments did not imperil Australasian security and to ensure that the Antipodean Dominions did not stop sending vital reinforcements to the Middle East.[24]

Meanwhile, Japan exploited the weakness of the European colonial powers, demanding that Britain close the Burma Road—a major supply route into China. In July, Halifax, the Foreign Secretary, was ready to call Japan's bluff; Churchill and the Chiefs of Staff wanted to give way in order to avoid a Far Eastern crisis when Britain was so committed in the Mediterranean. Eventually, in a compromise, Britain agreed to close the Burma Road for three months. Here was an ironic reversal of the familiar stereotype of Halifax the appeaser and Churchill the antiappeaser—a point the Prime Minister acknowledged privately at the time.[25] *Their Finest Hour*, however, makes no mention of these discussions. There is a brief allusion to the road being reopened in October but nothing about its closure in July—another example of hasty drafting and general inattention to the Far East.[26] On 27 September, the global crisis came into sharper focus with the Tripartite Pact between Germany, Italy, and Japan. In the memoirs, this warrants only a factual sentence belatedly added to the chapter "Relations with Vichy and Spain," followed by the cryptic comment, "This opened wider fields."[27] In volume 3, Churchill does pay more attention to Japan, but by then, as in 1941, it was too late.

By contrast, Churchill devotes six chapters of book 2 to the Mediterranean, from which three major topics emerge. Who should command the Middle Eastern theater? Could Egypt be reinforced against Italian attack, which began on 13 September? And should scarce forces be diverted from Egypt to Greece, after the latter was invaded by Italy on 28 October? Each theme spills over into 1941 and is addressed again in volume 3; the question of command also dominates much of volume 4, since it was not resolved until August 1942.

General Sir Archibald Wavell had been appointed commander in the Middle East in 1939. His wartime command extended from Egypt to the Persian Gulf, from Iraq down to Somaliland. After the Italians declared war on 10 June, their 200,000 troops in Libya enjoyed a four-to-one advantage on paper over British, Indian, and New Zealand forces in neighboring Egypt. Churchill wanted action, such as an amphibious landing behind enemy lines, whereas Wavell concentrated on building up his positions; he was summoned home by the frustrated Prime Minister in early August for "severe" discussions. In the end, though "not in full agreement with General Wavell's use of the resources at his disposal," Churchill writes, "I thought it best to leave him in command. I admired his fine qualities, and was impressed with the confidence so many people had in him."[28]

Underlying strategy lay a fundamental clash of temperament. Wavell was also a scholar and poet, and his persona was one of taciturn gravity. Churchill, by contrast, loved to argue: that was how he thrashed out ideas and got the measure of others. "Talk to him, Archie," begged Sir John Dill, Chief of the Imperial General Staff, but these rambling, disputatious meetings at London and Chequers drove Wavell farther into his shell.[29] Biographers have concurred that the visit was disastrous for his relationship with Churchill, and Eden's memoirs revealed in 1965 that Churchill came close to sacking Wavell, but the first draft of *Their Finest Hour* sheds further light on the story.[30] "For these three or four days and indeed for the next few weeks I poised upon his supersession. . . . My inclination was for General Freyberg. This meant the appointment of a very junior officer to one of the greatest positions in the war." Only the fact that the Middle East was not merely a field command but involved "an extraordinary amalgam of military, political, diplomatic and administrative problems of extreme complexity" eventually persuaded Churchill to stick with the senior and more experienced Wavell.[31]

The name of his possible successor is revealing. General Bernard Freyberg was Churchill's kind of general: confident, aggressive, and brave (he won a Victoria Cross on the Somme in 1916). Since November 1939, he had been commander of the New Zealand Army. Freyberg was on first-name terms with Churchill, who asked him in July 1940 to appraise "the dead-alive way the Middle East campaign is being run." His report was dismissive of German chances of invading Britain, critical of "the Defence of London School," which opposed reinforcement of the empire, and confident that even with German help an Italian invasion of Egypt could be "made to suffer a great reverse." Freyberg submitted his report on 30 July 1940 and spent the following weekend at Chequers—all of which was doubtless in the mind of Churchill when he met the cautious, reticent Wavell a few days later. There is no mention of Freyberg in volume 2, nor does Churchill quote any of these minutes about him. Yet this hitherto obscure story from 1940 illuminates the role Freyberg suddenly assumes in volume 3 as commander in the vital battle for Crete in May 1941.[32]

Action in Egypt required substantial reinforcements, some of whom, Churchill was sure, could come from the Middle East theater itself. He was particularly angry at the "mass of fine troops"—British, Australian, and New Zealander—still garrisoning Palestine. He adds that he wished to arm the Jewish settlers but "encountered every kind of resistance." A version from late February 1948 was positively vituperative: "All our military men disliked the Jews and loved the Arabs. General Wavell was no exception. Some of my most trusted ministers like

Lord Lloyd, and, of course, the Foreign Office, were all pro-Arab, if they were not actually anti-Semitic." These sentences were cut at the request of Norman Brook in June 1948. He said he was not disputing their validity but did fear they would be "taken out of their context and used, in the controversies over the Palestine question, in support of arguments which you could not approve."[33]

At the heart of the two chapters entitled "Egypt and the Middle East" and "The Mediterranean Passage" is the Cabinet's decision in August 1940 to send to Egypt three tank regiments, totaling 154 tanks—described by Churchill as "nearly half our best available tanks." He calls this "at once awful and right," "a bold and far-reaching step" taken "in spite of the invasion menace" although the armor constituted Britain's mobile reserve.[34] Over time, the decision became something of a cause célèbre. In February 1942, Churchill cited it when asking the Australian government to take a similar gamble and not call their troops home after the fall of Singapore. In August 1945, John G. Winant, America's wartime Ambassador in London, called it "the bravest thing" Britain did in the war. Gradually, the deed became identified exclusively with Churchill. In 1957, Jock Colville instanced it as an example of how "Winston would come to the right decision when everyone else was on the other side."[35]

In his memoirs, Churchill concentrates on the debate about how to get the tanks to Egypt. The Admiralty, reluctant to make so vital a convoy run the gauntlet of Italian air- and seapower, favored the safer route around South Africa. Churchill, fearful that the tanks would arrive too late for the impending battle, urged the navy to go straight through the Mediterranean. There are echoes here of his "Catherine" plan during the Phony War for forcing the Baltic with a special fleet supposedly immune to air attack. In the published version, Churchill admits "sharp argument" with Pound and the Admiralty, which he was "both grieved and vexed" not to win: "An exaggerated fear of Italian aircraft had been allowed to hamper operations." In the event, as Churchill admits, during the three weeks it took the convoy to arrive "no serious disaster did in fact occur in Egypt." More significant, his focus on how to send the tanks distracts from the deeper question of where credit should lie for the original decision.[36]

Sir John Dill, Chief of the Imperial General Staff, was no favorite of Churchill, who nicknamed him "Dilly-Dally." Yet after the war, Eden repeatedly said that Dill (who had died in 1944) deserved the main credit for this, the "boldest decision of the war."[37] In the initial draft, Churchill stood center stage with Dill—"Together we took the awful step as it then seemed of sending away half our tanks"—but when Eden read this he told Churchill on 1 September 1948, "As your Minister of the War Office at the time, I would naturally like it made clear that I, as well as Dill, had a hand in it together with you."[38] The result of this intervention is more Eden and less Dill. In emendations during the autumn of 1948, Churchill wrote a fuller paragraph on the whole issue in which the key sentence now read: "As a result of the Staff discussions on August 10 Dill, with Eden's ardent approval, wrote to me that the War Office were arranging to send immediately to Egypt" the three tank regiments.[39]

In these final revisions, Churchill also cut two minutes to Ismay from 26 and 31 August 1940 that showed his reluctance to send *any more* tanks to Egypt, with September looming as the month predicted for invasion. These minutes were consigned to the draft appendix, and only the second of them survives in the book.[40] Both are reminders that Churchill, understandably, was less sure about priorities in 1940 than in his memoirs. On 16 September, for instance, Eden recorded in his diary that Churchill was "vehement against sending anything more to the Middle East," exclaiming, "I do not know what you are thinking of." When Eden produced a hard-hitting memo advocating "a consistent policy of strengthening our forces in the Middle East," Churchill responded the next day, 24 September, that there was "no difference between us in principle, but the application of the principle raises issues of detail, and this is especially true of the denudation of this Island in the face of the imminent threat of invasion." Again, he insisted that there was a "shocking waste of troops" within the Middle Eastern theater.[41]

Eden proposed a personal visit to Egypt to develop plans for an attack. With Cabinet approval, he left London on 11 October and was away for nearly a month. He was therefore peeved to learn from Churchill's August 1948 draft of the chapter "Mr. Eden's Mission" that the initiative for both the trip and the offensive came from the Prime Minister. He suggested a sentence indicating that "my mind and those of the Commanders [in the Middle East] had been moving upon exactly parallel lines to yours at home." Churchill duly added an impersonal reference to the "harmony" of outlook "on the main issue" between those at home and on the spot. He also prints his memo of 24 September on wastage of troops but not the surrounding correspondence with Eden. All this serves to obscure his September anxieties about home defense and the leading role of Eden and the War Office in urging an offensive buildup in Egypt.[42]

It was during Eden's mission, on 28 October, that Italy invaded Greece. How to respond constitutes Churchill's third big Middle Eastern theme in *Their Finest Hour*. According to the memoirs, his disagreement with Eden and Wavell in Cairo about whether to send aid to Greece was based on misunderstanding. Secretly, they had concocted plans for a desert offensive and did not want to jeopardize them by a Balkan diversion. Left in ignorance and chafing at inactivity, Churchill pressed for aid to Greece as a way of striking at the Italians. It was not until Eden returned to London on 8 November, claims Churchill, that he revealed "the carefully-guarded secret which I wished I had known earlier." From then on, he tells us, they all concentrated on Wavell's strike against the Italians massing in the desert.[43]

What actually happened is less simple and more revealing. Before Italy invaded Greece, it was Leopold Amery, the Secretary of State for India, and Lord Lloyd, the Colonial Secretary, who were the leading Cabinet advocates of aid to the Greeks. On 27 October, Churchill told them firmly, "I do not agree with your suggestions that at the present time we should make any further promises to Greece and Turkey. It is very easy to write in a sweeping manner when one does not have to take account of resources, transport, time and distance." This minute was cut from the appendix to *Their Finest Hour* in December 1948. Amery and Lloyd also accused Churchill of deceiving the Cabinet. On the Prime Minister's instruction, the printed set of Churchill-Eden telegrams for Cabinet distribution did not include those that the two men exchanged via a special cipher. Amery and Lloyd knew this and complained formally to the Cabinet Secretary on 28 October.[44]

That same day, however, Italy invaded Greece, and Churchill immediately changed his tune, championing aid to the Greeks. This threatened Wavell's still-secret offensive, so Eden asked on 3 November to come home immediately: "It is impossible to explain the whole position and plans fully by telegram." Churchill tells us that "assent was given." In fact, his reply was exactly the opposite: "Do not return till you have received my telegram and considered it with all your advisers in all its bearings. When I have received your answer I will consult Cabinet about your returning. It would be most unfortunate if at this juncture action were to be paralysed here and in Egypt by your being in transit."[45] This forced Eden and Wavell to tip their hand. "Entirely for your own information," Eden cabled in the special code, "Wavell is having plans prepared to strike blow at Italians in Western Desert at the earliest possible moment, probably this month. . . . Margin is small and any withdrawal of troops or equipment would mean cancelling the plan and remaining on defensive." Churchill received this late on 3 November, five days before he claims he learned for the first time of these plans on Eden's return. He simply ignored the message. On the fourth, Cairo was told that the Chiefs of Staff and the Prime Minister had decided it was "necessary to give Greece the greatest possible material and moral support at the earliest possible moment." This support could come only from Egypt, so commanders there "will put this plan in train at once." That same day, Churchill informed the War Cabinet of this telegram, without mentioning Eden's preview of Wavell's plans. Only after the Greek commitment had been accepted in London and Cairo did Churchill authorize Eden's return home.[46]

At this stage, aid to Greece was limited—five air squadrons plus support services—and it did not jeopardize Wavell's offensive. But this was a portent of bigger struggles to come in the spring of 1941. The episode also illuminates how Churchill made policy and wrote history. He kept the Cabinet in the dark about his back channel to Eden and about the preview it provided of Wavell's plans. In his memoirs he represents what happened as misunderstanding rather than manipulation, yet the archival record, much of it in the Chartwell papers, told a different story.[47] The Greek debate of late 1940 was a blatant example of Churchill bypassing his Cabinet; not surprisingly, he bypasses it in his memoirs as well.

BRITAIN'S SUDDEN vulnerability in 1940 prompted new bouts of appeasement. On 16 June, the day the Cabinet agreed to union with France, it also approved secret talks in Dublin about the possibility of a united Ireland, and nine days later it endorsed a formal offer to the Irish government. In return, the Irish would join the Allies and allow British forces to use their bases. This proposal foundered on the refusal of the Irish leader, Eamon de Valera, to enter the war and of the Ulster Unionists to end partition. The talks were handled by Chamberlain, not Churchill, who made it clear he would not coerce the Unionists, but the Prime Minister approved the proposals and participated in several Cabinet discussions. Given the sensitivity, however, he did not mention the story even in drafts of his memoirs. The only hint in *Their Finest Hour* is buried in a letter to Roosevelt in December 1940.[48]

On India, too, the Cabinet was ready for some measure of appeasement in mid-1940, to mobilize Indian support for the war and free troops from internal policing. In July, Leo Amery urged the Cabinet to promise India a constituent assembly at the end of the war. Watered down by Churchill, his plan was published in August, only to be rejected, as with the Irish offer, by the principal parties—in this case, the Hindu-led Congress party and the Muslim League. Again, Churchill keeps silent in his memoirs. His 1947 drafts did contain a testy comment about how "in the most desperate moment of our struggle for life I was confronted with fine sentimental proposals for far-reaching constitutional changes in India." This was followed by a diatribe about India as "the greatest war profiteer" of the whole conflict: "We were charged nearly a million pounds a day for defending India from the miseries of invasion which so many other lands endured." This passage was dynamite, but Deakin persuaded him to defer discussion of India's role in the war to a later volume.[49]

Although understandable given Britain's predicament in 1940, the attempted appeasement of Ireland and India, like the temporary closure of the Burma Road, do not fit Churchill's theme of resolute and principled defiance in *Their Finest Hour*. By contrast, he does feature one of his most ruthless acts of that summer — the attack on the French fleet at the beginning of July in order to prevent it from falling into German hands. Under the armistice terms, most of France's navy was to be demobilized and disarmed, but the Germans promised not to use these ships themselves. Churchill deemed this a worthless pledge, given Hitler's record. Nor did he believe that Admiral Darlan, the French Minister of Marine, would be able to make good his assurance to scuttle the ships if the Germans tried to seize them. On 3–4 July, the Royal Navy took preemptive action. In Portsmouth and Alexandria, French warships were captured or demobilized by agreement, with little loss of life. But the bulk of the fleet was at Mers-el-Kébir, near the Algerian city of Oran. When negotiations broke down, Admiral Sir James Somerville's Force H from Gibraltar was ordered by the Cabinet to open fire, sinking one battleship and badly damaging two others. Nearly 1,300 Frenchmen died, and the resentment in France, whipped up by press and newsreel coverage of the funerals, was enduring.

Churchill calls this "a hateful decision, the most unnatural and painful in which I have ever been concerned." But he insists there was no alternative and says the British action "produced a profound impression in every country," particularly the United States, making plain that "the British War Cabinet feared nothing and would stop at nothing." He also notes an added political bonus: on 4 July, after he had told the Commons what had happened, the Tories dropped their former coolness and joined in the prolonged cheers.[50] But this picture of Cabinet, Commons, and country united in ruthless defiance is exaggerated to suit the theme of *Their Finest Hour*. "The War Cabinet never hesitated," Churchill tells us. In fact, it went through a week of indecision, exploring alternatives such as offering £100 million to buy the French fleet or (Churchill's own idea) asking the Americans to purchase it.[51] And although the politicians finally hardened their hearts, the admirals found the deed utterly abhorrent. Then and later, both Somerville and Andrew Cunningham (in command at Alexandria) were convinced that violence could have been avoided. Admiral North, Somerville's flag officer at Gibraltar, sent a formal protest to London on 4 July, infuriating Churchill and A. V. Alexander, the First Lord of the Admiralty. "It is evident that

Admiral Dudley North has not got the root of the matter in him," Churchill wrote Alexander on 20 July, "and I should be very glad to see you replace him with a more resolute and clear-sighted officer." Only Pound's intervention saved North, and no mention of this or of the depths of naval dismay were made in Churchill's chapter.[52]

Churchill's verdict on Oran—"the elimination of the French Navy as an important factor almost at a single stroke"—is also something of a distortion.[53] The battle cruiser *Strasbourg* escaped to join a powerful French squadron at Toulon, on France's southern coast. On 9 September, alerted by leaks that de Gaulle's Free French forces were on their way from Liverpool to seize the French West African port of Dakar, three Vichy cruisers and three destroyers slipped out of Toulon, eluded the British at Gibraltar, and beat the Anglo-French assault force to Dakar. On 23–25 September, they helped local troops repulse the attack, disabling a British battleship in the process. Dakar was a disaster for Churchill, undoing much of the effect of Oran at home and abroad, and there were mutterings about another Gallipoli. He accelerated a Cabinet reshuffle to divert discussion, though in his memoirs the two events are carefully kept separate.[54] In the Commons on 8 October, Churchill declined to give a detailed account of the operation on the grounds that it was "primarily French," but he dwelled at length on the escape of the Vichy warships. That, he said, "transformed" the situation at Dakar and was not the fault of the government but the result of "accidents" and "some errors" by subordinates.[55] A week later, Admiral North was removed from his command. He was left unemployed for a year, and was then formally retired. No charges, however, were brought, and his pleas for a formal inquiry were ignored. Opinions vary as to whether Alexander and Pound were responsible for North's fate or whether the Prime Minister added pressure of his own.[56]

Churchill's chapter on Dakar was therefore very sensitive, and he constructed it with particular art. He does not deny that he "undertook in an exceptional degree the initiation and advocacy" of the expedition, down to drafting the instructions for the British naval commanders, but presents it, like Oran, as a sign of British unity and resolve. Responsibility for its failure is shifted elsewhere. In part, he blames indiscretions by de Gaulle's Free French, retelling contemporary anecdotes about their toasts to Dakar in a Liverpool restaurant, though he cut from his galleys the sentence "Even the General bought his tropical kit himself from 'Simpson's' in Piccadilly."[57] Equally deftly, he allots some blame to the British admirals for pressing on even when the Vichy squadron had reached Dakar. At this point, he says, he and the War Cabinet were inclined to stop but felt that the local commanders should be the final judges. Perhaps aware that some readers might find his self-restraint implausibly uncharacteristic, he adds: "It was very rare at this stage in the war for commanders on the spot to press for audacious courses."[58]

Churchill reserves his main criticism for those who let the Vichy warships slip past Gibraltar, specifically North and an unnamed signals officer at the Admiralty. This passage was drafted with care, because North blamed Churchill's speech to the Commons in October 1940 for the stain on his reputation and lobbied hard after the war for vindication, sending several detailed letters to Churchill. In 1940, North was not in the know about the Dakar expedition, and his standing orders were to attack Vichy ships leaving the Mediterranean only if they seemed to be turning north — that is, toward Britain. Commodore Allen, asked by Churchill to investigate, therefore concluded in July 1947 that the Admiral was "guilty of an error in judgment but hardly of a failure of duty" and expressed doubt that the French ships "really affected the ultimate outcome" at Dakar.[59] Allen revised the passage, and Churchill toned it down even further after another letter from North in April 1948 that was probably intended as an oblique threat of legal action if he was damned in print.[60] In the chapter on Dakar, Churchill merely states that North "was *not* in the Dakar circle, and took no special action" when news of the Vichy movement was received. Despite further correspondence with Allen, North was unable to secure amendment in later editions. "It is a pity," he wrote with studied understatement, that a "false account" at the time, highlighted by Churchill's oratory in the Commons, "should go down as history."[61]

At the end of that chapter Churchill admits that "to the world at large" Dakar seemed "a glaring example of miscalculation, confusion, timidity and muddle." In America, "there was a storm of unfavourable criticism. The Australian Government was distressed." Robert Menzies, Australia's premier, first heard of the operation from the press, and Appendix D prints a forthright exchange of telegrams between him and Churchill, with Menzies denouncing "a half-hearted attack" and the "humiliating" lack of information from London. But Churchill omits his initial telegram on 27 September, disingenuously blaming "mis-chance and misfortune" plus the ardor of local commanders, thereby leaving the impression that Menzies had exploded out of the blue.[62] Norman Brook would have preferred to omit the whole correspondence for fear of damaging Commonwealth relations, but Churchill had adroitly secured Menzies's verbal permission to print it when the Australian was given a full-dress tour of Chartwell in August 1948.[63] He placated Brook by moving the exchange into the appendix and including only the one cryptic sentence in his text. Dakar was an intimation of greater headaches to come for the Cabinet Secretary when Churchill resurrected his 1941–1942 rows with Australia about imperial strategy in volumes 3 and 4.

Churchill rounds off his Mediterranean story for 1940 with the chapter "Relations with Vichy and Spain." He portrays them both as distasteful regimes, with which it was nonetheless strategically necessary for Britain to maintain contact. But whereas no defense is made of Pétain—Churchill quotes a memo he wrote in November 1940 saying that the Marshal had "always been an anti-British defeatist"—he goes out of his way to defend Franco. The reason is not hard to infer. The discredited Vichy leadership had been purged and tried in 1944–1945; Pétain spent the rest of his life in prison. Franco, by contrast, remained the unquestioned leader of a country that Churchill hoped in 1949 to make a valuable member of the Western Alliance. On the other hand, Attlee and the Labour party still nursed a bitter hatred of Franco dating back to the Spanish Civil War. Churchill's treatment of Franco in this chapter is particularly adroit. He does not question the left-wing stereotype—Franco is a "narrow-minded tyrant" who "thought only of Spain and Spanish interests," which meant "keeping his blood-drained people out of another war." But in Churchill's hands this becomes a virtue. Given Franco's debt to Hitler and Mussolini for helping him seize power in 1936–1939, the striking point is his consistent refusal to enter the war on the Axis side. "It is fashionable at the present time to dwell on the vices of General Franco," Churchill tells us, "and I am therefore glad to place on record this testimony to the duplicity and ingratitude of his dealings with Hitler and Mussolini."[64]

This is, of course, an indulgent view of Franco: in the autumn of 1940, the Caudillo came very close to throwing in his lot with Hitler. What restrained him was German unwillingness to satisfy his colonial appetite. Churchill also glosses over the secret campaign of bribery he personally sanctioned to buy the neutrality of key Spanish generals. His intermediaries were Captain Alan Hillgarth, a swashbuckling naval attaché, and Juan March, one of Franco's bankers, through whom $10 million in scarce British foreign exchange were channeled into the generals' Swiss bank accounts. "Relations with Vichy and Spain" contains only a passing reference to Hillgarth and his "profound knowledge of Spanish affairs." In his original draft, Churchill was less discreet: "Through Captain Hillgarth, whom I knew personally before the war, I maintained my Admiralty contacts with Juan March, who lay in the heart of many Spanish political affairs, and I was encouraged to believe that a game was being played with Hitler and that all would be well." It is unlikely that this passage would have survived Norman

Brook's scrutiny, but Churchill took it out long before it reached him: the imperatives of wartime secrecy and Cold War diplomacy both pointed in the same direction.[65]

OF ALL THE NEUTRALS, the one that mattered most to Britain was the United States. In the opening chapter of volume 2, Churchill describes and celebrates his "personal correspondence" with Roosevelt. "My relations with the President gradually became so close that the chief business between our two countries was virtually conducted by these personal interchanges between him and me. In this way our perfect understanding was gained."[66] His long passage on the correspondence in this scene-setting chapter conditions the reader for the rest of the work: the Anglo-American relationship was central to Britain's war effort, it was characterized by "perfect understanding," and its "chief business" was "virtually conducted" by the two leaders. Whatever may be said of other periods of the war, none of these three propositions is valid for 1940.

Since Churchill had tried to boost morale by speaking repeatedly after the fall of France about an imminent U.S. declaration of war, the second half of 1940 was intensely frustrating for him, as minutes omitted from his memoirs make clear. "We have not had anything from the United States we have not paid for," he told Halifax on 20 December 1940, "and what we have had has not played an essential part in our resistance." In trying to prise aid out of the United States, the Foreign Office urged a policy of calculated generosity, whereas Churchill favored hard bargaining, playing on American fears that the British fleet might fall into Nazi hands.[67]

Churchill does devote a chapter to "United States Destroyers and West Indian Bases." After weeks of haggling, the two governments agreed on 2 September that Britain would receive fifty American destroyers, World War I vintage, in return for leases on eight British possessions in the Caribbean and western Atlantic on which Washington could build naval and air bases. Although generally known as the Destroyers-for-Bases Deal, there was a third element: Churchill reiterated the pledge he made to the Commons on 4 June that the British fleet would never be surrendered but would, in extremis, fight on from elsewhere in the empire. This was, therefore, a complex diplomatic negotiation. Sir Orme Sargent in the Foreign Office considered Churchill's early draft "disjointed" and "arid"; Norman Brook urged him to convert documents into narrative and clarify the story for "the average reader."[68] Revisions were duly made, but Churchill never got on top of the documents. He even prints a telegram he never sent: his original draft was revised by the Foreign Office![69]

The Leader

Churchill greets the crowds outside 10 Downing Street on
10 September 1939, newly appointed as First Lord of the
Admiralty. Eight months later he would achieve his
lifelong dream and become Prime Minister, just as the
Nazis began their blitzkrieg on the West.

The first wartime meeting between Churchill and Franklin Roosevelt
at the Atlantic Conference, 10 August 1941. FDR's son Elliott (middle)
later published a 1946 memoir that was deeply critical of Winston.

In August 1942 Churchill had his first meeting with Stalin—pictured with Averell
Harriman, FDR's emissary (second from left), and Vyacheslav Molotov, the Soviet
Foreign Minister. Churchill felt that Stalin could be trusted and did not conceal this
belief in his memoirs.

Difficult Allies

Churchill and
Roosevelt watch
with pleasure as
Charles de Gaulle
reluctantly shakes
hands with his rival
for leadership of
the Free French,
General Henri Giraud,
at Casablanca,
24 January 1943.

On 17 August 1944,
while in Italy,
Churchill met Tito,
the Yugoslav Partisan
leader. His up-and-
down relationships
with de Gaulle and
Tito were both
carefully edited in
the memoirs to avoid
prejudicing
postwar diplomacy.

IMPERIAL WAR MUSEUM

The aftermath of the Dieppe raid of 19 August 1942. *The Hinge of Fate*
contains only a brief passage about the tragedy, largely written by
Admiral Lord Louis Mountbatten to cover up his own role.

DWIGHT D. EISENHOWER LIBRARY

On 6 June 1944 the Allies successfully landed in Normandy, where
U.S. troops are seen next day on Omaha Beach. In his memoirs
Churchill did not reveal the depth of his doubts about the operation.

After D-Day the Americans became the dominant partner in the transatlantic alliance, and when the Big Three met at Yalta in February 1945 Churchill felt Britain was like a "small lion" between the "huge Russian bear" and the "great American elephant."

Little of this was apparent to jubilant Britons in Piccadilly Circus on 8 May after Churchill's victory broadcast. Two weeks later, in the utmost secrecy, he asked his military advisers to assess the chances of fighting a successful war against Russia.

Churchill's leading military advisers during the war were Field-Marshal Sir Alan Brooke (glasses) and General Hastings Ismay (cigarette), pictured at Yalta in February 1945 with U.S. counterparts Admiral William D. Leahy (left) and General George C. Marshall. "Pug" Ismay would later help Churchill write his memoirs, but the diary kept by "Brookie," published in 1957–1959, punctured many Churchill myths.

Lord Moran, the eminent physician, helped keep Churchill alive from 1940 but also kept a record of Winston's "struggle for survival," which would prove even more controversial than Alanbrooke's diary when it was published in 1966.

U.S. NATIONAL ARCHIVES

Anthony Eden, Churchill, and Clement Attlee in a pensive mood as they leave Westminster Abbey on 10 April 1945 after the memorial service for Earl Lloyd George. Churchill measured himself against LG as a great war leader.

U.S. NATIONAL ARCHIVES

On 23 October 1945 Churchill joins Field-Marshal Montgomery at the Alamein dinner at Claridge's Hotel in London. Churchill's memoirs would celebrate Monty and his desert victory in November 1942 as the turning point of the war.

Churchill and Stalin with the new U.S. President, Harry Truman,
at the Potsdam conference of July 1945.

A few days later the British electorate had spoken, and on 1 August the Churchill family
was unceremoniously moving out of 10 Downing Street, with nowhere to go.

Churchill correcting proofs of his memoirs in the study of
Chartwell, his country house in Kent, in 1947. Additional
proofs are on the special desk behind him, under a 1916
portrait of his wife, Clementine, by Sir John Lavery.

Churchill hits the world headlines with his "iron curtain" speech at Westminster College, Fulton, Missouri, on 5 March 1946. President Truman is to his right (glasses).

After Fulton, Winston and Clementine (left) visit FDR's grave at the Roosevelt family home in Hyde Park, up the Hudson River from New York City, with the President's widow, Eleanor.

General Dwight D. Eisenhower, seen reviewing U.S. troops in Devon on 4 February 1944, was the Supreme Allied Commander on D-Day. His 1948 memoirs questioned Churchill's commitment to the cross-Channel invasion.

Robert Sherwood, the playwright and White House speech-writer, pictured on 28 March 1945, went on to publish a best-selling study in 1948 of Roosevelt and his closest aide, Harry Hopkins. Churchill feared this would scoop his own memoirs.

Vacations

Churchill relied heavily on his research assistants, especially the young Oxford historian Bill Deakin, seen here arriving at Marrakech in December 1947 for the first of several working vacations funded by Churchill's American publishers.

The Christmas 1947 party at the Mamounia Hotel includes Deakin (left facing) and (to his left) secretaries "Jo" Sturdee and Elizabeth Gilliatt. Churchill's daughter Sarah has her back to the camera.

Assistants

General Sir Henry Pownall, seen here in 1940, retired from the army in 1945 and became Churchill's military assistant on the memoirs.

Denis Kelly (left) and Gordon Allen, the other members of the "Syndicate" of researchers, are pictured with Churchill discussing the final draft of the chapter on the battle of Leyte at Chartwell in August 1953. Rufus II, a gift from *Life* magazine, is in the foreground.

Churchill's American publishers sign the deal of the century in May 1947—from the left, Henry Laughlin of Houghton Mifflin, Julius Ochs Adler of *The New York Times*, and Andrew Heiskell of *Life* magazine.

Daniel Longwell, the managing editor of *Life*, spent hours coaxing, cajoling, and often criticizing the magazine's most celebrated author. A dog lover, he helped pay for Rufus II.

Censors

Sir Edward Bridges, Cabinet Secretary from 1938 to 1946 and self-styled "guardian" of official secrets, facilitated Churchill's unique access to government documents.

Sir Norman Brook, his successor from 1947 to 1962, acted as official censor and unofficial editor of Churchill's memoirs. Several pages of *The Second World War* are almost entirely Brook's work.

Churchill greets American fans as he leaves a lunch hosted by Houghton Mifflin on
1 April 1949. "I am told that a Boston lunch party is greatly to be preferred to a Boston
Tea Party," he quipped. Henry Laughlin of Houghton Mifflin is behind.

A shop-window display in Copenhagen, October 1950, marks Churchill's visit to
Denmark, as guest of the King and Queen, and publication of volume 3 of his memoirs.

Throughout the negotiations, Churchill opposed the Foreign Office tactic of generosity, trying to minimize the number of leases offered and to keep them separate from the antiquated destroyers, since any explicit deal clearly weighed in America's favor. "It doesn't do to give way like this to the Americans," he told the head of the FO's American Department on 6 August. "One must strike a balance with them." But his chapter sounds the note he adopted in public at the end of the deal—lauding the offers of destroyers and bases as signs that "these two great organisations of the English-speaking democracies, the British Empire and the United States, will have to be somewhat mixed up together in some of their affairs for mutual and general advantage." This, of course, was the public Churchill of Harvard in 1943 and Fulton in 1946, but it was not the private Churchill of 1940.[70]

Churchill also opposed pressure from the Foreign Office and Service Departments to share Britain's advanced technology. "I am not in a hurry to give our secrets until the United States is much nearer war than she is now," he wrote on 17 July.[71] But eventually he capitulated. On 29 August 1940, a small, black metal box was carried onto a Canadian liner in the Liverpool docks—the most important luggage of a seven-man group of British scientists. Two weeks later, it was safely lodged in the wine cellar of the British Embassy in Washington. The box contained Britain's technological crown jewels—blueprints for rockets and gunsights, outline plans for the jet engine and the atomic bomb, and one of twelve prototypes of the cavity magnetron, which was essential for the next generation of miniaturized radar, small enough for use in an aircraft. Developed in 1941–1943 by American scientists, microwave radar became a war-winning weapon for the Allies. Yet Churchill says nothing about the British mission in his memoirs, even though relevant documents existed in his Chartwell files. His own position at the time may explain why: Churchill was initially opposed to the sharing idea and then wanted to link it closely to progress on the deal for the destroyers. In addition, the mission was led by Sir Henry Tizard, Lindemann's sworn enemy in the arena of government science. The two men had argued bitterly over air defense in the 1930s (see chapter 7, above) and over the beams in the summer of 1940. The mission may have been a convenient opportunity for Lindemann to remove Tizard from London. In any event, Churchill passes in silence over what has been called "one of the most important events of the Second World War," inaugurating a new era of transatlantic technological cooperation that proved crucial for ultimate Allied victory.[72]

In his chapter on the British origins of Lend-Lease, Churchill (prompted by Clementine) pays tribute to Lord Lothian, Britain's Ambassador in Washington. Lothian, Churchill acknowledges, urged him to present a full statement of

Britain's predicament to Roosevelt after his election victory on 5 November 1940, and so "I drew up, in consultation with him, a personal letter." After drafting and checking, this was dispatched on 8 December. Churchill prints almost the full text, calling the letter "one of the most important I ever wrote" and presenting it as the catalyst for the President's Lend-Lease bill to deal with Britain's dollar shortage. Yet in several respects this is a distortion of what actually transpired.[73]

As with the Destroyers-for-Bases Deal, Churchill had to be pushed to act. He was initially resistant to Lothian's suggestion of "putting all our cards on the table" for the President, and then he dragged his feet on revising and sending the letter. Moreover, Churchill wanted to concentrate on the impending shipping crisis, whereas Lothian favored a *tour d'horizon* of all of Britain's problems; they haggled over this for days. The text of the letter confirms that Churchill's primary emphasis was on shipping, which accounted for more than half the 4,000 words as well as a detailed statistical appendix setting out losses in 1940. Finance, by contrast, took up about 400 words at the end. Churchill warned FDR that "the moment approaches when we shall no longer be able to pay cash for shipping and other supplies" but told the President it was "in shipping and in the power to transport across the oceans, particularly the Atlantic Ocean, that in 1941 the crunch of the whole war will be found." The reason why this letter proved a catalyst for Lend-Lease is attributable less to its content or intent as to Lothian's calculated indiscretion to reporters in New York on 23 November. Whether he used the notorious words "Well, boys, Britain's broke, it's your money we want" is doubtful, but he certainly highlighted the urgency of Britain's dollar crisis, and his remarks put the issue at the center of American debate. This was the public atmosphere when Roosevelt left Washington on 2 December for a postelection cruise. And it was finance, not shipping, that the President seized on in Churchill's letter when it reached him a week later. Returning to the White House on 16 December, he gave a press conference the next day that launched the idea of Lend-Lease.[74]

Churchill's version of the origins of Lend-Lease has, however, proved influential: most historians follow him in depicting the 8 December letter as the intended trigger for Roosevelt's decision on British finance. Yet Churchill's insistence that shipping would be the "crunch" of the war in 1941 deserves closer attention. It was only under pressure from Gordon Allen, his naval adviser, that Churchill decided to devote a whole chapter, "Ocean Peril," to the deepening Battle of the Atlantic; early drafts were entitled "The Air and the U-Boats" and allotted half the space to strategic bombing. In this chapter, Churchill makes explicit what is buried in that letter to Roosevelt: "The only thing that ever really frightened me during the war was the U-boat peril. . . . I was even more anxious about this battle than I had been about the glorious air fight called the Battle of Britain."[75] He returns to the point in the sonorous ending of his volume: "The Battle of France was lost. The Battle of Britain was won. The Battle of the Atlantic had now to be fought."[76]

The definitiveness of Churchill's first two judgments are accentuated in "Germany and Russia," two chapters from the end, where he uses a collection of captured German documents to describe Hitler's plans to attack Russia, climaxing in the formal directive on 21 December. Churchill briefly admits that none of this was known in London at the time—"the main troop movements of the German armies eastward had not yet become apparent to our active Intelligence Service"—but the reader is left with a firm impression that by the end of 1940 a corner had been turned: "Hitler had failed to conquer Britain. It was plain that the Island would persevere to the end."[77] These remarks simplify Churchill's oscillating moods in 1941; his clear labels distort contemporary reality. Just as the Battles of France and Britain were intertwined, so the Battle of Britain was bigger than the epic dogfights of August and September 1940, continuing as long as the Battle of the Atlantic was undecided. At the time, Hitler's failure to subdue the British Isles by direct assault or maritime strangulation was less obvious than in retrospect. This matters even more in the first book of volume 3.

CHAPTER 13

HIS FINEST HOUR

F OR CHURCHILL'S PUBLISHERS, *Their Finest Hour* proved no less of
a challenge than *The Gathering Storm*. They faced the same impossible
deadlines, constant changes, and autocratic demands. Reviews were also
beginning to fit a mold, many being panegyrics rather than analyses. The big
exception was for the French edition, significantly retitled *L'Heure Tragique*,
because in France and Belgium 1940 was a time of national disaster and a running sore in postwar politics. As before, reception depended on audience as much
as intention.

EVER SINCE 1940, the British had been vilified by many on the Continent for
deserting their allies. Churchill therefore took pains to show that they did their
utmost in a situation that was already hopeless, emphasizing that the British
Expeditionary Force was ready to counterattack at Arras on 21–22 May 1940 but
insisting that it also had to protect its line of retreat to the sea. He deflected attention onto the precipitate Belgian surrender, quoting his speech to the Commons
on 4 June 1940 which followed Paul Reynaud, the French Prime Minister, in
placing the blame squarely on King Leopold. "Suddenly, without prior consultation, with the least possible notice, without the advice of his Ministers and upon
his own personal act, he sent a plenipotentiary to the German Command, surrendered his Army and exposed our whole flank and means of retreat."[1]

As he completed *Their Finest Hour*, Churchill found these comments coming back to haunt him. The stigma of surrender had marked Leopold. Unlike the

Dutch, Danish, and Norwegian monarchs, he stayed with his troops rather than join the government-in-exile in London and was taken to Germany when the Allies liberated Belgium in September 1944. With Leopold's brother acting as Regent, left-wing parties campaigned to block his return. The "Royal Question" became the most vexed issue in Belgian politics, and much of the debate revolved around interpretations of May 1940. In mid-January 1949, three weeks before serialization began, La Libre Belgique, an ultramonarchist paper, printed six front-page articles quoting and rebutting statements critical of the King by Churchill, Reynaud, and others.[2] Hurriedly, Pownall and Churchill checked their final draft of "The March to the Sea." On the German breach of the Belgian line on 24 May they had written, "The King of the Belgians considered the situation hopeless, and already thought only of capitulation." This was amended to say that he "soon considered the situation hopeless, and prepared himself for capitulation."[3] Churchill had also made reference to Reynaud's denunciation of Leopold's "treachery." After more research, Deakin advised him that Reynaud had never used the word "treachery"—this was a Vichy canard. The offending sentences were removed, as was the phrase "this pitiful episode" from the speech of 4 June 1940.[4] These and other last-minute revisions, resulting in six new pages of proofs, were all incorporated in the final text.[5]

Nevertheless, when the serial version appeared, Churchill was attacked for his 4 June 1940 comment about the King surrendering his army without prior consultation. Sixty-eight Belgian generals published a petition in February 1949 calling his remarks "neither accurate nor fair." After consulting the Prince Regent, who believed no amendments were necessary, Churchill stuck to his guns. "I am not attempting to write a History of the Second World War," he told one critic, "but only [to] give the story of events as they appeared to me and the British Government." Receiving no response, the petitioners took advantage of Churchill's visit to Brussels at the end of May to reissue their declaration, to which another twenty-two generals had added their names. Deakin warned that the document was "a manifesto destined for internal Belgian consumption" and that its probable intent was to "lure you into controversy round the position of the King." Following the Belgian elections in June 1949, a new coalition instituted a referendum on Leopold's return. As far as Churchill was concerned, the fuss then died down, except on the part of one fervent British partisan of Leopold, Olive Muir, who harangued him in letters and at public meetings about why he had not replied to the generals.[6]

In France, the reaction to Their Finest Hour was also intense. Le Figaro serialized the volume in forty-eight installments from 4 February to 30 March. The extracts on the fall of France provoked particular comment, with several major letters of rejoinder to the editor. General Gamelin claimed that on 16 May 1940, in response to Churchill's question about the strategic reserve, he did not claim there wasn't one ("*aucune*") but that it no longer existed ("*qu'il n'y en avait plus*"). He did not elaborate, Gamelin said, because the reserve of twenty-nine divisions had been committed piecemeal by local commanders, and he wanted to avoid recriminations in front of France's ally. In a more substantial piece, reprinted in *The New York Times* and the *Daily Telegraph*, Reynaud insisted that Churchill's incredulity on 15–16 May 1940 showed "how far he was from grasping the overwhelming danger" posed by armored warfare and how much his thinking "bore the imprint of the strategy of the previous war." Reynaud also noted that France's commitment to Belgium was made "at the request of the British," to deny the Luftwaffe bases within range of southern England. But after these dangerous openings, his piece became increasingly whinging in tone—the voice of a man who may have been right in 1940 but was certainly ineffectual. And Reynaud had no intention of prolonging the duel. "Having made this spontaneous and friendly response to the work of the great Englishman," he concluded, "I am glad to resume my place among his readers."[7]

This set the pattern for French reaction. Gamelin and Reynaud, like Weygand and the former premier Camille Chautemps, questioned points of detail and faulted Churchill on secondhand accounts of events he did not witness. But they did not dent Churchill's general argument. Assessing "The French Reply" in an editorial on 4 March 1949, *The New York Times* acknowledged that "Mr. Churchill views events from the British standpoint, and the full story of the French tragedy is still to be told. But judging from the replies received it may be doubted that history will differ much with Mr. Churchill's judgment." Of course, the paper said, 1940 marked the failure of a whole nation, not just "the petrified French military leadership," but the fact remained that "in its gravest hour, France was unable to produce a Gambetta, a Foch, a Clemenceau—or a Churchill."[8]

Two passing comments in the *Figaro* installments served to focus French anger about Churchill's depiction of 1940. One concerned General Gaston Billotte, commander of France's First Army Group, of whom Churchill wrote: "Neither the personality of this French general nor his proposals, such as they were, inspired confidence in his allies." Billotte was killed in a car crash in 1940, but his son defended his father in print in 1949 and complained bitterly to Churchill about these "inaccurate" and "very painful" comments. Paul Ramadier, the current French Defence Minister, agreed, telling Churchill it was rare to read an account of recent events from a pen that was so "sharp" (*acérée*). After consulting Pownall, Churchill again took the position that he was simply stating British impressions at the time, and nothing was changed in the book.[9]

More serious was a reference to General René Prioux, who, during the retreat to Dunkirk, according to the *Figaro* installment on 12–13 February, "gave the impression of wanting to surrender with all his army" — "*donnait l'impression de vouloir se rendre avec toute son armée.*" This sentence had, in fact, been amended twice in January 1949, after representations by *Life* and Plon, and Pownall intended the final version to state that Prioux "seemed prepared to surrender the entire force, but eventually he was prevailed upon to change his mind." In the last-minute rush, however, that correction was not sent to the serializers. A few days after the extract appeared in *Le Figaro*, the paper printed a statement by Prioux vigorously contesting Churchill's "defamatory remarks." Other generals weighed in, and Plon feared that Prioux would start legal action, thereby delaying book publication.[10]

A draft reply to Prioux was carefully vetted by Churchill's solicitor, but the legal threat did not materialize, and the letter was never sent. However, the offending sentence was removed from all book versions of the memoirs, and Churchill recognized that his narrative might have been couched more sympathetically. "I wish we had written in the French story a few accounts of the French fighting bravely," he told Pownall on 9 April. He decided to write a special preface to the French edition of *Their Finest Hour*, stressing that he was offering only the British viewpoint at the time. By the time this was drafted, however, the volume was in the shops, and the preface was held back for the second edition. Then, in January 1950, it suddenly appeared, without the author's approval, as a statement in the French and Belgian press. Reves told Churchill that "the campaign against volume II in France and Belgium was so strong that this volume sold less than half of Volume I," and Plon had issued Churchill's declaration in the hope of softening up the public for volume 3.[11]

The statement praised the "bravery" of French soldiers and the "skill" of their generals but argued that the French Army "never had the chance to fight it out with the Germans, front to front and face to face." In the draft, Churchill had offered two reasons but the first—that the army "was not given a good chance before the war by the politicians or the Chamber"—was deleted at Plon's request to avoid upsetting other interest groups in France. This left only the second reason: that the French Army "was ripped up by the incursion of the German armour on a scale and in a manner which few of us, whether in office or in a private station, could foresee." Thus, Churchill again slid over the Allied advance into Belgium. The Belgians, he said, "fought with gallantry and determination" but "were put into the war so late that they could not even occupy their own prepared front lines."[12] By now, Leopold was back on the throne, and his secretary wrote Churchill expressing the King's "profound astonishment" at an attack on "the honour of Belgium" and what amounted to a charge of "criminal negligence" on Leopold as Commander in Chief. Churchill, Pownall, and Reves all agreed that silence was again the best course, and the Belgian material was omitted when the statement finally appeared as the preface to the second French edition.[13]

The direct effect of this row on sales was probably not as grave as Reves suggested. He later said that, almost everywhere except Britain, the trend was sharply downward for each successive volume, mainly because of the surfeit of documents. Nevertheless, the French decline was particularly severe, and the row over *L'Heure Tragique* was a sobering reminder of how throwaway remarks that were tangential to Churchill's main argument could become central to the reception of his work. Keen to avoid any repetition, he told Reves he would like foreign publishers to scrutinize his text in advance, so he could avoid potential offense. But, given the perennial prepublication panic, this was pious hope rather than practical precept.[14]

IN THE UNITED STATES, *Life* squeezed no less than seven articles out of the book, starting on 7 February 1949. Again, these were lavishly illustrated, with photo spreads on Dunkirk, the Battle of Britain, and the Cabinet War Rooms, as well as sections on Churchill's summer 1948 vacation in Aix and on the Duke of Wellington—like Nelson for volume 1, a historic symbol of British resistance. *The New York Times* also followed its previous format, punctuating serialization with approving editorials. The final one, published on 12 March after the full thirty installments, reverted to Churchill's theme for volume 2: "How the British people held the fort alone till those who hitherto had been half blind were half ready." The paper called this "a harsh but accurate judgment on the rest of the free world in these years"; the volume underlined the lesson that "unless the democracies hang together they stand a very good chance of hanging separately." From here, it was an easy step to the negotiations for a North Atlantic Treaty just reaching their climax in Washington, which showed, the editorial claimed, that the lesson "so clearly stated" by Churchill was being taken to heart.[15]

For Houghton Mifflin, the book publication was again a desperate race against time. Ideally, it wanted at least five months from receipt of manuscript to books in the shops. In the event, it had three and a half—better than the eight weeks for *The Gathering Storm* but still painfully tight. One casualty was the index. Unhappy with the skimpy job done against the clock for volume 1, Nina Holton of the editorial staff turned to a retired minister who had worked for them in the past. Keen to produce an especially good index for "Winnie," he began on a grand scale but then had to cut corners as Churchill's overtakes rained down and the publisher's demands grew ever shriller. Alerted by C. C. Wood, Churchill was appalled to find on the very first page of the index that Field-Marshal Sir Harold Alexander was identified as both First Lord of the Admiralty and head of the British Army's Southern Command. Churchill regarded Alex as a superman, but not on that scale. In a letter of complaint to Henry Laughlin at Houghton Mifflin, he pointed out this conflation with the Labour politician A. V. Alexander as one of "many disastrous errors." Nina Holton tried to defend her indexer: "I guess it is a little tough to know that Lord Lothian was Philip Kerr and that Lord Templewood was Samuel Hoare." But Laughlin was not appeased. "Anybody who was alive there at the time and even faintly concerned himself with the world knew both of these things. If he didn't he ought not to have been indexing Churchill." When Houghton Mifflin published a revised edition of volume 2, it abandoned its original index and adapted the one from Cassell's.[16]

Part of the problem was that in mid-February Houghton Mifflin decided to advance the publication date by six days to 29 March. This was because Churchill had agreed to give a special lecture on 31 March for a conference at the Massachusetts Institute of Technology, just across the Charles River from their editorial offices on Beacon Hill. For the publishers, this was a heaven-sent opportunity. But Churchill had not come to promote his book or because of any passionate interest in the conference theme, "The World at Mid-Century." He envisaged the MIT speech as nothing less than a second Fulton.

What grabbed Churchill's attention was the invitation to share the podium with the President of the United States. The letter from Karl T. Compton, the MIT President, asked Churchill to reflect on the last fifty years and said that the following day Truman would preview the next fifty, in the other keynote address. Only after receiving confirmation from Truman that he had accepted Compton's invitation did Churchill commit himself. MIT offered to defray his travel expenses and "those of any members of your family who may wish to accompany you," but that was before Churchill explained that the cost of taking his party there and back on the *Queen Elizabeth* would be £2,100 (nearly $8,500). In the end, MIT paid £1,000, and *Life* magazine covered the rest.[17]

The trip became almost a state visit. Churchill sailed into New York on 24 March and went straight to the British Embassy in Washington, cheered along the drive by the entire staff. That evening, there was a reception attended by four former Secretaries of State (Hull, Stettinius, Byrnes, and Marshall), and then Truman hosted a small dinner in his honor. The next day, his party had a special coach on the lunchtime train to New York, where there were similar scenes and also the usual Churchillian anecdotes. Asked to confirm whether during the journey Churchill had indeed consumed a whole bottle of 1811 brandy (supposedly a gift of the railroad company), his valet quipped, "Don't you know Mr. Churchill is a teetotaller." Churchill gave two speeches in New York, one at a dinner hosted by Henry Luce, before continuing to Boston, where his party was accommodated on the top floor of the Ritz-Carlton Hotel. Churchill never set foot on the campus of MIT: his talk was moved to the Boston Garden, the city's 14,000-seat sports arena, because of the demand for tickets. Despite the distinguished academic cast, one journalist reported that Churchill "completely dominated the scene" and "demonstrated the reasons for his reputation as a doughty war leader, a skilled orator, and an individualistic showman." Most of the press coverage took a similar line. Dined as an equal by Harry Truman, whisked off the railroad platform in New York in "the Presidential Elevator," and housed in "the Presidential Suite" in his Boston hotel—the message was very clear.[18]

Too clear, in fact. At almost the last minute, on 21 March, Truman decided to pull out of his speech at MIT. Officially, the White House pleaded "increasing pressure of his official duties." Truman told Compton "the situation in Congress is a delicate one and I have to be available every minute from morning until late at night." In reality, the problem was more personal. Various senators wanted Churchill to be invited to address the U.S. Senate. But Dean Acheson, the Secretary of State, and Tom Connally, the Democratic leader in the Senate, both thought the Labour government in Britain "might not think favorably" of such treatment for the Leader of the Opposition. Truman agreed and also had second thoughts about his own speech at MIT. Ernest Bevin, Labour's Foreign Secretary, was about to visit Washington to sign the North Atlantic Treaty, and Truman decided that "making this speech the day following Churchill, perhaps on the very day that Bevin arrives in this country, might be undesirable."[19] Although not told the true explanation, Churchill was understandably peeved, since Truman's presence had been his real reason for coming. Even so, his speech was carried live on national radio networks, and, though lacking a sound bite comparable to the "iron curtain," it again attracted international attention for its claim that America's nuclear monopoly had prevented a third world war.

For Houghton Mifflin, Churchill's visit was worth "millions of dollars" of free publicity, and it would be "disastrous" if copies were not on hand in every bookshop before he spoke.[20] Henry Laughlin wanted to host a grand literary dinner in Boston and also invited Churchill to spend a quiet weekend painting at his home in Concord. But a weekend with the Laughlins hardly matched an evening with the Trumans. Eventually, Churchill did consent to a small, private lunch with Houghton Mifflin staff, held in the nearby Club of Odd Volumes on 1 April. "It is very kind of my American publishers to give this luncheon for me," he said with a twinkle in his eye. "I trust the date on which it occurs is purely coincidental." As the laughter died down, he added, "I am told that a Boston lunch party is greatly to be preferred to a Boston Tea Party."[21]

In the United States, therefore, serialization of *Their Finest Hour* could not have been better timed. Negotiation of the North Atlantic Treaty gave contemporary resonance to Churchill's story of a failed alliance; his triumphal progress along the Atlantic seaboard generated columns of comment and confirmed his standing as a world leader. The eventual book publication was almost an anticlimax. This volume "has probably been read by more people before its publication than any other ever printed," joked *The New Yorker*. "As the book was written by the only man in the world fitted for the task, and in a style commanded by only one man in the world, critical comment would seem unnecessary." Most reviewers managed to say the same at greater length. In the New York *Herald Tribune*, Walter Millis called it "a book scarcely paralleled in literature" which "almost defied review." This was "the story of one of the tremendous turning points of world history, told by a great master of English prose, who was himself the leader, the commander, the very heart and soul of the struggle." Professor Preston Slosson in *The American Historical Review* called it "an epic story" told "in epic fashion, as if Cromwell had written in the style of Milton."[22]

Most reviewers agreed with Vermont Royster of *The Wall Street Journal* that the Battle of Britain was "the heart of the story." Several singled out Churchill's visit to Keith Park's headquarters on 15 September 1940—"among the high spots of the book" in the view of Joseph Henry Jackson of the *San Francisco Chronicle*. By contrast, Churchill's chapters on the fall of France attracted much less attention, positive or negative. Wallace Duehl in the monthly *Survey* was rare in complaining that Churchill seemed "considerably less than fair to the French government and general staff and, even more conspicuously so, to King Leopold of the Belgians." Also attracting little comment was the war in North Africa and the Mediterranean—a theater of much less interest to Americans than Britons. John H. Thompson in the *Chicago Tribune* dwelled on the evidence Churchill provided for Roosevelt's nonneutrality, but this was obligatory for any writer in that obsessively anti-Democrat paper. Most who commented on Churchill's theme about America being "half blind" and eventually "half ready" accepted it as painful but just. "The text of history as well as this book, will bear him out," said the New Orleans *Times-Picayune*.[23]

A few reviews reflected on the significance of the volume. Ferdinand Kuhn in *The Washington Post* found "little that was new" about the war—the general story was already clear from Sherwood's *Roosevelt and Hopkins*, captured German documents, and Churchill's own war speeches. But Kuhn was among several perceptive reviewers to see how *Their Finest Hour* was trying to shift attention from the speeches to the minutes: "The most important disclosures are about WSC himself, and of the part he played in guiding, inspiring and galvanizing the British war effort." A. D. Emmart, in the Baltimore *Evening Sun*, agreed: "We remember, of course, Mr. Churchill's great speeches" that heartened Britain and the world, but in this book "we find more than the speeches"—the documentation of a man who had "concerned himself with every aspect of defense."[24]

As to style, James Newman in *The New Republic* felt the second volume fell short of the first. But most reviewers echoed Keith Hutchinson in *The Nation* in praising "a great masterpiece of English prose," with its "inimitable" style. Robert Minton of *The Indianapolis Times* thought the chapter on Dunkirk was "like a movie scenario, thrilling and beyond belief." (One wonders whether this review was read by Gordon Allen, the chapter's principal author.) Kuhn singled out "the best story ever told" of the British Army's desert comeback against the Italians—chapters that Henry Pownall had drafted. Attuned, one suspects, by the volumes of war speeches to expect Churchill the orator, this is what reviewers found in his latest book: great words, all written by the great man.[25]

Most reviewers picked up Churchill's implicit invitation to apply the tag "Finest Hour" to him. For Paul Jordan-Smith in the *Los Angeles Times*, 1940 was "Churchill's finest hour as statesman, war leader and inspirer of the English-speaking world." That summer, wrote Drew Middleton in *The New York Times*, "the man and the hour were one." In his book, Churchill had "made his own ideas, purposes and actions appear the core of the drama of our time," said Norman MacDonald in the *Boston Herald*. "Therein lies the essential part of his greatness."[26] In those American reviews, Churchill must have found ample vindication of his decision to leave the war to history but to be one of its first historians.

IN BRITAIN, the *Daily Telegraph* serialized forty-two installments from 4 February to 30 March 1949, each, as before, filling much of the editorial page. As in America, the book version was harder to produce, with the index a particular problem. Gleefully alerted by Charles Wood, Churchill told Cassell's in March

1949 that he did not think the compiler of the draft index "had a broad comprehension of the story." For instance, "British Empire, end of, 512," was "not quite according to the text," which read, "Germany foresees the end of." As for "B.B.C., rejection of Peace Offer by, 230," this, said Churchill, seemed to indicate "a startling enlargement of the B.B.C.'s functions." The eventual entry reads, "rejection of Peace Offer announced by."[27] Cassell's did not, however, have the same book-club linkage that brought pressure as well as profit to Houghton Mifflin. British publication took place on 27 June 1949, and this edition was free of the egregious errors that had proved so embarrassing in volume 1. When Wood tried to stir up Churchill against the workmanship of Cassell's printers ("a cheap, third-rate production"), he was firmly put in his place by Lord Camrose.[28]

British reviewers were even readier than Americans to adopt the Churchillian framework. For virtually all of them, 1940 *was* the country's finest hour, and most also accepted Churchill's unstated preemption of history's verdict on himself. "Whether or not 1940 was anyone else's finest hour," observed George Orwell, "it was certainly Churchill's." According to Wilson Harris in *The Spectator*, this was "perhaps the greatest story in English history; not impossibly, as these years show him, the greatest man." Woodrow Wyatt, MP, reviewing the volume for *Tribune*, wanted proper tribute to be paid to the British people, "whose determination threw up Mr. Churchill," but even he came grudgingly to the same conclusion: "Of all our Prime Ministers, Mr. Churchill was the most maddening, the most egotistical and the greatest."[29]

Many reviewers also picked up the turning points Churchill wanted them to note, especially his holding back of twenty-five squadrons from the Battle of France. "Mr. Churchill saved them to save us," wrote Malcolm Muggeridge in the *Daily Telegraph*, calling this "unquestionably one of the great decisions in our history." Another, he said, was the reinforcement of the Middle East when the Battle of Britain was nearing its height. In a half-hour radio discussion of the book, the journalists Chester Wilmot and William Clark praised Churchill's assiduous cultivation of Roosevelt—the way he saw "absolutely clearly things about the United States which many people missed." But their appraisal was more rounded than many—faulting Churchill, for instance, for slowness in grasping the nature of blitzkrieg warfare and the way that, despite "generous references" to Dowding, Dill, Eden, and the like, "we hear little of what they did." Churchill was "a giant," yes, "but those around him were not all pigmies."[30]

Another measured assessment came in *The Times Literary Supplement*, where, once again, Churchill's memoirs got front-page billing. Although the events of 1940 "offered him his finest hour as writer," Alfred Ryan, assistant editor of *The Times,* judged that Churchill had not fully taken his opportunity: "An air of hurried composition makes the whole read more like a brilliant exercise in journalism . . . than a balanced and considered work of history." But even this guarded verdict stoked one of Churchill's sensitive points in just the right way, describing him as "a colossus more gigantic than Lloyd George had ever been." And whereas "only students blow the dust from the many volumes" of Lloyd George's "source book" on the Great War, Churchill "still has time to write great history."[31]

Churchill's reaction to this review is not documented. But we do know his response to two others, each of considerable importance. One was by Alfred Duff Cooper, Churchill's wartime Cabinet colleague and himself a literary lion, having written acclaimed biographies of Talleyrand and Haig. Entitled "Winston Churchill and John Bull" and published in *The Listener* on 30 June 1949, it presented *Their Finest Hour* as a tale of two heroes. Churchill, "possessed of imagination and inventive genius, qualities which John Bull both lacks and distrusts, was able to draw out and to develop the slightly sluggish but quite indomitable courage which is fundamental in the character of John Bull." Duff Cooper's piece was an abbreviated version of a radio review of *L'Heure Tragique* that he had broadcast on the European Service of the BBC on 2 June 1949. In that, he elaborated on the themes that mattered most to Churchill, such as the commitment of tanks to the Middle East—"a very great man was required to take such a decision at such a time"—and his "intimate understanding" with Roosevelt. "We are accustomed to think of Mr. Churchill as a great orator and a great writer," Duff Cooper noted, "but this book proves beyond all argument that he is, above all and before all, a great warrior." He likened Churchill in 1940 to Pitt the Elder in the Seven Years War of 1756–1763—"a moment of far less danger"—who exclaimed, "I know I can save this country and that nobody else can." Duff Cooper sent Churchill the text of his talk in advance. "Deeply moved by your proposed broadcast," Churchill cabled. "Thank you so much." He noted for his secretary: "I should like to keep this. Show it to Mrs. Churchill NOW."[32]

It was the reference to William Pitt the Elder (the Earl of Chatham) that seems to have mattered most to Churchill. In the Whig histories by Lord Macaulay and George Macaulay Trevelyan, Chatham was one of the great saviors of the nation. In May 1946, as he embarked on the war memoirs, Churchill had written to Trevelyan, the Regius Professor of History at Cambridge, reminding him of "the inspiring letter that you wrote me in 1941 or 1942. In this you referred to the ill-success which attended Lord Chatham's first two years of war-direction; but how nevertheless later on everything worked out well." Churchill said he had been "much cheered" by the letter at the time, "after so many disappointments and reverses," and regretted he could no longer find it in his files. He went on: "You must not however suppose I am so conceited as to place myself with the great men of the past. It was only the crisis which stood at an equal or even higher level. Those were the days of great men and small events. We have endured an age in which the reverse proportions apply."[33]

This elaborate self-deprecation was transparently contrived. In his peroration to volume 2, Churchill recalls deadly moments of Britain's past, such as the Spanish Armada and the "famous period with Chatham" before asserting that "nothing surpasses 1940." This preoccupation with Chatham was almost a family obsession. His daughter Sarah wrote in her memoirs that "Randolph was everlastingly unhappy that he could not be as the younger Pitt to the elder"—an allusion to Chatham's son, who led Britain against Napoleon.[34] The significance of the Pitt comparison is heightened by two other points. In the past, Churchill had often been compared to Charles James Fox, archenemy of the younger Pitt and the supreme political spoiler. Now, as a modern-day Chatham, he had been welcomed into the national establishment.[35] And Churchill often spoke of the Seven Years War as "the first World War." He used that as a chapter title in his 1938 draft of *The History of the English-Speaking Peoples*, retaining it when the book was finally published in 1956.[36] If Duff Cooper likened him to Chatham in an earlier world war, Churchill could therefore feel confident that his place in the pantheon of British history was secure.

A second review that elicited a strong response from Churchill was by Isaiah Berlin. It appeared in the *Atlantic Monthly* of September 1949 and was a reflection on the man rather than a review of his book, with Churchill counterposed to Roosevelt and Europe to America. He was, said Berlin,

a gigantic historical figure during his own lifetime, superhumanly bold, strong and imaginative, one of the two greatest men of action his nation has produced, an orator of prodigious powers, the saviour of his country, a mythical hero who belongs to legend as much as reality, the largest human being of our time.[37]

Berlin had sent Deakin the twenty-eight-page typescript on 30 May 1949, asking him to show it to Churchill, "with the understanding that I shall not publish anything he might object to." This was partly because Churchill had "shown consideration" to Berlin in the past—presumably meaning the two hundred guineas paid for comments on the draft of *The Gathering Storm*—but more because

Berlin had no wish to "upset or annoy or even slightly irritate the Old Man, for whom my reverence, I discover with some surprise, is without limit." He need not have worried. Deakin told Berlin on 27 June that Churchill's "comment on the passages which he read in my presence was 'It's too good to be true'! And he asks me to thank you for sending it to him—and warmly!"[38]

Berlin commented that "President Wilson and Lloyd George yield in the attribute of sheer historical magnitude to Franklin Roosevelt and Winston Churchill." Here again was a historical marker that mattered to Churchill—equal to Chatham, greater than Lloyd George. But Berlin's central point was to link the man and the nation in a way no other reviewer had done so resonantly. Ignoring the minutes and directives, Berlin went back to Churchill the orator. His "dominant category, the single, central, organising principle of his moral and intellectual universe, is an historical imagination so strong, so comprehensive, as to encase the whole of the present and the whole of the future in a framework of a rich and multicoloured past." Whereas Roosevelt responded with "a kind of seismographic accuracy" to every tremor of his time, Churchill drew on the past "to impose his imagination and his will upon his countryman." Roosevelt reacted, Churchill acted—that was the true measure of his greatness. After he had spoken to the British people in 1940, "as no one has ever before or since, they conceived a new idea of themselves which their own prowess and the admiration of the world has since established as a heroic image in the history of mankind, like Thermopylae or the defeat of the Spanish Armada."[39]

As Berlin's biographer rightly remarks, this "panegyric" was "one of the essays that created the Churchillian myth."[40] Yet the ingredients came from Churchill. In his speech of 18 June 1940, he had identified "their finest hour"; in his book, he mapped out his finest hour. Most reviewers made the equation explicit. In Britain and America, even today, Churchill and 1940 are still inseparable.

AT THE END of October 1949, Churchill was one of two names mentioned in rumors about the Nobel Prize for Literature. In the event, no award was made that year by the Swedish Academy, but the gossip intimated things to come.[41] On 2 November, Churchill did receive the annual *Sunday Times* Literary Award for his first two volumes of memoirs, and Cassell's rushed out its revised edition of *The Gathering Storm*—larger type, better paper, no "poop"—to exploit the publicity. Churchill received his gold medal and check for £1,000 from Lord Kemsley, the paper's owner and also Camrose's brother, at the National Book Exhibition. Apart from some heckling about King Leopold of the Belgians in 1940 by the indefatigable Olive Muir, this was a celebratory and not too serious occasion. Churchill remarked that by the age of twenty-five he "had written as many books as Moses" and that he had "very nearly been keeping up that pace" ever since. But he also reflected, with some feeling, on the "adventure" of writing a book. "To begin with it is a toy, then an amusement, then it becomes a mistress and then it becomes a master and then it becomes a tyrant and, in the last stage, just as you are about to be reconciled to your servitude, you kill the monster and fling him to the public."[42]

Churchill felt that way about most of his books: initial enthusiasm, subsequent boredom, then joyful liberation. But by November 1949, the servitude of authorship was acute. Approaching seventy-five, with only two volumes of *The Second World War* flung to the public, Churchill felt real strain. Although still hoping to kill the monster, he was now secretly afraid it might kill him.

III.

THE GRAND ALLIANCE

1941–1942

1948–1950

"IN THE EVENT OF YOUR DEATH"

O N 3 N O V E M B E R 1949, the day after receiving the *Sunday Times* Literary Award, Churchill dictated a remarkable note to his secretary. "Reminder," it was headed:

To write to Lord Camrose about what arrangements are to be made about carrying on the work on the Book
  (a)   in the event of your return to Office, and
  (b)   in the event of your death . . .
You hope to get some work done in the way of collecting materials for Vols 5 and/or 6, but if either of the two conditions, as above, occurs, you would not be able to do any more work on it.
Keep adequate staff together. Somebody would have to be found to write it and also to do what is necessary to polish Vol. 4.[1]

There is no evidence that Churchill wrote a letter, but he discussed these matters at length with Camrose and with his legal advisers. Constitutionally, the Labour government had to call a general election before the end of July 1950, but Attlee's Cabinet seemed unlikely to last that long. Sluggish economic recovery, soaring defense spending, and a rash of strikes exacerbated the dollar deficit, and on 18 September 1949 the government announced that the pound would be devalued from $4.03 to $2.80. Heavy cuts in domestic spending followed, infuriating Labour backbenchers. An embattled government, running out of steam, was likely to go to the country earlier rather than later, with February 1950 a real possibility.

The electoral clock had always been on Churchill's mind, once he decided in 1945 not to retire from politics. But now it seemed that the grim reaper was also knocking at the gates. On the night of 23 August 1949, staying at Beaverbrook's villa near Monte Carlo, he played cards till two in the morning. Rising from the table, he grunted, "I've got cramp in my arm and leg." In the morning, the cramp was still there, and he found it difficult to write. Lord Moran, Churchill's physician, flew out from London that afternoon, ostentatiously carrying his golf clubs to allay the suspicions of the press. Churchill's speech seemed unaffected, and he could slowly write his name, but he complained of "a veil between me and things" and "a tight feeling" across the shoulder blades. "Have I had a stroke?" he asked. Moran was at pains to sound reassuring: "A very small clot has blocked a very small artery." Churchill stopped work for three days and kept out of the public gaze. He was able to return to England on 1 September.[2]

The press was told that Churchill had "contracted a chill while bathing," but it went down in Moran's diary as "the first stroke." Churchill certainly seems to have taken it seriously. According to Michael Wardell, a Canadian guest of Beaverbrook's who played cards with him on 23 August, Churchill said as he went to bed, "The dagger is pointing at me. I pray it may not strike." A day or so later, much improved, he told Wardell, "The dagger has struck, but this time it was not plunged in to the hilt. At least, I think not. But the warning is there, and I shall have to pay marked respect to it." Wardell's account was not published till after Churchill's death and may have ripened with age, but there is other evidence of Churchill's anxiety. On 24 January 1950, Moran was summoned again. "About an hour ago everything went misty," Churchill told him. "Am I going to have another stroke?" Once more, the doctor played it down: "You seem to get arterial spasms when you are tired." Churchill clearly felt he could not take his life for granted. Physical death as well as political resurrection threatened the completion of his war memoirs.[3]

The anxiety that autumn was evident in discussions about the Literary Trust. After intense scrutiny, the Inland Revenue concluded in February 1949 that the trust was not liable for income tax or surtax on the £375,000 it would receive from the book deal. Churchill told his legal advisers, Anthony Moir and Leslie Graham-Dixon, that this was "a complete vindication" of all their work. "I am pleased indeed and thank you so much." But the taxman could still get revenge if Churchill died within five years of the trust's establishment—in other words, before August 1951—because then the trust would have to pay at least two thirds of its income in estate duty. When the trustees met on 28 November 1949, Randolph and Sarah Churchill, both of whom had recently remarried, wanted larger payouts to the family, but Moir said no. Although Churchill was dissuaded from taking out life insurance against estate duty, because of the heavy premiums at his age, it seems the trust did insure itself against the possibility that the book might not be completed.[4]

The publishers, too, were worried that Churchill might not be able to finish the memoirs. Their insurance policy took a different form: identifying an alternative author. Among the research assistants, only Bill Deakin could have done the task, but he was too junior. The man penciled in by Camrose was Duff Cooper, who had written the review of *Their Finest Hour* that had so pleased Churchill. A former Cabinet minister and a prize-winning biographer, he had sufficient stature in the world of politics and letters to complete *The Second World War* if necessary.[5] In the event, Cooper (born in 1890) died in January 1954, before Cassell's had published volume 6. Churchill (born in 1874) survived him by a full eleven years. But few would have predicted that in late 1949—certainly not Moran, Moir, or Churchill himself. His own answer, characteristically, was to press on with the memoirs at increased speed, but from now on he was cutting corners in order to finish the race. Nowhere is this more evident than in volume 3. The year 1941 was certainly not Churchill's finest hour. Nor, it must be said, was *The Grand Alliance* his finest work.

CHURCHILL DREW UP the first detailed contents page for volume 3 on 23 February 1948. It envisaged two books totaling nineteen chapters (eleven plus eight); the final version was almost double the length (twenty and seventeen).[6] In March, he started sending selected minutes and telegrams to the printer as "the stepping-stones to the lay-out of Volume III." First drafts of early chapters were in circulation in May, and by the time Churchill turned back to complete *Their Finest Hour* in August, Pownall judged that the first book of volume 3 was "pretty firm" but that book 2 had "hardly gone any useful distance."[7]

After clearing *Their Finest Hour* in October 1948, Churchill concentrated on writing up the second half of 1941. "With the arrival of Russia as an ally," he told his assistants on 24 October, "the war has now broadened to such an extent that the scale of the narrative must be altered. It will become more general; operational details must be cut; the broad issues must dominate." He regarded book 1 as "very largely completed," and he had already done thirty or forty thousand words of book 2, mostly on his two meetings with Roosevelt.[8] As before, "completed" was a term of art what Churchill meant was material presentable enough to earn the next tranche from his publishers. He duly cleaned up his 1948 drafts for the May 1949 deadline, restructuring a few chapters in the process, and then got on with volume 4, but his American publishers were extremely unhappy with the result. William Jay Gold, who edited the memoirs for *Life*, considered this admittedly "very rough draft" as "a considerable disappointment" in light of the "very high standards" set by the first two volumes. The publishers had three main concerns: first, the amount of old documents rather than new narrative; second, the mass of material on British campaigns in the Mediterranean and the Middle East, which, Daniel Longwell warned, was "so remote from our public's interest" that *Life* would probably confine its serialization to "a few articles covering the highlights of the book"; third, the fact that the volume hardly got into 1942, making a sixth volume not only probable but almost essential if U.S. readers were to get the detail they wanted on what Henry Laughlin called the "American war."[9]

Churchill's American publishers were agreed that he must paraphrase more documents, cut the detail on the Middle East, and go further into 1942, ideally down to the North African landings in November. Jay Gold at *Life* suggested one rearrangement; Paul Brooks at Houghton Mifflin proposed another, on topical rather than chronological lines.[10] On 16 May, Longwell lunched at Chartwell and pressed the case for revision—so hard, in fact, that it proved counterproductive. A testy Churchill said there was "no question" of enlarging the scope of volume 3: this was "artistically impossible." All right, said Longwell, but would he extend volume 4 to the eve of D-Day? Churchill replied he could not make any decision on this matter for six months. Whereupon Longwell reminded Churchill that the original deal provided for only five volumes and said bluntly that *Life* and *The New York Times* were not willing to make a further payment if Churchill wrote a sixth. In which case, Churchill responded, there would be only five volumes and "a very great mass of important documents" would have to be omitted.[11]

It was clearly a rather unpleasant lunch. Emery Reves believed that Longwell and his boss Henry Luce had handled matters abysmally: "They tried to impose their will on Churchill by pressure. Not even Hitler succeeded in this." On 2 July, Reves found Churchill "inclined to revise considerably" volume 3 but not to extend its timespan. "In my opinion," Reves told Houghton Mifflin, "it would have been easy to convince him to do so, had our friends not tried to bully him, which nobody can."[12]

On 22 August 1949, after reading the galleys for volumes 3 and 4, Reves tried flattery. "Volume I was excellent. Volume II was better. Volume IV is superb," he added. "There is no reason why Volume III should not be a step in this crescendo," but at present it was "weaker than the first two." Reves felt it contained "far too much detail on the African campaign prior to Alamein, on the Middle East and on Naval operations"—in general, excessive minutes and telegrams on "day to day routine operations" sometimes involving "a few battalions." Instead, he wanted Churchill to build up the wartime conferences; because "Roosevelt is dead and Stalin will never publish his documents, you are the only man who can reveal the decisive issues of the last war" at the very top. Churchill's six chapters on his visit to Washington at the end of 1941 were, in Reves's opinion, "the most interesting section of this volume."[13]

Churchill intended to reshape volume 3 in the summer and autumn of 1949. But his vacation in Italy and southern France was initially devoted to volume 4 and then disrupted by his stroke. It was not until 30 September that revised chapters started going to the printers. Churchill worked through the whole volume during October and November but, with Parliament back in session and an election imminent, he had to spend more time in the Commons and on party business. By 8 November, he was ready to sign off. "I am counting on you to let me have this book free of serious errors of fact," he told his assistants. He also wanted further suggestions about "shortenings and transferences from chapter to chapter." With those in hand, he would give book 2 a final read. During this final phase, a good deal was cut and changed—Deakin, for instance, helped radically restructure the North African campaign of late 1941 and the chapters on the Washington conference.[14] But with the election looming, Churchill's health uncertain, and serialization set for the end of January 1950, he had to let go. The "final" text of book 2 was sent airmail to America on 16 December 1949.

"I think you will feel that very great improvements have been made," Churchill told Longwell on 27 December. "I shall be surprised if it does not lay its hold upon you. Hitherto you have seemed elusive to its charms." This was typically Churchillian, of course: the moral of his memoirs included the motto "In Defeat: Defiance." Volume 3 was hardly a defeat, but it could not be called a triumph. In April 1950, Churchill privately acknowledged as much, telling Camrose: "Most of us think that Volume IV is better than Volume III."[15]

ONE PROBLEM with volume 3 was the tension between content and form. Churchill had settled on "The Grand Alliance" as the volume title by 23 March 1948. This had been the name of the coalition against Louis XIV, marshaled by Churchill's ancestor Marlborough. But labeling the two component books was much harder. He started with "Still Alone" and "World War," then shifted to "Hard Trials" and "Mighty Allies." In April 1949, he adopted "Ding Dong" for book 1, printing as an epigraph a quotation from the eighteenth-century novel *Tristram Shandy*: "There is no way but to march coolly up to them—receive their fire, and fall in upon them pell-mell—Ding dong, added Trim." An exasperated Reves pointed out that "very few" foreign readers would recognize the reference or grasp its meaning. "Also the imitation of the sound of bells is different in many languages"—bim bam, for instance, in German. Reves wanted concrete titles expressing "the main event of each book." He favored "The Invasion of Soviet Russia" for book 1, and "War Comes to America" for book 2. Churchill accepted the second but countered with "Germany Drives East" for the first, perhaps because book 1 ends on the eve of the invasion in June 1941.[16]

In most of Churchill's drafts, the "Theme of the Volume" was the same: "How Soviet Russia and the United States were attacked and rallied to the Cause on which their hearts had long been set." At the end of August 1949, however, Norman Brook suggested that the last phrase was "scarcely apt" when applied to the Soviet Union; even "rallied to the Cause" was "not particularly happy." (He could have added that "on which their hearts had long been set" hardly applied to isolationist America either.) In any case, Brook continued, "the entrance of Russia and the United States into the war, though the outstanding events of 1941, are scarcely the theme of this Volume—a large part of which is concerned with our varying fortunes in the Middle East." He therefore suggested a different wording: "How the British fought on, with Hardship their Garment, until Soviet Russia and the United States were drawn into the Great Conflict." These lines were cut out of Brook's letter, pasted onto the late November proofs, and printed word for word in the published volume.[17]*

With this in mind, Churchill decided to mention Brook in his acknowledgments: "I must also thank the very large number of others, including particularly Sir Norman Brook, head of the Cabinet Secretariat, who have kindly read these pages and commented on them." When shown the proposed text, however, Brook was uncomfortable. "I have greatly enjoyed my share of the work on your book," he told Churchill on 28 November, and "I should have been very proud if my name could have been included in the Acknowledgments." But, "after reflecting very carefully upon this I have come to the conclusion that, in view of my official relations with members of the existing Government, it would be better that you should not make this public acknowledgment of my help." The Cab-

---

*Houghton Mifflin's promotion department had already incorporated the original phrase on the dust jacket. No one noticed the discrepancy until Churchill complained when he received an advance copy of the book on 23 March 1950. Laughlin sent an abject apology and arranged for the jacket to be amended once the first impression of 55,000 had been exhausted.

inet Secretary rested his case on "the old rule of anonymity in the Civil Service," but he was doubtless aware that his assistance to Churchill had gone far beyond the call of duty and that he had concealed its full scope from Attlee. Brook, like Bridges, believed he was promoting official history as well as official secrecy, but the Labour government might well have taken a less generous view of his endeavors.[18]

Churchill duly removed Brook's name from the acknowledgments, but the Cabinet Secretary had left his mark at many points. In particular, he had acted as a counterbalance to Reves and Longwell, who wanted to focus on what interested American readers in the depths of the Cold War—the entry of the Big Two into the war. Brook, by contrast, supported Churchill's emphasis on North Africa and the Mediterranean. Commenting in February 1949 on the opening of book 1, he argued that the Middle East provided "the hinge on which our ultimate victory turned" and that "it was in 1941 that the first significant moves in the Middle East began." Much of this book was concerned "with our efforts to maintain, with scanty resources, an effective front" in the desert, Greece, Iraq, Syria, and Crete. "And it was because we preserved our position there, despite all vicissitudes, that we were able to turn it to our advantage in the end." Was not this, the Cabinet Secretary asked, "the connecting thread" that tied together "the various episodes" of book 1?[19]

It is possible that Brook's characterization of the Middle East as "the hinge" of victory gave Churchill his title for volume 4—*The Hinge of Fate*. Certainly Brook's encouragement to sharpen the Middle Eastern theme strengthened Churchill's own intent in volume 3. Brook also urged

> a longer passage of sustained argument on the question of whether it was right to go to the aid of Greece. This has become a matter of public controversy. And, although the documents of the time have an important bearing on that controversy, I think your readers will also expect you to weigh up the arguments, looking back on the past.

Churchill's response was a firm no.[20]

Here Brook had trodden on sensitive ground. About appeasement or 1940 Churchill had few regrets, but there were episodes in 1941 that still nagged at his conscience. The disastrous campaign in Greece in April was one; another was the sinking of the *Prince of Wales* and the *Repulse* off Malaya in December. For these debacles, Churchill bore a large measure of personal responsibility, and he wrestled at length with them when writing his memoirs. He also had scores to settle. The desert war in 1941 had been a catalog of frustrations. He wanted to demonstrate that he had been right and that his generals, Wavell and Auchinleck, had been too cautious to fight—hence, "Ding Dong." At these and other such points volume 3 became an exercise in vindication—a point not fully appreciated by Brook and certainly not grasped by Churchill's American publishers. This personal agenda added more lumpiness to the texture of *The Grand Alliance*.

Thus, Germany versus Russia and even Japan versus America are largely offstage in volume 3. Churchill was frank about the marginality of the Soviet story, telling his assistants in October 1948 that "the gigantic struggle on the Russian front could not claim more than 1,000 to 1,500 words, up to the end of September [1941], and another 1,000 afterwards." Pownall was to "select the salient points," much as he had done for the material on the invasion of Poland in 1939. In his preface, Churchill admits that the Russian front involved "as many divisions on both sides as were engaged in the Battle of France" and on "a far longer front." (An early draft read, "as many or even more divisions.") But he tells his readers that he could not "attempt to do more than refer to the struggle" and that "the Russian epic of 1941 and 1942 deserved a detailed and dispassionate study and record in the English language." This paragraph in the preface seems to serve as absolution for what follows: one chapter, "The Soviet Nemesis," at the end of book 1 and three chapters in book 2. But the gap could have been partially filled if Churchill had not moved "Germany and Russia"—on Hitler's planning for Operation Barbarossa—into *Their Finest Hour*. In its original place, as the opening of *The Grand Alliance*, it would have complemented "The Soviet Nemesis" and firmly established the theme "Germany Drives East."[21]

Japan is accorded one chapter in book 1 and two in book 2. Here, too, the structure weakens the impact of this material. Churchill had omitted all but passing mention of Japan in volumes 1 and 2, and it is only in chapter 31 of volume 3 that he offers any background on the rise of Japan, the militarization of Japanese politics, and Tokyo's policies since the start of the European war. The historical perspective was largely the work of Bill Deakin; the analysis of 1939–1941 came from Geoffrey Hudson, an Oxford specialist on East Asia, who was paid fifty pounds for an essay that, like Deakin's, was printed without substantial change. This material would have been more effective, however, if it had come in chapter 10, where Churchill plunges straight into events in Asia in January 1941, details his warnings to the Japanese Ambassador on 24 February, and then describes at length Foreign Minister Matsuoka's visit to Moscow and Berlin in March and April. This chapter, "The Japanese Envoy," is an effective summary of Axis relations that spring—it originated in another Deakin paper based on published German documents. But without any background material of the sort printed later in chapter 31, it introduces Japan in an abrupt and opaque way.[22]

The ostensible big themes of volume 3 are therefore obscured in Churchill's actual account. The core of book 1 is the extended crisis in the Mediterranean in the spring of 1941, which Churchill documents at length but does not contextualize accurately. Book 2 is more diffuse: the North African campaign continues to bulk large, Russia and Japan now make serious appearances, but the swelling theme is Churchill's relationship with Roosevelt. Introduced by their first wartime meeting in August 1941 (which resulted in the Atlantic Charter), this culminates in Churchill's visit to America over Christmas and New Year's 1941–1942, where the two leaders concerted grand strategy. Again, Churchill documents the story at length; once more, he distorts its significance.

Churchill was essentially a Whig historian—not just because he saw British history as an unfolding story of popular liberties and parliamentary government but in the more technical sense that he wrote narratives of the past that led inexorably into the present. At times, particularly when writing about appeasement in volume 1, Churchill indulges his fascination for counterfactuals—the "what-ifs" of history. In volume 3, however, he is persistently Whig: knowing the outcome, he reads it back into the documents. Thus, knowledge of Barbarossa—Hitler's invasion of the Soviet Union on 22 June—serves to resolve the confusions of the first half of 1941, while anticipation of the victory at Stalingrad obscures the doubts about Soviet survival so prevalent in 1941 and 1942. Similarly, Pearl Harbor casts a long shadow back over his treatment of Asia in 1941, even though it was almost the last event Churchill expected at the time. And D-Day 1944 is the template against which he measures and, where necessary, trims the strategic blueprints he wrote in December 1941. Nowhere is Churchill's history more teleological than in volume 3. "Germany Drives East" and "War Comes to America" do not adequately describe the content of the two books, but these two motifs shaped Churchill's interpretation of what was in reality a most confused and confusing year.

CHAPTER 15

THE CRISIS OF SPRING 1941

A T THE START OF *The Grand Alliance,* readers are directed toward 22 June 1941. In chapter 1, Churchill prints a letter from Hitler to Mussolini on 31 December 1940 asserting that the war in the west was "won" except for "a final violent effort" to crush England and including a long paragraph about Russia and the need for a German army "sufficiently strong to deal with any eventuality in the East." In chapter 2, discussing British strategy in Greece and North Africa, Churchill says that "the main question" in ensuing chapters would be whether the action of the British government "influenced in a decisive, or even in an appreciable manner, Hitler's movements in South-East Europe" and "whether that action did not produce consequences first upon the behaviour of Russia and next upon her fortunes."[1]

Yet Churchill admits in chapter 20 that "up till the end of March I was not convinced that Hitler was resolved upon mortal war with Russia, nor how near it was." This statement simplifies his state of mind even in the period from April to June; in the first three months of the year, when the decision to aid Greece was made, Russia was far from the center of Churchill's strategy. Furthermore, as he again remarks in passing, Hitler intended 22 June as the start of a six-week blitzkrieg, after which German forces would be free for the final overthrow of Britain in the autumn. In the meantime, Britain would be worn down by the U-boat blockade and by aerial bombing.[2]

The bombing campaign is briefly described in a cut-and-paste chapter called "Blitz and Anti-Blitz, 1941: Hess," which runs from December 1940 to May 1941 and includes the British debate over German air strength, Churchill's visit to bomb-damaged Bristol on 12 April, and renewed British efforts to deflect the Luftwaffe's navigation beams. The place of the Blitz in the wider conflict is therefore easily lost. Churchill tells us that in April 1941 he did not regard invasion "as a serious danger" because "proper preparations" had been taken. While he *was* generally more sanguine about this than his advisers, he wobbled on a number of occasions, as Denis Kelly realized when going through the 1941 minutes: "Inconsistent views on invasion to be watched." Nowhere in the volume do we read, for instance, Churchill's minute of 15 February 1941, "Preparation of the Public Mind for Invasion," in which he urged that "the reduction in the population in the coastal zones should begin now." Also absent is his order on 23 June, the day after Hitler attacked Russia, that "our defences are to be brought to the very highest anti-invasion efficiency" by 1 September.[3]

Churchill is more candid about the war at sea: "dominating all our power to carry on the war, or even keep ourselves alive, lay our mastery of the ocean routes and the free approach and entry to our ports." He also notes how in March 1941 he coined the phrase "Battle of the Atlantic" to focus public attention on the problem and raise it to the same plane as the Battle of Britain in 1940.[4] In book 1, Churchill devotes consecutive chapters to the U-boat war—one on the Western Approaches, the other on growing support from the U.S. Navy—plus a third on the threat posed by the *Bismarck* in May. These were all drafted by Gordon Allen, who called the Battle of the Atlantic "perhaps the most important of all operational subjects." But a surfeit of documents clogs the narrative and, as Jay Gold of *Life* observed, the separation of the dramatic *Bismarck* chapter from the other two weakened the cumulative effect.[5]

Book 1, therefore, does not do justice to the continued threat from invasion or strangulation. It is mainly devoted to Britain's war in North Africa and the Balkans. Here Churchill had to address three major operational disasters in April and May 1941: the rapid eviction of British forces from Greece, Wavell's retreat to the borders of Egypt, and the German capture of Crete.

MUSSOLINI INVADED Greece in October 1940, expecting an easy victory, but his troops were quickly driven back into Albania—a spectacular reverse, which the Greeks inflicted almost unaided. Churchill admitted on 6 January 1941, in a memo printed in *The Grand Alliance*, that "the exploits of the Greek Army have been an enormous help to us. They have expressed themselves generously about the extremely modest aid in the air which was all we could give." After reading *Their Finest Hour*, one Greek businessman pointed out to

Churchill that the Greek story cast doubt on his whole theme of Britain standing alone in 1940.[6]

In April 1939, as part of its belated shift from appeasement to containment, Chamberlain's government had guaranteed Greece against aggression. When Italy invaded, Churchill was keen to send air support, against the preference of Eden—then Secretary of State for War and privy to Wavell's plans for a desert offensive. By January 1941, however, Wavell had won his victory, and there were signs that Hitler was turning to the Balkans: it therefore seemed both possible and necessary to stabilize the desert front and concentrate on Greece. Furthermore, Eden had now moved to the Foreign Office and was more sensitive to the diplomatic significance of the Balkans as a whole. In mid-February 1941, he and Dill, Chief of the Imperial General Staff, decamped to Cairo to assess the situation at first hand.

The decision to send troops to Greece, taken by the Cabinet on 7 March, was not made in isolation. Assistance from neighboring armies, particularly the Yugoslavs, would be vital to any successful defense; equally, Britain's readiness to aid Greece might galvanize Yugoslavia and Turkey into forming "a Balkan front"—with "effects upon Soviet Russia which could not be measured by us," Churchill cannot resist adding in chapter 6. "Our duty," he says, was to try to "aid the Greeks," but "our aim" was to "animate and combine Yugoslavia, Greece and Turkey."[7] Eden and Dill therefore kept shuttling among Cairo, Athens, Belgrade, and Ankara. But the Balkan front failed to materialize. British official historians later commented on the "surprising" amount of "wishful thinking" about it in Whitehall.[8] A British-engineered coup in Belgrade simply triggered a German invasion of Yugoslavia on 6 April. That same day, Hitler's troops attacked Greece, and by the end of the month 53,000 British, Australian, and New Zealand troops had been evacuated, with the loss of 11,000 men. The sixth of April was also a black day in the desert. Outflanked by newly arrived German armor, Wavell decided to pull his troops back three hundred miles to Tobruk. This humiliating retreat marked the dramatic entry of General Erwin Rommel into the North African campaign.

By the time Churchill wrote his memoirs, the twin debacles in Greece and the desert were already the subjects of public criticism, with the first often being cited as a reason for the second. General Sir Francis de Guingand's memoirs, published in January 1947, contained a scathing chapter, "The Greek Adventure." De Guingand, a senior planner at Wavell's Cairo headquarters in 1941, claimed the operation never had a chance of success, that the Greeks had been misled about Britain's capacity to help, and that by intervening in Greece "we brought about disaster in the Western Desert and threw away a chance of clearing up as far as Tripoli." De Guingand said he did not know whether "the politician forced the soldier's hand," but his text seemed to finger Eden.[9] In March 1948, the military historian Cyril Falls argued that the British government pushed help on the reluctant Greeks, who feared it would be "too small to be effective" but large enough to provoke Hitler. "Britain insisted in order not to lose face," claimed Falls; "the whole episode now appears a sorry tale of political and strategic frivolity."[10] Falls's history appeared just as Churchill was drafting these chapters. He and Ismay were very conscious of the need to address such charges as they refined book 1.[11]

Ismay's interventions were unusually forthright. He seems to have felt personally affronted by the charge that action in Greece was a political decision, taken against military advice, perhaps because this called into question his own role as Military Secretary to the Cabinet. In a long note for Churchill on 25 May 1948, he emphasized two themes from the printed telegrams. First, "it was the men on the spot, both statesmen and soldiers, who pressed vehemently for intervention in Greece." By this Ismay meant Eden, Dill, and Wavell. "Although you may not wish to mention it in the book," Ismay recalled that Dill's appraisal of the Greek campaign as "a reasonable military venture" carried "great weight" with the War Cabinet and Chiefs of Staff because he normally took "prudence, or might we say caution, to extremes." Ismay's second point was that Churchill, the War Cabinet, and the Chiefs of Staff "made no secret of their military anxiety, and frequently emphasised that we were in no way obliged to send assistance to Greece." But the advice from Eden, Dill, and Wavell made it "almost impossible for the War Cabinet to pull out."[12]

Churchill was inclined to the same interpretation. On 30 November 1948, he told his assistants that

> Wavell spoiled his African show for the sake of the Greek adventure in which he believed and in which he was much pressed by Eden, with the consent of Dill, on general political grounds. If he had refused to go to Greece, he would not have helped the general show, but would have secured his own, which was of great importance. His great mistake was allowing the desert flank to be broken in. I would never have gone to Greece if I had not thought the desert flank was secure.[13]

Yet Churchill had to be careful. Wavell and Eden were still alive—the latter being Deputy Leader of the Tory party—and their approval would be needed before Churchill could quote their telegrams. There was also a Dominion angle, since two thirds of the "British" troops in Greece were Australians and New Zealanders, and their governments had been keenly worried at the time. Deep down, Churchill himself had qualms about his own role. Shaping the story was therefore delicate.

The chapter "Decision to Aid Greece" was heavily reworked after Ismay's intervention in May 1948. Another version added a lengthy quote from Falls's indictment, which Churchill was inclined for a time to use at the start of the chapter. By midsummer, the chapter was becoming, rather as Norman Brook had urged, a full-scale defense of the decision to intervene. But then Churchill backed off. Both Clementine and Bill Deakin suggested he remove the quote from Falls—presumably because there was no reason to highlight the case for the prosecution.[14] And when Eden was sent the draft, he hit back hard against the evident attempt to shift the blame onto him, sending a detailed six-page memorandum on 26 August. "We were scrupulously careful not to impose ourselves on the Greeks," he insisted—implications to the contrary in some telegrams were just "bad drafting on my part." Nor was Eden happy at Churchill's attempts to distance himself from the decision, such as the claim that in late February "I did not feel finally committed to the Greek expedition." Eden also contested the link between Greece and North Africa. "Our failure in the Desert at this time was due to the defects of our armour," he argued, but Britain sent only one armored brigade to Greece, and its retention in North Africa would not have made much difference.[15]

In September 1949, Churchill reworked his discussion of Greece to take account of these objections. He does not highlight the agreement Eden unilaterally concluded with the Greeks on 4 March, which presented the War Cabinet with virtually a fait accompli. He also states, "I take full responsibility for the eventual decision, because I am sure I could have stopped it all if I had been convinced." These amendments blunted but did not remove the original point of the chapter: to reveal the doubts in London and the insistence of the men on the spot. To this end, Churchill prints the damning telegram from the Cabinet to Eden on 7 March 1941, saying that so far he had given "few facts or reasons" to justify the operation "on any grounds but noblesse oblige. A precise military appreciation is indispensable." No such appreciation was ever received. But, equally damning, the War Cabinet still authorized the operation later that day. Although primary responsibility is still left with Eden and Dill, the reader is bound to find Churchill and his colleagues at fault for not probing harder about the military chances.[16] It is interesting that Churchill intended to write a conclusion to the chapter, summing up the story, but could never bring himself to do so. In a draft response to Cyril Falls's verdict, he could say only that the Greek decision "may have been wise or unwise, but Agony rather than 'Frivolity' characterised the process by which it was reached."[17]

Jay Gold of *Life* wanted all the Balkan material to be concentrated in a single chapter, but Churchill keeps the story of Yugoslavia (chapter 9) separate from that of Greece (chapters 6 and 12).[18] As a result, the all-important regional dimension is lost. In August 1949, Eden said, "I have no doubt myself that it was the knowledge that we would help Greece that made the Yugoslav coup d'etat possible." And Churchill's cable to the Australians on 30 March 1941, printed in the text but without special comment, shows how the Yugoslav coup seemed, in turn, to vindicate the Greek decision.

> When a month ago we decided upon sending an army to Greece it looked rather a blank ["bleak" in the original] military adventure dictated by *noblesse oblige*. Thursday's events in Belgrade show the far-reaching effects of this and other measures we have taken on the whole Balkan situation. German plans have been upset, and we may cherish renewed hopes of forming a Balkan front with Turkey, comprising about seventy Allied divisions from the four Powers concerned. This is of course by no means certain yet. But it puts "Lustre" [the Greek expedition] in its true setting, not as an isolated military act, but a prime mover in a large design.[19]

Wishful thinking, of course. Within two weeks, most of Yugoslavia was in German hands; four weeks later, Greece had surrendered, and Turkey stayed on the sidelines. The Balkan front, one of Churchill's grand illusions in 1914–1918, proved equally chimerical a quarter century later. Yet this document, buried in the chapter on Yugoslavia, helps explain why Churchill allowed himself to be persuaded by Eden and Dill into the Greek adventure. It *was* a gamble, but he was playing for the Balkans as a whole, not just one country.

Was he staking Britain's position in North Africa as well? Churchill opens chapter 11 by telling us that "the Desert Flank was the peg on which all else hung, and there was no idea in any quarter of losing or risking that for the sake of Greece or anything in the Balkans." He also prints "an important considered reply" from Wavell on 2 March, when asked to assess the recent German and Italian reinforcement of Tripolitania. Wavell predicted little more than "offensive patrolling," judging that logistics and weather both made a serious Axis offensive unlikely "before the end of the summer." Churchill says that "in London we accepted Wavell's telegram of March 2 as the basis of our action." So far, so fair: Wavell never tried to deny his responsibility—"Looking back on it all, I took too big a risk in the Western Desert," he admitted to Pownall when reviewing the draft chapter in October 1949. Yet Wavell argued that "we might have held all right" but for the inferiority of tanks, both in number and quality, and the fact that "I had certainly not budgetted for Rommel after my experience of the Italians." On Rommel's genius Churchill and Pownall were in agreement—the chapter already included two pages extolling "this new figure" on "the world stage," who arrived in Tripoli in February 1941. On armored units, however, they did not see eye to eye. In chapter 11, Churchill does admit that there were problems but he usually blames poor commanders rather than mechanical defects when explaining Britain's desert disasters in 1941 and 1942.[20]

Nor did Churchill acknowledge how he contributed to Wavell's complacency about the desert front. By early 1941, he was receiving a large quantity of Ultra intercepts, and this encouraged confidence about German intentions. On 27 February, he told the War Cabinet that "there were no indications that the Germans were preparing to attempt the considerable operation of an advance across the Libyan Desert." This was before Axis reinforcements began flowing, but even after they arrived Ultra showed clearly that Hitler's priorities lay elsewhere and that Rommel was supposed to build up his strength rather than mount a substantial offensive. The problem was that these intercepts came mostly from the German and Italian air forces. Only army signals would have revealed that Rommel, still almost unknown to the British, was an audacious general who rarely allowed logistics or even orders to stand in his way. When his probes on 31 March exposed serious British gaps, he vigorously exploited the situation. As late as 7 April, Churchill was using the air force Ultra to tell Wavell that there was no German plan to invade Egypt. When Wavell defended himself in October 1949, he told Pownall, "I should have been more prudent, but no one knows better than Mr. Churchill that a little prudence is often a dangerous thing." One might say the same about the dangers of a little intelligence. This is another theme of the Mediterranean theater in 1941–1942.[21]

RESOURCES, COMMANDERS, and intelligence are equally central to Churchill's account of the battle for Crete, which fell to German paratroops in a week at the end of May 1941. In an early outline, probably from 1947, Churchill said bluntly that "the story of Crete is bad for Wavell. Eighteen days before the attack he had the fullest information. Repeatedly he was enjoined to make every effort to hold the island. I was vexed by the paltry progress." Churchill blamed the failures to turn Suda Bay into a strong naval and air base, to "rearm the large number of resolute soldiers who had arrived from Greece," and to implement his directive to "put a score of tanks in proximity to the airfields and thus destroy all foes who landed on them."[22] From this outline, Pownall's narrative on Crete, and the relevant telegrams, Churchill constructed a damning draft chapter in July 1948. "The resources were available but the mental strength and efficiency of Middle Eastern Command was not adequate for the gripping of these matters," he wrote. On Ultra, Churchill is particularly candid:

> At the end of April our Intelligence Reports gave us full and exact informa-
> tion of the German plan. We knew the general scale and the actual day of the
> impending attacks, both by land, air and sea. I took extraordinary measures
> not only to convey our information to General Wavell, but also to convince
> him of its truth. To General Freyberg, who commanded in Crete, I sent by air
> a special officer to show him the authentic evidence of the kind of attack he
> would have to meet.

In short, argues Churchill, the struggle "hung upon a feather-weight. Any effective addition to the British forces would have given us the victory."[23]

His first draft on Crete was therefore far more assertive than his first on Greece. Whereas Ismay toughened Churchill's Greek material, here Churchill was sharpening Pownall—probably because he never felt any doubts about his conduct during the Crete campaign. As with Greece, however, he faced weighty objections from men whom he could not ignore.

The most significant was Bernard Freyberg, the New Zealand general nearly appointed to replace Wavell in August 1940, whom Churchill personally sent to command Crete at the end of April 1941. In February 1949, Churchill invited Freyberg to comment on a draft of the fulsome biographical passage that introduced him to readers. Freyberg deducted ten scars from the thirty-seven with which Churchill credited him from 1914–1918 and six of the nine from 1939–1945. Having recently talked with Eden about volume 3, he also warned that "your book will be the first history dealing with Crete" and that the impending New Zealand official histories would be "controversial."[24]

Thus put on notice, Churchill sent Freyberg two draft chapters on Crete, to which he replied on 25 March with nine pages of typescript insisting that the campaign was always a forlorn hope. Even if defense preparations had started energetically in 1940, this would have prolonged resistance rather than ensured victory. The motley force salvaged from the Greek evacuation was "small, unequipped, unbalanced, immobile," amounting to "little more than a Division" in total, without a proper headquarters staff. A few more tanks and artillery would not have affected the outcome. Churchill's "featherweight" argument was only true, Freyberg asserted, because of two major German errors: landing their airborne troops on top of the static Allied garrisons and sending in the seaborne forces by night, when the Royal Navy could intercept them without fear of the Luftwaffe. Freyberg also reminded Churchill of the cables he sent to Wavell and his own government on 1 May, when assuming command, stating that the forces he had were "totally inadequate to meet attack envisaged" and urging that the "question of holding Crete should be reconsidered." He added that those cables of 1 May would soon appear in the New Zealand official history. Churchill marked this point in red.[25]

Revisions were made in April 1949 to accommodate most of the objections. The "featherweight" argument disappeared, and Freyberg's cables were given due prominence. Churchill also took account of queries from Wavell and Brook, who both argued that the problem was lack of means, not lack of foresight. Churchill deleted his comment that Wavell "had, in my view, the necessary resources" and also a biting reference to the absence of "three or four men of outstanding quality" at his Cairo headquarters.[26] In deference to "C," the intelligence material was also toned down. Churchill still claims that "at no moment in the war was our Intelligence so truly and precisely informed," and "in no operation" did he take such trouble to weigh the evidence and impart it to local commanders. But the reader is given the impression that the information came from "active and daring" agents in Athens where "German staffs preserved less than their usual secrecy."[27]

Although Freyberg said nothing explicitly about Ultra in his correspondence with Churchill, his reply exposed some of the problems of using secret intelligence.[28] "Nobody then thought that the Germans would use a whole airborne Force for Crete," Freyberg wrote on 25 March 1949. "What we feared most was a seaborne landing with tanks because we had no Anti Tank artillery." During May 1941, Freyberg was given the intelligence evidence showing that the Germans intended a major paratroop drop inland. According to his son, he was even told in strictest confidence by Wavell of the Ultra secret itself. But he was also warned that he must not change any dispositions on Ultra evidence alone, lest German suspicions be aroused, and this tied his hands. Although Freyberg clearly made tactical errors in his conduct of the battle, these in turn may be attributed partly to Ultra. From the few decrypts he saw, Freyberg (unlike Churchill) did not know the Führer's determination to clean up the Mediterranean quickly in preparation

MOST SECRET

A.M. FORM No. 1479
TO BE KEPT UNDER LOCK AND KEY AND NEVER TO BE REMOVED FROM THE OFFICE.
THIS FORM IS TO BE USED FOR AIR INTELLIGENCE MESSAGES ONLY.

NR. No.		GR. No.			OFFICE SERIAL No.	
DATE		TIME OF RECEIPT		TIME OF DESPATCH	SYSTEM	
TO:						
FROM:						

SENDER'S No:

TO AIR MINISTRY (COPY)

CX/JQ/923/T19.

S.E.EUROPE.

OPERATIONS.

FOLLOWING DOCUMENT SENT ON 6/5 BY SIEGFRIED 4. (ROMAN) IA,

TO KURFUERST, (ROMAN) I A, LUFTFLOTTE 4, VIENNA, OPERATIONAL STAFF:-

PROPOSED EXECUTION OF OPERATION MERCURY.

1) PROBABLE DATE FOR ENDING OF PREPARATIONS; 17/5.

2) PROPOSED COURSE OF OPERATION:-

AS PREPARATION, SHARP ATTACK AGAINST ENEMY AIR-FORCE,

MILITARY CAMPS AND A/A POSITIONS.

STAGES OF OPERATIONS FROM X - DAY ONWARDS:-

A) 7TH FLIEGER DIVISION, INCLUDING KORPS - TROOPS OF

FLIEGERKORPS (ROMAN) XI: PARACHUTE LANDING IN

ORDER TO OCCUPY MALEME, CANDIA AND RETIMO.

B) TRANSFER OF DIVE-BOMBERS AND FIGHTERS TO MALEME AND

CANDIA.

C) AIR-LANDING OPERATION BY REMAINDER OF FLIEGERKORPS (ROMAN)

XI, INCLUDING CORPS HEADQUARTERS AND SUBORDINATED UNITS

DISTRIBUTION:

DEGREE OF PRIORITY		TIME OF ORIGIN	SIGNATURE OF ORIGINATOR. NOT TO BE TELEPRINTED		OPERATOR'S RECEIPT

Bletchley Park decoded this Luftwaffe message outlining German plans to invade Crete at some date after 17 May 1941 and Churchill ordered it to be sent to commanders in the eastern Mediterranean. But in his memoirs, to protect the Ultra secret, he implied that the information came from agents in Athens.

MOST SECRET

A.M. FORM No. 1479
TO BE KEPT UNDER LOCK AND KEY AND NEVER TO BE REMOVED FROM THE OFFICE.
THIS FORM IS TO BE USED FOR AIR INTELLIGENCE MESSAGES ONLY.

NR. No.	GR. No.		OFFICE SERIAL No.
DATE	TIME OF RECEIPT	TIME OF DESPATCH	SYSTEM
TO:			
FROM:			
SENDER'S No.			

PROVIDE PROTECTION WITH ITALIAN TORPEDO BOAT

FLOTILLAS MINESWEEPERS SUBMARINE CHASERS AND POSSIBLY U-BOATS.

SEA TRANSPORT BY GERMAN AND ITALIAN VESSELS. OPERATION TO

BE PRECEDED BEFORE ZERO DAY BY SHARP ATTACK ON ROYAL AIR FORCE

MILITARY CAMPS AND ANTI-AIRCRAFT POSITIONS.

B/A/W   HD/DPL   0418/7/5/41.

RD AM 0418/7/5/41. IM
RD BB   " GL

C.

In view of the gt importance of
this I should like the actual text
transmitted by MOST SECRET
together with warnings about
absolute secrecy.
                                          WSC
                                          7.5

DISTRIBUTION:			
DEGREE OF PRIORITY	TIME OF ORIGIN	SIGNATURE OF ORIGINATOR, NOT TO BE TELEPRINTED	OPERATOR'S RECEIPT

for Barbarossa. This may explain why, as he put it to Churchill in 1949, "it never entered my head" that Hitler would commit the cream of his airborne forces to take what was "not really a vital position." For "C," protecting the source of Ultra was a fundamental axiom; Churchill accepted this. But only by letting Freyberg fully into the secret could the Prime Minister have really changed his thinking. Once again, a little intelligence could be dangerous.[29]

Freyberg and others had whittled away the original point of "Crete: The Advent." At the same time, however, Churchill sharpened its sequel, "Crete: The Battle." The German airborne corps, he tells us, was "the spear-point of the German lance. And this is the story of how it triumphed and was broken."[30] The July 1948 draft asserted that 4,000 Germans were killed and 2,000 wounded in the land and air battles, plus 4,000 drowned on troop convoys at sea. But in March 1949, Freyberg suggested 5,600 dead and 11,200 wounded (assuming two wounded for each man killed). Adding prisoners and those Germans lost at sea, "the numbers will be well over 20,000." Although Freyberg's figures were "largely speculative," Pownall told Churchill that "those in the text could safely be stepped up a bit." They were. In the book, we are told that "the enemy must have suffered casualties in killed and wounded of well over fifteen thousand." The British official history, published in 1956, judged that the total killed, wounded, and missing was little over 6,000. By inflating German losses, Churchill offsets the gloom of the previous chapter, almost squeezing victory out of defeat.[31] Even the critical Jay Gold was impressed, calling this "one of the best chapters of Book I."[32]

GREECE AND CRETE are the two epic dramas of book 1, and Churchill's palimpsest chapters testify to the finely balanced arguments for and against. He punctuates these set pieces with narratives of other campaigns in the Middle East. Although those chapters are easy to skim over, they reinforce his case against Wavell.

Chapter 5 narrates the "Conquest of the Italian Empire." Its aim is to show how Churchill prodded the cautious Wavell into attacking Abyssinia in February, rather than waiting until the end of the rainy season in May or June. Wavell secured some softening of the draft—troops standing "idle" in Kenya became "motionless"—but the thrust remains clear. The rapid success of British forces, says Churchill, "showed how unduly the commanders on the spot had magnified the difficulties and how right we were at home to press them to speedy action."[33]

This is also the theme of chapter 14 on "The Revolt in Iraq" in May 1941, when the Prime Minister, Rashid Ali, tried to hand this British client state over to the Germans. Fearful of overcommitment, Wavell urged a negotiated settlement, but, Churchill tells us, "the authorities at home, over whom I presided, directly overruled from Whitehall the judgment of the man on the spot." British reinforcements preempted a German takeover and crushed the revolt by the end of May. Churchill ends with a pregnant conclusion contrasting Wavell's reluctance with the readiness of General Sir Claude Auchinleck, the commander in India, to send troops to Iraq: "The episode could not pass without leaving impressions."[34]

Syria in June was almost a replay of Iraq. As German influence grew in this Vichy French territory, a reluctant Wavell (for a time threatening resignation) was prodded into action on 8 June. Within five weeks, the Allies were in control. The campaigns in Iraq and Syria, says Churchill, ended any German threat to the Persian Gulf and India. They also proved the merits of audacity—that golden rule of Napoleon, his great military hero. "There is always much to be said for not attempting more than you can do and for making a certainty of what you try," admits Churchill. "But this principle, like others in life and war, has its exceptions."[35]

In places, Churchill is unfair to Wavell. He does not make clear that only on 2 May was Iraq moved from the Indian command to that of the Middle East. With Crete, the desert, and Abyssinia all about to explode, Wavell was understandably furious at yet another problem being dropped in his lap, and this explains the asperity of some of his responses. "Your message takes little account of realities," he cabled London on 5 May when ordered into Iraq.[36] By spreading out these operations across separate chapters, Churchill does not convey the magnitude of Wavell's burdens in this vast Middle Eastern theater, despite a few asides about "the mass of business which four or five simultaneous campaigns imposed upon him."[37] He had in fact considered dismissing Wavell on 6 May, for insubordination over Iraq, but decided to await the outcome of the impending desert offensive, Operation Battleaxe. This eventually opened on 15 June, only to fizzle out in a couple of days. Within a week, Auchinleck was moved to Cairo, and Wavell took his place as commander in India.[38]

In Battleaxe, the British lost 87 tanks and suffered about 1,000 casualties, of whom only 400 were killed or missing. "Although this action may seem small compared with the scale of the Mediterranean war in all its various campaigns," says Churchill, "its failure was to me a most bitter blow." Success, he says, "would have meant the destruction of Rommel's audacious force," and the enemy's retreat "might have carried him back beyond Benghazi."[39]

Why had Churchill worked himself up into such a state about Battleaxe? Once again, a major reason is intelligence. Churchill tells us he had "accurate

information of the fearful difficulties of Rommel's assertive but precarious position." In the book, he attributes this information to "a spy in close touch with
Rommel's headquarters," but in fact his prime source was Luftwaffe decrypts.[40]
This created confidence, far greater than reports from a lone spy, that he was
reading Rommel's mail and could see the weak hand the German general was
playing. Hence his sense of hope in May and his desolation on 17 June. What
Churchill never admits—and seems not to have understood—is that although
the British had an advantage over the Germans in strategic intelligence, the
tables were reversed at the tactical level. Not only was British field intelligence
about German dispositions very poor, Rommel's air and land patrols and his
intercepts of radio traffic provided a good picture of British dispositions and
intentions. This point came out strongly in the British official history of the North
African campaigns of 1941, published in 1956, and evidence for it was already
accumulating in the Cabinet Office's Historical Section when Pownall was researching Churchill's drafts, but he never seems to have picked it up. Pownall's
"Comments on 'Battleaxe,'" dated 5 August 1948, note that "the enemy foresaw
the attack" but offer no elaboration.[41] The superiority of German field intelligence offset much of the value of Ultra in the desert war until mid-1942.

Churchill lays the primary blame for Battleaxe at the operational level.
"Rommel's glory was built up on our incompetence," he told Pownall in July
1948. The German "was then at his last impetuous gasp," desperately short of
fuel and ammunition, against an army "three or four times as strong with three
hundred brand new tanks." In the book, Churchill calls Wavell's attack "ill-
concerted" and faults him for failing to "make a sortie from the Tobruk sally-
port," under siege behind enemy lines, "as an indispensable preliminary and
concomitant" to the main advance. Pownall agreed that the "root cause of the
failure was that we were soundly beaten in battlefield tactics." But "even if the
available resources had been better used," Pownall doubted that Wavell could
have reached Tobruk, let alone Benghazi.[42]

In chapter 13, Churchill makes much of his determination to rush extra tanks
to Wavell in early May. He felt that these could have been put to better use in
Crete or the desert. Pownall, amplifying Wavell at the time, stressed the tanks'
mechanical problems, the shortage of trained crews, and the lack of time to prepare infantry for combined operations. After examining materials in the Cabinet
Office, Pownall suggested that the Germans had 300 tanks before the battle. But
Churchill "after studying no records at all, said they had 200." The final text says
"the Germans brought rather over 200 tanks into action against our 180." These
figures were all educated guesses from British reports—the Cabinet Office had

no relevant German documents—but the haggling shows Churchill's propensity to adjust the evidence to suit his case.[43]

To justify the changes in command, Churchill reiterates Wavell's recent failings: Crete, Battleaxe, the tardy intervention in Iraq, and above all "the beating in of the Desert Flank by Rommel, which had undermined and overthrown all the Greek projects on which we had embarked." Prompted by Ismay, he says that "at home we had the feeling that Wavell was a tired man." Churchill admits that he had considered Auchinleck far too cautious in the Norway campaign of 1940. But, as Ismay again noted, he had been greatly impressed by Auchinleck's alacrity in May over Iraq.[44] And so "the Auk" began his Middle Eastern command with a honeymoon that Wavell never enjoyed in 1940.

Churchill's impatience with the generals reflected his real yet limited experience of war—both adjectives should be weighted equally. As a young subaltern, he had served in Africa and India. He had fought and killed, had charged with the cavalry at Omdurman, and led daring patrols on the Western Front. But he did not command any formation larger than a battalion, had never attended Staff College and learned to plan operations, and had no interest in logistics—that essential science of supply. In other words, Churchill knew battle but did not really understand modern war—large-scale, resource-intensive operations involving the mobilizing and deployment of complex formations and different arms. Of course, the complexities of war could induce paralysis. Churchill believed the campaigns in Abyssinia, Iraq, and Syria, not to mention Rommel's success in the desert, showed what could be done by boldness and aggression. "The moral," he told Pownall in July 1948, "is that war consists of fighting, gnawing and tearing, and that the weaker or more frail gets life clawed out of him by this method. Manoeuvre is a mere embellishment, very agreeable when it comes off. But fighting is the key to victory."[45] This sums up his military philosophy.

THE DISASTERS in Greece and North Africa in April 1941 provoked rumblings of discontent about Churchill's autocratic decision making. "It is a complete dictatorship," Lord Hankey told Halifax. One of the Chiefs of Staff complained about "a great deal too much cigar stump diplomacy."[46] Many of these critics were longstanding foes of Churchill, and when the Commons divided on 7 May after a two-day debate on Greece and the Middle East, there was no repeat of the Norway vote a year before: the result was 447 for the government and only 3 against. After Crete, however, it was harder to give the Prime Minister the benefit of the doubt. Wags claimed that the initials "BEF" stood not for "British Expeditionary Force" but "Back Every Friday." "Chips" Channon,

MP, wrote in his diary on 6 June 1941: "On all sides one hears increasing criticism of Churchill. He is undergoing a noticeable slump in popularity. . . . Crete has been a great blow to him."[47] These were inchoate mutterings rather than a clear demand for change, but one wonders how the mood might have developed if Hitler had not relieved the pressure on 22 June by invading Russia.

Churchill originally outlined a separate chapter called "The Parliamentary Front." This featured several addresses he gave on the war situation in April and May 1941, culminating in his 7 May speech during the vote of confidence debate, which sought to answer his detractors, including Lloyd George, who had gone public for the first time. In the draft chapter, Churchill's tone was combative—the word "Front" was used in a military sense. He admitted that the spring of 1941 saw far larger disasters than the ones that toppled Chamberlain a year before yet insisted that his attackers had lost touch with reality: "they might have been criticising what went on in Mars." This brief draft was abandoned in the summer of 1949. Norman Brook wanted a full chapter on "parliamentary difficulties at this time," but such a chapter on 1942 was emerging in volume 4 ("Suspense and Strain"). In consequence, the vote of confidence on 7 May 1941 disappears entirely from *The Grand Alliance* and with it Churchill's defense of government policy—including a striking qualification of his pledge to the Commons a year before:

I have never promised anything or offered anything but blood, tears, toil and sweat, to which I will now add our fair share of mistakes, shortcomings and disappointments, and also that this may go on for a very long time, at the end of which I firmly believe—though it is not a promise or a guarantee, only a profession of faith—that there will be complete, absolute and final victory.[48]

One of the sternest critics of Churchill's war management in the spring of 1941 was Robert Menzies. The Australian premier arrived in England on 20 February and, apart from a few days in Ireland, did not leave until 3 May. He attended War Cabinet meetings, forming strong views about Churchill's courage, energy, and "genius" on the one hand and the dangerous dominance exerted over his colleagues on the other. "Oratorical even in conversation," Menzies wrote, "his real tyrant is the glittering phrase—so attractive to his mind that awkward facts may have to give way." Like Lloyd George, Menzies felt that "Winston is acting as the master strategist, without qualification and without really forceful chiefs of staff to guide him. . . . He has aggression without knowledge." In the Cabinet, Menzies found himself in the role of a "new boy" in "the first week of school," asking the School Captain the awkward questions that no one else would pose, in particular about Greece—an operation he came to question as Eden and Dill failed to send convincing analyses of the military prospects. He was furious at the fait accompli presented by Eden's agreement with the Greeks on 4 March and spoke out strongly two days later about the lack of consultation with Britain's Dominions.[49] This was, in fact, the basic reason for Menzies's visit to London. The New Zealand Prime Minister, Peter Fraser, arrived in England on a similar mission on 21 June.

The Dominions, however, are scantily treated in Churchill's memoirs. It is only from an aside in chapter 3 on the Blitz that we learn that Menzies is in the country at all in 1941. In "The Decision to Aid Greece" we are told that "Mr. Menzies, on whom a special burden rested, was full of courage," but that is all. Not until chapter 22 does Churchill say explicitly that Menzies had "sat through two critical months with the War Cabinet, and had shared many of our most difficult decisions." At this point, Churchill mentions Menzies's proposals for an Imperial War Cabinet, on the Great War model, but adds that the governments of Canada, South Africa, and New Zealand were not in favor.[50] This glosses over an issue of real substance at the time. Fraser's two-month visit to Britain gets even less mention, even though he, too, attended the War Cabinet. This was partly a matter of personality—Jock Colville, Churchill's private secretary, found the New Zealand premier "singularly unattractive and dull" on first acquaintance—but Fraser was making similar criticisms to those of the more charismatic Menzies.[51] Churchill cut from his draft Fraser's questioning telegrams about Greece and Crete but prints his own cables praising the New Zealanders and their "brilliant fighting."[52]

With most of their troops in the Middle East, the governments of Australia and New Zealand were especially anxious about the Far East—"to us the near north," as Menzies put it in 1939.[53] Churchill took little notice of their complaints about Britain's incoherent policy in Asia, but he could not ignore a remarkable blast about imperial strategy from Sir John Dill, Chief of the Imperial General Staff, on 6 May 1941. Although this is printed in *The Grand Alliance*, Churchill completely distorts the context.

On the night of 27 April, a well-lubricated Churchill lambasted General John Kennedy, Director of Military Operations at the War Office, about the vulnerability of Cairo. "Wavell has 400,000 men," Churchill shouted. "If they lose Egypt, blood will flow. I will have firing parties to shoot the generals." In the ensuing argument, Kennedy let slip that contingency plans existed for the evacuation of Egypt. "This comes as a flash of lighting to me," Churchill exploded.

"War is a contest of wills. It is pure defeatism to speak as you have done." The next day, he dictated a directive ordering all plans for the evacuation of Egypt to be recalled. The loss of Egypt and the Middle East, declaimed Churchill, "would be a disaster of the first magnitude to Great Britain, second only to successful invasion."[54]

It was this directive that Dill sought to rebut on 6 May. Although "the loss of Egypt would be a calamity," he did not regard it as "likely" and insisted it "would not end the war"—a "successful invasion alone spells our final defeat." Dill argued "that we have gone to the limit, if not beyond it, in respect of the security of Great Britain" and that no more tanks should be sent to the Middle East over the next three months. Norway, Belgium, Greece, and Libya had shown the danger of underestimating the Germans' capacity for surprise attack. "Egypt is not even second in order of priority," Dill went on, "for it has been an accepted principle in our strategy that in the last resort the security of Singapore comes before that of Egypt. Yet the defences of Singapore are still considerably below standard."[55]

On the next day, 7 May, as the vote of confidence in the Commons was coming to a head, all three Chiefs of Staff sent a formal reply to Churchill's directive. They questioned its priorities, stressing that Hitler might be "tempted to make the desperate gamble of invasion in the hope of gaining a knock-out blow before American help destroys his last hope of success." On 13 May, Churchill hit back at Dill, making clear he would rather lose Singapore than Egypt but arguing that there existed no conceivable Japanese threat. Dill was not cowed, responding the same day, paragraph by paragraph. He recalled that Churchill had himself given priority to Singapore over Egypt in the memo to the Cabinet on 17 November 1939. He agreed that the defense of Singapore required only a fraction of the troops needed to defend Egypt but added that this was "the very reason why I am so anxious not to starve Malaya." And he remarked on "how difficult it is for a soldier to advise against a bold offensive plan. . . . It takes a lot of moral courage not to be afraid of being thought afraid."[56] All this was typical Dill. He loathed verbal fisticuffs with Churchill but fought back hard on paper. This, says his biographer, "left Dill exhausted and Churchill unmoved."[57]

The Grand Alliance does not mention this row at the appropriate chronological place in book 1. It appears only at the start of chapter 23, "My Meeting with Roosevelt," to introduce similar criticisms of Churchill's obsession with Egypt made by the Americans in July. Churchill prints most of Dill's memo of 6 May and much of his own reply a week later but does not mention his 28 April directive, the Chiefs of Staff's paper of 7 May, or Dill's second rebuttal on 13 May. In fact, he totally misrepresents what happened, claiming, "I was of course supported by the Chiefs of the Navy and the Air. My views therefore prevailed." Churchill adds that Dill "must have been himself conscious of this consensus of opinion against him on this aspect, and having struck his note of warning he let the matter drop."[58]

Churchill added this material late. On 10 November 1949, he vaguely recalled "an important minute" from Dill about the Middle East and asked for it to be found. "Does Lord Ismay remember any of my divergences with Dill?" The next revision of "My Meeting with Roosevelt," printed on 14 November, included Dill's 6 May paper and Churchill's response of 13 May. Pownall sent him Dill's second paper, "in case there is anything you want to include in the text," but there is no sign Churchill looked at it. And Ismay, unable to locate the full exchange, encouraged him to believe that Dill's paper was only a "feeler" and that it was not backed by the other two service chiefs.[59]

Churchill's distorted account cannot be explained entirely by the last-minute rush to send off volume 3. He also fails to mention his formidable directive of 28 April—readily available in his files—presumably because that would have shown up his complacency about Japan (as would have the 1939 memos omitted from *The Gathering Storm*).[60] And featuring the full row with Dill would have highlighted the criticism of his leadership in May 1941. Instead, by printing his exchange with Dill well after Barbarossa, when the threat of invasion had receded, Churchill makes Dill's warnings seem almost risible. In the gloom and uncertainty of early May 1941, however, they were not, because at that point no one in Whitehall, not even Churchill, could be sure where Hitler would strike next.

CHURCHILL ENDS book 1 with a dramatic chapter, "The Soviet Nemesis." This opens with a blast about the Kremlin's "error and vanity" in allowing the Balkans to be overrun by Hitler. "Stalin and his commissars showed themselves at this moment the most completely outwitted bunglers of the Second World War."[61] After relating a string of British defeats, it doubtless was a relief to expose far greater follies by the Soviets. Churchill also argues that "a delay of five weeks was imposed upon the supreme [German] operation as a result of our resistance in the Balkans, and especially of the Yugoslav revolution" (which Britain had engineered). "It is reasonable to believe that Moscow was saved thereby." These assertions have been contested by subsequent historians, for whom the late thaw and a shortage of equipment were more significant than the Balkan campaigns in delaying Barbarossa.[62]

Another theme underlined in this chapter is Churchill's superior grasp of intelligence. A whole page is devoted to the slowness of the Joint Intelligence Committee in reaching its conclusion on 12 June, only ten days before Barbarossa, that Hitler intended to attack the Soviet Union without further negotiation. Here, for the first time, Churchill makes reference to the intelligence revolution of 1940–1941. Since the summer of 1940, he says, he had received "a daily selection of tit-bits" of raw intelligence from which he had formed his own opinion, "sometimes at much earlier dates" than the JIC. And so, Churchill goes on, it was

> with relief and excitement that towards the end of March 1941 I read an Intelligence report from one of our most trusted sources of the movement and counter-movement of German armour on the railway from Bucharest to Cracow. . . . To me it illuminated the whole Eastern scene like a lightning-flash. The sudden movement to Cracow of so much armour needed in the Balkan sphere could only mean Hitler's intention to invade Russia in May.

He immediately offered his reading of the intelligence to Eden in Athens and cast around for some way of passing it on to Stalin.[63]

"One of our most trusted sources" was, of course, Ultra, and this passage — so central to Churchill's argument — required a good deal of redrafting. The reference was actually to a Luftwaffe intercept dated 27 March, which he read on the thirtieth, but Pownall warned against giving an exact date, since "no *ordinary* agent could have got the message through in three days." From Churchill's telegram to Eden on 30 March Pownall removed the reference numbers of the intercepts, and a commendation of "searching and vigilant British intelligence" became a tribute to "our agents on the spot."[64]

Less justifiably, Churchill also distorts the debate in Whitehall: he claims that the Chiefs of Staff "were ahead of their advisers," citing a cable they sent on 31 May. But from that message he cut a sentence showing that the Chiefs were by no means sure that the Russians would fight if the Germans did invade. If Hitler got what he wanted by mere threat, or if the Soviets collapsed as soon as they were attacked, then he could turn back on Britain in a few weeks with impunity. Although Churchill was undoubtedly more confident about the Red Army than many of his advisers — he makes a point of quoting Dill on 22 June: "I suppose they will be rounded up in hordes" — he could not be sure. The memoirs do *not* quote his striking message to Roosevelt on 1 July: "I am asking that everything here shall be at concert pitch for invasion from September 1st."[65]

Jay Gold of *Life* considered this "an absorbing chapter." It addressed major issues and made big claims—none more so than Churchill's indictment of Sir Stafford Cripps, the British Ambassador in Moscow, for failing to pass on the "lightning-flash" intelligence of 27 March about the German threat. This had been conveyed to Cripps in a brief message on 3 April, for delivery in person to Stalin—the Prime Minister's first communication to the Soviet leader since June 1940. Churchill claims Cripps did not reply until 12 April and then to say he had already conveyed lengthy warnings of the German buildup to Andrei Vyshinsky, the Deputy Foreign Minister, and felt that delivery of Churchill's "short and fragmentary" message would weaken their effect. Churchill tells us he was "vexed" at this reply, pressing Eden for immediate delivery, but on 19 April Cripps sent the message to Vyshinsky, who transmitted it to Stalin. Thus, there was no personal meeting between Cripps and Stalin to drive home the point. "I cannot form any final judgment upon whether my message, if delivered with all the promptness and ceremony prescribed, would have altered the course of events," Churchill admits. But he suggests that if his instructions had been "carried out effectively," they "might perhaps" have saved Stalin from having "so much of his Air Force destroyed on the ground."[66]

This whole attack on Cripps is, however, misconceived, because the Ambassador had in fact been urging the Foreign Office for months to send Stalin a clear warning of the Nazi buildup. It is likely that Churchill grasped the import of the 27 March intercept only because he had taken charge of the Foreign Office while Eden was in Athens and was shown corroborative evidence, including the file from Cripps. Until then, his eyes still focused on Greece and Yugoslavia— hence the "lightning-flash." Churchill is also unfair to Cripps about the delay in transmitting the 3 April message. The Ambassador actually replied on the fifth to explain his reservations, and Churchill explicitly agreed that the cable should be sent to Russian Foreign Minister Vyacheslav Molotov instead. He later changed his mind, but this initial consent removes much of the sting from his barbs about Cripps's obstruction.[67]

Once again, we find Churchill in 1941 being less decisive than he imagined in 1949. When treating the episode in his memoirs, he did not go back to the original sources but relied on a digest of the telegrams drawn up by his staff in October 1941. This made no reference to Cripps's cable of 5 April and jumped straight to his message on the twelfth.[68] The digest had been commissioned when Churchill learned, to his anger, that Stalin had told Beaverbrook he could recall no warning in April. And so an unwarranted wartime grievance was transformed into a postwar historical "truth."

Did Cripps's failure to transmit the message promptly and personally to Stalin make any difference? Almost certainly not. The resulting delay was only a couple of weeks, and there was, in any case, plenty of high-grade intelligence coming to Stalin from his own sources. The problem was not one of information but of preconceptions—the Soviet leader believed that the evident German buildup was part of Hitler's war of nerves rather than a prelude to a surprise attack. This obsession with one cryptic message shows Churchill at his counterfactual worst.[69] Moreover, he fails to appreciate how any faint chance that the suspicious Stalin would heed information from the British was undermined by their handling of a far more important matter: the Rudolf Hess mission.

Why the Deputy Führer flew solo to Britain on 10 May 1941 remains a subject of absorbing interest. Conspiracy theories abound, intensified by the slowness of Whitehall in declassifying relevant files and by suspicion that it is still holding things back. The material currently available does, however, corroborate the essentials of Churchill's account. This was a crazy one-man peace mission, unauthorized by Hitler, and Hess did not disclose German plans for the attack on Russia. Churchill dictated his basic account in November 1948, treating Hess as "a medical and not a criminal case" whose story would not have merited much space but for the curiosity it had aroused. Hess's motives, he suggests, were a desire to get back into Hitler's affections by winning peace with Britain, adding that "such moods, however naïve, were neither wicked nor squalid."[70]

It is noteworthy that Churchill discusses the Hess mission in chapter 3 (on the Blitz) and not in its proper chronological place. The effect—like his misplacement of Dill's powerful papers of May 1941—is to imply that it has little relevance to the real history he describes. That is quite wrong. How the British handled Hess publicly was almost more important than what Hess said in private. In May 1941, everything seemed dire: Greece was lost, Crete about to fall, Rommel stood poised in the desert, and the U-boats were strangling Britain's lifelines. So desperate was Churchill that on 3 May (in a cable not printed in the memoirs) he asked Roosevelt for immediate American entry into the war—a plea he had not made since the darkest days of June 1940.[71] In the east, Hitler was clearly massing his forces, and, whatever Churchill's hunch about Soviet survival, the result might be a new Nazi-Soviet Pact rather than a war to the death. Even if the Red Army did fight, it seemed likely to go the same way as the French. Hence Churchill's new alert for preparations against invasion in September.

Onto this bleak stage, enter Hess. It quickly became clear that his mission was a nonevent, but at least for a moment Hitler had lost the initiative. How best to exploit this propaganda opportunity? In *The Grand Alliance*, Churchill fails to discuss his intense argument with the Foreign Office about what should be said in public. After the initial interrogation of Hess, the Prime Minister prepared a detailed statement for delivery to the Commons on 14 May that confirmed that Hess was sane, that he had not acted on Hitler's authority, and that his self-imposed goal was to persuade Britain to make peace, believing there was "a strong peace or defeatist movement" in Britain. Eden and Cadogan blocked Churchill's statement, arguing that it was much better to keep the Germans and the world guessing. If the Americans thought Britain was now so desperate as to consider a negotiated peace, that might move them closer to entering the war. To the Soviets, the Foreign Office represented the Hess affair as the result of a split in the Nazi leadership, thereby implying that Stalin should not be too confident of reaching a new deal with Berlin.[72]

The campaign backfired completely. Moscow was uncertain whether Hess presaged a new Nazi-Soviet Pact or an Anglo-German alliance against Russia. Such speculation further blurred the impact of intelligence about the German buildup and encouraged Stalin's suspicion that warnings about it from Cripps and Churchill were British misinformation, to drag him into the war. According to the 1995 version of Marshal Zhukov's memoirs, Stalin insisted on 12 June 1941 that "Germany is busy up to her ears with the war in the West and I am certain that Hitler will not risk creating a second front by attacking the Soviet Union. Hitler is not such an idiot."[73] Ten days later, the Panzers started to roll: Germany had turned east with a vengeance. But that was far clearer in retrospect than it seemed to British leaders, even Churchill, in the spring crisis of 1941.

CHAPTER 16

FORGING AN ALLIANCE

B OOK 2 of *The Grand Alliance* lacks a firm intellectual structure, particularly in the middle; in fact, chapters were being moved around until the very end. Churchill started it late, and plans for revision were overtaken by the election buildup and the need to press on with later volumes. He was now posing fewer questions to his assistants and nodding through more of their work—the important chapter "Closer Contacts with Russia" on the autumn of 1941, started life as a paper by Deakin and was published with few substantial changes.[1] Some questions did engage Churchill's mind and his heart, notably the sinking of the *Prince of Wales* and the *Repulse* by the Japanese in two hours on 10 December 1941. He also devoted a good deal of attention to his visit to Washington after Pearl Harbor, ensuring that the volume ended on a high note. But these efforts could not resolve his basic structural problem—namely, the emerging tension between autobiography and history. The two were one in 1940—Britain's finest hour was also his—but by late 1941 that unity had gone. Churchill's war, Britain's war, was waged in the African desert and the Atlantic sea-lanes, but a world war was boiling up across the plains of western Russia, the jungles of Southeast Asia, and the islands of the Pacific. Soviet survival and American belligerency were the decisive events of late 1941, yet Churchill had little impact on either. This was his problem as Prime Minister and also as historian eight years later.

THE OPENING CHAPTER of book 2, "Our Soviet Ally," includes an unusual amount of narrative, much of it from Churchill's 1947 dictation, "History of the

War." Here he sets out several key themes for his treatment of the Soviets in the rest of the memoirs. These include the unrealism of their demands for a second front, his efforts to establish a personal correspondence with Stalin akin to the one with Roosevelt, and the problem of how to reconcile the goals of Polish independence and Soviet security. Churchill argues that Soviet entry into the war "was welcome but not immediately helpful" because Britain had to make "very large diversions of our weapons and vital supplies of all kinds" and because much of the American aid sent to the USSR would otherwise have gone to Britain. In consequence, "we had to cramp all preparations which prudence urged for the defence of the Malay peninsula and our Eastern Empire and possessions against the ever-growing menace of Japan." Summing up, Churchill says,

> Without in the slightest degree challenging the conclusion which history will affirm that the Russian resistance broke the power of the German armies and inflicted mortal injury upon the life-energies of the German nation, it is right to make it clear that for more than a year after Russia was involved in the war she presented herself to our minds as a burden and not as a help.[2]

Yet Churchill also insists that throughout 1941–1942 "I took a more sanguine view than my military advisers of the Russian powers of resistance." This is prefigured at the end of book 1 in his radio speech on the evening of 22 June 1941, welcoming the Soviet Union as an ally and, although not renouncing his aversion to the Soviet system, insisting that Nazi expansion was far worse. In his memoirs, he quotes from an account provided by Jock Colville, who had remarked on 21 June about his U-turn. "If Hitler invaded Hell," retorted Churchill, "I would at least make a favourable reference to the Devil in the House of Commons."[3] In reality, Eden was the warmest advocate of aid to Russia, even calling for a big cross-Channel attack in 1941. Churchill was generous with words but stingy with hardware—as one might infer from occasional sentences in the mass of telegrams in the book, such as one to Beaverbrook on 30 August in which he said that "no large flow [of aid] can begin till the middle or end of 1942, and the main planning will relate to 1943."[4]

Churchill's claim to have been more confident than his Chiefs of Staff about Russian resistance, though strictly true, also requires qualification. On 24 October 1941, he estimated the chances of Moscow falling before the winter as "evens." The next day, he predicted that "in a month or so" the Soviet Union "will have been reduced to a second-rate military Power"—allowing Hitler to redeploy two thirds of his army to threaten Britain. And on 5 November he told the Chiefs of Staff, "I cannot feel any confidence that the Germans will be prevented from occupying the Baku oilfields." These three documents all appear in the memoirs, though only the last is printed in a chapter ostensibly about Russia.[5] In October 1949, he cut a reference to "the vague but increasing menace of a German passage across Turkey or break-through in the Caucasus" and also emasculated the text of a major paper he had written for the Americans in January 1942. This was done "for reasons of space," he tells readers, but the main removed passage urged an Anglo-American army of some fifteen divisions to defend the Persian Gulf. If the Red Army collapsed in the Caucasus, Churchill warned his allies, "the loss of the oilfields of the Caspian and Persia, and of all the regions between the present Russian front and the frontiers of India cannot be excluded from our thoughts."[6]

Meanwhile, Stalin kept demanding greater military help and agreements on postwar arrangements. Churchill tells us, "I proposed therefore to make a further attempt to smooth out relations between us by offering to send Mr. Eden himself on a mission to Moscow."[7] Again, this is misleading. It was Cripps who had been demanding such a visit for weeks, to help allay Russian suspicions. Frustrated by the lack of response in London and by his exclusion from top-level meetings, the Ambassador was now hinting at resignation. If this prominent left-wing politician returned home to denounce official policy, at a time of mounting popular support for Russia, he might seriously damage the government. On 15 November, Churchill drafted a telegram daring Cripps to come back and foment political opposition "by making out that we had not done enough" for Russia. "You must not underrate the case I could deploy in the House of Commons and on the broadcast," he warned. Eden dissuaded the Prime Minister from dispatching the telegram, and the Cabinet sent a more conciliatory message to Cripps, playing up Eden's readiness to come to Moscow.[8] None of this background appears in Churchill's memoirs, possibly because Deakin, who drafted the chapter, did not use the Prime Minister's working files, which contain the draft telegram to Cripps.[9]

Churchill's mood had changed markedly since June 1941. "After his first enthusiasm," Eden's private secretary noted on 27 October, "he is now getting bitter as the Russians become a liability." In his memoirs, Churchill admits that in October he could not rule out Hitler stabilizing the Eastern Front for the winter to allow a springtime invasion of Britain.[10] Yet, characteristically, his response to uncertainty was not paralysis but opportunism. Hitler might not remain in the east, but while he was there offensive action was possible elsewhere. As in 1914–1918, Churchill looked to the flanks: the Baltic and the Mediterranean. There are brief asides in *The Grand Alliance* to his ideas for an attack on Norway, which actually provoked a massive argument with the War Office in October over his demand for an immediate plan to seize Trondheim.[11] The memoirs are much fuller about the other flank, especially his scenario for a desert offensive to take British forces to Benghazi or even Tripoli. Not only would this, he assured Roosevelt with customary breeziness on 20 October, "alter the whole shape of the war in the Mediterranean" by prompting Spain and Turkey to shift to the Allies, but it would also permit the seizure of Sicily and perhaps Sardinia, from which "a heavy and possibly decisive attack" could be made on Italy by Allied bombers. But the window of opportunity seemed brief. For Sicily "it is probably a case of 'Now or never,'" he wrote on 25 October. "In my view by the end of December these prospects will be indefinitely closed."[12] Here is further evidence that Churchill never took Russian resistance for granted.

Any thrust at Sicily or Italy depended on Auchinleck's autumn offensive into Libya, code-named Crusader. Churchill recounts his disappointment that this was delayed until November, blaming "a disproportionate concern for our northern flank" toward the Caucasus and the Auk's belief that he needed 50 percent reserves in tanks. "Generals only enjoy such comforts in Heaven," Churchill observes caustically. "And those who demand them do not always get there."[13] Churchill's drafts were even more scathing, but Ismay, Pownall, and Norman Brook all enjoined moderation. "If I might be quite frank," pleaded Pownall in June 1949, "I think you are being overhard on Auchinleck." He argued that if the Auk had attacked with any less armor than was deployed on 18 November, he would have been defeated; further, his anxiety about the Caucasus was understandable given Russia's precarious situation. Pownall even quoted some of the Prime Minister's own missives on the latter subject. Under pressure, a grumpy Churchill removed phrases such as "an obstinate, high-minded man" and changed the chapter title from "A Costly Interlude" to "An African Pause." But he did not alter his basic conclusion: "I must record my conviction that General Auchinleck's four and a half months' delay in engaging the enemy in the desert was alike a mistake and a misfortune."[14]

By then, any hopes of exploiting the success of Crusader were dashed, as Churchill notes, by a succession of disasters for Britain's Mediterranean Fleet. In four weeks, it lost an aircraft carrier, three battleships, and two cruisers. These "fearful naval losses," says Churchill, plus Hitler's decision to transfer a whole air corps from Russia to Sicily meant that Britain lost control of the Mediterranean and allowed "the refit of Rommel's armies," which had been previously on "the brink of ruin."[15] The brief window of opportunity, through which he had hoped to squeeze, was slammed firmly shut.

Not surprisingly, Churchill's response to dashed expectations was to sack senior commanders. In October 1941, he chose Lord Louis Mountbatten to replace Admiral Sir Roger Keyes as head of Combined Operations for raiding the Continent. In December, Sir Alan Brooke took over from Dill as Chief of the Imperial General Staff. Both these changes are noted in book 2. In the case of Keyes, Churchill mentions the need for a younger man and the "friction" Keyes had generated in the Service Departments, but a draft was more candid, speaking of Keyes's unconcealed resentment at not having been made First Sea Lord. Dill's removal is mentioned only in passing, without explanation, but again a draft was more revealing—Churchill linked it directly to Dill's advocacy of Singapore over Cairo in their strategic battle in May 1941.[16] In the early draft of "An African Pause," he claims he also thought of sacking Auchinleck at the end of July 1941 for delaying the desert offensive but then realized he could not appoint yet another commander so soon after Wavell. It was only after persistent pressure from Ismay that this material disappeared.[17]

Apart from blaming commanders, Churchill also turned his mounting frustration on Australia, three of whose four infantry divisions were in the Middle East. In the first half of 1941, its Sixth Division was thrown into Greece, the Seventh spearheaded the campaign in Syria, and the Ninth had to sustain the siege of Tobruk. In the summer, the Australian government demanded that the Ninth be relieved and also consolidated into a single Australian corps, to avoid the Aussies being thrown piecemeal into yet more disasters. Its deeper concern, voiced by Menzies during the debate on Greece, was the lack of consultation by Britain over strategy. Auchinleck, equally understandably, did not want to pull the Ninth Division out of Tobruk—a potentially hazardous naval operation under enemy fire—and feared that to do so would delay his renewed offensive against Rommel. In 1941, Tobruk had therefore been very sensitive, and Churchill's handling of it in 1949 became an issue for the British and Australian governments.

At the time, there was bipartisan support in Australia for the relief of Tobruk. The first demands were made by Robert Menzies, and one brigade had been withdrawn before he was toppled as premier at the end of August 1941. His short-lived successor, Arthur Fadden, continued the pressure, as did the new Labor premier, John Curtin, from October until evacuation was complete. But Churchill's account of the story, originally a separate chapter entitled "The Relief of the Australians in Tobruk," throws the onus firmly on Fadden and Curtin. Deletions he made on a copy of one of Menzies's telegrams suggest that this was not accidental. Churchill began work on this chapter in the autumn of 1948, after Menzies's visit to Chartwell had set their personal relations on a very different footing from those of his last spell in Britain in 1941. In any case, Menzies's Liberals were far more congenial to Churchill than the Australian Labor party. Menzies was therefore built up in successive drafts of the Tobruk saga into the "ablest figure" in the Australian government and distanced from Fadden and Curtin, with whom "relations were not as easy." Churchill even suggests that Fadden made a fuss because of "hard pressure" from Labor, "a party Opposition thirsting for local power."[18] This leads him to a larger point: the failure of the Australians to form a coalition government. One draft contained the sentence: "It was astonishing that in the dire peril in which we all stood Party interests in Australia could not have been subordinated as in Britain to the general cause." With lengthy quotations he sets out his own attempts to make Fadden and Curtin relent and describes how, faced with their obduracy, he was forced to tell Auchinleck that the evacuation must proceed. "It has given me pain to have to relate this incident," he concludes. But "to suppress it indefinitely would be impossible. Besides, the Australian people have a right to know what happened and why."[19]

When Norman Brook read the draft chapter in February 1949, he grasped its diplomatic sensitivity, warning Churchill that he would have to consult Attlee and Canberra. Aware of acerbic comments elsewhere in Churchill's drafts about the Australians in Southeast Asia, Brook proposed an overview chapter about Australia and imperial defense from the siege of Tobruk to the fall of Singapore. Its approach could be reflective and retrospective, "showing how, as events proved, their fears were exaggerated." This would not require much wartime documentation or, in consequence, Canberra's approval. Brook feared that if Churchill published his own papers, the Australians would ask for their side of the story to be printed as well.[20] Brook was also worried about the upcoming Commonwealth Foreign Ministers conference, scheduled for January 1950, and the efforts by British military planners to draw a skeptical Australia into new defense commitments in the Middle East. This was not the time to reopen wartime wounds. The Cabinet Secretary's discreet persistence paid off. In October 1949, the separate chapter "Australia and Tobruk" was merged with its predecessor, on Auchinleck's postponed offensive, making its argument less visible. Churchill moved the most contentious telegrams to an appendix, cut some of his aspersions on Australian politics, and added a summary, composed by Brook, of why Canberra wanted to pull out its troops.[21]

Brook now told Attlee that, although Churchill had expressed himself "somewhat trenchantly" in early drafts with "some rather rancorous telegrams," the final version handled "these difficult episodes with moderation and restraint." Attlee duly approved Brook's message to Ben Chifley, Australia's Labor Prime Minister, which was deftly composed. Whereas Brook had shown Attlee relevant extracts from Churchill's text, Chifley was sent only the telegrams that Churchill wished to quote—all by Churchill. Making it even harder for Chifley to object was the tone of the message Brook had written for Attlee, which made it clear that London had no objection to his publishing any of the telegrams. Even so, Chifley did demur. On 26 November, he asked that Churchill quote Canberra's 1941 replies to explain more fully Australia's position not only on Tobruk but also on imperial consultation. He also noted that, since much of Churchill's 1941 correspondence was with Menzies and Fadden, he would have to consult them before giving a final response.[22]

This reply did not suit Churchill, faced with a looming publisher's deadline. Fortunately for him, Chifley was defeated in the election on 10 December 1949 by Menzies, now a close friend, and Brook was able to broker a compromise. Churchill moved the post–Pearl Harbor rows about Southeast Asia into the next volume, which gave time for further reflection, and assured Menzies that his own narrative (not sent) fully explained Australian views on imperial consultation. On that basis, Menzies and Fadden offered no objection to Churchill printing his own telegrams about Tobruk and did not push for more on Australia's position.[23] A possible Commonwealth crisis had been averted, thanks to Brook's finesse and the accidents of Australian politics, but Churchill's treatment of Australia's war would prove to be one of the most sensitive issues in volume 4.

OF ALL BRITAIN'S friends in 1941, the United States was the most important. Churchill starts the American theme strongly in the second chapter of book 1, describing the visits to London in January by Harry Hopkins, Roosevelt's confidant, and Wendell Willkie, the defeated Republican candidate in 1940, as well as the departure of Lord Halifax to be Ambassador in Washington. In chapter 8, on the Battle of the Atlantic, he discusses the extension of U.S. naval patrols as far as Greenland and the Azores—America, he tells us, was "moving ever nearer to war."[24] But enactment of Lend-Lease in March gets only the briefest mention, as does the replacement of British by U.S. troops in Iceland in July. Nor does Churchill mention the top-secret American-British staff conversations held in Washington from January to March 1941, which developed contingency plans for a combined strategy if the United States became Britain's ally. Some of the key documentation was included in his preliminary files for volume 3, but nothing appeared in the eventual text.[25]

This sporadic treatment of America is further evidence that Churchill did not really take a firm grip on volume 3. On 1 October 1949, Bill Deakin pointed out how the American theme faded away after January 1941, but Churchill did not respond.[26] Yet some of the neglect was intentional. The way Roosevelt maneuvered the United States into an undeclared naval war in the Atlantic during 1941, behind the back of Congress, had become political dynamite in the United States. Critics of the President, such as Charles Beard, and defenders, such as Robert Sherwood, had already revealed a good deal of evidence, and *The Grand Alliance* could have supplied much more. At their Atlantic meeting in August 1941, Roosevelt told Churchill that "he would wage war, but not declare it, and that he would become more and more provocative. If the Germans did not like it, they could attack American [naval] forces." Warned by Churchill of deteriorating British morale, the President "made clear that he would look for an 'incident' which would justify him in opening hostilities."[27] These extracts from Churchill's account of the meeting for the Cabinet do not appear in his memoirs, though he uses material from that account on other matters.[28] Presumably, he wished to avoid providing further ammunition to the President's critics.[29]

In consequence, however, Churchill distorts the significance of the Atlantic meeting on 9–12 August. He sailed to their rendezvous off Newfoundland excited to be meeting Roosevelt for the first time. He had forgotten their brief encounter in London in 1918—a source of some irritation to FDR as Robert Sherwood had noted in *Roosevelt and Hopkins*—and evidence of this misconception was deleted from the telegrams Churchill printed in the memoirs.[30] Of even greater excitement was his belief that at last the President was on the verge of declaring war. "I do not think our friend would have asked me to go so far for what must be a meeting of world-wide importance," he told the Queen just before leaving, "unless he had in mind some further forward step."[31] He and British opinion in general were seriously disappointed when, instead of a declaration of war, they got only a declaration of war aims. In his memoirs, Churchill spends some time on the resultant Atlantic Charter, not only because it proved to be one of the most celebrated documents of World War II but also because it had already been used as a centerpiece of Elliott Roosevelt's memoir attacking Churchill's outmoded imperialism. In "The Atlantic Charter," Churchill counters strongly: "Considering all the tales of my reactionary, Old World outlook, and the pain this is said to have caused the President, I am glad it should be put on record that the substance and spirit of what came to be called the 'Atlantic Charter' was in its first draft a British production in my own words." He prints the whole of this first draft as "my text."[32]

These assertions are misleading. On the first night of the conference, 9 August, Roosevelt suggested they concoct a joint declaration of principles. The next morning, Churchill demanded an immediate draft, telling Sir Alexander Cadogan of the Foreign Office, "in broad outlines, the sort of shape the latter should take." Over his eggs and bacon, Cadogan worked up a text, about which Churchill "expressed general but not very enthusiastic approval," but it was typed up virtually unchanged for the Prime Minister to give to the President. Churchill's reference to "my text" is therefore economical with the truth. It is hard to believe this was accidental because he had borrowed Cadogan's diaries in the spring of 1949, and the entry there for 10 August 1941 made clear the sequence of events.[33]

Churchill also misrepresents his own attitude toward the whole idea. For months, he had resisted pressure from Labour and Tory members of his Cabinet for a statement of British war aims. "I am very doubtful about the utility of attempts to plan the peace before we have won the war," he told Eden in May 1941.[34] His enthusiasm for the Atlantic Charter was therefore an about-face: he needed something to show from the meeting, and the Atlantic Charter could be represented as a tacit alliance. Yet in Britain afterward there was a real sense of letdown. On 28 August 1941, Churchill sent a cable to the White House reporting a "wave of depression" in the Cabinet and fears that the Russians would be out of the war by 1942. "Should be glad," he told Hopkins for Roosevelt, "if you could give me any sort of hope."[35] None of this appears in the memoirs.

Apart from the Atlantic Charter, the other big issue at the conference was the Far East. Again, the story is seriously distorted in the memoirs. Churchill says little of substance about Japan in book 1 of *The Grand Alliance*. He does not, for instance, print his angry minute rebuking the British planners in Washington for pushing the reluctant Americans to promise a fleet for Singapore. "The first thing is to get the United States into the war," he wrote on 17 February 1941. "We can then best settle how to fight it afterwards." This minute was originally slated for inclusion in chapter 10, but in early 1949 the Foreign Office feared that these sentences would provide ammunition for American opponents of the new NATO treaty, and the minute was first edited and then cut entirely, probably because it again revealed Churchill's complacency about the Far East: "We think it unlikely that Japan will enter the war against Great Britain and the United States. It is still more unlikely that they would attempt any serious land operations in Malaya . . . while a United States Fleet of adequate strength remains at Hawaii."[36]

During 1941, Britain's dilemma became ever more acute. The State Department failed to keep London properly informed of its contacts with Japanese emissaries about a possible Far East settlement. Nor was there prior consultation when the Roosevelt administration unilaterally imposed an oil embargo on Japan in July. Neither of these issues receives more than passing mention in *The Grand Alliance*. Churchill does print several telegrams he sent from Newfoundland indicating that the President had agreed to give Japan "a very severe warning." But then the Far East again recedes into the background—we are not told that the President reneged on his promises and produced yet another waffly statement of principles.[37]

It is only in chapter 31 that Churchill devotes himself fully to the problem of Japan. Long passages of historical background by Bill Deakin and Geoffrey Hudson precede Churchill's minutes and telegrams for the six weeks before Pearl Harbor. Linking these two sections is a reflective passage of dictation. "The reader has seen from the first day of the war our anxieties about Japan weighed relentlessly upon us," Churchill writes disingenuously. "I confess," he adds more honestly, "that in my mind the whole Japanese menace lay in a sinister twilight, compared with our other needs." Churchill reaffirms his priorities in 1941, arguing that "nothing we could have spared at this time, even at the cost of wrecking the Middle Eastern theatre or cutting off supplies to the Soviets, would have changed the march of fate in Malaya. On the other hand, the entry of the United States into the war would overwhelm all evils put together."[38]

Writing of Washington's final negotiations with Tokyo, Churchill admits that London was sometimes surprised and disconcerted by shifts in the American posture. But, in a passage of some importance, he implies that this was mostly because of delays in transmitting vital intelligence:

> From the end of 1940 the Americans had pierced the vital Japanese ciphers, and were decoding large numbers of their military and diplomatic telegrams. In the secret American circles these were referred to as "*Magics*." The "Magics" were repeated to us, but there was an inevitable delay—sometimes of two or three days—before we got them. We did not know therefore at any given moment all that the President or Mr. Hull knew. I make no complaint of this.

These sentences were some of the last to be finalized, on 22 December 1949.[39] This is because, amazingly, Churchill had only just discovered Magic. His 8 November proof included the first two sentences of this passage but then continued, "This deadly fact was not imparted to us. We did not know what the President knew." The revised chapter was referred by Brook to "C," Sir Stewart Menzies—

the head of MI6—who preferred to say that information was delayed rather than concealed. Churchill complied with this request and revised the passage into the form printed above. Menzies explained that in 1941 Churchill was not formally told about Magic but that decrypts from the Americans were passed to him by "C" in the daily selections of the juiciest intelligence. "I am not accepting this," Churchill exploded on 5 December 1949. "I should have been informed by them or you." He asked "what information about the 'magics' was actually in my possession during the ten days before Pearl Harbor." When Menzies checked his files against the messages printed in the congressional inquiry into Pearl Harbor, he concluded that both he and Churchill had not been sent some of the final intercepts: "I believe it was purely by mistake, and not intentional, that the Americans did not pass us the 'deadline' messages which appear in the Congressional Report."[40]

Churchill had by then lost interest in the problem. "I am returning the book and the telegrams which you so kindly looked out for me," he wrote Menzies on 27 December 1949. "I think the chapter is 'watertight' now."[41] But if it is true that Churchill was not indoctrinated into Magic in 1941 and some eleventh-hour intercepts were not shared with the British, this reinforces the impression that London failed to grasp the hardening of U.S. policy in late 1941 and the way this provoked rather than deterred Japan. It also renders even more dubious claims that Churchill withheld from Roosevelt information about an attack on Pearl Harbor. The existing evidence strongly suggests that by December 1941 both leaders were expecting Japanese aggression in Southeast Asia but not such an audacious strike on the U.S. Pacific Fleet at Hawaii.[42] As late as 2 December, Churchill told Eden it was "unlikely" that the Japanese would seize the Kra Isthmus, linking Thailand and Malaya—a phrase that he edited out of the minute when preparing the memoirs. He also excised references to the President's eleventh-hour promise to Lord Halifax that if the Japanese did attack Kra, in Halifax's words, "we could certainly count on their support." If British or Dutch possessions were attacked, the President added, then "we should obviously all be together." Such passages, the Foreign Office feared, might feed conspiracy theories that FDR allowed the Japanese to bomb Pearl Harbor in order to prod a reluctant America into war. On similar grounds, Churchill removed his comments that Roosevelt and his advisers "had long burned to take part in the war against Hitler" and saw in the Japanese attack on American possessions "a vast simplification of their problems and their duty."[43]

A vivid passage, dictated in 1947, tells how he learned of the attack on Pearl Harbor casually from BBC radio, in the company of Averell Harriman and John

G. Winant, the U.S. Ambassador. His first draft said the two Americans received the news with "exaltation—in fact they very nearly danced for joy," but he rewrote that to read more discreetly: "one might almost have thought they had been delivered from a long pain." He was, however, candid about his own response: "No American will think it wrong of me if I proclaim that to have the United States at our side was to me the greatest joy"—"in my life," the first draft went on. He was sure "we had won the war. England would live; Britain would live; the Commonwealth of Nations and the Empire would live." In this, the purplest passage of a rather monochrome volume, Churchill expatiates on the potential of the United States, recalling Sir Edward Grey's comment during the Great War that America was like "a gigantic boiler. Once the fire is lighted under it there is no limit to the power it can generate." Being "saturated and satiated with emotion and sensation," he concludes, "I went to bed and slept the sleep of the saved and thankful." His first draft continued: "One hopes that eternal sleep will be like that."[44]

THREE MORNINGS LATER, however, his mood was very different. In another vivid reminiscence, Churchill says that he was working in bed on 10 December when Dudley Pound, the First Sea Lord, came on the line: "His voice sounded odd. He gave a sort of cough and gulp, and at first I could not hear quite clearly." Then Churchill gathered that the *Prince of Wales* and the *Repulse*—Britain's only capital ships in Far Eastern waters—had been sunk by Japanese aircraft. "Are you sure it's true?" he asked. Pound said there was no doubt. "I put the telephone down. I was thankful to be alone. In all the war I never received a more direct shock. . . . As I turned over and twisted in bed the full horror of the news sank in upon me." Across the "vast expanse" of the Indian and Pacific Oceans, "Japan was supreme, and we everywhere were weak and naked."[45]

The Pearl Harbor passage is grandiloquent; here the words are short, the phrasing staccato. "Turned" and "twisted" are masterful verbs. The loss of these two great ships was a devastating blow for Churchill. In August, he had traveled on the *Prince of Wales* to his meeting with Roosevelt; the two leaders had shared in a moving act of worship on the battleship's quarterdeck. Weightier still, it was on Churchill's personal insistence that the *Prince of Wales* had been sent to Singapore. The decision reveals two of his greatest errors as a strategist: underestimation of Japan and complacency about naval airpower. It also tells us a good deal about Churchill's relations with his military commanders.

In his chapter "Japan," Churchill quotes minutes he sent the Admiralty in late August 1941 demanding "a deterrent squadron in the Indian Ocean" using "the smallest number of our best ships." Pound, the First Sea Lord, did not want to release any of the most modern battleships—the *King George V* class (*KGVs*)—which were needed nearer home. His aim was a balanced fleet at Singapore by early 1942, but Churchill demanded an immediate gesture to cow Japan. "Nothing would increase her hesitation more than the appearance of the force I mentioned," he told Pound on 29 August, "and above all a K.G.V. This might indeed be the decisive deterrent." After summarizing this exchange and printing the documents in an appendix, Churchill simply tells us that "it was decided to send as the first instalment of our Far Eastern fleet" the *Prince of Wales*, the *Repulse*, and four destroyers, plus the aircraft carrier *Indomitable*. "Unhappily the *Indomitable* was temporarily disabled by an accident," but it was agreed "to let the two fast capital ships go forward, in the hope of steadying the Japanese political situation." Accordingly, Admiral Sir Tom Phillips set sail on 24 October and proceeded via Cape Town to Singapore.[46]

Churchill's account does not conceal his confidence that a few modern battleships could deter Japan from war, but it distorts the process of decision making. When he first raised the issue in August, backed by Eden and the Foreign Office, Pound argued successfully that no *KGVs* could be spared. On 17 October, Churchill revived his proposal in the War Cabinet's Defence Committee, backed by Eden and Attlee; again, Pound stood his ground. But in another meeting three days later, the First Sea Lord agreed to send the *Prince of Wales*, on the condition that the position was reviewed when it reached Cape Town. This second debate is not mentioned in the memoirs. Churchill and his assistants might not be expected to dig deep into the Defence Committee records, but Pound's conditional agreement was clearly recorded in the telegram Churchill sent to the Australian and New Zealand governments on 25 October, which he prints in his chapter.[47]

Admiral Phillips reached Cape Town on 16 November. By that time, it was clear that the damaged *Indomitable* could not proceed to Singapore, thereby eliminating almost all air cover, yet there is no record of the promised review. When the official history of Britain's war at sea was being finalized in 1953, there was a long argument about this lacuna. Supporters of Pound claimed he had been overruled verbally by the Prime Minister; Churchillians such as Leslie Rowan insisted that this was not how the Prime Minister dealt with his military advisers on "matters of first-class importance," though he "might on occasion have induced them to acquiesce in a decision against their better judgement."[48] The gap in the records has never been filled or explained.

After two days at Cape Town, Phillips steamed on to meet the *Repulse*, and both ships reached Singapore on 2 December. Before leaving South Africa, Phillips had a brief meeting with the Prime Minister, Jan Smuts. Throughout his memoirs, Churchill makes extensive use of his correspondence with Smuts, but he does not print the latter's telegram on 18 November, after his meeting with Phillips about the danger of Britain and America having fleets at Singapore and Hawaii, each separately inferior to the Japanese Navy: "If Japanese are really nippy there is here opening for first-class disaster."[49] In his chapter on Pearl Harbor, Churchill describes a meeting late on 9 December to discuss the disposition of the two battleships in the light of the attack on the U.S. fleet. His thought now was that "they must go to sea and vanish among the innumerable islands" or perhaps "join what was left of the American Fleet." But he and his advisers "decided to sleep on it," and by the time they awoke next morning the two great ships were "at the bottom of the sea." Churchill's three and a half pages on their fate makes clear Phillips's complacency about the danger of air attack but also admits that this was a general failing in both London and Washington.[50]

Churchill's personal attitude toward these events was complex and seems to have shifted over time. In April 1948, he blamed the disaster on the absence of the *Indomitable*. In January 1950, he ascribed it to the novelty of torpedo bombers, which, he claimed, had never been used before in the Mediterranean or Europe. "This is a great defence of Tom Phillips," he wrote, only to be rebutted by a memo from Allen showing how and when torpedo bombers had been used by all the powers, including Britain. Japan's success, Allen insisted, was mainly due to strategic surprise and tactical skill.[51] At other times, Churchill seems to have blamed Phillips himself. In August 1953, he insisted that Phillips should have disappeared into the Malayan islands until the rest of the fleet arrived. The attempt to intercept the Japanese invasion force without air cover was, he claimed, "the last thing in the world that the Defence Committee wished." And by 1955 he was telling the anecdote of Phillips's running argument during the 1930s with "Bomber" Harris about the threat posed by airpower to seapower. "Tom," said Harris on one occasion, "there's no reasoning with you. One day you'll be on the bridge of your ship and you will be hit by bombs and torpedoes dropped from the air. And as you sink you will swear it was a mine."[52]

In August 1953, Churchill was reported by Norman Brook as still "very emotional" about the loss of the ships and of "his friend" Tom Phillips. In the memoirs he speaks of Phillips as being formerly "our trusted Vice-Chief of the Naval Staff."[53] Yet Phillips seems to have forfeited Churchill's affection by insisting earlier in 1941 that the diversion of troops and ships to Greece would jeopardize Egypt and Malta. After Churchill denounced Phillips as a "defeatist," the two men parted angrily, and one senior Admiralty official recalled that shortly before leaving on the *Prince of Wales* Phillips lamented that the Prime Minister had not spoken to him for eight months.[54]

The evidence for this is anecdotal, but Churchill had similar run-ins with other senior officers. In May 1941, he sacked Sir Arthur Longmore, the air commander in the Middle East, who had also criticized the intervention in Greece. Nowhere is this mentioned in *The Grand Alliance*: suddenly Longmore is gone, and Churchill is sending telegrams to Arthur Tedder. Nor does Churchill say that after Crete, Admiral Sir Andrew Cunningham, commander of the Mediterranean Fleet, was ready to resign, having complained without success about having to conduct the operation without adequate air cover.[55] Churchill did not learn the lesson: like Tom Phillips, he was still living in the battleship era. Phillips paid for such complacency with his life and those of 800 seamen; Churchill's twists and turns of anguish on hearing the news continued long afterward on paper.

DISASTERS IN THE Far East made it all the more urgent to concert global strategy with the Americans. "As soon as I awoke" on the morning after Pearl Harbor, Churchill tells us, "I decided to go over at once to see Roosevelt." He recalls his fears that Pearl Harbor would induce an "America First" policy in Washington—cutting back on aid to Britain to build up American strength and perhaps to concentrate on revenge against Japan. The first draft added, "I thought of staying at the British Embassy, as I did not know how stiff our discussions might be," but then the President sent "a cordial invitation" to stay in the White House.[56]

Churchill set out on 12 December aboard the *Duke of York*. The eight-day voyage gave him and his military advisers time to reflect on the new strategic situation. His chapter "Proposed Plan and Sequence of the War" prints the bulk of three magisterial surveys composed on the boat, which he entitles "The Atlantic Front," "The Pacific Front," and "The Campaign of 1943." The last, he says, would refute the "many tales" about his "rooted aversion from large-scale operations on the Continent" by presenting "the authentic and responsible documents written at the time." Churchill claims he "always considered that a decisive assault upon the German-occupied countries on the largest possible scale was the only way in which the war could be won, and that the summer of 1943 should be chosen as the target date."[57]

These words were carefully chosen and, read with equal care, are not inaccurate. But they do not mean that in December 1941 Churchill was envisaging the campaign of 1944. In his paper he wrote: "We have therefore to prepare for the liberation of the captive countries of Western and Southern Europe by the land-ing at suitable points, successively or simultaneously, of British and American armies strong enough to enable the conquered populations to revolt." As possible landing points he instanced Norway, Denmark, Holland, Belgium, the French Channel and Atlantic coasts, and also Italy and the Balkans (if North Africa was liberated in 1942). Eventually, three or four of these points should be specifically targeted, with troops hitting the beaches from specialized landing craft. "It need not be assumed that great numbers of men are required," he went on—perhaps forty armored divisions, or 600,000 men, of which Britain would supply half, plus one million backup troops: "If the incursion of armoured formations is success-ful, the uprising of the local population, for whom weapons must be brought, would supply the corpus of the liberating offensive."[58]

Armored landings at several points in occupied Europe to galvanize the local populations are not, of course, what took place on D-Day. The scenario owes more to 1940 than 1944, particularly the SOE conception of "setting Europe ablaze" and Churchill's renewed ardor for tank warfare after the Nazi blitzkrieg and the Wehrmacht's early success in Russia. Nor is "The Campaign of 1943" a blueprint for total victory. Summing up for the Chiefs of Staff, Churchill said the war could be divided into three phases: "closing the ring," "liberating the popula-tions," and "final assault on the German citadel." The first of these corresponds to his paper "The Atlantic Front" in 1942, the second to "The Campaign of 1943," but nowhere does he explain how the German citadel itself would be subdued, as distinct from the occupied territories. Perhaps the loss of the latter would have a domino effect on the homeland; perhaps he anticipated the sudden 1918-style collapse of German resistance that he talked about in 1940; maybe he felt he had looked ahead far enough. "He is an unwise man who thinks there is any certain method of winning this war," he wrote in October 1941. "The only plan is to per-severe." (Or, as he put it in private, KBO: Keep Buggering On.) At any event, nothing is spelled out here on the ultimate end of the Reich. Churchill's Decem-ber 1941 scenario ends with Allied armies back on the Continent, pressing against Germany from several sides—the equivalent of 1915 not 1918.[59]

The other paper from December 1941 that Churchill prints is entitled "The Pacific Front." Here some considerable sleight of hand is involved. Churchill actually wrote four papers, not three, on the voyage across the Atlantic, but for the memoirs he dropped the original "Pacific Front" paper (number 2) and gave that title to the fourth, originally called "Notes on the Pacific." Why the omission? He says in a draft (when planning to consign paper 2 to an appendix) that it was "a somewhat technical memo on the naval aspect," but that does not explain the subterfuge of claiming that he wrote only three papers. Perhaps he was embarrassed by what the paper revealed of his continued complacency about Singapore, which in December 1941 he still expected to hold out for six months: "A large Japanese army with its siege train and ample supplies of ammunition and engineering stores will be required for their attack." Talk of sieges and siege trains, redolent of the days of Marlborough, accorded ill with Japan's Pacific blitzkrieg, or for that matter with the plans for armored warfare Churchill himself was sketching out for Europe in 1943.[60]

The paper he does print on the Pacific is also revealing. This conceded that the Japanese had temporarily achieved naval superiority, though Churchill hoped that by May 1942 the Allies could form a superior battle fleet in the Pacific. In the interim, he refused to remain on the defensive, urging a concentration of aircraft carriers and "improvised carriers"—warships converted to carry even a dozen planes—to gain local air superiority for long enough to attack the enemy's new conquests. (As with tanks after the blitzkrieg in May 1940, so with naval airpower in the aftermath of Pearl Harbor: Churchill quickly seized on new developments in warfare to which he had previously been somewhat blind.) He accepted that this redeployment of airpower to Asia, against all his previous preferences, would retard the bombing of Germany in 1942. But a savage next paragraph, which he deliberately did not print, urged a massive air assault on the Japanese to deter them from further "overseas adventures" and shake domestic morale. "The burning of Japanese cities by incendiary bombs will bring home in a most effective manner to the people of Japan the dangers of the course to which they have committed themselves."[61]

Churchill presents all these papers to his readers as visionary and prescient scenarios for the eventual Allied victory. Because he does not print related material from his advisers, he conceals the fact that his papers were also intended to win a bureaucratic battle with the Chiefs of Staff. The Prime Minister was seriously concerned by what he saw as their apparent belief, after Pearl Harbor and the loss of the *Prince of Wales*, that nothing could now be done anywhere without air superiority. And he was appalled by their contention that "until we have disposed of Germany and Italy we must accept the fact that the Japanese will be able to run wild in the Western Pacific." Extravagant rhetoric about aircraft carriers and local air superiority was his response to such passivity. Nor would he accept their claim that "the attainment of air predominance will be a prerequisite to the invasion of the Continent and not a concomitant or result of such operations." Hence his refrain about "liberating offensives," unleashing the power of the subject populations. In other words, his papers of December 1941 were not really

Olympian surveys. They were framed to win an immediate debate in which, once again, he saw himself pitted against defensive-minded commanders and used hyperbole to overcome their caution.[62]

Churchill also had American opinion in mind. Talk of Japan simply being allowed to "run wild" would be disastrous in a vengeful Washington. His sudden enthusiasm for carrier strike forces reflected the need to persuade the Americans that they could still act in the Pacific while giving overall priority to the war against Germany. After some spirited exchanges aboard ship, the Chiefs of Staff recognized that further argument was pointless. "The important thing," they told the Prime Minister on 22 December, as the *Duke of York* neared the end of its voyage, "is that we speak to the Americans with one voice."[63]

This common line was one reason why the British got much of what they wanted in Washington, at a time when American planners were in disarray after Pearl Harbor. Confirmation of the "Germany First" strategy was particularly important. Overall, Churchill says, there was "complete agreement on the broad principles and targets of the war." Ismay wanted a special mention about setting up the Combined Chiefs of Staff, offering a draft saying that "when history comes to be written, the verdict will be that this decision had a greater effect on the conduct of the war than any other single decision that was taken either by the Higher Commands or in the field." Since that accorded the Combined Chiefs greater significance than Churchill himself, it was not surprisingly revised. Instead, we are told that the establishment of a shared machinery for directing the war, based in Washington but with permanent British representatives in close touch with London, "may well be thought by future historians" to be "the most valuable and lasting result" of the conference.[64]

Accentuating the positive as usual, Churchill slides over moments of friction during the American trip. He plays down the fury of Secretary of State Cordell Hull that "the so-called Free French," whom America did not recognize, had unilaterally seized the Vichy islands of St. Pierre and Miquelon. Churchill says that Hull, "for whom I entertained the highest respect," had "pushed what was little more than a departmental point far beyond its proportions." In draft, Churchill claimed that the Secretary cut "a rather pathetic figure" in an incident that "did not enter at all into our main discussions."[65] Also neglected in the memoirs is the long-running Anglo-American debate about the "Consideration" Britain would provide in return for Lend-Lease—never intended by Roosevelt as a gift. The State Department wanted an end to the special tariff preferences given to goods from the British empire and Commonwealth. Churchill did plan to print a minute on the matter that he sent to Lord Halifax on 10 January 1942 but then changed his mind. Kelly's comment "Explain how this arose" may have been one reason—Churchill did not have space for a lengthy contextual aside—but the content was also problematic. His minute assured Halifax that the idea of a Consideration was a product of prealliance diplomacy: "With every month that passes the fighting comradeship of the two countries as allies will grow and the haggling about the lend-lease story will wane." In the event, the haggling over economic relations got worse. This minute was not Churchill's most prescient, and that may explain its exclusion from *The Grand Alliance*.[66]

Despite a few such examples of cosmetic surgery, Churchill was justified in putting a good face on the conferences of December 1941 and January 1942. Driven together by shared disasters in Asia, the two governments found much to agree about, and relations at the top were notably close. Churchill prints parts of his acclaimed speech to the U.S. Congress, though not his splendid line that if his father had been American and his mother British, rather than the other way around, he might have reached Capitol Hill on his own. He does quote his remark on Christmas Eve that although far from his family he did not feel far from home. And he describes the close bond forged with the President while a guest in the White House. On reflection, however, he did not repeat the story, already published by Robert Sherwood, about Roosevelt being wheeled into Churchill's suite on one occasion only to find the Prime Minister emerging from his bath, "stark naked and gleaming pink." FDR started to withdraw, but Churchill called him back. "The Prime Minister of Great Britain," he announced, "has nothing to conceal from the President of the United States."[67] Why Churchill did not include this anecdote, much loved by Hopkins and also related by others, is not clear—perhaps he felt it lacking in dignity. But it epitomizes the mood of Anglo-American relations at that grim moment of the war.

CHAPTER 17

"MAN OF THE HALF-CENTURY"

THE WRITING OF CHURCHILL'S war memoirs was always inter-twined with his continuing careers as national leader and international prophet. At no time was this more evident than in the opening months of 1950. On 2 January, *Time* magazine, part of the Henry Luce empire, proclaimed Churchill its "Man of the Half-Century." On 26 January, *The New York Times* and the *Daily Telegraph* began serializing *The Grand Alliance*, followed by *Life* eleven days later. Over the next month, Churchill threw himself into a general-election campaign, on 23 February just failing in his bid to return to 10 Downing Street. Once again, he was making history in the present as well as the past. In 1950, as before, the reception of his memoirs was bound up with his current reputation.

TIME STARTED its Man of the Year award in January 1928, to celebrate Charles Lindbergh's solo flight across the Atlantic in 1927. Those subsequently honored were not always men—for instance, Wallis Simpson, the American divorcée who cost Edward VIII his throne. Nor were they all heroes: whereas *Time* shunned Osama bin Laden, the obvious choice in 2001, it had no qualms about choosing Hitler for 1938 and Stalin for 1939 and 1942. In January 1941, *Time* gave Chur-chill its accolade, praising his inspirational speeches of 1940 delivered in a "brandy-harsh" voice. "Those who write history with words sometimes forget his-tory is made with words," *Time* reminded its readers.[1]

In January 1950, *Time* declared that "Churchill's story comes closest" to summing up "the dreadful, wonderful years 1900–50." He was always at the heart of the action, from the Boer War to the trenches of Flanders, from defiance of Hitler to the Cold War against Stalin: "That a free world survived in 1950, with a hope of more progress and less calamity, was due in large measure to his exertions." Quoting liberally from the war memoirs, the magazine lauded his success in rallying Britain and the world against Hitler: "Some of the passages of his wartime speeches are as ready to the tongue of 1950 as anything in Shakespeare." It also made much of the Fulton speech—"one of his greatest services for Western civilization," in which he "flourished his membership card in the union of practicing prophets"—and brought the story right up to the present, with Churchill getting ready for his thirteenth British general election. "He would fight it—as he had fought all his other great battles—on the issue of freedom. Churchill likes freedom. He has been with freedom on some of its darkest and brightest days."[2]

The Man of the Half-Century as perennial man of the moment was a compelling theme in 1941 and in 1950. But it was also convenient. In 1941, Henry Luce was a vehement supporter of the Allied cause; in 1950, he was keen to promote Churchill's memoirs, on which he had spent more than three quarters of a million dollars. In both cases, boosting Churchill was not a disinterested act, but each Man of the Year essay shows how Churchill's own words, as orator and historian, helped form his reputation.

On 3 February 1950, Cassell's published *Europe Unite*, an edition of fifty-two of Churchill's speeches from 1947–1948. The title came from his keynote address to the Congress of Europe in The Hague in May 1948 and served as a reminder that Churchill was an apostle of European unity, not just of the Cold War alliance. There was plenty of domestic material as well. "By the time this book appears, a General Election may well be in progress," Randolph Churchill wrote in his editor's introduction. "These pages contain a formidable indictment of the Socialist Government and an urgent plea for new men and new measures." The contracts had been signed in July 1949, long before the election date was announced, but once again Churchill's timing was fortuitous, and *Europe Unite* fed directly into the election campaign.[3]

Churchill was also adding new rhetoric to his old. On 14 February 1950, in a speech in Edinburgh, he offered a formidable if partisan survey of world affairs. Where he praised Labour, it was because Ernest Bevin had "followed with steadfastness the line I marked out at Fulton." Mostly he blamed Labour for losing, at least "for the time being," Britain's rank as one of the "Big Three" and for failing to capitalize on all Britain's wartime research to build the country's own atomic bomb, calling it "one of the most extraordinary administrative lapses that has ever taken place." Yet Churchill also wanted to find "some more exalted and august foundation for our safety than this grim and sombre balancing power of the bomb." He urged "another talk with the Soviet Union at the highest level," so that the two countries might live "if not in friendship at least without the hatreds of the cold war." As at Fulton in 1946 and the Tory conference in 1948, Churchill exploited his status as sage and seer: "You must be careful to mark my words in these matters because I have not always been proved wrong. It is not easy to see how matters could be worsened by a parley at the summit, if such a thing were possible. But I cannot tell."[4]

Not surprisingly, the Tory press was full of praise. "One of his finest acts of statesmanship," editorialized Beaverbrook's *Evening Standard*. "There is only one man who could talk to Stalin. His name is Winston Churchill." Equally predictable was the Labour counterattack. "I am not enamoured of this individual business," snorted Bevin. "It was tried by Mr Chamberlain with Hitler and it did not work very well. It was tried at Yalta and did not work very well." Churchill was "a great master of words," Attlee told an audience in Nottingham, "but it is a terrible thing when a master of words becomes a slave of words." During the war, Churchill "in imperishable words . . . translated what the Nation felt. The trouble is now that because he feels frustrated he thinks that everybody else is frustrated."[5]

The man of words enslaved by words, the man of 1940 marooned by the tide of history—these were powerful charges. In London and Washington, Churchill's call for "a parley at the summit" was dismissed as election propaganda, perhaps with some justice, for he had committed himself to nothing. But Edinburgh was not all electioneering: the speech echoed Fulton in advocating negotiation from strength, with the shadow of a Soviet bomb making all the more urgent a "summit" conference (another term he added to the lexicon of international relations). The Edinburgh speech also offered a consistent view of recent events: things had started to go wrong in 1945 when Britain ditched him and turned to Labour. His search for political vindication was therefore buttressed by an interpretation of recent history. The conceit that he alone knew how to do business with Stalin was to run like a thread through the last three volumes of *The Second World War* and become a refrain of his second premiership.

Churchill's memoirs became entangled with election politics in other ways in 1950. As soon as the election date was announced, Churchill told Camrose it was "undesirable" for serialization to occur during the campaign. Arrangements in America were too far advanced, but Camrose did suspend the *Daily Telegraph*'s serialization from 8 February to 2 March while Parliament was dissolved.[6]

Churchill's attack on Sir Stafford Cripps's slowness in transmitting his April 1941 warning to Stalin also became politically sensitive. As Labour's Chancellor of the Exchequer, Cripps was one of Churchill's main political targets, and relations had become very strained. When Churchill impugned the Chancellor's integrity over devaluation in September 1949—he had promised on several occasions to maintain the value of the pound—a furious Cripps refused to accept an honorary degree from Bristol University, where Churchill was Chancellor. In his Edinburgh speech, Churchill paid tribute to Cripps's "brilliant intellect" but said it was "so precariously poised that his public life has been disfigured by lamentable and spasmodic utterances to which he falls victim in moods of excitement or moments of strain." Cripps accused Churchill of descending to the politics of "the gutter," but Churchill replied he had "suffered censure from a great many more substantial and solid and massive-minded critics than Sir Stafford Cripps."[7]

On 6 January 1950, Denis Kelly expressed concern that readers might "make too much" of Churchill's attack on Cripps in 1941, when taken out of context:

Cripps was personally asked by you if he objected to the publication of these documents and agreed. Which was sporting of him because you might not have told the story without his consent, and you hesitated even when he gave it. To publish it at all in inevitably fragmentary serials seems to me undesirable:

1. Because it might appear personally unfair.

2. Because the present Government has so far been friendly and co-operative and has raised no objection to publishing official documents. They might not be so helpful over future volumes if they thought that unfavourable doings of present ministers had been high-lighted in the Press.

3. It might be said that the book was being used for political tracts on the eve of an election and was not a historical work at all.

"Ismay agrees with this," Kelly added. "He said to me: 'I don't think we ought to make political capital out of those great days when we all worked together.'"[8]

Churchill took their advice, telling Kelly that the Cripps episode should not appear during the election campaign. He circled the words "political capital," but point two about the Labour government's acquiescence in the memoirs probably also carried some weight. Whatever his reasons, Churchill was receptive to Kelly's advice to maintain the ban even after the election was over: "I think that, taken out of their general context, these statements are undesirable, and I would be glad if other extracts could be chosen." But Camrose was resistant, and it took a personal word from Churchill before he agreed to keep Cripps out of the serials. The newspaper printed Churchill's telegram of 3 April 1941 but said nothing about the delay in its transmission.[9]

Across the Atlantic, *The New York Times* again squeezed thirty installments out of the volume, but *Life* was much less enthusiastic. As Longwell and Luce had warned, all the material on Britain's war in the Middle East did not resonate with Americans. According to John Shaw Billings, a senior editor at Time Inc., Luce was "terribly disappointed" by the excerpts and "shocked to find them so dull. The old boy is chiseling on us; if he were younger, we'd kick him in the shins. Luce had a wild idea that, by way of punishing him, we print only those parts of his work which refer to the U.S." Having carved seven installments from *Their Finest Hour*, *Life* extracted only three from *The Grand Alliance*, all centered on the volume's explicit theme, Britain's relations with America and Russia. Where *Life* did expand on Britain's war, it was in self-contained dramas such as Hess, Crete, the *Bismarck*, and the loss of the *Prince of Wales*. By contrast, Greece, the desert battles, and the siege of Tobruk were barely mentioned.[10]

In Australia, however, Churchill's account of the evacuation of the Ninth Division from Tobruk caused a minor dust storm. The Melbourne *Sun* sensationalized his account, with pictures of Prime Ministers Menzies, Fadden, and Curtin and the caption "Churchill Hits at These Men." The *Sun* and *The Herald*, also a Melbourne paper, printed letters of complaint from veterans, and there were calls for the Australian government to publish its own report on the evacuation. As in Britain, criticism of Churchill was often partisan in spirit—the Sydney *Sunday Telegraph*, for instance, also serialized the extracts but in a low-key way and, whereas Menzies, Fadden, and Chifley all refused to comment, H. V. Evatt, Labor's wartime Foreign Minister, denounced Churchill's criticism as "quite unjustified." Evatt landed some shrewd blows, rightly noting that evacuation from Tobruk had been the policy of three successive Australian premiers and complaining that Churchill had not printed the military and medical advice on which their demands were based. As usual, Churchill sat tight, and the row eventually blew over.[11]

THE BOOK VERSION of *The Grand Alliance* was published by Houghton Mifflin on 24 April 1950. Once more, it was a Book-of-the-Month Club selection; again, the reviews were prominent and generally laudatory. By now, the genre was well established, a tribute to the man as much as his book. Thus, Will Jarvis in *The Salt Lake Tribune* extolled "this Olympian figure," his "first-rate history," and his "stately prose." This was "not only a Book of the Month" but also "a book of all time." Henry Steele Commager, the eminent historian, struck a similar note in the New York *Herald Tribune*, commending a "magnificent book" about a "prodigious year." From the *Newark News* came the ritual comment—to warm the hearts of Deakin and Pownall—that Churchill's prose was inimitable: "A ghost-writer for Churchill would be the height of the incredible."[12]

There was, however, greater criticism than before about style and form. *Time* felt the volume seemed "more hurriedly written." Orville Prescott in *The New York Times* noted the mass of documents—"heavy and not easily digestible"—and found the prose "more pedestrian than usual." Churchill was very upset by Prescott's comments and genuinely puzzled that they appeared in the paper that serialized his memoirs. He kept asking, "Why would Sulzberger, who has made such a big investment, knock it in his own paper?"[13] Robert Sherwood in the Sunday *New York Times* made the same criticisms more obliquely—his draft was blunter—and the Cleveland *Plain Dealer* suggested that Churchill "placed too much emphasis" on the Middle East. Yet this latter criticism was offset for Cold War Americans by the rich material on the United States and the Soviet Union. For this reason, Sherwood found *The Grand Alliance* "much more interesting than its two distinguished predecessors." Reviewers in anti-Roosevelt papers such as the *Chicago Tribune* and *The Miami Herald* featured the material about Roosevelt's nonneutrality in 1941 and the administration's relief after Pearl Harbor.[14]

Once again, the most direct criticism came from the left—usually anonymously. *The New Republic*'s reviewer found this "the least satisfactory" volume so far. The weight of documents meant that "the story keeps stalling and the reader is overwhelmed." Although the narrative of the battles in Crete, North Africa, and the Atlantic were "by and large, as vivid and as comprehensive as the general reader could desire," the same could not be said about his handling of diplomacy. The chapters on Yugoslavia, the causes of Japanese entry, and especially Anglo-Soviet relations after June 1941 were, said the reviewer, "woefully incomplete." According to *The Nation*, "a generation from now readers are likely to wonder how a skilled historian could be so obsessed by the American side of the medal as to neglect, relatively and seriously, its opposite Russian side." Its reviewer was also ambivalent about Churchill's enthusiasm for war: "At his best he communicates nobility and virtue; at his worst he calls up images of adults enjoying warlike toys and puppetry." Although praising "a prodigious production," *The Nation* said the book might be retitled "Everyman His Own Napoleon."[15]

The British edition, published on 27 July 1950, also provoked some tart reviews from the left. The MP and journalist Michael Foot, who had attacked *The Gathering Storm* in *Tribune* under the title "Churchill's Mein Kampf," now skewered *The Grand Alliance*. His praise for Churchill's "wondrous vitality" and "fortitude in the face of disasters" was prelude to an extended attack on Churchill's "carefulness as an autobiographer" and his "carelessness as an historian," selectively printing his own documents and hardly ever reproducing any replies. This, said Foot, was a *Hamlet* totally dominated by the Prince of Denmark; "the only other characters left on the scene are Rosencrantz, Guildenstern, and an occasional grave-digger." But British criticism was not confined to the left. In the BBC weekly *The Listener*, the military historian Sir Basil Liddell Hart took on Churchill the strategist, being especially damning on Churchill's "relative blindness over the Far East" and his "excessive dispersion of effort" around the Middle East. *The Listener* did not print Liddell Hart's caustic summary of the consequences of strategic dispersion: "a second 'Dunkirk,' in Greece, and a bad setback in Africa."[16]

The bulk of British reviews were, however, much more positive; indeed, Foot claimed that his was "designed as an antidote to the gushing, hysterical applause with which Mr. Churchill's new volume has generally been greeted." The piece in *The Manchester Guardian*, a traditionally Liberal paper, said the narrative of 1941 was "less dramatic" than that of 1940, "but the artistry of the crowded canvas is hardly less" and the chapter on the *Bismarck* was one that Churchill had "never excelled in vividness and skilful compression." For most British readers, the detail of 1941 had more interest and appeal than it did across the Atlantic. They were intrigued by Churchill's accounts of Greece and Crete and by his appraisals of Wavell, Auchinleck, and Cripps—the story of the delayed telegram finally appeared in print and received a good deal of partisan attention. And if most concurred that this volume was "less arresting" than the one on 1940, to quote Wilson Harris in *The Spectator*, they were also agreed on the reason: "Churchill no longer stood alone in the forefront of the stage."[17]

There was a general note of letdown. Particularly revealing was the stance of *The Times Literary Supplement*. Unlike its treatment of volumes 1 and 2, it did not accord this one its lead review, and having suspended judgment in 1949 on *Their Finest Hour*—"he still has time to write great history"—its reviewer, Alfred Ryan, now offered a more categorical verdict: "His book will be a happy hunting ground for research workers in years to come. Parliamentary duties have evidently forced him to give the tools to future historians and to leave them to finish the job for which he himself is supremely qualified." This was "a great source book and a great self-portrait," said Ryan—clearly implying it was not "great history."[18]

For most reviewers, the most interesting source material and the most revealing self-portraits were in Churchill's accounts of his wartime summits—those authentic pieces of original work embedded in the documents and drafts. One such passage was his account of Sunday worship on 10 August 1941, during his Atlantic meeting with Roosevelt. The two leaders and several hundred British and American officers stood on the quarterdeck of the *Prince of Wales* on that bright sunlit morning. It was, says Churchill, "a deeply moving expression of the unity of faith of our two peoples"—Union Jack and Stars and Stripes "draped side by side on the pulpit," the crowded ranks sharing in hymns and prayers in the same language and tradition. "I chose the hymns myself," Churchill adds, ending with "O God, Our Help in Ages Past," which "Macaulay reminds us the Ironsides had chanted as they bore John Hampden's body to the grave. Every word seemed to stir the heart. It was a great hour to live. Nearly half those who sang were soon to die."[19]

The economy and power of those last few sentences still stir the emotions. The allusions to a classic hymn, a great historian, and a champion of freedom in the English Civil War summoned up the Whig historical tradition in which Churchill was steeped. His last two sentences, paired yet opposed, foreshadowed the fate of the *Prince of Wales* five months later, evoking the epic and the tragedy of war.

Another vivid story comes at the very end of the volume, as Churchill recounts his journey home in January 1942 after the Washington conference. He had traveled on a Boeing flying boat from Washington to Bermuda, with the intention of taking the *Duke of York* on to Britain. But, greatly impressed with the plane and its pilot, Captain Kelly-Rogers, he decided to continue home by air. Churchill allows himself four pages for the story, describing the doubts of Pound and Portal and his own second thoughts when it was too late. He builds up to the sense of growing anxiety in the cockpit as they neared the British Isles in thick cloud. After some huddled conversation with Kelly-Rogers, Portal suddenly announced that they were turning north at once. Within half an hour they broke through the cloud into brilliant sunlight and arrived at Plymouth. "I never felt so much relieved in my life as when I landed you safely in the harbour," the pilot remarked as his VIP left the plane. Only later, Churchill tells us, did he learn that if they had continued east for another five or six minutes they would have been over the German batteries at Brest. As it was, by coming into Plymouth from the south, they were identified as a hostile bomber, and six Hurricanes were scrambled to shoot them down. "However," says Churchill, "they failed in their mission." He ends the volume by quoting his laconic message to Roosevelt: "We got here with a good hop from Bermuda and a thirty-mile wind."[20]

In the twenty-first century, summitry is a matter of routine; in 1941, it was still a novelty. Although Churchill does not belabor the point, his readers could not fail to be aware that his two voyages across the Atlantic in 1941 were hazardous in the extreme, particularly the return legs, when the Germans knew where he was. The trip on the flying boat, intended to be safer as well as to reduce time, nearly ended in disaster, which he relates in this nicely understated way. The account of 10 August 1941 was Churchill at his most sonorous; the story of 17 January 1942 displayed his gift for dramatic simplicity.

Yet both these anecdotes attracted criticism as well as praise from reviewers and readers. One target was Churchill's reference to "O God, Our Help in Ages Past." "It may seem almost as captious as some art student calling attention to a false stroke of the brush on the Sistine frescoes," wrote historian W. E. Brooks in the Memphis *Commercial Appeal*, but "John Hampden had lain in that grave for 74 years before Isaac Watts sat down to write that hymn." The same point was made by other readers, one of whom also noted that Hampden died in 1643, before Cromwell formed his Ironsides. Churchill's passage about Sunday worship on the *Prince of Wales* was based on his account to the Commons on 24 August 1941. But then he had told it slightly differently: "We sang the hymn based on the psalm which John Hampden's soldiers sang when they bore his body to the grave." Such are the tricks and elisions of memory.[21]

As for the hazardous flight, Churchill's version was strongly contested by the pilot himself. After reading it in the serials, Kelly-Rogers submitted his own account, parts of which were printed in the *Daily Telegraph*. He insisted that the plane was never closer than ninety miles to Brest and that the zigzag course reflected changes in intended destination because of bad weather. Although Churchill displayed "exceptional skill in navigating the Empire through the uncharted seas of war," Kelly-Rogers said he showed "no more than a layman's interest in the art of aerial navigation." It should be noted that Portal supported Churchill's version in print and said he had been "extremely uneasy" for the last hour of the flight. This was also the contemporary record of Churchill's secretary, John Martin. But one is still left with the impression that here was another purple passage to which Churchill the artist had added a little too much color.[22]

WHATEVER ITS PROBLEMS, Churchill had completed volume 3. He had also lost another election. Defeat in July 1945, aptly dubbed by Clementine "a blessing in disguise," enabled Churchill to start his war memoirs, and Attlee's second victory in February 1950 allowed him to finish them. Had Churchill returned to 10 Downing Street then, he and his publishers would probably have had to activate their doomsday scenario—asking someone else to complete the work. Instead, Churchill had another year and a half before he climed back to the summit of British politics, and that was just enough. The manner of his defeat is also important. In January 1950, he assured Brendan Bracken that if he lost the election he would promptly retire.[23] That, of course, was the old, old story, but if Labour had notched up another hundred-plus majority even Churchill would have found it impossible to resist Tory pressure to retire. Instead, facing a tired government with a precarious Commons majority of five, he was able to justify staying on. As in July 1945, Churchill could eat his cake and have it, too—writing his memoirs while staying in politics. His appetite to command the past, the present, and the future was unimpaired.

IV.

THE HINGE OF FATE

1942–1943

1948–1951

"THE WORST MESS YET"

T HE HINGE OF FATE is the fourth and longest of Churchill's six volumes, exactly one thousand pages in the American edition. Its two books, "The Onslaught of Japan" and "Africa Redeemed," run from the middle of January 1942 to the beginning of June 1943. In this volume, declares Churchill in his preface, "we turn from almost uninterrupted disaster to almost unbroken success. For the first six months of this story all went ill; for the last six months everything went well." And, he adds, "this agreeable change continued to the end of the struggle." This volume is therefore the hinge of his whole work.[1]

LIKE ITS PREDECESSORS, *The Hinge of Fate* had a long lead time. As early as October 1946, Churchill had "pruned" the best of his 1943 papers for the Cabinet for printing. At the end of March 1948, he dictated a two-page note to General Pownall establishing his basic interpretation of the Desert War.[2] In April, August, and September 1948 he dictated recollections of his travels in 1942–1943 — particularly to Cairo, Moscow, and twice to Washington — which were printed as part of his outline "History of the War" and appear in much the same form in the published text. One of them is his account of hearing news of the surrender of Tobruk while meeting with Roosevelt and General Marshall at the White House in June 1942. Churchill recalled this "bitter moment" in stark and simple words that survive almost unchanged in chapter 22:

Nothing could exceed the sympathy and chivalry of my two friends. There were no reproaches; not an unkind word was spoken. "What can we do to help?" said Roosevelt. I replied at once, "Give us as many Sherman tanks as you can spare, and ship them to the Middle East as quickly as possible."

Despite the paucity of the American arsenal, 300 Shermans and 100 self-propelled guns were soon en route to Cairo. Churchill observes: "A friend in need is a friend indeed!"[3]

Once again, such anecdotes are a good indication of what had lodged in Churchill's memory. Many were remarkably accurate. His pilot for the 10,000-mile round-trip to Cairo and Moscow via Teheran was an American, Captain Bill Vanderkloot, who, Churchill records, had already flown about 1,000,000 miles in his career. *Life's* skeptical staffers eventually tracked down Vanderkloot, who explained that he had been an airline pilot for five years and had then ferried U.S. planes across the Atlantic for the RAF, making some seventy such crossings before the trip to Cairo.[4] In other cases, however, Churchill's memory seems to have been shakier. In successive drafts, the bulletproof glass in Molotov's Moscow limousine was reduced in thickness from an inch and a quarter to half an inch, before expanding again to two inches.[5] More seriously, Churchill confused his 1942 visit to America with later trips. Despite efforts by the methodical Ismay to sort things out, these confusions marred Churchill's account of his June 1942 discussions about the atomic bomb.[6]

During January 1949, seven chapters were printed in draft form, though many comprised only documents with skeletal narrative connections. Then Churchill reverted his focus to volume 3, so that he and the trust would receive their payments on 1 May, whereupon he announced that he would spend the next month identifying documents for the volumes on 1944–1945.[7] Unable to get clear guidance on volume 4, a frustrated Henry Pownall divided up the background work among the research assistants, envisaging some 26,000 words from himself on military matters and at least the same from Gordon Allen on aspects of the war at sea. Bill Deakin was allocated about half that wordage on diplomacy and politics. Ismay was given "a roving commission," mainly because he was hospitalized in May 1949 for a serious operation, but he provided the basic narrative for each of Churchill's meetings with the Americans in 1942–1943.[8]

Thanks to Pownall's initiative, when Churchill got down to volume 4 in earnest during the Commons recess in the summer of 1949, he had in front of him a series of background papers, as well as prints of his documents and recollections. Between the last week of June and the middle of September, twenty-seven chapters were printed in first draft. As usual, a Mediterranean vacation paid for by his American publishers expedited the work. Churchill's party flew to Lake Garda in northern Italy on 25 July. On 9 August, Churchill took the train to Strasbourg, where he attended inaugural meetings of the Council of Europe and delivered a major speech on the seventeenth. He then returned to the Mediterranean for the rest of August, staying in Beaverbrook's villa near Monte Carlo. The cost to *Life* and *The New York Times* was some $8,300.[9] As before, members of the Syndicate were enticed to accompany him. The Deakins came to Italy for the first week and the Ismays for the second. Deakin's presence was particularly important—"I want him very much indeed," Churchill exclaimed when it seemed that the Oxford don might not be coming.[10] Once more, bags of papers went to and from Hyde Park Gate almost daily—draft chapters for the printers, proof copies in return. Denis Kelly brought out bag 17 on 20 August and stayed for the rest of the month.

The trip took a somber turn with Churchill's stroke in the early hours of 24 August. He stopped work completely for several days and then resumed at a slower pace. Between 30 August and 15 September, proofs of seven more chapters were printed out by the Chiswick Press. Although four fifths of the volume was now in draft, many of the chapters were still mostly documents, with little connecting narrative. After Parliament resumed, book time during the autumn of 1949 was mostly devoted to finishing *The Grand Alliance*, so the Christmas vacation would clearly be important for *The Hinge of Fate*. Bryce Nairn, who, with his painter wife, Margaret, had made Churchill so welcome in southwest France in July 1945, was now British Consul in Madeira. Churchill cabled them on 19 November: "Please write soon about Madeira in January. Query warm, paintable, batheable, comfortable, flowery, hotels, etc. We are revolving plans. Keep all secret. Should so much like to see you both again." The Nairns sent encouraging letters, and the Churchills arrived at the capital, Funchal, by boat on New Year's Day 1950, with an entourage including Bill Deakin and the Pownalls. They were lodged in Reid's Hotel, recently reopened after the war and one of the world's finest. Again, *Life* and *The New York Times* footed the bill.[11]

Churchill had told Pownall beforehand that they would concentrate on volume 5, but he changed his mind on arrival, and they worked on nothing but volume 4. By 9 January, the first seventeen chapters had been dispatched to the printer, and there was still another week to go before departure. Again, however, fate intervened, this time in political form, because on 11 January Attlee announced the general election. Churchill and his secretary, Jo Sturdee, flew home the next day, leaving the rest of the party to come home later by boat as planned.[12] The next month was devoted to politics. As Tory leader, Churchill gave speeches all over the country. And, to quote R. A. Butler, he applied to the party manifesto "all that skill as a writer and proof-corrector, which he proudly says is his primary trade."[13]

Despite losing the election on 23 February, Churchill was absorbed in the new Parliament, and it was not until the Easter Recess that he could get back to volume 4 in earnest. Fortunately, this coincided with Oxford's spring vacation. In the month from 10 March, Deakin "dined and slept" at least ten nights at Chartwell, culminating in the whole Easter weekend. During that time, he read the chapters systematically, noting gaps and overlaps, reconstructing some and writing new material in Churchillian style for others. By the middle of April, volume 4 had been beaten into shape, at least for the 1 May deadline: in Churchill's preferred phrase, it was fit for the publishers if not for publication.[14]

The titles of the volume and of its two component books were still in flux. At an early stage in 1949, Churchill had jotted down for the volume "The Turn of the Tide" and "Preponderance of the Allies." His note to the publishers dated 3 April 1950 proposed "The Balance Turns," before he opted for "The Hinge of Fate" on 25 April. Henry Laughlin of Houghton Mifflin lunched with Churchill just after he had hit on the title: "He was as pleased as punch about it and so was I."[15] Churchill still dithered, however, about the component books. His August 1949 version envisaged "Defeat" and "Success"; in April 1950, it was "The Dark Valley" and "The Top of the Pass." The 1 May proofs used "The End of the Beginning" and "The Beginning of the End." These had been suggested back in August 1949 by Emery Reves, who wanted Churchill to make more of his own wartime phrases. Here Reves was quoting from the 10 November 1942 speech after Monty's victory at Alamein: "Now this is not the end. It is not even the beginning of the end. But it is, perhaps, the end of the beginning." It is, however, noteworthy that no reference to this speech appears in volume 4, or even in its drafts (see page 335). On 29 July 1950, Kelly told him "most of us" still preferred "The Dark Valley" and "The Top of the Pass" because Reves's titles were not "new" or "chronologically accurate." Only during the final push in August did Churchill come up with "The Onslaught of Japan" and "One Continent Redeemed" (from his address to the U.S. Congress on 19 May 1943) before amending the latter to "Africa Redeemed."[16]

CHURCHILL'S FOURTH INSTALLMENT was duly paid, but his American publishers were again far from happy with the drafts. Daniel Longwell at *Life* complimented Churchill on several chapters, including his meeting with Stalin, but estimated that only about one quarter of what he had seen was original writing. Henry Luce agreed that the volume would be "more readable" if the story were told as a connected narrative rather than through documents but admitted that the latter made fascinating reading. In other words, volume 4 was "fine as a book" but "not so well suited for magazine serialization," although "after a reasonable amount of editorial sweat" *Life* would probably be able to come up with "three or four admirable installments." Luce said he remained "a satisfied customer," but if Churchill wanted "a super-satisfied customer," then he should concentrate on some of those "great and dramatic episodes of history which have not yet been written as history by the Churchill who is unique in our time—historian and maker of history."[17]

Life was being more tactful than in May 1949, when it argued openly over volume 3, but Churchill was again very peeved and dictated sarcastic replies. Although never sent, these drafts offer an insight into his mind. To Longwell, he asserted that the original documents "far surpass in historical value anything that could be written in later years" and said that "no one connected with our joint enterprise has lost any money over it up to the present time." These were his standard ripostes to such criticism. "Of course," he added with heavy irony, recalling his irritation in 1946 about the book by Eisenhower's wartime aide,

I cannot compete for instance with Captain Butcher in personal reminiscence, nor can I at this juncture write a history of the World War in terms of Gibbon or Macaulay. We have just to go on as we are, with unprecedented sales, overwhelmingly favourable reviews, and authentic documents woven together to tell the tale as I have to tell it.

Churchill ended this draft with another reference to his anxieties about health: "I wonder that you are not surprised that I have had the life and strength granted to me to make this prolonged and intense effort at the advanced age which I have attained."[18]

Houghton Mifflin took a more positive view of volume 4, however—reflecting Luce's distinction between the interests of newspaper editors and those of book publishers. Having read the draft, Henry Laughlin wrote Churchill on 12 June 1950 that it was "the most engrossing of all your books." Despite more documents than ever, Laughlin agreed that these enhanced the interest, particularly in the meetings with Stalin, and welcomed the fact that Churchill was now printing more responses to his missives. "I am so glad you like THE HINGE OF FATE," Churchill replied on 20 June, adding in an echo of his comment to Camrose in April, "I myself think it is better than the preceding volumes."[19]

But any complacency was punctured by a hard-hitting letter on 5 July from Emery Reves. Outside Britain, he warned, sales figures had declined steadily for each successive volume. In France, the fall had been precipitous: 85,000 copies for volume 1, 45,000 for volume 2, and 28,000 for volume 3. "All your publishers are unanimous in pointing out the one and only cause of this reaction: an overdose of documents, and too many details of military operations." Reves estimated that two thirds of volume 4 was documents—probably four fifths including the appendixes. When Churchill sent a defensive reply about the value of original documents and the impressive American sales, Reves put him right:

NORTH AMERICAN SALES FOR VOLUMES 1 TO 3
(TO 5 JULY 1950)

	Houghton Mifflin	Book-of-the-Month Club	Thomas Allen (Canada)	Total
Vol. 1	111,700	377,500	24,400	513,600
Vol. 2	84,600	261,000	15,000	360,600
Vol. 3	55,400	213,000	7,500	275,900
Vols. 1–3	251,700	851,500	46,900	1,150,100

Source: Emery Reves to WSC, 20 July 1950, CHUR 4/12/74 (CAC).

Readers around the world were not interested in documents, said Reves, but in "your unequalled prose. They want to read Churchill the writer." If Churchill reduced this volume to the size of *Their Finest Hour* and transformed half of it into narrative, Reves believed "the tide can be turned," and *The Hinge of Fate* would prove as big a success as *The Gathering Storm*.[20]

Reducing the documents was one big challenge for the summer of 1950. The other was a much tighter deadline. In September 1949, Churchill still assumed that volume 4 would not appear in serial form until January 1951 or as a book until June. But in an effort to regain momentum and boost sales, *Life*, *The New York Times*, and Houghton Mifflin all wanted to publish volumes 3 and 4 in 1950, with 5 and 6 (if needed) in 1951.[21] Laughlin came to London to press his case, telling Churchill on 12 June that he wanted to publish on 27 November, in time for the Christmas market, and seeking permission to start setting the type immediately. Rather than send new galley proofs, Churchill should simply transmit specific corrections. On 20 June 1950, Churchill agreed.[22]

Five days later, North Korea invaded the south. It was assumed (rightly) that Stalin had given the nod to the North Korean attack, and President Truman rushed U.S. forces into the south to stem the surging communist tide. This became a United Nations operation, with the British government deeply involved. As Leader of the Opposition, Churchill faced a new and demanding political agenda, which cut deeply into the time anticipated for the book during the Commons summer recess. He had planned another working vacation, courtesy of his American publishers, this time at Biarritz on the southwest coast of France. Rooms were duly booked from 23 July at the Hotel du Palais, originally built by Napoleon III for the Empress Eugénie. Despite Churchill's enjoinders, the manager set about renovating his suite with softer beds, an "ultra modern" bath, and salmon-pink décor. ("We understand this is Monsieur Churchill's favourite colour," he told the press.)[23] But Churchill kept postponing his arrival and finally canceled completely. He did go as planned to the European Parliament in Strasbourg from 6 to 12 August but then returned straight home.[24] After a visit to Chartwell on 23 August, the *Daily Telegraph*'s deputy editor, Malcolm Muggeridge, noted that Churchill had "lost interest" in the memoirs and had "simply been stringing together masses of documents which he had written in the war. The Americans, who have paid a huge sum of money for the serial and book rights, have protested. In the course of conversation about them it slipped out that certain chapters have not been written by him at all, and I suspect that he is doing extremely little."[25]

Churchill, of course, claimed he was working very hard. "I have had to give up all my holiday and cannot even squeeze a tube," he told his cousin on 24 August. "Volume IV is a worse tyrant than Attlee." Once again, he turned to Bill Deakin and Denis Kelly—the latter to tie up the loose ends, the former to pull the volume together. During August, Deakin "dined and slept" nine nights, most of them at Chartwell, and Kelly five.[26] Together, they cut back the documentation, and Deakin rewrote several chapters—for instance, converting the original 1942 reports of Churchill's meetings with Stalin into a personal narrative and producing new material to fill serious gaps, such as for the unconditional-surrender declaration and the Katyn massacre. The result, of course, was a mass of corrections; in August, Kelly persuaded Churchill to reprint the whole text completely and distribute another set of 150 copies to newspapers and publishers all over the world.[27]

On 25 July, Laughlin requested final revisions in a month's time. He was now locked into a Book-of-the-Month Club deal for December. Pressure of the opposite sort came from Desmond Flower, who condemned the "juggernaut" mentality of Houghton Mifflin: "Where the production of an historic document is concerned I consider the setting of an arbitrary and premature date and the sweeping aside of all considerations of accuracy and the author's wishes for the sake of a Book Club are to be deplored." Since Cassell's was keeping, as planned, to a summer 1951 publication date, the gap between the two editions could be six months. Cassell's would look ridiculous, said Flower, and would lose substantial export sales. He begged Churchill to secure a delay on the American side.[28]

On 4 August, Churchill cabled Laughlin, pleading the pressure of world events: "I cannot see why the Book of the Month [Club] can only publish in December," he wrote. "Would not February be quite good?" Laughlin stuck to his guns, reminding Churchill of the declining sales figures and noting that $12,000 had already been committed to advertising. He also played on Churchill's concern about current affairs: publication before Christmas would "rekindle the flames" of Anglo-American cooperation at a critical moment in history. Laughlin now gave Churchill till 11 September, "or even a few days later," for the new text.[29] "I feel it my duty to do my utmost to meet his wish," Churchill told Desmond Flower. "Whether I can succeed or not depends on events outside my control." But he cabled Laughlin: "I hope you are setting up in galley proof." Laughlin was not. After further cabling, Churchill agreed in a long transatlantic phone call on 21 August that Laughlin could carry on with page proofs, leaving a set number of pages for problematic chapters such as the opening one about Australia. On that basis, to Laughlin's immense relief, Churchill said he expected to meet the 11 September deadline.[30]

Then, at the end of August, British printers went on strike. They might be out for two weeks, Churchill cabled Laughlin on 31 August. "Am sending you today by airmail my only duplicate of my master copy" of book 1. He said he hoped to dispatch book 2 before Parliament met on 12 September. But the master copy, though sent registered delivery by express airmail, disappeared in transit and did not reach Boston until 6 September. Laughlin's nerves could not stand a repeat performance. He arranged for an American friend, John Hunter, who was working in London, to collect the master copy of book 2 from Chartwell and personally get it onto a transatlantic flight on the evening of 11 September. Laughlin met the plane in Boston the next morning.[31]

The British printers' strike was an even bigger blow for Emery Reves, who had taken up residence in London to help Churchill and his Syndicate with their final push. Serial publication dates around the world had been set long before, and Reves feared he would be sued for breach of contract if the updated text was not available in time. In desperation, he mounted what he dubbed Operation Mimeo, mobilizing twenty-four secretaries from two agencies to work around the clock for three days in order to prepare new sets of book 1. This meant personally checking the text he had received at the beginning of August against the revised chapters; he found more than 1,000 alterations. Then, Reves told Churchill, "I had many passages—from 50 to 5,000 words—stencilled" and then run off as mimeographed copies. "Finally we had to paste and correct by hand 14,000 galley sheets!" Reves warned that "in doing this tremendous volume of corrections by hand the human element plays a certain role," so there would be a lot of queries from foreign publishers and, even then, mistakes in the final editions. Typically, Churchill chose to ignore the scarcely veiled criticism. "It is wonderful what you have done," he replied. "Thank you very much."[32]

Reves told Laughlin bluntly that the last two weeks in London had been "absolute hell" and "utterly unnecessary."[33] Still fuming, he departed on other business, telling Churchill to get book 2 mimeographed himself. The work was done by the *Daily Telegraph*, aided by proofreaders from the Chiswick Press, and copies of book 2 were duly distributed in mid-September.

Henry Pownall called the publication crisis over volume 4 "the worst mess yet. . . . We shall muddle through somehow but I shouldn't be at all surprised to find a lot of bloomers when the book comes out."[34] *The Hinge of Fate* was indeed pretty creaky in places—heavy with documents, short on narrative, and sometimes, as we shall see, seriously wrong. But Pownall was a congenital skeptic. Although the messiest production of all Churchill's volumes, surpassing even *The Gathering Storm*, it was as effective as volume 1, yet in completely different ways.

CHAPTER 19

ASIAN DISASTERS, DESERT VICTORY, AND THE SILENCE OF STALINGRAD

I N A VOLUME about the alchemy of victory, two names embody the dross of defeat. The surrender of Singapore to Japan on 15 February 1942 was, says Churchill, "the worst disaster and largest capitulation in British history."[1] And he calls the fall of Tobruk to the Germans and Italians on 21 June 1942 "one of the heaviest blows I can recall during the war." In both places, British armies surrendered to numerically weaker enemies: "Defeat is one thing; disgrace is another."[2] Most of the first quarter of *The Hinge of Fate* is concerned with Singapore and concomitant Japanese victories, which redrew the map of Asia and forced the Allies to reorient their whole strategy. The Asian hinge eventually turns with the American naval victory at Midway in June 1942; in North Africa, the volume pivots around the British victory at Alamein in November. Equally striking to present-day ears is the sound of silence: Stalingrad receives hardly a mention.

EXPLAINING THE SINKING of the *Prince of Wales* and the *Repulse* was an emotional matter for Churchill. He knew he had sent them to their doom, and the pain could never quite be assuaged. By contrast, the loss of British Southeast Asia in 1942 was rooted in a series of strategic decisions made during the 1920s and 1930s, mostly when Churchill was out of office. Drafts of *The Hinge of Fate* contain some musing about his degree of responsibility for the debacles of early 1942, but these came from the mind not the heart.

Churchill's research assistant Henry Pownall had a more direct interest in the Singapore disaster. He had been on the Cabinet Secretariat in the mid-1930s when many of the defining decisions about the base were taken, and then served as Vice-Chief of the Imperial General Staff in 1941. That December, he was appointed overall Commander in Chief in the Far East and might well have had to conduct the surrender of Singapore but for his sudden appointment as Wavell's Chief of Staff in the short-lived Allied command for the whole region. What's more, as Pownall's wartime diary makes clear, he believed he had been sent to the Far East mainly because Churchill now wanted Sir Archibald Nye to be Vice-Chief. Pownall even likened his situation to the biblical account of King David sending Uriah the Hittite out to the battlefront because of his affection for Uriah's wife, Bathsheba. Pownall's diaries had also been critical of the dispatch of Phillips's unsupported fleet and the priority Churchill gave to the Mediterranean. The entry for 20 December 1941 noted: "He didn't believe the Japs would come into the war—not yet at any rate. For once his long range vision was at fault, and badly. . . . I only hope we shall not pay dearly for the mistake."[3]

Pownall wisely concealed his 1942 diaries (like those of 1940) from Churchill, but all the military material about Asia in volume 4 closely follows drafts Pownall produced in 1949. Knowing that Churchill intended to criticize the lack of landward defenses at Singapore, Pownall prepared a special paper emphasizing that the base had originally been seen entirely in naval terms, to support the fleet if it was sent from the Mediterranean to deal with Japan. But, Pownall argued, this strategy was nullified by the unforeseen disasters of 1940. With France out of the war, Britain facing invasion, and Italy at war in the Mediterranean, there was no fleet to spare for the Far East. The Chiefs of Staff hoped that airpower could deter an attack on Southeast Asia, but there were never enough planes to spare because of home defense and North Africa. At very short notice, the burden therefore devolved onto the army—the service least prepared for war. Moreover, it was being asked to defend not only Singapore but also the whole of Malaya. When the Pacific war broke out in December 1941, General Arthur Percival, the hapless commander in Singapore, had only three quarters of the troops he had requested, most of them still only semitrained.[4]

Prompted by Pownall's material, in the summer of 1949 Churchill dictated several notes to himself about what had happened and how the disaster might have been avoided. Although believing the field commanders could have done much more to check the Japanese advance, he said he would in his book "emphasise very much my continuous demand not to risk troops in the long stretch of the Malay Peninsula" and "to keep everything for the defence of the Island." As to why the naval base had not been fortified on the northern side facing Malaya, he typically blamed individuals: "the people we sent out were an inferior troop of military and naval men. None of them thought of any of these things." Churchill did not deny his own failings—"Note," he scribbled on a print of one of his 1940 minutes, "I took for granted there was a permanent landward defence. Dreadful!"—and admitted that he failed to focus on the Far East until after Pearl Harbor. "I have no defence for it except that I had not the life and strength to light up the field of interest with the same intensity after I had done all I could in the West and Africa. Moreover I consoled myself by feeling that the Americans would be in it, and that would make amends for all." But even if he had addressed the problem earlier, Churchill reassured himself, these disasters "could not have been prevented," though "they might at least have been foreseen." On the big question about the importance of the Middle East versus that of the Far East, over which he had wrestled with Dill in 1941, Churchill was unrepentant: "The major dispositions were right."[5]

Some of Churchill's debate with himself survives in modified form in chapter 3 of *The Hinge of Fate*. There, he says it was "at least arguable" that they should have concentrated on defending Singapore rather than the whole of Malaya, but he admits he approved the commanders' decision to fight a delaying battle down the peninsula. An early draft criticizing the "inexcusable" failure of the navy to command the west coast of Malaya was toned down after vigorous objection from the Admiralty. Churchill even prints an unusually rebarbative minute from Pound in January 1942, which Allen had provided, saying that Churchill's criticisms of the navy ignored the impact of airpower and confused the conditions of 1942 with those of 1914. Churchill's shock and anger when he learned in mid-January 1942 about the lack of landward defenses at Singapore is one of the most vivid passages of the early part of the book. And his share of responsibility is also acknowledged: "My advisers ought to have known and I ought to have been told, and I ought to have asked." But "I had not asked" because "the possibility of Singapore having no landward defences no more entered into my mind than that of a battleship being launched without a bottom."[6]

A wonderful figure of speech, this obscures some larger points. First, Churchill's fixation with Singapore's defenses reflects his dated concept of warfare. He talks of "the famous fortress" and of his assumption that "a regular siege would be required," along the lines of the "glorious" resistance of Verdun in 1916. "I had put my faith in the enemy being compelled to use artillery on a very large scale in order to pulverise our strong points at Singapore" and in "the almost prohibitive difficulties and long delays" that would impede an artillery buildup "along Malayan communications." We shall see the same concept of almost Marlborough-era siege warfare underlying his account of Tobruk. Second, Churchill never took on board Pownall's paper about the chaos in British strategy in 1940–1941, as the burden of Far Eastern defense shifted first from the navy to the air force and then to the army. To do so would have reopened the sensitive issue of choosing between the Mediterranean and the Far East. Instead, there is simply a bland observation in chapter 3 that the resources to meet Far Eastern needs "were, as I have described, all used elsewhere." He prints Pownall's paper almost verbatim under the general's name as Appendix D but does not integrate its argument into his text.[7]

Singapore, suddenly and "hideously" revealed as "the almost naked island," is the dramatic centerpiece of Churchill's Asian disasters. But he has chapters on several others, including the loss of the Dutch East Indies, the invasion of Burma, and the April raids on Ceylon, which threatened a Japanese breakout into the Indian Ocean. These chapters convey the extent of the Asian crisis and also explain the British takeover of the island of Madagascar from Vichy in May 1942, to preempt a Japanese foothold near East Africa. In explaining the scope of Japan's victories, Churchill relies largely on the mix of arguments already made about the fall of Singapore: Allied complacency, unpreparedness, and poor leadership, plus the impossibility of facing three enemies at once. But he also tantalizes readers with counterfactuals, in this case turning some of his most savage fire in all six volumes on the Australian Labor government of John Curtin.

In January 1950, possibly following the advice of Norman Brook, Churchill prepared a new opening chapter (initially called "Australian Anxieties"), which pulled together the Australian material from the turn of 1941–1942.[8] This begins with Curtin's celebrated newspaper article of 27 December, announcing that in the present crisis "Australia looks to America, free of any pangs as to our traditional links with the United Kingdom." These words, says Churchill, "produced the worst impression both in high American circles and in Canada." Most of the chapter is devoted to the cables he exchanged with Curtin in January 1942, the latter demanding reinforcement of Southeast Asia while Churchill reiterated the need to defend Libya and aid Russia. Here and elsewhere in *The Hinge of Fate*, Churchill blasts Curtin, with his majority of two, for not forming a national government and imposing conscription. As in volume 3, Churchill goes out of his way to praise the New Zealand government for what he called at the time its consistently "helpful and realist attitude to the war," meaning its willingness to keep the bulk of its troops in the Middle East. By contrast, Curtin wanted to bring the Australians home to face the Asian crisis.[9]

Churchill returns to the issue in chapters 3 (about Malaya) and 9 (on Burma). Once he got over his initial angry shock at the feebleness of Singapore's defenses, he recognized that the island's fall was only a matter of time. On 21 January 1942, he suggested to the Chiefs of Staff that it might be wiser to cut Britain's losses in Singapore and divert reinforcements to Burma, the gateway to both India and China. Otherwise, by "hesitating to take an ugly decision," Britain could lose both Singapore and Burma. But Curtin learned of the idea, and on 23 January he sent an angry telegram saying that evacuation of Singapore would be regarded in Australia and elsewhere as "an inexcusable betrayal." Churchill implies that Curtin's accusation, though "not in accordance with the truth," resulted in a "hardening of opinion" in London against giving the impression of a "scuttle." "There is no doubt," wrote Churchill in 1950, "what a purely military decision should have been." And so the British Eighteenth Division sailed on to Singapore, arriving just in time to surrender.[10]

By this time, Australia had recalled two of its three divisions in the Middle East. Churchill correctly states that he personally initiated that move in December, in deference to Australian anxieties, though he is wrong to say that he suggested they return to Australia itself. He actually proposed their deployment to India or Singapore; eventually, the Australian government settled on the Dutch East Indies.[11] On 20 February, Churchill cabled Curtin again, claiming that the Australian leader's "inexcusable betrayal" message had led directly to the loss of the Eighteenth Division and asking him, in effect, to make amends. "Assuming a favourable response," Churchill unilaterally diverted the troop convoy toward the Burmese capital of Rangoon. Curtin was naturally furious, Churchill had to relent, and, with the Dutch East Indies by then lost, the Australian troops went home. This story is told in chapter 9, using many contemporary telegrams, in a tone of sorrow rather than anger: "I could wish it had not fallen to me to tell the facts, but the story of the Burma campaign requires it." He does not conceal his belief that the Curtin government was unreasonably panicked about an imminent invasion. (There is no mention in his book of the Japanese bombing of the northern Australian city of Darwin on 19 February, just before these exchanges over Burma.) Churchill also takes pains to rub in the contrast with Britain in August 1940, when "we had sent half our scanty armour to the defence of Egypt" despite a much more acute threat of invasion. Again, the tone is lofty, not censorious: "It was their duty to study their own position with concentrated attention. We had to try to think for all."[12]

In March 1942, there was more trouble when Churchill appointed Richard Casey, the Australian envoy in Washington, as Britain's Minister of State in Cairo. The appointment was announced on the BBC before a reluctant Curtin had given formal approval. His anger was leaked to the press, whereupon Churchill issued his own defense, and FDR had to intervene to warn that this row was playing into enemy hands. In January 1949, Deakin dug out the relevant telegrams; in an outline dated 12 July 1949, Churchill noted that "a paragraph is all that can be spared for this, nor need the correspondence be published." In the event, Churchill never mentioned the story at all, even in his drafts. Perhaps he forgot; perhaps he decided that there was enough bickering with the Aussies in the book.[13]

Even without the Casey affair, Norman Brook considered the Australian material the most contentious part of *The Hinge of Fate*. Churchill eventually agreed to include several of Curtin's replies to his telegrams and to remove some sniping—for instance, "The usual stream of complaint and reproach came from Mr. Curtin." Even so, the Commonwealth Relations Office was unhappy: Sir Percivale Leisching told Brook that the chapters would "revive memories of controversies with Australia which would be much better forgotten." But, Leisching admitted, "we can hardly suggest complete suppression of all references to these matters and, if mentioned at all, there seems to be no alternative to telling the full story." At Brook's request, "Australasian Anxieties" and "The Invasion of Burma" were submitted to Canberra for approval.[14] As with volume 3, Churchill benefited from the ousting of Chifley's Labor government by Menzies and the Liberals in December 1949. Menzies made no fuss, sending simply a one-sentence reply: "I have no objection to the reproduction of the messages you mention." He wrote this letter during an official visit to London in July 1950, which (perhaps not accidentally) included lunch at 28 Hyde Park Gate.[15]

Churchill's hints that diversion to Burma of the British Eighteenth Division or the Australian Sixth and Seventh Divisions might have made a difference are almost a malicious *jeu d'esprit*, because his overall account implies that little could be done by December 1941 to avert the Asian debacle. Thus, the chapters on the fall of Singapore ("The only question was how long") and what he calls the "forlorn battle of the Java Sea" are anticlimactic.[16] Likewise, in the case of Burma, Churchill has to admit that "no troops in our control could reach Rangoon in time to save it." But, he goes on, "if we could not send an army, we could at least send a man." There then follows a purple passage introducing General Sir Harold Alexander. "Alex" was handsome, courteous, and famously brave—personifying Churchill's ideal soldier: "Nothing ever disturbed or rattled him, and duty was a full satisfaction in itself, especially if it seemed perilous and hard.

But all this was combined with so gay and easy a manner that the pleasure and honour of his friendship were prized by all those who enjoyed it, among whom I could count myself." Near the end of chapter 9, Churchill's comments on Alex serve to top and tail Pownall's narrative of the Burma campaign, turning the latter into an encomium on Churchill's favorite general, who "showed all those qualities of military skill, imperturbability, and wise judgment that brought him later into the first rank of Allied war leaders."[17]

Thus, the Japanese tide is dammed in the west by a great man, but the turning point in the Pacific is a great battle, Midway. This was a purely American victory, though Churchill claims some credit for Britain because several Japanese carriers had to return home after heavy losses of aircraft during the raids on Colombo in April.[18] Chapter 14 provides a lively account of the battles of Coral Sea and Midway. In the first (8 May), both Japan and America lost an aircraft carrier, but the Japanese aborted their invasion of Port Moresby, on the southern coast of New Guinea, across from Australia. At Midway (4 June), four operational Japanese carriers were sunk, against the loss of one American. Unlike earlier chapters on the land war in Asia, "American Naval Victories" is full of vivid detail. A first draft appeared rather late, in March 1950, probably in response to criticism from Emery Reves, who wanted more about battles of interest to non-British readers. Reves was delighted, calling the draft "an excellent chapter" and a model for others.[19] Very little of "American Naval Victories" was Churchill's work, however. He rewrote the opening and sharpened some phrases but otherwise relied on the draft from Gordon Allen, who in turn had largely paraphrased volume 4 of Samuel Eliot Morison's history of U.S. naval operations in World War II.[20]

Once the tide had been turned at Midway, the Far East disappears from *The Hinge of Fate*. Again responding to Reves's criticism, Allen and Pownall drafted another chapter of interest to American readers, on Guadalcanal, but this got squeezed out of the volume in the rush to publish in August–September 1950.[21] The virtual absence of the Pacific War for the year after June 1942 has serious implications. Not only does it unbalance Churchill's account of 1942–1943, it also distorts his presentation of the strategic problems at the heart of the volume: North Africa and the Second Front.

THE FIRST QUARTER of volume 4 is mostly about Asia, and the Desert War is slow to appear. Only three of the twenty-three chapters in book 1 are allotted to the struggle between Rommel and Auchinleck. But four of the first ten chapters of book 2 are concerned with the retreat of the Eighth Army into Egypt, Churchill's shake-up of its command during his August visit to Cairo, and the ensuing victory at Alamein in November. Churchill's essential argument was clear from an early stage in a note to Pownall dated 30 March 1948:

> I consider Rommel a very great commander, beating us up at heavy odds, hurling us back hundreds of miles in 1941. The struggle was more equal with Auchinleck in 1942. But again, through Auchinleck's delays, Rommel won against odds by the narrowest margin. The capitulation of Tobruk, where 25,000 surrendered to about 4,000, is an awful story. . . . It was only after we got fine generals like Alexander and Montgomery, and they also got better weapons and equipment, that defeat turns into victory. Till then it is a melancholy story, the Germans out-manoeuvring and out-fighting us on almost every single occasion.[22]

Despite the aside about "better weapons and equipment," Churchill's explanation of both defeat and victory revolves around great leaders. That was also true at the time. On several occasions in 1942, Churchill paid public tribute to Rommel, calling him nothing less than "a great general." His aggressive spirit exemplified what Churchill prized in a commander; his related indifference to logistics was equally Churchillian. In July 1942, Hitler mused that "not a little" of Rommel's "world-wide reputation" was due to Churchill's speeches in the Commons, in which, "for tactical reasons of policy, the British Prime Minister always portrays Rommel as a military genius." Churchill did not wish to admit, said Hitler, that "the British are getting a damned good hiding from the Italians in Egypt and Libya."[23]

By January 1942, the victorious Eighth Army had conquered much of Cyrenaica. But then a probe by Rommel, vigorously exploited, led to the loss of Benghazi and a precipitate British retreat. In chapter 2, Churchill writes that this "military disaster," in some ways a repeat of Rommel's dramatic arrival on the scene a year before, "was to ruin the whole British campaign in the Desert for 1942." Auchinleck pulled back nearly 300 miles to Gazala and Tobruk, where, says Churchill, "pursuers and pursued gasped and glared at each other until the end of May." The Auk was determined to build up his strength before mounting a new offensive, but Churchill warned that if he waited too long, Rommel might strike first. In early May, Churchill claims—somewhat inaccurately—that the Chiefs of Staff and the War Cabinet, anxious to draw the enemy away from the vital island of Malta, sent Auchinleck "definite orders which he must obey or be relieved. This was a most unusual procedure on our part towards a high military commander."[24] Under such pressure, Auchinleck agreed to go ahead but warned on 19 May that "the narrowness of our margin of superiority over the enemy" meant that success could not "be regarded as in any way certain." This warning was deleted from Churchill's August 1950 draft.[25]

As Churchill predicted, Auchinleck's caution, however understandable, gave Rommel the chance to strike first. Chapter 24 describes the surrender of Tobruk on 21 June and the retreat of British forces another 300 miles to Alamein. For some time, Churchill had badgered the Auk to take personal command of the Eighth Army, and he attributes the eventual stabilization of the front at Alamein to Auchinleck belatedly doing so after the fall of Tobruk: "He should have done this when I asked him to in May."[26] In explaining Tobruk, Churchill makes much of the "ill-defined responsibility" between General Neil Ritchie, command-ing the Eighth Army, and Auchinleck, which led, he says, "to a mishandling of forces which in its character and consequences constitutes an unfortunate page in British military history." Earlier drafts had used the adjectives "discreditable" and "deplorable"; "unfortunate" emerged in the final proof after representations by Brook and Pownall.[27]

For Churchill, the fall of Tobruk was more awful than that of Singapore because he could blame the latter on the follies of the thirties, whereas the North African war was his overriding concern as Prime Minister. Worse still, Tobruk came as a total surprise. After Rommel's breakthrough at the end of May, Chur-chill issued clear instructions "to hold the place for certain" and left for America confident that the "fortress" of Tobruk was secure. Hence his shock in the White House on 21 June.[28]

Churchill remained genuinely puzzled as to why Tobruk fell and so did Pow-nall, who in early 1950 went very fully into the matter, using War Office and Cabinet records. At the beginning of 1942, with the victorious Eighth Army hun-dreds of miles to the west, Auchinleck had issued an order declaring that whereas Tobruk was an essential base for *offensive* operations, it should not be held if the enemy was again in a position to attack. Consequently, the defenses were in poor shape in May 1942—mines had been taken up, barbed wire removed, and the antitank ditches allowed to fill up with sand. Churchill's categorical orders in June to hold Tobruk came far too late for effective defense, but they had to be obeyed, and the last-minute reinforcement condemned thousands of men (mostly South African) to a lengthy spell in Italian prison camps. When Pownall unearthed Auchinleck's order in January 1950, Churchill asked him to make sure it was correct to say "at home we had no inkling that the evacuation of Tobruk had ever entered into the plans or thoughts of the commanders." After further research, Pownall said he found no evidence to the contrary in the available documents and added that both Brooke and Ismay could not recall any such plans.[29] In 1957, however, the memoirs of General Sir John Kennedy, Director of Military Operations in 1942, stated that Auchinleck's order had indeed been received in the War Office in early 1942. He opined that perhaps no notice was taken of it because at the time, after the Eighth Army's spectacular advance, a new siege of Tobruk seemed most unlikely.[30]

Whether or not London knew, however, is less important than the underlying tactical assumptions. Auchinleck was conscious of the fluidity of desert warfare. On such terrain, with few natural features, it was hard to establish secure defensive positions. Towns, even ports, were, in his view, intrinsically indefensible— and in any case it was not necessary to hold every mile at vast cost when ground could be easily regained, as in late 1941. The Auk fell back all the way to Alamein because there his southward flank would be protected by the impassable Qattara depression, leaving him only a thirty-five-mile front to defend, close to the supply port of Alexandria. Churchill, in London, was much more concerned with the politics of war, with the growing perception that the British Army could never secure a victory. From this perspective, retreat spelled defeat. And once again, Churchill's language betrays a dated conception of warfare, with frequent, almost medieval, reference to Tobruk as a "fortress" and a "sally-port" behind enemy lines. A very different impression is given by General Sir Michael Carver, who served in Tobruk and later published a study of the battle. "As the only sheltered harbour, capable of taking anything larger than a caique, between Benghazi and Alexandria, it had great logistic value," said Carver. But by no "stretch of the imagination could this village with its tiny quay be regarded as a port"—the normal limit of its capacity was six hundred tons per day, roughly twenty Sherman tanks.[31] In a sense, the "disaster" of Tobruk was self-inflicted: if Churchill had not made so much of its importance in 1942 and in his memoirs, judgments on its loss might have been much less severe.

In other respects, too, Churchill's account is less than fair on Auchinleck, especially by playing down the problem of poor British tanks, which Auchinleck had emphasized in his official dispatch on the Desert War, published in January 1948. Churchill ended the March 1949 draft of chapter 2 with a warning that the nation should not be "too easily satisfied with tales of technical inferiority of our tanks." This prompted his son-in-law Christopher Soames—who had served in the desert and was critical of Auchinleck's handling of the January battles—to warn that "at this time our tanks *were* technically inferior to the Germans, which put our armoured forces at a disadvantage in every tank-to-tank fight." Churchill accepted Soames's rephrasing and wrote that the British should not be "misled into thinking that the technical inferiority of our tanks was the only reason for this considerable and far-reaching reverse."[32]

Tanks or tactics, poor resources or poor commanders—Churchill and Pownall had waged the same battle during the composition of volume 3. In February 1950, Pownall wrote a lengthy background paper on tank design, based on War Office records. This emphasized that the embargo on tank production from the end of the Great War until 1936 had had a "crippling effect" and that the belated British prototype, the Crusader, was a rush job that simply could not compete in armor and firepower with German equivalents. The better though still problematic Grants and Shermans from America were not available in large quantities in early 1942.[33] At one stage, Churchill intended to write a chapter on tank design, based on Pownall's paper. When this idea was dropped, he still planned to print Pownall's memo as an appendix, as he had done with the paper on the defenses of Singapore. But Pownall felt himself on weaker ground here, telling Churchill it was "a highly controversial subject, even to facts and figures, and may lead to indignant comment from both sides, for there are two 'sides.'" The appendix was cut from the final version—perhaps to save words, possibly in deference to Pownall's sensitivity, probably because of Churchill's basic antipathy to the claim that poor armor was truly Britain's Achilles' heel.[34]

Apart from equipment problems, Auchinleck's 1948 dispatch also set out a second line of self-defense. Although always seeing victory in North Africa as his prime task, Auchinleck stressed that the "danger that Germany might attack Turkey and that Turkey might collapse was always present. Moreover, the German invasion of Russia, which progressed at first with alarming rapidity, meant that danger threatened the Northern Front from the Caucasus also." This concern for his northern flank decisively influenced Auchinleck's conduct throughout 1942, as the War Office reiterated when commenting on Churchill's draft of book 1.[35] It helps, for instance, to explain his unwillingness to mount a desert offensive in the spring, while the Germans were surging into southeast Russia and the Red Army was surrendering in droves. It also accounts for his reluctance to take personal command of the Eighth Army, lest he lose sight of the big picture. In chapter 21, Churchill notes the Auk's anxiety about the danger from the north, "to which he felt it his duty to attach an importance to which we at home, in a better position to judge, no longer subscribed." This statement is very misleading. In early August 1942, when Churchill arrived in Cairo, debate about future dispositions in the desert was paralyzed by uncertainty over the northern flank. This is clear from the diary of Sir Ian Jacob, Churchill's wartime military aide, which Churchill borrowed from January 1949 to October 1950.[36]

One aim of Churchill's visit to Moscow a few days later was therefore to form a judgment about the Caucasus. In his second chapter about the visit, Churchill records Stalin's assurance that the Red Army could hold the line for two months, after which winter snows would make the mountains impassable. He also prints his telegram to the War Cabinet, which includes the comment "my own feeling is that it is an even chance they will hold, but the C.I.G.S. [Brooke] will not go so far as this." This refers to a persistent divide: Brooke was very pessimistic about the northern flank, Churchill less so. "I did not believe the Germans would reach Baku," he writes later in the memoirs, noting that he had a standing bet with Brooke on the matter. But the personal telegram of 28 September that he cites immediately afterward is more nuanced, saying that "I have always felt that the Russians would hold the line of the Caucasus mountains *until the spring*, and that Baku would not be taken *this year*. I must admit that this view is temperamental rather than scientific." It is therefore clear that, although Churchill was more confident about the northern flank in 1942 than Brooke, as in 1941, he had real doubts. By dismissing this argument as special pleading for Auchinleck, he distorts the pervasive strategic uncertainty in the months before Stalingrad.[37]

When Churchill writes that "we at home" were "in a better position to judge" the threat from the north, he is making oblique reference to his decrypts from Axis signals. As usual, however, there is nothing explicit about the Ultra secret in the volume after the Secret Intelligence Service (SIS) had read the draft with its customary vigilance.[38] Nor could Churchill explain that in the early months Auchinleck remained largely in the dark about Rommel's dispositions and intentions. By June 1942, Bletchley Park was providing useful signals intelligence, but this was still not being handled effectively in the field. During the July battles around Alamein, however, Auchinleck was not only receiving high-quality, up-to-date information from "the other side of the hill" but also using it skillfully. All this became clear in 1981 when the official history of British wartime intelligence during 1942 was published, but these essential parts of the jigsaw are missing from Churchill's account in 1950.[39]

Tanks, the northern flank, and intelligence delineate the arena for subsequent debate among historians of the Desert War. But, when all has been said in Auchinleck's defense, 1942 could hardly be described as a success story: the Eighth Army had lost six hundred miles in six months. By the time Auchinleck stabilized the line at Alamein at the end of July, Churchill had no doubt that changes must be made in the High Command, and this was the main reason for his stopovers in Cairo in August, before and after Moscow. The result was the removal of Auchinleck from command of both the Eighth Army and the Middle East theater, and his replacement by Montgomery at the army level and by Alexander as theater commander. Not surprisingly, therefore, these events became known as the "sacking" of Auchinleck.

It is therefore important to note that it was not Churchill's intention at the time to sack Auchinleck. According to the War Cabinet minutes on 1 August 1942, a few hours before Churchill and Brooke left London, the Prime Minister "thought the time had now been reached when General Auchinleck could once more concern himself with the duties of Commander-in-Chief, Middle East, some other general being appointed to command the Eighth Army."[40] His first choice as army commander, "Strafer" Gott, was shot down and killed the next day while flying back to Cairo. Thereupon Churchill accepted Brooke's recommendation of his own protégé, Monty.

In Cairo, Churchill concluded that Auchinleck should be moved as well. On 6 August, he offered the Middle East command to Brooke, who, after anguished reflection, declined.[41] None of this appears, however, in the American edition of *The Hinge of Fate*. After the serials had been published, Lord Alanbrooke, as he then was, reminded Churchill, via Pownall, on 10 November 1950 of the original offer and also advanced two reasons why he had declined: first, his concern not to upset the smooth running of the machine in Whitehall, only eight months into his job there; second, having taken part in Auchinleck's removal, it might appear that he had come to Cairo to get the command for himself. Pownall told Churchill that "Brookie" particularly hoped his two points would be noted in the memoirs because "a biography of him is being planned. Mention is sure to be made therein and it would therefore be appropriate if you referred to it first." Churchill duly inserted these two points in the British edition, but it must have been galling to Alanbrooke that Churchill had clearly forgotten "one of the most difficult days of my life." This was part of a pattern: Churchill's memoirs are notable for their lack of praise or even mention of Alanbrooke, unlike hero generals such as Alexander. As we shall see, this became a source of deep grievance for Alanbrooke.[42]

Churchill then settled on Alexander for the post. But the Prime Minister still respected Auchinleck and proposed that the vast Middle East command, stretching from the Libyan desert to the Caucasus, be split in two. Alex would run the "Near East" (Egypt, Palestine, and Syria), Auchinleck the "Middle East," now redefined as Persia and Iraq. Churchill was trying to let the Auk down gently and also probably did not want to accentuate his own reputation as an autocrat. The new Middle East command was not a total sop. Churchill genuinely believed that Auchinleck had been fatally distracted by his schizophrenia between the Caucasus and the Western Desert. And, given the continuing worries about the northern flank, Churchill was not merely flattering when he told Auchinleck that his proposed command "may in a few months become the scene of decisive operations."[43]

Churchill's offer foundered on two rocks. First, Auchinleck regarded it as an insult. He met the Prime Minister for an hour on 9 August, in a conversation beautifully described by Churchill as "at once bleak and impeccable."[44] But even before that, the War Cabinet had revolted—a rare and therefore sobering occurrence—objecting to the divided command and especially to the retention of the title "Middle East" for Auchinleck's truncated theater. Twice on 7 August, the War Cabinet convened to discuss Churchill's reiterated arguments; twice, it rebuffed them. The essential point—toned down in the telegrams to Cairo but clear in the Cabinet minutes and the original notes—was the need for a political scapegoat: "The impression would be conveyed that this separate command had been created in order to let him down lightly." There would be "criticism at home" that they were "creating new posts for those who had failed to make good in their existing appointments." The Labour members of the War Cabinet were most outspoken on this point, especially Cripps, but Sir James Grigg, the Secretary of State for War, also wanted to remove Auchinleck completely.[45]

None of this appears in the memoirs. Churchill does not print the War Cabinet's replies to his telegrams, speaking only in vague terms of its concern that the proposed command arrangements would "lead to confusion and misrepresentation." In August 1950, he heavily cut his own justificatory telegram home on 6 August. Among the omissions are the following striking sentences:

> I have no hesitation in proposing Auchinleck's appointment to it [the Iraq-Persia command]. At the head of an army with a single and direct purpose he commands my entire confidence. If he had taken command of the Eighth Army when I urged him to I believe we should have won the Gazala battle [and thus Tobruk], and many people here think the same. He has shown high-minded qualities of character and resolution. He restored the Battle of Sidi Rezegh, and has only recently stemmed the tide at Alamein.

Churchill also cut another long passage beginning "Nor can I advise that General Auchinleck should be ruined and cast aside as unfit to render any further service."[46] Even if Churchill had been given a free hand, it is unlikely that

Auchinleck would have said yes, but the fact remains that his abrupt and total departure from the Middle Eastern war was not Churchill's original intention in August 1942.

That was not, however, the way it seemed by 1950 in Churchill's memoirs. The dominant impression that Auchinleck had been sacked as a failure is enhanced by the contrast Churchill paints between the old order and the new in the chapter about his return to Cairo in late August. He quotes at length from his telegram to the War Cabinet on 21 August:

> I am sure we were heading for disaster under the former régime. The Army was reduced to bits and pieces and oppressed by a sense of bafflement and uncertainty. Apparently it was intended in face of heavy attack to retire eastwards to the Delta. Many were looking over their shoulders to make sure of their seat in the lorry. . . . Since then, from what I could see myself of the troops and hear from their commanders, a complete change of atmosphere has taken place.

In the text, he also describes Monty's "masterly exposition of the situation, showing that in a few days he had firmly gripped the whole problem. He accurately predicted Rommel's next attack, and explained his plans to meet it. All of which proved true and sound. He then described his plans for taking the offensive himself."[47]

Each of these passages in "Return to Cairo" became the focus of intense historical argument in later years, so their provenance is therefore important. The telegram was actually based on comments made to Churchill at the time by Montgomery, but when Monty in his 1958 memoirs repeated the claim that the Auk was ready to retreat to Cairo, he was obliged to disavow it in future editions. As for Monty's "masterly exposition," this was another insertion suggested in November 1950 by Brooke, Monty's wartime patron. It would also form the basis of subsequent controversy, with claims both that Monty's foreknowledge of Rommel's plans was not, as Brooke asserted, a sign of "almost prophetic foresight" but a tribute to Ultra and also that his plans for defense and offense had been taken over from "the former régime." As we shall see, this controversy opened up sensationally in 1953, in the form of an action for libel against Churchill.[48]

Having installed the new team of Alexander and Montgomery, Churchill waited impatiently for their offensive at Alamein, which finally opened on 23 October, though it took a week of bitter fighting before Monty's forces broke through. In the book, the basic draft about the battle (and the four maps) came as usual from Pownall, supplemented by material from Alexander's long telegram of

9 November 1942. In his chapter, Churchill cannot acknowledge the vastly improved intelligence position, both at the command level and in the field. He does note the enhanced strength of the Eighth Army, including a two-to-one superiority in tanks (half of them now American). But the overall impression is that superior generalship was the key to victory: Alexander "cool, gay, comprehending all" and Montgomery "a great artillerist," concentrating his firepower in preparation for attack. Churchill plays down his disputes with the new command as he badgered them, no less than Auchinleck, for early action and was firmly told to wait. Some heated exchanges on 20–21 September 1942 were cut from the August 1950 draft because Churchill's emphasis in the memoirs was on partnership and success now that the right men were in place.[49] In similar vein, he slides over the near collapse of Monty's plans in the first few days of the battle, when it became clear that the British armor was unable or unwilling to mount a frontal attack down the narrow corridors cleared through the German minefields, whereupon Alamein became an infantry slugging match. Some of this story was readily available in the memoirs of Freddie de Guingand, Monty's intelligence officer, published in 1947, but Pownall does not seem to have used this source at all. Churchill's chapter leaves the impression that Alamein was a hard-fought but inexorable victory.[50]

In most of its drafts, the chapter on Alamein ended lamely with a jumble of congratulatory telegrams that left the last word with King Abdullah of Transjordan, hardly a world-historical figure. Noting this in July 1950, Norman Brook suggested adding an appreciation of Alamein "as one of the important turning points in the war" and also some account of "the invigorating effect" of Monty on the Eighth Army. Emery Reves reminded Churchill of "the words you used last year in one of our private conversations: 'Before El Alamein we never had a victory. After El Alamein we never had a defeat.'" Following these suggestions, Churchill added to the August 1950 version a conclusion about Monty and Alamein, ending with one of the great perorations of volume 4 about the turning of the hinge of fate: "It may almost be said [he added belatedly, in a prudent but oft-forgotten modifier], 'Before Alamein we never had a victory. After Alamein we never had a defeat.'" Here, in essence, was Churchill's story of the Desert War.[51]

MIDWAY AND ALAMEIN were the hinges of the war in 1942–1943: that was Churchill's judgment in 1950. Today, however, few would dispute that Stalingrad was the most important turning point of all. The epic siege began in August 1942 and General Friedrich Paulus's Sixth Army was soon in the heart of the city, fighting house by house, floor by floor. But the Red Army held on, and in

November a dramatic Soviet pincer attack around the German rear turned the besiegers into the besieged. On 31 January 1943, pictures of Paulus, gaunt, sick, and unshaven, signing the instrument of capitulation, were flashed around the world—almost a year after similar images of General Arthur Percival in his baggy shorts, trudging through the Japanese lines to surrender Singapore. In every respect, Stalingrad dwarfed Alamein. The Russians lost a half million men, the Eighth Army 13,500. Some 147,000 Germans had been killed by the Red Army and another 91,000 taken prisoner, whereas the grandest estimate of Axis prisoners after Alamein was about 30,000. Alamein could be brushed aside by German propaganda—after all, the majority of Rommel's army was Italian—but the disaster of Stalingrad could not be concealed from the German people. Official radio played solemn music for three days, including, time and again, Siegfried's funeral march from Wagner's *Götterdämmerung*, the Twilight of the Gods. The "Hitler Myth" never recovered.[52]

Yet Stalingrad is almost absent from Churchill's war memoirs. He allots it a total of four pages of text, plus two half-page maps. Moreover, this is divided up between two chapters more than 100 pages apart, further reducing the impact. This material came from Pownall not Churchill and was added in August 1950. The only Churchillian touches were a couple of introductory sentences about "the tremendous drama unfolding around Stalingrad" and a brief summing-up: "This crushing disaster to the German arms ended Hitler's prodigious effort to conquer Russia by force of arms, and destroy Communism by an equally odious form of totalitarian tyranny." Quoted in isolation, "tremendous drama" and "prodigious effort" might suggest that Churchill acknowledged the epic character of the battle. But measured against the bulk of *The Hinge of Fate*, he is almost silent about Stalingrad.[53]

Even these limited additions were largely due to Emery Reves. In the draft he read in July there were only two references to Stalingrad, both of them asides in Churchill telegrams. Reves said bluntly that this was not enough: "Everybody believes that Stalingrad was the turning point in the war together with Alamein. A description of the battle, in the manner you describe the Battles of the Coral Sea and Midway, seems indispensable." Ideally, a whole chapter should be devoted to it; at worst, five or six pages of narrative using the word "Stalingrad" in the chapter title. Otherwise, "most reviewers" would be critical. These comments on Stalingrad were part of a larger critique about the parochialism of Churchill's account. "I understand that you are telling in this work only the British story of the War," Reves wrote in August 1949. "But the great political and military events in America and Russia cannot be completely ignored." He wanted one or two pages each for the Philippines, Midway, Guadalcanal, Moscow, Leningrad, and Stalingrad, so the reader could see the unfolding story in "proper perspective." In particular, he urged Churchill "to begin this Volume with the big battles raging in Russia" rather than what he called in July 1950 "a minor family quarrel" with Australia.[54]

Probably in response to Reves, Allen produced the chapter on Midway, and until the last minute volume 4 also contained his rough chapter on Guadalcanal—eventually dumped untidily and unchronologically into volume 5 because of the rush to meet Houghton Mifflin's deadline. But Churchill made almost no effort to address Reves's point on the Soviet side. There is only this vestigial outline on Stalingrad and nothing on the three-year siege of Leningrad, where the Russian death toll of nearly one million exceeded that of Britain and America combined in the whole of World War II.

Why this imbalance? Churchill liked to say in his prefaces that he was not writing history but a contribution to history, told from his personal vantage point as Prime Minister. But he breached that principle with the chapter on Midway, in which he played no role and about which he had written no documents. On the Pacific War there was an ideal source to hand, Samuel Eliot Morison's history of U.S. naval operations, whereas nothing so convenient existed on the Soviet side. Nevertheless, there were already published sources available in English, particularly by the journalist Alexander Werth, and Pownall had dug some evidence out of the British official archives. Ultimately, the problem was lack of inclination. Pownall, who might have prodded Churchill, evinced no great interest in the Soviet war effort, whereas Allen was keen to write about the U.S. Navy as well as the British one. Deakin, who might have unearthed appropriate German sources as he had done to good effect on the Rome-Berlin axis, was by 1950 too deeply absorbed at Oxford to do more than clarify and consolidate the existing drafts. Above all, Churchill himself was probably resistant. Although he paid chivalric tribute to the Red Army on various occasions during the 1940s, the Cold War hung like a cloud over his memoirs. The comment he added to Pownall's draft about Nazism and Communism being "equally odious" forms of "totalitarian tyranny" is a reminder of this mood. Especially in August 1950, at a desperate moment in the Korean War, Churchill had no reason to feel generous toward Moscow.

Here, as in so many places in the memoirs, we see Churchill blazing a path for future English-speaking historians. The clamor of battle in Southeast Asia and North Africa was to echo through decades of historiographical debate. But it was only after the Cold War that the silence of Stalingrad was broken and Russia's war became the true centerpiece of the hinge of fate.

CHAPTER 20

SECOND FRONT:
WHEN, WHERE, AND HOW?

S ECOND FRONT NOW!" is the title of chapter 18 of *The Hinge of Fate*, echoing the popular slogan of 1942. The Americans and Russians argued that the Second Front could be opened only across the Channel in France. The British claimed this was impossible until 1943 and successfully pressed the case for North Africa in 1942. Landings in Algeria and Morocco eventually took place on 8 November. Throughout 1942–1943 there was also a deeper debate about whether a Second Front would be needed at all. Proponents of "strategic bombing" asserted that this could break Germany's will to fight and avoid the need for a major land operation. The time, place, and very necessity for a Second Front were vital issues for Churchill in 1942, and they lie at the heart of *The Hinge of Fate*.

THERE WERE TWO Anglo-American plans: Sledgehammer, an emergency attack by six to ten divisions in 1942, and Roundup, a full-scale invasion by perhaps forty divisions in 1943. Sledgehammer was proposed partly as a device to relieve the Russians, whose demands for an immediate Second Front feature in chapter 19; the British viewed it as a likely disaster. Yet Churchill was adamant that they could not simply sit back and build up resources for 1943. Roosevelt was even keener on some kind of action in 1942 and personally inclined to strike in northwest Africa. And so, despite the reservations of FDR's military advisers, the decision for Operation Torch was taken in July 1942.

All this is narrated in chapters 18 to 20 of book 1. Subsequent chapters describe the final planning, the successful landings, and the hard-fought struggle to evict the Germans from Tunisia, eventually achieved in May 1943. "Victory in Tunis," asserts Churchill, "held its own with Stalingrad." But because this victory was gained in the spring of 1943, not at the end of 1942 as originally hoped, it was too late to mount Roundup, the invasion of France, in 1943. At conferences in May 1943, Churchill again insisted that the Allies could not simply stand idle until the next year's campaigning season and urged that they capture Sicily and Italy in 1943. Despite the resistance of General George Marshall, the U.S. Army Chief of Staff, the Prime Minister again got his way. He ends his volume portraying the Allies as virtually at one: "I felt that great advances had been made in our discussions and that everybody wanted to go for Italy."[1]

But by pushing the Mediterranean theater twice in successive years, Churchill gained a lasting reputation as an obdurate opponent of cross-Channel attack. These charges were aired as early as 1946 by Ralph Ingersoll and Elliott Roosevelt. Churchill alludes to them in chapter 12 of *Their Finest Hour* and takes pains to address them head-on in *The Hinge of Fate*. He portrays himself as always skeptical about Sledgehammer but happy to let it stand or fall by a process of "Strategic Natural Selection"—out of many competing plans, the fittest would survive. A draft in August 1949 had been more candid: "None of us on the British side saw how a heavy attack across the Channel could be launched in 1942; but we were more than willing that this should be studied and worked out in goodwill and good faith."[2] The British feared that, after Pearl Harbor and the loss of the Philippines, the Americans would try to shift their main war effort to the Pacific. It was therefore important not to repudiate Sledgehammer outright. In the event, Roosevelt and Marshall, "rising superior to powerful tides of public opinion," confirmed the Germany First principle agreed on in 1941. (The August 1949 draft said "almost indifferent to public opinion.") But the growing American conviction that London had never been serious about Sledgehammer cast doubt on British good faith.[3]

What, then, of Roundup? Churchill is at pains to show that he was sincere about this plan for a major invasion of France in 1943. When Reves suggested that since the chapter "Strategic Natural Selection" mostly comprised four of his strategy papers from mid-1942 about "plans which were *not* carried out," it might be better to relegate them to the appendixes, Churchill wrote a firm no in the margin, presumably because this documentation was essential for his self-defense. Likewise, in "Problems of Victory" he prints documents from November 1942 showing his alarm when it seemed that the U.S. troop buildup in

Britain had tailed off. Torch was "no substitute" for Roundup, he told Roosevelt; to the Chiefs of Staff he wrote that North Africa was supposed to be "a spring-board and not a sofa." In fact, if Torch was "going to be made an excuse for lock-ing up great forces on the defensive and calling it a 'commitment,' it would be better not to have gone in there at all."[4]

But, as seen in his papers of December 1941, Churchill's conception of a cross-Channel attack was a far cry from the eventual D-Day plan. In a long paper about Roundup, dated 15 June 1942 and printed in "Strategic Natural Selec-tion," he talked of "at least six heavy disembarkations" at various points along the north and west coast of Europe, from Denmark and Holland down the Pas-de-Calais ("where the major air battle will be fought") to Brest and Bordeaux. He also advocated "at least half a dozen feints" to mystify the enemy. These armored landings would be followed by a second wave of heavier attacks at four or five strategic points, with the hope that three might be successful. "The moment any port is gained and open the third wave of attack should start," comprising not less than 300,000 infantry and supporting artillery.[5]

In his memoirs, Churchill calls this paper "my first thoughts" on such an operation, but that was also how he presented the invasion of the Continent later in the summer to Marshall and to Stalin. He does not mention that his paper was shot down by the land, sea, and air commanders of Home Forces two weeks after its composition, even though a copy of their critique existed in his working files. Deploring all talk of "feints," the home commanders insisted there should be only three or four large thrusts much closer together, with the foci at the Pas-de-Calais and the Seine port of Le Havre.[6] And once again Churchill glosses over his continued emphasis in 1942 on setting Europe ablaze. In the 15 June paper, he cited "rousing the populations" as a main aim of the first-wave attacks. In his "Review of the War Position" on 21 July—a major appraisal for the Cabinet printed only in his appendix—he looked forward to "mass invasion of the Conti-nent by liberating armies, and general revolt of the populations against the Hitler tyranny." On this theme, too, the home commanders were much more skeptical. Despite the "great potential value" of "patriot forces," they warned that much would depend on the speed and depth of the initial Allied penetration.[7] Although Churchill was therefore right to claim that in 1942 he had clear plans for a cross-Channel attack in 1943, these were at odds with those of his leading advisers and bore little resemblance to what was mounted in June 1944.

When Churchill cast around for possible theaters of action in 1942, he looked north as well as south, and his memoirs do not conceal his passion for Operation Jupiter, a landing in the north of Norway. In memoranda of the time he spoke of this as a way of rolling "the map of Hitler's Europe down from the top"—another example of his mind being seduced by a suggestive phrase. The Chiefs of Staff had no difficulty pointing out the flaws in such a plan, but that did not stop him from reviving Norway on numerous occasions, much to the fury of Brooke. "If I could have had my full way," admits Churchill in "Second Front Now!" the ideal would have been Jupiter *and* Torch in 1942, though never if the former should "queer the pitch of 'Torch.'" This underlines a point already made when discussing the Phony War: Churchill was always as ready to probe the Baltic as the Mediterranean. His strategic thought was opportunistic, and memory of the Dardanelles should not persuade us he had a rigid Mediterranean strategy.[8]

The principal attraction of northern Norway was the airfields from which Gemany menaced Arctic convoys, and this reflects one of Churchill's main motives for doing something in 1942: the need to reassure the Russians. His aim in visiting Moscow in August 1942 was to persuade Stalin that the Mediterranean could be a surrogate Second Front. At their first meeting, Churchill drew a picture of a crocodile to show that one could attack "the soft belly" of the enemy (the Mediterranean) as well as "his hard snout" (France). In describing the visits to Britain in May and June by Vyacheslav Molotov, Stalin's Foreign Minister, he is at pains to rebut the charge of deliberately misleading the Soviets. After Roosevelt had proposed a vague but potentially misleading communiqué stating that "full understanding was reached with regard to the urgent tasks of creating a Second Front in Europe in 1942," Churchill gave Molotov an aide-mémoire making clear that while the Allies would try their best, there were huge logistic problems to overcome, and "we can therefore give no promise in the matter." Whenever Russians later impugned Britain's good faith, Churchill adds, he always pointed to those words. But before publishing this document in volume 4, he cut the compensatory paragraph highlighting Anglo-American determination to land up to 1.5 million troops on the Continent the following year—a theme he also developed to Stalin in Moscow in August 1942. In other words, while protecting himself against possible imputations of bad faith about 1942, Churchill left hostages to fortune for 1943. The way he cut the 1943 promise from his memoirs suggests that he realized this.[9]

Why, then, was there no cross-Channel attack in 1943? This is a bigger and more significant question than the failure to mount what would surely have been a suicide mission, largely British and Canadian, in 1942. The answers are there in Churchill's chapters, though rarely underlined for our attention—and once again what he says or does not say staked out the terrain for later historians.

The basic problem was that the Allies did not take Tunis before the winter rains descended in December 1942, turning roads and airfields into quagmires. There would have been a greater chance of doing so if the Americans had been willing to land more U.S. forces inside the Strait of Gibraltar, thus reducing the distance to Tunis, but they feared Hitler would occupy Spain and mount heavy air attacks against landings on the opposite shore. Churchill describes American concerns at length in his chapter "The Final Shaping of 'Torch'" and is later discreetly critical of their consequences. He also blames Vichy's "caitiff decision" on 8 November to allow the Germans use of Tunisian airfields—"caitiff" being his own addition to Deakin's draft.[10]

But the main reason for the Allied failure to win a quick victory was Hitler's refusal to abandon North Africa. Churchill admits that, in retrospect, it seemed Marshall was right to warn that Torch in 1942 precluded Roundup in 1943— "Certainly this is what happened." But, he goes on, "no one could foresee at this time that Hitler would make his immense effort to reinforce the Tunisian tip," using nearly 100,000 of his best troops. That Churchill shared in this misconception by British planners is evident from his minutes at the time. On 9 November 1942, he told the Chiefs of Staff that the success of Torch is "now plainly in sight after one day's campaign. . . . In a month French North Africa should be comfortably and securely in Allied hands." On 3 December, he remained optimistic that "by the end of the year we may be masters of the whole of French North Africa including Tunisia." It was quite explicitly against this background that Churchill went on to elaborate his plans for a thirty-five-division invasion of France in July 1943. The chapter "Problems of Victory" prints passages from these memos that show his continued commitment to Roundup, while omitting the sections that expose his expectation of rapid victory in North Africa. This sleight of hand is important, because Churchill's enthusiasm for 1943 was dependent on his optimism about 1942.[11]

Although the failure to take Tunis in 1942 was the main reason why there was no cross-Channel invasion in 1943, the Pacific War was a contributory factor. By April 1942, Japan's spectacular victories had taken it to the edges of India and Australia, and Allied reinforcements were needed simply to hold the line, let alone turn the tide. Despite their concern to safeguard "Germany First," Churchill and his advisers feared that Japan might join forces with Germany in India and the Middle East.[12] April 1942 marked the peak of British anxiety, but the American concern for the Pacific lasted much longer. Churchill, quoting Sherwood's *Roosevelt and Hopkins*, says that 15 July 1942 was "a very tense day in the White House," where it was seriously suggested that if Britain would not mount

Sledgehammer then the United States should ignore North Africa and concentrate on Japan. "There is no evidence that either General Marshall or Admiral King harboured such ideas," Churchill tells us, but "there was a strong surge of feeling in the powerful second rank of the American Staff." These sentences were added in March 1950. The claims about Marshall and Ernest King (the U.S. Chief of Naval Operations) are at odds with documentary extracts published in this chapter—for instance, a telegram from Dill to Churchill on 15 July that he quoted on the previous page.[13]

Churchill's memoirs suggest that the Pacific First idea was finally scotched by the July decision for Torch. But, as later historians have shown, despite the Germany First rhetoric, the reality was Pacific First for the rest of 1942. Privately, King and even Marshall diverted resources to the Pacific, including fifteen air groups originally designated for Britain, as well as troops and landing craft that were redeployed to the escalating campaign on Guadalcanal. Had Churchill included a chapter on Guadalcanal in volume 4, some of this might have come to light. Instead, we simply have a side reference from November 1942 to the way the American buildup in Britain (code-named Bolero) seemed to have run out of steam. Churchill adds that this impression was a "misunderstanding, which had arisen at a lower level." But this is wrong: Bolero *had* run down, as much because of the Pacific as North Africa. Thus, the delay in invading France was not simply the fault of Britain's "Mediterranean strategy." By neglecting the Pacific after June 1942, Churchill's memoirs missed important evidence against his critics.[14]

One of the passages Churchill cut from Dill's cable of 15 July 1942 included the warning that "no one has faced the real dislocation of shipping which having two main theatres to maintain would involve, and how imports to Britain would be affected."[15] This was a prescient remark. Churchill does have a chapter called "The Shipping Stranglehold," in which he states that "shipping was at once the stranglehold and sure foundation of our war strategy." The new demands posed by U.S. belligerency and the Pacific War complicated the relatively simple picture of transatlantic supply in 1941, and the renewed success of the U-boats meant that sinkings in 1942 vastly exceeded Anglo-American new construction. Churchill makes these points, but, as Kelly rightly noted, they needed "a lot more rubbing in" to other chapters and are never fully developed even in the sections about shipping. The war at sea constitutes one of the weakest links in *The Hinge of Fate*.[16]

"The Shipping Stranglehold" is actually a ragbag chapter that started out as "Shipping and Strategy" because that was the theme of some March 1942 telegrams to Roosevelt around which the chapter was built. On 13 August 1950,

Churchill told his assistants he wanted to enlarge the discussion of strategy, "showing how shipping was the limiting factor and sole foundation," but despite some tinkering the chapter never broke free from its moorings in March 1942. On 31 August, Gordon Allen urged Churchill to incorporate the shipping paragraphs from his lengthy "Review of the War Position" dated 21 July 1942, which Allen had recently resurrected from the Cabinet Office. "It makes a fine climax to the subject under discussion," he told Churchill. "Without such a summary the whole chapter seems to me to lack the precision required." But it was too late for wholesale revisions, and on Churchill's instructions the review stayed in the appendix. This is a pity, because Allen was right about its value. In the review, after discussing the U-boat depredations and the danger of reducing imports yet further, Churchill informed the Cabinet that Britain needed "a solemn compact, almost a treaty, with the United States about the share of their new building we are to get in 1943 and 1944." This phrase would have led him naturally to his 31 October letter to the President, which identified the U-boat as "our worst danger," postulated 27 million tons of imports as Britain's essential minimum for 1943, and asked that U.S. shipping cover at least 7 million tons of that. The letter was carried to Washington by Oliver Lyttelton, Britain's Minister of Production, and on 30 November Roosevelt offered Lyttelton "definite assurance," with some qualifications, that "your requirements will be met."[17]

Bureaucratic confusion and rivalry in Washington nearly scuppered the whole deal, but eventually FDR kept his promise, and U.S. shipping proved invaluable to Britain in 1943. In other words, even though the full and tangled shipping story lay outside Churchill's interest and purview, he could easily have featured its essentials from his own documents in 1942. He did not do so in part, perhaps, because the sources were not readily available. The Cabinet paper was unearthed only very late, while the messages to and from Roosevelt on 31 October and 30 November were letters and therefore not printed in the annual runs of his personal telegrams. But there is a deeper reason. Logistics were largely a closed book for Churchill, both as war leader and as postwar historian. And opening it would have shown how the hasty decision for Torch, without attention to the logistical burden that fell on Britain, exacerbated the shipping crisis and further delayed the cross-Channel attack.

Churchill also has little to say about the Battle of the Atlantic, to which he had devoted several chapters in earlier volumes. What aroused him were battles to the death against great surface ships, such as the *Graf Spee* or the *Bismarck*. The U-boat war was less visible and exciting, and one of its most dramatic aspects—the loss and then recovery of the German naval codes during 1942—

could not be mentioned. (Churchill explains mastery of the U-boat mostly by reference to airborne radar, though he does make cryptic reference to "other measures.") As in volume 3, therefore, Allen had to fight hard for coverage of the Battle of the Atlantic, and there is only one substantive chapter about it in *The Hinge of Fate*, entitled "The U-Boat Paradise." This started out as a July 1949 paper by Allen on U-boats in American waters, where they ran amok in early 1942. Allen then prepared another paper, "The U-Boat Mastered," taking the story from July 1942 to May 1943. But both papers were short—as with the Coral Sea and Midway, Allen relied heavily on Morison's history—and in May 1950 they were fused. In the British edition, "The U-Boat Paradise" runs to twenty-three pages, of which four are maps or charts.[18]

Unlike the rest of the Syndicate, Allen was not invited on the working vacations. Churchill even avoided talking to him, though in March and April 1950 Allen twice asked in writing for a meeting.[19] A shy man, he lacked Deakin's incisiveness and conviviality or the forthrightness of Henry Pownall, and Churchill had possibly tired of his company. But their distance was probably also a measure of Churchill's lack of interest in the naval war by this stage in his memoirs. This was unfortunate. In fusing the two draft chapters about the U-boat, as Allen complained, Churchill did "rather less than justice to a phase of the war which, as you say, alone made possible the great events of 1944."[20] Without command of the Atlantic, Overlord would have been impossible.

IN 1942, there was much discussion in London about whether strategic bombing alone could bring Germany to its knees—perhaps the dilemma of how to open a Second Front could be answered from above? This debate appears only piecemeal in volume 4. One explanation is that Churchill did not yet have someone to research the air war. Pownall kept reminding him about this gap, but Churchill procrastinated, and it was not until the summer of 1950 that Air Marshal Sir Guy Garrod was recruited to write drafts on the strategic-bomber offensive. Consequently, this material, like Guadalcanal, was dumped into volume 5, even though much of it belonged chronologically in *The Hinge of Fate*.[21] But what fragments about the air war are in this volume do provide some stepping-stones through one of the most important strategic debates of 1942.

After the fall of France, the bombing campaign had become the only way for the British to strike back at Germany; this was enshrined in all British and Allied strategic documents. But in the first half of 1942, denunciations of Bomber Command became almost deafening in Whitehall. Critics said that Britain was producing an excess of heavy bombers and that too many of them were being wasted in ineffective mass raids over Germany. This debate surfaces briefly in chapter 10 of *The Hinge of Fate* when Wavell, Commander in Chief in India, warned in April 1942 that the Japanese naval drive menaced British control of the Indian Ocean and of India itself: "It certainly gives us furiously to think when, after trying with less than twenty light bombers to meet [an] attack which has cost us three important warships and several others and nearly 100,000 tons of merchant shipping, we see that over 200 heavy bombers attacked one town in Germany." Similar cries came from the Middle East, where Auchinleck wanted more air support for his troops, and from the navy, desperate to strengthen Coastal Command against the U-boats. Against them, Sir Arthur Harris battled to keep Bomber Command together. He was convinced that strategic bombing would be the winning weapon in the war, and he used massive and highly publicized assaults on Germany to boost popular support. The night of 30 May 1942 saw the celebrated Thousand Bomber Raid on Cologne, which Churchill mentions in passing when quoting from a speech to the Commons in the chapter entitled "Rommel Attacks." Reves, keen as ever for more drama and fewer documents, urged in August 1949 that the Cologne raid should be described in detail—"preparation, operation, results"—but although this idea was touted until the final stages of revision, nothing was added to the original ten lines.[22]

Thus, Churchill glosses over the bomber offensive and the criticisms of it, which came to a head in the Chiefs of Staff Committee and the Cabinet in July and August 1942. His position has been fairly described as "consistently ambivalent."[23] He wanted more planes for the army and particularly the navy, but not if that meant frittering away a major British asset in small packets. As he told Wavell in April, "One has to be sure that we do not ruin our punch here without getting any proportionate advantage elsewhere." This message is printed in volume 4, as is an exchange between him and Lord Trenchard, one of the pioneers of airpower, in August 1942, but these are scattered references, more than 300 pages apart, and Churchill offers only hints that a major row was in progress. As with the shipping issue, however, he could easily have traced its contours by reference to his own documents, particularly if the 21 July "Review of the War," written as part of that debate, had been located and used at an early stage, rather than being consigned to an appendix. In this paper, he noted that "when we were fighting alone we answered the question, 'How are you going to win the war?' by saying 'We will shatter Germany by bombing.'" Since 1941, the combination of Russian manpower and American munitions had "rendered other possibilities open"—namely, the mass invasion of the Continent by "liberating armies" and a general revolt by the captive populations. "All the same," Churchill went on, it would be a mistake to cast aside our original thought—which, it may be mentioned, is also strong in American minds—namely, that the severe, ruthless bombing of Germany on an ever-increasing scale will not only cripple her war effort, including U-boat and aircraft production, but will also create conditions intolerable to the mass of the German population.[24]

The comment about creating conditions "intolerable to the mass of the German population" touches on an especially delicate feature of the strategic-bombing debate: was it conceived as "precision attacks" on military-industrial targets or as "terror bombing" of urban areas, designed to break civilian morale? Churchill's comments in July 1942 suggest that the latter was in his mind, and he cut several similar remarks when editing documents for his memoirs. For instance, the British text of his first meeting at the Kremlin on 12 August 1942 recorded Churchill's assurance to Stalin that Britain looked on German civilian morale "as a military target" and "hoped to shatter twenty German cities as we had shattered Cologne." As the war went on, he said, Britain "hoped to shatter almost every dwelling in almost every German city."[25] Of course, Churchill needed to sound particularly bellicose when Stalin was accusing the British of inertia and even cowardice. But he took the same line in a paper about Italy for the War Cabinet in November 1942: "All the industrial centres should be attacked in an intense fashion, every effort being made to terrorise and paralyse the population." These remarks were also cut from the text during 1950. Churchill did not manage to sanitize everything—buried in his January 1943 letter to the Turkish President, occupying more than three pages of the book, is the pledge that "our intention is to destroy Italy; shatter her entirely." But at the end of volume 4, he is careful to present the rail yards in Rome as "an important and necessary military target," provided that "the attacks were made by day and due care was taken to prevent damage elsewhere."[26]

Although Churchill therefore played down the point in his memoirs, in 1942 he saw strategic bombing as the most plausible way to wear down Germany. Unlike Trenchard, he did not claim that it would make a land invasion unnecessary, but he viewed systematic air attacks on German cities as essential to create the conditions for successful Allied landings and for revolt by the conquered populations. Although "Victory in Tunis" contains some approbatory comments about tactical airpower in support of ground troops, these came from Pownall.[27] Churchill's opinion on the matter in 1942–1943 was more accurately conveyed in a long memo on 29 July 1942 to Clement Attlee—the Labour leader, Deputy Prime Minister, and a persistent critic of strategic bombing. This memo, cut from the final version of the appendixes, rebutted Attlee point by point, questioning the value of dive-bombers, defending an autonomous air force, and insisting that it would be "disastrous" to turn the RAF into "a mere handmaid of the Army."[28] Strategic bombing may not have been very successful, but what else was there to cling to as the means of victory? In mid-1942, the Russians were again being routed by the Wehrmacht, and the gloom that sometimes engulfed Churchill is evident in another passage from this memo: "Continuous reflection leaves me with the conclusion that, upon the whole, our best chance of winning the war is with the big bombers. It will certainly be several years before British and American land forces will be capable of beating the Germans on even terms in the open field." Not quite the line he took with the Americans about mounting Roundup in 1943.[29]

The corollary to waging a war of attrition with limited resources and no major allies was the likelihood of an eventual negotiated peace with a non-Nazi German government. As we have seen, Churchill did not rule this out as late as November 1941. But he admitted in his "Review of the War" on 21 July 1942 that alliance with Russia and America opened new paths to victory, and he sounded a correspondingly harsher note about a negotiated peace. "In the event of an overthrow of the Nazi regime it is almost certain that the power would pass to the chiefs of the German Army, who are by no means ready to accept the kind of terms which Britain and the United States deem essential to future world security."[30]

On the other hand, just as Churchill still did not abandon his hopes of strategic bombing, he was not ready to say publicly that there were no acceptable German alternatives to Hitler. But Whitehall was no longer a free agent on the matter of war aims: indeed, Roosevelt started staking out this ground in 1941, before the United States entered the war, with the Four Freedoms and the Atlantic Charter. At Casablanca in January 1943, the President promulgated the doctrine of unconditional surrender. Not only did this shape Allied policy for the rest of the war, it also cut across Britain's previous strategy. A negotiated peace was the best one could hope for from a war of attrition, waged mainly from the air. Unconditional surrender of the Axis could result only from total defeat of its armies, culminating in the conquest of Germany itself. In other words, when Churchill signed on to unconditional surrender, he made it almost impossible to avoid a full-scale land war across continental Europe.[31]

Nowhere in *The Hinge of Fate* does Churchill acknowledge this point. He does, however, devote more than five pages of his chapter about Casablanca to the doctrine of unconditional surrender, helped by a close critique of his draft from Norman Brook and additional research by Ismay and Deakin. One reason for this lengthy account was the need to rebut claims that the Casablanca declaration served to harden German resistance. He quotes from public statements he made later in 1943 and in 1944 to the effect that, although "the victors have a free hand," unconditional surrender did not mean they were "entitled to behave in a barbarous manner." Therefore, he says, "it cannot be contended that in the closing years of the war there was any misconception in Germany."[32]

Churchill was also prompted to set out the record because of an exchange he had in the Commons on 21 July 1949 with Ernest Bevin, a wartime member of his Cabinet and Labour's postwar Foreign Secretary. Bevin complained that the War Cabinet had never been consulted about the declaration, whereupon Churchill said he had never heard the phrase until the President suddenly uttered it at the Casablanca press conference. As Churchill later admitted to the House, he spoke in error. In his memoirs, he therefore put the matter straight, quoting telegrams and Cabinet minutes from January 1943 that Deakin had unearthed to show that Roosevelt had discussed it with Churchill at Casablanca before the press conference and that the Prime Minister in turn had cabled home for approval. Far from repudiating the idea, however, the War Cabinet wanted to include all three Axis powers, rather than omitting Italy "to encourage a break-up there." In other words, both Churchill and Bevin had been wrong in their 1949 recollections. The affair served, Churchill told his readers, only to validate the final advice of a dying professor to his pupils: "Verify your quotations."[33]

Churchill therefore admits that the doctrine of unconditional surrender had been discussed in advance, even though he was surprised when Roosevelt unveiled it in public at Casablanca. But he confines discussion of its significance to the effect on Axis resistance, rather than admitting how it undermined the by now shaky foundations of Britain's original wartime strategy. Here was striking evidence of the new realities for British diplomacy. The hinge had also turned from fighting alone to fighting with allies.

CHAPTER 21

FIGHTING WITH ALLIES—
AND COLLEAGUES

CHURCHILL LIKED TO SAY that there was only one thing worse than fighting with allies, and that was fighting without them.[1] The entry of the Soviet Union and the United States into the war meant that Britain now had to deal with difficult and powerful partners, not to mention minor allies but big headaches such as de Gaulle's Free French. Churchill also had to struggle with colleagues at home. The coalition he had formed in May 1940 had been vital in mobilizing the country for total war, yet by 1942, with defeat unlikely but victory remote, bipartisanship became severely strained. At the start of his war premiership and at the end, Churchill's leadership was virtually unquestioned, but at times in the middle of the war it seemed distinctly shaky. Fighting with allies and with colleagues was one of his main preoccupations in 1942, but this was less evident when he wrote his memoirs in 1950.

THE MOST DRAMATIC chapters of volume 4 are the two recounting Churchill's talks with Stalin in August 1942. These were a compound of recollections dictated by him in 1948 and the official record of their meetings, which Deakin turned into a first-person narrative. Churchill also used the diary of Ian Jacob, who had accompanied him, but not that of Sir Alexander Cadogan of the Foreign Office, which he had used for the Atlantic meeting in August 1941. The flight itself was an epic, since Churchill had to travel via Cairo and Teheran in a converted Liberator bomber. The plane was unheated, some blankets on a shelf suffered for a bed, and when flying over twelve thousand feet it was necessary to suck on oxygen tubes. At almost any point, German fighters might have shot him down: "Strafer" Gott, Churchill's first choice to take command of the Eighth Army, had been killed in just this way when flying back from the desert to Cairo. General Douglas MacArthur, no anglophile, said Churchill deserved a Victoria Cross for the journey alone.[2]

The chapters on Moscow are full of vivid vignettes, such as the luxurious air-raid shelter ninety feet below State Villa 7. (This was Stalin's so-called Near Dacha, placed at the Prime Minister's disposal during the visit.) But Churchill cut from his draft a more significant story. After lunch on the second day, 13 August, while dictating replies to some telegrams, he was warned that the room was probably bugged. Churchill's draft went on,

> I did not believe this because of my faith in Russian hospitality—at any rate at the top level. Lower down we were none too particular ourselves. However in case I was too confiding I broke off my message in order to say a few words to any secret eventual listeners. I cannot remember or print all these here, but they were to the effect that those who played low tricks on their guests should at least have the opportunity of hearing some home truths about themselves and that I hoped that they would tell Mr. Stalin personally what they had detected.

But, he concluded, "I am sure that this sterilising measure was quite unnecessary." Cadogan's diaries, published in 1971, made clear that Churchill's "home truths" included such lines as "The Russians, I am told, are not human beings at all. They are lower in the scale of nature than the orang-outang. Now then, let them take them down and translate it into Russian." Having inserted the bugging story in August 1950, Churchill then took it out of the final text, perhaps feeling his proclaimed faith in Stalin sounded too credulous. But it is clear from Cadogan's account that both Churchill and Brooke were surprisingly naïve about the danger of bugging. During all Churchill's visits to Russia, it is likely that Stalin was well informed about his "private" conversations.[3]

Particularly fascinating are Churchill's detailed accounts of his meetings with Stalin. The first, on the evening of his arrival, 12 August, might have been postponed until the next day, but Churchill, typically, could not bear to wait. Their encounter lasted nearly four hours, with the Prime Minister doing most of the talking as he explained why the Western Allies could not invade France in 1942 but would conquer North Africa instead. The meeting ended in "an atmosphere of goodwill." Churchill says he went back to his dacha exhausted but satisfied that "the ice had been broken and a human contact established." (Other accounts record his boasts that he could handle Stalin.) But the second meeting, late on 13 August, proved "most unpleasant," with Stalin insinuating that the British were scared of the Germans and were breaking promises about Sledgehammer. Churchill gave as good as he got, but after two hours of fruitless exchanges he returned to the dacha angry and shaken. (According to his physician, Lord Moran, he was ready to pack up and go home, and it took much persuasion to talk him around.) Seeking to explain the contrast between the two meetings, Churchill told the War Cabinet that probably Stalin's "Council of Commissars did not take the news I brought as well as he did. They may have more power than we suppose, and less knowledge. Perhaps he was putting himself on the record for future purposes and for their benefit, and also letting off steam for his own."[4]

This conception that Stalin was beholden to other, shadowy figures stands in marked contrast to what we now know of Kremlin politics, but it became an idée fixe for Churchill, helping him explain otherwise puzzling changes of mood by Stalin in person or on paper. It was reinforced by their final meeting on 15 August, billed as an early-evening talk lasting an hour. As Churchill prepared to leave, Stalin suggested going to his house for "some drinks." Churchill said he was "in principle always in favour of such a policy." So Stalin led him through a maze of corridors and across the Kremlin grounds to his own rooms—"of moderate size, simple, dignified, and four in number." For six hours they sat together as an ostensibly impromptu banquet unfolded. Picking at various dishes, sampling choice wines and spirits, they chatted via Churchill's interpreter about the war, history, and politics, even getting around to the kulaks and collectivization. After Stalin had hacked into "a considerable sucking-pig," the dinner ended at 2:30 in the morning. That left Churchill just enough time to get back to the dacha, change his clothes, and drive to the airport. He writes: "I had a splitting headache, which for me was very unusual." This was probably his euphemism for a severe hangover.[5]

Cadogan and the President's emissary, Averell Harriman, both of whom had visited Moscow in 1941, suggested that Churchill had been the victim of a standard Soviet ploy: friendly first meeting, nasty second, and final modus vivendi. In Churchill's mind, however, the final meeting was decisive. "For the first time we got on to easy and friendly terms," he told the War Cabinet. "I feel that I have established a personal relationship which will be helpful." From these words he drew the title of his second Moscow chapter, "Moscow: A Relationship Established." As we shall see, Churchill's moods about the Soviet Union swung to and fro, but the belief that he could forge a partnership with Stalin lay at the heart of his policy.[6]

Such optimism was hard to sustain in the winter of 1942–1943, as Stalin blasted the Western Allies for a Second Front and more supplies. In the ironically entitled "Soviet 'Thank You,'" Churchill details the "ceaseless affront" he and Roosevelt received for their attempts to help "a Government which had been hoping to work with Hitler, until it was assaulted and almost destroyed by him."[7] On a related Cold War controversy, Churchill was more circumspect. In April 1943, the Germans discovered the bodies of 15,000 Polish soldiers, buried in mass graves in the Katyn Forest, near Smolensk, and charged that they had been killed by the Russians in 1940. In response, Stalin blamed the atrocity on the Nazis after June 1941 and broke off diplomatic relations with the London-based Polish government in exile, which had endorsed the German accusation. In the summer of 1949, Churchill put together a lengthy account of this 1943 crisis for a chapter then entitled "Russia and the Western Allies. Katyn." This used his telegrams from the time to document Stalin's attack on the Poles, his own efforts to prevent a formal breach, and his intimation to Stalin that he was "examining the possibility of silencing those Polish papers in this country which attack the Soviet Government." These telegrams accurately depict Churchill's priority in April 1943, only a couple of months after Stalingrad, to maintain good relations with Moscow in the interests of victory over Hitler. He and the Foreign Office suppressed their suspicions that Stalin was responsible for the massacre, and the British press was instructed not to "play the German game."[8]

From a Cold War perspective, however, those 1943 concerns looked dubious. In November 1949, the American Committee for the Investigation of the Katyn Massacre was formed, with an advisory board that included wartime intelligence boss Bill Donovan and Clare Boothe Luce, wife of the owner of *Life*. The committee started badgering Churchill about what he knew and did in 1943, so in August 1950 Deakin rewrote the whole story, replacing the telegrams with a measured narrative. Although setting out the German and Russian claims, Deakin noted that the assumption behind the Russian version was "incredible": namely, that more than 14,000 Polish soldiers passed from Russian to German hands in the chaos of mid-1941 and were then liquidated without a single person escaping to reveal what had happened. In taking over much of Deakin's draft, Churchill nevertheless replaced the "incredible" comment with a more tempered statement that belief in the Soviet version required "an act of faith." At the end of the chapter, he writes that "everyone is therefore entitled to form his own opinion," noting that "there is no lack of material in the many books" published by Poles in exile. The account of Katyn in *The Hinge of Fate*, while clearly hinting at Churchill's verdict, therefore carefully avoids explicit judgments that would have cast a questionable light over his conduct in 1943 and exposed the contrast with his image as a robust Cold Warrior.[9]

Another controversy with allies from 1942–1943 posed equally delicate problems for Churchill's memoirs: Eisenhower's agreement with Admiral François Darlan on 10 November 1942. Once the Torch invasion forces were ashore, Ike's main concern was a rapid end to French resistance. Fortuitously, Darlan, then number two in the Vichy regime, was in Algiers visiting his young son who was stricken with polio, and he fell into Allied hands. Here was someone who would be obeyed by French forces, and Eisenhower unilaterally sanctioned negotiations with him for a cease-fire. But not only did this mean abandoning the Allies' intended governor of French Northwest Africa, General Henri Giraud, recently escaped from a German prison camp, it also blurred the moral lines between Allies and Axis, resistance and collaboration. To many in Britain, let alone de Gaulle's Free French, Darlan was a Quisling with an odious record. The British government felt obliged to endorse the Darlan deal, at least temporarily, in the interests of military expediency and Allied solidarity, but it was a difficult time for Churchill. Then, on Christmas Eve, Darlan was shot by a young Frenchman, Fernand Bonnier de la Chapelle. Giraud was promoted to replace him and immediately had the killer tried and executed. As historian François Kersaudy observed, rarely can a political assassination have been "so unanimously condemned and so universally welcomed."[10]

In his chapter "The Darlan Episode," Churchill treads very carefully, seeking to show his doubts about the deal but also to demonstrate its necessity. Thus, he defends Eisenhower and his staff, saying they showed "a high level of courage and good sense," while noting that their action "raised issues of a moral and sentimental character of cardinal importance to the peoples of the United States and Great Britain, and reverberated through the Allied world." And he prints his warnings to Roosevelt about the "very deep currents of feeling" stirred in Britain, on a par with Munich. Churchill admits that "Darlan's murder, however criminal, relieved the Allies of their embarrassment of working with him, and at the same time left them with all the advantages he had been able to bestow during the vital hours of the Allied landings." He concludes with nearly a page and a half in defense of Darlan, blaming anglophobia and "ambition" for his support of Vichy in 1940 but applauding his resolve that the French fleet should never fall into German hands. "Let him rest in peace," Churchill ends magnanimously, "and let us all be thankful we have never had to face the trials under which he broke."[11]

Behind this surprising tribute lies a tangle of emotions. In July 1940, Churchill had sanctioned the controversial attack on French naval vessels in North African ports, lest they be ceded to Germany. One piece of evidence used by French critics to show that the attack was unnecessary was the way the French fleet in Toulon, threatened by the Germans, was scuttled by its own officers in "a twinkling of an eye" on 27 November 1942. In January 1950, Gordon Allen recommended "a pacifying reference" about Toulon in volume 4, and Churchill may well have had this controversy in mind in April when drafting his tribute to Darlan.[12] On a human level, Churchill represents Darlan as an ardent French patriot, whose motives he could respect if not share, noting, too, that Darlan's great-grandfather had died at the Battle of Trafalgar and citing this as the root of his anglophobia. Moreover, the strange act of fate by which Darlan was in Algiers at the time of the Allied landings suited Churchill's sense of the contingency of history. He seems to have been genuinely moved by this family tragedy, as was Roosevelt. When FDR learned in November 1942 that Darlan's son had been stricken with polio, the same disease that had wrecked his own life in the 1920s, he sent Darlan a warm letter of sympathy and later invited Darlan's widow to bring the boy to Warm Springs, the therapy center for polio victims that the President had established in Georgia. Churchill's April 1950 draft ended with this story, taken from the just published memoirs of William Leahy, Roosevelt's wartime Chief of Staff. It was cut in August after both Denis Kelly and Charles Wood found it anticlimactic, but Churchill's inclination to include it is revealing.[13]

This leads us to a still deeper reason: Churchill may have felt guilt about Darlan's murder. In the published chapter, he is at pains to represent Bonnier de la Chapelle as a deranged, lone actor. Apart from "a small circle of personal friends" with royalist sympathies, he writes, "there was no open support in Algiers for his action." This was untrue: Bonnier was in league with the Gaullists, who were in turn supported by elements of Britain's Special Operations Executive. Moreover, Sir Stewart Menzies, head of Britain's Secret Intelligence Service, who rarely left London, just happened to be in Algiers at the time of the assassination. Leahy hinted at British involvement in his memoirs: "I had received from many sources information that the British might make an effort to get Darlan out of the picture." If, as seems likely, the British were implicated, this may have increased Churchill's tangle of emotions when writing in 1950.[14]

The assassination occurred at a time when Churchill was particularly antagonistic toward de Gaulle, as is evident from the diary of Oliver Harvey, Eden's private secretary. On 26 November, the Prime Minister told Eden that Darlan had "done more for us than de Gaulle." Two days later, after the French fleet had been scuttled, Harvey noted: "P.M. is getting more and more enthusiastic over Darlan." In Churchill's secret speech to the Commons on 10 December 1942, he combined defense of the Darlan deal with warnings that de Gaulle was by no means "an unfaltering friend of Britain." Churchill told MPs not "to base all your hopes and confidence upon him," adding, "I cannot feel that de Gaulle is France, still less that Darlan and Vichy are France. France is something greater, more complex, more formidable than any of these sectional manifestations." Churchill's opinion in 1942–1943 was that Britain should exploit whatever French support was forthcoming. This was, however, less easy to admit after de Gaulle's triumphant return to Paris in 1944 and his subsequent presidency of France, which was why Sir Edward Bridges asked Churchill to cut the attack on de Gaulle from his 1946 *Secret Session Speeches* and, presumably, why Churchill omitted all reference to him from the three pages devoted to that speech in *The Hinge of Fate*.[15]

On the other hand, subsequent chapters, and especially their drafts, give strong hints of Churchill's outlook at the time. In "The Casablanca Conference," Churchill derides the "rubbish" peddled by Elliott Roosevelt and others that he tried to stop de Gaulle from attending—"the telegrams dismiss it for ever"—and describes the "shotgun" marriage at Casablanca between de Gaulle and Giraud. Although knowing de Gaulle to be "no friend of England," Churchill says that "even when he was behaving worst, he seemed to express the personality of France—a great nation, with all its pride, authority, and ambition." (An early version continued: "I should be sorry to live in a country governed by de Gaulle, but I should be sorry to live in a world, or with a France, in which there was not a de Gaulle.")[16] During Churchill's visit to Washington in May 1943, Roosevelt and the State Department provided him with daily evidence of de Gaulle's machinations. "I brought all this forcibly to the notice of my colleagues at home," says Churchill, and it "hung in the balance whether we should not break finally at this juncture with this most difficult man. However, time and patience afforded tolerable solutions." These discreet sentences cloak a bitter struggle between Churchill and his colleagues back in London. On 21 May 1943, the Prime Minister cabled the Cabinet asking "whether we should not now eliminate de Gaulle as a political force." He cited as justification the general's anglophobia and his efforts to sabotage transatlantic relations, even casting aspersions on the general's courage and integrity: "He has never himself fought since he left France and took pains to have his wife brought out safely beforehand." This telegram, and others in a similar vein on 23 and 24 May, were printed for an early draft of this chapter but then cut. Churchill does not mention that the Cabinet, rallied by Eden as Foreign Secretary, flatly rejected his proposal.[17]

The War Cabinet found it much easier to say no to Churchill when he was out of the country—as over Auchinleck in August 1942—and it dug in on another foreign-policy issue during Churchill's Washington visit of May 1943: Portugal's Atlantic islands. Although Portugal was Britain's oldest ally, it remained neutral in the war; Churchill, under pressure from the Americans, favored a surprise military occupation of the Azores. The War Cabinet, however, again stiffened by Eden, successfully opposed such action until diplomatic means had been exhausted. An early draft described the face-off at some length, with extensive quotation from Churchill's cables on 21 and 23 May. But the whole story was then rewritten, without documents and in much more guarded tones, in the summer of 1950, after Norman Brook had passed on representations from the Foreign Office. While relaxed about Churchill's self-edited account of friction with de Gaulle—this was already in the public domain thanks to Sherwood and others—the Foreign Office feared that Churchill's revelations about how close the British came to military action in 1943 might be resented in Lisbon and "just possibly" used to justify denying Britain and NATO bases in the Azores.[18]

PORTUGAL AND EVEN France were relatively minor diplomatic concerns for Churchill in comparison with the United States. His return by plane from Washington in January 1942 opened up new vistas of speedy transatlantic travel. "Perhaps when the weather gets better I may propose myself for a week-end with you and flip over," he cabled Roosevelt on 1 April. "We have so much to settle that would go easily in talk." The idea of flipping over for a weekend was something of an exaggeration, but in 1942–1943 visits supplemented correspondence as never before. In the memoirs, Churchill remains keen to emphasize the overriding importance of his relationship with Roosevelt. After describing the deadlock in final planning for Torch, for instance, he writes: "As all agreement between the Staffs had failed, the issue had to be settled personally between the President and me."[19]

Churchill continues to play down many areas of controversy between the two governments. In this volume, as in the previous, he ignores the lengthy argument over State Department pressure to end the tariffs protecting British empire trade, even though he had to resolve it in direct correspondence with FDR. His indifference to economics was probably one reason—this volume, like the others, has very little on finance, industry, and trade—but it also reflects his desire to portray Anglo-American relations, like Lend-Lease, as an "unsordid act."[20]

Also expurgated from his book are criticisms of American troops, whose baptism of fire in northwest Africa had not been a happy one: ill-trained and poorly led GIs were routed at Kasserine in February 1943. This confirmed the British prejudice about the Yanks: bigger on words than deeds. Even King George VI observed that after the Americans' "sound defeat" in North Africa it looked as if the British would "have to do all the fighting there." When Churchill printed the King's letter in his memoirs, he discreetly cut this remark and also his own reply that "the enemy make a great mistake if they think that all the troops we have there are in the same green state as are our United States friends."[21] Nor did Churchill print telegrams from April 1943 that showed Eisenhower, in name the Allied supreme commander in North Africa, plaintively begging General Alexander, his nominal subordinate, for the "essentials of your broad tactical plan" for the attack on Tunis. In a "most secret and private" telegram, also omitted, Churchill told Brooke he would ask Alex to keep Ike more fully informed in future. "So much depends on going through the ceremonial processes."[22]

What Churchill saw as the reality behind the ceremony is hinted at in places in *The Hinge of Fate*. Once the campaigns in northeast and northwest Africa were fused in January 1943, the British had "three times as many troops, four times as many warships, and almost as many aeroplanes"—yet, to Marshall's amazement, they continued to accept an American in overall command. This was a calculated policy because in practice, says Churchill, "Eisenhower confided the entire conduct of the battle to Alexander," adding that "if you treat the Americans well they will always want to treat you better." This, he argued, made it easier to get his way over Mediterranean strategy. In the classical analogy favored by Harold Macmillan, Britain's political adviser at Ike's headquarters, the British should run "this American empire" like "the Greek slaves ran the operations of the Emperor Claudius."[23]

Looking back from 1950, at the nadir of the Cold War, one of the most striking features of the wartime Anglo-American alliance was the development of the atomic bomb. In 1940 and 1941 the British were well ahead of the Americans in theoretical research—and when they shared their findings with Washington in the autumn of 1941, Roosevelt was spurred to sanction a full-scale American atomic program. By late 1942, however, the Americans were ahead of the British, on account of their far superior resources, and the U.S. War Department wanted to cut Britain out of the project entirely. This became a vexed issue in Anglo-American relations in 1942 and 1943, prompting anguished complaints by Churchill at Casablanca; it was not resolved until his visit to Washington in May 1943. During the Quebec conference of August 1943, the two leaders signed a formal wartime partnership and followed this up in September 1944, at the President's home at Hyde Park in upstate New York, with another agreement about continued collaboration after the war.

In Churchill's account, he claims that his visit to America in June 1942 was made to reach agreements on military operations and on "Tube Alloys," the British code word for the bomb. He describes talks with the President and Harry Hopkins at Hyde Park on 20 June, in the President's tiny study, where, he says, they agreed to mount a joint and equal atomic project located in the United States. Thereafter, the bomb disappears from *The Hinge of Fate* until a telegram of May 1943 (added very late to the penultimate chapter), in which Churchill spoke of FDR's agreement in principle that "the exchange of information on Tube Alloys should be resumed, and that the enterprise should be considered a joint one." Nowhere has he indicated that the partnership had been ruptured. Not only is Churchill's account disingenuous, it is also inaccurate — indeed, this episode constitutes one of the most serious factual errors in *The Hinge of Fate*. In 1964, the official historian of the British atomic project, Margaret Gowing, had difficulty with Churchill's claims. She found no evidence in the official British files that Churchill was briefed about "Tube Alloys" before he left London or any record of an agreement with Roosevelt.[24]

Gowing's puzzlement is explained by the drafts of this chapter. In February 1949, Churchill asked Ismay, "what was my main purpose in crossing the Atlantic at this time? It must have been a very serious one. My own feeling is that it was about the atomic bomb and that other purposes were subsidiary." Ismay could find nothing in the archives — unsurprisingly, because Churchill seems to have conflated his visit to Hyde Park in June 1942 with that of September 1944. In the same letter, he told Ismay, referring to the 1942 visit, "Here at Hyde Park, in the tiny room the President worked in, we settled the questions of the atomic bomb and made the Treaty which lies in the Government archives." In a draft he wrote that he and Roosevelt "took this decision jointly and settled the basis of the agreement, which I drew up, at the White House a few days later and which we both initialled." Ismay persuaded Churchill that no treaty had been signed in 1942, unlike 1944, but he was in no position to contest the general claim about a decisive meeting that no other Briton attended. So the centrality of the bomb and the agreement were allowed to stand.[25]

In January 1950, Churchill suddenly asked Ismay for 1,000 words on the background to "Tube Alloys." Fortunately, Sir John Anderson, the Home Secretary, who had overseen the British atomic project during the war, came up with some relevant documents. Using Anderson's material, Ismay composed a draft that would "enable Winston to tell the story in his own inimitable language and with accuracy." Ismay was ever the courtier—as he could have anticipated, Churchill incorporated the draft with little amendment. This summarized the story up to 1941, as preamble to Churchill's confused memories of June 1942. What exactly happened at Hyde Park will probably never be known, but we may presume that Churchill and Roosevelt had a cursory discussion about the need for atomic cooperation, putting nothing on paper. The U.S. military was kept in the dark and cold-shouldered the British—hence the need for the formal agreements in 1943 and 1944.[26]

By late 1942, individuals in both governments were also beginning to look toward the postwar world. When sent a Foreign Office paper on this issue in October, Churchill told Eden, "I hope these speculative studies will be entrusted mainly to those on whose hands time hangs heavy, and that we shall not overlook Mrs. Glass's Cookery Book recipe for Jugged Hare—'First catch your hare.'" This neat one-liner, first used by Churchill in *The World Crisis*, does not appear in *The Hinge of Fate*. Instead, Churchill prints his reply of 21 October 1942 to the persistent Eden, which includes his lament that it "would be a measureless disaster if Russian barbarism overlaid the culture and independence of the ancient States of Europe." This sounded very prescient when viewed from 1950.[27] He also prints a five-page paraphrase of the postwar blueprint that he presented to American policymakers on 22 May 1943. This envisaged a World Council, directed by the great powers, backed by subordinate regional conclaves including a Council of Europe. His basic axiom was a "fraternal association" between the United States and the British Commonwealth, including a peacetime Combined Chiefs of Staff and the sharing of military bases. He anticipated eventually a common passport, perhaps common citizenship. On the other hand, Churchill's regional principle implied world in which America was internationalist but not globalist. He desired "a strong France" because he "could not easily foresee the United States being able to keep large numbers of forces indefinitely on guard in Europe." For the book, he cut the next sentence of the 1943 record, predicting that if U.S. troops did stay in Europe, such an "experiment" would not last for "more than one Presidential election." But he did include his other reason for reviving France: "the prospect of having no strong country on the map between England and Russia was not attractive."[28]

In May 1943, Churchill told the Americans he was willing to include China in the same rank as Britain, America, and Russia if they wanted, "but, however great the importance of China, she was not comparable to the others." For decades, the country had been wracked by civil war between Chiang Kai-shek's Nationalists and the Communists led by Mao Zedong, before both were driven inland by the Japanese invaders. In *The Hinge of Fate*, Churchill does not conceal his distaste for Chiang's regime or for his haughty wife, whom he nearly met while in the United States in May 1943. A cable to Eden on 21 May 1943 said, "the lady gives herself royal airs and considers herself co-ruler of China," adding that she was "always accompanied by an extremely masculine niece dressed as a boy." On this telegram, however, Churchill firmly wrote the words "Not print."[29]

Behind American enthusiasm for China as one of the Big Four, Churchill, as he told Eden in the memo of 21 October 1942, detected a bid for support in "any attempt to liquidate the British overseas Empire." Less than three weeks later, Churchill used that last phrase in his post-Alamein "End of the Beginning" speech at the Mansion House in London: "I have not become the King's First Minister in order to preside over the liquidation of the British Empire." However, he never uses these lines or even refers to the speech in *The Hinge of Fate*, probably because his famous phrase sounded very hollow in 1950, after India, Pakistan, and Burma had become independent and after Britain had withdrawn in chaos from Palestine.[30]

This is speculation. What is clear, however, is that Churchill's harshest words about Roosevelt in *The Hinge of Fate* are reserved for the President's interference in British affairs in India. In March 1942, with Japan's army deep into Burma and its fleet rampaging across the Bay of Bengal, the Cabinet feared for the survival of British rule in India. To placate the Hindu-led Congress party and mobilize Indian support for the war, Sir Stafford Cripps traveled to Delhi with proposals for greater Indian self-government. Roosevelt offered plenty of advice, quoted at length in the chapter "India: The Cripps Mission," telling Churchill that a move toward independence was "in line with the world changes of the past half-century and with the democratic processes of all who are fighting Nazism." When the talks collapsed, he cabled on 12 April that American opinion "almost universally" blamed Britain and warned of a backlash in the United States if, as a result, Indians refused to resist a Japanese invasion. FDR proposed a "temporary Dominion government" with power over domestic affairs as a wartime staging post to full independence and pressed the analogy of America's Articles of Confederation in the 1780s, which were precursors to the Constitution ratified in 1789. Churchill was convinced that Indian self-government at this stage would undermine the war effort and lay the country open to Japan. In his memoirs he was scathing about FDR's intervention, calling it "idealism at other people's expense and without regard to the consequences of ruin and slaughter." As for the historical analogies: "The President's mind was back in the War of Independence, and he thought of the Indian problem in terms of the thirteen colonies fighting George III." It is unusual for Churchill to be so damning about Roosevelt. A telegram he prints even hints at the threat he made openly to Harry Hopkins: if the President pressed the issue, he, Churchill, might resign.[31]

The chapter on the Cripps mission is also notable for Churchill's excoriation of India. Though praising "the glorious heroism and martial qualities" of Indian troops, he is vituperative about their politicians. The "peoples of Hindustan," he says, using material omitted from volume 2, were "carried through the struggle on the shoulders of our small Island," and "we were charged nearly a million pounds a day for defending India from the miseries of invasion," resulting in a debt to India "almost as large as that on which we defaulted to the United States after the previous struggle." In drafts, he also attacked Gandhi himself, asserting that the Mahatma "was willing to give the Japanese free passage across India to join hands with the Germans in return for Japanese military aid to hold down the Moslems." Ismay contested the claim that Gandhi wanted a Hindu Raj, and Norman Brook warned that the passage would "surely give offence to millions in India who revere Gandhi's memory." Churchill took their advice.[32] But he left in some aspersions on Gandhi's famous fast of February 1943, the publication of which did cause an uproar in India.[33]

BRITISH DOMESTIC POLITICS figure a little more in *The Hinge of Fate* than in volume 3. There are chapters on the vote of confidence Churchill solicited on 29 January 1942, after the disasters in the Far East, on the Cabinet reshuffle in February, and on the vote of censure he faced on 2 July, after the fall of Tobruk. But, he says, "I could count on the goodwill of the people for the share I had had in their survival in 1940," and he attributes the agitation to "the well-informed and airily detached criticism of the newspapers" and "the shrewd and constant girding" of no more than thirty MPs. When the critics were forced into the open, their support was pathetic: Churchill won the January vote by 464 to 1 and that of July by 475 to 25. Insofar as he discusses criticism *within* his government, it is almost entirely identified with Cripps, whose differences with Churchill, culminating in his November resignation from the War Cabinet though not from ministerial office, are examined in "Suspense and Strain." Churchill is at pains to stress that the coalition as a whole "was massive and overwhelming in its strength and unity," claiming that "all its principal Ministers stood together around me, with never a thought that was not loyal and robust."[34]

Political wrangling is thus discussed in *The Hinge of Fate* mainly as a fringe irritation. Sir Edward Bridges, the Cabinet Secretary during 1942, doubted "whether these chapters bring out as fully as they might the cutting edge of the various criticisms of the Prime Minister and of the administration current at this time."[35] The crux here is the political reshuffle of February 1942. Churchill says, "I disliked very much making changes under external pressure," but the demand for "new blood" was overwhelming.[36] What he does not make clear is the new party balance of the War Cabinet. Clement Attlee, the Labour leader, gained the title of Deputy Prime Minister; Cripps, then at the height of his popularity thanks to his advocacy of aid to Russia, was brought in as Leader of the Commons; while Ernest Bevin fought off Beaverbrook's bid to dominate war production and stayed as Minister of Labour. In a new War Cabinet of seven, the left therefore held three seats, all now occupied by political heavyweights, compared with three less powerful figures out of eight before. The January vote of confidence had been staged by anti-Churchill malcontents on the Conservative backbenches, but, as R. A. Butler observed, this "revolt of the Right had brought about a War Cabinet more to the Left."[37]

Nor does Churchill acknowledge that the Cripps mission to India was an immediate consequence of this Cabinet tilt to the left. Personally, he had hardly moved from his die-hard position on India in 1931–1935. But Labour leaders, especially Cripps, had long favored rapid moves toward Indian self-government and argued that the crisis of the war in Asia made this essential. "To mark time is to lose India," warned Attlee. On 25 February, Churchill established a special India Committee of senior ministers to advise the War Cabinet. He mentions this in his memoirs without noting how it was a concession to the new political balance. Nor does he say much about the political infighting over India during the next couple of months—how, for instance, he cannily convened a rare meeting of the Tory-dominated full Cabinet to counterbalance the more leftish War Cabinet, or how he opened a secret backchannel to the die-hard Viceroy, Lord Linlithgow, to undermine Cripps's position. While the intransigence of the Congress-party leaders was the main reason for Cripps's failure—they demanded independence immediately rather than after the war—Churchill's machinations certainly had some effect. But in *The Hinge of Fate* his remarks on the failure of the Cripps mission are breathtakingly disingenuous. Although "I was able to bear this news, which I had thought probable from the outset, with philosophy," he writes, "I knew how bitterly Sir Stafford Cripps would feel the failure of his Mission, and I sought to comfort him."[38]

Politics do make an appearance later in Churchill's account of Sir Stafford's resignation in November 1942. Cripps wanted to establish a War Planning Directorate to advise Churchill on broad strategy. For much of September 1942, says Churchill in "Suspense and Strain," they debated the merits of this idea, but with the Prime Minister adamantly opposed, Cripps eventually indicated that he had no option but to resign. Churchill admits that "severance between him and me during this period of oppressive pause [before Alamein and Torch] would have created a political crisis." In the interests of national unity, Cripps therefore agreed to stay in office until the battles in North Africa were decided: "his patriotism ruled his conduct," Churchill writes. Then, in the ministerial reshuffle of late November, Cripps accepted Churchill's offer of the Ministry of Aircraft Production, "an office which he held with increasing skill and effectiveness until the end of the war."[39]

Churchill's original version of "Suspense and Strain" had consisted mostly of correspondence from the time, but when Norman Brook, on Churchill's behalf, asked Cripps in July 1950 for permission to quote, the response was a flat negative. Brook told Churchill that Cripps considered the papers he had written in 1942 to be "specially confidential in character, as bearing on the relations between Ministers in their conduct of public business; and he takes the view that the publication of such documents while both authors are alive and actively engaged in politics is not likely to be helpful to the future of Cabinet government." Brook admitted that their omission would "involve your reconsidering the whole Chapter," and he offered to send a draft showing how this might be done. Churchill readily agreed, and twelve days later Brook sent a beautifully crafted paraphrase in smooth narrative as "an entirely unofficial contribution" that might be "of some use to you in your revision of this part of the book." Some use, indeed! Churchill incorporated Brook's pages straight into the typescript, without amendment. "I am most profoundly grateful," he replied. "The reconstruction of SUSPENSE AND STRAIN was a masterpiece. I do not know how you can find the time and energy to help me so much with all the other exacting work you have to do." And so some five pages of text in *The Hinge of Fate* are entirely the unattributed work of Britain's Cabinet Secretary—written, moreover, a month into the Korean conflict, when the country seemed on the brink of World War III.[40]

Like Bridges, Brook saw himself as helping expedite a quasi-official account of Britain's war, and he also wanted to keep on terms with the Leader of the Opposition, who might soon become his boss. On the other hand, Cripps was currently Chancellor of the Exchequer and a leading member of the Labour government, so Brook was certainly not going to offend him. Hence the need to find a literary modus vivendi.

Brook's sensitivity to his current political mentors was also evident in his firm request that Churchill delete from the appendix two minutes he sent to Attlee in February and July 1942. Both were responses to papers from Attlee, the first asking for a new directive to workers and civil servants, the second an extended critique of the current obsession with strategic bombing. Brook argued that since Churchill's replies suggested "some lack of confidence between yourself and Mr. Attlee," it was only fair to print the initial papers, adding firmly that, if Churchill did insist on printing his own minutes, the whole matter would have to be taken to the Prime Minister himself.[41] Churchill promptly cut both minutes. From the historical angle, this was regrettable. As Brook observed, the 1942 exchanges with Attlee showed that Cripps was not alone among ministers in questioning Churchill's conduct of the war. Attlee was in fact a sustained critic of strategic bombing, whereas Cripps was brought around by "Bomber" Harris, and any criticisms from the Deputy Prime Minister carried special weight.[42] Churchill never intended to enlarge his arguments with Attlee into a full-scale discussion in the text, but even printing his own minutes would have hinted at the extent of policy disagreement within the War Cabinet in those dark days of 1942.

After Cripps's resignation in November, the home front virtually disappears from *The Hinge of Fate*—a point noted by Denis Kelly in April 1950 but never taken up by Churchill.[43] Again, the omission is historically significant. Labour exploited its growing strength in the coalition from 1942 to advance its own reformist agenda, and here the Beveridge Plan for a postwar social-security system was of immense symbolic importance. Although Sir William Beveridge was a Liberal, Labour embraced his December 1942 proposals with enthusiasm, at a time when most Conservatives were critical or at best indifferent. In January 1943, Churchill wrote a paper about the Beveridge Plan for the War Cabinet, warning against "dangerous optimism" about what could be afforded after the war. When Labour MPs pressed for immediate legislation, he wrote a second paper accepting Beveridge's ideas in principle while proposing a special commission to refine proposals for a postwar parliament. Churchill makes no mention of the plan and the ensuing political row in the text of *The Hinge of Fate*. In June 1950, however, he decided to print his two papers for the Cabinet as an appendix, running to two pages of text. The second paper, seeking to defer legislation till after the war, had been strenuously contested by Attlee in 1943, but once again the Deputy Prime Minister's disagreements with Churchill do not appear in the memoirs.[44]

Churchill's overriding interest was the running of the war. In a splendid phrase, he writes that "all I wanted was compliance with my wishes after reasonable discussion," but for much of 1942 compliance was at best grudging.[45] Critics in Whitehall and Westminster wanted to trim his authority as Minister of Defence, the post he had created for himself in 1940. Many argued that a Lloyd George–style War Cabinet, comprising a few ministers without departmental responsibilities, could help the Prime Minister grapple with his burdens, whereas Churchill insisted that "exalted brooding over the work of others is too often the lot of a Minister without departmental duties." What he feared was that brooding would soon become plotting. Similar objections applied to the idea of a War Planning Directorate divorced from the Chiefs of Staff, which was advanced among others by Cripps. The aim here was to relieve the hard-pressed Chiefs and give a group of full-time planners the task of "helping" the Prime Minister with grand strategy. But Churchill was "resolved to keep my full power of war-direction. . . . I should not of course have remained Prime Minister for an hour if I had been deprived of the office of Minister of Defence."[46]

"Suspense and Strain" opens with a remarkably candid piece of dictation by Churchill about his fragile political position in the autumn of 1942: "I had now been twenty-eight months at the head of affairs, during which we had sustained an almost unbroken series of military defeats," from Dakar and Greece to Singapore and Tobruk—all "galling links in a chain of misfortune and frustration to which no parallel could be found in our history." Churchill goes on: "It is indeed remarkable that I was not in this bleak lull dismissed from power or confronted with demands for changes in my methods, which it was known I should never accept." Instead, says Churchill, he was sustained by the "unity and strength of the War Cabinet" and "the confidence which I preserved of my political and professional colleagues." Though this statement is disingenuous about the extent of criticism, Churchill is right on the main point: there was no real challenger for his post. Cripps, the only politician spoken of in this vein, did not behave as a serious rival. His most authoritative biographer, using Cripps's own papers, believes he was essentially honest about being a constructive critic.[47]

Even if no one was about to knife Churchill, many doubted he would last the distance. On 17 June 1942, just before the fall of Tobruk, Cripps privately told disgruntled Tories that he envisaged "a joint Government consisting of Oliver Lyttelton, Anthony Eden and himself. He implied that in due course Churchill would be pushed aside, because he did not understand the home front. He did not deny that Churchill was the best for the strategic war period." Such talk was typically vague—an alternative government in an indeterminate future. But the future could become the present with startling rapidity, as the sudden fall of Neville Chamberlain had made clear. No one could forget May 1940, least of all its surprise beneficiary, Winston Churchill—and in the autumn of 1942 he knew that the price of continuing defeat would be his own political extinction. If Torch failed, he told Eden on 1 October, "then I'm done for and must go and hand over to one of you."[48]

By persuading Cripps to defer resignation until after the desert offensive, Churchill neutered his opponent. The meteor that had burst over Westminster so dramatically in February had burned itself out, leaving hardly a trace. Although he did not admit it, the centrality of the Desert War in Churchill's memoirs reflected more than military considerations. Such was the political significance of Monty's victory. It would be too strong to rephrase Churchill's aphorism to read: "Before Alamein I never had a victory. After Alamein I never had a critic." But November 1942 proved the hinge of fate in the corridors of power as well as on the field of battle.

IN HIS MEMOIRS, Churchill pays tribute not only to colleagues in the War Cabinet but also to his military advisers: "Misfortunes only brought me and the Chiefs of Staff closer together."[49] Here, again, he is being economical with the truth because the supreme command was under acute strain in 1942. The Chiefs bore a double burden of running their respective services and also spending hours, often late at night, listening to Churchill's latest strategic fantasies (nicknamed Midnight Follies). Debate was made all the harder by the fact that Winston was a man of iron whim, jumping from one project to another in a desperate search for action, yet resolutely clamped to each idea while it engaged his attention. Sir Alan Brooke, Chief of the Imperial General Staff, fumed with rage but never buckled, using his diary as a safety valve. But Admiral Sir Dudley Pound, First Sea Lord since 1939, succumbed to the dual struggle against Hitler and Churchill, and this had serious consequences.

In early 1942, the Prime Minister tried to ease Pound out of his job through a remarkable exchange of letters, none of which got near even a draft of The Hinge of Fate.[50] On 4 March, Churchill proposed that Pound relinquish the chairmanship of the Chiefs of Staff Committee to Brooke, ostensibly to lighten his load, but asked Pound himself to propose that change rather than make it unilaterally. Churchill wanted Lord Louis Mountbatten to join the committee "as an equal member," with the title of Chief of Combined Operations and an appropriate rank in each of the three services. Pound had no objection about the chairmanship—he had done the job for a year and a half—but fiercely opposed Mountbatten's elevation. When Churchill persisted, Pound wrote back on 7 March about "a very widespread belief, not only in the Services but also in the country, that you do override the opinion of your professional advisers," which was "doing a great deal of harm in undermining confidence in the Service leaders." Pound hastened to add: "I can honestly say that in no case do I feel that my advice has been overridden in anything that matters." On the dispatch of the *Prince of Wales*, for instance, "I have been able to say quite definitely that it was in accordance with my advice." (This was simply not true.) But, said Pound, Mountbatten's promotion would be different: "I feel so strongly that it is wrong that I cannot shoulder this responsibility" and would not be able to deny it was "contrary to my advice." Some would attribute "a junior Captain in a shore appointment being given three steps in rank" to Mountbatten's royal blood.[51]

This was an extraordinarily frank letter, but Churchill simply ignored it. On 8 March, he reiterated his request that Mountbatten should enjoy "full and equal membership" of the Chiefs of Staff Committee, with the rank of Vice-Admiral and its equivalent in the other two services, Lieutenant General and Air Marshal.[52] Neither Brooke nor Portal had much time for Mountbatten, but Churchill's reforms were duly implemented. Mountbatten, backed by the Prime Minister, insisted he would attend War Cabinet meetings whenever the three Chiefs of Staff did so.

It seems clear that Churchill was trying to address the problem of Pound's deteriorating health. Around this time, Brooke's diary starts to comment on the First Sea Lord's tendency to nod off during meetings: on 3 February 1942, he "looked like an old parrot asleep on his perch!" But Pound was convinced Churchill wanted to get rid of him entirely and make Mountbatten First Sea Lord.[53] That is certainly a plausible interpretation of Churchill's letters in March. With the resignation of Admiral Fisher over the Dardanelles in 1915 still hanging around his neck, it is possible that Churchill intended to proceed step-by-step, replacing Pound first as chairman of the Chiefs of Staff and bringing Mountbatten onto the committee before administering the coup de grâce. Yet there is another way to interpret Churchill's conduct. His other reforms in March 1942 were responses to current political criticism from Cripps and others: more routine business passed to the Vice-Chiefs of Staff, more time for the Chiefs to discuss grand strategy under a new, efficient chairman. Mountbatten's enhanced status was testimony to the importance of Combined Operations HQ, charged with attacking Hitler's Europe. This would help convince America and Russia that Britain was serious about the war and also boost domestic morale. But in order to succeed the services had to be forced to cooperate — perhaps an aggressive and ambitious commander with royal connections might do the trick. All this is speculation. A less charitable view is that, as with General Alexander, Churchill was won over by a dashing young officer, whose royalty was an added attraction.

The Pound-Mountbatten affair has been neglected by historians, in part because Churchill omitted almost any reference to it in his memoirs. On 21 September 1942, Cripps told Churchill flatly that Pound was "past his work," but this letter disappeared in Norman Brook's rewrite.[54] As for Mountbatten, he is never introduced as a member of the Chiefs of Staff Committee. Instead, there is simply a passing mention of his rise in a telegram from Churchill to Roosevelt on 1 April 1942, buried in "The Shipping Stranglehold."[55] In any event, the tenacious Pound remained at the Admiralty, while the ambitious Mountbatten consolidated his position as Chief of Combined Operations. In both cases, fateful consequences ensued, neither of which is treated candidly in *The Hinge of Fate*.

The first of these was what Churchill calls "one of the most melancholy naval episodes in the whole of the war." Convoy PQ 17, en route from Iceland to Archangel with vital supplies for Russia, lost twenty-three of its thirty-four ships. This was a direct result of Admiralty orders, issued on 4 July, for the cruiser escort to withdraw and the convoy to scatter, on the mistaken belief that the German battleship *Tirpitz* had already left port in Norway to hunt the convoy. The PQ 17 disaster stunned the navy, and Churchill suspended Arctic convoys until September, to Stalin's fury. Although suggesting that some fault lay with the escort commander, Churchill's memoirs attribute most of the disaster to the Admiralty's instructions, which, he admits, came directly from Pound. He speculates that the First Sea Lord would probably not have sent "such vehement orders" if only British warships were involved but did not wish to risk two U.S. cruisers in one of the first large Anglo-American naval operations under British command. Churchill continues: "This is only my surmise from what I knew of my friend, for I never discussed the matter with him. Indeed, so strictly was the secret of these orders being sent on the First Sea Lord's authority guarded by the Admiralty that it was not until after the war that I learned the facts."[56]

This was untrue. Pound was instructed to report to the War Cabinet in person and did so on 1 August 1942, describing the intelligence about the *Tirpitz* and the orders to disperse. Throughout, according to the minutes, Pound referred to "the Admiralty" and did not assume personal responsibility. Nor did he indicate that he had overruled Admiralty Intelligence, which insisted there was no evidence on 4 July that the *Tirpitz* had put to sea, whereas Pound argued that there was no evidence to show that it hadn't. Churchill attended this Cabinet meeting.[57]

On the other hand, the meeting occurred at 11:30 A.M. on 1 August, a few hours before Churchill set off on his epic trip to Cairo and Moscow, and it is conceivable that it did not lodge in his memory. Certainly, Gordon Allen claimed that Churchill had been genuinely shocked when told in 1949 of Pound's personal responsibility. "I could see real pain and grief written across his face: he had not known about it," Allen recalled in 1963; he also believed that the sentences of extenuation in *The Hinge of Fate*, added by Churchill to Allen's draft, were an attempt "to make excuses for his old friend." Pound was always a hands-on commander, with a Churchillian readiness to micromanage operations, but one wonders now—as perhaps did Churchill in 1949—whether his declining health was a factor in this tragedy.[58]

Six weeks after the PQ 17 tragedy, there occurred a second, even greater, disaster: the Dieppe raid of 19 August, intended to boost Allied morale, placate the Russians, and probe German anti-invasion defenses. Most of the troops were Canadian, of whom 68 percent ended that day trip across the Channel dead, wounded, or captured. Churchill devotes little more than two pages to the story, sandwiched in the chapter about his return trip to Cairo, where he received the news.[59] The account is purely narrative, with no documents, in marked contrast to the original draft.

Gordon Allen produced a summary of the raid in February 1950. Churchill left this in the 1 May version of the book but added that it was "a very controversial issue and may conceivably need a chapter by itself." Ismay, however, wanted to say very little about Dieppe, ostensibly because "the military story has already been told so fully and accurately in other publications." (The only one he cited was the Canadian official military history.) He proposed the briefest of summaries, crediting Churchill with having approved the raid before leaving England, followed by an exchange of minutes between Churchill and himself at the end of 1942. Churchill's minute of 21 December began: "Although for many reasons everyone was concerned to make this business look as good as possible, the time has now come when I must be informed more precisely about the military plans." At first sight, he said, "it would appear to a layman very much out of accord with the accepted principles of war to attack the strongly fortified town front without first securing the cliffs on either side, and to use our tanks in frontal assault off the beaches." The Prime Minister wanted Ismay to ascertain the facts, after which he would decide whether to hold a more formal inquiry. Ismay's reply, on

29 December 1942, enclosed a copy of a detailed report already commissioned by Mountbatten and laid overall responsibility on Montgomery, then in charge of South Eastern Command, who, he said, "was the senior Army Officer concerned with the Raid from about the end of April onwards."[60]

Ismay's answer satisfied Churchill at the time—but not eight years later. In many matters, including PQ 17, Churchill did not become intellectually engaged in the complexities of 1942. Over Dieppe, however, he smelled a rat and was determined to find it. On 2 August 1950, he sent Ismay a searching inquisition, rightly noting that there had been *two* plans to attack Dieppe. The first, code-named Rutter, was ready in early July, with troops aboard ship, but was then abandoned because of bad weather and signs that the Germans had spotted the fleet. Monty advised strongly against remounting it and had nothing more to do with the operation, which went ahead under the code name Jubilee on 19 August. The question, said Churchill, was therefore "who took the decision to *revive* the attack after it had been abandoned and Montgomery had cleared out." On this, Ismay had given him no evidence.

> What we say about this [in the memoirs] is a matter for subsequent consideration, but we must at least know ourselves what the facts were—namely: did the Chiefs of Staff, or the Defence Committee or the War Cabinet ever consider the matter of the *revival* of the operation (a) when I was in England, (b) when I was out of England, or was it all pushed through by Dickie [Mountbatten] on his own without reference to higher authority?[61]

Ismay went through all the relevant files in the Cabinet Office. Now very flustered, he wrote Churchill on 14 August apologizing "for being so inadequate about the Dieppe Raid" but saying that it appeared that

> in the vital interests of secrecy, nothing was put on paper. Indeed, I can now recall the fury of General Nye, then V.C.I.G.S. [Vice-Chief of the Imperial General Staff, and in the absence of Brooke, accompanying Churchill in Cairo, the senior officer in command of the British Army], who had no idea that the operation was on until reports started to flow in from the scene of the action.

Churchill, Ismay added lamely, "must have approved the operation in principle" before leaving England because he cabled from Cairo two days before the raid using its code word.[62] Ismay also referred the matter to Mountbatten, who consulted his aides at the time, but they could not help. Admiral John Hughes-Hallett, the naval commander for Dieppe, did recall a meeting to discuss the raid with the Prime Minister, but he was not sure whether this occurred before Rutter was abandoned or prior to its remounting as Jubilee.[63]

Churchill decided to compose his own version. He moved the December 1942 minutes to the appendix and produced a more detailed account of Dieppe that opened up the issues at stake. This made clear that it was Mountbatten who decided to revive the operation and that there was "no written record of the revised plan being further examined, nor of any decision to launch it being taken by the Chiefs of Staff or by the Defence Committee of the War Cabinet." Churchill acknowledged that he was "in principle favourable to an operation of this character at this time." But, he added, he took no part in planning the operation and "naturally supposed it would be subjected to the final review of the Chiefs of Staff and the Defence Committee, before whom I should certainly have had the main issue brought prior to action had I not been abroad." His account also mentioned criticism of the raid from Canada, "whose gallant men had suffered such devastating losses," noting particularly that the Canadian Second Division "lost nearly seventy per cent of the five thousand men embarked."[64]

On 1 September 1950, Churchill sent his redraft to Mountbatten, who was seriously alarmed. He urged Ismay to prevent publication of his minute of 29 December 1942, on the grounds that Ismay held the copyright and "he cannot publish it without your permission." (It was, of course, Crown copyright.) Mountbatten also told Ismay he was "amazed" at Churchill "gratuitously" inserting the statement about the nearly 70 percent losses. Only 18 percent of the Canadians died, so the higher figure could only be reached by adding in all the killed, wounded, and prisoners of war, "which is the most pessimistic possible view to take and surely not one which our side should stress." (Listing killed, wounded, and POWs as "losses" in this way was, of course, standard military procedure.)[65]

Mountbatten compiled ten pages of answers to Churchill's questions and substantially rewrote the draft. He deleted all strictures on the lack of final review of the plan. Despite Hughes-Hallett's equivocation, he inserted a statement that he had discussed the remounting with Churchill personally. He also claimed that the Chiefs of Staff had given verbal approval, no records being kept for reasons of security. The aside about Canadian criticism disappeared, "nearly seventy per cent" Canadian casualties became 18 percent dead plus almost 2,000 prisoners, and a lengthy paragraph was added about the lessons gained from this "costly but not unfruitful reconnaissance in force," attributing "honour to the brave who fell. Their sacrifice was not in vain."[66]

Ismay, to whom Mountbatten had talked at length on the phone, sent Churchill a letter supporting this redraft: "I admit—with shame—that I still have no recollection of the meetings that he had with you on the question of re-mounting DIEPPE; but I am sure, having regard to the weight of evidence, that his story is substantially correct." He asked Churchill not to print his December 1942 reply to the Prime Ministerial minute and also expressed doubt about including the minute itself. Ismay said he felt sure that, in view of Mountbatten's account, Churchill would "drastically revise" the recent redraft, but, he added, "I am equally sure that you will drastically revise and curtail Dickie's suggested amendments." Churchill, however, had lost interest. With Houghton Mifflin importunate, he simply nodded through Mountbatten's rewrite. After Norman Brook pointed out that the December 1942 minutes were "very different from the considered judgement which you have given in the text," Churchill cut these out of the appendix. *The Hinge of Fate* therefore prints Mountbatten's self-serving answers, not Churchill's soul-searching questions.[67]

Whether or not Dieppe was genuinely an "unauthorized action" remains a matter of lively historical debate.[68] It seems clear that the Chiefs of Staff did not approve the final plan, as General Nye's anger suggests, but this may have been because revised procedures no longer required them to do so. On the other hand, if Mountbatten had been given authority to act alone, that makes him largely responsible for the shambles—hence his desperate efforts in 1950 to spread the blame. Yet Churchill could not wash his hands entirely. It was thanks to him that this egregious political climber had been so absurdly overpromoted. Mountbatten was a mere forty-one, with previous experience only with destroyers, and lacked the clout to obtain the essential support from the navy and the RAF. He probably pressed on with the flawed plan because the only way to consolidate his fragile position was by inflicting dramatic damage on Hitler's Fortress Europe. That was what the Prime Minister had asked him to do. Whether or not there had been meetings or records, Mountbatten was basically following the brief he had been given. When Churchill dropped his postmortem in September 1950, lack of time and energy were probably only part of the reason. It was not prudent for him to examine the Dieppe raid too closely—like many events in that dark tunnel between the surrender of Singapore and the victory at Alamein.

CHAPTER 22

"THE BEST OF WINNIE'S MEMOIRS"

THE WEAKNESSES of *The Hinge of Fate* will by now be evident. It was too long, too full of documents, and also seriously unbalanced because Churchill allots almost as much space to the first five and a half months as he does to the next eleven. Yet *The Washington Post* dubbed this volume "the best of Winnie's memoirs"—a verdict endorsed by many on either side of the Atlantic.[1] Explaining why takes us beyond what Churchill said about 1942–1943 to how it sounded in the depths of the Cold War.

IN THE FIRST FEW MONTHS of the Korean War, Allied troops were driven back to the southeast corner of the peninsula. But then General Douglas MacArthur mounted a devastating amphibious landing behind North Korean lines. "AMERICANS DRIVE FOR N. KOREAN CAPITAL," read the *Daily Telegraph's* headline on 10 October 1950, the day newspaper serialization of *The Hinge of Fate* began. "Today, in Korea and elsewhere," *The New York Times* editorialized, "it is the same old fight for freedom and the democratic way of life that Churchill led in the years he writes about in his memoirs."[2] On 25 October, just as serialization commenced in *Life*, Chinese forces clashed for the first time with South Korean troops. A month later, MacArthur began his final push to the Yalu River—China's border with North Korea—only to be routed by a massive Chinese counterattack on 26 November. The next day, Houghton Mifflin published *The Hinge of Fate*. On 30 November, President Truman indicated to reporters that use of the atomic bomb in Korea was under "active consideration." After uproar in Parliament, Clement Attlee flew to Washington on 2 December to urge restraint.

For many of Churchill's readers, therefore, the past was intertwined with the present. Transatlantic summitry, atomic diplomacy, even the Cold War itself—all had their roots in 1942–1943, and *Life* in particular played to the contemporary gallery in the four weekly installments that it extracted from the text. "How Our Russian Troubles Began" was the headline for the first. The second was called "Face to Face with Stalin," with the subtitle: "Mr. Churchill travels to Hyde Park for the atomic bomb decision and to Moscow for a lesson on how the Russians deal with the West." Most of the eight pages of text were devoted to Churchill's August 1942 visit to Moscow. The "atomic bomb decision" took up only eighteen lines at the start and, by accident or design, was edited to give a totally different impression from the one in the book. Whereas Churchill intended to show that the atomic-bomb decision was taken jointly by equal partners, *Life*'s heavily abbreviated version strongly implied that the President's "grave and fateful decision" was to develop the bomb solo. As we have seen, Churchill deceived himself about reaching a formal agreement with FDR in June 1942, but *Life*'s account was even more misleading—though it suited the current American mood of atomic unilateralism.[3]

Houghton Mifflin also played up the Cold War angle, putting a picture of Churchill and Stalin in August 1942 on the back cover of its edition. Initially, Henry Laughlin planned to use a photograph of the two men smiling at each other, but Churchill said no, so Laughlin offered "a gloomy and unhappy photograph" instead. "I would prefer the solemn picture," Churchill replied. Privately, Denis Kelly guessed his real objection was that "politically it is not very appropriate just now to show him embracing Stalin." Such a picture would encourage the impression that Churchill was "quite ready to suck up to Stalin when he wanted help." That charge "may be near the truth," Kelly went on, "but we don't want to give 'handles' to anyone in these critical days."[4]

Churchill's caution was probably wise because his Moscow visit of 1942 grabbed the attention of most reviewers. "In the light of today's world," wrote Drew Middleton in the Sunday *New York Times* on 26 November, "nothing in the book is so interesting as the report on Mr. Churchill's meeting with Stalin." Several reviewers were also struck by Churchill's sketch of Admiral Darlan—"as good as anything in the book," according to Walter Millis in the New York *Herald Tribune*. Donald Grant in the *St. Louis Post-Dispatch* found contemporary parallels even there, likening the Vichy turncoat to South Korea's leader, Syngman

Rhee: both received American support even though "neither satisfies our notion of a good democrat."[5]

Topicality alone did not explain the enthusiasm of the reviewers, however. Several were explicit that this volume was superior to its predecessor. "In *The Hinge of Fate* Churchill has undoubtedly resumed his literary stride," declared James R. Newman in *The New Republic*. "Unlike *The Grand Alliance*, it masters the complex technical task of presenting smoothly the great events occurring simultaneously in different parts of the world." Ferdinand Kuhn, in *The Washington Post*, agreed. Whereas *The Grand Alliance* "showed traces of slipshod work," this volume was "brimful of action, anecdote, and of history told for the first time. In content and style, it is by all odds the best volume of the monumental series." The transition from defeats to victories gave the volume its "inherent dramatic contrast," wrote J. B. Brebner in *The Nation*, and many reviewers built their articles around the hinge metaphor—vindicating Churchill's delight when he hit upon it. Even those who criticized the title did so by boosting its author. The hinge was "not a bad analogy," said Kuhn, but "Fate" suggested "something passive and foreordained"—whereas, in fact, the dramatic international changes owed at least as much to "Allied exertions[,] . . . enemy blunders" and "the dynamo inside Winston Churchill." Cleveland Rodgers, in the *Brooklyn Eagle*, said Churchill "did more than any living man to check the swing of the hinge and start its recession."[6]

There was much discussion of Churchill's relations with FDR. "One guesses that Mr. Churchill was at bottom contemptuous—the word is not too strong—of what he regarded as Roosevelt's naïve political idealism," wrote the Harvard political scientist Crane Brinton in *The Saturday Review of Literature*. Jim Dan Hill in *The Milwaukee Journal* admired the "magnificent, subtle" way in the book that "the Old Master" used FDR's own proposals to reveal him as "grossly uninformed" and "astoundingly provincial" about Indian politics. In general, though, comment on Churchill's coverage of Asia and the Pacific was rare, except for John H. Thompson in the *Chicago Tribune*. And on the Eastern Front reviewers were even more silent than Churchill's own volume, perhaps because of the frigid Cold War atmosphere in 1950.[7]

Volume 4 "strengthens the layman's opinion that this is the best of all the histories of the last World War," wrote Paul Jordan-Smith in the *Los Angeles Times*. Crane Brinton called it "one of the major pieces of writing of our time" and "the nearest thing" to a definitive history "we are likely to get for a long time." Orville Prescott in the weekday *New York Times* proposed that Churchill should be awarded the Nobel Prize for Literature "in recognition of his many other notable books as well as of his current masterpiece."[8] There was a sense of awe at how Churchill managed to do it. Ferdinand Kuhn, noting the "breathtaking episodes" in his globe-trotting of 1942–1943, said that "none was as amazing as Churchill's survival into old age, through all the accumulated perils of brandy and black cigars, to write his wartime story." As usual, it was taken for granted that the book flowed entirely from his pen. On Alamein (mostly written by Pownall), the Cleveland *Plain Dealer* praised "the finely phrased descriptive accounts and sidelights of a master of English."[9]

Perhaps the best of the American reviews came from Edward R. Murrow, the veteran CBS broadcaster, in the January 1951 issue of the *Atlantic Monthly*. He called Churchill "the most considerable man to walk the stage of world history in the last fifty years . . . an outstanding combination of gallant gambler, an aristocrat, an historian, and an early eighteenth century cavalry officer," with a sense of humor that marked him as "one of the world's indestructible juveniles." Murrow was sure "no other man of the century has made and written such history. . . . Later historians who have access to full documentation may amend or reverse his conclusions. But he is, and they will be, the prisoner of his experience." In this volume, Churchill again showed he was "a reporter without equal, a diplomat of great skill, a man of war with the habit of command heavy upon him." Throughout the conflict he "never quite regarded himself as a civilian" but saw himself as "a great commander, unavoidably and unfortunately prevented from commanding armies in the field because his services were more urgently needed for the central and supreme direction of the war."[10] Here was a more neutral version of what *The Nation* meant by dubbing volume 3 "Everyman His Own Napoleon." *The Hinge of Fate* highlighted as never before Churchill's double life as armchair strategist and would-be general.

IN BRITAIN, Cassell's did not publish *The Hinge of Fate* until 3 August 1951 — eight months after Houghton Mifflin. The lag was much longer than Desmond Flower would have liked, but he faced continued problems with paper and printers, not to mention Churchill's endless corrections. Flower, however, was convinced that Houghton Mifflin was killing the goose that laid the golden egg: "As their figures sink, ours rise," he told Churchill proudly on 29 August 1950, "so that of Volume III we have sold 25,000 more copies than they have including their Book of the Month edition." Rather than saturate the market by publishing volumes in too quick succession, Cassell's continued its stately progress and felt vindicated by the sales figures, which showed very little decline between volumes 2 and 3.[11]

Because of the delays, Cassell's edition appeared in a different climate from Houghton Mifflin's. The Korean War had stabilized after the dramatic swings of the pendulum in 1950, so *The Hinge of Fate* seemed much less a commentary on current international relations. On the other hand, with an exhausted Labour government staggering from crisis to crisis, the volume's reception was more intertwined with domestic politics. In the *Daily Mail*, George Murray welcomed "the fourth volume of the supreme literary-historical work of our time"—in itself "a big achievement" but still "only a sixth part of the immense history which to some men would be a life's work. Yet even this is only a fraction of the prodigy that is Winston Churchill." One senses here a reaction to the "WMG" whispering campaign then gaining momentum among Tory MPs: "Winston Must Go" because he was too old, too reactionary, and too prone to plow his own furrows. Murray, like some other Tory reviewers, seems to have been deliberately boosting the politician as much as the author.[12]

There was praise, too, for the content. The series "keeps up all its interest and fire," declared the anonymous review in *The Manchester Guardian*. "Though the purple patches are few and the documentation extensive there is no falling off in sweep or magnanimity."[13] *The Times Literary Supplement*, having consigned volume 3 to its inside pages, gave volume 4 top billing and high praise as a "breathtaking" work of much greater quality than the three "historic source-books" that preceded it. Developing this theme in a leading article, *The Times* said that the earlier volumes had been "marked by the steady pace of a melancholy epic," but the hinge motif gave Churchill full scope for his "true genius," which was "not epic but dramatic." Quoting Roosevelt's comment in January 1942—"it is fun to be in the same decade with you"—the editorial said many readers would "feel the same sort of exaltation as they turn the pages of this most graphic and revealing autobiography."[14]

Again, however, there were dissenting voices, such as Basil Liddell Hart in *The Listener* on 9 August 1951. He argued that Churchill was unfair to Wavell and Auchinleck, who lacked "the plenitude of equipment which smoothed the path of their successors," and that the volume failed to explain properly the sacking of Auchinleck in August 1942, a month after the Auk, "taking personal charge of the Eighth Army, had retrieved the June disaster and checked Rommel at Alamein." Climbing onto one of his hobbyhorses, Liddell Hart also tilted at the policy of unconditional surrender: "this was bound to leave England, and Western Europe, in utter dependence on America and confronted with Communist domination of the larger part of Europe and Asia."[15]

Despite what another reviewer called his "yapping" tone, Liddell Hart had identified some weak points in Churchill's account.[16] Others were probed in the *New Statesman* by Richard Crossman, the Oxford politics don and Labour MP—the Katyn massacre, for instance, where Churchill, "in startling contrast with his normal habit," quoted none of his own memoranda and offered only the briefest account of Russian culpability. "Right up to the end of the war, he was obsessed by the necessity of appeasing the Soviet Union—*but at a minimum cost in British lives.*" For Crossman, the Katyn cover-up was symptomatic of Churchill's larger dilemma:

> The statesman who turns chronicler, before he retires from active politics, is always seeking to adapt the past to the conveniences of the present. Mr. Churchill must portray himself simultaneously as a staunch ally of "Uncle Joe," and as a prophet who foresaw that Stalin would threaten Europe's liberties. He must answer those American critics, who assert that his heart was not in the Second Front; but he must also suggest that his own Mediterranean strategy, if only it had been accepted by Washington, would have prevented Russia from dominating Central Europe.

Without the sneering tone of Michael Foot, Crossman offered a perceptive analysis of Churchill's predicament as a politician-historian.[17]

CONSIDERING THE FINAL panic in which it had been produced in the summer of 1950, *The Hinge of Fate* was therefore a remarkable achievement, and the foreboding of Henry Pownall had proved excessive. Yet he was right to predict some "bloomers," and a few of these proved very controversial.

The installment in *The New York Times* on 17 October 1950 was devoted to the epic naval battles of the Coral Sea and Midway. Reading it, Samuel Eliot Morison, author of the already classic *History of United States Naval Operations in World War II*, experienced a keen sense of déjà vu and then mounting indignation. "It is transparently clear," he told his son-in-law, Brooks Beck, that Churchill had "obtained all his material from my volume four, of which he made a very accurate and intelligent summary." In itself, that was not cause for complaint, but "there was no acknowledgment or hint that he might have obtained this from my work." Beck was also Morison's attorney, and he immediately contacted Houghton Mifflin to demand proper acknowledgment in the book.[18]

With publication only a month away, Henry Laughlin passed the request on to Churchill as a matter of urgency. There was no dispute that the account in *The Hinge of Fate* was based on Morison, but the latter was wrong to assume Churchill's direct responsibility. Gordon Allen researched and drafted the material on the Pacific War, which was accepted with little amendment. Churchill's error was to ignore repeated reminders from Allen that Morison must be properly credited for his work, "which I used very freely." And that is why the acknowledgments of *The Hinge of Fate* contain this sentence, added hastily at the last minute: "I wish to acknowledge my debt to Captain Samuel Eliot Morison, U.S.N.R., whose books on naval operations give a clear presentation of the actions of the United States Fleet." Such reference to the work of another historian was unique in Churchill's volumes, but it was essential to head off an embarrassing charge of plagiarism. "I am most grateful to you for your generous acknowledgment," Morison wrote in March 1951, and the matter was closed. Churchill should have been equally grateful that Morison did not blow the whistle in public.[19]

The Hinge of Fate was widely serialized in Australia, though in different ways. The Sydney *Sunday Telegraph* rolled the first seven chapters into a massive twelve-page tabloid spread, thereby burying Churchill's row with Curtin amid all the setbacks in Malaya, Singapore, and the Western Desert. The Melbourne *Herald*, by contrast, offered a greater number of small installments, each with sharper focus. On 23 October 1950, it excerpted chapter 9 under the headlines "Australia refuses our request for aid" and "A Painful Episode in our relations," thus highlighting the rift. At the end of the twenty-five installments the *Herald* invited H. V. Evatt—in 1950 as in 1942 Australia's Minister for External Affairs—to defend Curtin's policy. Evatt was at pains to call Churchill "a greater war leader than Lloyd George, greater even than Pitt" but offered a blunt critique of his version of 1942. Curtin's resistance to diverting the Australian divisions to Burma was, said Evatt, entirely justified by the interests of Australian defense and the overall war effort in the Pacific. Placed in a similar position to Curtin, Churchill "would have done exactly the same thing" and "would have been much tougher and much rougher in the course of doing it." Evatt also said Churchill was "misinformed" when accusing Australians of partisan politics and flatly inaccurate in claiming that "conscription even for home defence was banned."[20]

On the first point, Evatt was on weak ground: the bipartisan War Council he cited was an advisory body and no substitute for a genuine coalition. On the second issue, however, he was quite right. The Tory Research Department told Churchill that in the autumn of 1939 Menzies had introduced conscription for home defense for single men between the ages of eighteen and thirty-five, and in December 1941 Curtin had extended it to married men of the same age and also singles up to forty-five. (The Research Department might have added that in 1943 Curtin persuaded the Australian Labor Party to send conscripts to the whole southwest Pacific, even though conscription for overseas service had split the party asunder in the First World War.) Churchill received this information on 28 November 1950 and apparently intended to correct the Cassell's edition, but nothing was altered. The claim that "conscription even for home defence was banned" was repeated without amendment on page 4 of the British edition of *The Hinge of Fate*.[21]

The book also ruffled a few feathers in India. Although Churchill had been persuaded to tone down his early drafts about Gandhi, he still cast aspersions in print on the Mahatma's three-week fast in February 1943 — claiming that he was "being fed with glucose whenever he drank water" and that he abandoned his fast once convinced of British obduracy. In September 1951, Gandhi's doctors responded with a public statement, claiming that he did not take glucose and that he always intended to fast for only twenty-one days. In December, Lord Ismay, by then Secretary of State for Commonwealth Relations in Churchill's new government, said that the "furore in India" had been allayed to some extent by a promise that the passage was being "carefully considered for future editions," and he strongly urged that it be cut out. Churchill agreed. This was "a *very* important amendment to the next edition," Kelly told Charles Wood in January 1952. "Could you hang on to it like grim death and make sure it is not forgotten."[22]

In Britain, it was Churchill's account of the Desert War that caused a backlash. As we have seen, his critique centered on the High Command: Wavell and Auchinleck were flawed; once he personally appointed Alexander and Montgomery in August 1942, victory followed inexorably. When the American edition appeared, General Sir Kenneth Anderson, a senior commander in northwest Africa, wrote to protest Churchill's remark in a letter to Alexander in February 1943 that his First Army lacked any "proper spirit or knowledge of what was going on" and was "very much in the condition of the Eighth Army when you and Monty took over." Churchill cut this sentence from the British edition.[23] When the latter was published, several officers and men from the First Armoured Division contested his interpretation of "The Setback in the Desert" in January 1942, emphasizing their lack of fuel and radios and the inferiority of British tanks. In chapter 2, Churchill had treated such claims as Auchinleck's excuses for failures in command, but they were genuine, insisted his correspondents, one of whom was a Tory MP, Christopher Peto. "I had better have a talk with him," Churchill noted. In the end, Peto and his fellows were mollified by the promise of amendment in future editions, but the correspondence showed how Churchill's memoirs had burnished the images of Monty, his Eighth Army, and its Seventh

Armoured Division—the "Desert Rats"—at the expense of all other generals and units.[24]

Another critic, however, was less easily placated, and his attack came totally out of the blue, after Churchill had again become Prime Minister. On 1 May 1953, Philip Smith, a solicitor in the provincial Irish town of Cavan, sent a letter to 10 Downing Street accusing Churchill of libel. He was acting for Eric Dorman O'Gowan, who, under his former surname of Dorman-Smith, had been Auchinleck's Deputy Chief of the General Staff in the summer of 1942 and had been sacked as part of Churchill's August purge in Cairo. According to Smith, Churchill's memoir had made "very grave charges that our client was incompetent and perhaps worse and that he was removed for incompetency." Readers of volume 4 will find only one reference to Dorman-Smith—a line in a telegram from Churchill to the War Cabinet on 6 August 1942, listing various personnel changes consequent on Auchinleck's replacement by Alexander. It simply states: "General Dorman-Smith to be relieved as Deputy C.G.S." The solicitor, however, claimed that this brought his client within Churchill's general strictures on Auchinleck's command, for example those in a telegram on 21 August in which he told the War Cabinet, "I am sure we were heading for disaster under the former régime." *The Hinge of Fate* had "spread the story of his incompetence to the ends of the earth," causing O'Gowan "untold pain and humiliation."[25]

Churchill's first response to the solicitor's letter was to say that these official telegrams were privileged documents, but Norman Brook quickly disabused him: any such protection had been lost once they were reproduced in his book. Churchill tried to enlist Camrose, only to be told that none of these extracts appeared in the serials, which left him and Cassell's on their own. Worse still, the Prime Minister was informed that O'Gowan had a plausible case: the cited passages implied that he had been sacked not for specific shortcomings but because he was unequal to the job, and this was defamatory. There were, said counsel, two possible defenses: that of "justification," which would require clear evidence of incompetence, or a plea of "fair comment," which depended on showing that Churchill's view was "honestly formed" from the facts at his disposal. Either mode would mean making public a mass of sensitive historical documents. Yet "any display of weakness in the face of this threat would be well calculated to encourage others who appear in an unfavourable light in this, or any of the other volumes of 'The Second World War' to launch proceedings for libel against Sir Winston and the publishers."[26]

This opinion was written on 11 May 1953, the day Churchill delivered a major speech to the Commons calling for a summit with Stalin's successors. It was therefore a very irritating distraction, but one that he had to take with the utmost seriousness. The Cabinet Office was asked to trawl through relevant papers. An exhaustive search produced "scant evidence," most of it general in nature, but suggested that Dorman-Smith was relieved for a combination of three reasons:

- "He was known to be an officer of difficult character and over-fertile imagination.
- "He was closely involved and personally associated with the policies of the outgoing Commander.
- "His brief tenure of an awkward and anomalous position at Eighth Army" as the Auk's personal adviser when the latter assumed its temporary command in June and July 1942.[27]

Pownall and Jacob assumed that the sacking had become a personal obsession for Dorman-Smith in the postwar years, exacerbated by a strain of anglophobia, now that he had retreated to Eire and assumed an old Irish family name.[28]

Both sides began to prepare for a hearing in court. In England, Churchill was being advised by Sir Hartley Shawcross, formerly Labour's Attorney-General and an outstanding advocate who had made his name as Britain's Chief Prosecutor at the Nuremburg war-crimes trials. Because O'Gowan was likely to sue in the Irish courts, Churchill had a legal team over there as well, including John Costello, a leading barrister and also Irish Prime Minister from 1948 to 1951. But the prospect of a trial in Dublin filled Churchill with dread. Not only was he a serving British Prime Minister, so the experience would be deeply humiliating, but he was also notorious in Ireland as the organizer of the brutal "Black and Tan" paramilitaries in 1920–1921. When Pownall wrote about what might happen "if the matter should come to court," Churchill scribbled in the margin: "It will not." Shawcross agreed that litigation ought, if possible, to be avoided. Not only would it have "many distasteful features" for Churchill personally, but questions of "constitutional importance might arise in regard to the disclosure of State documents."[29] On the other hand, O'Gowan wanted a public retraction, set out as an addendum to future editions, and this was more than Churchill would stomach. Shawcross hoped that, if the case came to court, the Prime Minister would not have to appear in person but could give written evidence to an examiner in London. This would be unusual, he told Churchill, "but this is a very unusual case and I should think that in view of your commitments over here, it is quite likely that an Order would be made." But, he added, "juries are always less impressed with evidence which is read out to them." Churchill did not want to appear in court, but he was even more determined to win. Whether or not the affair contributed to his stroke on 23 June 1953, it was certainly, as he said later, "a worry and a burden."[30]

Shawcross lined up Alanbrooke and Montgomery to testify against O'Gowan — the former had advised Churchill in the Cairo purge, while Monty had been its prime beneficiary. On the other side, it seemed clear that Auchinleck, though deploring O'Gowan's action, would support him if obliged to testify.[31] Also involved was Basil Liddell Hart, a longtime correspondent of O'Gowan. His newspaper articles had already questioned a simple transition in the Desert War from failure (Wavell and Auchinleck) to success (Alexander and Monty), and he was in fact an unwitting trigger for the whole affair. In April 1953, he had sent O'Gowan a copy of his edition of The Rommel Papers. O'Gowan replied a few days later, saying that for some time he had been considering legal action but had felt it would be difficult to overcome the general pro-Churchill prejudice. In the light of Rommel's praise of Auchinleck and Liddell Hart's editorial endorsement, however, the position had "greatly changed." This letter was sent on 13 April; on 1 May, his lawyers wrote to Churchill.[32] Like Liddell Hart, O'Gowan wanted to show that "the true turning-point of the African campaign" occurred not in November 1942 but in July—what he called "first Alamein," when the Auk stopped Rommel, making the Torch landings possible and "second Alamein comparatively superfluous." In Churchill's accounts the July battle was covered in only two sketchy paragraphs at the end of "The Eighth Army at Bay," taken from an outline of the North African campaign by Pownall. As O'Gowan said, his aim was nothing less than to "unhinge" The Hinge of Fate. No wonder that Churchill fought so hard or that Monty was so keen to assist him.[33]

"I don't see what more we can do," Churchill told Shawcross wearily on 24 April 1954. "I gather that the action is very likely not to take place until next year. Is this so? The longer it is put off the better."[34] Then, suddenly the logjam broke. Precisely why O'Gowan backed down from his full demands is not clear, but Churchill's lawyers were now threatening to air in public a good deal of embarrassing material about his military career if the case came to court. According to O'Gowan's biographer, Shawcross played on the former soldier's sense of chivalry by warning that he might cause Churchill a fatal stroke. At any event, after Shawcross made a second visit to Ireland at the beginning of May 1954, the two sides agreed to add in the next edition a footnote to Churchill's telegram of 6 August:

The references to the Officers whose names figure in this list are factual only. Neither they nor my later remarks are to be taken as imputing personal blame to any individual. These were the principal changes in Commands and Staffs at the time when General Auchinleck was replaced by General Alexander. Major General Dorman-Smith became Deputy Chief of Staff only on the 16th June, 1942, and thus bears no responsibility for the fall of Tobruk or the defeats at Gazala. From the 25th June to the 4th August he acted as General Auchinleck's Principal Operations Officer at Headquarters Eighth Army during the operation described in Chapter 24. My appreciation in that Chapter of the handling of the Eighth Army is supported by Rommel's remarkable tribute.[35]

An angry Churchill was no longer willing to pay a penny toward O'Gowan's legal costs, so Shawcross persuaded Cassell's to raise their offer to 250 guineas, without liability.[36] While the two sets of lawyers were negotiating an agreed statement, however, O'Gowan spoke unilaterally to the Irish press. His comments, published on 2 July, developed the theme of the two battles of Alamein and bluntly said that Churchill's Cairo purge was "wrong." The Prime Minister was then returning from America aboard the *Queen Elizabeth*, his mind full of a possible summit in Moscow. Suddenly, he had to deal with a series of cables from Shawcross, who wanted to issue a rebuttal to O'Gowan. This spoke of the footnote as factual clarification and claimed there was "no question" of legal victory for either side. Although most British papers reported the statements, they did so briefly and without comment. Shawcross called the coverage "very satisfactory."[37]

So what threatened to be the most deadly shell fired at Churchill's memoirs failed to go off. Again, a critic backed down in return for the promise of minor amendments in a future revised edition.[38] But the shell had a delayed fuse. Churchill had established an orthodoxy about the Desert War, built around his "great man" view of history and the centrality of Monty's victory at Alamein. This invited an equally categorical response, already sketched in Liddell Hart's review in August 1951, that Churchill knew "would stultify the whole story which I tell."[39] In 1958, Monty's memoirs affirmed the Churchillian line with his own self-promotional gloss, but two years later the young Correlli Barnett brought out *The Desert Generals*, a ferocious assault on the Churchill-Montgomery orthodoxy that popularized the idea of two battles of Alamein. One of Barnett's principal sources was Eric Dorman O'Gowan.

V.

CLOSING THE RING

1943–1944
1949–1952

DEADLINES

C LOSING THE RING spans the year from June 1943. It begins with planning for the invasion of Sicily; it ends with the capture of Rome on the eve of the Normandy landings. The two component books are entitled "Italy Won" and "Teheran to Rome," but taken together those phrases expose a contradiction.[1] If Italy was won in the first book, why are we only at Rome by the end of book 2? An earlier title, "Italy Surrenders," was more apt because, contrary to Churchill's expectations, Hitler did not abandon the peninsula after the Allies invaded in September 1943 but fought a war of attrition in central Italy, which forms the overarching theme of *Closing the Ring*. Churchill's most passionate prose is reserved for what he deems the fatal error of Allied strategy in 1943–1944: failing to exploit the Italian collapse by grabbing Aegean islands and thereby persuading Turkey to enter the war.

So *Closing the Ring* takes us from Sicily to Rome. Book 2 highlights the other main theme of the volume: Allied conferences, especially the Big Three summit at Teheran from 28 November to 2 December, to which he devotes four chapters. Teheran is doubly important. It is the first and arguably the more important of the two meetings of Churchill, Roosevelt, and Stalin. It also confirmed plans for the Normandy landings, bringing to an end Churchill's bid to exploit the Mediterranean opportunities opened up by Italy's collapse.

The volume is unbalanced. Two thirds of it is devoted to the first half of the period, June to December 1943—a comparable weighting to that in volume 4 and for similar reasons. In part, this was because the crux of the volume had passed: the agreement on Torch and the Cairo purge in July–August 1942 in *The Hinge of Fate* and the loss of the Aegean islands and the Teheran/Cairo decisions in October–December 1943 in *Closing the Ring*. The rest of each volume is depicted as a playing out of what had been decided. The difference is that in *The Hinge of Fate* Churchill could plausibly present the second half as vindication of the first: how his preferences in 1942 determined strategy in 1943. In *Closing the Ring*, however, he is struggling against the impression, evident in many American memoirs, that Overlord negated all he really wanted. In 1943–1944, Churchill was on the defensive strategically; by 1950–1951, he was also trying to defend himself against the historiography. This double defensiveness gives *Closing the Ring* a different tone to the more triumphal note struck in volume 4.

The imbalance between books 1 and 2 reflects pressures of the present as well as perspectives on the past. In 1951, Churchill was again racing against publishers' deadlines, and many later chapters received inadequate attention. Moreover, Attlee's Labour government had a fragile majority, making another election likely before long. Churchill knew that if he regained the premiership, his book time would virtually disappear, and he was therefore working hard on the final volume as well. The sixth of June 1944 was not the only D-Day on Churchill's mind as he raced to close the ring on volume 5.

ONCE MORE, CHURCHILL selected the main documents from his personal papers.[2] He also kept a firm hand on the conferences, and this was again where Ismay made his main contribution, correcting and amplifying Churchill's recollections. As before, Pownall handled military operations. The chapters on the battle for Monte Cassino and the advance on Rome, for instance, are built on a paper he wrote in December 1950. After repeated requests by Pownall, Churchill commissioned a paper on the strategic air offensive from Air Marshal Sir Guy Garrod. In general, however, there are far fewer research papers than in previous volumes—another sign of time pressures. Each member of the Syndicate, even Denis Kelly, was now writing drafts as if from Churchill himself (including Churchillian phraseology), rather than laboring over research memos for "Master" to distill into his own prose. As Jock Colville, Churchill's private secretary, observed in 1945 about wartime correspondence: "I often think how difficult it will be for future historians to know what is 'genuine Churchill' and what is 'school of.' We are all fairly good imitators of his epistolary style now." The same might be said of the Syndicate by the end of the war memoirs.[3]

Closing the Ring stayed largely within Churchill's inner circle. The main outside contributor was again Norman Brook, who helped clean up the Teheran chapters—a rewrite of conference minutes—apparently sharing Churchill's sense that these were important chapters and wanting to maximize their fluency. The future as well as the past mattered to both men. In August 1951, Churchill added some last-minute paragraphs to sum up the significance of Teheran for Germany and Eastern Europe. With one eye on a return to the premiership, he delayed submission to Houghton Mifflin until Brook had commented on whether these contained any hostages to fortune. His future Cabinet Secretary replied on 22 August: "My judgment is that there is nothing in this which could be embarrassing to you, either in the immediate or the more distant future."[4]

Churchill's personal memories remained a feature of the work. The post-Teheran chapters follow closely a vivid outline he dictated on 11 April 1950, running to nineteen pages of double-spaced typescript. After attacking the conduct of the Anzio landing, he jumps rapidly from the end of 1943 to May 1944, and then cites "The Eve of Overlord" as a moment of "great interest," for which he dictates ten pages of anecdotes. The content and the balance of this April 1950 note determined the second half of volume 5: Overlord overshadows all else.[5]

Yet memory remains Churchill's Achilles' heel. There was much that the Syndicate could not verify, particularly about wartime meetings. Consider this account of his visit to Roosevelt's home after the Quebec conference of August 1943:

> Harry Hopkins came to Hyde Park. He was obviously invited to please me. He explained to me his altered position. He had declined in the favour of the President. There was a curious incident at luncheon, when he arrived a few minutes late and the President did not even greet him. It was remarkable how definitely my contacts with the President improved, and our affairs moved quicker as Hopkins appeared to regain his influence. In two days it seemed to be like old times. He said to me, "You must know I am not what I was." He had tried too much at once. Even his greatness of spirit broke under his variegated activities.

This paragraph was published in *Life*'s serialization on 8 October 1951 and in the American book version the following month. But on 1 November, Robert Sherwood told Houghton Mifflin that, when researching his own biography of Hopkins, he was told by Churchill that this episode occurred after the *second* Quebec conference, in 1944. This message was hastily relayed to Churchill, and Deakin unearthed documentary evidence confirming that Hopkins had been present at Hyde Park in September 1944 but not in August 1943. There was still time to delete the passage from the British edition of *Closing the Ring*, but it was printed in almost exactly the same words in both editions of volume 6. Americans therefore read the same story twice — about events more than a year apart![6]

Having stayed at Hyde Park in June 1942, August 1943, and September 1944, Churchill understandably had difficulty separating the visits in his mind. This error about Hopkins parallels the far more serious confusion (described in chapter 21, above) about his understanding with Roosevelt concerning the atomic bomb.

CHURCHILL AND THE Syndicate did much of the basic work on volume 5 in the summer of 1950. Eighteen of the thirty-five chapters went into first proof during June and July. This period marked a lull between submission of the 1 May version of volume 4, to secure the next tranche of his advance, and the August push to prepare its final text for the press and book publishers. Once volume 4 was out of the way, Churchill laid down another eight chapters of volume 5 between September and December 1950. Christmas and New Year's were spent in Marrakech, again at the Mamounia Hotel. Churchill and his entourage flew out by private plane on 17 December and he did not return to England until 23 January 1951, the day Parliament resumed. Pownall, now a widower, was there for the whole time, Kelly stayed from 17 December until 3 January, and the Deakins arrived on the fifth for two weeks, so Churchill had continuous support. As usual, *Life* and *The New York Times* footed the bill. Walter Graebner, the head of *Life*'s London bureau, visited them and told Daniel Longwell that "the group has never worked so hard on one of these work-holidays abroad and the accomplishments are impressive."[7]

For the first couple of weeks at Marrakech, the Syndicate devoted itself to volume 6, but after Deakin arrived attention reverted to volume 5. For the rest of the trip, there was a steady flow of revised chapters to the Chiswick Press. Pownall, as usual, was carping in private, complaining to Ismay on 14 January that volume 5 had been "a horrid mess." After much "cutting and chopping and sticking," book 1 was almost complete, but work on book 2 was "only beginning and we haven't time to finish it." Pownall also told Ismay that Kelly was "quite hopeless. I had a very straight talk with him (it would be Christmas night!) but I don't suppose it will make any difference." Pownall wanted Kelly to collate comments, rather than draft and rewrite material on his own, but, given the preoccupations of the Syndicate, it was inevitable that the young barrister would assume a larger role.[8]

In fact, it seems that Kelly deserves credit for the title of volume 5. Back in January 1949, when Churchill still hoped to round off his history in five volumes, the title was *The Final Victory*, comprising "The Liberation of Western Europe" and "The End of the Cycle." This was abandoned once it became clear that volume 5 would carry the story only to D-Day. In a note for the Syndicate on 1 November 1950, Churchill gave its "provisional title" as "Closing In." But on 5 March 1951 he admitted to Norman Brook, "I have not yet found a name for Volume V."[9] *Closing the Ring* appears as the heading only with the May 1951 set of proofs. On 27 June, Kelly told Lord Portal, wartime Chief of the Air Staff, that "Mr. Churchill thinks that I invented the title, and has given me credit for it; but I am almost certain that I heard the phrase from him (and no one else) about a year ago." Portal drew Kelly's attention to its use in strategy documents prepared en route to Washington in December 1941 and reproduced in volume 3. Whether this originated from Churchill or the Chiefs of Staff is unclear. More interesting is that ten years later neither Churchill nor Ismay could recall hearing the phrase before.[10]

Choosing the title occurred during another frenzied April preparing the 1 May version. This was duly done thanks again to Churchill's parliamentary recess and Deakin's Oxford vacation. The summer of 1951 marked another financial milestone in the saga of Churchill's memoirs. During its first five years, the trust would have been liable for 65 percent estate duty if Churchill died, and Anthony Moir, his financial lawyer, blocked substantial spending and investment to cover this contingency. The passing of this deadline at the beginning of August 1951 was therefore celebrated in style with a champagne party at Chartwell (thirty-two people and thirty-two bottles). "This of course is the most important thing that could happen to our affairs," Winston told Clementine, "and relieves me of much anxiety on your account." Moir's stringency was now relaxed. The trust invested £127,500 in stocks and securities between December 1951 and February 1952, and starting in May it took over payment of Churchill's monthly allowances to his children.[11]

Meeting the deadline of 1 May 1951 did cause some strains on the home front, however. Charles Wood had gradually taken over the studio at Hyde Park Gate with his files, green pens, and reference books on English usage. Most of Churchill's female secretaries found him an insufferable pedant, and in February 1951, after months of lobbying by them, Clementine asked Wood to move into the front office on the grounds that the studio was needed to interview people who visited her husband. Once Clementine left on vacation, Wood went behind her back to Churchill himself, complaining that the front office was dark and cramped. Churchill ordered Wood back into the studio and said he would discuss the matter with his wife when she returned. Clementine pressed her case in two notes in April, but Winston was obdurate: "I will not have him turned out now. We are at the crisis of the book—I need him every hour of the day." She conceded defeat until after volume 5 went to the publishers in the autumn.[12]

With the May 1951 galleys in hand, Henry Laughlin began campaigning for rapid publication. This time, Houghton Mifflin wanted the November Book-of-the-Month Club slot, to maximize Christmas sales. Like Daniel Longwell at *Life*, Laughlin was now muted in his criticisms of content—partly because he, too, was genuinely pleased with the draft and its "wonderful" title but mainly because he wanted the final version as soon as possible. On 28 June, Churchill said he was aiming for delivery around 1 September.[13] Knowing what "delivery" meant in Churchillese and recalling the production nightmare over volume 4, Laughlin came to London, and they had a long and frank lunch on 18 July (lubricated by a 1928 Pol Roger). On the basis of their discussion, Laughlin established an installment plan, with the first ten chapters to be airmailed on 5 August and everything in his hands by 2 September.[14] He also sent Churchill the latest sales figures to demonstrate the financial imperative. These showed that the steady decline for volumes 1 to 3 had continued for book-club sales with volume 4, and had only just been arrested for Houghton Mifflin's own sales. Overall, the figures were still impressive—1.5 million copies sold in North America for the four volumes to date—but, having spent so much on the project, Laughlin was naturally concerned by the slide.[15]

NORTH AMERICAN SALES FOR VOLUMES 1 TO 4
(TO 24 JULY 1951)

	Houghton Mifflin	Book-of-the-Month Club	Thomas Allen (Canada)	Total
Vol. 1	119,260	385,000	26,070	530,330
Vol. 2	87,389	272,950	16,702	377,041
Vol. 3	54,963	241,700	9,727	306,390
Vol. 4	58,189	219,100	10,001	287,290
Vols. 1–4	319,801	1,118,750	62,500	1,501,051

Source: Margaret Minaham to Henry Laughlin, 24 July 1951, HM 318/4: Laughlin, 1951.

CASSELL'S SALES FIGURES
(TO 7 JUNE 1951)

Vol. 1 (4 Oct. 1948)	346,794
Vol. 2 (29 June 1949)	303,438
Vol. 3 (20 July 1950)	292,120
Vols. 1–3	942,352

Source: Desmond Flower to WSC, 7 June 1951, CHUR 4/24/458 (CAC).

Cassell's was far behind Houghton Mifflin on publication schedule—in the summer of 1951 it was bringing out volume 4—but the decline in their sales had been much less acute. Indeed, volume 3 had gone about as well as volume 2 and almost matched North American sales.[16] But Emery Reves, looking at the European and global market, shared Laughlin's concern. He warned Churchill that several of his foreign publishers were in serious difficulties. In Brazil, the four volumes had sold only two thousand copies, in Turkey a mere eight hundred, and Turkish book and serial publication had already been suspended. Worse still was the end of serialization in Argentina when *La Prensa*—the largest-circulation daily involved after the *Daily Telegraph* and *The New York Times*—was suppressed by the Perón regime. Reves told Churchill he preferred "not to offer the serial rights to one of the Fascist papers of Madame Evita." In Germany, volume 4 sold only 5,000 copies and resulted in a serious fall in circulation for those papers carrying the memoirs. This Reves ascribed to the "tremendous" resurgence of German nationalism and an organized boycott in the German book trade against English literature in general.[17]

August 1951 saw the final throes of revision. "I am virtually re-writing the early chapters of Volume V," Churchill told his wife, who was recuperating near Biarritz. "They take four or five hours apiece."[18] He also took pleasure in the first reviews of the British edition of volume 4, just appearing. And he was also looking ahead to volume 6. In early July, he cabled Walter Graebner, "Let me know about a month['s] holiday in France departing mid-August to make progress on Volume VI."[19] Although this was barely six months since the last working vacation, *Life*—conscious that an election was likely in the autumn—took the hint and offered to pay. On 6 August, Churchill told Camrose that he hoped to complete revisions of the whole of volume 5, book 1, before leaving on 15 August and that he would finish the rest in France by the end of August. But, as with volume 4, the dénouement did not go according to plan.

THIS TIME, Churchill went to Annecy in the French Alps, where his party was booked into the Imperial Palace Hotel on the lakeside. But the weather was so bad that after five days they decamped to the Excelsior in Venice, staying until 9 September. Returning via Paris, he arrived home on the twelfth. The cost to *Life* and *The New York Times* was $7,000, $2,000 more than their original budget.[20]

When Churchill left London he was keeping to his prediction to Camrose: all seventeen chapters of book 1 had been mailed to Houghton Mifflin by the night of 16 August. But then things began to slip. He was now hundreds of miles from his papers, and indeed from his Syndicate because none of them accompanied him this time. Kelly was supposed to join the party but decided to stay in England, partly for family reasons but mainly because "I feel I can serve you better by staying here at any rate till Volume 5 is finished," he wrote Churchill on 23 August.[21] It was just as well that he did. That morning, for instance, he discussed several sensitive points with Norman Brook and also searched the Cabinet Office records for a query about the first Cairo conference; in the evening, he had long phone conversations with Ismay and Pownall (on holiday in the north). But, with Churchill on the Continent and Kelly in England, communication between them became much slower. "Master" was now revising chapters, sending them to London to be checked and printed, and then often repeating the cycle before the final version could go to the publishers. When Kelly proposed major revisions, he had to communicate with Churchill by overnight airmail or telegram, rather than in person—agreeing on the guidelines for reconstructing "Burma and Beyond," for instance, took three days instead of three hours. Inexorably, Churchill slipped well past the 30 August deadline. The appendix of minutes for book 2 was not dispatched until 13 September. Even then, three chapters were still in provisional form, and they were not mailed until the night of 18 September.[22]

Churchill complained that his publishers had ruined his holiday, but this was hardly fair.[23] It was the delay in finalizing book 2, compounded by his absence from London, that was decisive. So why was he so determined to take a vacation in 1951? Partly because the Korean War had denied him a summer holiday the previous year; partly because he wanted to get on with volume 6 and, as usual, took a lofty view of the many details that have to be settled before any manuscript can go off to the publisher; and most of all, one suspects, because he knew that if he became Prime Minister it would be impolitic to accept *Life's* largesse when his countrymen were imprisoned in Britain by draconian exchange controls. A summer vacation, particularly if it was the last for some time, seemed essential to face the ordeal ahead.

Churchill was also genuinely worried about his health—the ultimate deadline. Although he recovered from the stroke of August 1949, it dealt a lasting blow to his confidence, and Lord Moran predicted further "arterial spasms" when he was very tired. On 20 September 1951, Churchill received a terse note from Attlee stating that an election would be held in five weeks' time. Moran warned that, if the Tories won, Churchill would have to consider how he was going to get through his work. "Oh, well," came the breezy reply, "I live most of the day in bed; dictating directives would be just like writing the book." But he was on edge and kept pacing up and down the hall at Chartwell. "It's a big job to take on at my age, but there's no alternative. It's my duty." For Churchill, "duty" was often a euphemism for "desire." The political vindication he had craved since July 1945 was now at hand, and that made the adrenaline surge again. But, deep down, he knew he was not the man he had been a decade before.[24]

Churchill's 1951 sensitivity about his health is fascinatingly reflected in the drafts of *Closing the Ring*. The second half of 1943 had seen no diminution in his globe-trotting, and nearly all of August and the first half of September were taken up with arduous travels to Canada and the United States. On 12 November, he set out again for conferences in Cairo and Teheran, a trip planned to last three weeks. Instead, he was out of the country for more than nine weeks, because he collapsed at Tunis on 11 December 1943, spent two weeks in bed with pneumonia, and then another two recuperating at Marrakech. "I never remember such extreme fatigue and weakness in body," he writes in his memoirs. "I could hardly walk at all" and "passed eighteen hours of every twenty-four prone." In February 1951, Moran was asked to comment on Churchill's draft account of his illness. This was actually a paraphrase of an upbeat December 1943 telegram that Churchill sent to well-wishers, insisting that "I did not feel so ill in this attack as I did last February" (on account of a bout of pneumonia) and that "I have not at any time had to relinquish my part in the direction of affairs." Against these words Moran noted: "Attack more severe than one in February with fibrillation of heart thrown in. Issue was at one time in doubt." But Churchill would have none of this. His final text reads: "Although Lord Moran records that he judged that the issue was at one time in doubt, I did not share his view. I did not feel so ill in this attack as I had the previous February." No reference is made to fibrillations, and a comment that on the flight to Marrakech "my heart behaved extremely well" became "I got along all right."[25]

Fibrillations had never been mentioned in public during Churchill's North African illness—beyond a vague reference to "some irregularity of the pulse"—because the merest hint of heart problems could be the kiss of death for a political leader. It was doubtless for the same reason that, on the eve of a new bid for the premiership in 1951, Churchill cited only pneumonia in his account of his illness in 1943–1944.

It is, of course, unusual for us to know so much about a political leader's health. But we do in this case because in 1966 Moran chose to publish a book about Churchill's "Struggle for Survival," based on his "diary" of the 1940s and 1950s.[26] This had started as jottings on odd scraps of paper in 1941–1942 but developed into systematic entries in a "Manuscript Book." Moran had always yearned to be an author, and his reflections on morale in the First World War, published in 1945 as *The Anatomy of Courage*, had been well received. Gradually, he came to see himself as Boswell to Churchill's Dr. Johnson and was sounding out possible publishers as early as the autumn of 1949. Freed from the Presidency of the Royal College of Physicians the following spring, Moran made rapid progress with his manuscript. In December 1950, he told his son John that he saw little prospect of publishing during Churchill's lifetime but added, "he is 76." Moran discerned "mounting evidence" that "Winston's long directives and memoranda" in *The Second World War* were "wearing down his reading public," whereas "a personal portrait of Winston" might be better received.[27] He even referred to the project in Churchill's presence, at a dinner on 10 July 1951 at the Royal College, when he was presented with a specially commissioned portrait. Churchill (an Honorary Fellow) paid brief but graceful tribute to Moran. The latter's more calculated reply included this passage:

> The undertones of history fall a little faintly on the ear, but there is a feeling, a very general conviction, that when we are all gone, Mr Churchill will live on as the Chatham of our age. One of my forebears, William Hazlitt, the writer, wrote a fine chapter on Chatham, and it would be fitting if one of his descendants were allowed to add a postscript on Mr Churchill.[28]

What Churchill made of these remarks is not known—probably they were too vague to be taken seriously—but by the autumn of 1951 Moran had finished his draft. As the two of them discussed Churchill's health on 20 September, with

Closing the Ring newly dispatched to the publishers, the authorized version of Winston's war was well established. But, ironically, their discussion that day, like many others, would eventually be recorded in one of the most trenchant pieces of Churchill revisionism. Two powerful histories—one public, the other still very private—were emerging in tandem.

CHAPTER 24

CHURCHILL AND "THE MEDITERRANEAN STRATEGY"

C HURCHILL'S MOST categorical statement in *Closing the Ring* concerns wartime strategy. He enjoins his readers not to be "misled by a chance phrase here and there into thinking (*a*) that I wanted to abandon 'Overlord,' (*b*) that I wanted to deprive 'Overlord' of vital forces, or (*c*) that I contemplated a campaign by armies operating in the Balkan peninsula. These are legends. Never had such a wish entered my mind."[1]

By the time Churchill got down to volume 5, it was an American commonplace that he had shunned a cross-Channel attack in favor of pressing on through Italy and the Balkans. In 1946, Ralph Ingersoll and Elliott Roosevelt had infuriated him with their bald statements of this thesis (see chapter 4, above). In 1948, Hull, Stimson, Sherwood, and Eisenhower developed it more temperately but with equal firmness, prompting Churchill's riposte in *Their Finest Hour* about how even in 1940 he was preparing for D-Day. In volumes 3 and 4 he used papers from 1941 and 1942 to try to prove he was always in favor of invading the Continent. But, as we have seen, his conception of that invasion was a far cry from the D-Day plan of 1944. Churchill envisaged several bridgeheads around the rim of Hitler's Fortress Europe, not one, established when the occupied peoples were ready to revolt and the Reich had been weakened by strategic bombing.

Early in 1950, the American military journalist Hanson W. Baldwin reopened this debate from a different angle. His *Great Mistakes of the War* blasted what he deemed the American propensity to wage war without considering the future peace. By contrast, he claimed, the British were always mindful of political imperatives—a classic case being their "soft underbelly" strategy, which Baldwin held might have preempted Russian control of much of Central Europe. In early April 1950, Churchill carefully read this part of Baldwin's book. He did not deny that he wanted to push northeast from Italy toward Vienna—indeed, that became a theme of volume 6. But Baldwin's assertions, many of them derived from Elliott Roosevelt, that Churchill wanted to mount a "Balkan invasion" or "jump eastward into the Balkans" provoked angry annotations in the margin: "rubbish," "wrong," even "crazy."[2] *Great Mistakes* argued that the British were right about strategy and the Americans misguided—a refrain of *The Second World War*—but Churchill was determined to distance himself from Baldwin on the Balkans, and this may help explain the passage quoted at the start of this chapter, which he wrote at the end of 1950.

In volume 5, Churchill also spars with Eisenhower, whose *Crusade in Europe* alluded to those who held that in war "opportunity should be exploited as it arises, and that if things went well in the 'soft underbelly' we should not pause merely because we had made up our minds to conduct the cross-Channel operation." In a draft of June 1950, Churchill quoted Ike's remark, adding, "I cannot agree that opportunism is a vice." Although this statement was later cut, it is revealing. In his memoirs, Eisenhower had asserted that "the doctrine of opportunism, so often applicable in tactics, is a dangerous one to pursue in strategy" and that this was why he and Marshall subordinated everything to Overlord. Churchill, however, believed that "major tactical needs must always have priority over strategic policy." These words from a November 1943 minute are quoted in *Closing the Ring* with reference to air operations in Italy, but they could serve as a motto for Churchill's approach as a whole. American critics were right about his resistance to a cross-Channel assault but wrong to indict him for an absolutely rigid "Balkan strategy." Churchill was a strategic opportunist—keen to seize what he deemed the possibilities of the moment.[3]

FOR CHURCHILL, the great opportunity of the second half of 1943 was the collapse of Italy and its potential ramifications across the eastern Mediterranean. Here we unearth two rooted assumptions of Churchill's strategy in 1943: first, that Hitler would allow Italy to surrender to the Allies, conceding most of the country, perhaps up to the Alps. In early October, however, the Führer changed his mind, ordering his forces to hold a line well south of Rome, and in *Closing the Ring* Churchill cites this U-turn as a major reason why deadlock in Italy ensued. In retrospect, it seems surprising that he ever entertained the hope that Italy would fall into his lap: after all, Hitler was not renowned for retreats (as Moscow, Stalingrad, and Tunis had shown). What Churchill cannot say in his memoirs is that his mistaken belief was based on a steady stream of signals intercepts. In *Closing the Ring*, he quotes a telegram he sent to Roosevelt on 8 October saying, "we know that the enemy is withdrawing to the north," and predicting that Rome would fall in October or November. The original version of this telegram read, "we know from BONIFACE that the enemy is withdrawing to the north" — "Boniface" being Churchill's favorite euphemism for Ultra. In other words, Churchill's initial confidence *was* justified, but — as with Tunisia in November 1942 so in Italy in October 1943 — Hitler suddenly reversed existing policy, turning what promised to be a quick victory into a hard slog.[4]

Churchill's second basic assumption of late 1943 was that the Italian collapse might shake Hitler's empire to its foundations. This harks back to his Great War fixations with the Bulgarian domino and the potential of Turkey — the latter being particularly on his mind in the autumn of 1939, the spring of 1941, and January 1943, when he made a personal visit to press for Turkish entry into the war.[5] His hopes surged again in the autumn of 1943. If the Allies took key islands such as Rhodes from the surrendering Italians before the Germans consolidated their grip, the psychological effects across the whole region could be dramatic. Such ideas must be understood against the background of hopes, encouraged at this time by the Joint Intelligence Committee, that Germany itself was starting to crumble. A minute that Churchill did not delete from Kelly's draft for the appendix hints at this. On 14 August 1943, he told Eden that if Franz von Papen replaced Ribbentrop as Hitler's Foreign Minister, this would be "a milestone of importance, and would probably lead to further disintegration of the Nazi machine." Harping on unconditional surrender would only discourage this process, whereas "a gradual break-up in Germany must mean a weakening of their resistance, and consequently the saving of hundreds of thousands of British and American lives."[6]

At this time of hope in Southern Europe, the outlook across the Channel seemed bleak. In the summer of 1943, the Overlord plan was very different from the operation eventually mounted in June 1944. An embryo staff, under General Sir Frederick Morgan, had been given tight guidelines by the Combined Chiefs of Staff about the limited availability of men and shipping. Working within that straitjacket, Morgan and his men ruled out any attempt to take Calais or some other big port and proposed an invasion of Normandy prior to driving west to take Cherbourg. The best Morgan could offer for D-Day was an assault by three divisions over a thirty-mile front. In reality, his plan was little more than a staff exercise. Once real commanders with political clout were appointed in early 1944, Eisenhower and Montgomery were able to secure additional resources and map out more ambitious operations. In the summer of 1943, however, reading Morgan's outline, Churchill's anxiety was hardly surprising.

"I do not believe that 27 Anglo-American divisions are sufficient for 'Overlord,'" the Prime Minister told the Chiefs of Staff on 19 July. He cited the "extraordinary fighting efficiency of the German Army, and the much larger forces they could so readily bring to bear against our troops even if the landings were successfully accomplished." In case Overlord proved beyond Allied strength in May 1944 and had to be postponed until August, he wanted other operations to be prepared, including Jupiter (his old hobbyhorse of northern Norway). He told the Chiefs:

I have no doubt myself that the right strategy for 1944 is: —

    a.   Maximum post-"Husky" [the invasion of Sicily] certainly to the Po, with an option to attack westwards in the south of France or northeastwards towards Vienna, and meanwhile to procure the expulsion of the enemy from the Balkans and Greece.

    b.   "Jupiter" prepared under the cover of "Overlord."

This minute was written nine days after the successful landing in Sicily, amid clear signs that Italy was crumbling. On the expectation that Germany would abandon most of Italy, Churchill was already talking of a thrust northeast into Austria. It is also noteworthy that he told the Chiefs he was working on the assumption "that Hitler and Mussolini are disposed of in 1944"—that is why the second part of his memo considered how Britain would then bring its forces to bear against Japan.[7]

Churchill had this minute of 19 July 1943 printed in December 1949, and Kelly collated it for the draft appendix, with a query "Transfer to text?" But then Churchill put a red line through the whole of part 1 (about Overlord) and later excised part 2 about the Far East.[8] His reticence is not surprising, for the 19 July minute called into question Churchill's claim of consistent support for Overlord. The allusions to Austria and the Balkans were now particularly embarrassing. On the other hand, what he wrote is more explicable when we take into account the success in Sicily, concurrent doubts about Morgan's plan for invading France, and hopes of an Axis collapse. It was reminiscent of that honeymoon period in November 1942 when it looked as if the Allies would take Tunis by Christmas.

A similar sleight of hand may be found in Churchill's account of the Quebec conference of August 1943. At the meeting, he says, "I emphasised that I strongly favoured 'Overlord' in 1944, though I had not been in favour of 'Sledgehammer' in 1942 or 'Round-up' in 1943. The objections which I had to the cross-Channel operation were however now removed." But he skates over "the lengthy discussions" in the Combined Chiefs of Staff, where the suspicious Americans tried to elicit a firm British commitment to give Overlord "overriding priority" over all other preparations in the European theater. Instead, he prints the eventual compromise stating that, where there was a shortage, "available resources will be distributed and employed with the main object of ensuring the success of 'Overlord.'" Although the Quebec conference confirmed the earlier decision to withdraw seven divisions from the Mediterranean in preparation for Overlord, this new phrasing gave the British flexibility. In addition, pressed by Churchill, the Americans accepted the three preconditions lain down by Morgan before any cross-Channel attack could be authorized:

1. "a substantial reduction" in German fighter strength over northwest Europe;
2. "not more than twelve mobile German divisions in Northern France"; and
3. "at least two effective synthetic harbours."

In other words, like previous conferences, Quebec produced formulas that each side could use to advance its strategic preferences. In what the Americans hoped would be a straitjacket, the British still discerned plenty of wriggle room.[9]

Churchill's position is also illuminated by his exchanges with Jan Smuts in early September 1943. The South African premier was the only Dominion leader for whom Churchill had real respect, so when he dissented from the Quebec conclusions, Churchill took time to respond. On 9 September, Smuts suggested that

our victories in Mediterranean should be followed up in Italy and Balkans instead of our now adopting a cross-Channel plan, which means switching on to a new theatre requiring very large forces and involving grave risks unless much more air softening has taken place. Preparations for Channel plan should be slowed down or put into temporary cold storage while bombing campaign is intensified to prepare for eventual military knock-out.

After reproducing this extract in his memoirs, Churchill says that it "required immediate correction from me" and then prints his reply: "There can be no question whatever of breaking arrangements we have made with United States for 'Overlord.' . . . I hope you will realise that British loyalty to 'Overlord' is keystone of arch of Anglo-American co-operation." But he added: "I think enough forces exist for both hands to be played, and I believe this to be the right strategy."[10] By that he meant that the Quebec guidelines gave enough flexibility to use the right hand (Italy) as well as the left (northern France) in striking the Axis. By indicating Smuts's extremism, Churchill leaves himself in the convenient position of a moderate, heeding Dominion concerns but faithful to the transatlantic contract. In fact, however, his fidelity was stretched almost to the breaking point in October 1943.

THE CHAPTER "Island Prizes Lost," about the Dodecanese, is one of Churchill's most biting criticisms of American strategists. In the power vacuum following Italy's surrender, "it seemed to me a rebuff to fortune not to pick up these treasures." This chapter prints copious extracts from Churchill's correspondence with Roosevelt between 7 and 10 October 1943, urging what he deemed a modest and brief diversion of troops and landing craft to secure Rhodes, Leros, and Cos. But FDR, bolstered by his Joint Chiefs and by Eisenhower in Italy, would have none of it. Churchill laments that "but for pedantic denials in the minor sphere," the Allies could have added "the control of the Aegean and very likely the accession of Turkey to all the fruits of the Italian campaign." This was, "happily on a small scale, the most acute difference I ever had with General Eisenhower." Rather than "risk any jar" in his "personal relations with the President," he submitted, albeit "with one of the sharpest pangs I suffered in the war." Early drafts were almost petulant. Of Roosevelt he wrote that "this was the only ungenerous act which I experienced in our long military partnership," though he laid much of the blame on the "prejudice" of the President's advisers. As for Eisenhower: "I thought he owed me much" — "much" later amended to "something."[11]

This was, in fact, a willfully inaccurate account. Having read the draft and checked its files in March 1951, the War Office told Norman Brook that Eisenhower had clearly done his best to help with plans to capture Rhodes: "Quite apart from considerations of policy at the present time [Ike was NATO Supreme Commander], we venture to suggest that in the interests of historical accuracy it is hardly right to characterise General Eisenhower's attitude as 'obdurate' and 'unreasonable.'" Brook—strongly backed by the Syndicate, who thought it was "a great pity to hit Ike so hard"—persuaded Churchill to remove these adjectives, as well as the reference to "prejudice" and the other petulant comments.[12] But the criticism of Eisenhower still stood, and Churchill failed to admit that his obsession with Rhodes defied his own military advisers who, like Ike, had had their eyes firmly on the advance in Italy. Alan Brooke's diary for those dog days of October 1943 are full of angry entries about "Rhodes madness" and Churchill's "frenzy of excitement" despite all rational argument. "He is in a very dangerous condition, most unbalanced, and God knows how we shall finish this war if this goes on."[13]

Churchill's account of this row creates a larger distortion. The focus on his maverick campaign over the Dodecanese early in October distracts from his more fundamental attack on Overlord later in the month, a critique that *was* encouraged by Brooke and the Chiefs of Staff. This barely figures in Churchill's account despite his proclaimed reliance on contemporary documents. As with the Hess mission of 1941, a breach in Churchill's basic principle, chronology, is telltale. Chapter 12, "Island Prizes Lost," breaks off the transatlantic argument on 10 October. Chapter 14, "Deadlock on the Third Front," picks up the documents again on 24 October. The gap is obscured by an intervening chapter entitled "Hitler's 'Secret Weapon,'" about the development of German flying bombs and rockets. During those missing two weeks, however, Churchill and the Chiefs came close to throwing Overlord overboard.

Smuts was now in London, a fact never mentioned in *Closing the Ring*. He started lobbying for an all-out Mediterranean strategy, even enlisting the support of the King, and Churchill was summoned to the Palace for dinner *à trois* on 14 October. At this stage, Churchill repeated the line he took with Smuts a month before, telling George VI that "there is no possibility of our going back on what is agreed. Both the U.S. and Stalin would violently disagree with us." Again, he added, "I think there are resources for both theatres."[14] This was also the line he took when the Chiefs of Staff, via "Jo" Hollis, asked him to commission a staff study of what could be done in the Balkans if "we were masters of our own destiny" and not bound to the Americans. Hollis's note, marked "Not to leave the office," indicated growing uneasiness "throughout the staffs" about the effect of the rigid Overlord timetable on the opportunities in the Balkans created by partisan resistance and weakening resolve in some of the Nazi satellite states. Although Churchill took up Hollis's suggestion and requested a staff paper, he added the rider "it may well be that we need not recant on OVERLORD except as regards emphasis and the balance of our effort."[15]

But when he and the Chiefs discussed the staff study on 19 October, with Smuts also present, Churchill's mood was more extreme. He warned that by being tied to Overlord the Western Allies risked fighting two campaigns of roughly equal strength in Italy and France, which the Germans could hold and then defeat at their leisure. In addition to the three preconditions already laid down for Overlord, he mentioned the need for a Soviet guarantee that they would continue to advance in the east. Cadogan suggested that "if we were afraid of the Russians easing up this might be prevented by stirring up action in the Balkans." Others present joined in attacking the rigid commitment to Overlord at a time when Southern Europe seemed so promising. Brooke lamented the policy of trying to wage war on the basis of "lawyer's contracts," while Smuts spoke of "a clear run in to victory" in the Mediterranean, "provided we did not blunder." Sir Charles Portal warned that if the British tried to reopen Overlord, the Americans might seek to divert larger forces to the Pacific, but Churchill said he was willing to risk this, provided the United States left their existing forces in Britain and maintained the air buildup already promised. The meeting agreed to reopen with the Americans the relative priorities given to the Mediterranean and Overlord. Summing up, Churchill said

it was clear that if we were in a position to decide the future strategy of the war we should agree

(i)   To reinforce the Italian theatre to the full.
(ii) To enter the Balkans.
(iii) To hold our position in the Aegean Islands.
(iv) To build-up our air forces and intensify our air attacks on Germany.
(v)   To encourage a steady assembly in this country of United States troops, which could not be employed in the Pacific owing to the shortage of shipping, with a view to taking advantage of the softening in the enemy's resistance due to our operations in other theatres, though this might not occur until after the spring of 1944.[16]

There is no mention in *Closing the Ring* of this meeting on 19 October 1943. The ideas discussed then are, however, revealed in fragments elsewhere—for instance, in a telegram to Eden, then in Moscow, on 20 October. This indicated Churchill's doubts about the current Overlord plan and his preference, "if it lay with me to decide," to withdraw no troops from the Mediterranean and engage the enemy strongly in central Italy, "while at the same time fomenting Balkan and Southern France disturbances." In a clear follow-up to the meeting on the previous day, he also asked Eden to find out what the Russians really wanted. Were they absolutely set on an invasion of France? Or would they be interested in

Britain "acting in the Aegean, involving Turkey in the war, and opening the Dardanelles and Bosphorus" so that British naval forces and supplies could move into the Black Sea, and "we could ultimately give them our right hand along the Danube?"[17]

Churchill prints this telegram in his chapter "Foreign Secretaries' Conference in Moscow" and notes Eden's reply that the Soviets were "completely and blindly set on our invasion of Northern France." In the next chapter, "Advent of the Triple Meeting," he prints extracts from a long telegram he sent Roosevelt on 23 October, questioning the rigid 1 May 1944 deadline for Overlord. He wanted a review of the timetable for withdrawing troops and landing craft from the Mediterranean for an operation that would not happen for at least seven months and then "only if certain hypothetical conditions are fulfilled." Churchill cut from the published version of this message his additional observation that these conditions "may very likely not be fulfilled."[18]

This telegram to FDR also lays bare his root fear about Overlord: "I do not doubt our ability in the conditions laid down to get ashore and deploy. I am however deeply concerned with the build-up and with the situation which may arise between the thirtieth and sixtieth day." In the meeting on 19 October he had been more explicit, saying that "he was not afraid of the Channel crossing or of the landing on the enemy coast. He felt we should probably effect a lodgement and in the first instance we might make progress." What worried him was the Germans' ability to concentrate substantial reserves after the first month, using their "excellent road and rail communications" to "inflict on us a military disaster greater than that of Dunkirk. Such a disaster would result in the resuscitation of Hitler and the Nazi regime." As we shall see, this was a recurrent refrain. What Churchill feared was not getting ashore but holding the bridgehead.[19]

These extracts from Churchill's telegrams to Eden and Roosevelt offer hints of the turmoil in his strategic thinking in October 1943. But by printing them in separate chapters and by making no reference to the crucial meeting of 19 October, Churchill conceals the intensity of feeling in London. After a Cabinet meeting on 27 October, Cadogan noted in his diary: "Winston will fight for 'nourishing the battle' in Italy and, if necessary resign on it."[20]

Churchill was also deceitful in the way he pressed his case on Stalin at this time. His cover-up of this in Closing the Ring is one of the most blatant pieces of distortion in his six volumes of memoirs.

"Deadlock on the Third Front" includes a lengthy appraisal of the Italian situation presented by General Alexander at Eisenhower's headquarters on 24 October 1943, in which he expressed grave concern about the scale of German reinforcements and the slowness of the Allied troop buildup. Churchill calls this "a masterly document, which touched all the gravest issues of our strategy" and says that it was so serious that Eisenhower sent the whole text to London and Washington. He adds that Ike "endorsed all that Alexander had said and described his statement as giving a clear and accurate picture." But Churchill prints only the first three parts of Eisenhower's telegram; a fourth part made clear that Eisenhower did not share Alex's gloomy view of the future: "Our buildup so far has at least equalled our estimates." He also emphasized Italy's subordinate place in his overall scheme of priorities: "If we can keep him [the enemy] on his heels until early spring, then the more divisions he uses in a counter-offensive against us, the better it will be for OVERLORD and then it makes little difference what happens to us if OVERLORD is a success."[21]

On 26 October 1943, Churchill sent parts 1 to 3 of the telegram to Eden in Moscow, for use with Stalin. Quite deliberately, part 4 was not sent. Similarly, in his memoirs Churchill uses the truncated version as evidence for the deadlock in Italy. Thus, Eisenhower's preamble, praising Alex's "clear and accurate" picture of the current battle was not offset by his more optimistic view of the future. In March 1951, the War Office pointed out the omission and asked that Churchill print part 4 of Ike's telegram. But nothing was done, thereby perpetuating Churchill's wartime deception.[22] What Churchill did not know, however, was that his duplicity had been detected in October 1943. General John Deane, head of the U.S. Military Mission in Moscow, saw the version of Ike's telegram that Churchill forwarded to Eden and also a copy of the full original sent to Washington. When Deane pointed out the discrepancy, Henry Stimson was furious, writing in his diary that this showed "how determined Churchill is with all his lip service to stick a knife in the back of Overlord." Hopkins shared his anger, and Roosevelt agreed that Churchill's conduct was "improper."[23] All this helps us understand the tone of many postwar American memoirs. It also explains the determination of U.S. policymakers at the Teheran summit to bring Churchill's strategic machinations to an end.

CHURCHILL, ROOSEVELT, and their staffs met at Cairo from 22 to 26 November and then proceeded to Teheran for their first tripartite meeting with Stalin. At Cairo, Churchill had hoped to forge a new Anglo-American strategy, taking account of the opportunities he discerned in the Mediterranean, but he says in Closing the Ring that their talks were "sadly distracted" by the presence of Chiang Kai-shek and the Chinese. (As we now know, that distraction was Roosevelt's deliberate intent.) On 20 November, en route to Cairo, Churchill prepared what he calls "an indictment of our mismanagement of operations in the Mediterranean" over the previous two months. He tells us that the Chiefs of Staff, "while agreeing in principle," persuaded him to soften it to avoid "giving offence to the Americans." It was from the revised version that he made his opening statement to the Teheran conference on 28 November.[24]

Even this "softer form" was deemed too harsh for the memoirs. Among many cuts, Churchill removed a paragraph listing proposals for action along the lines he suggested on 19 October. In order of priority, these read:

a). Stop all further movement of British troops and Allied landing craft from the Mediterranean.

b). Use all possible energy to take Rome.

c). Bring Turkey into the war. . . . Meanwhile prepare an expedition to take Rhodes before the end of January.

d). Seize a port or ports and establish bridgeheads on the Dalmatian coast, and carry a regular flow of airborne supplies to the Partisans. Use the British 1st Airborne Division and all the Commandos available in the Mediterranean . . . to aid and animate the resistance in Yugoslavia and Albania and also to capture islands like Corfu and Argostoli.

e). Continue and build up "Overlord" without prejudice to the above.

It should be noted that Churchill's idea of using British forces to create a Balkan bridgehead was opposed by the Chiefs of Staff, who argued that "we can do just as much, and, at the same time, avoid an unlimited commitment by smuggling in material at many points on the coast and by air." As for building up Overlord— Churchill's lowest priority—the American position was exactly the opposite: action in the Mediterranean only if it did not prejudice Overlord.[25]

That Churchill omitted his list of priorities from volume 5 is hardly surprising when we bear in mind the emerging historiography about Teheran. In 1948, Stimson's memoirs presented the conference as the triumphant culmination of a two-year "quarrel of brothers" over grand strategy: outvoted by Stalin and Roosevelt, the Prime Minister finally had to agree to a firm date for Overlord. The memoirs of Admiral William Leahy, FDR's Chief of Staff, published in 1950, stated bluntly that the British "finally fell into line" at Teheran. Churchill's account of the conference, four chapters in all, is therefore couched as a response to what he calls the "legend in America that I strove to prevent the cross-Channel enterprise called 'Overlord,' and that I tried vainly to lure the Allies into some mass invasion of the Balkans, or at least a large-scale campaign in the Mediter-ranean, which would effectively kill it." Churchill claims he always insisted "no strength which could be applied across the Channel should be absorbed" in the Mediterranean and simply wanted to use surplus local capacity to dominate the Aegean and induce Turkey into the war. "I could have gained Stalin, but the Pres-ident was opposed by the prejudices of his military advisers and drifted to and fro in the argument, with the result that the whole of these subsidiary but gleaming opportunities was cast aside unused." He goes on: "our American friends were comforted in their obstinacy by the reflection that 'at any rate we have stopped Churchill entangling us in the Balkans.'" But, he adds, "No such idea had ever crossed my mind." Only if one takes "entangling" in its most literal sense is Chur-chill's assertion accurate.[26]

He never saw the Balkans as an end in themselves. His strategic speculations in the autumn of 1943 still assumed that Turkey was ripe to enter the war and that this could set the dominoes falling across southeast Europe. In Cairo in early December, Churchill held another round of talks with Turkish leaders, renew-ing the pressure he had applied in January. The memos printed in *Closing the Ring* indicate his desire for Turkish entry by mid-February 1944 and his belief that an attack on Rhodes could trigger their decision. In a passage dictated in Jan-uary 1951, Churchill was candid that he wanted

> to bring Turkey into the war by dominating the Aegean islands, and thereafter
> enter the Black Sea with the British Fleet and aid the Russians in all their
> recovery of its northern coast, the Crimea, etc., as well as débouchements
> near the mouth of the Danube. No British or American army was to be
> employed in this. Naval and air forces alone might have sufficed.

This passage does not, however, appear in the published volume. It is not hard to imagine why. Sending a British fleet into the Black Sea was hardly a minor oper-ation. And it sounded a little too close for comfort to Gallipoli in 1915.[27]

IN THE AUTUMN of 1943, therefore, it was widely hoped in London that deci-sive action to exploit Italy's surrender might bring the war to a rapid conclusion. Overlord, not even scheduled until May 1944, was still a paper operation of lim-ited scope. Stalin put his finger on the central problem at Teheran on 29 Novem-ber, asking, "Who will command 'Overlord'?" He insisted that the operation would come to nothing unless one man was given charge of all preparations. Stalin's probing has generally been discussed by historians in relation to Roosevelt's uncertainty about whether to release Marshall for the job and his eventual conclusion that he "could not sleep at night" with the Army Chief of Staff out of the country. This remark was printed in Sherwood's *Roosevelt and Hopkins* in 1948 and has become the main explanation for FDR's decision to appoint Eisenhower. But Churchill also equivocated on the command question, both at the time and when writing his memoirs, and various renditions of this story in his drafts cast a revealing light on his grand strategy and on Roosevelt's own intentions.[28]

Churchill's version in *Closing the Ring,* spread out across the volume, may be summarized as follows. Since the United States held overall command in the Mediterranean, he and the President agreed Overlord should be under British leadership and, with FDR's concurrence, he had settled on Sir Alan Brooke, Chief of the Imperial General Staff. Brooke was informed early in 1943. As the year advanced, however, Churchill says he became "increasingly impressed" by the fact that although the landings themselves would be undertaken by equal numbers of British and U.S. troops, there would be a "very great preponderance" of Americans as the campaign unfolded. At Quebec in August 1943, he therefore proposed that Overlord should be under U.S. command, with the British leading in the Mediterranean. Thereafter, the ball was in Roosevelt's court, and Churchill understood that Marshall would be appointed.[29]

However, the issue aroused intense press speculation in Washington, with much comment that Marshall was going to be kicked upstairs to a minor role. One alternative being touted was that he might become commander for the whole of Europe, in charge of both Overlord and the Mediterranean. In "Advent of the Triple Meeting" Churchill prints extracts from his telegrams in the autumn of 1943 to show how he blocked this idea as violating "the principle of equal status which must be maintained among the great Allies." At Cairo on 25 November, the Americans revived the proposal for a Europe-wide chief, and in his chapter on the conference Churchill prints the renewed British rebuttals. He went to Teheran assuming that Marshall would command Overlord, Eisenhower would replace him as Chief of Staff in Washington, and Alexander would take over the Mediterranean. It was only during the second Cairo conference, on a drive to the Pyramids on 6 December, that Roosevelt remarked "almost casually" that he could not spare Marshall and would nominate Eisenhower to command Overlord.[30]

This was Churchill's published account, but at times in the drafting Churchill toyed with very different explanations. Take, for instance, his claim that he proposed an American commander for Overlord because of the "increasing preponderance" of U.S. troops as the operation unfolded. In the first draft of his "Cairo" chapter, printed on 1 June 1950, he stated: "I had the fear that if a bloody and disastrous repulse were encountered, far bigger than the first day's battle on the Somme in 1916, there might be an outcry in the United States. It would be said that another result would have attended the appointment of an American General." Hence his proposal at Quebec that the United States take command. "If he refused," Churchill adds, "our position would be invulnerable." And if he accepted, Churchill implies, then an American would carry the burden if their chosen operation ended in disaster.[31]

Other evidence not used in the memoirs suggests why Churchill was not unhappy to give the Americans command of Overlord. In a telegram he sent to Attlee on 2 September, he said that reciprocity would then dictate that the British would preside in the Mediterranean, "where it will be a great advantage to us to have our own Commander and to be able to correspond directly and constantly with him."[32] This fitted Churchill's conviction in the second half of 1943 that the Mediterranean was the key theater, with the curtain perhaps rising on the last act of the war, and as the autumn went on his view was reinforced by failure in the Aegean. For this, he blamed not only the inflexible American timetable for Overlord but also the division of the Mediterranean into two theaters, east and west, with Eisenhower calling the shots from Algiers. In his July 1950 draft of "Island Prizes Lost," Churchill writes that the loss of Rhodes and other islands "made me determine that the command in the Mediterranean in 1944 should be unified, and should pass into the hands of a British Commander in Chief free from the detailed control of Washington."[33] Of course, a British leader would still be under the authority of the Combined Chiefs of Staff, but Churchill had many ways of circumventing that.[34]

This brings us to what Churchill believed was the crux of the command issue. He and Ismay rejected Sherwood's claim that FDR felt he could not sleep easily without Marshall in America. Their explanation was "very different" — namely, that Roosevelt decided that "mere command of OVERLORD was not a sufficiently big job to justify General Marshall's removal from Washington." Churchill developed this theme in two outlines for *Closing the Ring:* "Early in October when I am pressing Roosevelt to agree to the urgent appointment, I begin to find out the reason for the American delay. They had this idea that they should have Marshall in command of everything. I won't have it." The crux was therefore the adamant British refusal to accept a "super supreme commander" for the whole of Europe. In his note of 11 April 1950, Churchill claims that Roosevelt made this point explicitly: "I well remember that when driving in his motor car from Cairo to the Pyramids he told me that, as Marshall was not to have the Mediterranean and OVERLORD in his hands, he would prefer to keep him in Washington. He could not spare him except to have this supreme direction of the final phase of the war." All that remains of this contention in the published memoirs is a brief sentence: "There can be little doubt that the President felt that the command only of 'Overlord' was not sufficient to justify General Marshall's departure from Washington."[35]

Once Roosevelt decided on Eisenhower for Overlord, the attendant British appointments could be made; in *Closing the Ring*, Churchill presents these as falling smoothly into place. The post of Supreme Commander in the Mediterranean "we confided to General ["Jumbo"] Wilson, it also being settled that General Alexander should command the whole campaign in Italy, as he had done under General Eisenhower." Montgomery would direct the cross-Channel attack until Ike could transfer his headquarters to France. "All this was carried out with the utmost smoothness in perfect agreement by the President and by me, with Cabinet approval." In fact, Eisenhower's appointment was not well received by the British. The War Cabinet predicted public opinion would be "surprised and rather uneasy at the substitution of Eisenhower for Marshall" and, in another act of self-assertion when Churchill was away, rejected the Prime Minister's desire that Alexander should command the invasion forces, proposing Monty instead. On 18 December 1943, Churchill cabled Roosevelt: "Eisenhower would have chosen Alexander, but I feel Cabinet are right as Montgomery is a public hero and will give confidence among our people, not unshared by yours."[36]

None of this is mentioned in *Closing the Ring*, however. In April 1951, Norman Brook asked Churchill to remove the reference to Eisenhower's preference for Alexander, as Monty had been appointed deputy to Eisenhower as NATO Supreme Commander in Europe.[37] The deletion was duly made. Churchill had already toned down criticisms of Eisenhower and the Italian armistice. An early outline note, for instance, implied that, but for Ike's caution, Allied paratroop forces could have seized Rome in September 1943.[38] Instead, Churchill tells us that, when asked by Roosevelt in Cairo for his opinion of Eisenhower as prospective Overlord commander, "I said it was for him to decide, but that we also had the warmest regard for General Eisenhower, and would trust our fortunes to his direction with hearty goodwill."[39] And although in April 1950 Churchill had not forgotten Eisenhower's "horrible bad temper" at dinner in Marrakech in January 1944 because, as he later learned, the general's "lady chauffeur had not been asked too," no mention of Ike's affair with Kay Summersby appears in the memoirs.[40] As Churchill and Brook were well aware, events had moved a long way in eight years. The genial but inexperienced wartime soldier was now NATO's Supreme Commander and, very possibly, the next President of the United States. Not for the first time or the last in Churchill's war memoirs, diplomacy took precedence over history.

WHAT, THEN, should we make of Churchill's categorical assertions quoted at the start of this chapter?[41] Is there evidence that he "wanted to abandon" Overlord, that he "wanted to deprive" it of "vital forces" and that he "contemplated a campaign by armies operating in the Balkan peninsula"? Or were these, as he claimed, "legends" put about by mischievous Americans?

Churchill was adept at arguing by reductio ad absurdum. He liked to overstate charges against him and then offer plausible denial. It is true that he did not try to challenge the principle of Overlord directly—recognizing, as he told Smuts, that by late 1943 it had become a touchstone of the Anglo-American alliance. Nor did he seek to deprive the operation of "vital" forces, couching his demands simply in terms of delaying redeployments from Italy or using idle resources in the Mediterranean. But, by giving priority to Italy and the Aegean, he was ready to risk delaying Overlord to August 1944—probably too late for mounting that year. And although he did not advocate a full-blooded "campaign" by "armies" in the Balkans, in late November 1943 he proposed using a British division to open a Balkan bridgehead. Ostensibly, this would have been a small, quick operation, but Gallipoli served as a grim warning about how big wedges start with thin ends.

In his memoirs, Churchill suppresses or doctors key pieces of evidence, such as the 19 October meeting, Eisenhower's telegram of 24 October, and the 20 November memo. As usual, however, some clues remain in documents he does print, such as the cables to Eden and Roosevelt on 20 and 23 October. But the underlying assumptions in London at the time make British resistance to the cross-Channel attack more understandable and less treacherous than it seemed in 1950–1951 when the road to victory ran so obviously across the beaches of Normandy. In late 1943, Overlord was still a flimsy paper plan, without commanders, whereas Italian surrender seemed to presage control of the whole peninsula, ripe pickings in the Aegean, Turkish belligerency, and an Axis collapse across southeast Europe. The Balkan domino thesis was how Churchill had explained victory in 1918, but Washington believed the critical factor in the collapse of Nazi Germany, as of the Kaiserreich twenty-five years before, would be the arrival of a massive American army on the Western Front. Churchill hoped the decisive blows could be struck under British command in the Mediterranean in 1943, rendering Overlord almost the coup de grâce, but by Christmas such hopes were clearly delusions. In 1944, he had to conform to America's strategy. So in 1951, he rewrote 1943 accordingly.

CHAPTER 25

THE TYRANNY OF OVERLORD

A FTER THE CAIRO AND Teheran Conferences, Churchill's narrative loses momentum. The remainder of *Closing the Ring* is a patchwork, with chapters on Yugoslavia, Greece, and strategic bombing, and two on the Far East. The deadlock in Italy and the buildup to Normandy are his main themes, but in neither can Churchill claim a heroic role. Allied armies were bogged down at Cassino, and the attempt to outflank the Germans by an amphibious landing at Anzio, south of Rome, in January 1944 produced another bloody stalemate. As for Overlord, though Churchill plays up facets in which he took special interest, such as the artificial harbors, it was not easy to conceal his continuing doubts about what was preponderantly an American strategic conception. Despite its variety, the last third of *Closing the Ring* is therefore over-shadowed by Overlord, in a mood of frustrated, fretful waiting.

THIS SENSE OF ANTICLIMAX is heightened by lengthy accounts of Churchill's pneumonia and convalescence in Tunis and Marrakech in December and January. It is as if the man as well as his plans had collapsed. Yet these weeks were also testimony to Churchill's resilience and sheer perversity. In defeat, defiance: what could be a more Churchillian road to recovery than planning a new military operation? This he did, with gleeful panache and almost disastrous consequences. And thus, two chapters of *Closing the Ring* are devoted to shifting responsibility for the Anzio debacle onto other shoulders.

On 9 September 1943, British and American forces, aiming to seize Naples, landed behind enemy lines at Salerno. Although ultimately successful, in the first few days the Allies were barely able to hold their beachhead. Eisenhower and Alexander discussed the possibility of another end run around enemy lines at their command conference on 24 October 1943, and it is mentioned in part 4 of Ike's telegram, which Churchill suppressed. During November, staff at General Mark Clark's U.S. Fifth Army headquarters produced an outline plan, but this was for only one division, with reinforcements, to land and exploit a breakout on the Allies' main front. The deadlock in southern Italy and the lack of landing craft meant that this operation, code-named Shingle, was dropped. It was Churchill who revived the idea as of 19 December.

In his memoirs, he is at pains to cite all the distinguished generals, from Eisenhower down, who attended the crucial staff conference on Christmas Day. He also, accurately, portrays Brooke as supporting the plan. In his chapter "In Carthage Ruins," Churchill tells how he persuaded the Americans to delay for a few weeks the move of crucial landing craft from Italy to Britain, so that a two-division assault could be launched and supplied. In "The Anzio Stroke," he describes the Fifth Army's supporting offensive around Cassino and the complete surprise achieved by the two Allied divisions that landed on Anzio beach early on 22 January 1944. By nightfall, 36,000 troops and more than 3,000 vehicles were ashore.[1]

"But now came disaster"; Churchill places the blame squarely on John P. Lucas, the U.S. general commanding the two divisions, one American and one British. Instead of pushing on, Lucas "confined himself to occupying his beachhead and having equipment and vehicles brought ashore." Churchill, following a dispatch from Jumbo Wilson, ascribes Lucas's caution to a "Salerno complex" — a belief borne of experience in the earlier amphibious landing that "the first task was to repel the inevitable enemy counter-attack." Lucas's inertia, says Churchill, gave Field-Marshal Albert Kesselring, the German commander in Italy, time to regroup, and his massive assault in mid-February nearly drove the Allies back into the sea. Churchill speaks of his bitter disappointment: "As I said at the time, I had hoped that we were hurling a wildcat onto the shore, but all we had got was a stranded whale." Primed by Deakin, he quotes a recent German memoir by Kesselring's former Chief of Staff that on 22 January "the road to Rome was open," apart from two German battalions, and that "no one could have stopped a bold advance-guard entering the Holy City. The breath-taking situation continued for the first two days after the landing."[2]

General John Lucas died in December 1949. After *Closing the Ring* was published, his brother, Charles, wrote to complain of "a grave injustice," asserting that John Lucas was "not the impotent, defense minded commander that your book portrays" but had "obeyed his orders to the letter at Anzio." Churchill passed the complaint to Pownall, who believed Churchill had "good reason" for his criticisms, adding that Mark Clark's recent memoirs had "four digs" at Lucas and that Alexander had "passed" the chapter "without comment." Charles Lucas was sent merely a formal acknowledgment.[3]

Pownall's response was, however, disingenuous. Clark's memoirs, published in 1950 and consulted for Closing the Ring, though critical of Lucas, portrayed Anzio as a political rather than military decision, inspired by Churchill's passion to seize Rome. Clark suggested that British intelligence in Italy deliberately made assessments of German intentions more optimistic, because the decision to attack had already been made at the Prime Minister's behest. Alexander's official dispatch on the Italian campaign, published in June 1950, admitted that progress in the first few days had been "rather too slow" but did not use this to attack Lucas. In fact, Alex argued that "the actual course of events was probably the most advantageous in the end." If the two divisions had pushed on toward Rome, he believed, they would have lacked the resources to hold the Alban Hills and also protect their communications some forty miles back to Anzio against the German counterattack. Privately, this was also the view of Sir Ronald Penney, commander of the British division at Anzio and generally a critic of Lucas: "We could have had one night in Rome and 18 months in P[risoner of] W[ar] camps."[4]

Not only was Churchill's account of Anzio at odds with the verdicts of senior commanders, it also diverged from his mood at the time. In September 1944, he told his doctor that Anzio was "my worst moment in the war. I had most to do with it. I didn't want two Suvla Bays in one lifetime." This was a reference to General Stopford at Gallipoli in 1915, consolidating his beachhead instead of pushing inland. Significantly, Churchill cut an allusion to "Suvla Bay all over again" out of his telegram to Smuts on 27 February 1944, which is otherwise quoted extensively in "The Anzio Stroke." In his first outline for volume 5, Churchill insisted that Lucas should have been removed on the opening day, when Alexander visited the beach and saw that the American general was "sticky." He quotes that part of his telegram to Smuts saying, "My confidence in Alexander remains undiminished" but not its continuance: "though if I had been well enough to be at his side as I had hoped at the critical moment I believe I could have given the necessary stimulus. Alas for time, distance, illness and advancing years."[5]

Churchill's statement that he wished he had been with Alex at Anzio in January 1944 is intriguing. It mirrors comments he made about the Salerno landings in September 1943. Churchill, then on a train in Canada, was gripped by anxiety about the landings and the need for speedy advance. In his book, he cites the sobering example of Stopford at Suvla Bay, adding, "I had the greatest confidence in Alexander, but all the same I passed a painful day while our train rumbled forward through the pleasant lands of Nova Scotia." Until almost the final draft he included a passage, originally suggested by Ismay, admitting that during the train journey "I had a strong impulse to fly to our headquarters in Italy. I restrained it, but not without some help from others."[6]

In other words, both at Salerno and Anzio—operations for which Churchill bore special responsibility and that he feared might turn out like Gallipoli—he was sorely tempted to go to Italy in person. Not only does this suggest a lack of confidence in Alex, it also reminds us that Churchill's supreme ambition was to be a general. "I envy you the command of armies in the field," he told Alex in August 1944. "That is what I should have liked." At Marrakech the previous January, he came closest to his ambition. Although Brooke supported a landing at Anzio, it is likely that a detailed staff study in London, with all the strategic, logistic, and intelligence resources of Whitehall behind it, would have exposed the crippling deficiencies of the plan. At Marrakech, staffs were small, resources limited, and skeptics easily cowed. Moreover, during a transitional period when Ike and Monty were moving out and Jumbo Wilson still moving in, there was a vacuum at the top. As Churchill remarked in another passage that did not make it into *Closing the Ring*, "although physically almost prostrate I wielded at this moment exceptional power." Certainly, he does not bear sole responsibility for the outcome, but Anzio would not have happened without him.[7]

AND SO, despite all Churchill's efforts, there was deadlock in Italy. At Anzio, and around the great stronghold of Monte Cassino, the Allies could not break through toward Rome. Attention and resources were now focused on Overlord, and Churchill had to make the best of the situation. In *Closing the Ring*, he admits that "memories of the Somme and Passchendaele . . . were not to be blotted out by time or reflection." While the Allies enjoyed air supremacy, enabling them to drop troops behind enemy lines and bomb his communications, "the firepower of the defence had vastly increased." On the other hand, he became more optimistic after the appointment of heavyweight commanders, committed to Overlord: "I was gratified and also relieved to find that Montgomery was delighted and eager for what I had always regarded as a majestic, inevitable, but terrible task." (An early outline was more candid: "I was not sure whether OVER-

LORD would come off. But when I saw how ready Montgomery was to take it on I felt much reassured.") He was also encouraged by Monty's insistence that he needed "more in the initial punch." In due course, the D-Day assault force was expanded from three to five seaborne divisions.[8]

The burden of the final chapters of *Closing the Ring* is therefore to demonstrate his keenness for Overlord, and he takes pains to rebut alternative interpretations. In his memoirs, Eisenhower had quoted Churchill on 15 May 1944 as saying, "I am hardening on this operation." Ike took this to mean that although Churchill "had long doubted its feasibility and had previously advocated its further postponement in favor of operations elsewhere, he had finally, at this late date, come to believe with the rest of us that this was the true course of action in order to achieve the victory." In *Closing the Ring*, Churchill quotes from a telegram he sent to General Marshall on 11 March 1944: "I am hardening very much on this operation as the time approaches, *in the sense of wishing to strike if humanly possible even if the limiting conditions we laid down at Moscow are not exactly fulfilled.*" These were the requirements about German strength and Allied logistics agreed in 1943.[9]

Even if Churchill was "hardening" on Overlord in early 1944, there were times when he clearly went pretty limp. The appendix to *Closing the Ring* includes a minute he wrote on 25 January 1944, warning that it was "very unwise to make plans on the basis of Hitler being defeated in 1944. The possibility of his gaining a victory in France cannot be excluded." Also in the appendix is a minute he sent the Chiefs of Staff on 19 February 1944, seeking to revive the idea of taking northern Norway, Operation Jupiter. He told them: "In the event of 'Overlord' not being successful or Hitler accumulating forces there quite beyond our power to tackle, it would perhaps be necessary to adopt the flanking movements both in Norway and from Turkey and the Aegean in the winter of 1944–45." As late as 19 April, a month after Churchill assured Marshall that he was "hardening" on Overlord, he told the Foreign Office that "this battle has been forced upon us by the Russians and by the United States military authorities. We have gone into it wholeheartedly, and I would not raise a timorous cry before a decision in the field has been taken." He quotes from this minute in the appendix, but only after removing these sentences.[10]

Churchill's preference for the operation was still at odds with the Normandy campaign that unfolded in the summer of 1944. The appendix contains a long minute dated 2 February 1944 urging seizure of Bordeaux "by *coup de main*" and then a drive inland using three spare British and South African divisions from North Africa: "A force of this character let loose in the south and centre of France would instantly arouse widespread revolt and would be of measureless assistance to the main battle." Churchill proposed that this operation, code-named Caliph, should be launched twenty or thirty days after D-Day, with the Germans totally preoccupied in Normandy. Airy talk of a coup de main and instant results was Churchill at his worst, and the Chiefs dealt firmly with his latest pipe dream. But one should not overlook the similarities between this idea and his papers of 1941–1943 about landings at several points to arouse local revolts, in the hope that one of them might prove decisive.[11]

What exactly did Churchill mean by "decisive"? Although at Salerno and Anzio he urged his commanders to advance as quickly as possible, in Normandy he did not expect dramatic progress. *Closing the Ring* is full of scathing comments he made in 1943–1944 about the teeth-to-tail ratio of British forces—in other words, the proportion of fighting troops to support forces. Learning that 18,000 vehicles were on the Anzio beachhead by 10 February, he cabled sarcastically: "We must have a great superiority of chauffeurs." In May, he chided Monty about an excess of vehicles in the plans for D-Day, recalling a story of dental chairs being landed at Algiers in the first wave of Torch in November 1942.[12] These were not casual gibes. On 21 May, just two weeks before the landings, he told Brooke (in a minute bowdlerized in the appendix): "I repeat that my great anxiety about this operation ("Overlord") is the comparatively small number of troops that will be landed." By that he meant specifically "the infantry component of the fighting troops" because he anticipated a slogging match, reminiscent of World War I, as the Germans tried to drive the Allies back into the sea. Here, Anzio served as a dreadful warning. In such a battle what were needed were not chauffeurs, let alone dentists' chairs, but what Churchill liked to call "bayonets."[13]

It was a tellingly antiquated word, redolent of Wellington or again even Marlborough and reminding us that Churchill completely failed to anticipate the pace of the breakout that did occur. In his memoirs, Eisenhower recalled Churchill telling him more than once in the spring of 1944 that if, by the end of the year, the Allies were established firmly on the Continent with the Cherbourg and Brittany peninsulas in their grasp, this would constitute one of the most successful operations of the war. Churchill added that if by Christmas the Allies had also taken the port of Le Havre and liberated Paris, "I will assert this victory to be the greatest of modern times." Although Churchill went out of his way to question Ike's interpretation of the phrase "I am hardening on this operation," neither he nor Ismay chose to contest this equally telling anecdote two pages earlier in Eisenhower's memoirs, perhaps because it accurately depicted Churchill's private prognosis at the time. On 16 February, he told the Chiefs of Staff that by the end of 1944 the Allied front would probably lie "somewhere in France," and it would "take all our strength to maintain it." Admittedly, the speed and scope of the Allied surge in late summer surprised almost everyone: when Eisenhower's forces reached the German border in September 1944, they occupied positions not anticipated by the Overlord planners until May 1945. But that was where all the chauffeurs came in—a liability on the beachhead, they transformed the breakout.[14]

In the final weeks before D-Day, Churchill was gripped with excitement, the warrior in him overcoming the strategist. His final chapter of *Closing the Ring* contains a long account of his ultimately fruitless dispute with the King about whether he should be allowed to witness D-Day in person from one of the bombarding cruisers. Churchill ends the volume on 5 June 1944, as "the greatest armada that ever left our shores set out for the coast of France," with a peroration about how "the hour was now striking" and Hitlerism was "doomed." Yet the whole previous year had been a rearguard action against what he called Overlord at Cairo: Tyrant. The tyranny of Overlord extended to his memoirs as well. Not only did he feel the need to present his strategy within that framework, he also found that the structure of *Closing the Ring* had to conform. Book 2 is entitled "Teheran to Rome," and it was always intended that the final chapter should record the triumphant Allied entry into the Holy City on 4 June 1944. But it was American not British forces that won the race, and Churchill, egged on by Pownall, does not conceal his belief that Mark Clark disobeyed Alexander's orders in a personal bid for glory, thereby allowing key German units to escape and establish a formidable new line of resistance to the north. Moreover, the fall of Rome, keenly anticipated throughout volume 5, could now come as only an anticlimax. For this was not September 1943 or January 1944 but a mere thirty-six hours before the Normandy landings. In the final proof of *Closing the Ring*, dated 4 September 1951, the fall of Rome was moved to the penultimate chapter, and the volume ends with the great armada setting out for D-Day. In 1951 as in 1944, Churchill had to concede defeat.[15]

OVERLORD CAST ITS SHADOW over the volume in many other ways. Domestic affairs, for instance, are again obscured. A minute dated 10 February 1944, which Churchill cut from the draft appendix, referred to proposed reforms of the medical services. "It is absolutely impossible for me even to read such papers," Churchill told Eden, "let alone pass such a vast scheme of social change through my mind, under present conditions."[16] But, even allowing for his strategic headaches, it is remarkable that Churchill's memoirs make no mention of the 1944 Education Act—the most durable social achievement of the wartime coalition—or of R. A. Butler, its architect.[17] Nor do they say anything about the string of by-election defeats inflicted on the coalition by independent candidates during 1943 and 1944.[18] These showed that the Tories were widely seen as indifferent to social reform, and it has been suggested that if Churchill had used the period after Alamein to forge "a popular post-war policy," wartime suspicions of the Conservative party might have been partially overcome. Failure to do so was a major reason for his crushing electoral defeat in 1945.[19]

The Eastern Front is another casualty of Churchill's preoccupation with war in the west. His preface mentions "the immense onslaught of Russia from the east"; his peroration notes that by 5 June 1944 Hitler had lost all the ground he had gained three years before, "with staggering losses of men and equipment." In between, however, the titanic struggle between the Wehrmacht and the Red Army is hardly mentioned. The Russian material that was included came again from Henry Pownall. The three "immense battles of Kursk, Orel, and Kharkov, all within a space of two months" in July and August 1943 are given a page and a half in a chapter mostly about Arctic convoys, even though, as Churchill/Pownall admits, they "marked the ruin of the German army on the Eastern Front." Likewise, the massive Russian offensives of early 1944, which finally liberated Leningrad and the Crimea and plunged into Poland, disappear in a single page at the end of the chapter on the fall of Rome. This chapter devotes eleven pages to the fortunes of twenty-three German divisions in Italy and only one to the fate of two hundred German divisions across Eastern Europe. In the post–Cold War era, such an imbalance would be unacceptable—Kursk, for instance, is now considered the greatest tank battle in history and the moment when the Red Army started rolling inexorably toward Berlin. But, as with Stalingrad in volume 4, Churchill knew his mind. Not only was he writing at the height of the Cold War, his emphasis was on "strategy rather than operations," with Overlord as top priority. He told the Syndicate in November 1950 to allow only 2,000 words to the Eastern Front, and neither Deakin nor Pownall demurred at such brevity.[20]

The air war in the west gets considerably more space, albeit largely in one chapter, "The Mounting Air Offensive." For this, prodded by Pownall, Churchill had recruited a special consultant, Air Marshal Sir Guy Garrod. "Master is now convinced that it was *most* important that the Strategic Bombing Offensive should have proper mention," Pownall told Ismay, tongue in cheek, after Garrod lunched with Churchill for the first time in November 1950. "It was good to hear him enlarge on that subject!" But Garrod was not a professional historian like

Deakin or even a staff officer like Pownall, used to writing reports. Morever, he spent the last two years of the war in the Far East and the Mediterranean and therefore lacked firsthand knowledge of the offensive over Germany. Given the passions aroused by "Bomber" Harris, the choice of Garrod may have been deliberate—Pownall commended Garrod to Churchill as "entirely level-headed on the subject" of strategic bombing—but in retrospect he was not the best choice.[21]

At the end of January 1951, Garrod produced eighteen pages of typescript, which Pownall reduced to three. Lord Cherwell, Churchill's scientific adviser, called Garrod's work "very pedestrian," and even Norman Brook, who habitually minced his words to make them more digestible, considered it "a rather flat statement." Brook urged Churchill to praise the bomber crews, which he did, and also highlight the British effort against that of America. But the latter idea was dropped when statistics from the Air Ministry indicated that while the RAF saw nearly 54,000 killed, wounded, missing, or taken prisoner, the American figure was over 94,000. Kelly settled on a rough total for both countries of over 140,000. Brook also asked if Churchill would offer a judgment on the value of strategic bombing, but the response was "not in this volume." At one stage, Churchill intended to pay tribute to "Bomber" Harris but ended up with only a brief reference to his "vigorous leadership."[22]

Behind the scenes, Cherwell and Garrod locked horns about the former's obdurate denials that German production actually rose in 1944. To admit this would have cast doubt on the efficacy of strategic bombing in its proclaimed role of destroying German industry and morale. As in the preparation of volume 4, contemporary documents indicating that civilians were targets were expunged— for instance, Churchill's call for the RAF to give Italians "all manner of hell" if they did not agree to an armistice. The critical point—today generally accepted despite all the problems with Nazi statistics—that the German production index rose in 1944 as Albert Speer belatedly mobilized the economy was dropped in the face of Cherwell's bluster: "If the 'index figure' rose I am sure it was faked. In any event I think this sentence should not be printed as it would encourage the Russians to believe bombing did not do much harm. After all these are your personal memoirs and you certainly knew nothing about the German 'index figure' at the time."[23]

So Churchill pulls his punches about strategic bombing—unlike Smuts, who is quoted in February 1944 asserting that the air offensive had had "even more far-reaching effects than the Russian land victories." But his chapter does make some reference to what historians would now consider the main achievement of the air campaign: namely, the diversion of German manpower, resources, and planes into the defense of the homeland. Whether or not that was "a decisive contribution to victory," as Churchill claims in the opening paragraph of his chapter, it was not unreasonable for him (following Garrod) to call it a "Third Air Front" to "the advantage of the Russians, and of ourselves in the Mediterranean."[24]

Another of Churchill's specialist chapters also reopened bitter wartime arguments. This was "Hitler's 'Secret Weapon,'" about how Whitehall tried to monitor and delay development of the V-1 pilotless planes and the V-2 long-range rockets. The initial draft was composed in December 1950 by Duncan Sandys, Churchill's son-in-law, who headed an investigation into the German V-weapons in April 1943 and then secured overall responsibility for handling intelligence about them. Sandys's draft mirrored his own wartime contribution, which highlighted the potential threat from long-range rockets, and climaxed with the 17 August 1943 raid on the V-2 research center at Peenemünde, on the Baltic. Quoting "Bomber" Harris's memoirs in support, Sandys claimed that this raid "may well have played a decisive part in the general progress of the war" and cited the comment in Eisenhower's memoirs that if the V-2s had been deployed on schedule Overlord "might have been written off." In 1943 and 1944, Sandys had crossed swords repeatedly with Cherwell, and their battle resumed in 1951. It was the Prof, scoffing at the idea of giant rockets, who had drawn attention to evidence of the V-1—of which Sandys was skeptical—and he secured due acknowledgment of his foresight in the revisions to Sandys's draft. Both Cherwell and Garrod encouraged Churchill to tone down the emphasis on Peenemünde, particularly since it had no effect on the more immediate threat from the V-1s in northern France.[25]

In March 1951, another wartime protagonist also entered the lists. In 1943, R. V. Jones had led the Air Ministry's Scientific Intelligence Branch, a rival to Sandys's organization, and he had already criticized Sandys in a published lecture in 1947. Jones had helped Churchill with "The Wizard War" in *Their Finest Hour*. When asked to comment on a draft of "Hitler's 'Secret Weapon,'" he further downplayed Peenemünde and insisted that Eisenhower had "much overstated" the possible effect on Overlord. Jones was particularly anxious to insert a passage giving credit to his own unit, observing that "the scientific picture was so complex that, if I may say so, Mr. Sandys' advisers were out of their depth."[26]

Sandys was given right of reply, and the resulting chapter, extended into early 1944, has a bit to satisfy everyone. Peenemünde, now shorn of all reference to Harris's memoirs, is no longer "decisive" but played "an important and definite part in the general progress of the war." Eisenhower's tribute, though quoted, is called "an overstatement." And most of the passage proposed by Jones is included, even though Sandys grumbled that it contained "nothing that has not already been said earlier." On the other hand, despite extensive credit to Cherwell for highlighting the V-1s, Sandys's own contribution in anticipating the V-2 still dominates the first half of the chapter. Churchill ends by saying that tribute must be paid to all because "when at length the blow fell upon us we were able . . . to ward it off, albeit with heavy loss in life and much damage to property, but without any effective hindrance to our war-making capacity or to the operations in France."[27]

The V-weapons were a serious threat to Britain, but a German atomic bomb would have been immeasurably worse. Yet the race to build the bomb is conspicuous by its absence from *Closing the Ring*. In "Hitler's 'Secret Weapon,'" Churchill confines himself to saying that by mid-1943 "no decisive progress had been made by the Germans towards the atomic bomb," and, according to the index of the British edition, he makes only two tangential references to "Tube Alloys," Whitehall's code name for the Anglo-American atomic project. There is, however, a third reference (noted by Houghton Mifflin's indexer), buried in a telegram Churchill sent after the Quebec conference in August 1943. "We have secured a settlement of a number of hitherto intractable questions," Churchill told Attlee, one of which he cited as "Tube Alloys." That is the only hint in *Closing the Ring* that Churchill and Roosevelt had reached an understanding on 19 August 1943 of major significance for the atomic program in both the war itself and the early Cold War.[28]

After months of British pressure in 1943, particularly from Churchill via Hopkins, Roosevelt decided that he had to sign a formal agreement on collaboration, along the lines he had vaguely promised at Hyde Park in June 1942 (see above, chapter 21). The text was negotiated by officials and then taken to Quebec for the two leaders to sign. It promised a pooling of "brains and resources" and established a combined committee to oversee the production of the bomb. Its most important provisions were article 2, stating that America and Britain would not use the bomb "against third parties without each other's consent," and article 4, in which Churchill disclaimed any interest in the industrial and commercial benefits of atomic energy "beyond what may be considered by the President of the United States to be fair and just and in harmony with the economic welfare of the world." This disclaimer was necessary to allay suspicion in Washington that the British were preoccupied with postwar economic advantage.[29]

The Quebec Agreement of 19 August 1943 constituted the foundation of Anglo-American atomic cooperation for the rest of the war. Why, then, was it not mentioned in *Closing the Ring*, especially given Churchill's (garbled) references to the atomic relationship in his previous volume? Bill Deakin did spot the lacuna during late revisions in August 1951: "Query insert passage on Tube Alloys." He had obtained a copy of the text from the Cabinet Office.[30] But nothing was done, because the Quebec Agreement had been censored not by Norman Brook but by President Truman.

To understand why requires a diversion into atomic history. The agreement served its immediate purpose—to get Britain back into the wartime bomb project—but it was much less acceptable after the war, when the American McMahon Act of August 1946 barred nuclear collaboration with any other state. Nationalism was one reason for the legislation; security another, given Britain's penetration by Soviet spies. But ignorance was also a factor—even senior members of Congress did not know of the Quebec Agreement until the spring of 1947. They were horrified at the veto accorded Britain by article 2, and pressed the Truman administration to have it annulled. Given the McMahon Act, the Attlee government decided that article 2 was a dead letter, and in a Modus Vivendi concluded in January 1948 it was formally surrendered in return for nullification of article 4, which fettered Britain's commercial use of atomic energy. This was all agreed in great secrecy, and Attlee did not even inform Churchill about the Modus Vivendi until 3 December 1950, just as he was leaving for Washington, impelled by fears that the Americans might resort to atomic weapons in Korea. Although Truman assured Attlee that he would not use the bomb without prior consultation, the President's advisers did not want that said in public. The official communiqué blandly recorded Truman's "hope that world conditions would never call for use of the atomic bomb" and his "desire to keep the Prime Minister at all times informed of developments which might bring about a change in the situation."[31]

Attlee told the Commons on 14 December 1950 that he considered these assurances "perfectly satisfactory," but Churchill was livid. He never forgave Attlee for, as he saw it, spinelessly surrendering the Quebec Agreement and, much to the Prime Minister's irritation, decided to raise the matter directly with the President. In a letter dated 12 February 1951, Churchill asked Truman to let the Quebec Agreement be published. Now that the United States had established air bases in East Anglia, he said he had "little doubt" that Parliament would not want them used by atomic bombers without British consent. "I believe that publication of the original document would place us in a position where this guarantee would willingly be conceded by the United States." But Truman's handwritten reply, four days later, asked Churchill not to press the matter. With the Senate challenging his troop commitments to Europe and many "Asialationists" urging him to concentrate on the Korean War, the President warned that reopening this discussion "may ruin my whole defense program both here at home and abroad. Your country's welfare and mine are at stake."[32] Faced with such a categorical request, Churchill told Truman, "I am not pressing the question any more at present."[33] He did not mention the Quebec Agreement in public nor, presumably for the same reason, in his memoirs.

IN CONTRAST TO *The Hinge of Fate*, in which Churchill laid into the Curtin government with gusto, Australia hardly gets a mention in *Closing the Ring*. Canberra's persistent efforts to find out British strategy and shift its emphasis to the Pacific are ignored, even though they resulted in long visits to Britain by Foreign Minister H. V. Evatt in June and July 1943 and by Curtin himself in May 1944. The Commonwealth Prime Ministers conference, at which Curtin pressed hard for closer consultation by London, gets only half a sentence.[34] Nor does Churchill have much to say about the Pacific War, apart from a few pages in his opening chapter, left over from *The Hinge of Fate*, and a couple more near the end.

Britain's own operations in the Far East fare little better. With Overlord his priority, Churchill told the Syndicate in November 1950 that he could not spare more than 3,000 words for Burma.[35] Much of that space is devoted to personalities, such as the jungle fighter Orde Wingate—the kind of eccentric warrior Churchill prized both for his personal qualities and for his galvanic effect on the military establishment. Also featured is Admiral Lord Louis Mountbatten, another favorite of the Prime Minister, overpromoted, as we saw, in 1942 to head Combined Operations. In *Closing the Ring* Churchill here provides the account of Mountbatten's appointment that he had omitted from *The Hinge of Fate*. He also plays up his role at Quebec in securing Mountbatten's elevation to head the new South-East Asia Command (SEAC), quoting his telegram to Attlee about the need for a "young and vigorous mind in this lethargic and stagnant Indian scene." In reality, Mountbatten was not the Prime Minister's first choice. Only when Air Chief Marshal Sir Sholto Douglas had been vetoed by Washington and Admiral Sir Andrew Cunningham had declined did Churchill adopt a suggestion from Leo Amery, Secretary of State for India, and propose Mountbatten.[36]

Mountbatten took over a theater that quickly became marginal thanks to the concentration of resources for Overlord and the Russian promise at Teheran of eventual belligerency against Japan—what Churchill calls a "decisive" event of "first-class importance" because the prospect of a Soviet invasion of Manchuria made operations in Burma much less important.[37] Churchill's interest in Southeast Asia was intermittent and usually prompted by events elsewhere. In August

1943, he fixated on seizing the northern tip of Sumatra (Operation Culverin). This, he tells us, would be the equivalent of Torch in the Indian Ocean or, in "its promise of decisive consequences," of the Dardanelles in 1915. In fact, Culverin was more a ploy to divert Roosevelt from a slogging campaign through Burma to aid the Chinese. At Cairo and Teheran, the President talked of seizing the Andaman Islands, off the coast of Thailand, as another way to help Chiang Kai-shek. This operation, code-named Buccaneer, was given the coup de grâce when SEAC demanded 50,000 troops, not 14,000, as Roosevelt claimed would suffice. Soldiers and landing craft on that scale could not be spared from Europe, and the demise of Buccaneer gave Churchill a new opportunity to push for operations in the Aegean. Perversely, he sent Mountbatten a coruscating cable saying that the demand for six-to-one superiority over the Japanese had created "a very bad impression" among the Americans and asking if "you are getting competent military advice."[38]

Mountbatten's chief adviser was, in fact, Henry Pownall, evicted from London by Churchill at the end of 1941 and then SEAC Chief of Staff. Pownall's diary for 1943–1944 is full of criticism of Churchill: Culverin was "a typically Winstonian project" proposed without adequate resources and advanced with the "usual fatuous obstinacy." Churchill's rebarbative cable about the "competent military advice" showed "he's at his old game of general-hunting and like a pi-dog he goes looking for dirts in which to roll." In 1951, Pownall resumed the argument face-to-face, albeit more politely. Supported by Brook and the War Office, he persuaded Churchill first to remove a passage suggesting that SEAC had proposed the 50,000 figure deliberately to sabotage Buccaneer and then to delete a scathing minute from the Prime Minister to Ismay about SEAC's "mobs of low-grade soldiery" and generals who were "unfit for further employment in this war."[39]

It was also Pownall, egged on by Mountbatten, who ensured that Churchill's memoirs contained some discussion of their campaigns. The chapter "Burma and Beyond" draws heavily on a paper by Pownall. Kelly reordered the material in early September, and all seemed ready for the publishers.[40] Then Churchill suddenly decided to have a separate chapter about the Whitehall row on Pacific strategy in the spring of 1944. To call this the eleventh hour would be too generous, since all of book 1 and most of book 2 had been airmailed to Houghton Mifflin. Moreover, the drafting had to be done at long range, with Churchill in Venice and the Syndicate in England. A new chapter eventually entitled "Strategy Against Japan" was printed on 5 September; this centered on what Churchill called "the only considerable difference which I and the War Cabinet had with our trusted military colleagues." The Chiefs of Staff wanted to act as the left flank of the main American advance, anchored on Australia, whereas Churchill and his Cabinet colleagues favored an assault from India to Malaya and the Dutch East Indies. Desperate to find a compromise, Ismay proposed a "middle strategy," starting from Australia into Borneo but diverging later to strike either at Singapore and Malaya or else at Hong Kong. On that basis, the dispute was eventually resolved. On 27 May 1944, Ismay wrote Pownall: "When history comes to be written I believe that the waffling that there has been for nearly nine months over the basic question of our strategy in the Far East will be one of the black spots in the record in the British Higher Direction of War, which has, on the whole, been pretty good."[41]

In his original draft of this chapter, Churchill ended with his minute of 20 March 1944. There, drawing himself up to his full constitutional height, he told the Chiefs it was his "duty, as Prime Minister and Minister of Defence, to give the following ruling": namely, that the Bay of Bengal should remain "the centre of gravity for the British and Imperial war effort against Japan." Now that this was settled, he told them, "we may bend ourselves to the tremendous and urgent tasks which are now so near, and in which we shall have need of all our old comradeship and mutual confidence." In the draft chapter, Churchill (from Venice) wrote that his "rulings were accepted and the subject dropped." This statement was quite untrue, so Gordon Allen produced an appropriate coda about the middle strategy proposed by Ismay. But Churchill brushed it aside. "I do not feel it is needed," he told Kelly; "the Chapter ends very well as it is." Meanwhile, Pownall had shown the draft to John Ehrman, engaged on the official history of British grand strategy for this period. In confidential comments, Ehrman demolished Churchill's version of events, noting that it was only from January to March 1944 that the Prime Minister had substantial Cabinet support and that once the middle strategy was proposed, he had "carried on virtually alone." Ehrman had no doubt that Allen's piece should be included, and this was duly done. He also asked why Churchill wanted to print his minute of 20 March 1944—many others in similar vein were available—since this was the only one that aroused the Chiefs' personal resentment. But, in the rush to get the book to Houghton Mifflin, the last point was ignored. That was very unfortunate, for in paragraph 2 of his minute Churchill had accused the Chiefs of Staff of going behind his back and reaching "settled conclusions" without "in any way endeavouring to ascertain and carry the views of the civil power under which they are serving." This was a grave accusation.[42]

Pownall suddenly grasped the import of this paragraph on 11 October 1951, when the volume was almost fully printed in Boston and Churchill was deep in the election campaign. He discussed it with Ismay, who then wrote a groveling letter to Churchill; he received a testy reply: "I was abroad when I wrote the chapter, and I understood that you had checked it and passed it." It seemed unlikely that the paragraph could be cut from the American text, and Ismay suggested that Churchill might write personal letters to Alanbrooke, Cunningham, and Portal in the hope of preempting their anger. In the event, Henry Laughlin and his Boston staff, rising to yet another challenge, managed to delete the offending passage, though some American readers may have wondered at the rather large gaps on page 579! For the Cassell's edition, Allen produced a longer account of the middle strategy, further blunting the sharpness of the preceding debate. The ending of "Strategy Against Japan" is therefore one of the major divergences between the American and British editions of *Closing the Ring*. A combined operation by the Syndicate and his publishers had saved Churchill from what could have been a most embarrassing row with his former colleagues.[43]

THAT CLASH BETWEEN Churchill and his Chiefs of Staff in early 1944 involved more than strategy. It was a contest of wills between opinionated men whose mutual patience had almost snapped under the incessant strains of war. Brooke's diary for that period testifies to his frustration. "I don't think I can stand much more of it," he wrote on 19 January, the day after Churchill returned from Marrakech. "My God how tired I am of working for him!"[44] Brooke had exploded in this way in his diary many times before, but by 1944 Churchill's military advisers were no longer willing to tolerate his "midnight follies."

Here a change in the Chiefs of Staff's Committee was of great importance. Admiral Sir Dudley Pound, the First Sea Lord, had suffered a severe stroke in September 1943 and died a few weeks later. In *Closing the Ring*, Churchill records the stoic dignity with which Pound faced the end but is deceitful about the question of Pound's successor. He admits his own preference was for Admiral Sir Bruce Fraser and that it was only when Fraser declined that he agreed to appoint Admiral Sir Andrew Cunningham (known from his initials as ABC). Churchill claims that Cunningham was "the obvious choice" but not easily spared from his command in the all-important Mediterranean. Yet his own minute of 25 September 1943, which Churchill chose not to reprint, came up with a variety of dubious objections: Cunningham was "an officer of the old school and the pre-air age"; and "we must move forward to younger men. Fraser is five years younger than Cunningham. These five years are important." Churchill also asserted that Cunningham "would not be well suited to the prolonged, ceaseless, detailed work of the C.O.S. Committee." As historian Stephen Roskill later observed, this was all camouflage. Churchill did not want Cunningham because the latter had stood up to him in the past, particularly over Greece and Crete in 1941. When finally giving in, Churchill exploded petulantly: "All right. You can have your Cunningham, but if the Admiralty don't do as they are told I will bring down the Board [of Admiralty] in ruins even if it means my coming down with it." Shades of Gallipoli in 1915 and his confrontation with Jackie Fisher![45]

Cunningham's appointment tilted the balance of the committee. "Peter" Portal, Chief of the Air Staff, rarely stood up to Churchill, and, given Pound's docility, this had left the burden of argument on Brooke. Now he had a ready ally in Cunningham, whose forthright views and short fuse were soon apparent. Churchill's critics were now in a majority on the Chiefs of Staff Committee and the protracted row over Pacific strategy in the spring of 1944 reflected that shift of power.

There were more personal reasons as well behind the row. In August 1942, Brooke had declined Churchill's offer of the command in North Africa, mainly because he felt that he (alone) could control the Prime Minister's strategic impetuosity. The consolation was that he had been promised command of the invasion of France—particularly gratifying since he had been a corps commander there in the dark days of 1940. But then, on 15 August 1943 in Quebec, Churchill told him that Marshall would command Overlord. "I remember it as if it was yesterday," Brooke wrote in the 1950s. They were walking up and down the terrace of the Citadel, surveying a panorama of the St. Lawrence River, where General Wolfe mounted his epic push for the heights of Quebec in 1759. As Churchill spoke, "that wonderful view" was "swamped by a dark cloud of despair." Brooke believed he had done his time as Winston's minder and yearned to take center stage in the culminating battle. Now the chance to be a twentieth-century Wolfe had been snatched from him because Churchill wanted to appease Roosevelt. It was, he said, a "crashing blow," from which it took several months to recover.[46]

Brooke remained Chief of the Imperial General Staff until his retirement in June 1946. Ennobled as Viscount Alanbrooke, he busied himself with various service charities but rejected all proposals to write his memoirs. Then suddenly in 1950 he consented to cooperate with a biography commissioned by the Royal Regiment of Artillery, his old unit, provided it was authored by the popular historian Sir Arthur Bryant and did not appear till after his death. In the spring of 1951, as an aid to his biographer, he started producing a transcript of the diary with his own retrospective commentary: "Notes on My Life."[47]

Why Alanbrooke changed his mind is not clear, but *The Second World War* was probably a powerful reason. First, Churchill had made a fortune—whereas Alanbrooke, despite some welcome directorships, was strapped for cash in retirement and had to sell his prize collection of bird books and even his Hampshire house, moving into the gardener's cottage. More important still, the egocentricity of Churchill's account had deeply offended him. Alanbrooke was sure that the Chiefs of Staff Committee had been essential for victory, both in coordinating the three fighting services and also in restraining Winston's flights of fancy. Yet Churchill's memoirs offer little praise for the Chiefs, except in the opening chapter of *Their Finest Hour*. There are also plaudits in that volume for Brooke's "singular firmness and dexterity" in France in 1940 and for "services of the highest order" in chairing the Chiefs of Staff Committee. But thereafter Alex and Monty take center stage as the military heroes of Churchill's memoirs. Brooke is appointed Chief of the Imperial General Staff at the end of volume 3 in only half a sentence.[48] He gets some brief references in *The Hinge of Fate*, including one about his declining the command in the Middle East, which, as we have seen, was inserted in November 1950 at Alanbrooke's request so it could then be quoted in his official biography. In *Closing the Ring*, when Churchill relates how he decided at Quebec in August 1943 that Overlord should have an American commander, he tells us only that Brooke, "who had my entire confidence . . . bore the great disappointment with soldierly dignity." Even this was an afterthought in July 1951, prompted by the Syndicate.[49]

Down in Alanbrooke's Hampshire cottage, where each volume of memoirs was read and carefully annotated, Churchill's account of 15 August 1943 was deeply resented. "Notes on My Life" explicitly cites the cursory reference in *Closing the Ring* as a mirror of Churchill's insensitivity at the time: "Not for one moment did he realize what this meant to me. He offered no sympathy, no regrets at having to change his mind, and dealt with the matter as if it were one of minor importance." Churchill's memoirs "hardened Alan's heart considerably," reflected his in-law and confidante Cynthia Brookeborough in 1954; Arthur Bryant, the official biographer, agreed that Alanbrooke was "hurt" by them.[50] And so 1951 saw the gestation not only of Lord Moran's "diary" but also of the two volumes that Bryant and Alanbrooke published in 1957 and 1959. In laying down so triumphantly the authorized version, Churchill had stirred up the revisionists.

CHAPTER 26

THE FUTURE OF EUROPE

IN 1943–1944, FINAL ALLIED VICTORY was still a long way off, but the Italian surrender opened up questions about the governance of liberated Europe, not only for Italy but also Greece, Yugoslavia, and France. The communist challenge was one of the biggest problems, but close scrutiny of Churchill's treatment of communism in *Closing the Ring* shows that opportunism, not ideological consistency, was his watchword. Debates about the postwar order created friction with Britain's two great allies. In this period, Churchill was more often at odds with the Americans than rhetoric about the "special relationship" might suggest and more ambivalent about the Soviet Union than one would expect from his image as a Cold Warrior. On both postwar policy and alliance relations, *Closing the Ring* is far from candid.

THE OVERTHROW OF Mussolini on 25 July 1943 was engineered by fascists and officers who had previously collaborated in his regime. When they signed an armistice with the Allies on 8 September, without calling for an uprising against the Germans, they created a power vacuum that enabled Hitler to seize two thirds of the country and also deport and intern 700,000 Italian military personnel. Italian troops who resisted the Germans on their own account, particularly in the Aegean, were shot. The events of 8 September played into the hands of the anti-Nazi resistance, whose leaders (and postwar historians) were predominantly communist. Casting the resistance as a revolutionary force battling a discredited ruling class, they waged a civil war as well as a war of liberation. Thus, September

1943 began a double tragedy for Italy that lasted until May 1945. The country became a battleground between the Allies and the Axis, on which was also waged a fratricidal struggle for postwar power.[1]

September 1943 is the equivalent in Italian political mythology of June 1940 for the French—for decades taken as a fundamental break in the political order. In *Their Finest Hour*, Churchill had written at length about "the French agony" of 1940 because he was genuinely fascinated by France and her collapse affected Britain directly. Italy was different on both counts, and his discussion of the Italian crisis of 1943–1944 is brief and sporadic, concerned mainly with strategy, not state building.

Book 1 is entitled "Italy Won," yet the Allies do not even take Rome until the penultimate chapter of the whole volume. Churchill's persistent illusion that the capital was about to fall is the prime reason why he stuck with the government set up in July 1943 under the King and Marshal Pietro Badoglio, even though it was unrepresentative of Italian opinion and packed with fascists and fellow travelers. (In 1935–1936, Badoglio had overseen Mussolini's brutal conquest of Abyssinia.) Churchill's obduracy about the Badoglio government testifies to two other convictions, both hinted at in *Closing the Ring*. First, it shows his continued pragmatism about the principle of unconditional surrender that FDR had publicly foisted on the Allies at Casablanca. "Merely harping on 'unconditional surrender' with no prospect of mercy held out even as an act of grace," he warned Eden in August 1943, "may result in no surrender at all." Second, it reflects his belief that Italy's recent history had been essentially a one-man show. Still ambivalent in 1951 about Mussolini, he credits him with saving Italy from Bolshevism and gaining "a position in Europe such as Italy had never held before." Conversely, because Mussolini had "almost absolute control," he "could not cast the burden" of failure on other institutions such as the monarchy or the general staff. Given this assumption, Churchill could justify the Badoglio government as a real improvement, worth working with, at least until Rome fell.[2]

As so often, however, *c'est le provisoire qui dure*. The Germans dug in, the Allies bogged down, and Britain was stuck with an increasingly embarrassing arrangement. The Roosevelt administration pressed for a broader government. It was particularly keen on Count Carlo Sforza, Foreign Minister in the prefascist era, who had built up a large American following during his exile in the United States and was now a vigorous critic of the Badoglio regime. In "The Broken Axis" and "Italy: Cassino," Churchill admits his differences with the United States on these points, without conveying their full force. In the autumn of 1943, he had been positively abusive about Sforza, calling him "a foolish and played-out old man" who wanted to be King.[3] From his February 1951 draft, Churchill cut parts of his telegram to Roosevelt on 8 March 1944 stating that he had "no confidence" in either Sforza or "the dwarf Professor," Benedetto Croce, as a possible "Lieutenant of the Realm" to ease out Victor Emmanuel III. Eventually, Churchill briefly records, a deal was struck in April 1944 whereby the King promised to hand over his powers to his son, and Badoglio "reconstructed his government to include leading political figures in the South, of whom Sforza and Croce were the most prominent."[4]

This passage was written by Bill Deakin, whose work here helped lay the basis for his 1962 classic on Mussolini, Hitler, and the fall of Italian fascism, *The Brutal Friendship*. It is therefore intriguing that *Closing the Ring* omits the most important feature of that new government of April 1944: the inclusion of the Communist party leader, Palmiro Togliatti, recently returned from exile in Moscow. There is no mention of Togliatti in volume 5, or of the essential precondition for his return: Soviet recognition of Badoglio's government on 8 March. The nearest hint is Churchill's telegram to Roosevelt five days later, in which he says of the Soviets that "their aim may be a Communist Italy, and it may suit them to use the King and Badoglio till everything is ready for an extreme solution."[5] But nothing is said explicitly of the Soviet diplomatic coup, which ensured the communists a place in Italian politics that the British and Americans had hitherto denied them. Togliatti's first speech on Italian soil, at Salerno, proclaimed an unexpected willingness to serve under Badoglio and the King. This turnabout, we now know, followed Stalin's injunction to seek a political path to power rather than revolution. *La svolta di Salerno*, as it is called in Italy, was a fundamental moment in the country's postwar history, in which the Communist party played such a major role. Yet in Churchill's book, Salerno figures only as the name of a battle not a speech, even though the latter proved far more significant. Possibly Churchill or Deakin decided that its inclusion would be embarrassing because Churchill's veto on Italian political reconstruction had frustrated the moderates and helped open the door to the Soviets.[6]

Churchill took a fairly complacent view of Italy's new coalition government, and it was not until May 1944 that he started to evince concern about Togliatti. This was in sharp contrast to his attitude at exactly the same time toward Greece, where he is at pains in *Closing the Ring* to demonstrate his vigilant opposition to communist power. His chapter "The Greek Torment" deals with the polarization of Greek resistance to German rule in 1943–1944 between the communist-led National Liberation Front (EAM) and anticommunist remnants of the Greek Army and local mountain bands (EDES), which combined under Colonel

Napoleon Zervas. Both groups were republican in sympathy, further undermining the authority of the exiled King. In "The Greek Torment," Churchill makes much of his minute to the Chiefs of Staff on 29 September 1943, ordering them to be ready with 5,000 British troops to preempt a communist coup if the Germans suddenly withdrew from Greece, commenting that this was "the first suggestion that we might be forced to intervene in Greek internal affairs at the moment of liberation." At the end of March 1944, EAM proclaimed an alternative communist-led government, sparking mutinies in the Greek armed forces under British command in Cairo. Churchill prints copious extracts from his telegrams enjoining the local British authorities to suppress the mutiny. His efforts in this chapter to highlight his anticommunist credentials stand in contrast to his silence on the communist issue in Italy. Moreover, he does not make clear that his initial minute of 29 September was not spontaneous brilliance but a response to prodding from Eden and the Foreign Office. It was Eden, in fact, who forced the pace over the Greek communists, urging a complete break with EAM in November 1943, long before the War Cabinet was ready to go that far.[7]

In neighboring Yugoslavia, however, Churchill was actually ready to back the communists. As in Greece, the resistance forces became polarized into the communist-led Partisans under Tito and the Cetniks, led by General Draža Mihailović, who were loyal to the exiled monarchy. Under pressure from constant German retaliation against civilians, Mihailović, says Churchill, "drifted into a posture whereby some of his commanders made accommodations with the German and Italian troops to be left alone in certain mountain areas in return for doing little or nothing against the enemy." (A September 1950 draft was blunter, saying that "Mihailović had obtained a kind of neutrality for his forces by an arrangement with the enemy.")[8] During the summer and autumn of 1943, Churchill shifted his weight to Tito, convinced that Mihailović was no longer worth Britain's support. His chapter "Marshal Tito and Yugoslavia" explains this change of policy largely in terms of information and advice about the situation on the ground from British emissaries to Tito, notably Fitzroy Maclean and Bill Deakin.

The account was, in fact, developed as a separate chapter by Deakin in April 1951, from an earlier and brief summary in a draft about "Convalescence at Marrakech."[9] Three points are of particular interest. First, Churchill does not draw attention to the contrast between his attitude to communists in Greece and in Yugoslavia. After reading the draft chapter, a former royalist exiled in London told Deakin: "The Jugoslav Partisans were supported in doing exactly the same thing that the Greek Partisans were being prevented from doing."[10] Nor does Churchill note that Eden and the Foreign Office were very reluctant to break with Mihailović and shift British aid to Tito, for their anticommunism in Greece was replicated in Yugoslavia, unlike Churchill's. This difference in attitude was related, third, to sources of information. Churchill was persuaded of the damage Tito was causing to the Germans by evidence from signals intercepts, a source not available to most of the Foreign Office. But, as usual, such evidence had to be purged from his memoirs. For instance, the words italicized below were cut from his telegram to Alexander on 22 July 1943: "I am sending you by an Officer a full account which I have had prepared *from Boniface and all other sources* of the marvellous resistance put up by the so-called Partisan followers of Tito in Bosnia and the powerful cold-blooded manoeuvres of Mihailović in Serbia."[11] Instead of crediting Ultra, he exaggerated the role of Maclean and Deakin. Undoubtedly, both men performed sterling service—Deakin's hazardous work in 1943 as an SOE operative in Yugoslavia earned him an award for gallantry—but the critical factor here was not human intelligence but signals intercepts.

Churchill's position on postwar Southern Europe was therefore pragmatic. In general, his sympathies lay with conservative governments, ideally monarchies, but his overriding concern was to win the war—hence his readiness to back Tito and his complacency about Togliatti. How, then, do we explain the greater candor in his memoirs about Yugoslavia than about Italy? Perhaps because Tito had been ostracized by Stalin in 1948 and was, at the time Churchill wrote *Closing the Ring*, almost a fellow traveler with the West. The powerful Italian Communist party, by contrast, was at the heart of Europe's Cold War.

In the case of France, communism was not yet an issue—but here, as in Italy, Churchill found himself at odds with both Eden and Roosevelt. In June 1943, a French Committee of National Liberation (FCNL) was established in Algiers, with de Gaulle and General Henri Giraud as uneasy cochairmen. By the end of the year, however, Giraud had been forced out by de Gaulle, and there was growing pressure in Britain from the Cabinet and the Commons to recognize the FCNL as the provisional rulers of postwar France. As in his account of Anglo-French relations in volume 4, Churchill admits he sought a middle ground between those views and Roosevelt's antipathy to de Gaulle. At Quebec in August, each government agreed to issue its own form of words. Churchill states that this constituted "recognition of the French National Committee," putting it "now on formal terms with the Allies as the representatives of France." In fact, even the British recognized the FCNL only as "administering those French territories which acknowledge its authority," and nothing was said about the eventual government of France itself. The American formula was even more guarded.[12]

As in *The Hinge of Fate*, Churchill deletes from the 1943 documents his strongest aspersions on de Gaulle—such as that he had "symptoms of a budding Fuhrer" or was "a combination of Joan of Arc and Clemenceau" and that "there is nothing this man will not do if he has armed forces at his disposal." Deakin, who reconstructed Churchill's draft, urged discretion, and Lord Cherwell warned that if de Gaulle came to power again "cooperation with him might be even more difficult if he had read some of these comments."[13] In the published text, Churchill also plays down his differences with Eden. He prints parts of a memo he wrote to the Cabinet on 13 July 1943, without mentioning that it was provoked by a paper from the Foreign Secretary pressing so strongly for some form of recognition of France that Churchill told Eden "we might be coming to a break." Eden argued that "our main problem after the war will be to contain Germany," and consequently Britain needed a strong France, which meant doing "everything to raise French morale" during the war. The Roosevelt administration, by contrast, seemed to view France as a minor power of no great importance, akin to Spain or Italy. Eden maintained that "in dealing with European problems of the future we are likely to have to work more closely with France even than with the United States."[14]

Churchill and de Gaulle clashed head-on in June 1944, and Churchill again conceals the passion of the argument. Eisenhower was keen to have a French provisional government-in-waiting when the Allies landed in Normandy, but Roosevelt remained adamant, and Churchill, despite strong domestic pressure, would not act alone. To make matters worse, for security reasons de Gaulle was not formally briefed about D-Day until the last minute, even though it was his country that was to be liberated. On 4 June, the Free French leader flew in from Algiers, and Churchill explained the operation. Their meeting began civilly enough, but when de Gaulle started to complain about the lack of official recognition, Churchill exclaimed angrily that, if there was a split between the FCNL and the United States, Britain would side with the Americans. This conversation is summarized at length in the chapter "On the Eve." But Churchill does not mention its sequel on the night of 5–6 June, when de Gaulle was asked to broadcast to the French people, even though not recognized as their leader-in-waiting. The general set certain conditions of protocol to maintain his sense of independence, which, relayed inaccurately to Churchill as a flat refusal, caused a volcanic eruption. All night, the Free French Ambassador, Pierre Viénot, shuttled between the two irate leaders, each tired and desperately anxious about the morning to come. In the early hours of 6 June, with Allied paratroops already dropping into Normandy, Churchill ordered de Gaulle to be sent back to Algiers, "in chains if necessary. He must not be allowed to enter France." It took all of Eden's finesse to have the order rescinded.[15]

Churchill had not forgotten the furor, as his April 1950 notes on "The Eve of Overlord" (as it was then called) make clear. Asserting erroneously that de Gaulle refused "to address a word to France," he recalled haranguing Viénot at two or three in the morning on 6 June: "I so beat up this poor man—de Gaulle of course would not come himself—that he practically collapsed. All his sympathies were with me. He was ashamed of de Gaulle. He died within a week." Yet Churchill's published version tells us nothing about how he actually spent the night before "the longest day."[16]

CHURCHILL'S WARNING to de Gaulle on 4 June 1944 that, if forced to choose, he would always side with America rather than France is hardly surprising. At Harvard on 6 September 1943, the Prime Minister had extolled the unity of the English-speaking peoples and urged its continuation into the postwar world. He quotes at length from this speech in chapter 7. What Churchill was now calling the "special relationship" was a matter very close to his heart. After Foreign Office Minister Richard Law told American businessmen in London in February 1944 that "a world that has suffered for four years under the Prussian jackboot will not want to exchange it for an Anglo-American governess," he received a pompous rebuke from Churchill for differing from "my publicly expressed views" with "so much casual levity." The Prime Minister went on: "It is my deepest conviction that unless Britain and the United States are joined in a special relationship, including Combined Staff organization and a wide measure of reciprocity in the use of bases—all within the ambit of a world organization—another destructive war will come to pass."[17]

Churchill's grand rhetoric—at Harvard in 1943 or Fulton in 1946—has often been taken as the definitive expression of his beliefs on Anglo-American relations. From that, it is a quick step to denouncing him for sentimental obsequiousness in the face of burgeoning American power and to extolling Eden as the advocate of "an independent foreign policy."[18] But we should not ignore Churchill's own readiness to stand up to the Americans—if necessary by outright deception, as in October 1943 over Mediterranean strategy. Churchill's interest in that theater reflected, in part, his search for a distinct British role. In similar vein, the documentary appendix to Closing the Ring includes a minute he sent to the War Office in November 1943 urging it to ensure that an equal number of British and U.S. divisions were landed on D-Day: "In this way we should maintain our right to be effectively consulted in operations which are of such capital importance."[19]

The search for balance in an increasingly one-sided relationship was a theme that preoccupied the economic ministries in Whitehall. Two important and long-running controversies concerned civil aviation, for which both countries had an eye on postwar bases and routes, and Britain's dollar holdings, which some Americans wanted to treat as part of a settlement of Lend-Lease and even as leverage over British trade policy. Churchill refers to neither of these in his text, though they do figure briefly in minutes quoted in the appendix. Another rumbling controversy was over oil rivalry in the Middle East. "Thank you very much for your assurances about no sheep's eyes at our oilfields in Persia and Iraq," Churchill cabled Roosevelt on 4 March 1944. "Let me reciprocate by giving you the fullest assurance that we have no thought of trying to horn in upon your interests or property in Saudi Arabia." But the only minute for 4 March in the documentary appendix is about a national day of prayer for Overlord. These sidelinings or omissions are partly reflections of Churchill's pervasive neglect of economic topics in his memoirs, but he probably also wanted to avoid the seamy side of wartime Anglo-American relations, at a time when transatlantic harmony was vital to NATO in the Cold War.[20]

But his memoirs *are* authentic testimony to his faith in the President: "My whole system is founded on friendship with Roosevelt," he told Eden in a confidential note in November 1942.[21] In wartime and in his memoirs, he was ready to blame the President's advisers, particularly the Joint Chiefs of Staff, rather than Roosevelt himself for obstruction of British wishes. A minute to Eden dated 4 March 1944, printed for the appendix but not eventually used, dismissed the recent spate of cables sent by FDR about areas of economic tension: "I cannot believe that any of these telegrams come from the President. They are merely put before him when he is fatigued and pushed upon us by those who are pulling him about."[22]

Churchill therefore had real problems explaining Roosevelt's wooing of Stalin in 1943. In the spring, the President tried, behind Churchill's back, to secure a meeting with Stalin alone. When Churchill discovered what was going on at the end of June 1943 and indicated as much, FDR brazenly lied that the meeting à deux was Stalin's idea. In *Roosevelt and Hopkins*, Robert Sherwood alluded to "Roosevelt's belief that he might be able to break the ice with Stalin more readily if Churchill were not present," but there is no mention of this episode or the related telegrams in *Closing the Ring*.[23] Churchill does not, however, ignore the President's conduct at Teheran at the end of 1943, admitting that

Roosevelt met Stalin privately while keeping him at arm's length. Again, though, he avoids blaming FDR directly: "There was emerging a strong current of opinion in the American Government circles which seemed to wish to win Russian confidence even at the expense of co-ordinating the Anglo-American war effort."[24]

The most blatant instance of Roosevelt deliberately siding with Stalin against Churchill occurred during their conference dinner on 29 November 1943. Churchill does discuss this episode at length—probably because of what he calls "a highly coloured and extremely misleading account" already published by Elliott Roosevelt, which insinuated that Churchill was drunk at the time and that he never forgot or forgave the contretemps. Churchill's version says that Stalin, who was in a teasing mood all evening, started to talk about breaking the German capacity for war by executing 50,000 key officers and technicians. Churchill took umbrage, whereupon FDR, with heavy-handed humor, proposed a compromise: to shoot only 49,000. While Eden desperately signaled that this was all a joke, Elliott Roosevelt spoke up to say "how cordially he agreed with Marshal Stalin's plan and how sure he was that the United States Army would support it." At this, Churchill stalked out, and it took Stalin and Molotov, "both grinning broadly," to draw him back.[25]

This turbulence at Teheran revealed a deeper undercurrent. Not only did FDR share Stalin's preference for a harsh peace, but according to Elliott's memoir he had gone to the dinner intent on taking Stalin's side in any badinage to signify that there was no Anglo-American axis. This was his tactic throughout the summit, and it helps explain why Churchill snapped—a storm in a wineglass, perhaps, but Churchill took it as a sobering sign of Roosevelt's apparent intoxication with Stalin.

IN GENERAL, friction with the Soviets does not bulk large in volume 5 except in a chapter entitled "Arctic Convoys Again." This centers on March to November 1943, when British supplies to the Russians were suspended once more because of the threat from the *Tirpitz* and other German warships during the long hours of northern daylight. Churchill prints various critical telegrams from Stalin and also documents Britain's repeated complaints about the treatment of their naval personnel in Russia. But he says nothing about the other big row of mid-1943, when Stalin learned for certain that there would be no Second Front that year. Churchill and Roosevelt sent a joint message after their Washington conference in May 1943, explaining plans to attack Sicily and Italy instead, and this sparked an acrimonious correspondence with Stalin throughout June.

The relevant telegrams were marked for printing when Churchill started work on his memoirs, and an early summary about the "Third Quarter of 1943" begins with "My correspondence with Stalin about 'no Second Front in 1943.'"[26] Deakin still had this theme in mind in February 1951, but no reference was made to it in the final text—possibly due to chapter reorganizations and the general rush but perhaps deliberately. In September 1950, Gordon Allen drew Churchill's attention to a "very interesting telegram" sent to the Prime Minister on 1 July 1943 by the British Ambassador to Russia. "I am the last to plead Stalin's case," Sir Archibald Clark Kerr observed of the recent exchanges, but he detected "a weakness" in Britain's defense: "not in our inability to open this second front but in our having led him to believe we were going to."[27] This pointed back to the Prime Minister's aide-mémoire given to Molotov on 10 June 1942, which contrary to the version of it given in volume 4, balanced a firm "no commitment" about invading France in 1942 with the clear impression that the Allies would do so in 1943.

Churchill also says little about his attitude to the Soviet Union itself, although he had been very forthright at the time. On 16 January 1944, he wrote Eden a long minute explaining why he was now, unlike in 1942, willing to recognize Soviet control over the Baltic states. His main reason was pragmatic—the Red Army was about to recover them by force—but there was more: "The tremendous victories of the Russian armies, the deep-seated changes which have taken place in the character of the Russian State and Government, the new confidence which has grown in our hearts towards Stalin—these have all had their effect." On 1 April 1944, by contrast, frustrated by arguments with Moscow over Poland and the treatment of British seamen, he told Eden: "Although I have tried in every way to put myself in sympathy with these Communist leaders, I cannot feel the slightest trust or confidence in them. Force and facts are their only realities." Neither of these minutes appears in Closing the Ring. The first probably sounded very naïve for the Cold War era, while the second invited a question about why, most of the time, Churchill sounded much more trusting about the Soviets.[28]

These two minutes from early 1944 show how the Prime Minister oscillated in mood about the Russians. The common thread, tied perhaps to Churchill's great-man theory of history, was his conviction that he could do business with Stalin. As with Roosevelt, Churchill tended to blame difficulties on Stalin's advisers. After a long and officious telegram from the Kremlin on 13 October 1943, Churchill cabled Roosevelt: "I think, or at least I hope, this message came from the machine rather than from Stalin." The image of a divided Soviet leadership, formed when he visited Moscow in August 1942, remained the lens through which he perceived the Soviet Union. He told the journalist Colin Coote on 27 January 1944 that "if only I could dine with Stalin once a week, there would be no trouble at all."[29]

One important issue on which Churchill tried to make progress with Stalin at Teheran was the future of Poland. This was a matter of particular sensitivity for Britain because Polish independence had been its ostensible casus belli in 1939, and the Polish government-in-exile in London was vehemently anti-Russian. Churchill offers a detailed précis of the discussions at Teheran, particularly his idea of "moving Poland westward" in order to compensate the Poles with German territory for having to cede much of the Ukraine to the Soviet Union. What he does not make clear is that he was fighting a lonely battle because Roosevelt was much more concerned about the future of Germany. According to Sir Archibald Clark Kerr, the President even said at one point, "I don't care two hoots about Poland. Wake me up when we talk about Germany." Churchill cut from his draft some passages indicating how he and FDR each kept trying to pull the discussion at Teheran about the future of Central Europe back to their preferred country.[30]

Teheran aside, Churchill has little to say on the Polish question in *Closing the Ring*. Personally, he was close to the Polish premier, General Wladyslaw Sikorski, and when Sikorski's plane was shot down on 5 July 1943, Churchill wept at news of his death and paid tribute to him in the Commons as a man of "calm dignity" and "remarkable pre-eminence."[31] Yet Sikorski is not mentioned once in this volume. Nor does Churchill say much about his persistent efforts in early 1944 to persuade the London Poles to accept the territorial formula he brought back from Teheran. This was a futile exercise—after the Katyn revelations in 1943, there was no hope of rapprochement between Stalin and the London Poles. In his appendix, Churchill prints part of a minute dated 30 January 1944 that shows he was still trying to find out what happened at Katyn, but he cut out a final sentence saying that "we should none of us ever speak a word about it."[32]

This silence is symptomatic of his treatment of Central and Eastern Europe as a whole in *Closing the Ring*. In particular, he fails to discuss the crisis in Anglo-Soviet relations in the spring of 1944, of which the Greek Army mutiny, Tito's growing power in Yugoslavia, and communist participation in the new Italian government were all manifestations. His agitated minute to Eden on 4 May— "are we going to acquiesce in the Communisation of the Balkans and perhaps of Italy?"—is deferred until *Triumph and Tragedy*.[33] For it is only in the final volume of his war memoirs that Churchill faces the problem of Eastern Europe head-on. Throughout *Closing the Ring*, Overlord remains tyrant.

CHAPTER 27

"ON THE DEFENSIVE"

C LOSING THE RING was born of defeat. If the Tories had won the general election of February 1950, Churchill would have been hard-pressed to produce the volume, as serious drafting did not begin until the summer of 1950. Even so, its completion was a close-run thing. The last three chapters were mailed to Houghton Mifflin on 18 September 1951, two days before Attlee announced another election on 25 October.

Churchill threw himself into the new campaign, telling Beaverbrook, "I hope we may both take our revenge for 1945." His reputation as a Cold Warrior became a major issue, with Labour insinuating that a vote for Churchill was a vote for war and the *Daily Mirror* pressing its question "Whose Finger on the Trigger?" with such crudity that Churchill sued for libel. The Tory majority was only eleven, and Churchill privately dubbed his victory "pyrrhic." But he was delighted to get back to Number 10 and immediately proclaimed himself, in wartime style, Prime Minister and Minister of Defence. "Extraordinarily maladroit . . . just folly," sputtered Harold Macmillan in his diary. "It almost justifies the *Daily Mirror!*"[1]

FOR CHURCHILL'S PUBLISHERS, the 1951 election campaign was timed to perfection. *The New York Times* began serializing *Closing the Ring* on 5 October, the day King George VI prorogued Parliament. Its front page showed Churchill in campaigning mode; page 29 excerpted "The Command of the Seas," with a careful footnote this time to Samuel Eliot Morison on Guadalcanal, "whose moving account I have followed." By the time *The New York Times* finished its coverage on 1 November, Churchill was back in Downing Street. "What sweet revenge life and the British people have given to Winston Churchill," the paper editorialized. The *Daily Telegraph*, still cramped by Britain's paper rationing, had to delay serialization until 5 November to ensure adequate space for covering the election, but it also played up the historical echoes. The international situation was "scarcely less critical" than in May 1940, declared Malcolm Muggeridge, the paper's deputy editor, under the headline "The Pilot That Weathered the Storm Takes Charge Again." British papers were full of talk about Churchill's plan to see President Truman in Washington in January. Summitry was back in fashion—another wartime echo.[2]

As it had with volume 4, *Life* squeezed only three articles from *Closing the Ring*, all featuring American themes: "Allied Discords" at Quebec and Cairo, "The Controversies of Teheran," and "Mounting History's Greatest Invasion." Alert for new visual angles, the magazine eschewed almost all photo illustration in favor of David Low's cartoons, most of them wartime but some specially commissioned. And the title page of its second installment featured a Stalin doodle retrieved from a Teheran wastebasket, full of weird shapes and searing lines. "Though one doodle is of course insufficient for personality analysis," *Life* told its readers, a psychoanalyst to whom this had been shown anonymously said it suggested a man "afraid of assassination" who "surrounds himself with a wall."[3]

Houghton Mifflin again faced big, largely self-imposed, problems. The Book-of-the-Month Club judges were not overwhelmed by Churchill's early galleys, and Henry Laughlin had to pull out all the stops: "I think Volume 5 is one of the best volumes because it is a more intimate portrait of Churchill." Having persuaded the club to take it for November 1951—ideal for Christmas sales at a time when Houghton Mifflin faced serious cash-flow problems—Laughlin watched with mounting dismay as Churchill failed to honor the deadlines agreed on in July. The last chapters did not arrive until 19 September, seventeen days late, and were followed by the usual barrage of corrections. Lanius D. Evans, Houghton Mifflin's veteran editor, was aghast at the "devastating" overtakes for book 2 that arrived in late September, requiring new plates for no fewer than twenty-eight pages: "God help us one and all." Even working around the clock, Houghton Mifflin had to postpone publication until 23 November, on the Thanksgiving holiday weekend, which meant missing the deadline for November Book-of-the-Month Club shipments. Fortunately, it was possible to take the December slot, and Laughlin put the best face on matters, noting that the club intended to offer all five volumes as a special Christmas package.[4]

Once publication day came, Houghton Mifflin benefited from the fact that Prime Minister Churchill was much in the news. A typical article in the *Los Angeles Times* was headlined "CHURCHILL VIGOR SETS TOUGH PACE. Aides Pushed to Keep Up with Leader. Nears 77th Birthday Carrying Heavy Work Load." *The New Republic* suspected he could be elected President of the United States. Labour's defeat, pontificated the left-of-center weekly, had freed Churchill "to act on a world scale, so that his bold imagination and incomparable prestige can serve world peace as in the days of the Grand Alliance."[5]

American reviews of the latest volume of memoirs fell more sharply than before into two camps. On the one hand, there was plenty of effusive praise. For Charles J. Rolo in the *Atlantic Monthly*, it was "a majestic triumph of order imposed on chaos—the most enthralling non-fiction reading of the year." As the work "rolls towards its thunderous and victorious climax," wrote Joseph G. Harrison in *The Christian Science Monitor*, "it assumes more and more the form of a great literary symphony." Walter Millis, in the New York *Herald Tribune*, believed the whole oeuvre would stand as "one of the greatest studies of modern war, as it is a great record of an amazing personality." How Churchill worked in 1943–1944 to hold the alliance together, he said, formed "an absorbing struggle in statesmanship" and merited a place on "the basic shelves, along, say, with Machiavelli or Clausewitz."[6]

But others adopted a cooler tone. Ferdinand Kuhn, in *The Washington Post*, considered this "the most defensive of all Churchill's volumes"—both at the time during "a year of bitter quarrels" and in retrospect as he tried to rebut the charges of advocating a Balkan strategy and opposing Overlord. In *The New Republic*, James R. Newman found *Closing the Ring* "less interesting and less finished" than its predecessors and bluntly said it "would have benefited from respectful but vigilant editorial attention." In contrast with Churchill's "superb narration" of his August 1942 meetings with Stalin, his account of Teheran was "prosaic," and although the author was in "fine form" when chronicling military operations, his "political comprehension" was "as usual less impressive"—as shown by support for the Badoglio regime in Italy. Robert Sherwood, in the Sunday *New York Times* book section, confessed to finding the volume "in some respects less interesting, more contentious and much more self-defensive than its predecessors." Sherwood added that "it is all Winston Churchill and it could therefore be nothing less than great" but said he detected "understandable signs of strain in the writing" and made clear that he was not persuaded by Churchill's strategic apologias. "The Prime Minister, while never opposing 'Overlord' outright, worked tirelessly for its postponement to permit various minor operations in the Eastern Mediterranean."[7]

Sherwood's private correspondence about this review reveals the degree of self-censorship that was now routine for any would-be critic of Churchill. He deleted, for instance, the statement that there was "evidence of hastiness, cursoriness, even impatience in 'Closing the Ring,' as if the author wanted to get it down on paper as quickly as possible without benefit of his own matchless elegance and passion for detail." He even wrote to George Marshall, then Truman's Secretary of Defense, to ask advice about including evidence showing "Mr. Churchill's extraordinary ability to reverse himself completely" within a few days. (Marshall replied judiciously that Sherwood was the best judge of what should be said in print.)[8] To Henry Laughlin, Sherwood admitted he was "very disappointed in this fifth volume of Mr. Churchill's great work. It seemed to me that in it he spends far too much time snarling back at various critics or Allied leaders" who disagreed with him and "far too little time setting forth the nature and background of the events themselves." In writing the review, Sherwood said, "I dislocated several vertebrae in the attempt to lean over backwards out of respect for this great man, but he could and should have done much better than this." Laughlin had expected a much more "shattering" review and was very relieved. Send us the osteopath's bill, he told Sherwood cheerfully.[9]

American interest in Churchill was sustained by his visit to Washington, where he met Truman over two days, 7 and 8 January 1952. Although cordial, their talks demonstrated that the era of Anglo-American equality was long gone. Churchill, for instance, vehemently opposed the idea that an American should assume NATO's Atlantic command—"I realize that England is a broken and impoverished power," he told his advisers, "but these fellows bungled the U-boat war and had to come to us for help"—yet eventually he had to give way. And Truman dealt briskly with what one British diplomat called Churchill's "emotional declarations of faith" in Anglo-American relations: "Thank you, Mr. Prime Minister. We might pass that on to be worked out by our advisers." The President, despite affection and respect for an elder statesman, felt Churchill was "increasingly living in the past and talking in terms of conditions no longer existing."[10]

There was some justice in this putdown. Churchill was in many ways trying to relive his finest hour. Preferring familiar faces, he included in his Cabinet men from the war, including Cherwell, Ismay, and Alexander, often in posts for which they were ill suited. He also blocked Norman Brook's move to the Treasury to keep him as Cabinet Secretary and pressed Jock Colville back into service as a

Principal Private Secretary.[11] But Churchill was not simply living in the past. After the Soviets tested their own bomb in 1949, he was keen to reach agreement on when and how America might use nuclear weapons, particularly from bases in Britain. The final communiqué from the Washington conference stated that "use of these bases in an emergency would be a matter for joint decision" by the two governments "in the light of the circumstances prevailing at the time." The Truman administration felt it had retained its freedom of action, but for Britain this formula was an improvement on the previous vacuum. For good or ill, it has governed Anglo-American relations on this matter ever since.[12]

Churchill also hoped to persuade the Americans that they had broken the letter and spirit of wartime agreements by cutting Britain off from postwar nuclear collaboration. He brandished a copy of the 1943 Quebec Agreement in Washington and again thought about making it public—only to be persuaded by Cherwell that this would embarrass Truman and "impair the prospects for U.S. cooperation" at a time of apparent improvement.[13] But these hopes proved vain. In May 1952, Britain tested its own atomic device in Australia. The Australians could provide not only space for testing but, together with South Africa, also essential uranium, and by the end of the year many in Whitehall felt it was time, as Cherwell put it, to stop chasing "the will-of-the-wisp of full American cooperation" and develop a "great Commonwealth enterprise." Churchill agreed that alternatives should be explored but remained hopeful of real transatlantic cooperation. "You must remember that our lives depend on the atomic power of the United States," he told Cherwell in May 1953, "and that many years must pass before we can become independent of them. By that time the Russians will be far more powerful than they are now or we are likely to be." The subsequent history of Britain's self-styled "independent" nuclear deterrent suggests that Churchill was more realistic than Cherwell.[14]

In other ways, too, Churchill had not lost his grip. Behind the scenes, he tried to turn his publishing contacts to national benefit. On 10 January 1952, his old New York friend Bernard Baruch arranged a lunch for Daniel Longwell of *Life* and Arthur Sulzberger and Julius Ochs Adler of *The New York Times*. Mixing rhetoric and reason, Churchill pressed on these leading opinion-formers the merits of British policy on such questions as Egypt and a European army. Having sold them his version of the past, he was now peddling his vision of the future.[15]

In January 1952, Baruch's apartment on East Sixty-sixth Street was also the venue for a casual encounter of long-term consequence. Henry Laughlin was invited to a gathering there in Churchill's honor, where he fell into conversation with Lord Moran. The doctor mentioned he was writing a book about Churchill, to appear after his death, and the publisher began courting him by letter and then in person. On 25 July 1952, Laughlin lunched with Churchill at Chartwell to discuss volume 6 and then, two days later, unknown to Churchill, drove to Moran's country home, near Uckfield in Sussex. After dinner, he was shown three notebooks containing the manuscript Moran had written, running to some 150,000 words. Moran said he wanted to cut that in half because one of the essentials of good writing was selectivity, adding that *The Second World War* was "not comparable in quality with some of Churchill's earlier books" because Churchill had lost "his power of selectivity." The two men sat up until 1:30 in the morning, as Moran read extracts. "I was simply fascinated," Laughlin told his staff. "He sees Churchill's weaknesses as well as his strengths and it is his opinion that in the long run when these become well known there will be an entirely different appraisal of Mr. Churchill than the present." But, said Laughlin, Moran believed that "Mr. Churchill will still stand out as the greatest man of our time and will be no less of a figure for the revelation of his qualities."[16]

Laughlin was ready to sign a contract, offering an advance of £2,000. Moran said he preferred to concentrate on the text, which he hoped would be ready by the following spring. He reiterated that he did not intend to publish until after Churchill's death. But, given the Prime Minister's age and infirmities, neither he nor Laughlin thought that that would be far in the future.[17]

ONCE CHURCHILL WAS BACK in Downing Street in October 1951, Denis Kelly tied up the loose ends for the British edition of *Closing the Ring*. Clementine reclaimed the studio at Hyde Park Gate, moving Charles Wood first into the front room and then out of the house completely in December. Much to his chagrin, Wood had to check the Cassell's proofs from his home in Golders Green.[18]

Cassell's did not publish until 3 September 1952, ten months after serialization in the *Daily Telegraph*, because of the usual combination of paper rationing and printers' strikes. The price had now risen from twenty-five shillings per volume to thirty. This, Desmond Flower of Cassell's assured Churchill, was solely because of increased production costs. Since publication of volume 1 in 1948, the price of paper had doubled, and printing rates had risen by 30 percent. Flower said that only the enormous print run of over 275,000 kept the price as low as it was. By now, Cassell's had arranged with the Reprint Society, a subscription club with 120,000 members, to bring out a special edition more cheaply. That version of *The Gathering Storm* appeared in the autumn of 1950; *Their*

Finest Hour followed in 1951, and *The Grand Alliance* a year later. Each was priced at seven shillings and sixpence, helping to bring Winston's war to a wider audience.[19]

Despite the delay, 3 September 1952 was an auspicious date for publication, being the thirteenth anniversary of the start of the war, and as usual a Churchill volume attracted considerable attention, including two leading articles in *The Times* and editorials in *The Manchester Guardian* and *The Scotsman*. At the political extremes, reaction was predictable: a diatribe from the communist *Daily Worker*, a rhapsody in the Tory *Yorkshire Post*, whose reviewer called it "the master-work of a master-mind. Distinction shines on every page." In the middle ground, too, there were plenty of plaudits: A. J. Cummings in the *News Chronicle* praised the "gusto and freshness" of the narrative, while *The Evening News* called it a "tremendous story" told with "dignity, humour, magnanimity and forebearance." Both pieces paid tribute to Churchill's double act as maker and writer of history. As usual, reviewers were oblivious to the Syndicate's contribution. "Scrutator" in the *Sunday Times* noted that it was unprecedented to complete a major book while Prime Minister. How did he find the time? "Mr. Churchill chooses his titles with the greatest care," said the *Western Mail*; they were "the envy of the best newspaper caption writers." As we have seen, Churchill credited Denis Kelly for suggesting "Closing the Ring."[20]

Yet one detects in some quarters a mood of anticlimax. Writing in the *Daily Mail*, Alfred Duff Cooper, now ennobled as Viscount Norwich, felt the volume was "less enthralling" than its predecessors. But this, he added, was "no fault" of Churchill's: "Bad news makes better reading than good news and the news that this volume contains is almost entirely good." *The Manchester Guardian*'s reviewer also found "less that is exciting and less that is new" in the latest volume, ascribing this to the scale and diversity of the war by 1943–1944, so that "the treatment is, almost necessarily, episodic rather than consecutive and comprehensive." But for many reviewers in Britain, as in America, the root reason for a feeling of letdown was that in this volume Churchill was "on the defensive," to quote Alfred Ryan in *The Times Literary Supplement*, and "more markedly autobiographical," according to Chester Wilmot in *The Observer*. The need to justify himself against wartime and postwar critics required more documents and argument, which, said John Connell in *Time and Tide*, made the book "less attractive and romantic" than his "unforgettable" volume on 1940, though "far more engrossing for the contemporary historian."[21]

As in America, several reviewers were not persuaded by Churchill's self-defense. Milton Shulman, in a lengthy piece for the *Evening Standard*, examined the Prime Minister's "serious doubts" about Overlord, citing evidence in the documents that contradicted Churchill's professed commitment to the plan. For Roger Rider in *Tribune*, Churchill's contrasting policy toward communists in Greece and in Yugoslavia showed that he was "a man for whom principles are less important than day-to-day practice." For Richard Crossman, the Oxford don, it all showed the dangers of "Totalwarmanship." He argued in *The New Statesman and Nation* that Churchill's volume gave the lie to books by Hanson Baldwin and Chester Wilmot arguing that the Americans were so obsessed with victory that they played into Stalin's hands despite warnings from the farsighted British. In reality, suggested Crossman, Churchill was little wiser than Roosevelt. "Far too busy and far too happy" planning Anzio, he never bothered about "the political consequences in Italy of his mulish support for Badoglio." Obsessed with "amateur generalship," he failed to see the contradiction between his attitudes toward communists in Greece and in Yugoslavia. Whereas Sir James Squire in *The Illustrated London News* portrayed Roosevelt as an "Innocent Abroad" when dealing with Stalin, Crossman asserted that "nearly all the tragic blunders which led up to Yalta and Potsdam were committed in perfect Anglo-American accord."[22]

Crossman had already sketched this theme of Churchill the appeaser when reviewing volume 4, but it was not his hobbyhorse alone. *The Times*'s leading article on publication day found it striking how Churchill and Roosevelt consistently "smoothed out" friction with Stalin and wondered whether, "without harm to the war effort," the Soviet leader could have been "handled with more resolution." Sir James Grigg felt when Secretary of War in 1943 that "Winston gives in to [the Americans] too much" and was "too polite to the Russians," and he made the same point in 1952 when assessing volume 5 for the *Daily Telegraph*. Churchill was "much clearer-eyed than Roosevelt" but "not so single-eyed as Stalin," Grigg said. Looking back, he "should have been more wary of his two co-adjutors." This would be a major issue for volume 6.[23]

The sense of frustration, even anticlimax, expressed by several reviewers of volume 5 was tempered by hope for things to come. The "reader will look forward with impatience to the climax of the next volume," concluded Alfred Ryan. Robert Sherwood told Henry Laughlin he hoped Churchill would "take a lot more trouble over the next tremendous volume." But Churchill, age seventy-seven, was now back in Downing Street. "It will be a miracle if he finishes it in the midst of all his new responsibilities," wrote Ferdinand Kuhn in *The Washington Post*. "But Churchill himself is a miracle; shall we ever look on his like again?"[24]

VI.

TRIUMPH AND TRAGEDY

1944–1945
1950–1954

A VERY DIPLOMATIC HISTORY

T HE FINAL VOLUME of *The Second World War* was published in America on 30 November 1953 and in Britain on 26 April 1954. In the preface, dated 30 September 1953, Churchill stated that "the original text was completed nearly two years ago. Other duties have since confined me to general supervision of the processes of checking the statements of fact contained in these pages and obtaining the necessary consents to the publication of the original documents." In the newspaper serials, he wanted it said that "the book was finished before I took Office."[1]

This claim was completely untrue. The "original text" printed out on the eve of Churchill's return to 10 Downing Street was a far cry from the version eventually published.[2] After October 1951, the Syndicate undertook a vast amount of work to turn an annotated set of documents into a publishable text. And Churchill made numerous revisions to ensure that his account of the last year of the war conformed to current diplomatic imperatives. His supreme goal as premier was to defuse the Cold War; as historian, he therefore had no desire to exacerbate East-West tension. So Churchill ended his history of the Second World War as he had begun it, with his eyes on the present as well as the past. The result was a fascinating but very diplomatic account of the origins of the Cold War.

ALTHOUGH CHURCHILL'S 1947 deal with the *Daily Telegraph* spoke of five volumes, it noted that "Mr. Churchill does not bind himself to such number," though there would be no additional payment for more than five.[3] The issue of a sixth volume emerged starkly in May 1949 when the publishers had their first sight of the draft of volume 3. This hardly extended beyond U.S. entry into the war, so Churchill would clearly need more than two volumes to cover the rest of the conflict. Cassell's and Houghton Mifflin had already done so well financially from the memoirs as to be almost embarrassed and were quite ready to pay for a sixth volume even though not contractually obliged. *Life* and *The New York Times*, on the other hand, had agreed to pay a massive $1,150,000 for American serial rights to the five volumes, as well as to fund Churchill's "working vacations." Disappointed with volume 3—from which *Life* eventually squeezed only three installments—they were ready to wind up the whole project. Unable to persuade Churchill to extend volume 3 up to the North African landings of November 1942, Daniel Longwell said *Life* and *The New York Times* would reluctantly publish portions of a sixth volume if Churchill was obdurate, but they would stick to the contract and not offer any further payment.[4]

Churchill was indeed obdurate—as Longwell discovered in their confrontational lunch on 16 May 1949 (see chapter 14, above)—and the Americans backed off, aware that the author held most of the cards.[5] By April 1950, an understanding had emerged. Camrose, Reves, Cassell's, and Houghton Mifflin were ready between them to offer £50,000 for the last volume (now worth $140,000, since the pound was devalued to $2.80 in August 1949). Even if, as Churchill noted, £35,000 of that would be needed to pay the Syndicate and his printers at Chiswick Press, the sixth volume was now financially worthwhile, whatever the opinions in New York. By the time Churchill took office in October 1951, the package had grown to £60,000, with up to £35,000 payable on 1 May 1952 for an acceptable draft and the rest a year later.[6]

Emery Reves in particular stood to gain from additional volumes. His original 1947 deal with Houghton Mifflin gave him half the income from any U.S. book-club sale and 15 percent on the trade edition once Houghton Mifflin had recouped its $250,000 payments to the author for the original five volumes. This they had almost done by November 1950, even before volume 4 was published.[7] Thus, Reves would gain substantially from a sixth American volume. On the other hand, *Triumph and Tragedy* placed Reves in a difficult position in his capacity as agent for the translation rights. Most of the foreign-language publishers had issued *The Second World War* on a subscription basis, offering readers a fixed price for five volumes. If his story were not finished within that compass, he opined, the publishers would probably be in breach of contract and might have to give subscribers the last volume free. In November 1950, Reves therefore urged Churchill to complete the military story of the war in volume 5, "mentioning only *briefly*, whatever is *unavoidable*, of the Yalta meeting." Churchill, already deep into *Closing the Ring*, dismissed the suggestion as "quite impossible."[8] The following spring, Reves secured a letter from Churchill for circulation to the foreign publishers. Dated 24 May 1951, it explained that a sixth volume had become "indispensable if the tale is to be told properly." This was not the virtual apology that Reves had wanted, but he had to be content.[9]

Life's top executives feared that Churchill might be "stringing out the book to eight or ten volumes." It might never be finished if, as seemed likely, he returned to power. The working vacations also grated: by March 1951, *Life* and *The New York Times* had paid out nearly $52,000, and Daniel Longwell felt strongly that "some provision or settlement should be made for these expenses."[10] In May 1951, he flew to Britain determined to hold Churchill to the contract, which obliged them to make the fifth payment only on delivery of whatever was the final volume. "To my agreeable surprise," he cabled Henry Luce, "our industrious friend has volume six blocked out in galleys with enough work done to make some sort of publication possible." Longwell and Julius Ochs Adler of *The New York Times* were so relieved that they agreed, on receipt of volume 5, to release two thirds of the final installment of $230,000. This, Longwell told his colleagues, "puts us in a good position to really drive for [volume] VI."[11] This split deal—$150,000 in the summer of 1951 for volume 5 and the remaining $80,000 on delivery of volume 6—gave Churchill some money up front while safeguarding the position of his American serial publishers that he should not be rewarded for verbosity.

SERIOUS WORK on volume 6 had begun in late 1950. An outline dated 20 November summarized highlights of the last year of the war, running from D-Day to when "I am kicked out" (a phrase that shows how the election defeat of July 1945 still rankled).[12] In six weeks during the Commons recess and at Marrakech over Christmas, twenty-three chapters were outlined by Churchill and Kelly. But, as Winston admitted to Clementine, most were largely "a stringing together of telegrams, minutes and other documents with their introductions and tail pieces."[13] Work on volume 6 then languished, until on 20 September 1951 Churchill received Attlee's announcement of a general election.

Suddenly, Churchill told the Syndicate that, if the Tories won, he wished to submit "a provisional version" of volume 6 "on or soon after October 26"—the day after the election. Allen, Deakin, Ismay, and Pownall worked flat out to finish their various contributions. Then Churchill changed his mind, telling Kelly on 19 October that the matter was "no longer urgent."[14] The reason for this panic spasm is unclear, but it probably signified his desire to claim that the volume had been "complete," at least in the form of a "literary property," before he became Prime Minister. This was also Norman Brook's concern as Cabinet Secretary. "Whatever the rules," he told Churchill on 16 November 1951, "many people will be disturbed if they thought you were devoting any substantial amount of time to the book now that you are in office again." Brook favored a preemptive statement that before the election volume 5 had been delivered to the publishers and volume 6 had been "submitted to the appropriate authority for scrutiny on behalf of the Government," though "some revision" would be required before publication. Churchill refused to issue such a statement, but he did sanction the disclaimer in the eventual preface.[15]

In the first months of his new premiership, Churchill had very little time for the book, leaving it to the Syndicate to complete a full revision of the volume during the winter of 1951–1952. Known as the "First S Revise," this was intended to meet Churchill's contractual obligation to submit some kind of text by 1 May 1952 in order to trigger the first £35,000 of the extra payment arranged for volume 6. During the summer of 1952, Kelly reworked numerous chapters, trying to reduce the documents and tighten the prose, and this gave Churchill plenty to deal with while vacationing with Beaverbrook on the French Riviera in September—so much so that he felt able to wind up the Syndicate (and stop paying Allen, Deakin, and Pownall) at the end of October. "There will be no more group work on the book after this month," Churchill told his assistants, "as I shall not be able to do anything more on it until just before it is published. I cannot at this stage say when that is likely to be, or whether indeed it will be published while I am in office." As a token of his appreciation, he invited Allen, Deakin, and Pownall to dinner at Number 10 on 27 October. It was a splendid evening, to judge by their letters of appreciation, and in the afterglow all three volunteered to do anything they could, gratis, to see the volume through to publication.[16]

Because of Churchill's political burdens, more of the text than ever before was drafted by the Syndicate as if from him. The chapters on the war in Burma and the Pacific were largely the work of Allen and Pownall, the latter produced all the basic military narrative on the war in Europe, and Deakin devoted a great deal of time to the final conferences, especially Yalta. "The German Surrender" was written almost entirely by the Syndicate—Churchill's only substantial addition was two paragraphs prefacing his victory broadcast on 13 May 1945. Ismay was no longer an effective member of the Syndicate, for in October 1951 Churchill had appointed him Commonwealth Secretary in the new government and then, six months later, sent him to Paris as NATO's first Secretary General. Afterward, Ismay contributed anecdotes on Yalta and Potsdam and hastily read some draft chapters in his spare time—his comments on book 2 are dated "Boxing Day 1952"—but, overall, his role in *Triumph and Tragedy* was marginal.[17]

By contrast, Denis Kelly had now become a central figure. Not center stage, because he was still very much the backroom boy—on the invitation list for the Syndicate dinner at Downing Street Churchill instructed firmly "*Not* Kelly"— but certainly in the role of stage manager.[18] In November and December 1950, he helped Churchill assemble the documents, often providing the connecting narrative skeleton himself. In May and June 1951, he went through the transcripts of the Yalta and Potsdam conferences, laboriously turning reported speech into first-person memoir—"Marshal Stalin asked what were the Prime Minister's views about Hungary," for instance, became "Stalin asked what I thought of Hungary."[19] Kelly's summer 1952 abridgments of numerous Syndicate chapters were usually accepted by Churchill, sometimes with explicit commendation, in the tone of schoolmaster to pupil.[20] These rewrites were mostly mechanical labor— Kelly's intellectual input to the book did not compare with that of Pownall, Deakin, or even Allen—and some chapters never fully transcended their origins in official transcripts, as Norman Brook kept saying about those on Potsdam. But the hours Kelly put in were essential to the production of a readable narrative. Discarded in one file is a note he scrawled to Churchill's secretaries after a late night at Chartwell: "JEP & Co. Please do not call me till 8.0. V. sleepy.—Den."[21]

Despite all their labors, the members of the Syndicate maintained the fiction that this was Churchill's book. "I hope my contribution will be of help," observed Kelly in August 1952, enclosing the Syndicate's rewrite of book 1, "and you will enjoy reading what I feel is one of the best books you have yet written."[22] Yet the fiction did rest on a foundation of fact. As before, Churchill made a first selection of his wartime minutes and telegrams for printing during 1949 and found time to come back to them again in the spring of 1952 to glean additional documents for the appendix. This was not merely a cursory glance—from a minute of 6 August 1944 he carefully removed a reference to "Boniface No. 5034" in order to safeguard the Ultra secret.[23] Working from the documents, he dictated many paragraphs of reminiscences—for instance, about his October 1944 meeting with Stalin or about witnessing the Rhine crossing on 23 March 1945. Back in office, Churchill reviewed Kelly's revision of the text in September 1952 and had another go at it after Christmas, continuing on the *Queen Mary* en route to the United States. "I have spent three mornings on this tangled Chapter, but I think it is greatly improved," Churchill wrote Kelly on 2 January 1953 after grappling with "A Fateful Decision."[24] In Washington, he and President-elect Eisenhower discussed prospects for a new conference with Stalin, then Churchill spent the rest of January in Jamaica reworking chapters on the Potsdam conference of July 1945—the last Western summit with the Soviet leader. In short, this was still Churchill's book. He may not have written most of the words, but he decisively set its tone and determined when—and even whether—it would be published.

CHURCHILL'S MAIN OBJECT in *Triumph and Tragedy* was to prove he had been a farsighted prophet of the Soviet threat. This was not easy, for two reasons. First, he had been in charge of British foreign policy in 1944–1945, carving up the Balkans with Stalin in Moscow in October and reaching a Polish settlement with him at Yalta the following February. Both these actions needed considerable explanation. Second, he wanted to shift responsibility for Western mistakes onto the Americans. Nothing, he said in August 1950, would convince them of the reality of the Russian danger.[25] He let Roosevelt down gently as a dying President, heroic but no longer effective, and concentrated on his successor, Harry Truman, and the military commander in Europe, Eisenhower. Yet at the time of writing Truman was still the serving U.S. President, who might run again, and Ike a much-touted though undeclared presidential aspirant. Consequently, Churchill was emphatic that volume 6 could not appear before the November 1952 election, and reports of his veto started appearing in American and European newspapers.[26] On 17 March 1952, Churchill sent the fretful Emery Reves a letter for distribution to foreign publishers stating that volume 6 was "already in a very advanced state" and would definitely be published, but it was "too early yet" to give an exact date.[27]

In early 1952, perhaps in some desperation, he had revived Reves's idea, dismissed out of hand in 1950, to publish book 1 soon and book 2 much later. This would give publishers something to go on with, while deferring all the sensitive material about the period from Yalta to Potsdam. He tried the idea on Daniel Longwell while in New York in January 1952, giving him a quick read of book 1, but the editor of *Life* was not persuaded. "Much as I like this book," he wrote Churchill on 21 January, "I don't think it would stand as a separate book, and I would seriously advise you against the idea of seven volumes." Kelly told Churchill that the Syndicate was "confident that a suitable version" of book 2 could be produced, albeit "with care and time."[28] *The Struggle for Europe* by Chester Wilmot, deeply critical of the Americans in 1945 for their credulity about Stalin and their withdrawal from Central Europe, had just appeared, and the Syndicate felt it had "eased our path by letting a number of cats out of the bag," which meant that Churchill did not have to hammer those points so hard.[29] When starting his memoirs, Churchill had benefited from the absence of rival accounts. When finishing them, he could shelter where necessary behind the verdicts of others.

The November 1952 election did clarify the American situation. Truman had decided not to run, and Churchill therefore felt freer to be candid about the President. On the other hand, he did want to quote extensively from their correspondence in 1945, and that required Truman's permission. On 30 March 1953, he asked to reproduce "a dozen personal messages" from the President. Although willing to paraphrase them, he told Truman disingenuously, "I prefer to be judged by what I wrote at the time, rather than rely on present narrative and argument which is liable to be influenced by after-events." His letter caught up with the ex-President in Hawaii. Truman promised a proper reply when he returned home from vacation but was "sure that as soon as I have an opportunity to look at my files there will be no difficulty about granting your request." A month later, however, Truman's tone had changed. Back in Independence, Missouri, he had talked with William Hillman, a local journalist advising him about his own memoirs, who noted that Churchill had not supplied texts of his messages, so Truman could not judge the "meaning and significance" of his own responses. Although Churchill was "a most honorable man," Hillman added, he was "a British Statesman with typical retrospective flexibility, no matter what he says in his letter to the contrary." On 20 May, Truman asked Churchill to paraphrase the telegrams, making a lame excuse about not being able "to get at the originals at the present time" because his files were "not in shape." And so Denis Kelly spent a good deal of time turning Truman's messages into third-person narrative.[30]

A bigger issue after November 1952 was what to say about Truman's successor. Churchill asked Brook, who had already read several versions of the volume, to go through the text yet again in the light of Eisenhower's election. The Cabinet Secretary identified two chapters, relating to the race for Berlin and Prague, which he thought should be softened, and most of his detailed suggestions were adopted.[31] Brook also drafted a letter for Churchill to send to the new President, and this was dispatched, virtually unchanged, on 9 April 1953. "Now that you have assumed supreme political office in your country," Churchill wrote, "I am most anxious that nothing should be published which might seem to others to threaten our current relations in our public duties or to impair the sympathy and understanding which exist between our two countries." With that in mind, he said he had gone over his text again with "great pains." "There was in fact little controversy in those years; but I have been careful to ensure that the few differences of opinion which arose are so described that even ill-disposed people will be unable now to turn them to mischievous account." Even so, Churchill offered to send "those passages which refer directly to yourself," if the President wished.[32]

Although Eisenhower said he was too busy to look at the extracts, he asked Churchill to send them to Walter Bedell Smith, his wartime Chief of Staff and now an Undersecretary at the State Department. The long-suffering Brook went over the material yet again, and in the end eight whole chapters were sent, rather than short extracts—another indication of how anxious Churchill was to avoid transatlantic friction.[33] And, as we shall see, when polite reservations were expressed by Bedell Smith about two chapters on the invasion of southern France in August 1944, Churchill went further than "Beetle" asked (or Brook advised) in further revisions.[34] This solicitude is all the more striking since he was not impressed with the new President. After their talks in January 1953, Churchill dubbed Eisenhower "a real man of limited stature"; by July, he considered him "weak and stupid" and bitterly regretted the Democrats' defeat in 1952.[35] But scoring historical or personal points now mattered less to Churchill than not damaging his beloved special relationship.

THE DELICACY of *Triumph and Tragedy* for Anglo-American relations explains much of Churchill's procrastination in 1952–1953, but not all of it. On 29 April 1953, Camrose apprised Laughlin, also chafing at the bit, of a recent dinner with Churchill:

> What is worrying him today is the Russian aspect. He does not think now that the book in its present form is likely to be injurious to Anglo-American relations, but if the U.S.S.R. peace and disarmament overtures assume serious form and conferences take place, he feels a grave doubt as to the propriety of the Prime Minister of England publishing a book which contains strong criticism of Russia's conduct of the past.[36]

Over dinner, Churchill had focused on the chance of talks with Stalin's successors, following the dictator's sudden death on 5 March. It is clear, however, that the hope of a new summit with the Russians leading to détente, on which Churchill had been speaking since 1950, had influenced his approach to *Triumph and Tragedy* from the beginning.

Once Germany was defeated, Churchill tells his readers near the start of the chapter "Western Strategic Divergences," "Russian imperialism and the Communist creed saw and set no bounds to their progress and ultimate dominion. . . . Soviet Russia had become a mortal danger to the free world." These sentences were dictated by Churchill at Marrakech on 23 December 1950. So was another forceful passage, intended for "The Final Advance" though eventually not used, which described how "at every point" in the spring of 1945 "the Russians were seen to be thrusting forward with utmost strength, and endeavouring to peg out the largest possible claims."[37] Many of the most trenchant criticisms of Soviet policy in *Triumph and Tragedy* date from around Christmas 1950, and this is not surprising. At the end of November, Communist China had entered the Korean War, driving back the American-led UN forces deep into the south. In the West, it was generally assumed (rightly, as we now know) that both the North Korean attack and the Chinese intervention had Soviet blessing. Churchill hoped the UN forces had prepared a proper defensive line and would "teach the Chinese the sort of lessons we learned upon the Somme and Passchendaele." He sent a cable in this vein on 27 December to General Douglas MacArthur, the UN commander based in Tokyo. The collapse of the UN line deeply distressed him. "There must be something very wrong in the whole lay-out," he told Anthony Eden. According to recollections of Denis Kelly in 1985, one evening at Marrakech Churchill became so agitated that he even talked of flying to Tokyo to sort things out, before thinking better of the idea the next morning.[38]

Churchill's depiction of Soviet policy in *Triumph and Tragedy* therefore reflects the mood of 1950–1951 as well as the events of 1944–1945. Yet that is not the whole story. Even in the most stridently anti-Soviet passages, Churchill generally avoids attacking Stalin personally. In his "Notes on Volume VI," Churchill recalled how the Yalta agreements were broken but suggested that this "probably was due not to bad faith on the part of Stalin and Molotov, but that when they got back home they were held up by their colleagues." This intriguing observation echoes his wartime comments about Stalin being a not entirely free agent.[39] Volume 6 actually contains some very positive asides about the Soviet leader. In "Prelude to a Moscow Visit" Churchill tells us, "I felt acutely the need to see Stalin, with whom I always considered one could talk as one human being to another." The draft of this passage was sent to the printer on 26 November 1950, just as China entered the Korean War. And at the end of May 1951, revising his account of Stalin at Potsdam, he added that it "was the last time I saw this amazing and gigantic personality."[40]

On 4 November 1951, little over a week after returning to Downing Street, Churchill sent a cable to Stalin. "Now that I am again in charge of His Majesty's Government, let me reply to your farewell telegram from Potsdam in 1945, 'Greetings. Winston Churchill.'" Stalin replied the next day with a short note of thanks, and Churchill cabled Truman, "we are again on speaking terms." On

6 November, the Prime Minister read the Commons a message he had sent to Stalin on 29 April 1945, warning that a quarrel between "the English-speaking peoples" and "you and the countries you dominate" would "tear the world to pieces." He then promised "a supreme effort to bridge the gulf between the two worlds, so that each can live its life, if not in friendship at least without the fear, the hatreds and the frightful waste of the 'cold war.'"[41]

The 1945 documents were live in his mind from working on the memoirs, and his message to Stalin was almost saying, "Let us resume from where we were so rudely interrupted six years ago." This was, however, easier said than done. Concerting policy with Washington came first, and that was complicated by Truman's reluctance for a special relationship with Britain and then by the paralysis of the election. But on several occasions during 1952, Churchill spoke privately of his desire for, after the U.S. election, a joint approach to Stalin, leading perhaps to a modern Congress of Vienna at which the Potsdam conference would be reopened and concluded. He also observed in June 1952 that "while Stalin was alive we were safer from attack than if he died and his lieutenants started scrambling for the succession." Reminiscing with Soviet Ambassador Andrei Gromyko in February 1953 about wartime summits, he said his meeting with Stalin in Moscow in October 1944 was "the highest level we ever reached."[42]

There are signs, however, that Churchill's hopes of doing business with the Soviet dictator had waned by early 1953. He was shaken by the purges in Eastern Europe and declared that "under these conditions the chances of achieving anything with Stalin were almost nil, whereas the dangers of failure would be very great."[43] And he responded with alacrity to the sudden news of Stalin's death on 5 March, sensing a relaxation of tension under the new reformist leadership. Churchill also felt freer to act now that the skeptical Eden was away from the Foreign Office for major surgery. On 11 May 1953, after lengthy preparation, the Prime Minister outlined his ideas to the Commons for a "conference at the highest level" between "the leading powers," unburdened by a "ponderous or rigid agenda" and "hordes of experts"—his preferred mode of summitry throughout the war. If Soviet-German relations could be improved, he hoped Moscow would then relax its grip on Eastern Europe, allowing Poland, at the heart of the Allied breakdown in 1945, to be "a friendly power and a buffer" for the Soviet Union while no longer "a puppet state."[44]

Churchill did not expect to end the Cold War, but he hoped for an "easement" of tension—what would later be known as détente. His goal, however illusory, was to unmake, or at least to remake, history—to pick up the pieces of 1944–1945 and build a stable, more peaceful Europe. Hence his reservations about volume 6: nothing must be said about the evils of the past that could prejudice a better future.

So Churchill reviewed his text once more, with an eye now to the Soviet side of the Cold War divide. In the summer of 1953, he modified a couple of tendentious chapter titles. "A Soviet Insult" became "Soviet Suspicions" and "A Soviet Trap" was changed to "Growing Friction with Russia." He also rejected part of Kelly's draft preface explaining that the volume was called *Triumph and Tragedy* because "the complete victory of the most successful combination in modern times condemned more than half of Europe to a tyranny no less terrible and perhaps more enduring than that which had been vanquished by the Grand Alliance." Instead, Churchill adapted Kelly's alternative: "the overwhelming victory of the Grand Alliance has failed so far to bring general peace to our anxious world."[45]

A related sensitivity concerned the Polish communists, led by Boleslaw Bierut, brought to power by the Red Army in 1944 and 1945 but ruling a country whose historic russophobia and ardent Catholicism made it a loose brick in the Soviet edifice. The Poles, for instance, were working with neutral countries such as Switzerland to resolve the Korean impasse. It therefore seemed prudent for Churchill to tone down some of his comments about those leaders. In his November 1950 dictation about meetings with the Polish communists in Moscow in October 1944, Churchill said Eden had described Bierut and his colleagues as the Skunk, the Rat, and the Snake. "I liked this very much," Churchill added. But after queries by both Eden and Norman Brook, he scribbled in August 1952: "I will delete if I am in office."[46] He also took out a reference in a letter he wrote in October 1944 to Bierut's group as "the greatest villains imaginable."[47]

Equally important for *Triumph and Tragedy* was Churchill's postwar rethinking about Yugoslavia. In May 1945, it seemed that the race between Tito's Partisans and British troops to seize Trieste might trigger a new war. As Churchill noted in a draft of 23 December 1950, Tito was then viewed as the Soviets' "spear-head."[48] In reality, however, Tito was his own man, with distinctive regional ambitions. After breaking with Stalin in 1948, he developed his own model of socialism and opened up to the West. In February 1953, he signed a treaty of friendship with Greece and Turkey—both members of NATO—and the following month he made a state visit to London, where Churchill found him "full of commonsense" but "very anxious" about what would happen if he was attacked by the Soviets. A few days later, the Prime Minister asked his Cabinet Secretary to review the text yet again, in case it contained anything "unduly sharp" about Tito. Brook found "little, if anything, which you need to be concerned about" but made minor suggestions, most of which were incorporated.[49] In consequence, volume 6, unlike its predecessor, has very little to say about Yugoslavia, even though the country was central to Churchill's "percentages" agreement with Stalin in October 1944 about spheres of influence in the Balkans and his subsequent alarm about the iron curtain closing across Eastern Europe. His account of the Trieste crisis treats it largely as a long-standing territorial dispute and avoids denigrating Tito. A measure of how times had changed was Churchill's redefinition of where the line of the iron curtain should be drawn. At Fulton in March 1946 he used the sculpted phrase "From Stettin in the Baltic to Trieste in the Adriatic," but in January 1953 he noted that this was no longer appropriate—"Tito has come over and Trieste is certainly not Russian." After much tinkering he settled on an alliterative revision: "from Lübeck to Linz."[50]

CHURCHILL'S ACCOUNT of the origins of the Cold War was therefore written with one eye on his bid to transcend it—if not to restore the Grand Alliance then at least to strengthen ties with Washington and reduce tension with Moscow. "I don't want to do anything which will make things worse," he kept telling Denis Kelly.[51] At times, he thought silence might be the best policy, but his publishers were becoming deeply frustrated—"the more time that passes, the more remote the events and personalities become," Daniel Longwell reminded him in December 1952.[52] Moreover, the remaining money for volume 6 would not be paid until final delivery and, as usual, Churchill was short of ready cash.[53] He kept juggling these conflicting arguments and also the burdens of office—in the spring of 1953 he was preparing his 11 May speech, making arrangements for the Queen's Coronation on 2 June and planning a summit with Eisenhower in Bermuda in July. But on 15 May, with the big speech over, Camrose cabled Houghton Mifflin: "Unless anything at present unforeseeable happens in world politics, am now promised release [of] proofs in June."[54]

Nothing momentous occurred in world politics, but disaster overtook Churchill. On 23 June, after entertaining the Italian Prime Minister over dinner at 10 Downing Street, he slumped in a chair. "They have put too much on me. Foreign affairs"—his voice trailed off. Discreetly, the guests and waiters were shuffled out, and Churchill was helped upstairs to bed. Lord Moran diagnosed another cerebral spasm, this time on a massive scale. Amazingly, the Prime Minister got through a Cabinet meeting the next morning, with colleagues noting only that he seemed very white and unusually quiet. But Friday, 26 June, he was almost completely paralyzed down his left side. Moran did not think he would survive the weekend, and newspapers prepared their obituaries. "Great Leader in War and Peace" ran the intended editorial in Camrose's *Daily Telegraph,* which said millions around the world would mourn his passing, "for they know well that if he had never lived they might not be alive to-day."[55]

Once more, however, Churchill displayed his formidable appetite for life. As he began to rally, a cabal of press lords and friends—Beaverbrook, Bracken, and Camrose—conspired to keep news of his stroke out of the papers. Medical bulletins said only that the Prime Minister needed "a complete rest" from his "very arduous duties."[56] His private secretaries plus Norman Brook and son-in-law Christopher Soames kept the business of government ticking along. The story of this remarkable cover-up—inconceivable in current politics—is now well-known. Less often appreciated is that it was also the context in which Churchill finished his war memoirs.

The latest proof of "Crossing the Rhine" was initialed by him in a very shaky hand with the date 29 June. That day, he also read "Western Strategic Divergences." This was not serious work, but it was evidence of mental activity.[57] Churchill was trying to be a model patient—even abstaining from brandy for a month (he drank Cointreau instead)—and by mid-July Moran discerned real progress. On the seventeenth, Churchill wrote Eisenhower again about their postponed summit; four days later, he reviewed Bedell Smith's comments on the chapters about Ike's wartime strategy. Recuperating over the next few weeks, he kept up his efforts on both fronts. "I can do something with the Russians which no one else can do," he told Moran on 16 August. "That is the only reason why I am clinging to office. But I have no mental zeal. I don't want to do things." Then he added, "I can correct proofs, of course; that is no effort," and he showed Moran a galley about his "percentages" deal with Stalin over the Balkans in 1944. That was transacted, he said, "on the spot in a few minutes. You see, the people at the top can do these things, which others can't do."[58]

During August, Churchill tinkered with the latest set of proofs. Even at this stage, his historical curiosity was not dulled. On 20 August, Walter Graebner was one of the lunch guests at Chartwell. After the second bottle of champagne had been emptied and the cigars lit (Churchill had now renounced abstinence), work commenced on "The Battle of Leyte Gulf." This was probably the least important chapter of *Triumph and Tragedy*—even Churchill had no input into U.S. naval tactics in the Philippines—but it was a complex battle, which Allen's account and Kelly's revisions had still not clarified to his satisfaction. "To read again with maps with Commodore Allen," he had scribbled on the previous draft. That was the purpose of the lunch. They did not adjourn until a quarter to five.[59]

Churchill continued fiddling with chapters into September. But newspaper serialization was now set for the end of October, and Houghton Mifflin was locked into a Book-of-the-Month Club publication in December. "As has been the case so often in the past, we are in desperate straits in our efforts to meet our schedule," moaned Henry Laughlin on 20 August, hoping to wheedle the latest set of proofs out of Churchill's secretaries. Yet desperation did not cloud his satisfaction. "All who have read Volume Six think it magnificent," he cabled Churchill, "perhaps the best, a fitting triumph to your personal narrative of [the] Second World War."[60] Laughlin's pleasure was genuine, and Churchill indeed had cause for satisfaction. His book told how triumph crumbled into tragedy. Its completion, against all the odds, was a story of tragedy ending in triumph.

CHAPTER 29

OVERLORD AND UNDERDOG

I N B O O K 1 of *Triumph and Tragedy*, Churchill takes his readers from
D-Day on 6 June 1944 to "Christmas at Athens." This was a time of spectacular Allied victories in both Eastern and Western Europe but also of mounting strain among the Big Three, and Churchill became increasingly aware of his
inferior position in the triumvirate. In February 1945, he talked of Britain as a
"small lion" in the company of "a huge Russian bear" and "a great American elephant," but he hoped it "would prove to be the lion which knew the way."[1] In the
memoirs, however, the second half of 1944 is presented as a period of promise —
"The Tide of Victory" — in contrast to his increasing disillusion in 1945. (In the
May 1951 draft, the two books were entitled simply "Triumph" and "Tragedy.")[2]
Although there is some truth in his dichotomy, many of the problems of 1945
were actually rooted in the events of 1944.

IN MAY 1951, Churchill told the Syndicate that three chapters must suffice to
take the military story from D-Day to the Battle of the Bulge.[3] Eventually, there
were four, but this is only a small proportion of the nineteen chapters in book 1.
As usual, Pownall provided the operational narrative, into which Churchill
added his own documents and reminiscences of visits to the front. Some of the
latter are readable and vivid — such as the anecdote about Churchill badgering
the navy to open fire on German batteries from a destroyer off the Normandy
coast on 12 June 1944. "This is the only time I have ever been on board a naval
vessel when she fired 'in anger,'" he remarks. It rounded off "a most interesting

and enjoyable day."[4] But Churchill was not intellectually engaged in writing about the Normandy campaign. The great battles in France, Belgium, and Holland—though much larger in scale than Tobruk or Alamein—are described in a fraction of the space, and in Churchill's files one finds nothing of the animated argument conducted between him and Pownall over commanders, tactics, and tanks in the Desert War. Norman Brook regretted the lost opportunities—"You will probably wish to heighten the key in which the Arnhem story is told," he noted in August 1951—and Denis Kelly pressed the same point. Given his earlier interest in counterfactuals, Churchill might have been expected to reflect on the narrow failure of the Allied airborne landing across the lower Rhine. But there is only a brief aside that the "daring stroke" at Arnhem was "the greatest operation of its kind yet attempted."[5] This was a far cry from his extensive treatment of the German paratroop assault on Crete in volume 3.

Parts of the military story still could not be told. Although Churchill comments on the "remarkable" success of Allied deception operations in persuading the Germans that the main attack would be mounted across the Strait of Dover, he gives the impression that this was mostly due to the destruction or jamming of German radar stations. Nothing is said about Operation Fortitude—the use of dummy divisions, false messages, signals intercepts, and Nazi double agents to suggest that the main threats were to Calais or Norway. Pownall and Churchill had been equally discreet about all this at the end of volume 5—"It would not be proper even now to describe all the methods employed to mislead the enemy"— and for good reason.[6] Operation Fortitude lay at the heart of the Ultra secret, and it had also spawned an extensive Cold War program of strategic deception. In the interval between publication of volumes 5 and 6, however, Chester Wilmot published what the Ministry of Defence privately called "a full and accurate account of Operation Fortitude" in *The Struggle for Europe*. So complete was this that initially the ministry feared an internal leak, until discovering that most of the material came from published sources, and it admitted that "the fullness of Wilmot's account" made Churchill's and Eisenhower's references to the matter "look rather jejeune" (*sic*).[7]

Churchill's reticence about the campaign in northwest Europe probably also reflects his desire not to damage current transatlantic relations. A succession of American memoirs by Butcher, Ingersoll, Patton, and others had attacked Montgomery for slowness in breaking out of Normandy in June and July and then for insubordinately demanding a British-led northern thrust into Germany rather than an Anglo-American advance along the whole front. Monty did not publish his memoirs until 1958, on retirement from the army, but behind the scenes he was assiduous in self-defense, opening his papers to biographer Alan Moorehead and then to Chester Wilmot. Although not a whitewash of Monty—there were references to his autocratic manner and "professional vanity"—Wilmot's book mounted a sustained critique of Eisenhower as field commander and sided firmly with Monty on the big strategic issues. It particularly lamented the "lost opportunity" of September 1944, when "a single, powerful thrust" could have reached the Ruhr at "no real risk." That might not have ended the war in 1944, Wilmot conceded, but it would have ensured that Berlin, Prague, and Vienna were liberated by the Western Allies and not the Red Army.[8]

Privately, Churchill agreed with Monty, who commented on many of the draft chapters of volume 6, that Eisenhower's broad-front strategy had "prolonged the war, with dire results, to the spring of 1945." This was one of the five "capital" military mistakes made by the Americans during the war over which the two men ruminated at Chequers on 8 August 1953.[9] But the British case had now been well set forth, particularly by Wilmot, and Churchill had no desire to add fuel to the flames of transatlantic controversy with inflammatory comments in his memoirs. On Normandy, he contented himself with Pownall's brief statement of the Montgomery line: "the whole plan of campaign was to pivot on the British front and draw the enemy's reserves in that direction in order to help the American turning movement." And on the narrow- or broad-front controversy, he relied on Pownall's carefully crafted summary, adding judiciously, "Strategists may long debate these issues."[10]

Whatever he said to Monty at Chequers, it seems likely that Churchill did not attach as much importance to the narrow-front strategy in August and September 1944 as he did in early 1945. This was partly because he had spent most of those two months in Italy or North America and did not give the campaign his full attention. He admits in chapter 13 that it was only on his return from Canada on 25 September that he was "able to understand all that happened."[11] For much of the summer, he focused on the dangers rather than the opportunities in Normandy—his lurking fears of another Dunkirk were aggravated by the failure to break out of the beachhead all through June and July. With hindsight, it is clear that both sides in the battle of the books in the late 1940s were distorting the truth. Whatever Monty claimed, he was supposed to take Caen quickly as part of an offensive drive on the left, not as a holding operation to allow the Americans to pivot for a right hook. On the other side, American accounts usually glossed over the original goal of the Normandy campaign—a drive *west* to capture the vital ports of the Cherbourg and Brittany peninsulas, which were deemed essential to supply the vast Allied armies, before they regrouped on the Seine for the next phase. Patton's wheel eastward, quickly sanctioned by Bradley and Monty on 3 August, was inspired improvisation, but it transformed the whole campaign.[12] Trapping at least 60,000 Germans in the Falaise pocket, the Allied armies raced on against crumbling resistance to Paris (25 August) and Brussels (3 September).

Even the daring Patton was surprised: on 19 June, he had privately lamented that the Allies would probably not be able to repeat "the kind of armoured drives the Germans had achieved in 1940" and would "have to go back to 1918 methods" with the infantry taking the lead.[13] But the caution shown by Churchill was extreme. There is considerable evidence, not just from Eisenhower's memoirs, that in June and July 1944 he considered crossing the Seine to be part of the next year's campaign. Despite a passion for tanks, his military mind was still mired in the trenches of 1916 and had not yet grasped the full potential of mobile armored warfare once the enemy's line was breached. Learning on 7 August 1944 that twelve U.S. divisions were surging through the Avranches gap, he exclaimed, "Good Heavens, how do you feed them?" General Omar Bradley replied he was running trucks up to the front, "bumper to bumper, 24 hours a day."[14] Given this cast of mind, on the other hand, Churchill was not seduced by the exaggerated hopes of late summer. With justice, he prints his response of 8 September 1944 to a bullish intelligence report from the JIC. "It is at least as likely that Hitler will be fighting on January 1 as that he will collapse before then. If he does collapse then," Churchill added, "the reasons will be political rather than purely military."[15] In short, Churchill probably did not see the narrow-front option as a lost opportunity—*in August and September 1944*.

By winter, however, with the war bogged down on all fronts, his tone was changing. In chapter 17 he prints lengthy extracts from a telegram he sent to Jan Smuts on 3 December 1944, including:

> we have of course sustained a strategic reverse on the Western Front. Before the offensive was launched we placed on record our view that it was a mistake to attack against the whole front and that a far greater mass should have been gathered at the point of desired penetration. Montgomery's comments and predictions beforehand have in every way been borne out.

This passage is interesting for a couple of reasons. First, the telegram was carefully edited in August 1953. The opening words originally read, "Eisenhower has of course sustained a strategic reverse." At the end, after saying that Monty's criticisms had been borne out, Churchill continued, "I have the greatest regard for Eisenhower and am sure we must back him up"—but this sentence was also removed. Second, the telegram went on to remind Smuts, caustic as ever about U.S. strategy, of the new diplomatic realities: "You must remember however that our armies are only about one-half the size of the American and will soon be little more than one-third. . . . It is not as easy as it used to be for me to get things done."[16]

In the opening chapter of volume 2, Churchill had tabulated the changing balance of the alliance, showing that until July 1944 the British empire had more divisions than the United States in "fighting contact with the enemy."[17] In *Triumph and Tragedy* he makes only occasional allusion, as in the telegram to Smuts, to the new balance of power, yet it was fundamental to operations in that last year of the war. Not merely were the American divisions now coming into the line en masse, but the British were now running out of combat troops. There are occasional hints of this in Churchill's appendixes, but the point is never integrated into the argument of the book, although this manpower crisis is essential for understanding British conduct of the campaign in northwest Europe.[18] At the tactical level, it explains Monty's preference for firepower over manpower, to minimize casualties, and his caution in following up success. This style of warfare, exemplified at Caen and derided in American memoirs, was rooted in warnings from the War Office in the summer of 1944 that they had scraped the bottom of the barrel as far as infantry replacements were concerned.[19]

There was a corollary at the strategic level, which Kelly noted as they were revising the material on the second Quebec conference, in September 1944. Kelly suggested that to sharpen up the chapter, which Norman Brook had found rather dull, "you may wish to stress that this period was one of the turning points of the war." When Churchill set out for Quebec on 5 September, many in London and Washington expected that the European conflict would be over before Christmas. By the time he arrived back in Britain on 25 September, Arnhem had failed and the Allied offensive had stalled. That meant that Britain had to go on for another eight months, "with declining manpower and declining production" and thus diminishing influence over the United States. "Neither at Yalta or at Potsdam could we any longer speak as equals," Kelly concluded. "Hence perhaps our failure to reach Berlin and Prague before the Russians, and the withdrawal to our zones of occupation before having a show-down with the Russians."[20]

This was indeed the implication of Churchill's argument in *Triumph and Tragedy*, but he did not take Kelly's advice and make it explicit. Perhaps with an eye on the transatlantic alliance of 1953, he did not wish to draw attention to the long-term reality of British decline. In any case, he believed profoundly that the power of leadership could tilt the balance of power. This was the central conceit behind the British concept of a special relationship with America. In the words of an anonymous verse penned in 1945 during negotiations for a postwar loan from the United States:

> *In Washington Lord Halifax*
> *Once whispered to Lord Keynes*
> *"It's true they have the money bags*
> *But we have all the brains."*[21]

In North Africa, Churchill and Brooke had been willing to let Eisenhower be overall Allied commander, as long as Alex and Monty could do the fighting. In France, they advocated the same arrangement, successfully at first, for Monty was made overall ground-force commander during the first three months of the French campaign. On 1 September, however, Eisenhower took over, relegating Monty to command of the Twenty-first Army Group, and thus to parity with American counterparts such as Omar Bradley. With the popular British press baying about Monty's "demotion," Churchill had him raised to the rank of Field-Marshal, effective 1 September. "I consider this step necessary from the point of view of the British nation with whom Montgomery's name is a household word," he told *General* Eisenhower, adding disingenuously: "It, of course, makes no difference in the military relations prevailing between Montgomery and other high-ranking American officers."[22]

Although this cable appears in Churchill's printed telegrams for 1944, it is not reproduced in *Triumph and Tragedy*. Nor does Churchill mention that Monty pressed Ike on several occasions that autumn to be reinstated as ground-force commander or that in early 1945 he personally tried to get Alexander accepted for that post. He does state that during the Battle of the Bulge, when the German thrust cut off Bradley from part of his army group, Eisenhower "very wisely placed Montgomery in temporary command of all Allied troops in the north." But he says nothing about Monty's tactless press conference and the exaggerated reports of it, suggesting that the British Field-Marshal was "claiming that he had moved in as the savior of the Americans," in the words of Eisenhower's memoir.[23] Again, Churchill could shelter behind the mounting pile of books because Ike's version of these disputes was supplemented in 1951 and 1952 by more partisan accounts, from opposite angles, by Bradley and Wilmot. In any case, his intent, as usual with volume 6, was irenic not polemic. At the end of his chapter on the Bulge, he and Pownall were at pains to praise the Americans, quoting his own tribute in the Commons on 18 January 1945 to U.S troops who had "done almost all the fighting" and "suffered almost all the losses" and also Monty's final dispatch: "The Battle of the Ardennes was won primarily by the staunch fighting qualities of the American soldier."[24]

"IF SUCH AN IMPORTANT BATTLE as that of Caen is not described in detail (and rightly so!) there is no need to describe individual battles in Burma," Emery Reves complained about the proofs he read in September 1952. But Churchill's assistants had a personal interest here: Pownall had been Chief of Staff for South-East Asia Command from 1943 to 1945 and Kelly had won a Military Cross in Burma in 1944.[25] Veterans of General Sir William Slim's Fourteenth Army had complained that there was no explicit reference to their "Forgotten Army" in volume 5, and Slim raised the matter personally with Churchill in November 1952. Then Chief of the Imperial General Staff and soon to become Governor-General of Australia, Slim was not a figure to ignore. Pownall promised that the Fourteenth Army would be "adequately 'featured'" in volume 6, and Churchill told him to make sure.[26] Hence the generous discussion in *Triumph and Tragedy* of the Burma campaigns, conducted by what Churchill personally called "the famous Fourteenth Army, under the masterly command of General Slim."[27]

Proportionate to the forces engaged, Italy is the campaign that receives the most attention in *Triumph and Tragedy*. Churchill devotes four full chapters to Alexander's slog from Rome to Florence in the summer and autumn of 1944 and then, after the winter mud and snow had cleared, up the northeast coast to a face-off with Tito's troops in Trieste. He puts the best possible gloss on events — "Gleaming successes marked the end of our campaigns in the Mediterranean" — but for him Italy was the real "lost opportunity" of summer 1944, rather than the failure to mount a narrow thrust into the Ruhr. "Not until the spring," he tells us, were the Allied armies in Italy "rewarded with the victory they had so well earned, and so nearly won, in the autumn."[28]

For that failure he explicitly blames the American determination to mount an invasion of southern France. This had been agreed in principle at Teheran in December 1943, but the plan gained new urgency, as far as Marshall and U.S. planners were concerned, in mid-1944 because of the struggling campaign in Normandy and the lack of major ports through which to funnel reinforcements and supplies. Hence the attractions of Operation Anvil—landings on the Riviera and then a drive up the Rhone valley to pull German reinforcements away from Eisenhower. But the troops and matériel for these landings would come from the Italian theater. Once again, Churchill struggled to prevent the emasculation of Alexander's armies, just as he had in the winter of 1943–1944. Blocked by Eisenhower and the Joint Chiefs in mid-June 1944, he took the argument to Roosevelt, only to receive a firm rebuff, and another when he reopened the issue in early August. Anvil, renamed Dragoon, began on 15 August. Within two weeks, Toulon and Marseilles had fallen, by 3 September the U.S. and French forces, encountering minimal opposition, reached Lyon, and on the eleventh they linked up with Eisenhower's forward units near Dijon.

Churchill's row with the Americans over Anvil was his most passionate of the war — exceeding even that over the Greek islands in the autumn of 1943 — but it echoed familiar themes. One was his somewhat antiquated conception of warfare, evident in the detailed case he set out for the President on 28 June 1944 and in an impassioned plea to Hopkins on 6 August, both of which appear in *Triumph and Tragedy*. In these messages, he spoke of Toulon and Marseilles as "fortresses" and repeatedly used the verb "to march" — language once again more suited to the era of Marlborough. Pointing out on 28 June that Marseilles was four hundred miles from Paris, he told Roosevelt that "even with great success" a landing in southern France could not "directly influence the present battle in 1944." As Churchill conceded, "very great hazards" menaced a "march" up Italy as well — that was evident from the succession of false hopes since the Allies had landed in September 1943.[29] The decisive point was that in the Italian theater the British were still dominant, both in command and troops. Victory there, unlike in France, would redound to the credit of Britain, and this mattered for reasons of domestic politics and international influence.

By June 1944, British policymakers could discern another reason for concentrating on Italy. Alexander and Jumbo Wilson, the overall Mediterranean commander, wanted to drive north through the Po valley to the head of the Adriatic, seizing the port of Trieste and pushing on through the Ljubljana gap into Austria and Hungary, where they could link up with the Russians. They made the case on purely military grounds — to accelerate Germany's defeat — but Churchill, egged on by Smuts, began to see the postwar benefits. Unless the Western Allies took "an important part in clearing the Balkans and invading Germany from the south," Smuts argued on 30 August 1944, "the role of Russia in South-Eastern Europe will be all the greater." He urged Churchill from now on "to keep a very close eye on all matters bearing on the future settlement of Europe."[30]

The Anvil debate was therefore complex and important, impinging not just on Anglo-American relations but also on the postwar balance. Forced to concede defeat in the summer of 1944, Churchill made his familiar quip that he would leave the controversy to history but intended to be one of the historians.[31] In the early 1950s, however, he found his contribution difficult to write. On the one hand, he was determined to state his case about the disastrous effect of Anvil on the Italian campaign and the early Cold War. On the other hand, he did not want to offend Eisenhower, and he also had to face the awkward fact that the operation he had so vehemently opposed proved a spectacular success.

The draft chapter on Anvil was the chapter on which Ismay made the greatest contribution. (It was originally intended for volume 5.) When he and Pownall worked on it in 1950–1951 they couched their material as an explicit rebuttal to Eisenhower's memoirs. Pownall argued that "it was Overlord that helped Anvil, not the other way round"—in other words, that German absorption in Normandy explained why the Americans could race up the Rhone. Ismay drew Churchill's attention to supportive passages in the memoirs of General Mark Clark, the senior U.S. commander in Italy in 1944, showing that "he was just as vehemently opposed to ANVIL as you and we were."[32] But by 1953 Churchill was more concerned about Eisenhower the President than Eisenhower the general. The chapters on the Riviera landings were among the eight he sent to Eisenhower's proxy, Bedell Smith. And these were the two on which Beetle tactfully drew a line. "I fear that such a strong presentation may result in another 'Americans vs. British' controversy," he told Churchill on 14 July. "I have taken the liberty of underlining a few phrases and sentences which it seems to me might be made somewhat less positive."[33]

The reactions of Brook and Churchill to this letter are revealingly different. The Cabinet Secretary dismissed much of Bedell Smith's letter as special pleading. "You cannot be expected to gloss over your dislike of 'Anvil' or your attempts to stop it," he told Churchill. "Nor should you conceal your view that, looking back, you were right." In *Crusade in Europe*, Eisenhower was "arguing from the view of a theatre commander" whereas Churchill saw the "wider strategic angle." Brook thought it "tactful" to make some verbal alterations in passages that Bedell Smith had particularly queried but felt "you should not consider for a moment making any major changes in these two Chapters."[34] Churchill, however, went much farther than Brook in his last flurry of revision in August 1953. He cut several passages overtly locking horns with Eisenhower and also removed his most inflammatory judgments, such as "ruining the Italian front for the sake of 'Anvil'" and "I still regard it as the major error of our Allied strategy." Also excised were all the quotations from Mark Clark's memoirs, which he had used as a powerful, non-British buttress for his own arguments.[35]

Even with these cuts, Churchill's case was firmly stated, and in the final stage Pownall added a carefully worded summation. This reiterated his original argument that Anvil "caused no diversion from the forces opposing General Eisenhower. In fact, instead of helping him, he helped it by threatening the rear of the Germans retiring up the Rhone valley." Pownall admitted that the result was another army on Eisenhower's right flank and new supply lines from the south. But for this "a heavy price was paid. The army of Italy was deprived of its opportunity to strike a most formidable blow at the Germans, and very possibly to reach Vienna before the Russians, with all that might have followed therefrom."[36]

AS USUAL, domestic affairs do not bulk large in Churchill's account. The main exception is chapter 3, "The Pilotless Bombardment." The first V-1 hit East London on 13 June, a week after D-Day, and the barrage continued until the launching sites in northern France and Belgium were overrun by Allied forces in early September. But then the Germans started firing long-range rockets, the V-2s, in a campaign that lasted some seven months. As Churchill remarks, prompted by the Home Office, these attacks imposed on Londoners "a burden perhaps even heavier" than the Blitz, being random, isolated, and almost without warning.[37]

Exactly what to say about the V-weapons was largely a replay of the battle waged when writing volume 5. Duncan Sandys again tried to highlight his own contribution, particularly the warnings about the V-2. Lord Cherwell pressed for the inclusion of evidence showing he was right about the threat from the V-1. When R. V. Jones was brought in to write a compromise version in April 1953, he added details boosting his own role. Sandys was Churchill's son-in-law, Cherwell his veteran science adviser and close friend, and Jones his favorite young scientist. Balancing between them was therefore not easy. Churchill left Kelly to broker a deal, but it was not until 19 September that the Prime Minister could report that "a version has at last been agreed between all the parties on this tangled matter."[38] Not surprisingly, this handed out bouquets to everyone. Sandys earned praise for moving the antiaircraft batteries nearer the coast in July 1944, vastly enhancing their success, and for his prescience about the long-term danger from "guided missiles." Cherwell was said to have been "strongly vindicated" in his predictions about the flying bomb. Over Sandys's objections, Churchill also retained a postwar comment from Albert Speer, Hitler's Armaments Minister, saying that Germany should have concentrated on V-1s, twenty of which cost the same as one V-2. And Jones secured some credit for himself and his unit at the Air Ministry. Although this politicized redrafting muddied the waters in places, the result of so much informed labor, abetted by advice and statistics from the Air Ministry, was a piece of cutting-edge research—the analogue for volume 6 of Pownall's narratives of the Desert War.[39]

Near the end of "The Pilotless Bombardment," Churchill includes a paragraph about the damage to Belgium. Antwerp, the main target, was hit by more than 10,000 V-weapons, and the statistics in his chapter indicate that this was comparable to the strikes against London. The Belgian people, he tells us, "bore this senseless bombardment in a spirit equal to our own."[40] This tribute was probably prompted in part by the anger in Belgium over his account of their capitulation in May 1940. One might sense similar motives in Pownall's gratuitous reference in chapter 2 to the role played in the liberation of Paris by "Colonel Billotte, son of the commander of the First French Army Group, who was killed in May 1940." In 1949, Pierre Billotte, by then a senior French general, had complained to Churchill about the "inaccurate" and "very painful" criticisms in volume 2 of his father's conduct in 1940.[41] In September 1952, Churchill was informed by Emery Reves of "widespread resentment in Holland that in your Memoirs you have neglected the Dutch," unlike the French, Belgians, or Poles. Churchill did not insert "a paragraph or two" of extenuation as Reves suggested but, reminded by Deakin and Kelly, he added to his account of Arnhem a reference to the courage of the Dutch resistance. And in book 2 he devotes a couple of pages to the "bravely borne afflictions" of the Dutch people during the grim winter of 1944–1945, which they, unlike the liberated Belgians, endured under continued Nazi occupation.[42]

Churchill was being nice to those offended by earlier volumes, but these insertions also reflect his diplomatic approach to volume 6. France, Belgium, and the Netherlands were now Britain's NATO allies—a far cry from Churchill's expectations in the last year of the war. On 25 November 1944, he blasted Foreign Office ideas for a British commitment to a "Western European bloc": "The Belgians are extremely weak, and their behaviour before the war was shocking. The Dutch were entirely selfish and fought only when they were attacked, and then only for a few hours." In July 1951, before resuming the premiership, Churchill intended to include this minute but with the sneers at Belgium and the Dutch toned down. In August 1953, he decided to cut the whole thing.[43]

In November 1944, Churchill did not anticipate that even France would revive as a military power for five or ten years.[44] Nor, as long as de Gaulle was its leader, could he imagine an entente cordiale to match his special relationship with Roosevelt. Indeed, the one seemed at odds with the other; not until October 1944 did the Roosevelt administration capitulate to reality and recognize de Gaulle's Committee of National Liberation as the provisional government of France. In chapter 16, Churchill describes the sequel: his own triumphant and emotional progress down the Champs Elysées with de Gaulle on Armistice Day, 11 November, and the latter's trip to Moscow the following month to forge a worrying relationship with the Soviets. In content and balance, the chapter is therefore a reasonably faithful rendition of Churchill's ambivalence toward the new France. But its tone does not do justice to his periodic explosions of rage about de Gaulle. "Remember that there is not a scrap of generosity about this man," he told Eden on 13 June 1944, in a minute he first elided and then cut completely from the memoirs. "I am sure he will make all the mischief he can" was likewise removed from a cable to Roosevelt on 22 October. After the Paris visit in November, we learn that he told FDR of reestablishing "friendly private relations with de Gaulle," but he does not print the phrase that followed: "who is better since he has lost a great part of his inferiority complex." The rationale for such editing, as in volume 5, was to avoid unnecessary offense to a probable future leader of France.[45]

On Germany itself, Churchill has little to say in book 1: the country figures simply as backdrop to the endgame of Hitler's war. To the modern eye, however, two omissions seem particularly striking.

One concerns the attempted coup on 20 July 1944, when Colonel Claus von Stauffenberg detonated a bomb in Hitler's headquarters in East Prussia. The Führer survived, and the coup crumbled in an orgy of Nazi revenge. Churchill summarizes this story in one paragraph, covering only one third of a page. Such brevity cannot be explained by lack of material. Several accounts had already been published; in 1949, the journalist Ian Colvin had been paid fifty guineas by Churchill for a 5,000-word paper on "The Twelve Hour Plot"; and in 1951, both Bill Deakin and Norman Brook urged a longer narrative. But Churchill was quite firm: "A paragraph is all that needs to be given," he told the Syndicate.[46]

Though unstated, the reasons for his insistence may be inferred. Back in volume 1, Churchill had featured the German resistance, but this was to argue that Chamberlain's visits to Hitler in September 1938 cut the ground from under a generals' plot to topple the Führer. In 1940–1943, he toyed at times with the possibility that the Reich might disintegrate through pressures from within. But by the summer of 1944, such hopes had evaporated, and an unconditional surrender of Germany, now made possible by Soviet and American arms, was preferable to a hand-tying compromise with German nationalists. In the Commons on 2 August, he noted that "the highest personalities in the German Reich are murdering one another, or trying to" but warned MPs not to put their faith in "these manifestations of internal disease" but "in our own strong arms and the justice of our cause."[47]

After 1945, however, the 20 July plot took on a new complexion as various German memoirs asserted that more Western support for the anti-Hitler resistance could have engineered a negotiated end to the war and preempted Russian control of Central Europe. By the late 1940s, the Foreign Office was sufficiently concerned to consider putting out a collection of documents in refutation, and Churchill had second thoughts about his own role. In the summer of 1949, he told one of the survivors of the German opposition, who had secretly visited Chartwell ten years before, that he now realized that "during the war he had been misled by his assistants about the considerable strength and size of the German anti-Hitler resistance."[48] Moreover, the bomb plot represented an embarrassing failure by British intelligence, which consistently denied that there was a viable German opposition, whereas U.S. intelligence in Switzerland was well informed about the German resistance and plans for the July plot.[49] Although this did not change the "unconditional surrender" line in Washington, the superiority of American over British intelligence was probably another reason for Churchill to move quickly over 20 July 1944 in his memoirs.

His hardening attitude to Germany in 1944 may have been influenced by what he learned during the summer about the quickening pace of Nazi genocide. *Triumph and Tragedy* prints the damning minute he sent Eden on 11 July 1944:

> There is no doubt that this is probably the greatest and most horrible crime ever committed in the whole history of the world, and it has been done by scientific machinery by nominally civilised men in the name of a great State and one of the leading races of Europe. It is quite clear that all concerned in this crime who may fall into our hands, including the people who only obeyed orders by carrying out the butcheries, should be put to death after their association with the murders has been proved.

Churchill could hardly have been more forthright. But this minute is relegated to the appendix to volume 6, and there is nothing in the text about the Nazi extermination camps, about which he is much more outspoken in volume 1. Nor does this issue, unlike the bomb plot, seem to have come up in correspondence with the Syndicate.[50]

Churchill's original printed minutes for July 1944 contain other expressions of concern. On pleas by the Jewish Agency to bomb the rail lines to Auschwitz and the gas chambers, he told Eden on 7 July, "You and I are in entire agreement. Get anything out of the Air Force you can and invoke me if necessary." The next day, in response to the Foreign Secretary's proposal for a public Allied protest, he noted, "I am entirely in accord with making the biggest outcry possible." Neither of these minutes appears even in the appendix to volume 6.[51] In November 1954, an Israeli reader wrote to ask whether "the desire for Anglo-German friendship was so strong as to compel you to withhold essential knowledge and information about the greatest mass murder in history." Denis Kelly replied that "in general Sir Winston tried to confine himself to happenings on which he could either throw some personal light or could provide an account which was not readily accessible to the general public. The happenings you mention were so deeply impressed in the mind and imagination of the world that he felt it was unnecessary to reiterate them in his volumes."[52]

This was lame stuff. So why the omission? Perhaps because nothing came of Churchill's demands for action. The Foreign Office dragged its feet, the Air Ministry pleaded technical difficulties, the U.S. War Department considered the idea impractical, and Churchill lost track of it during his foreign travels in August and September 1944. On 1 October, he sent Eden a brief minute (again omitted from the memoirs) supporting a public denunciation of German crimes. This might, he said, "have a chance of saving the multitudes concerned."[53] But then he was off to Moscow, followed by Paris in November and Athens for Christmas. To print his exhortations of July 1944 would therefore draw embarrassing attention to how little was actually done. And it might also have hinted at the Ultra secret, source for some of the detailed evidence of the Final Solution available to the Allies in 1944.

Churchill does have something to say about the Morgenthau Plan for a postwar "pastoralised" Germany, which he and Roosevelt approved in outline at Quebec in September 1944 but then quickly repudiated. In chapter 10 it is presented as an idea foisted on him by the "insistent" U.S. Treasury Secretary, which he had no time to examine in detail. Churchill hints at a deeper reason why he succumbed to pressure from Henry Morgenthau, "from whom we had so much to ask"—an oblique reference to the concurrent discussions about postwar financial aid to Britain. This passage was largely the work of Deakin and Cherwell, who had been at Quebec, and Churchill did little with it. He needed to say something about the Morgenthau Plan, because it had become a cause célèbre in America. But Morgenthau had made clear to Churchill that he felt he had unfairly been made the "whipping boy" for this punitive project. And, as with the

July plot and the Holocaust, Churchill did not need to stir up controversy among Germans who were now vital Cold War allies.[54]

THE DEEPENING CRISIS in Germany in July 1944 can be summed up in one word: "Bagration." This was the code name, appropriated by Stalin from a hero of the Napoleonic war of 1812, for the Red Army's summer offensive in Belorussia. It commenced on 22 June 1944, three years to the day after Hitler began Operation Barbarossa, his invasion of the Soviet Union. The similarities do not end there, for Bagration was fought across many of the same battlefields, it achieved an equally complete intelligence surprise, and it also resulted in overwhelming victory. The big difference from Barbarossa was that this time the Red Army steamrollered the Wehrmacht, totally destroying its Army Group Center and inflicting more than double the losses of Stalingrad. By the end of July, Soviet forces were five hundred miles farther west, on the outskirts of Warsaw. Bagration was only the centerpiece of five major offensives that rippled down the Eastern Front that summer. In June and July, the Red Army surged back into the Baltic states, reaching the borders of East Prussia. On 20 August, it invaded Romania, securing the whole country in two weeks and taking Hitler's last major oil fields. Soviet troops drove on through Bulgaria and Yugoslavia, and in early October they invaded Hungary.[55]

Bagration is still little known in the West, even though its success was more dramatic than Overlord and totally eclipsed the campaign in Italy, where the Germans fielded about as many divisions as Army Group Center *lost* in a month (thirty). Churchill's memoirs did nothing to educate his readers because, as usual, he allotted minimal space to the Eastern Front. Henry Pownall's basic narrative of the Soviet campaigns from June 1944 to February 1945 amounts to about 1,000 words. This was then chopped up to form parts of chapters 5, 14, and 20—as with the account of Stalingrad in volume 4 further weakening any impact on the reader. On the other hand, Churchill says enough to make clear the essential point, helped by Pownall's map and phrases such as "sweeping success" and "crushing" losses.[56]

The Soviet surge to the edge of Warsaw emboldened the Polish Underground Army to rise up against Nazi rule on 1 August. The Underground was loyal to the London government-in-exile, and its rising was intended to preempt a Soviet takeover. Chapter 9 narrates the ensuing "Martyrdom of Warsaw"—how the Red Army held back, pleading logistical overstretch, until the Germans had regained control of the city and exacted terrible revenge. Churchill prints his exchanges with Roosevelt and Stalin, in which he urged that Allied aircraft from Italy drop supplies into Warsaw and then use Soviet landing fields to refuel, and makes clear FDR's unwillingness to press the issue. He says he does not recall any occasion during the war when "such deep anger" was shown by the War Cabinet and adds that he would have liked to threaten suspension of convoys to Russia if the Soviets did not allow British planes to land. But, Churchill continues, "terrible and even humbling submissions must at times be made to the general aim." As with his treatment of Katyn in volume 5, he avoids making explicit judgments on Soviet conduct or identifying Stalin by name. We were dealing, he says, "with men in the Kremlin who were governed by calculation and not by emotion."[57]

Churchill was now desperate to reach an understanding with Stalin about Eastern Europe as a whole. A deal had been outlined in May 1944, when Eden and Feodor Gusev, the Soviet Ambassador in London, reached an informal understanding that the British would let Moscow take a lead in handling Romania's transition from the war while Britain, in turn, would take the lead with Greece. The latter was what mattered to Churchill; conceding Romania to the Russians was a paper sacrifice—as Churchill told Eden in a minute of 10 July that Deakin advised cutting from this chapter, "the Russians will take all they want in Roumania whatever we say."[58] But the chapter does make clear the real alarm in Washington that the Romania-Greece division of labor presaged a long-term Anglo-Soviet carve-up of the Balkans into "spheres of influence." The President pressed the point with unusual persistence, and Churchill proposed on 11 June that the Big Three should review the Romania-Greece arrangement in three months.

By the time Churchill flew to Moscow in October, the three months had expired. Moreover, Ultra showed that the Germans were about to evacuate Athens, leaving a power vacuum that communist partisans might speedily fill. "The moment was apt for business," Churchill tells us, and he took the initiative in his opening meeting in the Kremlin at 10:00 P.M. on 9 October. "Let us settle about our affairs in the Balkans," he told Stalin. "How would it do for you to have ninety per cent. predominance in Roumania, for us to have ninety per cent. of the say in Greece, and go fifty-fifty about Yugoslavia?" As this was being translated, he tells us, he wrote out on a half sheet of paper those figures plus a fifty-fifty split in Hungary and a division in Bulgaria of 75 percent for the Russians and 25 percent for "the others." He pushed the paper across the table to Stalin. "There was a slight pause. Then he took his blue pencil and made a large tick upon it, and passed it back to us. It was all settled in no more time than it takes to set down." A long silence ensued. "Might it not be thought rather cynical," Churchill eventually

Churchill's half-sheet of paper, scribbled in the Kremlin on 9 October 1944, dividing up the Balkans into proposed spheres of influence. Stalin's check of approval is at the top right. The note above is by John Martin, Churchill's private secretary.

remarked, "if it seemed that we had disposed of these issues, so fateful to millions of people, in such an offhand manner? Let us burn the paper." Stalin demurred. "No, you keep it."[59] This dramatic anecdote, one of the most famous in all the war memoirs, was dictated at the end of November 1950. (As with Churchill's account of meeting the dejected French leaders on 16 May 1940, the official record indicates a long and complex conversation.) Churchill intended to repro-duce a facsimile of the original sheet of paper in his book and only changed his mind in August 1953, much to the regret of *Life*.[60]

The basic deal—trading Romania for Greece—had already been outlined in May; now Churchill tried to enlarge it to all the Balkans. The percentages for-mula, however, came from nowhere—it does not seem to have been discussed with Eden in advance, nor did Churchill use it again. Perhaps he thought that figures would give precision to his proposals, rather than vague terms such as "predominance" or "taking the lead." Possibly he imagined that quantification would appeal to Marxist-Leninists—those men of "calculation" not "emotion." In any event, he played the numbers game, Stalin joined in, and what Churchill privately called this "naughty document" governed his Balkan policy in the remainder of the war.[61]

But what did it mean? Eden had no idea—he seems to have been as surprised as the Russians by Churchill's ploy. Back home, the Foreign Office was unhappy, and the Cabinet requested explanation. Churchill replied that the percentages were "not intended to prescribe the numbers sitting on commissions" but rather to act as a general "guide" to "the interests and sentiments" with which the two allies approached the individual Balkan countries. With America in mind, he insisted that the percentages did not establish "a rigid system of spheres of inter-est" and were only "an interim guide for the immediate war-time future." In an unsent letter to Stalin dictated on 11 October and also printed in volume 6, he indicated two premises on which he operated: "We feel we were right in inter-preting your dissolution of the Comintern [in May 1943] as a decision by the Soviet Government not to interfere in the internal political affairs of other coun-tries"; and,

> we have the feeling that, viewed from afar and on a grand scale, the differ-ences between our systems will tend to get smaller, and the great common ground which we share of making life richer and happier for the mass of the people is growing every year. Probably if there were peace for fifty years the differences which now might cause such grave troubles to the world would become matters for academic discussion.[62]

This was a remarkable profession of faith and certainly not what might be expected from the Cold Warrior of Fulton. But Churchill was now intent on presenting himself as the advocate of détente.

What Churchill really wanted on 9 October was a free hand in Greece, so that British troops could land in Athens in the next few days and preempt a communist coup without fear of Soviet recrimination. He says as much later in volume 6, quoting his comment to Eden on 7 November 1944, "having paid the price we have to Russia for freedom of action in Greece, we should not hesitate to use British troops to support the Royal Hellenic Government," and also noting in the text that "at the Moscow conference I had obtained Russian abstention [from Greece] at a heavy price."[63]

What was this "heavy price"? Churchill does not say, but Romania was surely part of the accounting. Churchill had already written it off in his minute to Eden on 10 July—the Russians would take what they wanted regardless of what Britain said—but at Moscow he gave them carte blanche to do so. Given Russian cooperation on Greece, he told Eden in an unpublished minute on 11 December, "we really must not press our hand too far in Roumania. Remember the percentages we wrote out on paper. . . . It is an awful thing we cannot have it both ways."[64]

Another Balkan country may also have been on Churchill's mind. In October 1944, Yugoslavia was designated an area of equal influence between the British and the Soviets—but whereas Churchill has much to say about Greece in volume 6, he is tight-lipped about Yugoslavia. One reason, noted above in chapter 29, is that by 1953 Churchill had no desire to offend Tito. But he also became conscious during 1944 and 1945 that he had been taken for a ride by the expansionist Yugoslav leader. "I have come to the conclusion that in Tito we have nursed a viper," Churchill told Eden on 19 December 1944, adding that now "he has started biting us" and not the Germans. Churchill deleted this minute from Kelly's June 1951 draft appendix. In January 1953, he also cut a lengthy passage, based on his 29 April 1945 complaint to Stalin, that "the way things had worked out in Yugoslavia certainly did not give me the feeling of a fifty-fifty interest and influence between our two countries. Marshal Tito had become a complete dictator."[65]

Another striking omission from Churchill's account is Italy, where the communist role in the postwar order was a major issue in 1944 and 1945. In chapter 7, relating his visit to Rome in August 1944, Churchill mentions in passing that he talked with various politicians including "Comrade Togliatti who had returned to Italy at the beginning of the year after a long sojourn in Moscow."

The reference to the communist leader was added by Deakin.[66] The Oxford don also reminded Churchill he had done nothing to explain the "Italian political tangle" of mid-1944 and appended some pertinent telegrams. These disclosed how on 9 June 1944, after the Allies had liberated Rome, the leaders of Italy's fractious political parties combined to topple Marshal Badoglio, the Churchill-backed hangover from the fascist era, and establish a new coalition under Ivanoe Bonomi. After a week of diplomacy, Churchill reluctantly accepted a fait accompli. When Attlee wrote to complain that the Prime Minister was conducting this business without consulting the Cabinet, Churchill replied that it would have caused "great inconvenience" to hold a meeting on a Sunday afternoon. (Such unwonted solicitude must have made Attlee smile wryly.) Given the embarrassing documentary record presented by Deakin, it is not surprising that Churchill says virtually nothing about the mess he had helped create in Italy.[67]

He does, however, have much to say about the Anglo-American row over Greece in December 1944. The coalition government formed in October collapsed, and the communists proclaimed a general strike. Street clashes followed, and when the British commander, General Scobie, ordered the communists out of Athens they tried to seize the capital by force. "At this moment," Churchill tells us, "I took a more direct control of the affair. . . . It is no use doing things like this by halves." He ordered Scobie "to hold and dominate Athens . . . without bloodshed if possible, but also with bloodshed if necessary." This cable was despatched at 4:50 on the morning of 5 December. An exhausted Jock Colville, Churchill's secretary, failed to write on it the word "Guard," to ensure it was not copied to the Americans. The State Department received a paraphrase, which was leaked to the columnist Drew Pearson and plastered across American newspapers.[68]

Churchill did not mention Pearson in his book, on the advice of *Life*, nor did he reveal Colville's faux pas. Otherwise, he tells the story in detail in chapter 18, indicating the storm of criticism across the Atlantic but placing most of the blame for the policy clash on the State Department: "In the main, the President was with me." Meanwhile, in Athens, British troops gradually gained the upper hand. On Christmas Eve, Churchill suddenly decided to fly there and supervise the construction of a new government. "If the powers of evil prevail in Greece, as is quite likely," he told Smuts, "we must be prepared for a quasi-Bolshevised Russian-led Balkans peninsula, and this may spread to Italy and Hungary." He ends book 1 with a colorful account of his flying visit to Athens. Back in London, he persuaded the King of the Hellenes not to return to Athens until invited by a plebiscite. By mid-January 1945, the military situation was stable, and the communists had accepted a truce.[69]

Churchill's virtual silence about Yugoslavia and Italy in *Triumph and Tragedy* suggests he recognized that his policies had contributed to the communist problem in these countries. Greece, on the other hand, could be represented as vindication of his stance, and this was done in two ways: first, by contrasting the "vehement attacks" to which he was subject at the time with the way his policy had been "completely" justified by later events. "Myself, I never had any doubts about it, for I saw quite plainly that Communism would be the peril civilisation would have to face after the defeat of Nazism and Fascism." And he juxtaposes the judgment of the State Department in December 1944 with what Dean Acheson, the Acting Secretary of State, told Congress in March 1947: "A Communist-dominated Government in Greece would be considered dangerous to United States security."[70] Churchill's second point in self-defense was that Stalin "adhered strictly and faithfully to our agreement of October, and during all the long weeks of fighting the Communists in the streets of Athens not one word of reproach came from *Pravda* or *Izvestia*." This mirrors comments he made at the time. On 3 December 1944, to Eden, he called Stalin "that great and good man." On 11 December, he told the Foreign Secretary, "I am increasingly impressed, up to date, with the loyalty with which, under much temptation and very likely pressure, Stalin has kept off Greece in accordance with our agreement." Both of these minutes appear in the appendix to volume 6.[71]

Spain is another country about which Churchill says virtually nothing in *Triumph and Tragedy*. But on 10 November 1944, he wrote a lengthy minute denouncing Labour pressures within the Cabinet to try to engineer Franco's downfall, which he predicted would lead to "revolution in Spain." Churchill decided to omit this minute in June 1951, but it encapsulates his policy toward Stalin:

> Should the communists become masters of Spain we must expect the infection to spread very fast both through Italy and France. . . . At this time every country that is liberated or converted by our victories is seething with communism. All are linked together and only our influence with Russia prevents their actively stimulating this movement, deadly as I conceive it to peace and also to the freedom of mankind.[72]

Stalin's adherence to the percentages deal on Greece came to serve as Churchill's talisman for "our influence with Russia." When the two men met, it seemed that business could be done. Paraphrasing a telegram he sent to the Cabinet on 17 October 1944, Churchill writes: "There is no doubt that in our narrow circle we talked with an ease, freedom, and cordiality never before attained between our two countries. Stalin made several expressions of personal regard which I feel sure were sincere. But I became even more convinced that he was by no means alone. As I said to my colleagues at home, 'Behind the horseman sits black care.'"[73] Here again was Churchill's idée fixe about Stalin as a relative moderate, battling shadowy extremists. He gambled on Uncle Joe because the alternatives seemed much worse. It was in this spirit that Churchill entered 1945.

CHAPTER 30

THE UNNECESSARY COLD WAR

CHURCHILL DID NOT WANT to write about 1945. The Cold War was not the outcome he had intended for the Grand Alliance, and—as with his account of the origins of the Second World War in volume 1—he resorted to a series of counterfactuals to explain why the East-West rift occurred. His argument was that the Yalta agreements, like the percentages deal, were right in themselves, or at any rate were the least bad option, but that things went wrong thereafter, in large measure because his policies were not pursued. Developing that argument, however, required care because Prime Minister Churchill was seeking to defuse the Cold War, the origins of which he, as a historian, was trying to explain.

ACCORDING TO Denis Kelly, Churchill found Yalta "an intensely painful memory he would have preferred to forget." When finally prodded to dictate some "rough notes" about the summit, Churchill spent fourteen pages of typescript on anecdotes about his visit to the battle-scarred Crimea and his stay in the half-Gothic, half-Moorish Vorontsov villa, before adding on the last half page:

> Please note the heavy stuff of the Yalta Conference. How Stalin and Molotov promised to come into the war against Japan, and the Americans paid a heavy price in the Kurils, etc. But how I was on Poland, and we fought for Poland and reached agreement, and how these agreements were broken in the

succeeding months. . . . We had the world at our feet. Twenty-five million men marching at our orders by land and sea. We seemed to be friends.

Churchill left Kelly to paraphrase the "heavy stuff" from the official minutes of the conference and asked the Syndicate to work his notes into that text.[1] He was, therefore, rather detached from the account of Yalta published in *Triumph and Tragedy*. On the other hand, his notes conveyed what he deemed the essentials of the conference: a deal on the Far East, a promise about Poland, and the conviction of continued Big Three unity.

In France, Yalta was already becoming "the most enduring, most widespread, most deeply rooted myth" of Cold War politics—"symbol of a world system run by the two superpowers" at the expense of Europe.[2] This interpretation was rooted in de Gaulle's exclusion from the conference. Even though Churchill succeeded in getting the French a zone of occupation in Germany, he had no doubt that the general's presence "would have wrecked all possible progress, already difficult enough." This remark, and the whole telegram to the War Cabinet in which it was embedded, was removed from volume 6 at Norman Brook's suggestion. The Cabinet Secretary also persuaded Churchill to excise some table talk on 4 February about the rightful predominance of the Big Three over the rest.[3]

Another version of the Yalta myth was peddled in America by the Republican right, especially after the exposure of Alger Hiss, a senior State Department aide at Yalta, as a likely Soviet agent. In the party's 1952 campaign, Yalta became a synonym for the Democrats' betrayal of Eastern Europe and Nationalist China to the communists through "secret understandings" made "without the knowledge or consent of Congress or the American people." The Democrats' defense was voiced in *Roosevelt and the Russians* (1949) by Edward R. Stettinius, Jr., FDR's Secretary of State in 1944–1945. He argued that at Yalta it was the Soviets who "made greater concessions," calling the agreements "on the whole, a diplomatic triumph" for America and Britain. "The real difficulties with the Soviet Union came after Yalta when the agreements were not respected." Stettinius claimed it was "essential" that Roosevelt and Churchill had made "an honest attempt at Yalta to work with the Russians. . . . Until clear agreements were made and tested, the world could not clearly know the difficulties of securing Russian compliance." Deakin thought Stettinius had made the case "very successfully," telling Churchill, "I think you will find his account very helpful when you come to deal with these matters."[4]

A high priority for Roosevelt at Yalta was a Soviet pledge to join the war against Japan. The U.S. military was adamant that the participation of the Red Army was essential to minimize American casualties, and the President believed that Soviet assistance had to be bought. He discussed the matter privately with Stalin on 8 February; then Molotov and Harriman drew up a document, which was presented to Churchill for signature. This promised Soviet entry against Japan within two or three months of the defeat of Germany in return for the Kurile Islands and "restoration" of territories lost by the Tsarist government in the Russo-Japanese War of 1904–1905. Since most of these concessions were at China's expense, it was left to Roosevelt to square the deal with Chiang Kai-shek. For this reason, and because the Far Eastern agreement pledged Russia to break its neutrality pact with Japan, the deal was top secret, and nothing was said in the conference communiqué. The text was made public only in 1947, prompting Republican accusations about "secret covenants," and in 1951 Harriman testified at length about it to a Senate committee. When drafting, Deakin had this testimony before him, and he took particular care to sanitize the published documents and urged Churchill to avoid adding fuel to the flames.[5]

Churchill concurred—up to a point. By the early 1950s, the Yalta agreement on the Far East looked naïve even to Roosevelt apologists such as Robert Sherwood. In *Great Mistakes of the War*, the military journalist Hanson Baldwin headed his section on Yalta bluntly "Appeasement in Asia." These accounts treated Churchill as a bit player in an essentially American tragedy, but in 1952 Chester Wilmot's *Struggle for Europe* had turned the spotlight on the Prime Minister. Wilmot claimed that "Eden did all he could to dissuade the Prime Minister from setting his signature to the terms agreed upon by Roosevelt and Stalin." He called the Far Eastern deal "the most controversial" and "least defensible" agreement made at Yalta; his chapter on the conference is entitled "Stalin's Greatest Victory."[6]

In his memoirs, Churchill was therefore keen to deflect any blame. "I must make it clear that though on behalf of Great Britain I joined in the agreement, neither I nor Eden took any part in making it," he wrote. "In the United States there have been many reproaches about the concessions made to Soviet Russia. The responsibility rests with their own representatives. To us the problem was remote and secondary." This is disingenuous. Ever since Teheran he had been ready and willing to buy Russian entry into the Asian war. After his October 1944 visit to Moscow, he told Eden, in a minute removed from the draft of his memoirs, that Stalin's promise to "march against Japan . . . on the day that the

German armies are destroyed" was "the most important statement at the Conference" and that it would be "absolutely necessary to offer Russia substantial war objectives in the Far East."[7] On 27 January 1945, Eden warned that Soviet claims in Manchuria and Korea could "only be satisfied at the expense of incessant friction with the Chinese." But Churchill was dismissive: "A speedy termination of the Japanese war, such as may be procured by the mere fact of a Russian declaration of war against Japan, would undoubtedly save us thousands of millions of pounds. The Staffs see no particular harm in the presence of Russia as a Pacific Power. I should not be able to oppose the kind of Russian wishes which you mention, especially as the *quid pro quo* far outvalues anything we are likely to get out of China." Unsurprisingly, this exchange never got near drafts of *Triumph and Tragedy*.[8]

Whereas Churchill's account of Yalta is discreet about the Far East, he devotes a whole chapter to "The Soviet Promise" on Poland. He tells us that the Polish question was "the most urgent reason" for the conference and that it was to prove "the first of the great causes which led to the breakdown of the Grand Alliance." Unlike in the assertive passage about the Far East, Churchill's tone on Poland is defensive: "The painful tale is still unfinished and the true facts are as yet imperfectly known, but what is here set down may perhaps contribute to a just appreciation of our efforts." In an unusually schematic paragraph, probably drafted by Kelly, he sets out four major issues at stake:

- "How to form a single Provisional Government for Poland," given the bitter rivalry between the London government-in-exile and the Soviet-sponsored Lublin Poles, now installed in Warsaw as de facto rulers.
- "How and when to hold free elections."
- "How to settle the Polish frontiers, both in the east and in the west."
- "How to safeguard the rear areas and lines of communication of the advancing Soviet armies" from attacks by the Polish Underground, loyal to London and outraged by Soviet passivity during the Warsaw rising.[9]

Poland's eastern border was settled relatively easily; Roosevelt and Churchill had already indicated broad approval of the so-called Curzon Line. Under pressure from the British Cabinet, they reserved the question of Poland's western border with Germany for the peace conference. For Churchill, "a strong, free, and independent Poland was much more important than particular territorial boundaries," and he stressed Britain's debt of honor to the Poles, whose independence it had ineffectually guaranteed in 1939. Stalin replied that Poland was "a matter of life and death for the Soviet State" because German armies had marched through it to attack Russia twice in the last thirty years. Kelly's lengthy paraphrase of the 6 February plenary discussion brings out clearly this clash of views. Given the Red Army's presence in Poland, Churchill and Roosevelt were in a weak position; their goal could be only to ameliorate Soviet control, not to eliminate it. After lengthy haggling, the three leaders announced that the existing Polish government should be "reorganised on a wider democratic basis, with the inclusion of democratic leaders from Poland itself, and also from those living abroad." Molotov would consult with the British and U.S. Ambassadors in Moscow on how this should be done. Once a new government had been formed, it would hold "free and unfettered elections as soon as possible on the basis of universal suffrage and a secret ballot." This would also allow Britain to extend diplomatic recognition, reopen its embassy in Warsaw, and get some inside information on what the Soviets were doing within Poland.[10]

All depended on whether Stalin delivered on his promises. Here, Churchill derived comfort from the rest of the conference. In "Yalta: Plans for World Peace," he makes much of Stalin's concessions in order to agree on establishing the United Nations. After lengthy clarification, and perhaps to help strengthen their hand over Poland, Stalin and Molotov accepted the American voting formula for the Security Council. They also withdrew their demand that all sixteen Soviet republics should be represented in the General Assembly—in part to off-set the effect of Britain's Dominions and the South American clients of the United States—and asked for only two or three seats. Continuing deadlock would have prevented the inauguration of the United Nations in San Francisco on 25 April, for which the Roosevelt administration was busy preparing. The Soviet concessions were therefore, in Churchill's words, "a great relief to us all" and a sign that Stalin was capable of cooperation. He also derived comfort from the Soviet leader's remarks at dinner on 8 February about the importance of working together. "In the history of diplomacy I know of no such close alliance of three Great Powers as this," Stalin told his two counterparts. "May it be strong and stable; may we be as frank as possible." Churchill adds: "I had never suspected that he could be so expansive."[11]

It was the spirit of Yalta as much as its content that Churchill took home with him to London. Whatever the difficulties, it seemed that one could do business with Stalin.[12] And what were the alternatives? At the first plenary session, Roosevelt made clear that America's military presence in Germany would be limited to two years. In his memoirs, Churchill calls that "a momentous statement. . . . Formidable questions arose in my mind."[13] This helps explain why he felt it vital to keep on reasonable terms with the Soviet Union. At Yalta, he read a bleak memo from the Moscow embassy about the likelihood of the Grand Alliance falling apart once Germany was defeated and the consequent need to work more closely with Western Europe. In a sharp rejoinder, not used in the memoirs, he wrote:

Query? Moral!

1. The only bond of the victors is their common hate.
2. To make Britain safe she must become responsible for the safety of a cluster of feeble States.

We ought to think of something better than these.[14]

Although seeing no alternatives to cooperation with Stalin, Churchill was uneasy. At Chequers on the evening of 23 February, he asked, "What will lie between the white snows of Russia and the white cliffs of Dover?" and mused about Russia possibly turning against Britain, observing that Chamberlain had trusted Hitler as he himself was now trusting Stalin. The analogy of 1938 was much on his mind. He had told a meeting of ministers earlier that day, "Poor Neville Chamberlain believed he could trust Hitler. He was wrong. But I don't think I'm wrong about Stalin." Preparing his speech for the Commons, he wrote, "Soviet Russia seeks not only peace, but peace with honour." Jock Colville scribbled against that phrase, "? omit. Echo of Munich." It was omitted, but Churchill told the Commons on 27 February that he was sure Stalin and the Soviet leaders wished "to live in honourable friendship and equality with the Western democracies. I feel also that their word is their bond." Printing this in the memoirs, Churchill seeks to explain it away: "I felt bound to proclaim my confidence in Soviet faith in order to procure it. In this I was encouraged by Stalin's behaviour about Greece."[15]

In the Commons, a vocal minority of MPs, mainly Tory right-wingers, mobilized against what was seen as a complete sellout of the Polish government and its brave army. Twenty-five MPs dared to vote against the government, eleven ministers abstained, and one of them later resigned. Churchill notes these statistics in his memoirs but does not convey the intensity of feeling aroused: Lord Cranborne, the Dominions Secretary, for instance, told him on 3 April that the Yalta agreement on Poland was "a fraud which will very soon be exposed." Nor does

Churchill print his instruction that "C," the head of MI6, should find out if some leading Tory critics of Yalta were being secretly funded by the Polish government-in-exile. Instead, he ends "Yalta: Finale" with a passage he had dictated long before and then pondered where to place. This speaks with feeling of the responsibilities of men in power, who cannot merely pontificate but must make decisions. What, he asks, "would have happened if we had quarrelled with Russia when the Germans still had two or three hundred divisions on the fighting front? Our hopeful assumptions were soon to be falsified. Still, they were the only ones possible at the time."[16]

WHY, THEN, were these hopeful assumptions not borne out? First and foremost, Churchill blames the Soviet failure to implement the Yalta agreements as he had expected. The discussions in Moscow about an enlarged Polish government made little progress, and representatives of the London Poles were excluded. "It was plain as a pikestaff," says Churchill, that the Soviet tactic was "to drag the business out while the Lublin Committee consolidated its power." At the same time, the Soviets dismissed the all-party coalition in Romania and installed their own government on 6 March. "I was deeply disturbed by this news, which was to prove a pattern of things to come," Churchill writes. But "we were hampered in our protests" by the percentages deal the previous October, to which "Stalin had kept very strictly" in Greece. Because of this, Churchill says he wanted Roosevelt to take the lead in protesting about Romania.[17]

Although documenting Soviet bad faith, Churchill is again at pains in his memoirs to avoid attacking Stalin personally. When relating the deadlock over Poland, Molotov is the person constantly named, while the coup in Romania is blamed on his deputy, Andrei Vyshinsky. As we saw earlier, this reflected wartime attitudes as much as 1950s diplomacy. In a telegram to Roosevelt on 5 April 1945, quoted in the memoirs, Churchill used the phrase "the Soviet leaders, whoever they may be." Ernest Bevin, soon to be Labour's Foreign Secretary, suggested in the Cabinet on 6 March that Molotov, not Stalin, was responsible for Soviet obstruction on Poland. Likewise, in May, Sir Orme Sargent, Deputy Under-Secretary at the Foreign Office, noted the Soviet leader's tendency "to take a broad and statesmanlike line on matters put to him directly" and blamed the hard line in Eastern Europe on "influences in Russia working independently of Stalin"—either "the Party bosses behind the scenes" or "the victorious Soviet Marshals" who wanted to run their own show without Allied interference. Churchill ticked the reference to the Marshals. These assumptions help explain his continued hope that an appeal to Stalin or a new summit might resolve matters.

Whatever we may think today, Churchill saw Stalin not as the problem but the answer.[18]

Soviet betrayal of Yalta was the main explanation for the origins of the Cold War offered by apologists for the Roosevelt and Truman administrations. But Churchill was much readier than they to cite American policy as a contributory factor—and this was the second prong of his explanation. In March 1945, he repeatedly urged Washington to take a firm, joint line on the Polish question, only to receive temporizing replies from the President. He also urged a rapid thrust toward Berlin, spearheaded by Monty, but again got nowhere. As with his critique of Soviet policy, Churchill avoids fingering the man at the top—or in this case, men, for the death of Roosevelt on 12 April catapulted his inexperienced Vice President, Harry Truman, into the White House. He writes of "the deadly hiatus which existed between the fading of President Roosevelt's strength and the growth of President Truman's grip of the vast world problem. In this melancholy void one President could not act and the other could not know." Thus, Churchill shifts responsibility for U.S. policy to "the military chiefs" and the State Department, claiming that "the former confined themselves to their professional sphere" while "the latter did not comprehend the issues involved." With no one explicitly blamed, he is able to indict American policy, or lack of policy, as a secondary reason for the unfolding tragedy: "These were costly weeks for all."[19]

For this argument, "Western Strategic Divergences" is the key chapter in the first half of book 2. Churchill's peg is a cable from Eisenhower announcing that, after encircling the Ruhr, his "main thrust" would be through central Germany toward Kassel and Leipzig. This would be delivered by Bradley, with Montgomery "protecting his left flank." At about this time, Churchill adds, "we learned that Eisenhower had announced his new policy in a direct telegram to Marshal Stalin," without informing his British deputy, Air Chief Marshal Sir Arthur Tedder, or the Combined Chiefs. The Soviet leader readily agreed, declaring that Berlin had "lost its former strategic importance," and the American military backed Eisenhower, arguing that it was an "operational necessity" to keep the Russians informed of Allied plans, since they were converging on the same area from the other side. But Churchill was furious at the apparent demotion of Monty, the neglect of Berlin, and the way Ike had tipped off the Soviets. At considerable length, he prints his exchanges with Roosevelt and Eisenhower from the ensuing week. He did, however, omit any quotation from Ike's memoirs, following Norman Brook's advice to portray his differences as being with Washington and not Eisenhower personally.[20]

In his chapter, Churchill presents the argument as an issue of strategy. At the time, however, what really incensed him in Eisenhower's cable on 30 March was the phrase "Montgomery will be responsible on patrol tasks," suggesting a complete marginalization of British forces. This was a coding error for "on these tasks," as Churchill learned by 2 April, but that detail is omitted in the memoirs. Kelly clearly thought Churchill was making too much of the episode—"the dispute only arose out of a mistake in signalling," he noted—but Churchill was also angry about the sidelining of Tedder.[21] This was a particularly sore point, because Churchill wished him to function as a personal emissary, pressing British views, whereas Tedder became well-known for taking an "Allied" view of policy. Unable to influence Eisenhower's strategy, Churchill sent a scorching indictment of Tedder to the Chiefs of Staff, which Alan Brooke privately considered one of his worst minutes ever—"he must have been quite tight when dictating it." The Chiefs replied that such abuse of Tedder was totally unjustified, but Churchill refused to withdraw the minute. It was only on 28 December 1945 that he asked Ismay, still Military Secretary to the Cabinet, to destroy all copies. "This does not mean that my view is altered in any way," he added defiantly, "but there is no need to keep it on the record." Churchill says nothing about the furor in his memoirs, but it helps to explain his passion at the time.[22]

As for Eisenhower's strategy, there are signs that Churchill became less sure of his ground when he reread the documents. "I still hold that Ike should have made Berlin his main objective," he noted on 26 January 1953. "I am however impressed by the fact that the Russians started a month earlier than we had been led to expect and I wonder whether we could in fact have got there, whatever had been done." As evidence he cited a message he had sent Eden on 19 April 1945, which is printed in the book, noting that the Russians had 2.5 million troops poised on the edge of Berlin, compared with some twenty-five American divisions on "an immense front" and "at many points engaged with the Germans." He told Eden, "It would seem that the Western Allies are not immediately in a position to force their way into Berlin."[23]

This was not the impression Churchill leaves with his readers, however. At the start of "The Final Advance," he states that, at the moment when Roosevelt died, "there seemed nothing to stop the Western Allies from taking Berlin." Although the Russians were "only thirty-five miles from the city," they were not ready to attack and still had to cross the Oder, where the Germans were entrenched and for which "hard fighting" was to ensue. This portrayal of the situation is clearly at odds with the line he took on 26 January 1953. But these words were nicely chosen: "there seemed nothing to stop the Western Allies from taking

Berlin" can be read as signifying appearances that were later contradicted—witness his message to Eden on 19 April 1945. Without overt deception, Churchill contrives to mislead his readers.[24]

And so we come to "The Climax: Roosevelt's Death"—the most poignant chapter of *Triumph and Tragedy*. Churchill conceived of it very late, in mid-September 1952. Roosevelt's death, he told Kelly, was "really the 'supreme climax' of the War," and this would be "the key chapter" of the volume.[25] Kelly and Deakin collected relevant material, and Churchill worked on it during his New Year's vacation in Jamaica, but the result was disappointing. Charles Wood, the proofreader, felt it did not do justice to "the close personal relationship" between the two leaders and their "long and important collaboration," while Kelly told Norman Brook, "The Roosevelt chapter is a rough first draft and I hope you will be able to persuade the P.M. to go over it later." Churchill was aware of the defects, telling Brook on 18 February he hoped to "find time and strength" to improve it, perhaps over the summer holidays. But before the holidays came the stroke. The stricken premier did not return to the dying President until the end of August 1953, by which time only minor changes were possible.[26]

In "The Climax: Roosevelt's Death," Churchill tells us the news came like a "physical blow. My relations with this shining personality had played so large a part in the long, terrible years we had worked together." He prints much of his Commons valediction on 17 April, which paid tribute to the disabled leader's personal courage, his foresight about the Nazi threat, and the lifeline he extended to Britain through Lend-Lease. Roosevelt, he told MPs, was "the greatest American friend we have ever known, and the greatest champion of freedom who has ever brought help and comfort from the New World to the Old."[27] But the rest of the chapter is taken up with plans for the funeral and cables about Truman. The Roosevelt-Churchill relationship is never summarized and celebrated as the Syndicate had hoped.

Nor is Churchill able to justify his claim that the President's death was the "supreme climax of the war." Despite admitting that FDR arrived in the Crimea looking "frail and ill," Churchill tries to present him there as an active, engaged participant in the negotiations. His rough notes for the volume had been more candid: "I thought he was very frail. . . . He was a tragic figure. You only have to look at the photographs. . . . He was transparent . . . he really was only a pale reflection almost throughout." On Kelly's suggestion, he removed a damning comment by Hopkins about Roosevelt, transmitted via Ambassador Halifax on 16 April 1945: "At Yalta Harry doubted if he had heard more than half of what went on round the table, and hardly anything of his late messages to you had been his own."[28] Churchill concedes the latter point in his memoirs, speculating on whether certain sentences might have been written by FDR, but a December 1950 draft said bluntly, "I was in fact talking to a friendly but darkening void."[29] All this serves to downgrade the significance of 12 April: if Roosevelt was already a spent force, did his demise make any difference?

Perhaps one should allow that "Roosevelt's death" is really shorthand for the President's loss of grip in his final months—what Churchill calls "the deadly hiatus" in American policy. In retrospect, it is clear that congestive heart disease, high blood pressure, chronic anemia, and other ailments had dragged Roosevelt down ever since Teheran, sometimes causing an insufficient supply of blood to the brain—hence, perhaps, the gaping-mouth photos of him at Yalta. But would a fit, sentient Roosevelt have behaved very differently? While some scholars have espoused this line—even asserting that "a more alert President Roosevelt might have prevented the debacle of the Vietnam War a generation later"—it seems clear that FDR's basic policies on the postwar world had been set long before 1945.[30] He did not intend to let Poland jeopardize cooperation with Stalin. Nor would he permit any impression of an Anglo-American axis against Russia. These had been axioms of his policy since 1943, they guided his conduct at Yalta, and they were generally supported by the State Department and the Joint Chiefs.

In his memoirs, Churchill notes the President's telegram to Stalin on 5 April, concerning contacts in Berne between the Office of Strategic Services (OSS) and the Nazi SS commander in Italy about a possible German surrender. Stalin had taken these as evidence of Western duplicity, and FDR expressed "bitter resentment" at "such vile misrepresentations of my actions." Churchill tells us he was "deeply struck" by this last sentence, and thought the President "might well have added this final stroke himself. . . . [I]t seemed like Roosevelt himself in anger." But Hopkins specifically told Halifax, in the passage not quoted from the telegram of 16 April 1945, that not even that sentence came from Roosevelt. By contrast, we now know that FDR *did* draft the whole of his penultimate message to Churchill on 11 April:

> I would minimise the general Soviet problem as much as possible, because these problems, in one form or another, seem to arise every day, and most of them sort themselves out, as in the case of the Berne meeting. We must be firm, however, and our course thus far is correct.

This message is printed at the end of "Soviet Suspicions" without any comment. Yet it is authentically the voice as well as the hand of Franklin Roosevelt.[31]

—

THUS, CHURCHILL'S DEPICTION of a fading President overshadowed by misguided staff is difficult to sustain—likewise his corollary, about a neophyte successor whose natural firmness was restrained by isolationist elements in Washington.[32] Truman did not deny his lack of experience—a former Missouri senator, chosen to balance the Democratic ticket in 1944, he knew little about foreign affairs and had received no induction from Roosevelt. But he was a feisty little man, determined to show he was no pushover. After a tough briefing from Averell Harriman, who had flown back from Moscow specially, he lectured Molotov on 23 April about the need to honor the Yalta agreement on Poland. "I've never been talked to like that in my life" was how Truman's 1954 memoirs reported Molotov's reaction. Although that quote was probably a later embellishment, there is little doubt that the encounter was blunt. Churchill mentions this meeting only obliquely in his memoirs, though he had received a full report on it from Eden, who, like Molotov, was in Washington en route to San Francisco for the inauguration of the United Nations. It does not square with his assertion in the chapter on Roosevelt's death that had he attended Roosevelt's funeral—rather than being dissuaded from going because Attlee and Eden were out of the country—he could have brought the new President around to a firm line. In fact, Truman started tough in April but then softened. And he, like Roosevelt, did not intend to be manipulated by Churchill.[33]

In the last days of the war, Churchill was desperate for the Western Allies to acquire as much territory as possible—not for indefinite retention but to use as bargaining counters in future diplomacy. Monty's forces, urged on from London, just beat the Russians into Denmark. On the other hand, Churchill had now given up hope of reaching Berlin. And, he tells us sourly, the chances of forestalling the Russians in Vienna had been "abandoned" eight months earlier when Alexander's forces had been "stripped" in order to invade southern France. In early May, the open city was Prague, about which there existed no firm agreement with the Soviets. Mindful of the March row about Berlin, Churchill was careful not to press the Americans too hard. "I am hoping that your plan does not inhibit you to advance to Prague if you have the troops and do not meet the Russians earlier," he cabled Eisenhower politely on 7 May. But, he tells us, the Russians "reacted strongly" to proposals for U.S. troops to move into the city, and so the Americans "halted while the Red Army cleared the east and west banks of the Moldau and occupied Prague." This last was a quotation from Eisenhower's final report to the Combined Chiefs. At Brook's suggestion in December 1952,

Churchill removed most of his overtly critical comments about the general who was now becoming President, such as his comment on 25 April 1945 that Eisenhower "had never conceived of Prague as a military, still less as a political objective" and the fact, already in U.S. memoirs, that Ike had again been in direct contact with Moscow.[34]

It is in this chapter, "The Final Advance," that one detects some of the sharpest differences of emphasis between Churchill and his researchers. In the Syndicate redraft in April 1952, Pownall wrote that the dying Roosevelt "had counted and staked so much on Stalin's good faith and his own powers of persuasion. Now all his gains were slipping away." Churchill deleted these sentences. On Truman's inexperience, Pownall said that "the purely military view" received "an emphasis beyond its proper proportions," citing Marshall as "the principal," but this phrase was also cut. Nor did his judgment on Stalin (and by implication on Churchill) survive into the book: "He had not only defeated the enemy on his front, but had also outwitted his Allies."[35] In September 1952, Denis Kelly drafted a new introduction to this chapter, intended to sharpen its thrust. Much of it appears in the published work but, despite the advice of Norman Brook, Churchill cut the punch lines: "Berlin, Prague and Vienna were needlessly yielded to the Soviets. Here may be discerned the Tragedy in our hour of Triumph" and "the reader may well conclude that it was an unnecessary one." This, of course, was what Churchill wanted his readers to infer, but it was not politic to be so blunt.[36]

On 8 May 1945, V-E Day, Londoners rejoiced in the streets, but Churchill's mood was now somber. Four days later, in a message highlighted in *Triumph and Tragedy*, he told Truman that "an iron curtain is drawn down upon their front. We do not know what is going on behind. There seems little doubt that the whole of the regions east of Lübeck-Trieste-Corfu will soon be completely in their hands." Churchill probably took the phrase "iron curtain" from Nazi propaganda in the dying days of the Third Reich, but the idea had been forming in his mind weeks before as he struggled for diplomatic access to Poland. On 16 March, he spoke to Roosevelt about "an impenetrable veil"; on 1 April, he complained to Stalin that "a veil of secrecy" had been "drawn over the Polish scene." Both these telegrams are quoted in the memoirs.[37] On 18 May, he used the phrase "iron screen" in "a brisk talking to" of Feodor Gusev, the Soviet Ambassador. Common to all these references is the theme of concealment: the Western Allies did not know what the Soviets were up to. But the imagery had gradually hardened — from "veil" to "curtain" and then to "screen" — and by May the "iron" had entered Churchill's rhetoric and his soul. He told Gusev bluntly that the British "refused to be pushed about" and had postponed the demobilization of the Royal Air Force so as "to enter upon discussions about the future of Europe with all the strength they had."[38]

A few days later, Churchill recalled all copies of the record of this 18 May meeting. His ostensible reason was that the coalition was now breaking up, but it is likely that he had second thoughts about drawing attention to his reference to delaying demobilization of the RAF. In his memoirs, he prints the orders he issued on 17 May about keeping the air forces intact and conserving all service-able German aircraft in Allied hands but without indicating the deeper thinking behind them.[39] For at this very time, Churchill secretly instructed his military planners to examine Operation Unthinkable—how to "impose upon Russia the will of the United States and British Empire" in order to get "a square deal for Poland." The hypothetical date for the start of hostilities was 1 July 1945.

The planners were told to assume that such a war would have "the full sup-port" of British and American public opinion and that they could "count on the use of German manpower and what remains of German industrial capacity." (Attacking a popular ally just three months after the end of the war, using the troops of the former enemy, was, of course, truly unthinkable.)[40] Plowing on, nonetheless, the planners highlighted the strength of the Allied fleets and strate-gic bombers but had to acknowledge massive Soviet superiority on land—roughly four to one in infantry and two to one in tanks. They proposed a surprise attack by forty-seven American and British divisions around Dresden and envis-aged achieving some limited political objective, such as a more acceptable Polish government. But this would not be "a lasting result." The Allies would have to accept the prospect of "total war," which could be won only by penetrating far more deeply and durably into the Soviet Union than the Wehrmacht had man-aged in 1942. Even if up to 100,000 Germans were mobilized in the long term, this would make no substantial difference to the imbalance of forces. And, added the Chiefs of Staff on 8 June, if the Americans wearied of the struggle and turned to the Pacific War, then the odds would change from "heavy" to "fanciful." Alan Brooke wrote in his diary that the whole idea was "fantastic and the chances of success quite impossible. There is no doubt that from now onwards Russia is all powerful in Europe."[41]

Faced with this grim scenario, Churchill not only conceded defeat but did a complete somersault. Abandoning any idea of the West imposing its will on Rus-sia, on 9 June 1945 he told the planners to consider how "we could defend our Island" if the Americans withdrew to the Pacific leaving the Russians with "the power to advance to the North Sea and the Atlantic." By retaining the code word

"Unthinkable," he added, "the Staffs will realise that this remains a precautionary study of what, I hope, is still a purely hypothetical contingency."[42] Unthinkable was so unmentionable that Churchill makes no reference to it in the text or drafts of his memoirs, though the discussion of German rearmament lodged in his memory—with embarrassing results, as we shall see, in November 1954.

Part of Churchill's alarm in May 1945 may be explained by the confrontation over Trieste, on which Alexander's armies and Yugoslav forces had converged. On 12 May, before receiving the "iron curtain" telegram, Truman cabled Churchill to propose a joint display of force to make Tito retreat. Like Churchill, Truman assumed that the Yugoslav leader was backed by Stalin. The problem was therefore "whether our two countries are going to permit our Allies to engage in uncontrolled land grabbing or tactics which are all too reminiscent of those of Hitler and Japan. . . . If we stand firm on this issue, as we are doing on Poland," Truman told Churchill, "we can hope to avoid a host of other similar encroachments." The President's message was "most welcome," Churchill tells us in the memoirs, going on to quote his own telegram to Alexander that "this action if pursued with firmness may well prevent a renewal of the World War." He also prints part of his enthusiastic reply to Truman, urging a "standstill" on movements of the U.S. Army and Army Air Forces from Europe to the Pacific "at any rate for a few weeks." But he omits the paragraph asking Truman to confirm that Alexander could use the seven U.S. divisions currently under his command "in the event of hostilities against Yugoslavia."[43]

Then Truman drew back from a confrontation over Trieste. Churchill speculates that there was a "somewhat violent reaction" in Washington to the President's "bold telegram to me" and blames neo-isolationists and Pacific Firsters. He admits that his suggestion of a "standstill" might have "raised this issue abruptly in the President's circle" but denies that he was envisaging "a war with the Yugoslavs." Again, Churchill portrays Truman as a right-minded but malleable figure, restrained by advisers from his innate boldness. He does not seem to have appreciated the fundamental shift in the President's attitude in mid-May, as the deadlock on Poland and the face-off in Trieste threatened a total breakdown in relations with Moscow. Unhappy that toughness had not worked, Truman was now listening to Joseph E. Davies, Ambassador to Moscow in 1937–1938, who advocated patiently allaying Soviet suspicions. He was also persuaded by James F. Byrnes, his new Secretary of State, that the Yalta agreements on Poland were ambiguous and that Churchill's hard-line interpretation of them was not tenable. At the end of May, Truman sent Davies to London to restrain Churchill and dispatched the ailing Hopkins to Moscow to sort out Poland. The President told

Davies he was "having as much difficulty" with Churchill as with Stalin and felt that "each of them was trying to make me the paw of the cat that pulled the chestnuts out of the fire."[44]

Davies visited Chequers on 26–27 May. He left convinced that, although "a very great man," Churchill was "more concerned over preserving England's position in Europe than in preserving Peace." He told Truman that this attitude "does undoubtedly account for much of the aggressiveness" of the Soviets since Yalta. Davies also said Churchill was furious to learn that Truman wanted a personal meeting with Stalin as a precursor to a Big Three summit.[45] As Churchill indicates in his memoirs, he gave Davies a memo for the President saying that the British government flatly refused "to attend any meeting except as equal partners from its opening." Truman duly backed off the idea of a personal meeting with Stalin, but the thrust of U.S. policy was painfully clear.[46]

As for Hopkins's mission to Moscow, Churchill covers that in a couple of pages. In early May, he had been incensed at the fate of the sixteen noncommunist Poles who traveled to Warsaw for talks about a new government, only to be taken to Moscow to face trial for "diversionary tactics in the rear of the Red Army." A month later, he could only acquiesce as Hopkins secured Stalin's agreement to invite Stanislaw Mikolajczyk, premier of the Polish government in London, and two colleagues, plus some noncommunists from Poland, to Moscow for consultations. The sequel is described in two terse sentences: "I persuaded Mikolajczyk to go to Moscow, and in the upshot a new Polish Provisional Government was set up. At Truman's request this was recognised by both Britain and the United States on July 5." Not surprisingly, he does not print the congratulatory telegram he sent to an uneasy Mikolajczyk on 26 June:

> How right you were to take the momentous decision you took in my room barely ten days ago. The results that have been achieved seem to me to give the greatest hope of a reconstitution of the Polish National Power. This can only be done through friendship to Russia. The Soviets will, I am sure, appreciate [the] kindly action on your part as helping to bring them and the Western Democracies together.

Churchill must have choked on these words as he dictated them in 1945, and they were not regurgitated in his memoirs. Instead, he ends with gloomy reflection: "It is difficult to see what more we could have done. For five months the Soviets had fought every inch of the road. They had gained their object by delay. . . . So far only dust and ashes had been gathered, and these are all that remain to us to-day of Polish national freedom."[47]

For weeks, Churchill had also tried to prevent the Western pullback in Germany, arguing that they should retain the most eastwardly positions possible as bargaining chips for a new summit. "Surely it is vital now to come to an understanding with Russia, or to see where we are with her," he wrote to Truman in his "iron curtain" telegram on 12 May, "before we weaken our armies mortally or retire to the zones of occupation." A month later, the President told Churchill he had carefully reviewed the Yalta agreement on occupation zones in Germany. He could see no justification for delaying its implementation and had been advised that to do so would harm Soviet-American relations. "This struck a knell in my breast," Churchill tells us. But, with America's forces three million to Britain's one, "I had no choice but to submit." In this way, "Soviet Russia was established in the heart of Europe. This was a fateful milestone for mankind." And "in the moment of victory was our best, and what might prove to have been our last, chance of durable world peace allowed composedly to fade away."[48] (He does not make clear that, under the same agreement, the Russians relinquished three quarters of Berlin to their allies.)

Churchill's hopes of a settlement with the Soviets were now pinned on the delayed summit in the Berlin suburb of Potsdam, which convened on 17 July. His two chapters on the conference are not very satisfying. This is partly because, unlike the discussion of Yalta, much of it never really transcended Kelly's paraphrases of the official minutes. Neither the Syndicate nor Churchill had time or energy to do as Norman Brook repeatedly urged and abandon narration for analysis.[49] At root, however, Churchill's account of Potsdam is disappointing because it was, for the British, a disappointing conference. Their dependence on America was now acute. Churchill mentions a talk with Truman on 18 July about the "melancholy" financial position of Britain, "who had spent more than half her foreign investments for the common cause when we were alone, and now emerged from the war with a great external debt of three thousand million pounds." Truman "said he would do his very utmost" to help but stressed his own domestic difficulties.[50] This is a rare reference in volume 6 to Britain's financial plight. Churchill does not discuss the talks at Quebec in September 1944 about postwar aid or Truman's abrupt termination of Lend-Lease in mid-August 1945 to propitiate Congress. As before, this neglect presumably reflects his general indifference to economic policy and his desire to represent Britain as much as possible as America's equal.

—

WHEN CHURCHILL FLEW to Berlin, he could see for himself the effects of Allied saturation bombing. "Bomber" Harris had become almost an independent operator, whom the Chief of the Air Staff, Sir Charles Portal, vainly tried to divert to specific strategic targets, notably the German oil industry. Area bombing had reached its now notorious apogee in the RAF's incineration of Dresden on the night of 13 February 1945, followed by an American raid the next morning. In all, at least 50,000 Germans died. Articles about "terror bombing" surfaced in the U.S. and British press, starting a debate that still rumbles on and from which Harris's reputation has never recovered. Yet the climax of the air war receives less than two pages in Churchill's chapter on "The German Surrender." Harris is not named, the debate between oil and area targets is ignored, and we are told only that in February 1945 British bombers "made a heavy raid" on Dresden, "a centre of communications of Germany's Eastern Front." A judicious summing-up of the strategic-bombing campaign admits that "we certainly under-estimated the strong latent reserve in Germany's industry" but argues that in the latter part of the war the Nazis were forced to divert "a large proportion of their total war effort" to air defense and that British and U.S. bomber forces "played a major part in the economic collapse of Germany."[51]

Virtually all this section, indeed most of the chapter, was drafted by the Syndicate in 1952. Churchill made only minor verbal changes—for instance, adding a reference to the "courage" as well as the "discipline" of German civilians.[52] When asked by the historians of Bomber Command in May 1950 for his recollections of Dresden, Churchill wrote, "I cannot recall anything about it. I thought the Americans did it." In fact, he had taken the lead in prodding Bomber Command to attack eastern German targets as a token of support for the Russians prior to Yalta, but when the furor about Dresden erupted publicly, he sent the Chiefs of Staff a stern minute on 28 March 1945 instructing that

> the moment has come when the question of bombing of German cities, simply for the sake of increasing the terror, though under other pretexts, should be reviewed. . . . I feel the need for more precise concentration upon military objectives, such as oil and communications behind the immediate battle-zone, rather than mere acts of terror and wanton destruction, however impressive.

After a protest from Portal, Churchill agreed to withdraw his "rough" minute and accepted a redraft by Ismay. It is the latter that is quoted in the war memoirs and then only the part relating to Churchill's argument that area bombing would prove counterproductive "if we come into control of an entirely ruined land" in which there was "a great shortage of accommodation for ourselves and our Allies."[53]

One historian opines that Churchill's original minute was a "calculated political attempt" to distance himself from the furor about Dresden and area bombing. Be that as it may, the memoirs do say that on 6 April Bomber Command was told to stop attacking industrial centers. They do not print Churchill's one-sentence minute of 19 April — "What was the point of going and blowing down Potsdam?" — after he had seen a report about a 500-bomber raid on the night of 14 April.[54] This was a facet of the war over which the Prime Minister had lost effective control; it was also one that became immensely controversial after 1945. On both accounts, one can understand why the memoirs are so tight-lipped.

Whatever Churchill's belated qualms about area bombing, he tells us he had no doubts, then or later, about the rightness of the dropping of the atomic bomb.[55] But, as we have seen, he had great difficulty in telling the background story in his memoirs.[56] In September 1949, after a lunchtime tutorial from Lord Cherwell, he dictated a survey of basic nuclear physics and the British research program of 1939–1941, but this was never taken further.[57] In volume 1 he prints a letter he claims (erroneously) that he sent to the Air Ministry in August 1939 questioning the chances of an atomic bomb in the next several years.[58] In volume 4, he prints a confused and inaccurate account of what he had discussed with FDR at Hyde Park in June 1942, leading to the full-scale development program in the United States. In volume 5, he says nothing about the Quebec Agreement that he and Roosevelt signed on 19 August 1943 because in 1951 President Truman refused to make the agreement public. And in volume 6 he is equally silent about the aide-mémoire he and FDR initialed at Hyde Park on 19 September 1944. This stated that when a bomb was ready, "it might perhaps, after mature consideration, be used against the Japanese" and also affirmed that "full collaboration" between the two governments in developing atomic energy for military and commercial purposes "should continue after the defeat of Japan unless and until terminated by joint agreement."[59]

The Syndicate did debate whether to include some reference to the Hyde Park discussions. Ismay told Churchill in October 1950, "I have a note that you had a talk with the President before dinner on Tube Alloys [the British code word]. In his book Leahy, who was evidently present at this talk, says that no agreement was reached about its use for military purposes." This was not an accurate representation by Ismay of the memoirs of Roosevelt's Chief of Staff, who actually said, "To my knowledge, no agreement was made in regard to sharing its use for military purposes." And Leahy himself was totally wrong in his next sentence: "There have been reports since that Roosevelt agreed to share the bomb's secret with Britain, but no such understanding was reached at this particular conference." On the basis of Ismay's misleading note, Bill Deakin drafted a sentence for inclusion in the December 1951 Syndicate redraft: "That evening I had a long talk with the President about Tube Alloys but we reached no agreement as to its use for military purposes." Cherwell pointed out that the sentence was incorrect but also noted that volume 5 had said nothing about the Quebec Agreement. He therefore suggested it was better to omit the Hyde Park Agreement from volume 6, and Churchill concurred. Thus, the two crucial wartime agreements on Anglo-American nuclear cooperation do not appear in Churchill's memoirs.[60]

But Churchill's options in 1950–1951 had already been constrained by the decision he made back in July 1945, in deference to the Americans, to not mention either document in his forthcoming statement to Parliament about the genesis of the atomic bomb. Cherwell had warned that to do so "would only lead to demands for publication, which would be very embarrassing to the Americans and perhaps even to us." He added that Henry Stimson and his staff at the U.S. War Department were "anxious that this particular aspect should be handled with considerable care as very difficult political issues may be involved."[61] Churchill acquiesced, and the agreements remained secret, which in turn made it easier for the U.S. Congress, without opposition from Truman, to negate their provisions for Anglo-American cooperation in the McMahon Act of 1946. It was this act that Churchill sought to overturn in his second premiership. Arguably, his silence in 1945 as much as the Attlee government's apparent spinelessness thereafter helped create the problem he was trying to solve in the 1950s.

Why had Churchill been so diffident in July 1945? This takes us back again to the imbalance of transatlantic relations in the last third of the war. The Quebec Agreement had been concluded over fierce opposition from the American military bureaucracy running the bomb project and in the knowledge that, whatever had been Britain's contribution in 1939–1941, it was now very much the junior partner. "I am absolutely sure that we cannot get any better terms by ourselves than are set forth in my secret agreement with the President," Churchill told Cherwell in May 1944, in a reference to Quebec. "It may be that in after years this may be judged to have been too confiding on our part. Only those who know the circumstances and moods prevailing beneath the presidential level will be able to understand why I have made this Agreement."[62] But Quebec and Hyde

Park were Executive Agreements, signed by the President without reference to Congress. Because of their sensitivity and Roosevelt's casual administrative habits, they were not widely known even at the top of his administration. FDR's copy of the Hyde Park Agreement was found some years later misfiled in the papers of his naval aide because "Tube Alloys" suggested it was about submarines. Stimson, the Secretary of War, was not aware of its existence until June 1945 and had to request a photocopy from the British.[63] Here was a shaky foundation on which to base such an important relationship, but Churchill felt it was the best he could get.

With all this unsaid, therefore, he takes up the story in "Potsdam: The Atomic Bomb" at the point when Stimson gave him news on 17 July 1945 that a successful atomic test had taken place in the New Mexican desert. "British consent in principle to the use of the weapon had been given on July 4, before the test had taken place," Churchill tells us. While in Jamaica over New Year's 1953, he brooded a good deal on this point. "I do not ever recall that the Cabinet or the Defence Committee were ever informed that matters were so imminent," he wrote Cherwell on 10 January. "Had I known that the Tube Alloys were progressing so fast it would have affected my judgement about the date of the election."[64]

Here was another ingenious counterfactual, but Pownall was unimpressed: "First I have heard of any qualms of this kind." The original documents show that Churchill was kept well informed about the timetable for the American test; the problem was that no one could predict what effect the bomb would actually have. The decision for an early election was made, as Churchill indicates in "The End of the Coalition," largely on the assumption that Labour would benefit from the new register of voters, which came into effect in October 1945. The domestic political point about the bomb project was therefore not what Churchill knew but what he told his colleagues. Cherwell's reply on 28 January 1953 made clear that the Prime Minister had the information but deliberately never took it to the Cabinet, the Defence Committee, or the Service Ministers. Cherwell also noted that Churchill, when giving his consent to using the bomb, had not pressed for proper "machinery" of Anglo-American cooperation to be set up: he expected that this would be discussed at Potsdam.[65] Once again, he was putting his faith in a personal relationship. Truman and Churchill discussed the bomb at length at Potsdam, but they concentrated on questions about its use and about what to tell Stalin. Perhaps Churchill intended to raise the Anglo-American aspect later in the conference; if so, his election defeat put an end to the idea. Like Roosevelt, he had treated atomic diplomacy as a personal fiefdom, only to be dispossessed by events.

Churchill tells us that "the decision whether or not to use the atomic bomb to compel the surrender of Japan was never even an issue" at Potsdam. Echoing an exaggerated claim in Stimson's memoirs, he mentions the prospect of saving "a million American lives"—and "half that number of British," he adds—by not having to invade the Japanese Home Islands. A further attraction was not needing Russian help in the Pacific War, which meant that "the array of European problems could therefore be faced on their merits." Churchill also says that, following hints from the Japanese to the Russians about possible capitulation on terms somewhat less than unconditional surrender, Truman agreed to spell out the Allies' demands in the Potsdam Declaration of 26 July. Churchill adds, "These terms were rejected by the military rulers of Japan, and the United States Air Force made its plans accordingly to cast one atomic bomb on Hiroshima and one on Nagasaki."[66]

This stark sentence masked an important debate within the Syndicate in September 1952. Briefed by Cherwell, Kelly advised Churchill (inaccurately) that on 2 August 1945 the Japanese Cabinet "told the Russians that they would accept the Potsdam ultimatum," but "the Russians concealed this from us" because they knew that, without declaring war, they would not get all the "benefits which we had promised them at Yalta." In the margin, Churchill wrote, "I knew this. Little doubt that it is true." Kelly added, however, that the evidence came mostly from secondary sources and "might be difficult to defend and justify if the story were published. Pownall and I feel that as most of this happened after you left office you may prefer to omit it. But if you wish to explore it further you will no doubt get in touch with Lord Cherwell direct."[67] This last sentence was ticked by Churchill, and Cherwell alluded to the matter again in January 1953, but nothing more was done.[68]

Churchill's final chapter contains a sparkling account of the Soviet dictator's reaction when Truman, as agreed with Churchill, mentioned the atomic-bomb test with studied casualness after the plenary meeting at Potsdam on 24 July.

> I can see it all as if it were yesterday. He seemed to be delighted. A new bomb! Of extraordinary power! Probably decisive on the whole Japanese war! What a bit of luck! This was my impression at the moment, and I was sure that he had no idea of the significance of what he was being told.

Churchill dictated this passage in May 1951, and it survives unchanged in his printed text. He clung to it in defiance of the evidence piling up in public from 1950 about the way Klaus Fuchs and other Soviet agents had betrayed the Manhattan Project to Moscow. Pownall raised this evidence with Kelly, who noted in September 1952 that "if Fuchs and Co. had told Stalin about it, this whole paragraph would make the Prime Minister and Truman look rather silly." Cherwell's response was that the Soviets had plenty of information about the bomb, but "Stalin did not comprehend its significance." Pownall reopened the issue in March 1953 after another exposé of Fuchs in Alan Moorehead's book *The Traitors*; again, Cherwell was dismissive. With "the Soviets" amended to "Stalin," Churchill stuck with his firm declaration about that moment at Potsdam: "I was certain therefore that at that date Stalin had no special knowledge of the vast process of research upon which the United States and Britain had been engaged for so long."[69]

The opening of Soviet archives has cast new light on these statements. Whether or not Stalin fully grasped what he was told on 24 July, immediately after the bomb fell on Hiroshima he galvanized the Soviet atomic project by putting it under the direct control of his secret police chief, Lavrenti Beria. The information from Fuchs provided the prototype for the bomb the Soviets eventually tested in August 1949.[70] Yet Churchill says nothing in his memoirs about the extent of Soviet espionage. He will not countenance the thought that Stalin was playacting. This would have undermined his most cherished belief or illusion—both in 1945 and in the memoirs—that the Soviet dictator was, at heart, a man who could be trusted. These reflections on the genesis of the nuclear age bring us back again to the overriding theme of his memoirs: history was determined by the men at the top.

CHAPTER 31

"IT SEEMS INCREDIBLE"

O N 10 OCTOBER 1953, Churchill addressed the Conservative party conference at Margate. The fifty-minute speech was designed to dispel rumors about his health and reiterate the case for a Cold War summit. A few days later, he was told he had won the Nobel Prize. His private secretary, Anthony Montague Browne, said Churchill received the news with "touching joy," but his mood turned to "indifference" on learning it was the prize for literature and not for peace. As Churchill finished his great work, the future still mattered more than the past.[1]

CHURCHILL TOLD the Swedish Ambassador on 15 October that it would be "a very great pleasure" to come to Stockholm to receive the prize, but much would depend on "how my duties will go." According to Montague Browne, Churchill was not really keen to attend, and his Bermuda summit with Eisenhower, rescheduled after the June stroke, provided a perfect excuse. Nor did Churchill devote much energy to the acceptance speech, which was brief, flat, and more about peace than literature—to the disappointment of Houghton Mifflin, which had expected a tour de force suitable for publication. The text was read for him on 10 December by his wife, who, accompanied by daughter Mary, captivated Stockholm. At one point, a student choir serenaded her with "My Darling Clementine."[2]

The presentation speech was delivered by the noted Swedish author Sigfrid Siwertz. It was "very seldom," he said, that "great statesmen and warriors have also been great writers." Churchill's political and literary achievements were of such magnitude that it was as if Caesar had been "wielding Cicero's stylus." He quoted from the biography of Marlborough: "Words are easy and many, while great deeds are difficult and rare." Yes, said Siwertz, but "great, living and persuasive words are also difficult and rare. And Churchill has shown that they can take on the character of great deeds." Siwertz praised *My Early Life*—"one of the world's most entertaining adventure stories"—and *Great Contemporaries*—"one of his most charming books." He lauded *Marlborough* for its "vivid battle scenes" and as "a penetrating study of an enigmatic and unique personality." *The World Crisis* received a brief mention, but there was nothing about *The Second World War*. Instead, Siwertz ended with the speeches: "Behind Churchill the writer is Churchill the orator. . . . With his great speeches he has, perhaps, himself erected his most enduring monument."[3]

Here was almost a second anticlimax: not only was the Nobel Prize for literature not peace, but also it made no allusion to his crowning work. Indeed, Siwertz's elevation of the speeches ran counter to the aim of *Their Finest Hour*. But Churchill was not displeased. "It is a very remarkable appreciation," he told Henry Laughlin. "I did not know I wrote so well!" The money was also welcome—"£12,100 free of tax. Not so bad!" he told Clementine. And he must have been struck by Siwertz's final tribute, added impromptu at the end of his formal text: "Generally the Nobel Prize gives lustre to the prizewinner. In this case the prizewinner gives lustre to the prize."[4] What hit the headlines was simply that Churchill had joined an elite group containing Britons such as Kipling, Shaw, and T. S. Eliot, and only one other historian, Theodor Mommsen, the German chronicler of ancient Rome. For Churchill's publishers, this was the best possible publicity with which to launch *Triumph and Tragedy*. *The New York Times* ran thirty installments, six days per week from 23 October to 26 November, and the *Daily Telegraph* ran thirty-seven on a more leisurely schedule to 18 December, which overlapped the Stockholm ceremonies and the Bermuda conference. At the end, the *Daily Telegraph* stated that volumes 1 through 5 had already sold six million copies, in many languages, while excerpts had appeared in fifty other papers in forty countries. "No book has ever so swiftly achieved such dissemination."[5]

Daniel Longwell of *Life* told colleagues that *Triumph and Tragedy* was "far and away the best book we have had from Churchill." The magazine generated five installments from the last volume of what it called Churchill's "Nobel Prize–Winning Memoirs," far more than from volumes 3, 4, and 5. Throughout, it featured Cold War angles, with headlines such as "A 'divergence' with U.S.

helps Reds clamp hold on the Balkans" (about the row over southern France), "Freedom wins a skirmish" (on Greece), and "The Russians win a battle" (at Yalta). Roosevelt's death appeared on a separate page about "one of the great personal friendships of this century." This ended with a comment Churchill had made (to Longwell) at Chartwell back in 1947, when he paused, looked out the window, and murmured, as if to himself, "How I loved that man!"[6]

Houghton Mifflin published the American edition of the book on 30 November 1953. As usual, they were squeezed between Churchill's late delivery and constant revisions and their Book-of-the-Month Club deadline. But they had longer for the task than on some earlier volumes—about three months—and also benefited from what had become a harmonious relationship with their publishing partners. *Life* and *The New York Times*, once so jealous about keeping a full week between the end of serialization and the publication of the book, were now willing for Houghton Mifflin to publish one day after the newspaper had finished. Laughlin, on his side, had stopped insisting that the serials must print no more than 40 percent of the total text, while, across the Atlantic, Desmond Flower was no longer apoplectic that Houghton Mifflin's publication date was six months before Cassell's. And Camrose, initially very resentful at being junior partner to *Life*'s moneybags, now had an almost warm relationship with Longwell.[7]

It had proved a particularly profitable venture for Cassell's, Houghton Mifflin, and Emery Reves. The British publishers were committed to paying £40,000 to Churchill for five volumes, as noted earlier (chapter 9), but they earned perhaps double that in net profit on volume 1 alone. Houghton Mifflin cleared their $50,000 commitment with volume 3, thereby allowing Reves to share in their profits in addition to the money he was making from the foreign-language rights. By September 1953, the North American edition had sold 1,833,000 copies (see the table on page 493), so volume 6 pushed sales well over the two-million mark. Cassell's had already sold 1,750,000 copies, and it also passed the two-million milestone, in a much smaller market, when it published volume 6 in April 1954.[8] *Life*, the biggest paymaster, did less well financially for its three quarters of a million dollars' investment, plus more than $60,000 in "expenses" for Churchill's working vacations. Daniel Longwell admitted that "a lot of our readers may have been bored with the whole series" but added that "a lot more of them were enormously complimented even if they never read them." The kudos of publishing the memoirs was why *The New York Times* was so desperate not to be left out in 1946. Both it and *Life* were happy to use Churchill's account of the war as a peg for their editorial views on the Cold War. Longwell told Beaverbrook contentedly in November 1953 that the memoirs "turned out to be a fine serial after all."[9]

NORTH AMERICAN SALES FOR VOLUMES 1 TO 5
(TO 4 SEPTEMBER 1953)

	Houghton Mifflin	Book-of-the-Month Club	Thomas Allen (Canada)	Total
Vol. 1	123,396	400,000	27,132	550,528
Vol. 2	90,817	286,000	18,022	394,839
Vol. 3	58,916	252,900	10,938	322,754
Vol. 4	63,569	233,600	9,727	306,896
Vol. 5	53,387	193,900	10,801	258,088
Vols. 1–5	390,085	1,366,400	76,620	1,833,105

Source: Smith to Moseley, memo, "Total Sales, Churchill Vols,"
4 Sept. 1953, HM 318/4: Churchill Memos, 1953.

American reviewers had plenty of praise for this last volume of Churchill's "magnificent and inspiring narrative" (New Orleans *Times-Picayune*), "his great prose epic of the war" (*The American Historical Review*), "one of the greatest studies in statesmanship our times are likely to see" (New York *Herald Tribune*). Rare stylistic criticism came from the historian Dexter Perkins, in the *Saturday Review of Literature*, who thought it lacked "the brilliance that has frequently characterised his style" and hardly justified "from the literary point of view" the Nobel Prize. But even Perkins considered the volume to be "a source of primary importance," raising questions that would be "debated again and again in the years ahead."[10]

The overriding question for American reviewers had to do with the origin of the Cold War. Most felt that Churchill was writing what *The Nation* called "subjective history," setting down "the present Prime Minister's position on the past — for posterity's sake," according to William B. Ruggles in *The Dallas Morning News*. Few were convinced by Churchill's counterfactuals about the effect of capturing Vienna, Berlin, and Prague or of delaying the troop withdrawal in Germany. Thomas Sherman in the *St. Louis Post-Dispatch* considered it "unlikely, in view of what we know now about the Russian will to power" that "any arrangement — short of a crippling blow delivered against the Russian armies by their then allies — would have materially changed the present uneasy relationship between Russia and the West." Dexter Perkins noted that the percentages agreement and the Yalta deal on the Far East did not easily fit Churchill's stated concern to stand up to Russia.[11]

A few reviewers seemed to swallow the Churchill line. Paul Jordan-Smith in the Los Angeles Times said, "Churchill is historian rather than apologist. He sets down the story of events as they occurred." But only Hanson Baldwin really went to bat for him in a long essay in the Atlantic Monthly entitled "Churchill Was Right." And this was surely because Triumph and Tragedy echoed Baldwin's thesis in Great Mistakes of the War that American "blindness to post-war political aims . . . was partially responsible for the establishment of Communism in the heart of Europe." He argued that Churchill saw the danger and warned against it "much sooner than did Roosevelt or the top echelons of the U.S. government" and that FDR's "one-man decision" to demand unconditional surrender and the American opposition to Churchill's "Balkans strategy" were fatal mistakes. Yet even Baldwin wanted to prevent Churchill from "washing his hands" completely, noting, for instance, his expressions of trust in Stalin.[12]

Americans in the know were certainly not persuaded. Averell Harriman, American Ambassador in Moscow in 1944 and 1945, went over volume 6 with care. He remained puzzled as to what Churchill thought he was accomplishing by the percentages agreement, doubted that his policy reversal after Yalta was so abrupt and rapid, and did not think that pulling back to the occupation zones in Germany made much difference—the result of standing firm would still have been an iron curtain, farther east. Robert Sherwood, reviewing the book for The New York Times, wrote in his draft that "some present day readers to whom the word 'Yalta' is synonymous with 'betrayal' may be surprised to read of the Churchill meetings with Stalin in the fall of 1944." But, careful as ever since his 1948 clash with Churchill over Roosevelt and Hopkins, Sherwood was laudatory in print, calling volume 6 "a gigantic contribution to history by a historical giant."[13]

On a lighter note, many American reviewers noted what Lewis Gannett in the New York Herald Tribune called the flashes of "puckish wit"—a favorite being Churchill's account of his lunch with the Saudi leader, Ibn Saud, in Egypt in February 1945. Churchill had been warned that tobacco and alcohol were forbidden in the royal presence but announced that his own "rule of life prescribed as an absolutely sacred rite smoking cigars and also the drinking of alcohol before, after, and if need be during all meals and in the intervals between them." The King, says Churchill, "graciously accepted my position."[14]

AND SO, Triumph and Tragedy was finally released in America, flanked by news of the Nobel Prize and the Bermuda summit. Back in England, Churchill had recovered from his stroke and still clung to office, stringing along Eden and his Tory colleagues with insinuations that retirement was only a matter of months away. Some quarters of the press were now openly calling for his resignation—"A Story without an Ending" editorialized *Punch*, juxtaposed with a vicious cartoon of Churchill as a living corpse. The Prime Minister's justification for clinging on remained the same—that he could exert a special influence "on what I care about above all else, the building of a sure and lasting peace"—and he found a new pretext in British anxiety about the American hydrogen-bomb test on 1 March 1954. Churchill was genuinely horrified at the enhanced power of the H-bomb and its collateral damage from radiation, telling Jock Colville that mankind was now as far from the atomic age as the atomic bomb was from the bow and arrow.[15]

Public anxiety in Britain about the bomb was mingled with anti-American feeling, whipped up by the Labour left. Churchill used this to justify finally publicizing the 1943 Quebec Agreement, which, he told Eisenhower, would "prove decisively that the Opposition, not I, are responsible for our present position."[16] Ike agreed, unlike Truman in 1951, and Churchill read out the text to the Commons on 5 April 1954. But he did so as part of a partisan attack on the Labour government for selling out the agreement after 1945, in sharp contrast with Attlee's speech just before, which took a statesmanlike, bipartisan line on the need for a summit about nuclear weapons. Churchill succeeded in incensing the Opposition and embarrassing his own party. At one point, amid calls of "Resign, resign," he stopped and asked Eden what they were saying. Lord Woolton, the Tory party chairman, called it "a most extraordinary flop." Even Churchill privately admitted he should have thrown away his notes and welcomed Attlee's support for a summit. "When one gets old," he told Moran, "one lives too much in the past."[17]

On 23 November 1954, another historical controversy exposed Churchill's waning powers. Speaking to his constituents at Woodford in Essex, he claimed credit for anticipating the current plans to bring West Germany into NATO: "Even before the war had ended and while the Germans were surrendering by hundreds of thousands, and our streets were crowded with cheering people, I telegraphed to Lord Montgomery directing him to be careful in collecting the German arms, to stack them so they could easily be issued again to the German soldiers whom we should have to work with if the Soviet advance continued."[18] The *Daily Herald* called it "an astonishing statement." "What a gift that is to Communist propaganda," editorialized the *Daily Mirror*. Predictably, most of the criticism came from the left, but *The Times* also found it "impossible to see what purpose or good" these remarks could serve.[19]

The furor took some of the gloss off Parliament's celebrations of Churchill's eightieth birthday on 30 November 1954. Several Labour MPs refused to sign the birthday book presented to him because he had been willing to "use Nazi soldiers against our war allies," in the words of Barbara Castle. Churchill's reaction was again muddled. Critics who asked for evidence were initially told to consult the last volume of his war memoirs. But Labour's Emanuel Shinwell told the House on 1 December that no such telegram appeared there. Churchill quoted back other parts of *Triumph and Tragedy*, but in the end had to eat humble pie. Asked for the text of the telegram, he said, "I shall be very glad to give that to the House—when I find it," and he conceded, "I might have been confused in my mind" and mixed up one telegram with another. Over the next week, the newspapers were full of "hunt the telegram" articles and cartoons, but nothing ever turned up. "I made a goose of myself at Woodford," Churchill admitted to Moran.[20]

There was more to the Woodford affair than met the public eye. Contrary to the impression sometimes created, this was not a brief, off-the-cuff speech but a long, carefully crafted address.[21] And the bombshell claim was one Churchill had tried to verify years before. On 18 March 1950, Bill Deakin told Denis Kelly that "Mr. Churchill has asked for a telegram sent by him to Montgomery in 1945 telling M. to stack German equipment and arms in case they should be needed." After a fruitless search at Chartwell, Henry Pownall was brought in. He told Churchill, "There is no trace in Cabinet Records Section of a telegram from you to Montgomery on the subject." All that could be found was an exchange between Churchill and Eisenhower on 9–10 May 1945 about not destroying German planes, and this was later printed in Churchill's chapter "The Chasm Opens." After the Woodford speech, Norman Brook initiated an extensive search of official papers but again drew a blank.[22]

What, then, had actually happened? Was this one of Churchill's idées fixes, like the claim he made in the Commons in July 1949 and then had to retract in *The Hinge of Fate*, that he had never heard of unconditional surrender until Roosevelt suddenly announced it to the world's press at Casablanca? Or did he have some subliminal memories of the contingency plan for war with the Soviet Union—Operation Unthinkable—which he had commissioned from the Chiefs of Staff in May 1945? Both are possible; the whole episode reminds us again of the vagaries of human memory.

Yet Churchill may not have been as confused as it seems. In the United States when the Woodford row erupted, Monty said publicly that he had received such a telegram. Back home, unable to find anything in his files, he told Churchill that his wartime intelligence chief remembered seeing the message but said it had come on "the very secret link" (via SIS) and was therefore destroyed after being read. Then, in June 1959, Monty wrote a private memorandum for the record saying that he had met Churchill at Downing Street on 14 May 1945 to discuss the military government of Germany. Churchill "got steamed up about the Russians" and told Monty not to destroy the weapons of the million Germans who had surrendered to him a week before because "we might have to fight the Russians with German help." This was a verbal order, Monty stated, with "no written confirmation." On 14 June, concerned at the number of troops thereby diverted to guarding weapons dumps, he asked the War Office to confirm or rescind these instructions. A week later, having received no reply, he gave orders for the destruction of the German weapons. Monty never heard any more about the matter until Churchill's Woodford speech. "He said he had sent me a telegram. It could not be found. There was no telegram!! The true facts are as above."[23]

Monty was not the most reliable of witnesses—and he had changed his tune since his message to Churchill in December 1954—but his private statement fits other evidence of the Prime Minister's near panic in mid-May 1945 about a third world war. On the other hand, as the press observed during the Woodford affair, it made little sense for Churchill to talk about those fears if he was trying to reassure the new Russian leadership.

All through 1954, Churchill kept pressing for a summit, but the reaction in Moscow was consistently negative. The Kremlin suspected Churchill's intentions and doubted his influence in Washington—the key to any thaw in the Cold War. The leading skeptic was Vyacheslav Molotov, still Soviet Foreign Minister, who had dealt with Churchill throughout the war. When Molotov met Eden in January 1954, his comments on the Prime Minister were "by no means cordial." He said "with some feeling" that Churchill had "some very hard things to say about the Soviet Union after the war, as any reader of Volume VI of his War Memoirs could see for himself." In 1957, the Russians published an English edition of Stalin's wartime correspondence with Churchill and Roosevelt. According to the foreword, it was produced because "tendentiously selected parts of this correspondence were published outside the Soviet Union at different times resulting in a distorted picture of the Soviet attitude during the war." Surely this was a barbed reference to the unauthorized use of Stalin's telegrams in *The Second World War*. For, although the Cabinet Office was punctilious about getting approval for Churchill to quote messages from Roosevelt and Commonwealth leaders, it decided back in 1948 that there was no point in asking Moscow. Here is another example of how Churchill's version of history provoked its own backlash.[24]

CASSELL'S EDITION of *Triumph and Tragedy* appeared on 26 April 1954, three weeks after Churchill's disastrous Commons speech about the Quebec Agreement. Some Tory papers saw publication as a chance to pump up the Prime Minister's deflated image, but much of the praise was apolitical and unfeigned. "Churchill has done the impossible," declared William Barkley in the *Daily Express*, "he has left the best wine till last." Robert Waithman in the *News Chronicle* called it "the ultimate book by the greatest Englishman of modern times," and *Reynolds News* extolled "the world's greatest non-fiction best-seller after the Bible." Most reviewers followed the *Triumph and Tragedy* motif—underlining how, as with *The Gathering Storm* or *The Hinge of Fate*, a compelling title could seduce reviewers.[25] Unusually, the Glasgow *Evening News* printed photos of Pownall, Ismay, and Garrod as "three of the men who collaborated with Sir Winston." But most reviewers, as before, assumed a one-man show. The chapter on Leyte, touched up by Churchill in August 1953 but largely the work of Allen and Kelly, was singled out as "a masterpiece" in *The Yorkshire Observer* and as a "brilliant example" of "first-rate Churchillian narrative" by the historian R. C. K. Ensor in the *Sunday Times*.[26]

The big contrast with reactions across the Atlantic was that British reviews overwhelmingly endorsed, even relished, Churchill's critique of American policy. (The growing sense of British decline in the world, exacerbated by the current row about America's unrestrained nuclear testing, doubtless played a part.) The "inevitable conclusion," wrote Sir Edward Spears in the staunchly imperialist *Daily Mail*, "is that American leaders, by disregarding Churchill's advice, allowed Russia to rend Europe, an error which has cost them as much as it has us." The *Financial Times* declared that "time has more than proved him right," a theme echoed by the historian Robert Blake under an *Evening Standard* headline "You can't blame Winston for losing the peace—the blame lies with U.S." A rare antidote appeared in *The Observer*, but this came from the Harvard professor Arthur M. Schlesinger, Jr. He argued that a settlement at the summit in 1945 would have gone the way of Yalta and that an iron curtain a hundred miles farther east would not have "terminated the Soviet impulse to aggression."[27]

The left, as usual, was harsh. In the *Daily Herald*, Emanuel Shinwell called the volume "a novel with Winston Churchill as the hero." Keith Waterhouse in the *Daily Mirror*, echoing the paper's editorial line that Churchill was passé, said the book showed "what a great man Winston Churchill was—in those great days ten to fifteen years ago." In similar vein but weightier was "Portrait of the Artist as a Great Man" by the Labour MP and Oxford don Richard Crossman, who had also savaged volumes 4 and 5 in the *New Statesman. Triumph and Tragedy,* he said, "reveals the role in world politics which Sir Winston would have played if history had let him do so." Crossman argued that by restraining Stalin in Greece, Churchill allowed the Russians a free hand elsewhere, especially in Poland, and that if he had been determined to stop Soviet expansion he should have opposed the dismemberment of Germany. Look, said Crossman, at the single paragraph about the anti-Hitler plot of 20 July 1944 or the disingenuous account of the Morgenthau Plan. Instead of accepting the story of the farsighted Churchill versus the myopic Americans, Crossman claimed that Churchill, like Roosevelt, had "become enamoured of total war as an end in itself." He only saw "when it was far too late" that the "consequences of the total victory which he had blindly sought would be a vacuum in Europe which democracy was ill-equipped to fill."[28]

The lead review in *The Times Literary Supplement* on 30 April 1954 was written by the diplomat and author C. M. "Monty" Woodhouse, who had served with the SOE in Greece during the war. He considered the oeuvre as a whole, judging it to be literally "incomparable"—it was more than the lightweight reminiscences often penned by political and military leaders, including Lloyd George, yet less than pure history, for Churchill was too close to the events he described. He was too close, for instance, as "an Englishman" for whom his country's contribution to the war could never be less than paramount; too close as a man so accustomed to occupying center stage that events in which he played no direct part are scanted. The volumes were also arbitrary in places: Woodhouse cited Churchill's recent exposé in the Commons of the 1943 Quebec Agreement on the bomb, about which there had been no mention in volume 5. Churchill was also dealing with events that were still unfinished and took on "a different aspect almost from year to year"—his shift toward Tito looked right in 1943, wrong in 1945, right again by 1950. "What will they say in 1960, or in twenty or a hundred years' time?" For all these reasons, Woodhouse accepted Churchill's own estimate of his work as "a contribution to history." But it was indeed unique, "a class apart" from either memoir or history, "as if the Iliad had been written by Agamemnon."[29]

Never one for false modesty, Churchill basked in the glow. "Looking back," he told Desmond Flower on 12 May 1954, "it seems incredible that one could have got through all these six volumes and I suppose nearly two million words."

(The best estimate, made by some poor soul at Cassell's, was 1,631,000 words of text and 278,000 in the appendixes, making 1,909,000. Adding the indexes pushed the total to 2,050,000.) When Flower went to Chartwell for a celebratory lunch, Churchill was still bursting with pride: "You must admit, Desmond, that I have made a prodigious effort." His publisher agreed. Lubricated by champagne, port, and brandy, Churchill kept returning to this theme all through the afternoon, with his guest happy to concur. They were still agreeing solemnly on the prodigiousness of the effort as Flower stepped somewhat gingerly into a taxi.[30]

Although Flower's story was probably embellished, Churchill clearly felt a justifiable sense of achievement. Awarded a Nobel Prize as a modern Caesar writing in the style of Cicero, lauded by Britain's premier literary journal for an *Iliad* composed by Agamemnon, and back in Downing Street, this time as a man of peace not a war leader—it was such a long way from the gloom of August 1945. He had triumphantly vindicated his intention to leave the war to history but to be one of its earliest historians. There is a striking contrast here with the memoirs of World War I by Churchill's old mentor and rival, David Lloyd George. In the 1930s, his six volumes had been compared with Caesar and Clarendon, his achievement as leader likened to that of the Younger Pitt. Despite the work of subsequent revisionist historians, the reputations of the generals never recovered from his denunciation of their follies. But in the 1950s, the man and his memoirs were rarely mentioned in the same breath as Churchill. Lloyd George had written as an embittered old man whose political career was over. His partisanship was transparent, whereas Churchill's was colored by literary skill, varnished by current diplomacy, and illuminated by a philosophy of history. The difference is summed up in their titles. Lloyd George had published his *War Memoirs*; Churchill had written *The Second World War*.[31]

YET CHURCHILL'S VOLUMES were not timeless—they bore the marks of so much else he had done in that remarkable yet neglected eighth decade of his life. It is now time to pull that story together.

What for shorthand we call "Churchill's memoirs" are a complicated literary text—not entirely Churchill's work and not simply memoirs. The prime ingredients were the "three Ds": documents, dictation, and drafts. Churchill's wartime minutes and telegrams formed the core, but these were interlinked with reminiscences he dictated at various times from 1946 and by drafts on the historical background from the Syndicate of research assistants. After laying down the documentary base—what Churchill called the track—he would incorporate the other two elements in successive rewrites of the chapters, which often ran to a dozen galley versions. Many of the chapters were radically revised in the process, but in some the three main ingredients were not really blended together, and it was a common complaint of his American publishers that the volumes contained too much unrefined documentation. In this sense, *The Second World War* was a lesser literary accomplishment than, say, his four volumes on Marlborough published between 1933–1938.

But in the 1930s, Churchill was on the margin of British politics; from 1945 to 1951, he was Leader of the Opposition as well as a world statesman, delivering clarion calls at Fulton and Zurich in 1946 or at MIT and Strasbourg in 1949. Even with his prodigious energy, there was insufficient time for the memoirs. This was particularly evident with volume 3, which was rushed to the publishers at the end of 1949 after Churchill's first major stroke and before the election of February 1950. Intent on a second term in Downing Street, Churchill knew he had to complete the bulk of the memoirs within five years of July 1945—the ultimate constitutional term of a single Parliament. That was why he usually juggled at least three volumes at once, laying the track far ahead and then rushing back to fill in the stations. And that is also why he was so reliant on his assistants, particularly Bill Deakin, Henry Pownall, and Gordon Allen, to provide much of the diplomatic, military, and naval background. Pownall's accounts of the fall of France and the desert battles of 1940–1942, drawn extensively from the draft narratives of the official histories being prepared in the Cabinet Office, were "state of the art" pieces of military history—likewise, Allen on the hunt for the *Bismarck* and the chapters on the V-weapons that emerged from the rival drafts of Cherwell, Sandys, and Jones. Deakin wrote several cutting-edge syntheses of the literature on German-Italian relations and Vichy France and, as the Syndicate's sole professional historian, also provided the critical and structural vision to revise a whole volume, particularly *The Hinge of Fate*, when Churchill lacked the time to do so.

If these volumes were not entirely Churchill's work, does that diminish his achievement? Not in my opinion. The writing of history and biography is often the work of a lone scholar, but in science it is the norm for a major figure to direct a research group, the output of which is published as collaborative papers in which he or she is listed as the last author. *The Second World War* is hardly a set of research papers, and Churchill was billed as sole author, but there is a sense in which he was running a large, well-funded research group on a par with the barons of modern science. He did not do all the work personally, but he set its parameters, guided its direction, and sustained its momentum, aware of the political timetable governing the whole. Denis Kelly, the Syndicate's factotum, remarked in 1985 that he was often asked how much of Churchill's books did the great man really write himself. That, said Kelly, was "almost as superficial a question" as asking a Master Chef: "Did you cook the whole banquet with your own hands?"[32] It was an apt analogy. Churchill did not chop the vegetables, and he did not lay the tables or mix all the sauces, but he knew how to get a six-course meal on the table in the right order and at more or less the right time—not just a meal, but a feast.

The Syndicate's contribution is one reason why these volumes were more than memoirs. Another, even more important, was the documentary base at their core—those papers that Churchill removed from 10 Downing Street in July 1945 under his remarkable bargain with the Cabinet Secretary, Sir Edward Bridges. These were what he gave to the Chartwell Trust and it in turn sold to Lord Camrose, as part of the clever legal device to avoid the punitive taxation that would have made the memoirs financially pointless. This rich documentation is part of the reason why his books commanded attention for so long. In the 1940s, it seemed unlikely that British government papers on the Second World War would be open to private researchers (as distinct from selected official historians) until well into the twenty-first century. Not until 1958 did Parliament enact a fifty-year rule, thereby opening up government documents on the origins of the *First* World War, and it was only in 1967, after Churchill's death, that Harold Wilson's Labour government reduced the time limit to thirty years—hence the fascination of readers and scholars with the minutes, telegrams, and directives that took up so much of Churchill's text.

Yet what they read were not pristine documents but material carefully edited for public consumption. The other side of Churchill's bargain with Bridges was that, although the papers were his property, their publication had to be approved by the government of the day—hence the vetting of his draft chapters by Whitehall departments, skillfully orchestrated by Norman Brook, Bridges's successor as Cabinet Secretary. Sometimes changes were made to make the other side of the case—for instance, in defense of desert generals such as Wavell and Auchinleck; sometimes to smooth current diplomacy, such as relations with Franco's Spain or Tito's Yugoslavia. The most sensitive issue was protecting the work of the Bletchley Park code breakers. The intelligence authorities feared that if Churchill pulled back the veil on Ultra, however slightly, this would encourage other would-be memoirists, chafing under the Official Secrets Act, to rip it apart. By accepting the censorship of his volumes, even over stories where intelligence was critical, such as the battle for Crete in 1941, Churchill made a considerable sacrifice. His grasp of the importance of signals intelligence had been one of his greatest contributions as war leader, yet virtually nothing is said about it in his memoirs.

The Cabinet Office acted as unofficial expediter of his memoirs as well as official censor. It allowed his researchers uniquely privileged access to much of the Whitehall archives. And Norman Brook spent hours helping Churchill improve the prose and argument, reading three or four versions of some of the volumes and sometimes writing whole passages himself (as on the sinking of the *Graf Spee* in 1939 or the resignation of Cripps from the Cabinet in 1942). For Brook, like Bridges, this was not just another political memoir, of the sort the Cabinet Office had tried to police during the war. They regarded it as almost *the* British official history of the war, written by the man supremely qualified to do so, both as leader and author. Here is another reason why Churchill had produced something more than a mere memoir.

In many other cases, the documents were edited by Churchill and his assistants. Sometimes this was done to obscure his blind spots, such as his complacency in 1939–1941 about the threat from Japan and the vulnerability of Singapore. Sometimes the editing was to defend himself against the emerging historiography of the war, notably American accounts of the Second Front debate. With those in mind, Churchill devotes a chapter of *Their Finest Hour* to his prescience in 1940 about the need for landing craft and artificial harbors. In volume 5, he jumps over his attempts in October 1943 to renege on the commitments to invade France the following spring because of the new opportunities he saw opening up in the Mediterranean after the surrender of Italy. (Had he been able to discuss the intelligence story, it would have enhanced his self-defense.) Often the editing reflected contemporary political concerns—Churchill pulled his punches over the Greek campaign of 1941 in part because Anthony Eden, whom he privately blamed as one of the prime architects of the fiasco, was Churchill's deputy as Tory leader. Likewise, he did not reveal the full extent of Cabinet criticism of his leadership in 1942 because Clement Attlee, one of his most acute critics, was currently Prime Minister. Instead, volume 4 concentrates almost entirely on Cripps.

Throughout the writing, Churchill was guided by his vision of an Anglo-American "special relationship"—centerpiece of speeches such as Fulton in 1946. His harshest blasts against Chamberlain are prompted by the Prime Minister's indifference to FDR's initiative in January 1938, and he deliberately establishes his own link with Roosevelt in the scene-setting chapter at the start of volume 2, asserting that through this personal correspondence "our perfect understanding was gained." In keeping with the propensity of readers and scholars to look at the text and skip the documents, that passage has often been quoted, sometimes to suggest that Churchill sacrificed British power on the altar of a romanticized special relationship. Such claims often imply that the British empire could have been maintained by brute force or that a viable peace with Hitler was possible in 1940–1941, both, to my mind, fallacious notions.[33] Churchill's conduct of Anglo-American relations was more complex than this one passage suggests. The romanticization is usually to be found in his public statements, couched to move hearts rather than change minds. In private, Churchill could fight very hard, as the ferocious rows over Mediterranean strategy in the autumn of 1943 and the summer of 1944 make clear. In doing so, he had no compunction about trying to deceive the Americans. Undoubtedly he was more optimistic about the United States than was Eden; quite clearly, his American roots pulled him toward "the Great Republic." But, to quote the contemporary quip, Churchill was half American and all British, and that becomes clear in the war memoirs if we scrutinize the documents as well as the dictation.

Churchill also presented his documents from World War II in the light of the evolving Cold War. As confrontation with the Soviets escalated in 1946–1948, so he enlarged his discussion of 1919–1939 from five chapters to the whole first book of *The Gathering Storm*. His theme as historian was how the Second World War broke out because his policies were not adopted; his theme as statesman was the danger of a third world war if his warnings were again ignored. This intertwining of past and present, history and diplomacy, gives *The Gathering Storm* a special power, but *Triumph and Tragedy* exhibits a similar pattern. The difference was that in volume 1 Churchill exaggerates his stance in the 1930s, to score points against domestic leaders who were dead (Baldwin and Chamberlain). In volume 6, he tones down some of his arguments to avoid offending foreign leaders with whom he would have to deal, such as Eisenhower and Tito. Even so, he makes clear his view that this had been an unnecessary Cold War. It is no accident that *The Gathering Storm* and *Triumph and Tragedy* are the two volumes in which Churchill's love of counterfactuals is given fullest rein. In the 1930s, he was out of power, in 1945 he was losing power—at neither moment could he make history.

This persistent counterpoint of historian and statesman can also be turned on its head. It was not just that Churchill the Cold Warrior wrote his history in the glare of the present; Churchill the wartime statesman sometimes acted with one eye on the history he was going to write. He composed *The World Crisis* after his tenure in office in 1914–1918 and it is hard to believe that he did not intend in 1939–1945 to do the same on a grander scale for what was indubitably his finest hour. The care with which he had his wartime documents printed and then labeled "Personal Minutes" or "Personal Telegrams" suggests as much. It was certainly the assumption in Whitehall during the Phony War that Churchill was writing memoranda for inclusion in future memoirs—as noted above in chapter 8, "another one for the book" became a private joke. There was less time for historical self-consciousness once he became premier, but several historians have guessed that later documents might have been written for the historical record. Two examples are the Auschwitz memorandum of 11 July 1944 and the injunction against terror bombing on 28 March 1945.[34]

On the other hand, we should not make Churchill seem too Machiavellian. During most of his time as war leader he was trying to win the war, not to write history. Likewise, when composing the memoirs, some of the distortions were not deliberate. A case in point is the blast at Cripps in volume 3 for failing to deliver his warning to Stalin in April 1941 about an imminent German attack. This became an obsession that autumn, after learning via Beaverbrook that Stalin did not recall any warning and after his hard-pressed officials had produced an erroneous chronological dossier. In writing up this episode in the memoirs, Churchill and his assistants simply used that dossier, rather than dig back into the original files.

There is a further reason to caution against always assuming deliberate deception. Often the documents, even after editing, do not square exactly with the argument in Churchill's text. Thus, the big papers on wartime strategy that he prints in various chapters of volumes 3 and 4 do not, on close inspection, foreshadow a cross-Channel attack on the lines of Normandy in June 1944. Instead, they talk of several landings at various points around the rim of occupied Europe, to be mounted when the occupied nations were ready to revolt and the Third Reich had been weakened by strategic bombing. Likewise, the claims in volume 6 about his foresight of the Soviet threat are at odds with the contemporary record of his faith in Stalin. Many other examples could be cited where the documents, read against the grain of the text, tell their own story. Fortunately for Churchill, most of his readers tend to skip the quotations and jump to the next piece of narrative.

What particularly attracts their attention are his personal reminiscences—those passages of postwar dictation that provide some of the most vivid and moving passages in the whole work. The defeatist Quai d'Orsay on 16 May 1940 and the dynamic RAF headquarters on 15 September serve as the two emotional poles of *Their Finest Hour*. In volume 3, no reader can fail to be affected by the story of how an anguished Churchill "turned over and twisted in bed" on hearing of the loss of the *Prince of Wales* and the *Repulse*. And in volume 4 there is Roosevelt's simple question, "What can we do to help?" when Churchill was devastated and humiliated in his presence by news that Tobruk had surrendered.

These pieces of dictation recall some of the most intimate moments of the war. But, in consequence, they were difficult for his assistants to check and, like most reminiscences, improved over time. The official records suggest, for instance, that his meeting with the French on 16 May 1940 and his percentages negotiations with Stalin on 9 October 1944 were more complex and less dramatic than stated in the memoirs. Moreover, some of his dictated memories were simply wrong. The most remarkable slip is that Churchill secured the premiership on the afternoon of 9 May and not the morning of the tenth—he obstinately misdated his crucial meeting with Chamberlain and Halifax. The most substantive error is Churchill's confusion of his first meeting with Roosevelt at Hyde Park in June 1942 with his third in September 1944 when the aide-mémoire on atomic collaboration was initialed, thereby seriously confusing historians of the atomic bomb. And the most blatant mistake is when Churchill confused his meetings at Hyde Park in August 1943 and September 1944, with the result that virtually the same paragraph about Roosevelt and Hopkins appears in the American editions of volume 5 and volume 6.

Reflecting on the past also aroused Churchill's emotions, at times even a sense of guilt. Intervention in Greece in 1941 is a notable example—the ebb and flow of the drafts seem to reflect his unresolved doubts about the campaign, in marked contrast with his decisiveness about the battle for Crete. He remained distressed about the loss of the *Prince of Wales* and the *Repulse*, seizing on various explanations that might reduce his own responsibility. And, more briefly, he was angered by the Dieppe disaster of August 1942—but then he let Mountbatten write his own cover-up, abetted by an embarrassed Ismay.

Dieppe is a reminder of how the pace of writing and the pressure of politics in the late 1940s and 1950s often prevented Churchill from trying to untie knotty historical problems in the way he had done for the *Marlborough* volumes. While preparing *The Gathering Storm*, he did do so to some extent—for instance, debating with Pownall how the Battle of Britain would have gone if fought a year earlier or speculating on the outcome if the French Army had invaded Germany at the start of war in 1939. With later volumes, he did not have much time to indulge his historical curiosity. But it is a tribute to Churchill's intense if erratic mind that in January 1953, in Jamaica, he was suddenly rethinking his interpretation of the race to Berlin and the dropping of the atomic bomb. And in August

1953, still recovering from his stroke, he devoted a whole afternoon to clarifying his understanding of the Battle of Leyte Gulf.

At other points, Churchill was obliged to take pains because of the sensitivity of the issue. He and Gordon Allen labored over the stories of Oran and Dakar in 1940, aware of the possibility of legal action from Admiral North. Guided by Norman Brook, he worked and reworked his clashes with successive Australian governments in 1941–1942 over North Africa and the Far East, for fear of a row that might shake the Commonwealth. Sometimes his care was insufficient—last-minute revisions in his account of May 1940 could not forestall the politically motivated protests of Belgian generals. And a throwaway line about the desert command in volume 4 blew up in his face in 1953 when an embittered general suddenly threatened to sue for libel. Only his equally abrupt climbdown a year later saved a serving British Prime Minister from the possibility of having to defend himself in a Dublin law court.

THE SECOND WORLD WAR was therefore a vast and intricate work, composed over a period of seven years. Each volume was different, reflecting a distinct phase of the war and also a distinct phase of Churchill's postwar life, which is why I have written about each one in turn. But taken together, they offered unique personal impressions of the war and its leaders, voluminous documentary evidence that scholars could not then expect to see until the next century, and (especially in the first three volumes) informed narratives of key battles and diplomacy. Their cumulative effect was to highlight Britain's contribution to victory at a time when a tide of American memoirs and movies gave the impression that Uncle Sam had won the war single-handed. But Churchill's deepest objective in writing them (apart from making money) was the search for vindication. Like most political memoirists, he wanted to show that he was right, or at least as right as it seemed credible to claim. On appeasement, he succeeded spectacularly—the reputations of Baldwin and Chamberlain have still not recovered.[35] Likewise on 1940, his stark contrast between the feeble French and the defiant British has shaped English-language history ever since. On the Second Front and D-Day, he offered a plausible but not compelling defense; on the origins of the Cold War, as the contrasting reviews of volume 6 indicate, he satisfied his own countrymen but not Americans as to the myopia of U.S. policy.

The most enduring image from the memoirs is of Churchill as leader. He was trying to shift perceptions of himself from the man of words to the man of deeds, to balance the war speeches that, through broadcasts, records, and texts, had become the basis of his public persona. The documents he prints at such length in the chapters and the appendixes show an omnipresent, almost omniscient, leader, directing every aspect of the war. The speeches and the directives were mutually reinforcing: they buttressed the image of bulldog Winston—resolute, robust, and authoritative. But they served to mask that volatility inherent in Churchill's relentless drive and iron whim—his tendency to swing from one idea to another—which frayed Eden's nerves and drove Alanbrooke to distraction. This, after all, had been the central feature of Churchill's image before the war as the "mercurial" man of ferocious energy but flawed judgment. One can see it at times in the documents he prints in *The Second World War,* but much of the volatility has been edited out—for instance, his frequent oscillations in focus between the Baltic and the Mediterranean.

Here lay the seeds of revisionism. Many of Churchill's wartime colleagues were irritated by the one-sidedness of his own account—"my" minutes but not their replies—and by the two-dimensional impression conveyed of Churchill himself. In the 1950s, some of them started to speak out. It is time to look at the battle for history during Churchill's final decade.

•

CHAPTER 32

LEAVING IT TO HISTORY, 1955–1965

C HURCHILL LIKED SAYING THAT he would stay in the pub until closing time. His political colleagues finally called time in April 1955, but departure from Downing Street left him more opportunity on the literary front. He returned to *The History of the English-Speaking Peoples*, drafted in the late 1930s but put aside in 1940, and joked, "I shall lay an egg a year." He was better than his word, with two volumes appearing in 1956, another in 1957, and the last in 1958. This project took to extremes the Syndicate method of the war memoirs, with much of the old draft rewritten after comments by a team of eminent historians, including J. H. Plumb, Asa Briggs, and A. L. Rowse.[1] The *English-Speaking Peoples* proved his literary swan song, but the battle for history went on.[2] During the last decade of his life, the Churchillian version of World War II was hammered home in an abridged edition of the memoirs and a major TV series. At the same time, however, serious criticism was beginning to hit the headlines.

"I READ THE WHOLE of 'The World Crisis' in the full-length edition," Denis Kelly told Churchill in September 1952. "I then carried—and read—the single-volume abridgement through the last campaign in Burma. Could you not give the world a similar short version of 'The Second World War'?" Churchill did nothing with the idea at the time, but he discussed it with his publishers in 1954–1955 and work got going in the winter of 1956–1957. The plan was to reduce nearly two million words by three quarters and add an "aftermath" essay by Churchill, surveying events since 1945. The publishers felt this would greatly enhance the volume's selling power.[3]

The epilogue was composed in February 1957 in great haste, prompted by Churchill's decision to retire from his profession as an author at the end of the tax year in April. This would bring considerable benefits in reduced tax liability on the £20,000 fee he was being paid for the epilogue.[4] Most of the work was done at La Pausa, Emery Reves's home in the south of France. Churchill dictated a few paragraphs, mostly on his Fulton and Zurich speeches of 1946, before handing the job over to Denis Kelly and his private secretary Anthony Montague Browne (a diplomat on what became permanent assignment from the Foreign Office). Dividing up the topics, they produced about 9,000 words in four days, which Churchill read in a couple of versions before it was finally dispatched to the printers on 16 February.[5]

Although largely written by others, the essay expressed Churchill's views. He does not claim full credit for the postwar Western alliance, paying tribute to "the stout-hearted and wise" Ernest Bevin and "the far-sighted and devoted" American Secretary of State George Marshall. But ample quotation from his Fulton and Zurich speeches was designed to show how his visions of the special relationship and European unity anticipated the new order. The epilogue also spends some time on nuclear issues, referring more candidly than in *Triumph and Tragedy* to the way "secrets were soon disclosed to the Soviet Union, which greatly helped Russian scientists in their researches." It also discusses for the first time the Quebec Agreement of August 1943—which Churchill says he still felt at the end of the war was "the best possible arrangement" that could have been made with America—and the McMahon Act of 1946, which then severed almost all atomic cooperation. The epilogue contains further hard words about Labour's "violently factional view" on India and suggests that the end of empire was premature and unnecessarily bloody.[6] There was also a powerful section on Israel, drafted by Montague Browne, stressing Churchill's commitment to Zionism but his abhorrence of Jewish terrorism. This admitted that "a race that has suffered the virtual extermination of its national existence cannot be expected to be entirely reasonable" but called the assassination of British officials and soldiers "an odious act." Churchill retained this condemnation of "the activities of terrorists" over objections from Emery Reves.[7]

The rest of the epilogue was largely taken up with the Soviet Union: "Stalin's death was a milestone in Russian history. His tyranny had brought fearful suffering to his own country and to much else of the world." This passage, also drafted by Montague Browne, presented Churchill's final effort at summitry as a response to the new men in the Kremlin. Kelly produced some balancing sentences saying that "Soviet leaders must not be judged too harshly" because Borodino, Tannenberg, and Stalingrad were "not things you forget in a hurry." With slight amendment, both points were retained in the final version.[8] In keeping with this harsher line on Stalin, compared with his original memoirs, Churchill declined to include the remark he was still making in private in 1956–1957, that Stalin always kept his word—a reference back to the percentages agreement of 1944.[9] But he ends on the note of optimism that had animated his last efforts at détente: commerce would erode the harshness of the Soviet system, opening up vistas of prosperity unimagined by Marx "in his hovel." "And when war is itself fenced about with mutual extermination it seems likely that it will be increasingly postponed." Providing "the free world holds together," he concludes, it may well be that in time, "Opportunity-for-All will conquer the minds and restrain the passions of Mankind."[10] Not a bad prediction of how the Cold War ended!

To abridge the six volumes, Cassell's and Houghton Mifflin initially approached Herbert Ziman, the *Daily Telegraph* editorial writer who had edited them for serialization. But in April 1957, they turned the work over to Kelly, now largely free of the *English-Speaking Peoples* and, as he put it, "comparatively unoccupied at the Bar."[11] He was offered £2,000, from which he was to find any payments needed to Deakin and others for specialist advice. The task was formidable, even after making the obvious cuts such as removing all the documents and appendixes. By February 1958, according to Desmond Flower, Kelly could "no longer see the wood for the trees"—his marked and mutilated set of old page proofs was about two feet high—and so Cassell's had the whole thing printed in galleys to expedite cuts of another two hundred pages.[12] "It has been hard going," Kelly told Churchill, "rather like killing someone else's child." By the end of July, the work was complete, resulting in a text of 436,000 words that Flower considered "a very well-balanced condensation."[13] Returning, somewhat, to Churchill's original conception of the memoirs, Kelly divided the work in four:

BOOK I   **Milestones to Disaster, 1919 to 10 May 1940**
BOOK II   **Alone, 10 May 1940 to 22 June 1941**
BOOK III   **The Grand Alliance, June 1941 to June 1943**
BOOK IV   **Triumph and Tragedy, June 1943 to July 1945**

In the process, some sensitive episodes from the original text disappeared, such as the Dieppe raid, the sacking of Dorman-Smith, and the Katyn massacre.[14]

The publishers were keen not to highlight Kelly's work. Cassell's kept his name well off the title page but featured Churchill's epilogue. On the other hand, Churchill wanted a clear statement somewhere that Kelly had done the abridgment—otherwise his tax status could be prejudiced—so the publishers made the necessary references in the prefatory material. Also with an eye toward tax, they dated the epilogue 10 February 1957.[15] With all parties content, the abridged *Second World War* was published in February 1959, and in November *Life* brought out a two-volume *Picture History of "The Second World War,"* combining Kelly's abridged text with illustrations from their out-of-print *Picture History of World War II.*[16]

TV producers were equally keen to acquire Churchill's name and, after one false start, Churchill signed up with Jack Le Vien, a U.S. Army public-relations officer in North Africa during the war and subsequently editor in chief of Pathé News. After lengthy negotiations conducted by Anthony Montague Browne, in June 1959 Churchill sold the film and TV rights to *The Second World War* for an advance of $75,000 against royalties of 5 percent, rising to 10 percent after the proceeds had grossed $1,000,000. Part of the deal was that he would encourage friends and colleagues such as Monty and Eden to give interviews for the series, but his demand to vet the sponsors' advertisements (to avoid being brought into "disrepute" or "ridicule") was not successful.[17]

Le Vien was a man who thought big—Montague Browne had to disabuse him of the hope that Prince Philip, the Queen's husband, might act as narrator—and he wanted to recount Churchill's whole life instead of sticking closely to *The Second World War.* "We must stay away from that title as much as possible if we want to make a commercial success of this venture," he told Montague Browne. Whereas Churchill's name would attract sponsors, he felt that reference to World War II would drive them away—a striking comment on how popular interest in the war had waned by the end of the 1950s. Eventually, Le Vien agreed to keep reasonably close to the war, while entitling his series *Winston Churchill: The Valiant Years.*[18]

The treatment also proved problematic. Le Vien's first producer, Edgar Peterson, was a veteran of TV westerns. His sample scenario in April 1960 wanted to dramatize Churchill's graphic account of the fall of France, with an actor playing the great man in bed on 15 May 1940 when phoned up by Reynaud and then at the Quai d'Orsay the next day as Gamelin announced there was no strategic reserve. Next, Peterson wanted film footage of Dunkirk, including what he called "the wild moors" of Dover, then the "white glow" in Britain after the troops returned home safely, followed by "that magnificent aerial clip of the Mosquito

Armada setting off in the very early morning." He felt it also important to have a photo of Churchill "in that zipper over-all (and any other strange clothes he wore during the war)." Montague Browne read the scenario with mounting indignation. Leaving aside the confusion of Kent and Scotland, of authentic history with the finale of Hollywood's *Mrs. Miniver,* he made it clear that they would accept no actor impersonating Churchill.[19] Peterson bit the dust in August 1960, and his successor as producer, Bob Graff, was more to Churchill's taste. (The fact that on his first visit he brought a bottle of vintage cognac probably did no harm.)[20]

The series began on American TV on 27 November 1960, with Richard Burton speaking Churchill's words and with music by Richard Rodgers. Shown in twenty-six half-hour episodes, it proved a huge financial and critical success, winning several awards, and British diplomats in Washington considered it did "a great deal" for the country's prestige in the United States. When aired in Britain by the BBC in the new year, over four Saturday nights, reaction was somewhat mixed—there were questions about why it had been done by an American—but the series was eventually shown to general acclaim in some twenty countries.[21]

THE ABRIDGED MEMOIRS and *The Valiant Years* served to weld Churchill's name, image, and words ever more firmly onto World War II. Meanwhile, for most of the 1950s, there were no rival interpretations or even dissenting voices.

In 1955–1956 Harry Truman published two volumes of memoirs about his presidency. The first dealt solely with 1945, that *Year of Decisions,* but it stuck close to (edited) versions of the documents arranged in chronological order and did not highlight his differences with Britain. In any case, this overlapped with only the last four months of Churchill's war premiership. A more substantial international challenger was Charles de Gaulle. Frustrated in his plans for a political comeback, in 1952 the general retreated to his country house in the village of Colombey-les-Deux-Eglises and there wrote the three-volume *Mémoires de Guerre.* In this case, unlike Churchill's, "wrote" is the operative verb. Day after day, de Gaulle shut himself in his study in a remote tower, scrawling out the pages, which were then deciphered and typed by his daughter—a far cry from the production line at Chartwell. In consequence, progress was slow. The French volumes were published in 1954, 1956, and 1959 and, although the first appeared in English in 1955, translation of the second languished until de Gaulle's return to power in 1958. The last two volumes came out in English in 1959 and 1960, by which time the Churchillian version of history was entrenched in the English-speaking world. And although de Gaulle's memoirs had plenty of candid things to say about Churchill, their overall tone was one of respect. Despite "the friction of our two characters" and "the unfair advantage taken by England of wounded France," the general tells his readers, "Winston Churchill appeared to me, from one end of the drama to the other, as the great champion of a great enterprise and the great artist of a great history."[22]

In Britain, the appeasers remained in the coffin that *The Gathering Storm* had nailed tightly shut. G. M. Young's biography of Baldwin, published in 1952, did nothing to enhance its subject's reputation—on the contrary, it reinforced the familiar stereotypes of indolence, inertia, and insularity. Young was essentially an essayist, and he made little effort to work through the mass of Baldwin's papers.[23] More effective was the memoir of 1931–1940 by Lord Templewood, entitled *Nine Troubled Years*, which appeared in October 1954. As Samuel Hoare, he had held most of the great offices of state during the 1930s and had been close to Chamberlain, whose record he felt had been distorted in *The Gathering Storm*. He was given access to Chamberlain's personal papers and also used a young historian, Reginald Bassett, as research assistant. The result of all this material, plus Templewood's skill as a writer, was a readable memoir with a powerful punch, not least at Churchill's expense—for instance, on the damage caused by his Ten-Year Rule to naval rearmament and his pressure in 1939–1940 for "premature action," which led to the disastrous Norway campaign. Overall, the book advanced what *The Manchester Guardian* called "the fullest apology for the appeasers that has appeared," a verdict echoed even by Frank Owen, one of the trio who wrote *Guilty Men* in 1940. Yet Owen remained convinced that Chamberlain was "utterly wrong," and this was the consensus among reviewers: Malcolm Muggeridge in the *Daily Telegraph* called the appeasers "more Cervantes heroes than Guilty Men—equipped with old-fashioned diplomacy to do battle with new-fashioned gangsters."[24]

The only British politician whose memoirs might have come close to rivaling Churchill's had blown his chance. Back in 1946, Anthony Eden embarked on an account of his foreign secretaryships, with his own research assistant working in the Cabinet Office, but little progress had been made by the time Eden returned to the Foreign Office in 1951 (see chapter 7). Eden's working methods were diametrically opposite to Churchill's. He did not chivy his research assistant, Harry Hinsley, whose draft material, when finally produced, was far too academic for his purposes, in marked contrast to Bill Deakin's. He did not dictate his own recollections at an early stage, which would have made it much easier for a researcher to fill out the story. And he allowed himself to be dragooned by Churchill into handling most of the Tory party's routine business in the Commons. From October 1951, Eden was continually in office, first as Foreign Secretary and then as Churchill's successor in Downing Street. Forced by ill health to resign after the Suez debacle of 1956, Eden naturally turned first to defending his shattered reputation as premier. He set up a literary trust on Churchillian lines, using Anthony Moir, Churchill's lawyer, to design it, and asked first Deakin and then Pownall to act as research assistant. When both declined, he used Denis Kelly for a few disastrous months in 1958. It was not until 1962 and 1965 that his two volumes on the 1930s and World War II appeared, by which time Eden was largely crossing the i's and dotting the t's of established historiography.[25]

In writing history, as in making it, Eden therefore lived in Churchill's shadow to the end. Just as he seethed at the way Winston blocked his own path to the premiership, so he was enraged at times by the way Churchill's carefully crafted reputation now carried all before it. In November 1954, Conservative Central Office produced a draft for Eden to use in a radio tribute for Churchill's eightieth birthday. This lauded the Prime Minister's consistently "prophetic voice": before the war in awaking the country to the Nazi threat, during it in foreseeing the Russian challenge, and afterward in calling for European unity and an Atlantic alliance. Eden read the script with growing fury. Where it credited Churchill for laying the groundwork for the United Nations, he noted: "He wouldn't listen to it!" Against a sentence on how Churchill anticipated the rift between "Soviet imperialism and the Western democracies," Eden wrote: "He was the last to take up F.O. warnings (see Yalta)." Finally losing his cool completely, he scrawled in red: "This is almost all untrue & quite nauseating! . . . I am not going to stand up & tell a series of colossal lies." Eden was notoriously petulant, but his comments are revealing. He knew he was losing the battle for history.[26]

Some of Churchill's military advisers could have sounded a dissenting note. But of the Chiefs of Staff, both Dill and Pound were dead, and Portal, an intensely private man, never wrote his memoirs. Viscount Cunningham, First Sea Lord in 1943–1945, did go into print in March 1951 with *A Sailor's Odyssey*, which did not conceal the fact that he had stood up to Churchill on occasions during the war. Cunningham remained sure, for instance, that the French fleet could have been neutralized by negotiation in 1940 and said he felt at the time that the onslaught at Oran was "almost inept in its unwisdom." He also complained about the "prodding messages" the Prime Minister was wont to send to commanders, "often so ungracious and hasty" in tone that they were "not an encouragement, merely an annoyance."[27] This reference was noted by some reviewers, but most featured Cunningham's own life story, and his rows with Churchill were lost in the detail of a 700-page book. Moreover, Cunningham ended with an ample tribute to his war leader: "We had not always seen eye to eye, and had our occasional disagreements and arguments. But never for a moment could I lose my profound admiration and respect for that most remarkable and courageous Englishman who by his energy, obstinacy and sheer force of character led Britain and her people through the greatest perils the country had ever experienced."[28]

Academic historians were still barred from access to government documents for 1939–1945. The only exceptions were those writing the official histories of the British war effort—the project promoted so assiduously by Sir Edward Bridges. In 1947, Churchill agreed that the official historians could have access to his "personal minutes and telegrams," but he wished "to be shown beforehand any extracts which it is proposed to publish." By January 1951, this proviso had been enlarged to include his approval before "substantial use is made of information from these papers which is not on official record elsewhere."[29] What really upset Churchill were the criticisms of him in the draft history of *The War at Sea* by Captain Stephen Roskill. Asked to approve quotation of extracts on the Norway campaign of 1940 and on the decision to send the *Prince of Wales* and the *Repulse* to Singapore in late 1941, Churchill complained that "the object of the writer is evidently to show that everything that went wrong was due to civilian interference." Gordon Allen, another official historian but also drafter of the naval sections of Churchill's memoirs, was brought in to broker a compromise. It was not until Christmas Day, supposedly after two or three double brandies, that the Prime Minister approved Roskill's account of the *Prince of Wales* and the *Repulse*.[30]

The bad opinion Churchill formed of Roskill was carried over to his fellow authors. "He is convinced," wrote Norman Brook, "that the Histories are all being written by retired officers of the Services who never rose to high rank while on the active list and harbour, in consequence, grievances and prejudices of various kinds which colour their present work." In Churchill's last year as premier, this animus delayed production of several of the military-history volumes, with John Ehrman's study *Grand Strategy*, on 1943–1944, the prime target. After Pownall and Ian Jacob read it "on behalf of Sir Winston Churchill" and brought some thirty-five pages of typescript to his attention, the Prime Minister demanded to see the whole book. Brook was warned of "the strong language" and "acute sense of disappointment and frustration" felt by Ehrman and James Butler, the series editor, who complained that Churchill had "no interest in the Official Histories except to obstruct them." Brook waited till after the Prime Minister's resignation and then had a long talk with him in June 1955. Churchill was now insisting that any official historian who wanted to quote from his papers must print the full document, to prevent distortion—a condition he never applied to his own memoirs, whether quoting himself or others. He would not budge about this, but Brook did get him to relent on a demand to see any passages that related to him personally. On the basis of these new guidelines, promulgated in August 1955, Churchill left the vetting to Pownall and Jacob, monitored by Brook, and the logjam finally broke.[31]

In 1956, Ehrman published his two-volume *Grand Strategy* on 1943–1944 and 1944–1945; the following year, Butler produced his own volume on 1939–1941. Each had some hard things to say about Churchill. Ehrman noted the progressive emasculation of the War Cabinet, as the Prime Minister and the Chiefs of Staff ran strategy and operations, and also the way that in the last two years of the war Churchill "seldom had his way on an important strategic position" because of growing American dominance. He wrote of Churchill's "massive and uneven genius," of how "the virtues were on a grand scale, and the defects were particularly those of the virtues." Likewise, Butler noted that the main feature of Churchill's "cherished projects was audacity. . . . He seemed not always to remember that what is operationally desirable may not be administratively possible." For this reason, said Butler, "while in large issues Mr. Churchill's instincts were sound, he did not in this early period of the war show greatness as a strategist in the narrower sense." This comment was picked up in some reviews— "SIR WINSTON IS CRITICISED OFFICIALLY," trumpeted the *Daily Mail*—but the *Sunday Times* noted Butler's counterbalancing evaluation of his war leadership, calling it "one of the most remarkable tributes ever paid by an official historian to a living man."[32] Churchill was, said Butler, a greater national leader than Lloyd George, "who had not the same understanding of either the technique of war or the Service mind." There had, in fact, been "no one like him since Chatham . . . and Mr. Churchill possessed the human quality which Chatham lacked." Here again were Churchill's own markers in the ranking of great Britons, with himself measured superior to either of them.[33]

The detailed, nuanced analysis of an official history was unlikely to attract a vast readership at the best of times. And March 1957 proved notably unpropitious for Butler's volume. The historian Michael Howard observed that its reception was rather like the one given to Arturo Toscanini at Victoria Station before the war, when the great conductor was reputedly knocked down by "a horde of bobby-soxers crowding to welcome Mr. Robert Taylor."[34] In this case, the media star was the most unlikely figure of Field-Marshal Lord Alanbrooke.

—

CHURCHILL'S NEGLECT of Alanbrooke and the Chiefs of Staff in his memoirs caused deep hurt (see chapter 25, above). This was one reason why "Brookie"
started writing "Notes on My Life" to complement his diaries and assist Sir
Arthur Bryant, the official biographer commissioned by his old regiment. It was
intended that the biography should appear after Alanbrooke's death, but in the
autumn of 1954 Bryant looked through the diaries and notes and, finding them
"fascinating" and of "immense importance," suggested writing a "preliminary"
account before the public "lost all interest in the War." Alanbrooke agreed, so
Bryant set aside his popular history of England and embarked on *The Turn of the
Tide*. This was built around Alanbrooke's material about the Allied conferences
of 1941–1943, but the first third of the text covered the period before he became
Chief of the Imperial General Staff in November 1941.[35]

The reason why was made clear early on, where Bryant insisted that the
"miracle" of the Dunkirk evacuation depended on a prior miracle: "the Army
reaching the coast at all." This was "due mainly to one man": General Brooke,
then a corps commander covering the long exposed flank opened up by the Belgian surrender. His "lightning action" averted "the greatest disaster of British military history." Yet, said Bryant, "the man who saved the Army at Dunkirk and
helped to chart the road to victory is best known to-day as a lecturer on bird films
and ex-President of the [London] Zoo." This was the first and most important
objective of Bryant's book: to ensure that the spate of memoirs did not swamp the
contribution of what he called Britain's "greatest soldier" of the war.[36] His larger
purpose was to show what the British had contributed to victory, not just by
heroic survival in 1940 but by shaping the strategy that, he argued, won the war
by grinding down Germany in North Africa and Italy before thrusting across the
Channel. This "concentric" approach prevented Hitler from using his strategic
reserve to destroy a premature cross-Channel attack of the sort advocated by Marshall and the Americans, whose "experience of modern warfare was very small."
Although not "the sole originator" of this strategy, Brooke "took the lead" in pressing it on the Americans at wartime conferences. He did this, the book emphasized, at great personal cost—turning down the Middle East command in 1942
because he felt he was needed in London, only to be passed over for the Normandy invasion because Roosevelt and Churchill decided in 1943 to appoint an
American.[37]

In such a book, Bryant had to deal head-on with Churchill. He did so right at
the start in a "Prelude" entitled "A Partnership in Genius," which presented

Brooke as "the necessary counterpart" and "complement" to his great leader. "No statesman save Alfred has done England such service as Churchill," Bryant asserted. Among his "immense" virtues as war leader were courage, imagination, oratory, and humor. He always looked to attack; he "would never take No for an answer." But those virtues, pushed too far, became failings. The "tireless energy" bred "impatience," the "soaring imagination" led to "impetuosity," prompting Churchill "to essay enterprises which, had he not been dissuaded, would have ended in disaster." It was Brooke's role to say no, or at least "not yet"—to see the war as a whole and in sequence, persuading Churchill not to dissipate Britain's forces in premature or peripheral operations.[38]

Having sketched this portrait in the prelude, Bryant then develops it with color and detail from Alanbrooke's diaries and notes. There are references to Churchill's propensity to make decisions by "intuition" not logic, his tendency "to stick his fingers into every pie before it was cooked," and his "eagerness to do everything simultaneously instead of concentrating on one thing at a time." We read of Brooke's irritation as he tries to wean Churchill away from pet projects such as attacking Norway and learn that it is he, not the Prime Minister, who is the truly consistent advocate of a Mediterranean strategy.[39] All this, however, is balanced by frequent tributes from Bryant or Brooke's diary to Churchill's supreme achievements—his courage and decisiveness after the fall of France, his wooing of Roosevelt and the Americans in 1940–1941, his fortitude in the desperate weeks after Pearl Harbor—"The Prime Minister never flinched. Disaster brought out all that was greatest in him." At the end of the book, after chronicling Brooke's anguish at losing the D-Day command, Bryant quotes the diary entry on Churchill for 30 August 1943: "He is quite the most difficult man to work with that I have ever struck, but I would not have missed the chance of working with him for anything on earth."[40]

Bryant submitted his manuscript to Norman Brook, who read it in September 1956 (as the Suez crisis neared its climax). The Cabinet Secretary made no objection on official grounds; in fact, he said he had "enjoyed the book very much," particularly Bryant's own part, which had "a splendid sweep." But in what he called "an informal expression of my personal views," Brook registered real concern about the effect of the book on Churchill's public image. Although he felt that Bryant's prelude offered a "very fair and balanced judgment of the complementary roles" of Churchill and Alanbrooke, the same could not be said of the isolated diary entries, written, as Bryant himself noted, as "a safety valve for repressed irritation." Yet it was these momentary explosions that would be picked up by the press. "Praise of Winston Churchill is not 'news'; any criticism of his conduct of the war, however slight, is material for headlines." For this reason, Brook concluded, "I could have wished that the book was not to be published in Sir Winston Churchill's lifetime. And I cannot refrain from asking what steps are being taken to prepare him for the kind of publicity which (if I am not mistaken) it will receive."[41]

Brook admitted that he was "looking at it purely from Winston's point of view," but his sage advice spurred a belated response.[42] In December 1956, Alanbrooke added a foreword about his relations with Churchill, noting that a diary was "necessarily an impulsive and therefore unbalanced record of events" and insisting that "scattered expressions of irritation and impatience at the defects that arose out of his very greatness are insignificant when set against the magnitude of his achievement." In February 1957, the month of publication, Alanbrooke sent Churchill an advance copy with an inscription proclaiming "unbounded admiration, profound respect, and deep affection" and asking him to discount a few "momentary" criticisms, "written at the end of long and exhausting days." This embarrassed note was too little, too late. "Brookie trying to have it both ways," observed Clementine Churchill tartly.[43] Ismay felt Bryant had done Alanbrooke "grievous injustice" by presenting him as a combination of "Marlborough and Napoleon" who thought that he alone was winning the war, "with occasional assistance from the Almighty." Churchill sent Alanbrooke a brief note on 12 March: "On the whole I think I am against publishing day to day diaries written under the stress of events so soon afterwards. However, I read it with great interest, and I am very obliged to you for what you say in your inscription."[44]

Privately, several of Churchill's wartime contemporaries believed that the portrait in *Turn of the Tide* was apt and essentially fair. Clement Attlee told Bryant, "We who worked with him know how quickly he could change from the great man to the naughty child." Sir James Grigg, Secretary of State for War in 1942–1945, felt "it was necessary to reduce him from a god before he could be appreciated as a great man." The historian G. M. Trevelyan also found that the book had raised rather than lowered his estimation of Churchill. Although "not very considerate of his advisers," he "asked for advice and very often took it, sometimes contrary to what he had first thought himself," whereas Napoleon and Hitler treated their generals as "servants" and eventually paid the price. Churchill's "habit of taking counsel," said Trevelyan, "combined with his own personal qualities, is what won the war."[45]

These were private comments, however, and few would say as much in print. A rare exception was Raymond Mortimer, who felt the book showed Churchill as "nothing if not human—a self-centred genius with faults that he seeks neither to curb nor to conceal." But this was in the *Sunday Times*, which was serializing Bryant's work. Some reviewers took up the theme of the "partnership in genius," but others dwelled, as Norman Brook feared, on irreverent trivia, such as the image of Churchill upturned, like Humpty Dumpty, by the Mediterranean surf. The impression conveyed, said Robert Pitman in the *Sunday Express*, was of "a lovable, rumbustious but rather naughty child when it came to the art of war . . . just the front-man behind whom a greater strategist performed his quiet work." In a caustic piece, "Meet General Superman," "Cassandra" in the *Daily Mirror* claimed that Alanbrooke had jumped from total obscurity to occupy "the highest literary military pedestal built within living memory." Bryant had heaped on him "a sickening, sweetened slime of unending praise" while presenting Churchill as "muddle-headed, impetuous, abusive and positively dangerous when it came to the major decisions of the war." Considering this chronicle of "violent and continuous disagreement" between Churchill and his generals, Alan Tomkins in the *Sunday Dispatch* felt it "a wonder that Britain won the war."[46]

Despite the critics, *The Turn of the Tide* proved a bestseller. It was a Book-of-the-Month Club selection in America, and the British print run reached 135,000 within a month.[47] Alanbrooke gained financial security at last (creating a Churchill-style trust into which his half-share of the royalties was paid as a tax-free capital sum) and he became, for the first time, a household name. November 1957 saw publication of another edited diary, that of General Sir John Kennedy, a senior staff officer at the War Office in 1940–1944, which echoed Alanbrooke's complaints about working with Churchill. Serialization was even more sensational than for the Bryant volume: the *Evening Standard* billed the theme as "Churchill or the Generals—Who Knew Best?" But most reviewers, thus invited to take sides, came down firmly against the soldiers. Kennedy's memoirs, said Henry Fairlie in the *Daily Mail*, confirmed the picture of Churchill as "the goad of his executives" but also showed "why the goad was needed."[48]

When Bryant published his second volume, *Triumph in the West, 1943–1946*, in November 1959, he devoted much less space to criticisms of Churchill and concentrated his fire, and that of Alanbrooke, on the supposed strategic ineptitude of the Americans, particularly Eisenhower. Bryant even claimed that the chance of victory in 1944, made possible by British strategy in 1942–1943, was "thrown away by the inexperience of the American High Command." This chimed with Monty's memoirs, published in November 1958, which rebuked Eisenhower for not fully backing his own thrust into the Ruhr and on to Berlin. The ensuing furor in America highlighted the diplomatic tact with which Churchill had treated Ike in *Triumph and Tragedy*.[49] It also gave some reviewers the chance to go public with some blunt talk about Churchill. In expressing distaste for volume 2 and its incessant Eisenhower-bashing, Attlee slipped in that there had, however, been "ample justification" for the material in volume 1. "Sir Winston had given his own story at great length and it was time that what he had said to those who served him should be supplemented by what they said to him. There was no harm in letting the world know that the great leader in war was a difficult man to manage and that genius has it drawbacks." Grigg was even sharper:

> There is something ludicrous in the prevailing attitude towards Sir Winston. In earlier life he was one of the most unjustly belaboured politicians and at the end of the war with Hitler which he had done so much to win, he was repudiated at the polls. Now, after his withdrawal from public life, he has been raised to the skies and accorded what amounts to a retrospective immunity from criticism. But he is not a god and, if Brooke's diaries deprive him of that status, they leave him with all his rich humanity and make him not less admirable and even more lovable in our eyes.[50]

These were isolated voices, however. The last decade of Churchill's life was the period in which his status as a national icon became secure. Longevity was part of the explanation, as were the deaths of the other top-rank war leaders, and, after his retirement as Prime Minister, partisan rancor was transformed into cross-party reverence.[51] This was reverence for the moment as well as the man. The idea that World War II was indeed Britain's "finest hour" became ever more attractive as the costs of victory were exposed by the pinched years of postwar austerity, the retreat from empire, and the new hegemony of Ike's America. (Resentment at the latter, particularly after Suez, surely affected the tone of Bryant's second volume.) During the fifties, therefore, the years 1939–1945 were viewed with growing nostalgia by many Britons of that generation, and *The Second World War* had made "Winston" and "the war" virtually synonymous. The boys' comic book *The Eagle* ran an extended cartoon life of Churchill, revealingly entitled "The Happy Warrior," using it as a vehicle to narrate the war.[52]

To help cement his place in history, Churchill had long envisaged an authorized biography. Back in 1932, when Randolph Churchill was offered a £450 advance for a commercial life of his father, Winston cabled home from the United States: "Strongly deprecate premature attempt. Hope some day you will make thousands instead of hundreds out of my archives." In 1946, when setting up the Chartwell Trust, he expressed the wish that five years after his death the trustees should appoint a biographer, with full access to his papers, proposing Randolph or grandson Winston for this role.[53] Yet the father-son relationship remained tempestuous. Randolph desperately wanted Winston's approbation, but he failed in politics, his journalistic career bobbed up and down, and he found it hard to control his fiery temper or his addiction to alcohol. Throughout the 1950s, Winston declined to give his imprimatur to the idea that Randolph should write his life, just as he had for his own father. In an effort to prove his fitness, Randolph accepted the Stanley family's commission to write a life of Lord Derby, the nineteenth-century Tory magnate. Six years' work by Randolph, three "young gentlemen," and two secretaries resulted in a tome of some 600 pages, published in April 1960. The reviews were good, and the following month Randolph received the letter he had long craved. "I think your biography of Derby is a remarkable work," Winston told him, "and I should be happy that you should write my official biography when the time comes. But . . . I do not want anything to be published until at least five years after my death." Randolph replied that since first reading Winston's biography of his father, as a fourteen-year-old at Eton, it had "always been my greatest ambition to write your life." He promised to "devote my declining years exclusively to what will be a pious, fascinating and I suppose, a remunerative task."[54]

In keeping with his filial conception of the work and Winston's own approach to historical writing, Randolph adopted the motto of John Gibson Lockhart, author of a life of Sir Walter Scott: "He shall be his own biographer." Winston's own words would take pride of place in the anticipated five volumes and spill over into companion volumes of documents. A special strong room was built at the back of Randolph's country house in Essex to accommodate more than one million pages from Churchill's archives, and the top floor was cleared to provide space for four or five researchers and a team of four secretaries. In 1961, the "young gentlemen" got down to work, while the Chartwell Trust negotiated sale of the biography to publishers and newspapers around the world. For the first time in his life, Randolph had a secure income, and, entering his fifties, he finally found a mission: to build a literary monument to a parent he revered but to whom he could not relate. Like Winston before him, he hoped to meet his father in the mausoleum.[55]

THE FUROR over Alanbrooke's diaries had a sobering effect on unofficial Churchill biographers. "With Winston aged 82," Lord Moran told Henry Laughlin at Houghton Mifflin, "there was a feeling that Alanbrooke ought to have waited until he was gone." His own intention was still to publish a year after the funeral.

He anticipated "a spate of overpraise" when Churchill died, followed by a reaction, so that his book would "come in between as a balanced appraisement." Meanwhile, he carried on revising his own manuscript, stimulated by Monty's TV appearances and ABC's *The Valiant Years* into imagining a television series of his own.[56]

Yet there was more to Moran than an old man's frustrated ambition. He also offered a powerful interpretation of Churchill's life and work:

It is roughly this: that his services in 1940 cannot be exaggerated. It is true that the nation as a whole was ready to fight to a finish, but the small political world was of a different temper. All three parties had shown before the war weak knees and I can conceive, if there had been no Winston, a separate peace with Hitler. By that I mean a fixed up settlement at the last moment. I therefore see Winston as a kind of Joan of Arc, nerving the political world.

On the other hand before the war the nation and the three parties had no use for Winston. And once the survival of England was assured, Winston tended to revert to the old Winston with many of the peacetime faults. Even in 1944 he was always quarrelling with the White House. While after the war he was a complete failure leading the Opposition and it is now I think generally agreed that he was not up to his job when he became Prime Minister for the second time. Finally, his record since he retired in 1955 is a rather dismal, self-centred picture.

Now it would be possible to write a remarkable book on Winston's fight with old age and disease. But this would have twice the significance if Winston had been shown first of all with his full powers and immense energy and terrific will-power. I therefore conclude that it is absolutely essential to my book that he should be described as a war leader.[57]

Yet Moran faced major problems. One, as he admitted, was his limited knowledge of the war years. He saw Churchill only when the latter went abroad to conferences. Even then, he did not attend official meetings and had to rely on secondary accounts of what happened. Nor did his account fill the gaps between the conferences or give much sense of what happened before 1940. And whereas most manuscripts benefit from rewriting, Moran's got worse. He added material, sometimes repeating himself, moved passages around, and became confused about what he had written at the time and what was added later. The book got bigger and bigger, yet Moran seemed unable to escape from his Sisyphean task.

Churchill, though frail, kept defying death, while Moran, eight years his junior, was in decline. "I have come to the conclusion that Sir Winston is going to live longer than either of us," Laughlin wrote him in January 1962. A year later, Moran told Laughlin, "I'd back myself against him if I were a racing man" but admitted that "anyone who has had a coronary as I have may go any night."[58] By now, Moran's literary trustees (modeled on Churchill's) had signed contracts for the book, and news of it was leaking into the press, to the distress of Churchill's staff and family. When Clementine learned that this was a book about Winston, not simply Moran's memoirs, she wrote in stern indignation in July 1964: "I had always supposed that the relationship between a doctor and his patient was one of complete confidence. . . . I do not see how you can justify your present course." Moran made no reply.[59]

Also in limbo was a very different study of Churchill. Violet Bonham Carter had first met Churchill in the summer of 1906 when she was nineteen and he thirty-two. Her father, Herbert Asquith, was a Liberal Cabinet minister and future premier. Violet was captivated by the dynamic young politician; despite his marriage and change of political allegiance back to the Tories, they remained close friends. In June 1955, the publishers Eyre and Spottiswoode invited her to write a set of portraits of Churchill at various stages of his life. They had in mind a book to offset the official biography, in which the personality of the man would probably be "overshadowed by the tremendous series of events in which he played a leading part." Attracted by the idea but uncertain she could pull it off, Bonham Carter wrote a trial chapter over the summer, on her first meeting with Churchill. Eyre and Spottiswoode professed themselves "more than delighted" and gave her a contract. The project soon mushroomed in scale, so it was agreed she would finish with Gallipoli, leaving the rest of Churchill's life for a projected second volume.[60]

As with Moran's book, Bonham Carter's memoir was intended to appear after Churchill's death. Since this could occur at any moment, publishers wished to be ready. By June 1961, the *Daily Telegraph* had the first seven installments for serialization set in type. After Churchill broke his hip in June 1962, Bonham Carter's American publishers, Harcourt Brace Jovanovich, produced a complete set of galleys for the book—"Because of the recent unhappy news of W.S.C. . . . we do not want to be caught unprepared."[61] But it was not yet closing time for Churchill, and Bonham Carter, like Moran, began to fear that she might go first. So in 1964 she pressed for the book to appear as a ninetieth-birthday tribute to Winston. Clementine, to whom she showed the proofs, thought this a wonderful idea, but Colin Coote of the *Daily Telegraph* insisted it would be impossible to publish "over a dozen articles about somebody still alive," while William Jovanovich feared the book might get only "polite and perfunctory attention" on Churchill's birthday.[62]

So Moran and Bonham Carter were both waiting for Winston. Their books, though very different in tone and character, were acute and nuanced portraits, which each author yearned to see in print. But the Alanbrooke furor was a powerful deterrent, demonstrating Churchill's hold on history. He was still sitting in the pub. They could only nurse their drinks and watch the clock.

PROLOGUE | *January 1965*

BEFORE WORLD WAR I, Churchill was captivated by what he called the "fascinating new art" of flying. In the summer of 1919, he made a determined effort to gain his pilot's license, until a near-fatal crash persuaded him that this was irresponsible to his family.[1] But he never forgot the experience of piloting a plane. In 1937, he wrote of "those human beings whose pace of life was faster and more intense than the ordinary. Just as an aeroplane only flies by its speed and pressure against the air, so he flew best and easiest in the hurricane." Churchill was writing about Lawrence of Arabia, but he was surely also thinking of himself.[2] It was an image to which he kept on returning. At the very end of *Triumph and Tragedy*, describing his sudden premonition early on 26 July 1945 that he had lost the election, he writes: "All the pressure of great events, on and against which I had mentally so long maintained my 'flying speed,' would cease and I should fall."[3]

Churchill was always in a hurry. For him, to live was to move. That was why he was so keen to stay in office—in 1945 and again in the 1950s—and to keep on writing.[4] Retirement, however comfortable, would be a living death.

ON 6 AUGUST 1953, six weeks after Churchill's massive stroke, Lady Violet Bonham Carter had lunch at Chequers. Winston was in good form, ruminating about politics and fulminating against the BBC: "it kept me off the air for eleven years. It is run by reds." But she drove home "feeling an unutterable sense of tragedy, at watching this last—great—ultimately losing fight against mortality. The light still burning—flashing—in its battered framework—the indomitable desire to live & act is still militant and intact. Mind & will at bay with matter. At best a delaying action—but every instinct armed to fight it out until the end."[5]

Many in 1953 thought the end was nigh. In November, the Queen left instructions that if Churchill died during her absence on a tour of the Commonwealth he should be given "a public funeral on a scale befitting his position in history—commensurate, perhaps, with that of the funeral of the Duke of Wellington." In the summer of 1957, at the behest of Prime Minister Harold Macmillan, research was conducted into the four great nineteenth-century state funerals for commoners: those for Nelson in 1805, Pitt the Younger in 1806, Wellington in 1852, and Gladstone in 1898. The two politicians had been buried in Westminster Abbey; Nelson and Wellington were interred in St. Paul's. It was decided to follow a simplified version of Wellington's funeral, except that Churchill, like Gladstone, would lie in state first in Westminster Hall and would then be interred privately. In a rare moment of candor on the subject, Churchill said he wished to be buried under the croquet lawn at Chartwell, but this was thought inappropriate—"Shouldn't we have to consecrate the turf?" asked a flustered Macmillan. Winston eventually settled on the churchyard at Bladon, near Blenheim, where his parents lay. In March 1958, the Cabinet Office drew up its first detailed master plan for his funeral—known privately as Operation Hope Not.[6]

The plan went through eight revisions over the next few years because, in Mountbatten's words, "Churchill kept living and the pall-bearers kept dying."[7] After his resignation, the old man spent a good deal of time out of the country, as a guest of Emery Reves on the French Riviera or cruising the Mediterranean with Aristotle Onassis. In May 1959, he managed a final trip to Washington and was entertained with affection and kindness by Eisenhower at the White House. But he now needed a full-time male nurse to provide round-the-clock care. He was also shaky on his legs, and a fall in June 1962 left him with a broken hip, which took time to mend. It required an enormous family battle before he resigned his parliamentary seat, which for some years he had been unable to represent properly. At Churchill's last appearance in the Commons in July 1964, his own words were used as a political obituary. Harold Macmillan, recently retired as premier, quoted the epigraph to each volume of *The Second World War:* "In War: Resolution. In Defeat: Defiance. In Victory: Magnanimity. In Peace: Goodwill." Churchill called these words "The Moral of the Work." In fact, said Macmillan, "they are the story of his life."[8]

Although crumbling, his body remained intact—whereas, to the sadness of family and friends, his mind was increasingly vacant. There were still flashes of the old wit—at one lunch, conversation turned to Pierre Mendès-France, the

French premier. "I am disappointed," said Churchill, "I thought he could really do it." Do what? he was asked. "Mend his France," came the reply, with a broad grin of satisfaction. But often, now, meals passed in almost total silence, made even more poignant at the end by a mumbled apology: "I am sorry, my dear, for having been such poor company." For the man of words, it was indeed a sad declension. In those last years, he retreated into himself. He sat for long periods in summertime on a garden chair at Chartwell, gazing across his beloved Kentish Weald. Or staring into the winter fire—as his daughter Mary put it, "finding faces in the quivering glow."[9]

What images did he discern in the embers? What gathering storms and finest hours, what past triumphs and tragedies? Sometimes, it would seem, very little. At one dinner he did not even want to talk about the Second World War, so Bob Boothby tried the Battle of Jutland in 1916. "I used to know a lot about that," came the plaintive reply. "Now I have forgotten." His mood was often melancholic. "I would like to die," he repeatedly told his private secretary, "and I wish I had died in 1945." Once, during a somber dinner, he said, "I have worked very hard all my life, and I have achieved a great deal—in the end to achieve NOTHING," the last word falling like lead.[10]

In 1925, when Clementine's mother died, Winston had told his wife, "An old and failing life going out on the tide, after the allotted span has been spent and after most joys have faded, is not a cause for human pity. It is only a part of the immense tragedy of our existence here below against which both hope and faith have rebelled. It is only what we all expect & await." And in 1938 he wrote of the death of his ancestor, the First Duke of Marlborough, "It is foolish to waste lamentation upon the closing phase of human life. Noble spirits yield themselves willingly to the successively falling shades which carry them to a better world or to oblivion."[11] As far as Churchill was concerned, there was no better world, only oblivion, "black velvet," eternal sleep. His egoistic belief in a Providence that had prepared him for some special task—memorably articulated at the end of *The Gathering Storm*—did not transcend the grave. The idea of eternal life appalled him. "How terrible if we did—if we went on for ever. It's a dreadful thought," he mused in July 1960, adding that in the last five years "I have had no appetite for life. No—when it comes to dying I shall not complain. I shall not miaow."[12]

What, then, endured? Churchill's response accorded with his classical sense of history—a saga of great men immortalized by great deeds. Unlike Neville Chamberlain, he was not one for quoting Shakespeare—more to his taste were Tennyson and Macaulay—yet he surely empathized with Michael Cassio in *Othello,* who called his reputation "the immortal part of myself." But such immortality depends on words: if great deeds are not told and retold, then they perish. Hence Churchill's determination not to await the verdict of history but to be his own historian—and hence his conviction, as he said in 1938, that "words are the only things that last for ever."[13]

That is why the decade after 1945—often neglected by biographers—is so important for Churchill's place in history. As the Oxford historian Max Beloff observed in 1964, there was no statesman of the twentieth century "whose retrospective accounts of the great events in which he has taken part have so dominated subsequent historical thinking." Likewise, J. H. Plumb from Cambridge, who noted in 1969 how subsequent writers had adopted the phases and phrases he used to structure the conflict. "Churchill the historian lies at the very heart of all historiography of the Second World War, and will always remain there."[14]

As the Alanbrooke diaries made clear, however, it was not possible to hold back the tide of revisionism forever. As Churchill suffered a massive stroke on 9 January 1965 and slipped into his final coma, biographers in waiting now saw the green light. Randolph Churchill had only ten chapters written and, to the ire of his publishers, these consisted largely of extracts from Winston's *My Early Life*. After the funeral, the trustees decided they must "call Randolph to order," and he and a research assistant departed for six weeks' literary purdah with a car full of files, typescripts, and galleys. (In a further act of filial piety, he installed himself in the Mamounia Hotel in Marrakech.) Within two years he had published two volumes taking Winston to 1914, but then died in his sleep in June 1968—on the anniversary of D-Day—tobacco and alcohol having taken a far greater toll of him than of his father. What Randolph had hoped would be his crowning achievement was completed in six magisterial volumes by the historian Martin Gilbert.[15]

Violet Bonham Carter was quicker off the mark and much more successful than Randolph. With her book all in proof, she drafted the preface on 18 January 1965, four days after learning of Churchill's coma, and the final version went to press on the twenty-first. *Winston Churchill As I Knew Him* was published at the end of March 1965, opening with its colorful version of her first encounter with the mesmeric young politician in a hurry. "Curse ruthless time! Curse our mortality!" erupted Churchill, age thirty-two. "How cruelly short is the allotted span for all we must cram into it!" And then words she never forgot: "We are all worms. But I do believe that I am a glow-worm."[16]

While Bonham Carter was writing her preface, Lord Moran knew his own long wait for immortality was also drawing to a close. During that last illness, Churchill's doctor emerged from the shadows into the glare of the world's media, giving twice-daily bulletins from the steps of 28 Hyde Park Gate until Winston's end came on the morning of Sunday, 24 January—his father's birthday. Moran could now add some final, poignant paragraphs to the account over which he had labored for a decade and a half. The slow ebbing of Churchill's strength, "as if he was still loath to give up life." Three days lying in state in Westminster Hall, as thousands queued across Lambeth Bridge to pay their respects. The coffin drawn on a gun carriage to St. Paul's, where the monarch—against all protocol— awaited her subject. And the final journey by rail to Bladon, where, "in a country churchyard, in the stillness of a winter evening, in the presence of his family and a few friends, Winston Churchill was committed to English earth, which in his finest hour he had held inviolate."[17]

Winston Churchill: The Struggle for Survival was published in the spring of 1966, igniting a furious row about the ethics of a doctor writing about his patient. It also stimulated a much more positive appraisal of Churchill in a book of essays by some of his closest professional associates, including Edward Bridges and Norman Brook.[18] The battle for history had begun in earnest: what was past had become prologue. But Churchill had dominated the field for a quarter century— through speeches and deeds in wartime and, even more, by what he wrote afterward. And he must surely have known, as he finally slipped away, that he had won the immortality he craved. In death, as in life, Winston Churchill continues to glow. He remains in command of history.

ABBREVIATIONS

ADM   Admiralty papers (NA)

AHR   *The American Historical Review*

AIR   Air Ministry papers (NA)

Alanbrooke   Field-Marshal Lord Alanbrooke, *War Diaries, 1939–1945*, ed. Alex Danchev and Daniel Todman (London, 2001)

"C"   Head of SIS

CA   Confidential Annex

CAB   Cabinet Office papers (NA)

CAC   Churchill Archives Centre, Churchill College, Cambridge

Cadogan   David Dilks, ed., *The Diaries of Sir Alexander Cadogan, OM, 1938–1945* (London, 1971)

CCS   Combined Chiefs of Staff (U.S.-U.K.)

CHAR   Chartwell papers, pre-1945 (CAC)

CHPC   Churchill press cuttings (CAC)

CHPH   Churchill press photographs

CHUR   Churchill papers, post-1945 (CAC)

CHWL   Chartwell additional papers (CAC)

CIGS   Chief of the Imperial General Staff

Colville   John Colville, *The Fringes of Power: Downing Street Diaries, 1939–1955* (London, 1985)

COS   Chiefs of Staff (U.K.)
C-R   Warren F. Kimball, ed., *Churchill and Roosevelt:*
           The Complete Correspondence, 3 vols.
           (Princeton, 1984)
C-Reves   Martin Gilbert, ed., *Winston Churchill and Emery*
           Reves: Correspondence, 1937–1964 (Austin, Tex., 1997)
CSC   Clementine Spencer Churchill
CV   Companion volume [to Gilbert biography]
CWP   Martin Gilbert, ed., *The Churchill War Papers,* 3 vols. to
           date (London, 1993–2000)

DDEL   Dwight D. Eisenhower Library, Abilene, Kans.
DH   *Diplomatic History*
DS   *Diplomacy and Statecraft*
DT   *Daily Telegraph* (London)

EHR   *The English Historical Review*

FCNL   French Committee of National Liberation
FDRL   Franklin D. Roosevelt Library, Hyde Park, N.Y.
FO   Foreign Office papers (NA)

Gilbert   Martin Gilbert, *Winston S. Churchill,* vols. 3–8
           (London, 1971–1988). Abbreviated as Gilbert + volume
           number.

HC   House of Commons, *Debates*
Hinsley   F. H. Hinsley et al., *British Intelligence in the Second*
           World War, 4 vols. (London, 1979–1990)
HJ   *The Historical Journal*
HLRO   House of Lords Record Office
HM   Houghton Mifflin, Trade Editorial Files, Houghton
           Library, Harvard University, Cambridge, Mass.
HSTL   Harry S Truman Library, Independence, Mo.

IA   *International Affairs*
IHR   *The International History Review*
IWM   Imperial War Museum

JCH	*Journal of Contemporary History*
JCS	Joint Chiefs of Staff (U.S.)
JIC	Joint Intelligence Committee
JMH	*The Journal of Modern History*
KCL	Liddell Hart Centre for Military Archives, King's College, London
KGV	*King George V*–class battleship
Kimball	Warren F. Kimball, *Forged in War: Roosevelt, Churchill, and the Second World War* (New York, 1997)
Langworth	Richard M. Langworth, *A Connoisseur's Guide to the Books of Sir Winston Churchill* (London, 1998)
LC	Library of Congress, Washington, D.C.
LG	David Lloyd George
MOD	Ministry of Defence, London
Moran	*Winston Churchill: The Struggle for Survival, 1940–1965. Taken from the Diaries of Lord Moran*, paperback edn. (London, 1968)
NA	National Archives, Kew (formerly Public Record Office)
NAA	National Archives of Australia, Canberra
NYHT	New York *Herald Tribune*
NYT	*The New York Times*
PREM	Prime Minister's files (NA)
Sherwood	Robert E. Sherwood, *Roosevelt and Hopkins: An Intimate History* (New York, 1948)
SIS	Secret Intelligence Service (MI6)
Soames	Mary Soames, *Clementine Churchill*, rev. ed. (London, 2002)
Soames, ed.	Mary Soames, ed., *Speaking for Themselves: The Personal Letters of Winston and Clementine Churchill* (London, 1998)
SOE	Special Operations Executive

Speeches	Robert Rhodes James, ed., *Winston S. Churchill: His Complete Speeches*, 8 vols. (New York, 1974)
SWW	WSC, *The Second World War*, 6 vols. (London, 1948–1954)
SWWUS	WSC, *The Second World War*, 6 vols. (Boston, 1948–1953)
TLS	*The Times Literary Supplement*
USNA	United States National Archives
WC	WSC, *The World Crisis*, 6 vols. (London, 1923–1931). This is strictly five volumes, since volume 3 is published in two parts.
WM	War Cabinet minutes
WO	War Office papers (NA)
WP	War Cabinet papers
WSC	Winston S. Churchill

CHURCHILL'S SIX VOLUMES

Readers may find it helpful to see a summary list of the six volumes, each with its two component books, showing the dates of publication of the American and British editions, and also a table giving the word count for each volume.

I. THE GATHERING STORM

    1. *From War to War, 1919–1939*
    2. *The Twilight War, September 3, 1939–May 10, 1940*

Published in the U.S.A. on 21 June 1948 and in the U.K. on 4 October 1948.

II. THEIR FINEST HOUR

    1. *The Fall of France*
    2. *Alone*

Published in the U.S.A. on 29 March 1949 and in the U.K. on 27 June 1949.

III. THE GRAND ALLIANCE

    1. *Germany Drives East*
    2. *War Comes to America*

Published in the U.S.A. on 24 April 1950 and in the U.K. on 20 July 1950.

IV. THE HINGE OF FATE

1. *The Onslaught of Japan*
2. *Africa Redeemed*

Published in the U.S.A. on 27 November 1950 and in the U.K. on 3 August 1951.

V. CLOSING THE RING

1. *Italy Won*
2. *Teheran to Rome*

Published in the U.S.A. on 23 November 1951 and in the U.K. on 3 September 1952.

VI. TRIUMPH AND TRAGEDY

1. *The Tide of Victory*
2. *The Iron Curtain*

Published in the U.S.A. on 30 November 1953 and in the U.K. on 26 April 1954.

WORD COUNT OF THE SECOND WORLD WAR

	Text	*Appendices*	*Total*
Vol. 1	261,000	41,000	302,000
Vol. 2	246,000	43,000	289,000
Vol. 3	284,000	57,000	341,000
Vol. 4	331,000	58,000	389,000
Vol. 5	248,000	36,000	284,000
Vol. 6	261,000	43,000	304,000
Totals	1,631,000	278,000	1,909,000

Source: undated and unsigned memo in Cassell and Company papers:
Churchill correspondence, file on SWW, vol. 6.

A NOTE ON MONEY

Churchill's original book deal in May 1947 for five volumes was worth £555,000 or more than $2.23 million (see chapter 5, above). But estimating what that money was worth in today's values is extremely hard. The exchange rate has fluctuated, inflation rates have been different in the two countries, and there are several measures of relative value, each of which yields different results.

Using the Consumer Price Index, £1,000 in 1947 is roughly the equivalent of £24,000 in 2002 and $1,000 the equivalent of $8,000. The same sums of money in 1951 translate into £17,000 and $7,000 in 2002. But the CPI is most useful for assessing the cost of goods and services over time. Better for comparing different incomes over time is gross domestic product per capita, which is an index of the economy's average output per person. On that measure, $1,000 in 1947 is the equivalent of nearly $22,000 in 2002, while $1,000 in 1951 works out at $17,000.[1]

Thus, the value of the book deal in today's money might be estimated at anything between $18 million and $50 million. And the $60,000 that Time Inc. and *The New York Times* paid for Churchill's "working vacations" translates into a range from $420,000 to more than $1 million.

On the other hand, Churchill was not an average person in terms of output or income. One might discern more about the value of the book deal by noting the annual official salary of the Prime Minister: £10,000 in 1940 and the same amount when he retired in April 1955. Thus, a deal amounting to £575,000 over six years was worth roughly ten times the income he could have expected if he had remained at 10 Downing Street over the same period. (Top managers in the mid-1950s received about £9,000; Sir Edward Bridges, as Permanent Secretary to the Treasury, was paid £5,000—comparable to the earnings of the top 10 percent of barristers and ten times the pay of a bricklayer.)[2]

Another variable to be kept in mind when reading the text is that the sterling-dollar exchange rate changed dramatically during these years. Although fixed in those days by governmental agreement and not floating against the movements of the money markets, the devaluation of the pound in August 1949 cut the rate from $4.03 to $2.80.

For all these reasons, it is hard to estimate with any precision the value of Churchill's earnings from the memoirs. But there is no doubt that he made money as well as history.

A GUIDE TO SOURCES

My researches have taken me to numerous archives in England and also to a number in America and Australia—they are listed below. But my principal source has been the drafts and working papers for *The Second World War* contained in Churchill's post-1945 "Literary Papers" in the Churchill Archives Centre at Churchill College in Cambridge (class CHUR 4). There are nearly four hundred files directly relating to the memoirs—one for almost every chapter of the six volumes and others containing correspondence with his research assistants, publishers, readers, and critics. These are cited in the notes by class, file, and folio number: e.g., CHUR 4/83/104. There is also important correspondence in Churchill's personal papers (CHUR 1), particularly on finance and the working vacations; in his public and political correspondence (CHUR 2); and in the drafts of his speeches (CHUR 5). The press cuttings (CHPC) and additional papers (CHWL) contain many reviews of the six volumes, and Denis Kelly's unpublished memoirs (DEKE) offer insights. I have also made extensive use of the pre-1945 literary papers in CHAR 8, which help us understand Churchill's closet life as an author during the Second World War, and of other classes of CHAR that contain wartime papers drawn on in the memoirs.

Beyond Cambridge, the papers of Lord Ismay at King's College, London (particularly the 2/3 files) offer insights into the workings of "the Syndicate" that are not available in Cambridge. The wartime papers of the Prime Minister's Office (PREM 3 and PREM 4) at the National Archives in Kew, Surrey, provide a check on what Churchill said in the memoirs. And the voluminous Cabinet Office files at Kew, especially in CAB 21, are essential for understanding how

Churchill crafted his special deal about official documents and how his memoirs were both vetted and facilitated by officialdom. Among many collections in Oxford, the papers of Churchill's scientific adviser Lord Cherwell (Nuffield College) were particularly useful on Churchill's postwar years.

The other most valuable collections have been in the United States, notably the files of Houghton Mifflin's trade editorial department in the Houghton Library at Harvard University, which reveal a great deal about relations among his American publishers and about the problems of producing these volumes under such tight time pressures. Also illuminating on both counts are the papers of *Life* magazine in the Time Inc. archives in New York, and of *Life*'s editor Daniel Longwell at Columbia University.

The papers of Churchill's British publisher, Cassell's, in Littlehampton, Sussex, are unfortunately much less full. Sir William Deakin, the only surviving member of Churchill's research Syndicate when I began this book, most kindly allowed me to consult his papers at his house in the south of France.

1. **CHURCHILL ARCHIVES CENTRE,**
   CHURCHILL COLLEGE, CAMBRIDGE (CAC)

> Attlee, Lord (ATLE)
> Burgis, Lawrence (BRGS)
> Cadogan, Sir Alexander (ACAD)
> Churchill, Lady Clementine (CSCT)
> Churchill, Sir Winston
>> Chartwell papers, 1874–1945 (CHAR)
>> Chartwell additional papers (CHWL)
>> Churchill papers, post-1945 (CHUR)
>> Churchill additional papers (WCHL)
>> Churchill press cuttings (CHPC)
>> Churchill press photographs (CHPH)
> Colville, Sir John (CLVL)
> Cunningham, Admiral Lord (CUNN)
> Eade, Charles (EADE)
> Godfrey, Admiral Sir John (GDFY)
> Grigg, Sir James (PJGG)
> Hankey, Lord (HNKY)
> Jacob, Sir Ian (JACB)
> Jones, R. V. (RVJO)

Kelly, Denis (DEKE)

North, Admiral Dudley (NRTH)

Pound, Admiral Sir Dudley (DUPO)

Roskill, Stephen (ROSK)

Vansittart, Lord (VNST)

2. NATIONAL ARCHIVES, KEW, SURREY (NA)

Admiralty (ADM)

Air Ministry (AIR)

Cabinet Office (CAB)

Foreign Office (FO)

Government Code and Cypher School (HW)

Prime Minister's Office (PREM)

War Office (WO)

3. ARCHIVES IN LONDON

House of Lords Record Office (HLRO)

Beaverbrook, Lord

Lloyd George, David

Imperial War Museum (IWM)

Montgomery, Field Marshal Lord

Liddell Hart Centre for Military Archives, King's College, London (KCL)

Alanbrooke, Field-Marshal Lord

Bryant, Sir Arthur

Ismay, General Lord

Kennedy, General Sir John

Liddell Hart, Sir Basil (LH)

Wilmot, Chester

Wellcome Institute for the History of Medicine

Moran, Lord

4. OTHER ARCHIVES IN ENGLAND

Birmingham University Library

Avon, Lord (AP)

Chamberlain, Neville (NC)

Cambridge, Trinity College
> Butler, J. R. M.
> Butler, R. A.

Cambridge University Library
> Baldwin, Lord
> Templewood, Lord

Greenwich, National Maritime Museum
> Chatfield, Admiral Lord

Littlehampton Book Services (LBS), Sussex
> Cassell & Company

Oxford, Balliol College
> Nicolson, Sir Harold

Oxford, Bodleian Library
> Berlin, Sir Isaiah
> Bonham Carter, Lady Violet
> Macmillan, Harold (Lord Stockton)
> Normanbrook, Lord
> Woolton, Lord

Oxford, Nuffield College
> Cherwell, Lord

York, Borthwick Institute
> Halifax, Lord—Hickleton papers

5. **UNITED STATES**

Butler Library, Columbia University, New York, N.Y.
> Longwell, Daniel—Churchill collection

Churchill Memorial, Westminster College, Fulton, Mo.

Dwight D. Eisenhower Library, Abilene, Kans. (DDEL)
> Bedell Smith, Walter
> Eisenhower, Dwight D.

Franklin D. Roosevelt Library, Hyde Park, N.Y. (FDRL)
> Hopkins, Harry L.
> Morgenthau, Henry, Jr.
> Roosevelt, Franklin D.

Harry S Truman Library, Independence, Mo. (HSTL)
> Acheson, Dean G.
> Ross, Charles G.

Truman, Harry S

Harvard University Archives, Cambridge, Mass.

Morison, Samuel E.

Houghton Library, Harvard University, Cambridge, Mass.

Houghton Mifflin Co., Trade Editorial Files (HM), 92M-51

Sherwood, Robert E., bMs Am 1847

Library of Congress, Washington, D.C. (LC)

Davies, Joseph E.

Frankfurter, Felix

Harriman, W. Averell

Leahy, William D.

Time Inc. Archive, New York, N.Y.

Sterling Library, Yale University, New Haven, Conn.

Baldwin, Hanson W.

Stimson, Henry L.

U.S. National Archives, College Park, Md.

Department of State, decimal file

6. AUSTRALIA

National Archives of Australia, Canberra (NAA), Department of Defence papers

Central Files, series A816

Shedden, Sir Percy, series A5954

University of Melbourne

Robinson, W. S.

NOTES

INTRODUCTION

1. For publishing details, see Langworth, pp. 254–82, and, on serials, *DT*, 18 Dec. 1953, p. 6. *NYT* produced only twenty-four installments from *Closing the Ring*.
2. J. H. Plumb, "The Historian," in A. J. P. Taylor et al., *Churchill: Four Faces and the Man* (London, 1969), p. 149.
3. The main exception is Robin Prior, *Churchill's "World Crisis" as History* (London, 1983), a fascinating and perceptive critique of his memoirs about World War I. But Prior dealt with only part of the six-volume work, for reasons of space neglecting the origins of the war and its aftermath, and did not fully locate the work within Churchill's personal and intellectual biography during the 1920s.
4. For an overview and evaluation of this literature see T. G. Ashplant, Graham Dawson, and Michael Roper, eds., *The Politics of War, Memory and Commemoration* (London, 2000), chap. 1. The essays in Jan-Werner Müller, ed., *Memory and Power in Post-War Europe: Studies in the Presence of the Past* (Cambridge, 2002), explore the connection of memory and politics, but with little reference to political memoirs.
5. Conversely, the effect of the absence of a political memoir for public memory is dramatically shown by two studies in reputation: David Dutton, *Neville Chamberlain* (London, 2001), and Philip Williamson, "Baldwin's Reputation: Politics and History, 1937–1967," *HJ* 47 (2004): 127–68.
6. A rare and very important exception to this general neglect is John Ramsden, *Man of the Century: Winston Churchill and His Legend Since 1945* (London, 2002).
7. Although the chapters that follow are not burdened with theory, my approach has benefited from two methodologies: the canons of "genetic criticism" developed by students of French literature and the methods of the so-called Cambridge school for analyzing the history of political thought. Both insist, though from different perspectives, that literary and political texts must be understood in their fullest historical contexts. For a useful introduction to genetic criticism, developed particularly by Almuth Grésillon and Louis Hay, see Marion Schmidt, *Processes of Literary Creation* (Oxford, 1998), pp. 3–47. On methodology for the history of political thought, see the collected

essays in Quentin Skinner, *Visions of Politics*, vol. 1: *Regarding Method* (Cambridge, 2002), and the debates in James Tully, ed., *Meaning and Context: Quentin Skinner and His Critics* (Cambridge, 1988).

EPILOGUE: JULY 1945

1. Principal sources for this chapter include Gilbert 8, chaps. 4–6; Soames, chap. 24; Moran, chaps. 26–28; Richard Lovell, *Churchill's Doctor: A Biography of Lord Moran* (London, 1992), chap. 15; and R. B. McCallum and Alison Readman, *The British General Election of 1945* (London, 1947).
2. Colville, p. 610.
3. Gilbert 7:1347.
4. Moran, pp. 282, 284, 285.
5. Gilbert 8:61.
6. Cadogan, p. 762; Moran, pp. 293, 295, 301, 303.
7. Soames, p. 424; *SWW* 6:583 and *SWWUS* 6:675.
8. Colville, p. 611.
9. Lord Avon, *The Reckoning* (London, 1965), p. 551.

CHAPTER 1: TO WRITE OR NOT TO WRITE?

1. Blanche E. C. Dugdale, *Arthur James Balfour*, 2 vols. (London, 1936), 2:337; Colville, p. 310.
2. Camrose to Seymour Berry, 14 Nov. 1941, *CWP* 3:1453. According to Anthony Eden's diary for 30 Oct. 1940, Churchill "reiterated that he was now an old man, that he would not make LG's mistake of carrying on after the war, that the succession must be mine." Avon papers, AP 20/1/20 (Birmingham Univ. Library).
3. CHAR 8/636/132 (Butterworth); CHAR 8/663/8 (1940); CHAR 8/687/7–10 (1941); cf. HM 318/4, "Churchill—Curtis Brown, 1941–3."
4. See the massive correspondence in CHUR 4/6, quoting Hill on fo. 43; also, Reves to WSC, tel. received 27 July 1945, CHAR 8/721/3.
5. WSC to Sir Newman Flower, 24 Nov. 1944, CHAR 8/713/97–99.
6. Bridges, note on "Mr. Churchill's Papers," 28 July 1945, CAB 21/2824; Gilbert 8:132, quoting Camrose; Charles Eade, diary, 31 Aug. 1945 (CAC). The sixpence line is also in Moran, *Struggle*, p. 313. See also WSC to Lady Randolph, 25 Oct. 1897, in Randolph S. Churchill, *Winston S. Churchill*, vol. 1 (London, 1966), p. 356.
7. Moran, p. 314; Soames, p. 429.
8. WSC to CSC, 5 Sept. 1945, in Gilbert 8:138; Moran, pp. 319–20, 328, and diary 13 Sept. 1945.
9. Moran, pp. 318–19, 2 Sept. 1945; see also CHUR 4/6/141–50, quoting from J. Kingsbury Smith to WSC, 27 Sept. 1945.
10. *Life*, 7 Jan. 1946, pp. 44–52; cf. correspondence in CHUR 4/15/544–70.
11. CHUR 4/5/247–52; Gilbert 6:188 (Luce); Eade diary, 20 Dec. 1945.
12. Correspondence in CHUR 4/6, fos. 232, 241–44. For the approved version of his 10 Dec. 1942 speech, see CHAR 9/156B/217–47, marked "Returned by Sir Edward Bridges." The cut pages are at fos. 256–59.
13. Attlee to Chifley, 31 Jan. 1946, NAA A5954 676/1.

14. See Shedden to Menzies, 6 Feb. 1946, and Chifley to Cameron, 20 Feb. 1946, NAA A5954 676/11; Attlee to Chifley, 15 Feb. 1946, and Shedden, note, 21 Feb. 1946, NAA A5954 676/1.

15. See press clippings in CHUR 4/5/63–87, quoting *Daily Mirror*, 2 Feb. 1946; also HC, 5th series, 14 Feb. 1946, 419:521–22.

16. *The Sunday Sun*, 3 Feb. 1946 ("no comment"), copy in NAA A5954 676/1; *News Chronicle*, 28 Jan. 1946; CHUR 4/5, fos. 6–12, 22–24 (Eade) and 197–205 (books to MPs); cf. Eade diary for Jan. and Feb. 1946.

17. Moran, pp. 332–35; Gilbert 8:32; Michael David Kandiah, "The Conservative Party and the 1945 General Election," *Contemporary Record* 9.1 (1995): 22–47; Steven Fielding, "What Did 'The People' Want? The Meaning of the 1945 General Election," *HJ* 35.3 (1992): 623–39.

18. Gilbert 8:174 (to Windsor); Moran, p. 334; John Ramsden, "Winston Churchill and the Leadership of the Conservative Party, 1940–1951," *Contemporary Record*, 9.1 (1995): 99–119, esp. 106–7; Cranborne to Eden, 8 Jan. 1946, Avon papers, AP 20/43/1.

CHAPTER 2: CONTRACTS: CHURCHILL AGAINST THE PUBLISHERS

1. Quoted in Norman Rose, *Churchill: An Unruly Life* (London, 1994), p. 201. See also David Cannadine, "Winston Churchill as an Aristocratic Adventurer," in Cannadine, *Aspects of Aristocracy: Grandeur and Decline in Modern Britain* (London, 1994), pp. 130–62.

2. Gilbert 5:835, 844.

3. For the weight, see CV 5/3:742–43.

4. For an overview of Churchill's literary work in this period, see Roy Jenkins, *Churchill* (London, 2001), pp. 420–32, 447–56.

5. Desmond Flower, *Fellows in Foolscap: Memoirs of a Publisher* (London, 1991), p. 148; cf. CHAR 8/308.

6. See CHAR 8/710/13.

7. For 1939–40 see esp. CWP 1:345–46, 526, 577, 611–12, 622, 791.

8. CHAR 8/658, esp. Flower to Bracken, 16 April 1940, fo. 47, and Hill to Bullock, 24 April 1940, fo. 17.

9. CHAR 8/803, esp. Bracken to WSC, 26 June 1940, fo. 169, contract of 26 Nov. 1940, fos. 2–3, and June 1942 royalty statement, fo. 10. The debate over titles is at fos. 128–43. See also Flower, *Fellows in Foolscap*, p. 172.

10. CHAR 8/686, esp. Bracken to WSC, 30 May 1941, fos. 28–30, and contract of 3 Aug. 1941, fos. 13–16.

11. CHAR 8/708, esp. Daniel Macmillan to Kathleen Hill, 1 April 1943.

12. See CHAR 8/709; also Hannen Swaffer's article in *Daily Herald*, 16 Nov. 1943, and *Daily Express*, 20 Dec. 1943.

13. See CHAR 8/708 on Macmillan's, and CHAR 8/713 on Korda, esp. Nicholl, memo, 18 April 1944, fos. 23–26. See also Charles Eade diary, 14 Oct. 1943 (CAC).

14. CHAR 8/714, esp. Hill to WSC, 14 April 1944, fo. 26, and WSC to Daniel Macmillan, 27 April and 10 Aug. 1944, fos. 32, 50.

15. CHAR 8/710, esp. WSC n.d. notes [1944], fos. 3–6, WSC note, 4 Sept. 1944, fos. 112–13, and Walter Harrap to WSC, 7 Sept. 1944, fo. 117.

16. CHAR 8/713, esp. the two letters from Sir Newman Flower to WSC, 24 Nov. 1944, at fos. 97–99, 100. On the film deal, see CHAR 8/720.

17. Hannen Swaffer's article in the *Daily Herald*, 28 Sept. 1944. The same deference was shown by Churchill's solicitors, who had undergone a huge amount of inconvenience and lost work because of these negotiations but who asked for (and therefore were paid) almost nominal fees. See CHAR 8/720, esp. Nicholl to Hill, 26 April 1945, and WSC to Nicholl, 2 Aug. 1945.

18. Flower, *Fellows in Foolscap*, p. 148.

19. CHAR 8/715, esp. Albert Curtis Brown to Hill, 22 Sept. 1944, and Hill to Curtis Brown, 22 Dec. 1944; cf. note of 25 Aug. 1945, CHUR 4/6/117.

20. This is Bracken's own phrase—see his letter to Flower, 4 Jan. 1940, CHAR 8/658/55.

21. See the biography by his son, Lord Hartwell, *William Camrose: Giant of Fleet Street* (London, 1992), pp. 305–6, 330.

22. Hartwell, *William Camrose*, p. 333; cf. WSC to Arthur Christiansen, 13 Sept. 1947 (not sent), CHAR 4/6/32: "Some years ago, after a conversation at the Other Club, I promised Lord Camrose the first refusal of any memoirs which I might publish after the war."

23. WSC to Camrose, 29 Dec. 1945, in Gilbert 8:176; see also pp. 255–56, 304.

24. WSC to Sir Newman Flower, 24 Nov. 1944, CHAR 8/713/100; WSC to Camrose, 17 Oct. 1945, CHAR 8/718/4. See also CHAR 8/626 and CHAR 8/658.

25. WSC, memo, [17 Oct. 1945], CHAR 8/718/5–9.

26. CHAR 8/719, esp. WSC to Brogan, 30 Oct., 20 Nov., and 11 Dec. 1945.

27. Stated in WSC, memo, 17 Oct. 1945, CHAR 8/718/5.

28. Eade to WSC, 2 Feb. 1946, CHUR 4/5/29.

29. CHUR 4/6, esp. Marshall Field to WSC, 19 Sep. 1945, fos. 165–66, Kingsbury Smith to WSC, 29 Oct. 1945, fos. 142–45, and WSC to Camrose, 15 Oct. 1945, fo. 147.

30. CHUR 4/41/17–18. WSC's son, Randolph, also urged him to seek the advice of a tax expert. See Gilbert 8:131.

CHAPTER 3: PAPERS: CHURCHILL AGAINST
THE BUREAUCRATS

1. Moran, p. 318.

2. C 1 (19) 3, 4 Nov. 1919, CAB 23/18; cf. Stephen Roskill, *Hankey: Man of Secrets*, 3 vols. (London, 1970–1974), 1:127, and John F. Naylor, *A Man and an Institution: Sir Maurice Hankey, the Cabinet Secretariat and the Custody of Cabinet Secrecy* (Cambridge, 1984), pp. 67–69.

3. For the LG deal, see Frank Owen, *Tempestuous Journey: Lloyd George and His Life and Times* (London, 1954), pp. 699–701, and George W. Egerton, "The Lloyd George War Memoirs: A Study in the Politics of Memory," *JMH* 60 (1988), esp. 57–61.

4. Gilbert 4:757–58; cf. WC 1:358n1.

5. WSC to Bonar Law, 3 March 1923, in CV 5/1, 32–36; WSC to LG, 28 Feb. 1923, LG papers, G/4/4/4 (HLRO). See also Naylor, *Man and an Institution*, pp. 117–18, and CHAR 8/44, fos. 26–27, 35, 81.

6. Churchill's approach is set out in a draft letter to Baldwin, 18 Nov. 1926, prepared at his behest by his private secretary at the Treasury, P. J. Grigg, CHAR 8/204/39–40. It is not clear from the files whether this became a formal letter or whether, more likely, Churchill spoke about it to Baldwin, his next-door neighbor.

7. Hankey to WSC, 8 Dec. 1926, CHAR 8/204/145–59.
8. WSC to Hankey, 9 Dec. 1926, and Hankey to WSC, 10 Dec. 1926, CHAR 8/204/160–69.
9. Cf. LG papers, G/212 (HLRO), esp. Hankey to LG, 8 April 1933, and LG to Hankey, 10 April 1933.
10. See CAB 21/391; cf. Edgar Lansbury, *George Lansbury—My Father* (London, 1934), pp. 194, 199.
11. Cab. 11 (34) 5, CAB 23/78, and CP 69 (34), CAB 24/248.
12. Cab. 35 (34) 4, 17 Oct. 1934, CAB 23/80; cf. CAB 21/1230 and LG, *War Memoirs*, vol. 3 (London, 1934), chap. 52, quoting p. 1588.
13. Quotations from Howorth to H. G. Vincent, 5 Nov. 1934, CAB 21/2161. For the paper chase, see CAB 21/457, esp. Howorth memo, 20 Nov. 1935. There is a good account of the 1934 row and its consequences in Naylor, *Man and an Institution*, chap. 6, though this was written before many of the Cabinet Office files were opened.
14. WSC to Howorth, 19 Nov. 1934, and WSC to Hankey, 18 June 1935, in CV 5/2:925, 1195–97, 1198–99.
15. CAB 21/2824, esp. Hankey to WSC, 27 June 1935, and Hankey, memo, 19 April 1936. In his unpublished memoirs, Burgis offered a colorful account of his well-lubricated lunch at Chartwell and of Churchill's lengthy oratory on politics and Napoleon, lasting from 12:45 to 2:45. When Burgis finally summoned up courage to mention the papers he had been sent to collect, Churchill supposedly said, "Don't you bother about them my dear boy! I'll give you the abridged version of my World Crisis instead." He then escorted Burgis to his car, mission unaccomplished. See Lawrence Burgis, TS. memoirs, p. 35, BRGS 1/1 (CAC). This agreeable story is rather dented by Burgis to WSC, 22 April 1936, CAB 21/2824, which acknowledges receipt of the Cabinet papers, adding: "The suitcase which you lent me to take these Conclusions away in, I will return during the weekend."
16. "Recovery of Cabinet documents: Position 6th January 1938," CAB 21/790.
17. WDW to Howorth, 21 April 1940, and Howorth, note, 22 April 1940, CAB 21/2824.
18. WSC to Bridges, 30 Apr. 1945, and Brook to Bridges, 18 May 1945, CAB 21/1652.
19. WSC, "War Cabinet Documents," WP (45) 320, 23 May 1945, CAB 66/65; Charles Eade diary, 31 Aug. 1945 and 20 Dec. 1945 (CAC).
20. Bridges to Cripps, 1 July 1942, CAB 21/2677. See generally Sir John Winnifrith, "Edward Ettingdean Bridges—Baron Bridges, 1892–1969," in *Biographical Memoirs of Fellows of the Royal Society* 16 (1970): 36–56.
21. CAB 21/2165, esp. Bridges to WSC, 22 Nov. 1941, WSC to Bridges, 23 Nov. 1941, and Bridges to Chatfield, 28 Nov. 1941; WM 118 (41), 24 Nov. 1941, CAB 65/20.
22. CAB 21/2677, quoting Bridges, note, 15 May 1942, and WSC to Bridges, 7 June 1942.
23. WM 75 (42) 1, 16 June 1942, CAB 65/26, and WM 90 (42), 9 July 1942, CAB 65/27. The haggling between Cripps and Bridges is in CAB 21/2677.
24. See CAB 21/2677, quoting Bridges to Barnes, 9 July 1942, and also CAB 21/2678, quoting Londonderry to Bridges, 11 March 1943.
25. See CAB 21/2193, and Hankey papers, HNKY 25/2 (CAC).
26. CAB 21/2193, esp. Hankey to WSC, 8 Dec. 1944, Bridges to WSC, 9 Dec. 1944, WSC, "Lord Hankey's Book," 22 Jan. 1945, and official note of the 29 Jan. 1945 meeting; letter to author from Lord Bridges, 3 March 2004.
27. CAB 21/2193, esp. Bridges's note of 27 March 1945, Hankey to Bridges, 29 March 1945 and enclosure, and WSC to Bridges, 4 June 1945. Cf. WC, 2:10.

28. See Neville Chamberlain papers (Birmingham Univ. Library), NC 11/15/122–34, quoting Keith Feiling to Horace Wilson, 31 July 1941, NC 11/15/129.

29. CAB 21/2166, esp. Bridges's memoranda of 8 Oct. 1941, 5 Dec. 1941, and 26 Sept. 1944, and Hector McNeil to Norman Brook, 29 June 1951.

30. Bridges to Feiling, 13 March 1945, CAB 21/2166; WSC to Feiling, 16 Oct. 1944, PREM 4/16/4.

31. CAB 21/2166, esp. Laithwaite to Brook, 20 July 1945, Bridges to Cadogan, 20 Aug. 1945, and Cadogan to Bridges, 12 Oct. 1945.

32. Quotations from Feiling to Anne Chamberlain, 22 Feb. and 22 March 1945, NC 11/15/12 and 11/15/4.

33. Churchill to Bridges, minute C51/5, 7 July 1945, PREM 4/83/1A.

34. See CAB 21/4476, esp. Bridges to Laithwaite, 9 July 1945, and Laithwaite, note of meeting on 20 Aug. 1945. Sir Norman Brook, Bridges's successor as Cabinet Secretary, observed in 1952: "I have always been a bit nervous about the special facilities accorded to Mr. G. M. Young, by Mr. Churchill's direction." Brook to Strang, 14 Aug. 1952.

35. Martin Gilbert, *In Search of Churchill* (London, 1994), pp. 105–6; Gilbert 8:1327.

36. CAB 21/2824, esp. Bridges note, 28 July 1945, and Wood to Fraser, 2 April 1947.

CHAPTER 4: REPUTATION: CHURCHILL AGAINST MORTALITY

1. HC, 5th series, 365:1617, 12 Nov. 1940.

2. David Lloyd George, *War Memoirs* (London, 1934), 3:1067–72. Reviewing a draft, Hankey told LG that, despite "its dazzling brilliancy and truth," the passage about the defect in the machine would hit Churchill dreadfully. "It will be quoted against him if he is ever in, or aspires to get into, office again." LG, promising to "tone down the acerbities of truth," made some amendments, but the essential indictment remained. See LG papers, G/212 (HLRO), esp. draft of vol. 3, chap. 1, pp. 22–24b, Hankey to LG, 16 April 1934, and reply, 18 April 1934.

3. Gilbert 5:741, 1081.

4. Harold Nicolson, *Diaries and Letters*, ed. Nigel Nicolson, 3 vols. (London, 1966–1968), 2:479, 1 Aug. 1945.

5. Moran, pp. 334–35.

6. Quoted in Malcolm MacDonald, *Titans and Others* (London, 1972), p. 89; WSC to Stalin, unsent draft, 31 Jan. 1944, PREM 3/396/11, fo. 320. For other examples, see Herbert L. Stewart, *Sir Winston Churchill as Writer and Speaker* (London, 1954), p. 102, and Colville, p. 509, 6 Sept. 1944.

7. Gilbert 8:126.

8. Moran, pp. 440–41, 2 July 1953.

9. Harry C. Butcher, *My Three Years with Eisenhower* (New York, 1946), pp. 75, 639, 644, entries for 26 Aug. 1942, 11 and 15 Aug. 1944. Churchill had already written about the folly of keeping a diary in an essay on Haig — see *Great Contemporaries* (London, 1941 ed.), p. 191.

10. Eisenhower to WSC, 18 Dec. 1945, and WSC to Eisenhower, 26 Jan. 1946, Eisenhower 16/52 file, box 22 (DDEL).

11. *Chicago Tribune, Chicago Sun* (Reynolds), *The Milwaukee Journal*, all 28 April 1946, copies in Harry C. Butcher papers, box 7: reviews file (DDEL); cf. Butcher, *My Three Years*, p. 319.

12. Ralph Ingersoll, *Top Secret* (London, 1946), pp. 41 (Marshall), 51 ("magnet"), 169 (Ike), 265 (Monty), 272 ("nonsense"), 274–76 (Russia).

13. Ibid., pp. iii-iv, 263 ("prepared"); Colville to Hill, 17 Aug. 1945, CHUR 2/3/29.

14. WSC to Attlee, 29 May 1946, CAB 21/3740.

15. Moran, p. 332, 4 Jan. 1946.

16. McCluer to WSC, 3 Oct. 1945, CHUR 2/230/350, and WSC to Truman, 8 Nov. 1945, CHUR 2/230/166–67; *Kansas City Star*, 20 Jan. 1946, p. C1.

17. WSC to Truman, 29 Jan. 1946, CHUR 2/158/68–69; William E. Parrish, *Westminster College: An Informal History, 1851–1969* (Fulton, Mo., 1971), p. 211; Charles G. Ross diary, 7 March 1946, Ross papers, box 22 (HSTL).

18. References in what follows are to the published text in *Speeches* 7:7285–93, and the drafts in CHUR 5/4. Two valuable interpretations of the speech are Henry B. Ryan, "A New Look at Churchill's 'Iron Curtain' Speech," *HJ* 22 (1979): 895–920, and John Ramsden, "Mr. Churchill Goes to Fulton," in James W. Muller, ed., *Churchill's "Iron Curtain" Speech Fifty Years Later* (Columbia, Mo., 1999), pp. 15–47—though my account differs in important respects from each of these.

19. *Speeches* 7:7214, 16 Aug. 1945.

20. Alan Foster, "The British Press and the Coming of the Cold War," in Anne Deighton, ed., *Britain and the First Cold War* (London, 1990), p. 13.

21. See David Reynolds, "Rethinking Anglo-American Relations," *IA* 65 (1989): 94.

22. WSC to Attlee, 17 Feb. 1946, CHUR 2/210; Halifax diary, 10 and 11 Feb. 1946, Hickleton papers, A 7.8.18 (Borthwick Institute, York).

23. Churchill to McCluer, 14 Feb. 1946, CHUR 2/230B; cf. *DT*, 5 March 1946, copy in CHPC 23. The official British Information Services advance text of the speech, given to the press, does not contain this sentence about the sinews of peace: see copy in W. Averell Harriman papers, box 991 (LC).

24. *NYT*, 14 March 1946, pp. 1, 4; William Taubman, *Stalin's American Policy: From Entente to Détente to Cold War* (New York, 1982), pp. 141, 144.

25. HC, 5th series, 420:759–61, 11 March 1946; cf. Attlee to WSC, 25 Feb. 1946, CHUR 2/210.

26. Leahy diary, 10 Feb. and 3 March 1946, William D. Leahy papers (LC); WSC to Attlee, 7 March 1946, CHUR 2/4; Fraser J. Harbutt, *The Iron Curtain: Churchill, America, and the Origins of the Cold War* (New York, 1986), pp. 280–85.

27. Second draft of 15 March 1946 speech, p. A2, in CHUR 5/4.

28. HC, vol. 420, cols. 231, 236, 5 March 1946; Salisbury to Eden, 13 March 1946, and Eden to Salisbury, 15 March 1946, Avon papers, AP 20/43/17, 17A (Birmingham Univ. Library).

29. *The Evening News*, 15 March 1946, *Daily Mail* and *The Star*, 18 March 1946, all in CHPC 23.

30. Moran, p. 277; Truman to WSC, 30 July 1945, CHUR 2/142/212.

CHAPTER 5: TAKING THE PLUNGE

1. *DT*, 27 March 1946, p. 6.

2. Gilbert 8:221; Ismay to WSC, 13 Apr. 1946, CHUR 4/23B/366; cf. diary for April 1946 in CHUR 2/616.

3. See Moir's memo "Schemes," n.d., and Graham-Dixon, "Opinion," 18 Feb. 1946, CHUR 4/41A/11–14.

4. WSC, memo, 11 April 1946, CHUR 4/41A/127–31; cf. Sturdee, note [May 1952], CHUR 4/41B/289–90.

5. Settlement, 31 July 1946, CHUR 4/41A/52. WSC's accompanying memorandum is at fos. 59–60, but see also fo. 56.

6. WSC to Camrose, 4 Aug. 1946, CHUR 4/42/124–25.

7. Correspondence of 7–11 April 1946 in Avon papers (Birmingham Univ. Library), AP 20/43, docs. 25, 25A, 27, 27A; David Dutton, *Anthony Eden: A Life and Reputation* (London, 1997), p. 233. See also David Carlton, *Anthony Eden: A Biography* (London, 1981), pp. 266–67.

8. Avon papers (Birmingham Univ. Library), AP 33/1/1–5; Harold Nicolson, MS. diary, 20 and 31 May, 4 June, and 22 Oct. 1946 (Balliol College, Oxford). Some of these entries were published, in expurgated form, in Harold Nicolson, *Diaries and Letters*, ed. Nigel Nicolson, 3 vols. (London, 1966–1968), 3:63, 65, 79.

9. Note of 30 Aug. 1946, R. A. Butler papers, G17/33 (Trinity College, Cambridge); Moran, p. 339; Bracken to Beaverbrook, 16 Oct. 1946, Beaverbrook papers, C/56 (HLRO).

10. *Speeches* 7:7379–82; Gilbert 8:266–67.

11. Elliott Roosevelt, *As He Saw It* (New York, 1946), esp. pp. xii–xviii, 36, 38–39, 184, 253.

12. Arthur M. Schlesinger, Jr., *A Life in the Twentieth Century: Innocent Beginnings, 1917–1950* (Boston, 2000), pp. 435–36; Beaverbrook to WSC, draft tel., n.d. [Sept. 1946], Beaverbrook papers, C88 (HLRO). Although this was not sent, one may assume that Beaverbrook eventually passed on its contents verbally.

13. Frankfurter to Sherwood, 7 Oct. 1946, and, in similar vein, Halifax to Frankfurter, 7 Nov. 1946, in Felix Frankfurter papers, 102/2112, 62/1204 (LC).

14. Moran, p. 340.

15. Correspondence in CHUR 2/155/103–34, quoting from WSC to Sherwood, 17 Aug. 1946, and enclosed answers.

16. Truman to Sherwood, 23 May 1946, and Sherwood to Matthew J. Connally, 23 Jan. 1948, PPF 1685: Hopkins (HSTL). There is a copy of Truman's letter in CHUR 2/155/119.

17. CHUR 4/23B/250–57, quoting WSC to Eisenhower, 3 Feb. 1947, at fo. 251.

18. See CAB 21/2165 (Chatfield) and FO 370/1195 (Vansittart).

19. Armstrong to Brook and Bridges, 21 March 1946, CAB 21/2162; Attlee to Bevin, 27 March 1946, FO 370/1309.

20. "It is surely indefensible for a politician to use all the *recent* state secrets that he wants to make a book—and a fortune, while the diplomatist may not even use *ancient* ones. I was told at the time that Lloyd George made £100,000 out of his war memoirs, and there is no doubt that Churchill's war-book will have an even greater sale and be even fuller of what were once official secrets. (He had also a considerable sale of his secret speeches during the war which were of course more secret and more modern than anything I contemplate saying of a distant past.)" Vansittart to Sargent, 2 Nov. 1946, Vansittart papers, VNST I, 4/9/3 (CAC).

21. CP (46) 188, 10 May 1946, CAB 129/9.

22. Bridges to Brook, 21 May 1946, CAB 21/2392; Bridges to Attlee, 24 May 1946, and WSC to Attlee, 29 May 1946, CAB 21/3740. Much of WSC's letter is quoted in Gilbert 8:235.

23. Ismay to WSC, 15 Aug. 1946, CHUR 4/23B/359; WSC to Bridges, 23 Sept. 1946, CAB 21/3747—the latter reproduced extensively in Gilbert 8:268.

24. OIP 1 (46) 3, 24 Sept. 1946, CAB 134/548; and papers in CAB 21/3747, quoting from Bridges to Attlee, 7 Oct. 1946.
25. CP (46) 369, 8 Oct. 1946, CAB 129/13; CM 85 (46) 7, 10 Oct. 1946, CAB 128/6; Bevin to Attlee, 9 Oct. 1946, and Bridges to WSC, 10 Oct. 1946, CAB 21/3747.
26. CHUR 4/23B/348–73, quoting from Ismay to WSC, 15 Aug. 1946, fo. 359, and Bridges to WSC, 28 Sept. 1946, fos. 356–57.
27. See CAB 103/263, quoting from COH (U) 3rd meeting, minute 3, 12 May 1943; also COH (44) 1 and COH 2 (44) 2, CAB 98/11.
28. Ismay to Bridges, 30 Sept. 1946, CAB 21/3747; Bridges to WSC, 2 Nov. 1948, CHUR 4/49/53. On Sherwood, see PREM 8/155.
29. CAB 21/3747, quoting S. E. V. Luke to Bridges, 26 July 1947 ("exceptional"), D. F. Hubback, "Note for the Record," 9 Oct. 1947 ("category"), Hubback to Murrie, 10 April 1947 ("Deakin"), Allen to McGrigor, 11 July 1947, and Brook to Helsby, 25 Aug. 1947.
30. This biographical sketch draws heavily on the introduction to *C-Reves*.
31. *C-Reves*, pp. 264–71.
32. Quotations from *C-Reves*, p. 266, and CHUR 4/12/282. Cf. Walter Graebner (*Life's* bureau chief in London) to Daniel Longwell, 20 Nov. 1946: "Our friend very emphatically says that Lord Camrose (assisted by Reves) is only person with whom discussions and negotiations can be carried out." Longwell papers/Churchill, box 2, "Contract Negotiations" (Butler Library, Columbia Univ., New York, N.Y.).
33. CHUR 4/42/148–50.
34. *C-Reves*, pp. 267–70, and Laughlin to Reves, 27 Nov. 1946, HM, 318/1: H. J. Frank file.
35. Although this is not evident from Reves's 1966 recollections, it follows Reves to Brooks, 28 Nov. 1946, HM 318/1: Frank.
36. CHUR 4/42, fos. 140–41, 135–36 (Camrose) and 4/12/261 (Reves). See also Heiskell to Camrose, 28 Nov. 1946, Time Inc. papers (New York, N.Y.): WSC Memoirs.
37. Heiskell to Adler, 13 Dec. 1946, Time Inc. papers: WSC Memoirs.
38. CHUR 4/41A, esp. statement, 6 Jan. 1947, fo. 119. For slightly different figures, see Lord Hartwell, *William Camrose, Giant of Fleet Street* (London, 1992), pp. 334–35.
39. Quotation from Hartwell, *William Camrose*, p. 335. This paragraph draws on papers in HM 318/1: Frank; and Time Inc. papers: WSC Memoirs.
40. Quotations from Reves to Brooks, 6 Jan. 1947, Reves to Laughlin, 3 May 1947, and Laughlin to Reves, 14 May 1947, all in HM 318/1: Frank.
41. Heiskell to London office [April 1947], Time Inc. papers: WSC Memoirs.
42. For the public announcement see CHUR 4/42/260–92; cf. *NYT*, 15 May 1947, pp. 1, 18; *Time*, 19 May 1947, p. 67; Hartwell, *William Camrose*, p. 325.

I | THE GATHERING STORM, 1919–1940, 1946–1948

CHAPTER 6: SETTING A COURSE

1. CHUR 4/74/24–28.
2. Cf. CHUR 4/146/84.
3. "Note on Volume III," 25 March 1948, Ismay papers, 2/3/45 (KCL).
4. See CHUR 4/75/1 and CHUR 4/74, fos. 29, 31, 54.
5. Walter Graebner, *My Dear Mister Churchill* (London, 1965), p. 69.

6. Maurice Ashley, *Churchill as Historian* (London, 1968), pp. 27–28. Ashley's book is the fullest study of Churchill's working methods, but see also Martin Gilbert, *In Search of Churchill* (London, 1994), chaps. 8–9, and F. W. Deakin, "Churchill the Historian," *Schweizer Monatshefte* 49.4 Sonderbeilage (1969–1970): 1–19.

7. See Deakin papers, "WSC: Drafts and Correspondence" and CHUR 4/91/3–51 (Czech crisis); CHUR 4/140, fos. 256–63, 340–48 (Pownall).

8. *SWW* 4:41 and *SWWUS* 4:52; cf. "The Rise of Hitler," in Deakin papers: Deakin-Churchill drafts (privately held) and revision in CHUR 4/78, fos. 1–10.

9. CHUR 4/24A/145.

10. See WSC to Pownall, 11 Nov. 1946, CHUR 4/20B/428, and WSC to Joll, 21 Dec. 1946, CHUR 4/23B/318.

11. CHUR 4/20, fos. 417, 395.

12. Pownall to Ismay, 10 May 1948, Ismay papers, 2/3/50/1.

13. WSC to Ismay, 4 Nov. 1946, Ismay papers, 2/3/11.

14. For background, see CHUR 4/20/395–98 and 4/18/66–67.

15. For this paragraph and the next, see Denis Kelly, TS. memoirs (1985), chap. 1 (CAC), and his summer 1947 memo on the archives, CHUR 4/42/191–202. The "Cosmos out of Chaos" quote occurs in both accounts.

16. CHUR 4/42, esp. fos. 181–89, 194 (fire), and 247 (bank charges).

17. Ibid., fos. 198–201, 243–45, 285–86.

18. CHUR 4/145/1–90, quoting fos. 18, 21, 87–88.

19. CHUR 4/19/84–94 (Cripps) and CHUR 4/22/2–15 (Carter).

20. CHUR 4/20/157–58; cf. Christopher Hassall, *Edward Marsh: Patron of the Arts* (London, 1959), pp. 498, 542, 653.

21. CHUR 4/131/243.

22. Michael Ignatieff, *Isaiah Berlin: A Life* (New York, 1998), pp. 124–27. See also FO 371/38537/236 and PREM 4/26/10/922.

23. CHUR 4/14/472–73 and comments on Brooks to Laughlin, 15 Oct. 1947, in 318/4: Churchill. For anecdotes about their relationship, see Henry A. Laughlin, "Glimpses of Winston Churchill," *Proceedings of the Massachusetts Historical Society* 77 (1976): 67–82.

24. HM 318/4: Churchill, quoting from letter of 17 Sept. 1947.

25. CHUR 4/14/457–60 and Reves to Laughlin, 4 March 1948, HM 318/1: Reves.

26. CHUR 4/15/231–32.

27. Longwell to WSC, 27 Aug. 1947, and Longwell to Camrose, 30 Aug. 1947, Time Inc. papers: WSC Memoirs. The marked set of galleys is in CHUR 4/133.

28. A copy of the memo is in HM 318/4: Churchill. Although no author is identified, internal evidence strongly suggests that it was Longwell.

29. *C-Reves*, pp. 274–79.

30. CHUR 4/12/232–33; cf. Langworth, pp. 278–82.

31. See CHUR 4/15, quoting from CHUR 4/15, fos. 221–22, 207. On Rufus, see Graebner, *My Dear Mr. Churchill*, pp. 99–102, and the line entry "miniature poodle $158.68" in "Vacation Payments to Winston Churchill," memo [Nov. 1950], Daniel Longwell papers, Churchill collection, box 4: Payments (Butler Library, Columbia Univ., New York, N.Y.).

32. CHUR 4/15/511.

33. Letter of 18 Dec. 1947 in Soames, ed., p. 547.

34. Figures from memo, "Vacation Payments," in Longwell papers/Churchill. My main

sources for this account of the visit to Marrakech are Gilbert 8, chap. 21, and the papers in CHUR 1/68–69.

35. CHUR 4/15/203 (to Longwell); Gilbert 8:383 (Deakin); CHUR 4/25/126 (Luce).

36. Gilbert 8:392–94, with fuller texts in *C-Reves*, pp. 279–85. For Kelly's comments of 16 Jan. 1948, see CHUR 4/141/271.

37. The correspondence is in CHUR 4/141, esp. fos. 98, 239–60.

38. *C-Reves*, p. 284 and CHUR 4/145/199–200; cf. CHUR 4/74/55, 4/119/138. The poet and critic William Empson titled a volume of poems he published in 1940 *The Gathering Storm*.

39. CHUR 4/74/46; cf. Colville, p. 342.

40. For acute pen-pictures of the two, see Peter Hennessy, *Whitehall* (London, 1989), pp. 138–49.

41. WSC to Brook, 10 Dec. 1947, CAB 21/2174. This file is the main source for what follows about Brook and volume 1.

42. "I appreciate all the care and thought you have given and are giving to the text of my book," Churchill wrote on 2 Feb. 1948 (CHUR 4/18/338).

43. Brook to Bridges, 19 Dec. 1947, and Brook to WSC, 24 Dec. 1947, CAB 21/2174.

44. Brook to WSC, 24 Dec. 1947, CAB 21/2174; cf. CHUR 4/76/264.

45. CAB 21/2174, esp. Scorgie to Brook, 22 Jan. 1948, and Brook to Attlee, 23 Jan. 1948. For the Cabinet, see CAB 128/12, CM 7 (48) 4, 26 Jan. 1948, and Brook to WSC, 11 Feb. 1948, CAB 21/2186.

46. Brook, memo of conversation on 27 Jan. 1948, CAB 21/2174.

47. CHUR 4/18/339–40; cf. Brook's notes for the record, 11 and 13 Feb. 1948, and Brook to WSC, 11 and 13 Feb. 1948, CAB 21/2186.

48. See PREM 8/1321, quoting from Attlee to Brook, 27 Jan. 1948, and Brook to Attlee, 26 Feb. 1948.

49. Brook, note, 6 Feb. 1948, CAB 21/2174.

CHAPTER 7: THE UNNECESSARY ROAD TO MUNICH

1. *SWW* 1:vii–ix and *SWWUS* 1:iii–v, ix. The comment to FDR was probably made during Churchill's Washington visit at the end of 1941.

2. "Cato," *Guilty Men* (reprint edition; London, 1998), p. xv.

3. CAB 21/4476/17.

4. This is stated explicitly in Dixon's minute of 31 July 1947, FO 370/1444B/L3607. In general, see CAB 21/3750 and Avon papers, AP 33/1 (Birmingham Univ. Library).

5. Dunglass to Cadogan, 30 Dec. 1946, Neville Chamberlain papers, NC 11/15/50 (Birmingham Univ. Library). For the reviews, see NC 11/15a, docs. 1, 2, 15.

6. "Minister of 'Appeasement' in the Gathering Storm," *The Times*, 10 Dec. 1946, p. 5. Churchill acknowledges borrowing "The Twilight War" from Feiling (who took it from a letter by Chamberlain)—see *SWW* 1:330, *SWWUS* 1:422, and Keith Feiling, *The Life of Neville Chamberlain* (London, 1946), pp. 419–20, 424.

7. On 30 Oct. 1940, Churchill called it "the most unnecessary war in history . . . a war far harder to win than to avoid." He used the phrase again on 29 Dec. 1943. See Colville, pp. 278, 459. For fuller detail on what follows in this chapter, see my "Churchill's Writing of History: Appeasement, Autobiography and *The Gathering Storm*," in *Transactions of the Royal Historical Society*, 6th series, 11 (2001): 221–47.

8. *Speeches* 7:7251, 7292–93.

9.   Gilbert 8:357–58.

10.   *SWW* 1:8, 12 and *SWWUS* 1:10, 14–15.

11.   *SWW* 1:12–13 and *SWWUS* 1:15–16.

12.   *SWW* 1:21, 25 and *SWWUS* 1:25, 31.

13.   *SWW* 1:30, 52 and *SWWUS* 1:37, 66.

14.   *SWW* 1:26, 187 and *SWWUS* 1:33, 240.

15.   *SWW* 1:173–74 and *SWWUS* 1:221–22.

16.   *SWW* 1:52, 148 and *SWWUS* 1:67, 189; cf. CHUR 4/85/4.

17.   On Baldwin, see *SWW* 1:94 and *SWWUS* 1:119. "If Lee Had Not Won the Battle of Gettysburg" is reprinted in Michael Wolff, ed., *The Collected Essays of Sir Winston Churchill*, 4 vols. (Bristol, 1976), 4:73–84.

18.   *SWW* 1:147–48, 186; *SWWUS* 1:188–89, 237; cf. CHUR 4/87/65.

19.   *SWW* 1:169–71; *SWWUS* 1:215–19; cf. drafts in CHUR 4/81.

20.   Paul Addison, *Churchill on the Home Front, 1900–1955* (London, 1992), p. 323.

21.   *SWW* 1:169 and *SWWUS* 1:216; cf. CHUR 4/81, fo. 175, and WSC, *Arms and the Covenant* (London, 1938), pp. 385–86. Reginald Bassett drew attention to Churchill's editing in "Telling the Truth to the People: The Myth of the Baldwin 'Confession,'" *The Cambridge Journal* 2.1 (Oct. 1948): 95 n1, but Bassett was not aware of the original distortion in *Arms and the Covenant*. For fuller evidence, see Reynolds, "Churchill's Writing of History," pp. 230–31.

22.   CHUR 4/141/126 (Sargent, drawing on the comments of his colleague Ivone Kirkpatrick, who had served in the Berlin Embassy in 1933–1938) and CHUR 4/91, fos. 98, 120–21 (Pownall and Deakin).

23.   *SWW* 1:243–46, 250 and *SWWUS* 1:310–13, 319; cf. CHUR 4/91/113.

24.   For instance, Sir Ian Kershaw highlights the importance of the Rhineland occupation in 1936 for the Führer's domestic position and, while admitting it is "an open question" whether the "ill-coordinated" plotting in 1938 "would have come to anything," argues that the "legacy of Munich was fatally to weaken those who might even now have constrained Hitler." Ian Kershaw, *Hitler*, 2 vols. (London, 1998, 2000), 1:589–91, 2:123–25.

25.   David Zimmerman, *Britain's Shield: Radar and the Defeat of the Luftwaffe* (Stroud, Gloucestershire, 2001), pp. 108–9. See also Adrian Fort, *Prof: The Life of Frederick Lindemann* (London, 2003), pp. 140–41, and Thomas Wilson, *Churchill and the Prof* (London, 1995), pp. 34–42. For Churchill's text, see *SWW* 1:115–24 and *SWWUS* 1:147–58.

26.   *SWW* 1:120 and *SWWUS* 1:153; cf. CHUR 4/83/48–54.

27.   Zimmerman, *Britain's Shield*, pp. 150–52.

28.   CHUR 4/83/51B.

29.   *SWW* 1:124 and *SWWUS* 1:158. On Churchill and the tank, see Robin Prior, *Churchill's "World Crisis" as History* (London, 1983), chap. 13.

30.   R. J. Overy, "German Air Strength 1933 to 1939: A Note," *HJ* 27 (1984): 465–71, esp. n5; cf. Wilhelm Deist et al., *Germany and the Second World War*, vol. 1 (Oxford, 1990), p. 503; *SWW* 1:180 and *SWWUS* 1:231.

31.   Basil Collier, *The Defence of the United Kingdom* (London, 1957), p. 528.

32.   WSC, *Arms and the Covenant*, pp. 172–73; CV 5/3:273–74; cf. *SWW* 1:93–94, 178–79, 541–42, and *SWWUS* 1:118–19, 227–29, 685–86. Churchill was not alone in such fears, of course. In October 1936, the Joint Planning Sub-Committee of the Chiefs of Staff estimated that 20,000 casualties might be expected in London in the

first twenty-four hours of an air attack, rising within a week to around 150,000. See Uri Bialer, *The Shadow of the Bomber* (London, 1980), p. 130.

33. Wesley Wark, *The Ultimate Enemy: British Intelligence and Nazi Germany, 1933–1939* (Oxford, 1986), esp. pp. 59–69, 202–11.

34. Pownall blamed "Air Panic," whipped up by Churchill and others, for the July 1934 cutback in funds for the army expansion program. See Gilbert 5:553 n.

35. *SWW* 1:179 and *SWWUS* 1:229.

36. N. J. Crowson, *Facing Fascism: The Conservative Party and the European Dictators, 1935–1940* (London, 1995), pp. 158–63; "Future Safeguards of National Defence," *The News of the World*, 1 May 1938, in Wolff, ed., *Collected Essays*, 1:402.

37. Donald Cameron Watt, "Churchill and Appeasement," in Robert Blake and William Roger Louis, eds., *Churchill* (Oxford, 1993), p. 204.

38. Brian Bond, *Liddell Hart: A Study of His Military Thought* (London, 1976), p. 68; figures from Klaus A. Maier et al., *Germany and the Second World War*, vol. II (Oxford, 1999), p. 279.

39. Quoted in *SWW* 1:59 and *SWWUS* 1:75.

40. *SWW* 1:67–69, 168, 598 and *SWWUS* 1:86–88, 215, 747–48; cf. CHUR 4/19/65, 4/141/311–13.

41. Robert Rhodes James, *Churchill: A Study in Failure* (Harmondsworth, 1970), pp. 328–29.

42. *SWW* 1:144 and *SWWUS* 1:185; cf. Graham Stewart, *Burying Caesar: Churchill, Chamberlain and the Battle for the Tory Party* (London, 1999), p. 243.

43. *SWW* 1:167 and *SWWUS* 1:214.

44. Rhodes James, *Churchill*, pp. 406–9, quoting p. 407; Gilbert 5:785, 854. See also David Carlton, *Churchill and the Soviet Union* (Manchester, 2000), pp. 50–61.

45. *SWW* 1:151 and *SWWUS* 1:185; cf. Anthony Adamthwaite, *Grandeur and Misery: France's Bid for Power in Europe, 1914–1940* (London, 1995), pp. 222–31, and Martin Thomas, *Britain, France and Appeasement: Anglo-French Relations in the Popular Front Era* (Oxford, 1996), pp. 229–35.

46. *SWW* 1:239–40 and *SWWUS* 1:304–5. See also Igor Lukes, *Czechoslovakia Between Stalin and Hitler: The Diplomacy of Edvard Beneš* (Oxford, 1996), chaps. 4, 7; Zara Steiner, "The Soviet Commissariat of Foreign Affairs and the Czechoslovakian Crisis in 1938: New Material from the Soviet Archives," *HJ* 42 (1999): 751–79.

47. *SWW* 1:224–26, *SWWUS* 1:288–89, and CHUR 4/22/57–58 (Berlin) and CHUR 4/90/45 (Deakin). For a fuller account, see Reynolds, "Churchill's Writing of History," pp. 239–40.

48. *SWW* 1:196–99 and *SWWUS* 1:251–55; cf. David Reynolds, *The Creation of the Anglo-American Alliance, 1937–1941: A Study in Competitive Co-operation* (London, 1981), pp. 16–23, 31–32, 297.

49. CHUR 4/76, fo. 13 and (a later version) 161, and 4/20/377 (Brook). For "the biggest blunder," see Moran, p. 330.

50. CV 5/1: 306; cf. Stephen Roskill, *Churchill and the Admirals* (London, 1977), pp. 77–80.

51. CHUR 4/76/111; cf. *SWW* 1:40 and *SWWUS* 1:50–51.

52. R. A. C. Parker, *Churchill and Appeasement* (London, 2000), pp. xi, 65, 261–62.

53. Stuart Ball, *Baldwin and the Conservative Party: The Crisis of 1929–1931* (London, 1988); Stewart, *Burying Caesar*, esp. chaps. 4–6.

54. *SWW* 1:141, 157 and *SWWUS* 1:181, 201–2.

55. Parker, *Churchill and Appeasement*, pp. 82–85. Baldwin had used a similar tactic during the crisis over the Hoare-Laval Pact the previous December, preempting a possible assault from Austen Chamberlain, the Tory elder statesman, by hinting that Austen might succeed Samuel Hoare at the Foreign Office. Once the parliamentary crisis had passed, the post was then offered to Eden. See Crowson, *Facing Fascism*, pp. 58–65.

56. For the outline, see CHUR 4/145/156–94, quotations from fos. 156, 169, 186, 189; cf. CHAR 8/528/104–10 and 8/536/39.

57. SWW 1:201 and *SWWUS* 1:257–58; drafts in CHUR 4/88.

58. Correspondence in Avon papers, AP 19/4/1–14.

59. CHUR 4/145, fos. 181, 192–93.

60. Lord Avon, *The Reckoning* (London, 1965), pp. 251, 425; Halifax diary, 23 May 1943, Hickleton papers, A 7.8.12, also diary 7 March 1946, A 7.8.18 (Borthwick Institute, York); Moran, p. 261.

61. CV 5/3:11; Cecil H. King, *With Malice Toward None: A War Diary*, ed. William Armstrong (London, 1970), p. 22.

62. N. J. Crowson, "Conservative Parliamentary Dissent over Foreign Policy During the Premiership of Neville Chamberlain: Myth or Reality?" *Parliamentary History* 14 (1995): 322–23.

63. Ibid., pp. 326–27. More generally, see Parker, *Churchill and Appeasement*, chaps. 8–10, and Stewart, *Burying Caesar*, chaps. 11–13.

64. SWW 1:280 and *SWWUS* 1:358; cf. CHUR 4/119/108 and CHUR 4/144/38–40.

65. SWW 1:271, 283–84 and *SWWUS* 1:347, 362–63; cf. Kershaw, *Hitler*, 2:192, 208.

66. SWW 1:218, 263–65 and *SWWUS* 1:279, 336–39; cf. CHUR 4/92/118–20. Interestingly, this runs against Ismay's own analysis on 20 September 1938, when he was Military Secretary to the Cabinet, that Britain would be better advised to fight Germany "in say 6–12 months time" (CAB 21/544). Ismay did not draw that document to Churchill's attention ten years later.

67. Cf. Williamson Murray, *The Change in the European Balance of Power, 1938–1939: The Path to Ruin* (Princeton, 1984), chap. 7. On French tank production, see Robert Frankenstein, *Le Prix du Réarmament Français (1935–1939)* (Paris, 1982), p. 228.

68. CHUR 4/141, fos. 99–115, 384–89; cf. Vansittart papers, VNST II/1/29 (CAC). For revisionist surveys of Vansittart's own policies in the 1930s, see the set of articles in *DS*, 6 (1995): 1–175.

CHAPTER 8: TWILIGHT FOR CHAMBERLAIN, NEW DAWN FOR CHURCHILL

1. SWW 1:320 and *SWWUS* 1:410.

2. SWW 1:384 and *SWWUS* 1:488.

3. Neville Chamberlain to Hilda, 17 Sept. 1939, NC 18/1/1121, and Halifax to Chamberlain, 15 Jan. 1940, NC 7/11/33/132 (Neville Chamberlain papers, Birmingham Univ. Library). Cf. SWW 1:359–60, 438 and *SWWUS* 1: 456–57, 554–55. Even at the start of Churchill's premiership, the same suspicion was aroused. On 16 May 1940, as France collapsed, he pontificated about "the mortal gravity of this hour." Arthur Rucker, one of the private secretaries at Number 10, murmured, "He is still thinking of his books" (Colville, p. 132).

4. Neville Chamberlain to Ida, 8 Oct. 1939, NC 18/1/1124; SWW 1:382–83 and *SWWUS* 1:485–87.

5. *SWW* 1:388–89 and *SWWUS* 1:494–95; cf. original dictation in CHUR 4/100/29–32 and Clementine's annotation on CHUR 4/131/94.

6. *SWW* 1:345 and *SWWUS* 1:440–41.

7. Sherwood to Beaverbrook, 16 May 1948, Robert E. Sherwood papers, file 973 (Houghton Library, Harvard Univ., Cambridge, Mass.); Sherwood, pp. 350–51. On 3 Aug. 1941, before leaving London, Churchill cabled the Dominions Prime Ministers that "I have never had the pleasure of meeting President Roosevelt." According to Churchill's aide Tommy Thompson a few weeks later, it was decided conclusively at the meeting that they had met before. See FO 371/26151, A6944, and PREM 4/71/88. Even in 1943, perhaps to make amends, Churchill was taking the line he adopted in the memoirs; see *C-R* 2:355–56, 419.

8. Brook, note, 1 April 1948, CAB 21/2174.

9. Churchill insisted on printing FDR's original letter of 11 September on the grounds that this was "a purely personal and private document, and I have obtained Mrs. Roosevelt's permission to use it." See Brook, note, 7 April 1948, CAB 21/2175; WSC to Brook, 12 April 1948, CHUR 4/23/137; *SWW* 1:405, 418–19 and *SWWUS* 1:513–16, 529–30. The paraphrases are at CHUR 4/120/79–93. *Life*'s fourth installment of *The Gathering Storm* (10 May 1948, pp. 61–62) featured the 11 September letter under the headline "President Roosevelt sends an encouraging letter to the First Lord of the Admiralty."

10. *SWW* 1:321, 329 and *SWWUS* 1:410, 421; cf. CHUR 4/96/18. On the relationship, see Arthur Marder, "Winston Is Back: Churchill at the Admiralty, 1939–40," *EHR*, supplement 5 (1972): 4–5.

11. "The Naval Memoirs of Admiral J. H. Godfrey," TS. (1965), vol. 5, pp. 63, 111–12, and vol. 7, pp. 225–26 (CAC); *SWW* 1:343, 389, 448 and *SWWUS* 1:437, 495, 567.

12. Godfrey, "Naval Memoirs," 5:63; *SWW* 1:342–43 and *SWWUS* 1:436–38; Harold Nicolson, *Diaries and Letters*, ed. Nigel Nicolson, 3 vols. (London, 1966–1968), 2:37.

13. CHUR 4/96, fos. 56–65, 80–83A. The original is in PREM 1/345 and a copy is printed in CV 5/3: 1414–17. Dated 25 March 1939, it was sent to Chamberlain on the twenty-seventh, and Gilbert follows Churchill in using the latter date.

14. Quotations from Chatfield, note, 29 March 1940, and Chatfield to Churchill, 3 April 1940, Chatfield papers, CHT 6/4, fos. 16–17, 28 (Royal Naval College, Greenwich); cf. Reynolds D. Salerno, "The French Navy and the Appeasement of Italy, 1937–9," *EHR* 112 (1997): esp. 89–90, 97–98.

15. CHUR 4/96/56, cf. fos. 103–5, 158–59; *SWW* 1:324–27 and *SWWUS* 1:415–18. In similar vein, Churchill printed and then omitted a paper he submitted to the Cabinet on 17 Nov. 1939 entitled "Australian and New Zealand Naval Defence." Again dismissing the prospects of a siege of Singapore—the Japanese were "a prudent people" and would not "embark upon such a mad enterprise"—this paper stressed the added benefit of Italian neutrality, which meant that "the British Fleet has become again entirely mobile." See CHUR 4/96/236–337.

16. *SWW* 1:363–65, 550–52 and *SWWUS* 1:462–64, 692–94; also *WC* 2:23.

17. *SWW* 1:363–65, 434–35 and *SWWUS* 1:462–64, 550–51; cf. drafts in CHUR 4/98, quoting fos. 36, 86, and Marder, "Winston Is Back," pp. 31–38.

18. WSC to Eden, 18 Oct. 1938, in CV 5/3:1231; WM (39) 2, 18 Oct. 1939, printed in *CWP* 1:258–59; *SWW* 1:381, 384 and *SWWUS* 1:484, 487; cf. CHUR 4/100, fos. 7–8, 55.

19. *SWW* 1:351–53; cf. CHUR 4/98, fos. 49, 57. *SWWUS* 1:448, published four months

earlier, prints only the first paragraph of this paper, about Russia, and none of the paragraphs about the Balkans and Turkey.

20. *CWP* 1:497, 629; on the two naval schools see WC 2:511–15.

21. See Robin Prior, *Churchill's "World Crisis" as History* (London, 1983), pp. 231–37.

22. Michael Wolff, ed., *The Collected Essays of Sir Winston Churchill*, 4 vols. (Bristol, 1976), 1:424–25, 394–95.

23. *SWW* 1:374, 566–68 and *SWWUS* 1:475, 713–15; cf. CHUR 4/99/82–83.

24. *SWW* 1:459 and *SWWUS* 1:581. "Thrall" replaced "obsession" in an earlier draft—see CHUR 4/105/26.

25. CHUR 4/104, fos. 56–57, 82–83; cf. *SWW* 1:441 and *SWWUS* 1:558. Also deleted was another confession: "The picture I formed in my mind of warfare on the western front was governed by my impressions of the previous war. The defensive was still predominant. . . . I still believed that field-artillery had the mastery over armoured vehicles in close quarters and in the open" (CHUR 4/99/82).

26. David Reynolds, *The Creation of the Anglo-American Alliance, 1937–1941: A Study in Competitive Co-operation* (London, 1981), pp. 73–75; for the intelligence assumptions, see Hinsley 1:59–73.

27. Instead, he inserted a robust passage about Hitler's failure to grasp that Chamberlain and all the British empire "now meant to have his blood or perish in the attempt." See *CWP* 1:224–26; cf. CHUR 4/141/308, *SWW* 1:381, and *SWWUS* 1:484–85.

28. *SWW* 1:434–35 and *SWWUS* 1:549–51; *CWP* 1:629–30.

29. *SWW* 1:429–33 and *SWWUS* 1:543–47; cf. Patrick Salmon, "Great Britain, the Soviet Union and Finland at the Beginning of the Second World War," in John Hiden and Thomas Lane, eds., *The Baltic and the Outbreak of the Second World War* (Cambridge, 1992), pp. 96, 109, 113–14.

30. *SWW* 1:438 and *SWWUS* 1:554–55.

31. Hinsley 1:115–25.

32. *CWP* 1:826, also 926; *SWW* 1:461–62 and *SWWUS* 1:583–85.

33. *CWP* 1:951; CHUR 4/106/12–14; *SWW* 1:467–68 and *SWWUS* 1:591–92; cf. S. W. Roskill, *The War at Sea, 1939–1945*, vol. 1 (London, 1954), pp. 155–62; Stephen Roskill, *Churchill and the Admirals* (London, 1977), pp. 98–99.

34. The distances "came as a complete shock to me," Denis Kelly told Churchill in January 1948, and he asked "in all humility" if they had been considered when the plan was adopted (CHUR 4/141/278).

35. CHUR 4/141/348 and 4/142/59.

36. *SWW* 1:482–88, 511 and *SWWUS* 1:610–18, 649.

37. In a later chapter, barely 6,000 Germans are set against some 20,000 Allied troops. *SWW* 1:487, 510–11 and *SWWUS* 1:617–18, 649; cf. CHUR 4/142, fos. 75, 102–3, 212–18. In 1970, Mackesy's son, a military historian, dissected Churchill's account (before the documents were made public). See Piers Mackesy, "Churchill on Narvik," *Journal of the Royal United Services Institution* 660 (Dec. 1970): 28–34.

38. CHUR 4/142/68–69 (deletions as in draft); *SWW* 1:510 and *SWWUS* 1:649. Churchill uses the word "Namsossed" in a memo of 3 Sept. 1940, printed in *SWW* 2:407 and *SWWUS* 2:460.

39. *SWW* 1:510–11 and *SWWUS* 1:648–49; CHUR 4/109/44.

40. *SWW* 1:458, 500 and *SWWUS* 1:580, 634. Cf. Correlli Barnett, *Engage the Enemy More Closely: The Royal Navy in the Second World War* (London, 2000), p. 133, on Scandinavia as "an enfeebling diversion from the crucial theatre of France and the Low Countries."

41. *SWW* 1:463 and *SWWUS* 1:586 ("equals"); CHUR 4/142/58–59 (Forbes).
42. Soames, pp. 141–44; CHUR 4/131, fos. 155 ("ruined"), 183 (Narvik); CHUR 4/189/42 ("a quarter of a century").
43. *SWW* 1:511 and *SWWUS* 1:649–50; CHUR 4/109/42–43.
44. John D. Fair, "The Norwegian Campaign and Winston Churchill's Rise to Power in 1940: A Study in Perception and Attribution," *IHR* 9 (1987): 429.
45. *SWW* 1:522–24 and *SWWUS* 1:661–63.
46. *SWW* 1:523 and *SWWUS* 1:663.
47. L. S. Amery, *My Political Life*, vol. 3 (London, 1955), p. 371; CHUR 2/179/216–24.
48. Gilbert 6:301 printed Churchill's account as occurring on 9 May, adding in a footnote that in his memoirs "Churchill has mistakenly placed this interview on 10 May 1940." In his set of companion documents—published in 1993, ten years later—Sir Martin prints the Halifax and Cadogan accounts plus extracts from Churchill's memoirs for other events on 9–10 May, but he does not include the "long silence" passage at all. See *CWP* 1:1257–90.
49. The accounts are set out in Andrew Roberts, *"The Holy Fox": A Life of Lord Halifax* (London, 1991), pp. 204–6.
50. They had particular difficulty verifying events in May 1940 because Churchill's printed minutes stopped for a couple of weeks while he was in transition from the Admiralty to Number 10, and his table of engagements for that month had disappeared. A reconstruction by Leslie Rowan in September 1946, helped by various Whitehall departments and back issues of *The Times*, had Churchill at Number 10 at 6:00 P.M. on 9 May to see Halifax, Chamberlain, and the Labour leaders, and nothing on the morning of the tenth. See CHUR 4/23, fos. 162–63, 167–68, 171, 188–89.
51. Roberts, *"Holy Fox,"* pp. 198, 203; letters of 8 and 15 Oct. 1939, NC 18/1/1124 (Winston), 1125 ("loathe").
52. *SWW* 1:511, 527 and *SWWUS* 1:650, 667; CHUR 4/131/207.
53. *SWW* 1:526–27 and *SWWUS* 1:667.

CHAPTER 9: PROPHET OF THE PAST AND THE FUTURE

1. Longwell to Graebner, 4 Feb. 1947, Longwell papers/Churchill, box 2: Contract Negotiations, and Graebner to Longwell, 10 Oct. 1947, ibid., box 2: Daily Telegraph, Camrose (Butler Library, Columbia Univ., New York, N.Y.).
2. Figures from Longwell to Laughlin, 21 and 29 June 1948, HM 318/1: Life, 1947–51.
3. John Bright-Holmes, ed., *Like It Was: The Diaries of Malcolm Muggeridge* (London, 1981), p. 270.
4. It was read on Churchill's behalf by his secretary, Jo Sturdee, who considered it "friendly and, in my opinion, well written and interesting." Nothing was changed. See CHUR 4/25/299–327; *Life*, 15 March 1948, pp. 94–106, quoting p. 95; Harold Nicolson, *Diaries and Letters, 1945–1962*, ed. Nigel Nicolson (London, 1968), p. 111.
5. CHUR 4/24/298 (Flower) and 4/12/181–82 (Reves).
6. *Time*, 10 May 1948, pp. 75–76, 78; CHUR 4/15/483–88.
7. Quotations from HM 318/4: Gathering Storm; CHUR 4/14/432–33.
8. CHUR 4/24/306–9; cf. Desmond Flower, *Fellows in Foolscap: Memoirs of a Publisher* (London, 1991), pp. 275–76.
9. CHUR 4/24/305.
10. *SWW* 1:56, 611; Denis Kelly, TS. memoirs, chap. 3, p. 3 (CAC); CHUR 4/25/328.

11. CHUR 4/12, fos. 195–97, 201, 238–39; cf. Langworth, pp. 278–82.

12. CHUR 4/19/161–63, 4/145/224–25.

13. Cf. Flower to Laughlin, 19 March 1948, HM 318/4: Cassell.

14. *DT*, 17 June 1948, p. 4; *NYT*, 1 May 1948, p. 17, and 20 May 1948, p. 28.

15. *Speeches* 7:7671, 7709.

16. WSC, *The Sinews of Peace*, ed. Randolph S. Churchill (London, 1948), p. vii.

17. *NYT*, 9 May 1948, sec. 4, p. 8.

18. For figures, see Langworth, p. 289.

19. WSC to Macmillan, 9 Feb. 1948, copy in Avon papers (Birmingham Univ. Library), AP 19/1/27E; Harold Nicolson, MS. diary, 18 Dec. 1947 (Balliol College, Oxford).

20. John Ramsden, "Winston Churchill and the Leadership of the Conservative Party, 1940–1951," *Contemporary Record* 9 (1995): 108; Stuart Ball, ed., *Parliament and Politics in the Age of Churchill and Attlee: The Headlam Diaries, 1935–1951* (Cambridge, 1999), pp. 544–45, 561.

21. Margaret A. Minahan to Henry Laughlin, 24 July 1951, HM 318/4: Laughlin 1951. Cf. CHUR 4/14/113.

22. *NYT*, book review, 20 June 1948; *Newsweek*, 21 June 1948; *The Christian Science Monitor*, 24 June 1948; *Chicago Tribune*, 27 June 1948; *Time*, 28 June 1948; *The Miami Herald*, 4 July 1948. These are all in a special leather-bound folder of American reviews sent to Churchill by Houghton Mifflin—see CHWL/PE, box 5, 80a.

23. *NYT* and *Washington Star* reviews, 20 June 1948.

24. *NYT*, 9 May 1948, sec. 1, p. 16 (Baldwin); *NYHT*, 21 June 1948; *AHR* 54 (1948): 103; *JMH* 21 (1949): 358.

25. *NYT*, 26 Sept. 1948, sec. 4, p. 8, and 17 Oct. 1948, sec. 4, p. 10; cf. CHUR 4/20/81, 86–89. Deakin's source on Strang was the historian Lewis Namier.

26. *Philadelphia Bulletin*, 20 June 1948; *Newsweek*, 21 June 1948; *Time*, 28 June 1948; *The New Yorker*, 10 July 1948; *JMH* 21 (1949): 358. For the Ribbentrop lunch/lynch, see SWW 1:211–12 and SWWUS 1:271–72.

27. *The Saturday Review of Literature*, 19 June 1948; *NYT*, 20 June 1948, sec. 7, p. 19, and 21 June 1948, p. 19.

28. SWWUS 1:322–23.

29. CHUR 4/48, fos. 115–17, 235–63, quoting Edward E. Plusdrak to WSC, 19 June 1948, fo. 259, and CHUR 4/2/34–42, quoting James Stewart Murray to Edward Marsh, 6 July 1948, fo. 36.

30. Gilbert 8:418; CHUR 4/144/357.

31. Gilbert 8:418; CHUR 4/92, fos. 59, 103–4; SWW 1:252–53.

32. *Evening Standard*, 1 Oct. 1948; CHUR 4/24/334. Much of the press comment cited below may be found in the cuttings file CHPC 28.

33. *DT*, *The Manchester Guardian*, and *The Evening News*, all 4 Oct. 1948; *The Spectator*, 8 Oct. 1948, p. 453 (Amery); *The Fortnightly* 163 (Oct. 1948): 227.

34. *The Listener*, 7 Oct. 1948, pp. 533, 535.

35. Halifax to Anne Chamberlain, 13 May 1948, Hickleton papers, A 4.410.18.4 (Borthwick Institute, York).

36. SWW 1:249 and SWWUS 1:318; Keith Feiling, *The Life of Neville Chamberlain* (London, 1946), pp. 381–82; *The Times*, 28 Oct. 1948, p. 5; CHUR 4/19, fos. 227–36, 265–66.

37. *The Times*, 2, 5, 9, 13, 15 Nov. 1948, all p. 5; E. C. Castle to Hankey, 15 Nov. 1948, and reply, 20 Nov., Hankey papers, HNKY 24/4 (CAC); WSC drafts in CHUR 2/157, fos. 68–88.

38. Admiral Lord Chatfield, *It Might Happen Again,* vol. 2: *The Navy and Defence* (London, 1947), pp. 10–11; Liddell Hart to Hankey, 20 Sept. 1948, HNKY 24/4. For Liddell Hart's syndicated review, see, e.g., *Oxford Mail,* 4 Oct. 1948.

39. E.g., *TLS,* 28 Aug. 1948, p. 485; *The Spectator,* 22 Oct. 1948, p. 527; *The Times,* 13 Nov. 1948, p. 5.

40. CHUR 4/141/299–300; cf. Robert P. Shay, Jr., *British Rearmament in the Thirties: Politics and Profits* (Princeton, 1977), and G. C. Peden, *British Rearmament and the Treasury, 1932–1939* (Edinburgh, 1979).

41. *Daily Herald,* 4 Oct. 1948; *Tribune,* 8 Oct. 1948, pp. 7–8.

42. Bridges to Martin, 24 June 1944, and Bridges to Laithwaite, 10 July 1944, CAB 103/286. For background, see David Reynolds, "The Origins of the Two 'World Wars': Historical Discourse and International Politics," *JCH* 38 (2003): 29–44.

43. HC, 5th series, vol. 428, col. 608, 30 Oct. 1946; CHUR 4/41, fos. 52, 84, 127, 130.

44. CAB 134/105, esp. meeting of 21 Jan. 1948, minute 7, and Attlee endorsement of 27 Jan. 1948; cf. Cyril Falls, *The Second World War: A Short History* (London, 1948), and J. F. C. Fuller, *The Second World War, 1939–45: A Strategical and Tactical History* (London, 1948).

45. CHUR 4/23/336 (Wood) and 4/24, fos. 355–56, 383–84; cf. *The Spectator,* 4 Feb. 1949, p. 141.

II | THEIR FINEST HOUR, 1940, 1946–1949

CHAPTER 10: BETWEEN MEMOIR AND HISTORY

1. SWW 2:81–83 and SWWUS 2:92–95; cf. CHUR 4/150/161–62 and Brian Bond, ed., *Chief of Staff: The Diaries of Lieutenant-General Sir Henry Pownall,* vol. 1: *1933–1940* (London, 1972), pp. 333–34.

2. On Allen, see particularly CHUR 4/195.

3. Ismay papers, 2/3/2 and 2/3/21 (KCL).

4. SWW 2:307–9 and SWWUS 2:348–50; cf. CHUR 4/201/308. For the amendment, see the Reprint Society edition (London, 1951), p. 286.

5. CHUR 4/194/34–36; cf. SWW 2:17–19 and SWWUS 2:18–20; Bridges to WSC, 5 March 1949, CHUR 4/22/84–86.

6. Denis Kelly, TS. memoirs (1985), chap. 2, pp. 3–5 (CAC); correspondence in CHUR 1/65/294–316.

7. Gilbert 8:435.

8. CHUR 4/24, fos. 336–38, 347–68; Kelly, Memoirs, chap. 2, pp. 4–5 ("indefatigable").

9. CHUR 4/194/39–40.

10. Quotations from Pownall's letters in Ismay papers, 2/3, docs. 60, 82, 104.

11. CHUR 4/22/131–36.

12. CHUR 4/184/178.

13. Brooks to Laughlin, 7 July 1948, and reply, 22 July, HM 318/1: "Their Finest Hour"; Gold to Longwell, memo, 7 July 1948, copy in CHUR 4/197/100–101.

14. Pownall to Ismay, 5 July 1948, Ismay papers, 2/3/64.

15. Note of phone conversation on 30 June 1948 and Brooks to Laughlin, 7 July 1948, HM 318/1: "Their Finest Hour."

16. This paragraph and the next are based on the files in CHUR 1/70–72 and differ in some details from the account of the trip given in Gilbert 8:424–35.

17. Deakin to Ismay, 14 Sept. 1948, Ismay papers, 2/3/98/1; Graebner to Longwell, 5 Sept. 1948, Longwell papers/Churchill, box 2: Graebner (Butler Library, Columbia Univ., New York, N.Y.); WSC to Luce, [end of Sept. 1948], CHUR 4/25/217.

18. CHUR 4/23/67–69.

19. CHUR 4/13/11–18, quoting Reves's cable and WSC reply, 5 Dec. 1948, fos. 11–12.

20. CHUR 4/199/30.

21. *The Observer*, 3 Oct. 1948; Paul Reynaud, *La France a sauvé l'Europe*, 2 vols. (Paris, 1947). France had saved Europe, Reynaud asserted, because if she had denounced her alliance with Poland in 1938–1939, Britain would not have dreamed of committing itself to Poland and intervening alone on the Continent. From that British commitment, he said, eventually followed the decisive involvement of America and Russia. See esp. 1:29–30.

22. *TLS*, 3 July 1948, pp. 365–67; WSC to Ismay, 8 July 1948, CHUR 4/46/121. For Namier's authorship of the review, see the *TLS* Centenary Archive at http://www.tls.psmedia.com.

23. *The Memoirs of Cordell Hull*, 2 vols. (New York, 1948), 1:870, 2:1473–74.

24. Henry L. Stimson and McGeorge Bundy, *On Active Service in Peace and War* (London, 1948), pp. 7, 236–37; cf. Kai Bird, *The Color of Truth: McGeorge Bundy and William Bundy: Brothers in Arms* (New York, 1998), chap. 5.

25. Eisenhower to WSC, 6 June 1948 (DDEL); also Stephen E. Ambrose, *Eisenhower*, 2 vols. (New York, 1983–1984), 1:473–75. Ike had always planned to write his memoirs—the stimulus in 1948 was a deal, similar to Churchill's, to sell all rights in the manuscript and so pay capital-gains tax but not personal income tax, leaving Ike richer by nearly half a million dollars.

26. Dwight D. Eisenhower, *Crusade in Europe* (Garden City, N.Y., 1948), esp. pp. 61–62, 194–95, 243, 245, 281–84. For more on Ike's memoirs and their reception in Britain, see G. E. Patrick Murray, *Eisenhower Versus Montgomery: The Continuing Debate* (London, 1996), chap. 3.

27. WSC to Eisenhower, telegram, 17 Aug. 1948, Eisenhower 16/52 box 22 (DDEL).

28. SWW 2:213–24 and SWWUS 2:242–54; cf. CHUR 4/158, esp. fos. 24–30, 86–89, 108–10.

29. Sherwood, pp. 262, 591, 965; Kenneth Young, ed., *The Diaries of Sir Robert Bruce Lockhart*, vol. 2: 1939–65 (London, 1980), p. 674 ("very annoyed").

30. CHUR 2/155, esp. fos. 159–63, 170–74.

31. Correspondence in FO 115/4373, quoting from Lovett to Inverchapel, 24 April 1948, and in CAB 21/2175, quoting from WSC to Brook, 12 April 1948.

32. CHUR 2/155/146–47.

33. WSC to Leahy and to Truman, 5 May 1948, CHUR 4/23, fos. 118, 120–24.

34. Memos by Leahy and Hickerson, 11 and 14 May 1948, and Truman to WSC, 18 May 1948, all in President's Secretary's General File box 115 (HSTL). See also Ambrose, *Eisenhower*, 1:459–60, and Robert J. Donovan, *Conflict and Crisis: The Presidency of Harry S Truman, 1945–1948* (New York, 1977), pp. 86–87, 338, 386–90.

35. CHUR 4/23/113.

36. CHUR 2/155/230–53, quoting telegram of 15 June, fos. 240–41.

37. Memo, dated 14 June 1948, of conversation with Beaverbrook, and Sherwood to Marshall, 18 June 1948, Robert E. Sherwood papers, folders 1843, 1359 (Houghton Library, Harvard Univ., Cambridge, Mass.). Privately, the Foreign Office made repeated but unsuccessful overtures to the State Department to stop Sherwood from

publishing British documents in his book without permission. See FO 370/1589 and FO 370/1759.

38. Sherwood to Marshall, 18 June 1948, Sherwood papers, folder 1359; WSC to Brook, 8 July 1948, CHUR 2/155/209.

39. Douglas Jerrold to Sherwood, 22 April 1948, and Sherwood to Jerrold, 4 Aug. 1948, Sherwood papers, folders 266, 1131.

40. CAB 21/2175 — Brook, Note for the Record, and letter to Sargent, both 28 Jan. 1948; Sargent to Brook, 7 Feb. 1948.

41. CAB 21/2175, esp. Brook, "Points for Consideration," 9 Feb. 1948, and Brook to WSC, 26 Feb. 1948.

42. Note [1947?], CHUR 4/201/151.

43. See CAB 21/2185.

44. CAB 21/3749, quoting Cornwall-Jones to Brook, 10 June 1948; SWW 2:viii and SWWUS 2:vii.

45. JIC (45) 223 (0), 20 July 1945, and JIC (48) 14 (0), 11 Feb. 1948, copies in CAB 103/288; Richard Aldrich, *The Hidden Hand: Britain, America and Cold War Secret Intelligence* (London, 2001), pp. 1–4, quoting p. 3.

46. CAB 104/282, quoting from Brook to Hubback, 27 Jan. 1948, and Hastings to CSS [Menzies], 3 Feb. 1948.

47. Brook, "Points for Consideration," on book 2, chap. 15, 7 April 1948, CAB 21/2176.

48. SWW 1:539 and SWWUS 1:611.

49. CHUR 4/196/47–48.

50. Cornwall-Jones to Brook, 12 Feb. 1948, CAB 21/2175.

51. F. H. Hinsley, "British Intelligence in the Second World War," in Christopher Andrew and Jeremy Noakes, eds., *Intelligence and International Relations, 1900–1945* (Exeter, 1989), p. 218; see also Gilbert 7:609–12, and Hinsley 1:160, 293–96.

52. F. H. Hinsley, "Introduction," in F. H. Hinsley and Alan Stripp, eds., *Codebreakers: The Inside Story of Bletchley Park* (Oxford, 1993), p. 12; Christopher Andrew, "Churchill and Intelligence," *Intelligence and National Security* 3 (1988): 181–93, quoting p. 181.

CHAPTER 11: "VICTORY AT ALL COSTS"

1. Chamberlain diary, 15 May 1940, NC 2/24A (Birmingham Univ. Library); Halifax diary, 25 May 1940, Hickleton papers, A 7.8.4 (Borthwick Institute, York). See, more generally, David Reynolds, "1940: Fulcrum of the Twentieth Century," *IA* 66 (1990): 325–50, and Julian Jackson, *The Fall of France: The Nazi Invasion of 1940* (Oxford, 2003).

2. SWW 2:31–35 and SWWUS 2:34–38; cf. figures on p. 99.

3. Hinsley 1:127–29; Ernest R. May, *Strange Victory: Hitler's Conquest of France* (New York, 2000), pp. 308–14.

4. See CHUR 4/148, fos. 109–12, 151. One explanation may be that his account of the Battle of France relied heavily on the work of General Pownall, whose firsthand experience of the conflict was that of a staff officer in the field rather than as a participant in the strategic debates in London.

5. SWW 2:38–44 and SWWUS 2:42–49.

6. CHUR 4/148, fos. 49, 106, 162, 193 (on the French version) and 142–46 (WSC's dictation which refers to Gamelin's "hopeless shrug of the shoulders"); cf. SWW 2:43n and SWWUS 2:47–48n; CWP 2:53–60.

7. SWW 2:38, 189 and SWWUS 2:42, 215. On Dowding, see CHUR 4/196/453–54.

8. *SWW* 2:162, 189 and *SWWUS* 2:182–83, 215; cf. CHUR 4/155/76.

9. CHUR 4/22/227–44, quoting from de Gaulle to WSC, 17 Sept. 1948, fo. 242.

10. *SWW* 2:180–88, 194–96 and *SWWUS* 2:204–14, 221–23; Avi Shlaim, "Prelude to Downfall: The British Offer of Union to France, June 1940," *JCH* 9 (1974): 62.

11. FO 371/24298, C4444/9/17; Shlaim, "Prelude to Downfall," pp. 31–32.

12. Churchill uses very similar words in chapter 11. See *SWW* 2:157, 199 and *SWWUS* 2:177–78, 227.

13. The records are in CAB 65/13, CA, WM (40) 139/1, 140, 141/1, 142, 145/1, quoting from fos. 151, 179. Halifax's bottom line of terms not "destructive of British independence" is also in his draft appeal to Roosevelt, ca. 25 May 1940, Hickleton papers, A4.410.4.1. For further detail, see David Reynolds, "Churchill and the British 'Decision' to Fight On in 1940: Right Policy, Wrong Reasons," in Richard Langhorne, ed., *Diplomacy and Intelligence During the Second World War* (Cambridge, 1985), pp. 147–67.

14. Quotations from Chamberlain diary, 26 May 1940, NC 2/24A, and CAB 65/13, fos. 180, 187.

15. Thomas Munch-Petersen, "'Common Sense Not Bravado': The Butler-Prytz Interview of 17 June 1940," *Scandia* 52 (1986): 73–114, quoting from p. 74.

16. Andrew Roberts, *"The Holy Fox": A Life of Lord Halifax* (London, 1991), chaps. 22–24, quoting from p. 227; John Lukacs, *Five Days in London, May 1940* (New Haven, 1999), pp. 126, 136, 187–90.

17. Hugh Dalton, diary, vol. 23, p. 93 (British Library of Political and Economic Science, London).

18. Hickleton papers, A 7.8.4, quoting pp. 119, 130, 142.

19. *SWW* 2:109 and *SWWUS* 2:124.

20. CHUR 4/152, fos. 52, 70.

21. CHUR 4/194/31; cf. Ismay papers, 2/3/96b (KCL).

22. *SWW* 2:109–10 and *SWWUS* 2:124–25; Paul Reynaud, *La France a sauvé l'Europe*, 2 vols. (Paris, 1947), 2:200–2. The chapter also gave a footnote reference to Reynaud's account, which itself depicts Halifax at odds with Churchill, Attlee, and Chamberlain.

23. *SWW* 2:24 and *SWWUS* 2:26; WSC, *Into Battle*, comp. Randolph S. Churchill (London, 1941), p. 210.

24. WSC to Baldwin, 4 June 1940, Baldwin papers, 174/264 (Cambridge Univ. Library); notes of interview with Ismay, 11 July 1946, and Ismay to Sherwood, 23 July 1946, Robert E. Sherwood papers, folders 1891 and 415 respectively (Houghton Library, Harvard Univ., Cambridge, Mass.).

25. *SWW* 2:81, 144, 231 and *SWWUS* 2:91, 162, 262.

26. CAB 65/24, WM 120 (41) 5 CA; also CAB 65/19, WM 66 (41) 5-CA.

27. Hickleton papers, A 7.8.4, pp. 174–75; memo of 12 Sept. 1940, LG papers, G/81 (HLRO). LG's opinion in 1940 stands in marked contrast to his biographer's assertion that 1917 was a graver crisis than 1940 — see John Grigg, *Lloyd George: War Leader, 1916–1918* (London, 2002), chap. 1.

28. CAB 65/13/147, 149 (26 May references); WSC, *Into Battle*, p. 233. The two COS papers are CAB 66/7, WP (40) 168 and CAB 66/11, WP (40) 362, quoting paras. 44, 47, 218. On Bulgaria in 1918, see WC 2:510, 3.2:509–10, 536.

29. CAB 66/11, WP (40) 362, para. 214.

30. See the pioneering article by David Stafford, "The Detonator Concept: British Strategy, SOE and European Resistance After the Fall of France," *JCH* 10 (1975): 185–217, quoting p. 202.

31. WSC to Beaverbrook, 8 July 1940, in Beaverbrook papers, D 414/36 (HLRO); WSC, memo, 3 Sept. 1940, CAB 66/11, WP (40) 352. They are printed in *CWP* 2:492–93, 762–64. For fuller discussion of this theme, see Reynolds, "Churchill and the British 'Decision,'" pp. 155–60.

32. *SWW* 2:78–79, 405–6, 567 and *SWWUS* 2:87–89, 458, 643.

33. CHUR 4/196/614–15 (home resistance); David Stafford, *Britain and the European Resistance, 1940–1945* (London, 1980), p. 2.

34. CAB 66/7, WP (40) 168, para. 1 (emphasis in original).

35. Charles de Gaulle, *War Memoirs*, trans. Jonathan Griffin (London, 1955), 1:108; Colville, p. 283.

36. Supreme War Council (39/40), 13th meeting, p. 12, CAB 99/3 (NA). For fuller discussion, see Reynolds, "Churchill and the British 'Decision,' pp. 161–63.

37. WSC, *Secret Session Speeches*, comp. Charles Eade (London, 1946), p. 14; *SWW* 2:174, 246 and *SWWUS* 2:196, 279.

38. *SWW* 2:9–10 and *SWWUS* 2:9–10; cf. CHUR 4/147/29.

39. WSC to Chamberlain, 10 May 1940, Chamberlain papers, NC 7/9/80; Cecil King, *With Malice Toward None: A War Diary*, ed. William Armstrong (London, 1970), p. 50.

40. *SWW* 2:503 and *SWWUS* 2:569–70.

41. Diary, 9 Sept. 1940, NC 2/24A; Colin Cross, ed., *Life with Lloyd George: The Diary of A. J. Sylvester, 1931–1945* (London, 1975), p. 281, entry for 3 Oct. 1940.

42. *SWW* 2:438–39 and *SWWUS* 2:496; Clementine and Hoare are in *CWP* 2:927–29.

43. Eden diary, 30 Sept. 1940, Avon papers, AP 20/1/20A (Birmingham Univ. Library); *SWW* 2:503–5 and *SWWUS* 2:569–71.

44. Colville diary, 10 May 1940, in *CWP* 2:1280; John Wheeler-Bennett, ed., *Action This Day: Working with Churchill* (London, 1968), pp. 48–49, 161–62; Soames, pp. 325–26.

45. *SWW* 2:70–73 and *SWWUS* 2:79–82. This story was clearly etched in his memory—he had told it, for instance, to Moran in September 1945—and Ismay's 1960 memoirs recalled Churchill's deep sadness that evening. See Moran, p. 318; *The Memoirs of General the Lord Ismay* (London, 1960), p. 131.

46. CHUR 4/155/88.

47. *SWW* 2:14–16 and *SWWUS* 2:15–17.

48. *SWW* 2:16–17, 589 and *SWWUS* 2:17–18, 665–66; Reves to Laughlin, 24 Nov. 1950, HM 318/1: Reves.

49. Correspondence in CHAR 20/10. More generally, see D. J. Wenden, "Churchill, Radio and Cinema" in Robert Blake and William Roger Louis, eds., *Churchill* (Oxford, 1993), pp. 215–26.

50. Langworth, pp. 202–11. See also the discussion in chapter 2.

51. Ibid., pp. 203–4.

52. Ronald Hyam, "Winston Churchill Before 1914," *HJ* 12 (1969): 172–73.

53. Moran, pp. 317–18, 2 Sept. 1945.

CHAPTER 12: THE BATTLE OF BRITAIN AND THE MEDITERRANEAN GAMBLE

1. *SWW* 2:198 and *SWWUS* 2:225.

2. *SWW* 2:104, 233, 250–52 and *SWWUS* 2:118, 264–65, 284–86; cf. David J. Newbold, "British Planning and Preparations to Resist on Land, September 1939–September 1940," Ph.D. diss. (London University, 1988), chaps. 7–8.

3. *SWW* 2:252–56 and *SWWUS* 2:286–90; cf. CHUR 4/159/151 (1947 draft), CHUR 4/160, fos. 47–48, 57–58 (Pound memo), CHUR 4/193/111 (Brook request).

4. In his sentence "Our excellent Intelligence confirmed that the operation 'Sealion' had definitely been ordered by Hitler," the verb had originally been a blunt "reported" (CHUR 4/160/104). See *SWW* 2:252, 261–62, 267 and *SWWUS* 2:286, 296–97, 302; cf. Hinsley, 1:26–30, 168–85.

5. See *SWW* 2:293–97 and *SWWUS* 2:332–37.

6. Moran, p. 324, 5 Sept. 1945; CHUR 4/198/36–43. WSC asked Park to review the draft.

7. CHUR 4/190/195.

8. *The Battle of Britain: An Air Ministry Account of the Great Days from 8th August–31st October 1940* (London, 1941), pp. 5, 35; cf. *La Bataille de Grande-Bretagne* (London, 1941), p. 34; Richard Overy, *The Battle of Britain* (London, 2000), pp. 130–31. On sales, see minutes by Peck to Sinclair and to Peirse, 5 and 9 April 1941, AIR 19/258.

9. For Goodwin, see CHUR 4/162/147, 4/19/380–83, quoting from WSC to Ismay, 22 Nov. 1946, and Ismay papers, 2/3/19–20, 22–25. Apparently unknown to Ismay, Goodwin was not the real author of the Air Ministry pamphlet, who was Hilary Saunders, Assistant Librarian to the House of Commons, seconded to the Air Ministry in 1940–1942. See Peck to Peirse, 9 April 1941, AIR 19/258.

10. *SWW* 2:286, 297 and *SWWUS* 2:325, 337.

11. For the original contexts of these phrases, see WSC, *Into Battle*, comp. Randolph S. Churchill (London, 1941), pp. 234, 259; for 13 May, see *Speeches* 7:7158.

12. This point is emphasized in Overy, *Battle of Britain*, p. 41.

13. Williamson Murray, *Luftwaffe: Strategy for Defeat, 1933–1945* (London, 1988), pp. 75–77.

14. *SWW* 1:519 and *SWWUS* 1:657; similarly, *SWW* 2:268 and *SWWUS* 2:303.

15. CHUR 4/169, fos. 17, 105–6.

16. *SWW* 2:300 and *SWWUS* 2:340.

17. *SWW* 2:294, 338 and *SWWUS* 2:333–34, 383; see also CHUR 4/165, fos. 61–65, 96, and David Zimmerman, *Britain's Shield: Radar and the Defeat of the Luftwaffe* (Stroud, Gloucestershire, 2001), chap. 12, esp. pp. 196–98.

18. See correspondence in CHUR 4/22/254–69 and the narrative in CHUR 4/197/104–94. Commenting in August 1947 on the first part, Pownall called it "a very full story which contains, no doubt, much useful material" but was "far from being in the shape it should ultimately take" (CHUR 4/197/163–64).

19. WSC to Jones, 14 Dec. 1946, CHUR 4/20/7; see also R. V. Jones papers, RVJO B 216 (CAC). On the Aberdeen chair, "it was your praise of his work and vigour which decided the vote," the Vice-Chancellor told Churchill afterward. See M. Hamilton Fyfe to WSC, 1 May 1946, Cherwell papers, K69/2 (Nuffield College, Oxford).

20. CHUR 4/201/181; see also CHUR 4/197/244–305.

21. CHUR 4/190/3.

22. *SWW* 2:390, 563 and *SWWUS* 2:440, 639.

23. Quotations from J. R. M. Butler, *Grand Strategy*, vol. 2 (London, 1957), p. 301, and Correlli Barnett, *Engage the Enemy More Closely: The Royal Navy in the Second World War* (London, 2000), p. 213.

24. *SWW* 2:385–87 and *SWWUS* 2:435–37; cf. David Day, *The Great Betrayal: Britain, Australia and the Onset of the Pacific War, 1939–1942* (North Ryde, New South Wales, 1988), pp. 54–55, 74–75.

25. W. P. Crozier, *Off the Record: Political Interviews, 1933–1943*, ed. A. J. P. Taylor (Lon-

don, 1973), p. 176, interview of 26 July 1940. On the Burma Road crisis, see Peter Lowe, *Great Britain and the Origins of the Pacific War: A Study of British Policy in East Asia, 1937–1941* (Oxford, 1977), chap. 5.

26. An August 1948 draft includes the marginal query, "Explain about its closing," and Churchill's response, "Have I not done?" (CHUR 4/171/32). The nearest he comes to doing so is the comment that Japan "pointedly requested" its closure. See *SWW* 2:225, 440 and *SWWUS* 2:256, 497.

27. CHUR 4/172/182. There are also some side references, particularly in the chapter "Germany and Russia." See *SWW* 2:440, 463, 514–15, 518–19 and *SWWUS* 2:497, 523, 581–82, 587.

28. *SWW* 2:376 and *SWWUS* 2:425.

29. Ian Beckett, "Wavell," in John Keegan, ed., *Churchill's Generals* (London, 1992), chap. 4, quoting p. 76.

30. John Connell, *Wavell: Scholar and Soldier* (London, 1964), pp. 254–55; Ronald Lewin, *The Chief* (London, 1980), p. 39; Lord Avon, *The Reckoning* (London, 1965), pp. 129–33, where Eden says that Claude Auchinleck (who eventually replaced Wavell in June 1941) was mentioned as a possible successor.

31. CHUR 4/167/127–28.

32. Freyberg's report and the surrounding correspondence are in PREM 3/295/2 (NA), quotations from fos. 43, 26, 30.

33. *SWW* 2:373 and *SWWUS* 2:421–22; cf. CHUR 4/167/154–55, 4/193/132.

34. *SWW* 2:378–79, 395 and *SWWUS* 2:428, 446.

35. *SWW* 4:138 and *SWWUS* 4:156 (Australia); Kenneth Young, ed., *The Diaries of Sir Robert Bruce Lockhart*, vol. 2: *1939–1965* (London, 1980), p. 496 (Winant); Moran, pp. 758–59 (Colville).

36. *SWW* 2:397, 399 and *SWWUS* 448, 450; cf. CHUR 4/168/94–95.

37. Young, *Diaries of Sir Robert Bruce Lockhart*, 2:675, 1 Sept. 1948; similarly on pp. 496, 548.

38. CHUR 4/167, fos. 117 ("together"), 5a (Eden); cf. Avon papers, AP 19/4/15B (Birmingham Univ. Library).

39. CHUR 4/167, fos. 22, 30–31, 68; *SWW* 2:378 and *SWWUS* 2:428.

40. CHUR 4/167/209 and CHUR 4/185/251–52; cf. *SWW* 2:588 and *SWWUS* 2:664.

41. The diary entries of 16 Sept. 1940 (and in similar vein, 19 Sept.) in AP 20/1/20A were partly reproduced in Avon, *Reckoning*, pp. 137–38. For the memos of 23–24 Sept. 1940, see PREM 3/296/11, fos. 251–67.

42. CHUR 4/171/39a; *SWW* 2:442–43, 448 and *SWWUS* 2:449–51, 506.

43. *SWW* 2:474–75, 479 and *SWWUS* 2:536–37, 542.

44. CHUR 4/185/272 (to Amery and Lloyd); PREM 3/308/6 (instruction); John Barnes and David Nicholson, eds., *The Empire at Bay: The Leo Amery Diaries, 1929–1945* (London, 1988), p. 665.

45. PREM 3/308, fos. 87, 94; *SWW* 2:478 and *SWWUS* 2:540; cf. Colville, pp. 285–87, 3 Nov. 1940.

46. PREM 3/308/14, fos. 101–2; *CWP* 2:1036–40.

47. See CHAR 20/14.

48. *SWW* 2:498–99 and *SWWUS* 2:564. For accounts, see John Bowman, *De Valera and the Ulster Question, 1917–1973* (Oxford, 1982), pp. 218–39, and Robert Fisk, *In Time of War: Ireland, Ulster and the Price of Neutrality, 1939–1945* (London, 1985), pp. 186–219.

49. CHUR 4/154, fos. 61–62, 82–83 and CHUR 4/197/81 (Deakin). On the proposals, see Barnes and Nicholson, *Empire at Bay*, pp. 604–10, and R. J. Moore, *Churchill, Cripps and India, 1939–1945* (Oxford, 1979), pp. 31–37.

50. Quotations from *SWW* 2:206, 211–12 and *SWWUS* 2:232, 238–39.

51. *SWW* 2:206 and *SWWUS* 2:232; cf. P. M. H. Bell, *A Certain Eventuality: Britain and the Fall of France* (Farnborough, Hampshire, U.K., 1974), chap. 7.

52. Stephen Roskill, *Churchill and the Admirals* (London, 1977), pp. 150–60, quoting p. 160.

53. *SWW* 2:211 and *SWWUS* 2:238.

54. *SWW* 2:326–27, 438–39 and *SWWUS* 2:369–70, 495–96; see also Sheila Lawlor, *Churchill and the Politics of War, 1940–1941* (Cambridge, 1994), pp. 107–8.

55. WSC, *Into Battle*, pp. 287–88.

56. Cf. Arthur Marder, *Operation "Menace": The Dakar Expedition and the Dudley North Affair* (Oxford, 1976), pp. 263–64, and Roskill, *Churchill and the Admirals*, pp. 163–64.

57. *SWW* 2:422–23 and *SWWUS* 2:477–78; CHUR 4/170/210.

58. *SWW* 2:428 (quotation), 435–36 and *SWWUS* 2:484, 492. Originally, he wrote "very rare in this war" but Clementine remonstrated, "Isn't this rather unfair to Alex, Monty & some of our Admirals?" (CHUR 4/170/99).

59. Allen's report of 18 July 1947 is in CHUR 4/195/36–42; compare his 1973 account of it in Marder, *Operation "Menace,"* pp. 231–32.

60. The WSC-North correspondence is in CHUR 4/20/217–45. On the motives behind North's letter of 19 April, see Marder, *Operation "Menace,"* p. 231, and Mountbatten to North, 25 June 1948, Dudley North papers, NRTH 2/6/34 (CAC).

61. *SWW* 2:425 and *SWWUS* 479–80; North to Allen, 16 Aug. 1952 (draft), North papers, NRTH 2/6/41.

62. *SWW* 2:437, 645–49 and *SWWUS* 2:493, 718–22; cf. CHUR 4/170/150.

63. Brook to Machtig, 6 Oct. 1948, CAB 21/2176 (NA); John Ramsden, *Man of the Century: Winston Churchill and His Legend Since 1945* (London, 2002), p. 496.

64. *SWW* 2:459, 467, 469 and *SWWUS* 2:519, 527, 530. WSC made a similar defense of Franco in the Commons on 10 Dec. 1948, praising his treatment of Hitler and Mussolini as "a monumental example of ingratitude. We cannot say that Spain injured us or the United States at all in the late war." *Speeches* 7:7768.

65. *SWW* 2:459 and *SWWUS* 2:518–19; cf. CHUR 4/172/118. On Franco and Hitler, see Paul Preston, *Franco: A Biography* (London, 1993), pp. 393–400; on Hillgarth's operations, see Denis Smyth, "'Les Chevaliers de Saint-George': La Grande-Bretagne et la corruption des généraux espagnols (1940–1942)," *Guerres mondiales* 162 (1991): 29–54.

66. *SWW* 2:22 and *SWWUS* 2:23. His draft, until the autumn of 1948, continued: "In another generation, the whole correspondence should be put together" (CHUR 4/147/177).

67. WSC to Halifax, 20 Dec. 1940, PREM 4/25/8, fo. 502. For background, see David Reynolds, *The Creation of the Anglo-American Alliance, 1937–1941: A Study in Competitive Co-operation* (London, 1981), chaps. 4–5.

68. Sargent to Brook, 4 May 1948, and p. 10 of the comments enclosed with Brook to WSC, 1 June 1948, CAB 21/2176. Clementine, however, found this "a deeply interesting and significant chapter" (CHUR 4/166/57).

69. *SWW* 2:359 and *SWWUS* 2:405 ("I now cabled Lothian"). For the fate of his 7 Aug. draft, see FO 371/24241, A3670 (NA).

70. Sir John Balfour, *Not Too Correct an Aureole* (London, 1983), p. 77; WSC's Commons speech of 20 Aug. 1940, quoted in *SWW* 2:362 and *SWWUS* 2:409. See also Reynolds, *Creation*, pp. 121–32.

71. WSC to Ismay, 17 July 1940, PREM 4/475/1, fos. 33–34.

72. See David Zimmerman, *Top Secret Exchange: The Tizard Mission and the Scientific War* (Stroud, Gloucestershire, 1996), esp. pp. 3 (quotation), 83–85. On 1 Aug. 1948, Kelly provided some "suggested headings" for a "Wizard War" chapter in volume 3, including "sharing of our knowledge with the U.S.A.—who later mass-produced our inventions," but the theme was never followed up (CHUR 4/197/205).

73. The phrase "which was one of the most important I ever wrote" was added after the American edition went to press. *SWW* 2:489–90, 493, 501 and *SWWUS* 2:553, 555, 558, 567. For Clementine's representations on Lothian, see CHUR 4/174, fos. 4, 16, 56, 65.

74. For the detailed evidence see David Reynolds, *Lord Lothian and Anglo-American Relations, 1939–1940* (Philadelphia, 1983), chap. 6.

75. *SWW* 2:529 and *SWWUS* 2:598; cf. CHUR 4/176/102.

76. *SWW* 2:555–56 and *SWWUS* 2:628–30.

77. *SWW* 2:509, 524 (troop movements) and *SWWUS* 2:576–78, 593.

CHAPTER 13: HIS FINEST HOUR

1. *SWW* 2:84 and *SWWUS* 2:96 (and chaps. 3–4 generally). Cf. WSC, *Into Battle*, comp. Randolph S. Churchill (London, 1941), pp. 213–14, 217.

2. *La Libre Belgique*, 12–17 Jan. 1949; cf. CHUR 4/198/2–6. The correspondence was forwarded by the Prince Regent's private secretary André de Staercke, with whom WSC was on very friendly terms—see CHUR 2/142/73–75.

3. *SWW* 2:74 and *SWWUS* 2:82; cf. CHUR 4/150, fos. 38, 53.

4. CHUR 4/150/143 and CHUR 4/199, fos. 92–95, 98.

5. CHUR 4/18/122–56; cf. *SWW* 2:80–81 and *SWWUS* 90–91.

6. CHUR 4/52/17–78, quoting from fos. 19 (Deakin), 36 ("hurt"), 40 (generals), 51 (WSC to Baron Carton de Wiart, 12 May 1949). See also *La Libre Belgique*, 28 May 1949. Olive Muir did not desist until Leopold finally abdicated in 1951.

7. *Le Figaro*, 16 Feb. 1949, p. 1 (Gamelin). For Reynaud, see *NYT*, 2 March 1949, p. 27, and *DT*, 2 March 1949, p. 4.

8. *Le Figaro*, 4 March 1949, pp. 1, 6 (Weygand); *NYT*, 3 March 1949, p. 24 (Chautemps) and 4 March, p. 20 (editorial).

9. *SWW* 2:48 and *SWWUS* 2:54. For the French versions, see *Le Figaro*, 9 Feb. 1949, and *L'Heure Tragique* (Paris, 1949), p. 57. Cf. CHUR 4/16, fos. 152–53, 160–66, quoting letters from Billotte, 15 Feb. 1949, and Ramadier, 8 March 1949, fos. 164, 160. For the gesture made to Billotte in volume 6, see below, chap. 29.

10. *Le Figaro*, 12–13 Feb. 1949, p. 6. For drafts and postmortem, see CHUR 4/16, fos. 179–87, 205–11; also *Le Figaro*, 18 Feb. 1949, p. 6 (Prioux).

11. CHUR 4/20B/319 (to Pownall). For the preface, see CHUR 4/16, fos. 84–94, 107–38, quoting Reves, fos. 122, 107, 86.

12. Quotations from the original English text, revised to satisfy Plon; see CHUR 4/16, fos. 73–74, 130. The French translation was again somewhat loose—see *Le Soir* (Brussels), 25 Jan. 1950, p. 3.

13. Jacques Pirenne to WSC, 3 March 1950, CHUR 4/16/93–94, see also fos. 84–88, 131, 135.

14. For sales, see Minahan to Laughlin, 24 July 1951, HM 318/4: Laughlin; for Reves references, see CHUR 4/12, fos. 92–93, 123.
15. *NYT*, 12 March 1949, p. 16. As with the *DT*, the first installment appeared on 4 February.
16. WSC to Laughlin, 20 June 1949, CHUR 4/14/309–10, and Holton to Laughlin, 18 April 1949, with Laughlin annotations, HM 318/1: Shipherd. See also correspondence in HM 318/1: Their Finest Hour.
17. Compton to WSC, 4 Jan. 1949, WSC to Compton, 26 Jan. 1949 and CHUR 2/265: MIT; Truman to WSC, 2 Feb. 1949, CHUR 2/266.
18. *NYT*, 26 March 1949; *The Christian Science Monitor*, 1 April 1949.
19. Matthew Connelly to Karl Compton, 21 March 1949, Truman to Compton, 25 March 1949, PPF 4719: MIT, and Lucius Battle and Dean Acheson, memcons, 21 March 1949, in Dean G. Acheson papers, box 64: memcons (HSTL).
20. Moseley to Brooks and to Cross, 17 and 18 Feb. 1949, HM 318/1: Their Finest Hour.
21. See memo about 1 April 1949 in HM 318/4: Churchill.
22. *The New Yorker*, 16 April 1949; *NYHT*, 3 April 1949, book review, p. 1; *AHR* 54.4 (July 1949): 858. Most of the U.S. reviews quoted in this section may be found in CHWL/PE/Box 5, 80a and/or CHUR 4/200.
23. *The Wall Street Journal*, 29 March 1949; *San Francisco Chronicle*, *Chicago Tribune*, and the New Orleans *Times-Picayune*, all 3 April 1949; *Survey*, April 1949.
24. Baltimore *Evening Sun*, 2 April 1949; *The Washington Post*, 3 April 1949.
25. *The Nation* and *The Indianapolis Times*, both 2 April 1949; *The Washington Post* (Kuhn), 3 April 1949; *The New Republic*, 2 May 1949.
26. *Los Angeles Times*, 3 April 1949; *NYT*, 3 April 1949, sec. 7, p. 1; *Boston Herald*, 6 April 1949.
27. See WSC to Flower, 7 March 1949, CHUR 4/24B/389–90.
28. "Messrs. Cassell's is the responsibility, for commissioning cheap, third-rate printers," Wood told Churchill on 13 June 1949. He added in a postscript: "Should this matter be mentioned to Mr. Desmond Flower, might any reference to myself be omitted, please?" Camrose looked through several copies and told Churchill he could not discover any bad printing. See CHUR 4/13/27–29.
29. *The Spectator*, 1 July 1949, pp. 6–7; *The Tribune*, 8 July 1949, pp. 16–17. Orwell reviewed the American edition for *The New Leader*, 14 May 1949.
30. *DT*, 27 June 1949, p. 4; transcript of discussion on BBC Third Programme, 2 Aug. 1949, in Liddell Hart papers, LH 15/15/125 (KCL).
31. *TLS*, 1 July 1949, pp. 421–22.
32. *The Listener*, 30 June 1949, pp. 1116–17. The radio text is at CHUR 4/19/76–82, with WSC's comments, 26 May 1949, on fo. 73.
33. WSC to G. M. Trevelyan, 18 May 1946, WCHL 1/11 (CAC). I have not been able to trace the original Trevelyan letter in Churchill's papers.
34. Sarah Churchill, *Keep on Dancing: An Autobiography*, ed. Paul Medlicott (London, 1981), p. 22. In December 1948, Churchill recalled that twenty-five opposed him in the Commons vote of censure on 2 July 1942. This, said Churchill, was the same as the heaviest vote against Pitt in his War Ministry: "Mark coincidence." WSC to Deakin, 7 Dec. 1948, Deakin papers: WSC-FWD minutes.
35. See proofs in CHAR 8/790. On 10 May 1940, R. A. Butler complained that "the good clean tradition of English politics, that of Pitt as opposed to Fox, had been sold to the

greatest adventurer of modern political history." By May 1943, Butler spoke very differently in public: "Never since the time of Chatham had Britain occupied so prominent a position in the countries of the world nor had any Prime Minister led the armies and navies and air forces of the world towards saving civilization as Mr. Churchill was now doing." John Lukacs, *Five Days in London, May 1940* (New Haven, 1999), pp. 24–25.

36. Churchill scribbled a note about Chatham on the opening page of his 1938 proofs, probably in early 1946 when he had taken up the book again: "He had to wait 2 years for success. Cf. Trevelyan's letter to me." CHAR 8/790/1.

37. Isaiah Berlin, "Mr. Churchill," *Atlantic Monthly*, Sept. 1949, pp. 35–44, quoting p. 44; subsequently published as "Mr. Churchill and F.D.R.," *The Cornhill Magazine* 981 (winter 1949–1950): 219–40, quoting p. 240. Who was that other, unnamed "greatest man of action" Britain had produced? John Ramsden suggests Berlin had in mind Oliver Cromwell—see his *Man of the Century: Winston Churchill and His Legend Since 1945* (London, 2002), p. 138.

38. Michael Ignatieff, *Isaiah Berlin: A Life* (New York, 1998), p. 197, citing an interview with Deakin in 1997, slightly misdates this. Cf. Berlin to Deakin, 30 May 1949, and Deakin to Berlin, 27 June 1949, MS. Berlin 119, fos. 78, 180 (Bodleian Library, Oxford).

39. Berlin, "Mr. Churchill," pp. 36–37, 39, 40–41 and "Mr. Churchill and F.D.R.," pp. 222–23, 228–29, 231–33. Fifteen years later, John Murray, the publisher of *The Cornhill Magazine*, issued the article, slightly revised, as a small book. Incredibly, they described it as a review of *The Gathering Storm*! See Isaiah Berlin, *Mr. Churchill in 1940* (London, 1964), p. 15.

40. Ignatieff, *Isaiah Berlin*, p. 195; see also Ramsden, *Man of the Century*, pp. 115–16.

41. The other name mentioned was the Italian philosopher Benedetto Croce, whom Churchill cordially detested. See *NYT*, 26 Oct. 1949, p. 30, and *The Times*, 4 Nov. 1949, p. 4.

42. Transcript of speech in CHUR 5/28/6–9. For Muir, see CHUR 4/52/74–76.

III | THE GRAND ALLIANCE, 1941–1942, 1948–1950

CHAPTER 14: "IN THE EVENT OF YOUR DEATH"

1. CHUR 4/13/33.

2. Quotations from Moran, pp. 357–59; see also Gilbert 8:485–88.

3. Kenneth Young, *Churchill and Beaverbrook: A Study in Friendship and Politics* (London, 1966), pp. 284–85; Moran, p. 360.

4. See CHUR 4/41B, esp. fos. 194, 211–12, 248 (quoting WSC to Moir, 3 March 1949); also Moir to Clementine, 28 April 1952, copy in Cherwell papers, K77/4 (Nuffield College, Oxford).

5. Lord Hartwell, *William Camrose: Giant of Fleet Street* (London, 1992), p. 334. See also Henry Laughlin to Paul Brooks, 14 July 1949: "when the time comes for Duff Cooper or someone else to finish it . . ." in HM 318/1: Book of the Month, 1948–9.

6. CHUR 4/202, fos. 53, 65.

7. WSC note, 25 March 1948, and Pownall to Ismay, 29 July 1948, Ismay papers, 2/3/45 and 2/3/76 (KCL).

8. WSC note, 24 Oct. 1948, Ismay papers, 2/3/107.

9. Gold to Longwell, telegram, 12 May 1949, CHUR 4/63/727–28; Longwell to WSC, 9 Sept. 1949, CHUR 4/15/96; Laughlin to Brooks, 14 July 1949, in HM 318/1: Book of the Month, 1948–9.

10. Gold to WSC, 17 June 1949, CHUR 4/15/102; Brooks to Laughlin, 22 July 1949, in HM 318/1: Book of the Month, 1948–9.

11. See Longwell to WSC, 17 May 1949, and WSC, General Note, 16 May 1949, CHUR 4/63, fos. 729, 731.

12. Reves to Laughlin, 4 June 1949, and to Brooks, 5 July 1949, HM 318/1: Reves.

13. Reves to WSC, 22 Aug. 1949, printed in *C-Reves*, pp. 297–300.

14. WSC, note, 8 Nov. 1949, CHUR 4/19/290; for Deakin, see CHUR 4/231/283–87 and CHUR 4/238/66.

15. WSC to Longwell, 23 Sept. and 27 Dec. 1949, CHUR 4/15, fos. 89–94, 74–75; WSC to Camrose, 3 Apr. 1950, CHUR 4/13/42–44.

16. CHUR 4/202, esp. fos. 3–4, 12, 33, 53, 65; Reves to WSC, 27 Oct. 1949, and WSC to Reves, 27 Nov. 1949, in *C-Reves*, pp. 306–7.

17. Brook, "Comments on Book 5" [26 Aug. 1949], p. 1, CAB 21/2177 (NA); cf. CHUR 4/202, fos. 161, 188. For the American dust jacket, see HM 318/4: Grand Alliance, esp. cable from WSC to Laughlin, Laughlin to WSC, and Holton memo, all 23 March 1950.

18. CHUR 4/202, fos. 157, 172; Brook to WSC, 28 Nov. 1949, CHUR 4/18/234.

19. Brook, comments on book 1, 22 Feb. 1949, p. 1, CAB 21/2177.

20. Ibid., p. 10; also CHUR 4/208/60.

21. WSC note, 24 Oct. 1948, Ismay papers, 2/3/107A; SWW 3:ix–x and *SWWUS* 3:vi, CHUR 4/202/173 (preface) and CHUR 4/203/180–209 ("Germany and Russia").

22. See CHUR 4/232 ("Japan"), CHUR 4/19/249–52 (Hudson), and CHUR 4/212, esp. fos. 37–64. ("The Japanese Envoy").

CHAPTER 15: THE CRISIS OF SPRING 1941

1. *SWW* 3:10–12, 27 and *SWWUS* 3:11–14, 29–30.

2. The latter passage originally stood at the opening of chapter 3; instead, four pages into the text, it is much less prominent. *SWW* 3:37, 317 and *SWWUS* 3:42, 354; cf. CHUR 4/205/54–55.

3. CHUR 4/203/105 (Kelly); for the unused minutes see *CWP* 3:225, 842.

4. *SWW* 3:98, 106 and *SWWUS* 3:111–12, 122.

5. CHUR 4/209, fos. 71, 88 (WSC), and 173 (Allen); CHUR 4/219/36 (Gold). For Allen's role, see also CHUR 4/248.

6. *SWW* 3:8 and *SWWUS* 3:9; E. H. Athanassoglou to WSC, 30 June 1949, CHUR 4/199/173–74.

7. *SWW* 3:83–84 and *SWWUS* 3:95.

8. J. R. M. Butler, *Grand Strategy*, vol. 2 (London, 1957), p. 459; Hinsley 1:359.

9. Francis de Guingand, *Operation Victory* (London, 1947), chap. 3, quoting p. 80. De Guingand was able to publish his memoirs with impunity because he had retired from the army and moved to Southern Rhodesia.

10. Cyril Falls, *The Second World War: A Short History* (London, 1948), p. 91. This passage was enlarged and somewhat toned down in Falls's second edition, published later that year. As early as the summer of 1942, similar criticisms had been bruited about in the

press. Such was their sensitivity that they were subjected to considerable analysis by the Prime Minister's Office and the Cabinet Office's Historical Section—see PREM 3/288/7.

11. See Ismay to WSC, 25 May 1948, CHUR 4/208, fos. 85–89, 113, and WSC to Ismay, 26 May 1948, CHUR 4/205/223.

12. Ismay to WSC, 25 May 1940, CHUR 4/208/85–89.

13. CHUR 4/221/95. Cf. WSC to FDR, 11 June 1944, "by denuding Cyrenaica to help Greece we also lost the whole of Wavell's conquests in Cyrenaica," SWW 6:67 and SWWUS 6:76.

14. CHUR 4/208, fos. 81, 140, 238.

15. CHUR 4/206/44–46 and 4/208/70–84. A copy of Eden's memo is also in Avon papers, AP 19/4/15B (Birmingham Univ. Library).

16. SWW 3:90, 93–94 and SWWUS 3:101, 105–7; cf. CHUR 4/208/276. The significance of Eden's fait accompli is stressed in Sheila Lawlor, Churchill and the Politics of War, 1940–1941 (Cambridge, 1994), p. 252, chaps. 9–13 of which provide the fullest archivally based analysis of the Greek decision.

17. CHUR 4/208, fos. 126 (conclusion) and 264 (Falls).

18. At one point he did think of narrating the German conquests of both countries in a single chapter but then seems to have been carried away by the rich material that Deakin found on Yugoslavia. See CHUR 4/211, esp. fos. 61 (Gold) and 163 (single chapter). This larger Balkan dimension is emphasized by Lawlor, Churchill and the Politics of War, and Martin van Creveld, "Prelude to Disaster: The British Decision to Aid Greece, 1940–41," JCH 9 (1974): 65–92.

19. Avon papers, AP 19/4/15B (Eden); CHUR 4/211/131 (20 March cable); SWW 3:142, 152 and SWWUS 3:161, 171. On British complicity in the coup, see Hinsley 1:369–70, which updates the more agnostic appraisal by David A. T. Stafford, "SOE and British Involvement in the Belgrade Coup d'Etat of March 1941," Slavic Review 36 (1977): 399–419.

20. SWW 3:173–75, 177 and SWWUS 3:196–99; Wavell to Pownall, 25 Oct. 1949, CHUR 4/213/9–10.

21. CWP 3:272; Hinsley 1:388, 395; CHUR 4/213/10. See also the Ultra deletions from WSC to Wavell, 2 March 1941, CHUR 4/213, fos. 35, 214.

22. CHUR 4/217/245.

23. CHUR 4/217, fos. 302 (intelligence) and 321 (Cairo command, featherweight).

24. CHUR 4/19, fos. 26–27, 223; cf. SWW 3:241–42 and SWWUS 3:272–73. In this passage, Churchill hints cryptically that "in September, 1940, I had toyed with the idea of giving him a far greater scope."

25. CHUR 4/217/12–20. See also his covering note, fo. 11, and his annotated copy of "The Advent," fos. 65–77.

26. CHUR 4/217, esp. fos. 56–58, 60–61, 93, 418.

27. CHUR 4/217, fos. 94–95, 285a; SWW 3:240 and SWWUS 3:270.

28. Freyberg had referred to Ultra the previous year when commenting on a draft War Office history of the Crete campaign: "Our intelligence was excellent: without it Crete would have gone much earlier. These accurate estimates came from War Office Intelligence and most secret intercept sources." Freyberg to Director of Public Relations, War Office, 27 Aug. 1948, CAB 106/761.

29. Freyberg quotations from CHUR 4/217, fos. 69, 18. See also Anthony Cave Brown, The Secret Servant: The Life of Sir Stewart Menzies, Churchill's Spymaster (London, 1988), pp. 338–40, as amended by Paul Freyberg, Bernard Freyberg, VC: Soldier of Two Nations

(London, 1991), esp. pp. 268, 284. The remark about intercepts in the previous note, though from 1948, supports Paul Freyberg's claim that his father knew the Ultra secret.

30. *SWW* 3:253 and *SWWUS* 3:285. The July 1948 draft accorded most of the credit to Freyberg's New Zealand division, but Pownall noted that there were nearly as many Australians as New Zealanders on Crete and "more British than either." Churchill duly made some adjustments—see CHUR 4/218/299–300.

31. CHUR 4/217, fos. 17, 64; CHUR 4/218, fos. 132, 184; *SWW* 3:268 and *SWWUS* 3:301. Cf. I. S. O. Playfair, *The Mediterranean and the Middle East,* vol. 2 (London, 1956), pp. 128–29, 147. The most recent scholarly study, using Allied and Axis documents, says 6,700 casualties, of whom half were killed: Callum MacDonald, *The Lost Battle: Crete, 1941* (London, 2002 ed.), p. 301.

32. CHUR 4/218/64.

33. CHUR 4/207, fos. 68, 96; *SWW* 3:73, 75 and *SWWUS* 3:81, 84.

34. *SWW* 3:236–37 and *SWWUS* 3:266–67.

35. *SWW* 3:296–97 and *SWWUS* 3:331–32.

36. *SWW* 3:228 and *SWWUS* 3:257.

37. *SWW* 3:239 and *SWWUS* 3:270. For other examples, see *SWW* 3:236, 296–97 and *SWWUS* 3:266, 331–32.

38. In August 1950, Norman Brook wrote that Churchill "revised his opinions of Wavell's capacities as a Commander—very substantially, I believe—as a result of re-reading the telegrams and other material while he was at work on Volume III." In December 1948, after an exchange with Churchill about Auchinleck, Pownall told Ismay, "I feel sure he will come round a lot in time, but we shall have to continue the hunt on every suitable occasion. He's now almost soppy about Wavell, perhaps in the end he'll be the same about the Auk." See Brook to Laithwaite, 9 Aug. 1950, CAB 21/2178; Pownall to Ismay, 14 Dec. 1948, Ismay papers, 2/3/129 (KCL).

39. *SWW* 3:307–8 and *SWWUS* 3:342–43; CHUR 4/221/122.

40. *SWW* 3:299 and *SWWUS* 3:334. Until October 1949, he went on to say that this spy later "lost his life in trying to come over to our lines." See CHUR 4/221/101.

41. CHUR 4/221/44; cf. Hinsley 1:393–99.

42. CHUR 4/221, fos. 44–47 (Pownall) and 88–89 (WSC); *SWW* 3:308 and *SWWUS* 3:344.

43. Pownall to Ismay, 12 Aug. 1948, Ismay papers, 2/3/82; cf. CHUR 4/20/349–51 and CHUR 4/221/76–77, 134. For the text see *SWW* 3:305 and *SWWUS* 3:340.

44. *SWW* 3:308–9 and *SWWUS* 3:343–45; for Ismay, see CHUR 4/221, fos. 91a, 91b.

45. CHUR 4/221/89–90.

46. Hankey to Halifax, 1 May 1941, Hickleton papers, A 4.410.4.5 (Borthwick Institute, York), and Richard Stokes, MP, to LG, 14 May 1941, LG papers, G/19/3/27 (HLRO). Stokes does not name which of the Chiefs of Staff said this to him.

47. *"Chips": The Diaries of Sir Henry Channon,* ed. Robert Rhodes James (London, 1993), p. 307; see also Kevin Jefferys, *The Churchill Coalition and Wartime Politics, 1940–1945* (Manchester, 1995), pp. 86–88.

48. CHUR 4/239, fos. 17 (Gold), 34 (WSC), 41, 46 (Brook); WSC, *The Unrelenting Struggle* (London, 1942), p. 131.

49. Quotations from A. W. Martin and Patsy Hardy, eds., *Dark and Hurrying Days: Menzies' 1941 Diary* (Canberra, 1993), pp. 63, 66, 71, 119.

50. For references, see *SWW* 3:39, 69, 94, 365 and *SWWUS* 3:44, 76, 107, 409. I am not

persuaded by the argument that Menzies had actually "set his sights" on Number 10. See David Day, *Menzies and Churchill at War* (North Ryde, New South Wales, 1986), p. 252.

51. Sir John Colville, diary, 21 June 1941, CLVL 1/5, p. 32 (CAC); cf. the published version in Colville, pp. 403n, 405, and 429, where the entry for 21 June simply calls Fraser "dull."

52. *SWW* 3:95, 244–45 and *SWWUS* 3:108, 275–76; cf. CHUR 4/217/289–90 and 4/219/81–82.

53. See Alan Watt, *The Evolution of Australian Foreign Policy, 1938–1965* (Cambridge, 1968), p. 24.

54. Sir John Kennedy, *The Business of War*, ed. Bernard Fergusson (London, 1957), chap. 13, quoting pp. 106, 109. The directive is also printed in *CWP* 3:556–57.

55. Dill to WSC, 6 May 1941, WO 216/5.

56. All these documents are in WO 216/5.

57. Alex Danchev, "'Dilly-Dally,' or Having the Last Word: Field Marshal Sir John Dill and Prime Minister Winston Churchill," *JCH* 22 (1987): 27.

58. *SWW* 3:373–77 and *SWWUS* 3:419–24.

59. CHUR 4/225, fos. 49–55, 129–30 (WSC), 132, 111 (Pownall), 115–20; Ismay comments of 1 Dec. 1949, Ismay papers, 2/3/190/2a.

60. *SWW* 3:677 and *SWWUS* 3:761; cf. CHAR 23/9, fos. 1, 24.

61. *SWW* 3:315–16 and *SWWUS* 3:352–53; cf. CHUR 4/211/29–30.

62. Pownall had to restrain Churchill from adding rather dubious statistics on German tank strength to bolster his argument. See *SWW* 3:316 and *SWWUS* 3:353–54; CHUR 4/222/321; cf. Martin L. van Creveld, *Hitler's Strategy, 1940–1941: The Balkan Clue* (Cambridge, 1973), pp. 182–83, and the German official history by Horst Boog et al., *Germany and the Second World War*, vol. 4 (Oxford, 1998), pp. 315–16, 376.

63. *SWW* 3:317–20 and *SWWUS* 3:354–57. For the raw intelligence, see HW 1/3 (NA).

64. CHUR 4/222, fos. 185, 217, 317.

65. *SWW* 3:318 and *SWWUS* 3:355–56; CHUR 4/222/228; cf. Hinsley 1:429, 476, 482 and *C-R* 1:216.

66. CHUR 4/222/43 (Gold); *SWW* 3:320–23 and *SWWUS* 3:357–61.

67. For this defense of Cripps, see Gabriel Gorodetsky, *Grand Delusion: Stalin and the German Invasion of Russia* (London, 1999), pp. 159–68. See also Peter Clarke, *The Cripps Version: The Life of Sir Stafford Cripps, 1889–1952* (London, 2002), pp. 214–17.

68. The digest of telegrams is in PREM 3/395/2 and was printed as an annex to Churchill's "Personal Telegrams" for Sept. 1941. See also Rowan to WSC, 13 Oct. 1941, PREM 3/403/7, fo. 250.

69. In volume 4, somewhat contradictorily, Churchill quotes a conversation with Stalin in Moscow in August 1942 about the April 1941 telegram: "I remember it," said Stalin, "I did not need any warnings. I knew war would come, but I thought I would gain another six months or so." *SWW* 4:443 and *SWWUS* 4:493.

70. An early draft went on: "If all Germans had had the same impulse at the same moment how many more millions of people would have been spared violent, untimely death." *SWW* 3:43–49 and *SWWUS* 3:48–55; CHUR 4/205/446–61, quoting fo. 461.

71. Text and draft in *C-R* 1:181–82.

72. Gorodetsky, *Grand Delusion*, chap. 12. WSC's draft statement is in PREM 3/219/6–11.

73. Gorodetsky, *Grand Delusion*, p. 279.

CHAPTER 16: FORGING AN ALLIANCE

1. CHUR 4/229/105–32.
2. *SWW* 3:350–52 and *SWWUS* 3:393–95. For the draft, see CHUR 4/223/52–54.
3. *SWW*3:331 (Colville), 350–51 (advisers) and *SWWUS* 3:370, 393–94; CHUR 4/222/210.
4. *SWW* 3:403 and *SWWUS* 3:453. On WSC and Eden, see Sheila Lawlor, "Britain and Russian Entry into the War," in Richard Langhorne, ed., *Diplomacy and Intelligence During the Second World War* (Cambridge, 1985), pp. 168–83.
5. *SWW* 3:745, 486, 466 and *SWWUS* 3:829, 548, 525. In the second of these, WSC added "(temporarily)" after "reduced."
6. CHUR 4/228/30 and 4/238/47; cf. *SWW* 3:619 and *SWWUS* 3:700.
7. *SWW* 3:471 and *SWWUS* 3:531.
8. Steven Merrit Miner, *Between Churchill and Stalin: The Soviet Union, Great Britain, and the Origins of the Grand Alliance* (Chapel Hill, N.C., 1988), chap. 6, quoting pp. 172, 179; see also Martin H. Folly, *Churchill, Whitehall and the Soviet Union, 1940–1945* (London, 2000), pp. 32–38. The full text of WSC's draft of 15 Nov. 1941 is printed in *CWP* 3:1458, but without indication that the message was never sent.
9. CHUR 4/229/105–32. The draft message is in PREM 3/170/1, fos. 67–68.
10. John Harvey, ed., *The War Diaries of Oliver Harvey, 1941–1945* (London, 1978), p. 57; *SWW* 3:445–46 and *SWWUS* 3:501–2.
11. *SWW* 3:412, 479, 483, 732, 766 and *SWWUS* 3:464, 540, 544, 817, 852; cf. Alanbrooke, pp. 183, 187–91.
12. *SWW* 3:484, 486–87 and *SWWUS* 3:545–46, 549.
13. *SWW* 3:356–58, 487 and *SWWUS* 3:399–401, 549.
14. CHUR 4/224, quoting fos. 285–88; *SWW* 3:364 and *SWWUS* 3:409. Left to himself, "I suppose he would have waited another year," Churchill observed sarcastically on another of Pownall's apologias for the Auk. CHUR 4/231/190.
15. *SWW* 3:512–13 and *SWWUS* 3:575–77.
16. *SWW* 3:480–81, 555–56 and *SWWUS* 3:542, 626; cf. CHUR 4/225, fos. 132 (Dill), 211 (Keyes).
17. See CHUR 4/224, fos. 109, 122–23, 283–84; also CHUR 4/251/192–93. Ismay said he did not believe that Churchill "seriously thought of changing Auchinleck almost from the moment that he took over his command" (CHUR 4/224/283), but that was exactly what had happened with Wavell in August 1940.
18. *SWW* 3:366–67 and *SWWUS* 3:410–12; CHUR 4/224/408. See also John Ramsden, *Man of the Century: Winston Churchill and His Legend Since 1945* (London, 2002), pp. 495–98.
19. *SWW* 3:372 and *SWWUS* 3:418; cf. CHUR 4/224/70.
20. CHUR 4/18, fos. 212 (WSC), 267–71 (Brook).
21. CHUR 4/224, fos. 53–73, 344
22. PREM 8/1321, esp. Brook to Attlee, 26 Oct. 1949, Attlee to Chifley, 27 Oct. 1949, and Canberra tel. 767, 26 Nov. 1949 (NA); cf. Shedden to Chifley, 8 Nov. 1949, A5954, 676/12 (NAA).
23. CHUR 4/18, fos. 220–24, 227–28 and 231 (Churchill quotation); cf. Shedden to PM, 6 Feb. 1950, A5954, 676/12 (NAA).
24. *SWW* 3:126 and *SWWUS* 3:146.
25. CHUR 4/251/326–28.

26. CHUR 4/251/162–63.

27. Minutes of 19 Aug. 1941 in CAB 65/19, WM 84 (41) 1, CA (NA).

28. CHUR 4/227, fos. 114, 149. He also sanitized passages in his draft about FDR's pre-emptive naval patrolling and the "anomalous" situation that this created for the U.S. Navy. See CHUR 4/228/42.

29. Once again, however, his text is sometimes at variance with his documents. Much later, in his chapter "Japan," Churchill prints a cable to Smuts on 9 November 1941 in which he recalls the President saying in August, "I may never declare war; I may make war" because of the difficulty of persuading Congress to approve a formal declaration of U.S. belligerency. SWW 3:528 and SWWUS 3:593. The original text of the cable used "shall" rather than "may" in both places, but Churchill gradually reworked it. See CHUR 4/232, fos. 33, 65, 316, 55.

30. Sherwood, pp. 350–51; cf. CHUR 4/228/42.

31. Letter of 3 Aug. 1941, PREM 3/485/6, fo. 16.

32. SWW 3:385–86 and SWWUS 3:453–54. Cf. Elliott Roosevelt, As He Saw It (New York, 1946), p. 38: "Father grunted. 'A real old Tory isn't he?'"

33. Cadogan, TS. (1960) "Atlantic Meeting," ACAD 7/2 (CAC); Cadogan, p. 398; cf. CHUR 4/225, fos. 46, 92–93, 148, 150.

34. WSC to Eden, 24 May 1941, PREM 4/100/5.

35. SWW 3:394 and SWWUS 3:444; WSC to Hopkins, 28 Aug. 1941, PREM 3/224/2, fo. 37. See more generally David Reynolds, "The Atlantic 'Flop': British Foreign Policy and the Churchill-Roosevelt Meeting of August 1941," in Douglas Brinkley and David R. Facey-Crowther, eds., The Atlantic Charter (New York, 1994), pp. 129–50.

36. CHUR 4/212, fos. 67, 160–61, 262; cf. CWP 3:234–36.

37. SWW 3:379–80, 389–91, 399 and SWWUS 3:426–27, 438–41, 448–49. For fuller discussion, see David Reynolds, The Creation of the Anglo-American Alliance, 1937–1941: A Study in Competitive Co-operation (London, 1981), chap. 9.

38. SWW 3:522–23 and SWWUS 3:587–88. In his first draft, Churchill developed this point by noting that Britain won back its Asian colonies in 1945. The British empire, he snarled at the Attlee government's postwar policy of decolonization, was "successfully defended against everyone but the British." See CHUR 4/232/288–89.

39. SWW 3:532 and SWWUS 3:598; CHUR 4/232/486.

40. Correspondence in CHUR 4/20/185–94; also CHUR 4/232/192–93.

41. CHUR 4/20/194.

42. See the judicious analysis in Richard J. Aldrich, Intelligence and the War Against Japan: Britain, America and the Politics of Secret Service (Cambridge, 2000), chap. 5.

43. SWW 3:534–36 and SWWUS 3:600–603; CHUR 4/232, fos. 91, 215–16, 488; Reynolds, Creation of the Anglo-American Alliance, p. 246.

44. SWW 3:537–40 and SWWUS 3:604–8; CHUR 4/233, fos. 134–35, 137.

45. SWW 3:551 and SWWUS 3:620.

46. SWW 3:523–24, 768–74; SWWUS 3:588–90, 854–59.

47. SWW 3:525 and SWWUS 3:590; cf. CAB 69/2, DO 65 (41) 1 and CAB 69/8, DO 66 (41) 1.

48. See Roskill papers, ROSK 4/79, esp. Waller to Roskill, 7 Feb. 1953, and A. B. Acheson to J. R. M. Butler, 19 Feb. 1953, quoting Rowan (CAC).

49. Smuts to WSC, 18 Nov. 1941, PREM 3/163/3, fos. 8–9.

50. The original material was provided by Gordon Allen, whose first draft was harsher on Phillips, but after further discussion with the official naval historians Allen decided that

the case "might be made more favourable to Admiral Phillips," and this was duly done. *SWW* 3:548–51 and *SWWUS* 3:616–19; cf. CHUR 4/233, fos. 8, 76–78, 120, 435.

51. CHUR 4/247, fos. 31–38 (1950) and 63 (1948).

52. WSC to Allen, 11 Aug. 1953, copy in ROSK 4/79; Anthony Montague Browne, *Long Sunset* (London, 1996), p. 201.

53. Butler to Roskill, 20 Aug. 1953, ROSK 6/26; *SWW* 3:524 and *SWWUS* 3:590.

54. See the entry on Phillips in *The Dictionary of National Biography, 1941–1950* (Oxford, 1959), p. 668. One source for this was apparently Admiral J. H. Godfrey—see Thursfield to Godfrey, 24 May 1954, and reply 28 May 1954, Dudley Pound papers, DUPO 6/1 (CAC).

55. For Longmore and Tedder, see *SWW* 3:200–201, 221, 249–50, 300 and *SWWUS* 3:227, 249, 281, 335; for Longmore and Cunningham, see Callum MacDonald, *The Lost Battle: Crete, 1941* (London, 2002), pp. 123, 127, 252–54.

56. *SWW* 3:540, 567–71 and *SWWUS* 3:608, 641–43; CHUR 4/234/68.

57. *SWW* 3:581–82 and *SWWUS* 3:655; CHUR 4/235, fos. 1–15, 24–25; cf. CHUR 4/202/65.

58. *SWW* 3:574–78, 582–84 and *SWWUS* 3:646–51, 655–58. For earlier comments on strategy, see *SWW* 3:106, 451–52, 767–68 and *SWWUS* 3:122, 508–9, 853.

59. *SWW* 3:452, 585 and *SWWUS* 3:509, 659.

60. CHUR 4/235/91–92; cf. the original documents marked for printing at CHAR 23/10/10–17.

61. *SWW* 3:578–81 and *SWWUS* 3:652–55; cf. CHAR 23/10. The memo is printed in full with its proper title in *CWP* 3:1649–53.

62. See material in PREM 3/499/2, quoting fos. 22, 27.

63. PREM 3/499/2, fo. 3.

64. *SWW* 3:608–9 and *SWWUS* 3:686–88; CHUR 4/237, fos. 2–5, 10–14. Deakin suggested a parallel passage about the importance of the Anglo-American Combined Boards to manage the economic side of the war, but Churchill did not respond. See CHUR 4/238/134–35.

65. *SWW* 3:590–91 and *SWWUS* 3:666–67; cf. CHUR 4/234/78–79.

66. CHUR 4/237/259.

67. CHUR 4/237/114; cf. Sherwood, p. 442. For variants of the story, see *CWP* 3:1676 and Ian Jacob diary, entry for 1 Jan. 1942, JACB 1/13 (CAC).

CHAPTER 17: "MAN OF THE HALF-CENTURY"

1. *Time*, 6 Jan. 1941, pp. 23–26. A full run of the Person of the Year cover stories may be found at http://www.time.com/time/personoftheyear/archive/stories/index.html.

2. *Time*, 2 Jan. 1950, pp. 28–29, 40–41.

3. WSC, *Europe Unite: Speeches 1947 and 1948*, ed. Randolph S. Churchill (London, 1950), pp. v–vi; for contracts, see CHUR 4/53.

4. *Speeches* 8:7942–44.

5. *Evening Standard*, 15 Feb. 1950 and *Daily Herald*, 16 Feb. 1950 (Attlee), both in CHPC 31; *NYT*, 21 Feb. 1950, p. 12 (Bevin). Attlee also derided the claim that Labour's foreign policy was simply a poor imitation of Churchill's: "while he talked, Mr. Bevin worked—building up Western Union and the Atlantic Pact." To huge cheers, Attlee said Churchill was "like a cock that crows and thinks it produced the dawn."

6. CHUR 4/13/34–36.

7. *Speeches* 8:7941, 7945. See also Peter Clarke, *The Cripps Version: The Life of Sir Stafford Cripps, 1889–1952* (London, 2002), pp. 519–21.
8. CHUR 4/250/535–36.
9. CHUR 4/250/532–34; cf. *DT*, 13 March 1950, p. 4. Kelly and Churchill also hoped to exclude the account of Wavell's sacking after Battleaxe, but Camrose did not agree to that.
10. *Life*, 6 Feb. 1950, pp. 46–64; 20 Feb. 1950, pp. 66–82; 27 Feb. 1950, pp. 62–76; John Shaw Billings diary, 6 Dec. 1949 (Univ. of South Carolina, Columbia). I am grateful to Prof. Alan Brinkley for this latter reference.
11. NAA, A5954, A676/2, quoting Melbourne *Sun*, 16 and 18 Feb. 1950; see also 1950 papers in A585/12 and the file of cuttings in A2054/1.
12. *The Salt Lake Tribune*, NYHT, and *Newark News*, all 23 April 1950, copies in CHWL/PE, Box 5, 80a.
13. *NYT*, 24 April 1950; *Time*, 1 May 1950, both in CHWL/PE 80a. WSC is quoted in Graebner to Longwell, 2 May 1950, Longwell papers/Churchill, box 2: Graebner (Butler Library, Columbia Univ., New York, N.Y.).
14. *NYT* (Sherwood), Cleveland *Plain Dealer*, *The Miami Herald*, all 23 April 1950; *Chicago Tribune*, 30 April, all in CHWL/PE 80a. For Sherwood's draft, see Robert E. Sherwood papers, folder 2092 (Houghton Library, Harvard Univ., Cambridge, Mass.).
15. *The New Republic*, 5 June 1950; *The Nation*, 6 May 1950, both in CHWL/PE 80a.
16. *The Tribune*, 28 July 1950, pp. 17–18; *The Listener*, 27 July 1950, p. 137; cf. drafts in Liddell Hart papers, 10/1950/18a, pp. 7, 9–10 (KCL). Liddell Hart had already used the "second Dunkirk" tag in a strong attack on "The Great Greek Blunder" in *Sunday Pictorial*, 19 Oct. 1947, pp. 4, 10.
17. *The Manchester Guardian*, 20 July 1950, p. 4; *Tribune*, 28 July 1950, p. 17; *The Spectator*, 21 July 1950, p. 88.
18. *TLS*, 1 July 1949, p. 422, and 21 July 1950, p. 447.
19. *SWW* 3:384 and *SWWUS* 3:431–32.
20. *SWW* 3:625–29 and *SWWUS* 3:706–11.
21. Memphis *Commercial Appeal*, 23 April 1950, sec. 4, p. 12, and Brooks to Churchill, 9 May 1950, CHUR 4/55/5–6; correspondence in CHUR 4/249, fos. 150–51, 168.
22. Letter from J. C. Kelly-Rogers in CHUR 4/249/206–7, excerpts printed in *DT*, 15 April 1950, p. 4; cf. CHUR 4/54, fos. 85, 88–89, 100–103, and PREM 4/71/2, fos. 643–44.
23. Bracken to Beaverbrook, 10 Jan. 1950, Beaverbrook papers, C57 (HLRO).

IV | THE HINGE OF FATE, 1942–1943, 1948–1951

CHAPTER 18: "THE WORST MESS YET"

1. *SWW* 4:ix and *SWWUS* 4:vi.
2. CHAR 23/11; CHUR 4/20B/366–67.
3. CHUR 4/274/164; cf. *SWW* 4:344 and *SWWUS* 4:383.
4. *SWW* 4:408–9 and *SWWUS* 4:453; cf. CHUR 4/278/27–28.
5. *SWW* 4:428–29 and *SWWUS* 4:476; cf. CHUR 4/274/24, 4/279/449.
6. See CHUR 4/295/10–11.
7. CHUR 4/20B/318.
8. See esp. Pownall to WSC, 5 May 1949, CHUR 4/300C/595–99, and Pownall to Ismay, 7 May 1949, Ismay papers, 2/3/156 (KCL).

9. Marston notes on finance, 6 Sept. and 11 Oct. 1949, CHUR 1/75.

10. Note on Marston to WSC, 16 July 1949, in CHUR 1/77: Plans.

11. CHUR 1/81, esp. Churchills to the Nairns, 19 Nov. 1949 (Nairn file), and CHUR 1/80: Finance.

12. Pownall to Ismay, 23 Jan. 1950, Ismay papers, 2/3/196; also CHUR 1/80–81, esp. CHUR 1/80: Lists of Homeward Bags.

13. Note on Churchill and Policymaking, ca. May 1950, R. A. Butler papers, G22/20–22 (Trinity College, Cambridge).

14. CHUR 4/300/396–402; cf. diary for March and April 1950, CHUR 2/616.

15. CHUR 4/252, esp. fos. 110, 128, 154; Laughlin to Longwell, 24 May 1950, HM 318/1: Life. Churchill's official biographer credits "The Hinge of Fate" to Norman Brook, the Cabinet Secretary (Gilbert 8:552). I have not been able to find any evidence to back up this statement, but in February 1949 Brook did press the idea of the Desert War as "the hinge on which ultimate victory turned." See his comments on vol. 3, book 1, CAB 21/2177.

16. CHUR 4/252, esp. fos. 7–8, 71–72, 77, 83, 87, 110; CHUR 4/300, fos. 618 (Reves) and 696 (Kelly); WSC, *The End of the Beginning* (London, 1943), esp. pp. 214–15.

17. CHUR 4/15/60–61 (Longwell) and CHUR 4/25/276–77 (Luce).

18. Draft reply to Longwell, CHUR 4/15/57–58; cf. draft to Luce, CHUR 4/25/274–75.

19. CHUR 4/14, fos. 255, 257–58; cf. CHUR 4/13/42–44 (to Camrose). Laughlin's praise was genuine: he told Daniel Longwell that volume 4 was "the most interesting book of the lot." Letter of 24 May 1950 in HM 318/1: Life.

20. CHUR 4/12, fos. 74–76, 86–89, 92–94.

21. CHUR 4/15, fos. 81–82, 89.

22. CHUR 4/14, fos. 255, 257–58, 264–67.

23. *Sunday Dispatch*, 23 July 1950. See generally CHUR 1/79.

24. CHUR 2/275, esp. WSC notes of 13 July and 1 Aug. 1950.

25. John Bright-Holmes, ed., *Like It Was: The Diaries of Malcolm Muggeridge* (London, 1981), pp. 409–10.

26. Gilbert 8:548; diary for Aug. 1950 in CHUR 2/616.

27. See Kelly to WSC, 22 Aug. 1950, CHUR 4/300C/357–9.

28. CHUR 4/24/432–39, quoting Flower to WSC, 2 Aug. 1950, fo. 433; cf. Laughlin to Reves, 25 July 1950, HM 318/1: Reves.

29. CHUR 4/24, fos. 425–26, 431.

30. CHUR 4/24, fos. 416–26, quoting WSC to Flower, 16 Aug. 1950, fo. 423.

31. CHUR 4/14/222–38, quoting WSC to Laughlin, 31 Aug. 1950, fo. 238. Hunter's role was intended as a one-shot, but Churchill was so taken with the arrangement that he demanded repeat performances, to Laughlin's embarrassment. See HM 318/4: Churchill, 1950, esp. Laughlin to Hunter, 3 Oct. 1950.

32. CHUR 4/12/67–69; also CHUR 4/14/239.

33. Reves to Laughlin, 2 Sept. 1950, HM 318/1: Reves.

34. Pownall to Ismay, 26 Sept. 1950, Ismay papers, 2/3/228. There were indeed some bloomers. For instance, the chapter "Adana and Tripoli" purports to cover Churchill's meeting with the Turks at Adana and the capture of Tripoli in January 1943. Yet the Tripoli material had been moved to another chapter during the August revisions, and new material about Stalingrad was added after that, but neither change was reflected in the chapter title.

CHAPTER 19: ASIAN DISASTERS, DESERT VICTORY,
AND THE SILENCE OF STALINGRAD

1. *SWW* 4:81 and *SWWUS* 4:92.
2. *SWW* 4:343 and *SWWUS* 4:383. His 1948 dictation read "the heaviest single blow I can recall during the war." Only after a query from Ismay, reminding him of the loss of the *Prince of Wales* and the *Repulse*, did he amend this. See CHUR 4/274, fos 83, 137 (Ismay), 164. In 1945, he had been more dismissive, telling Moran on 10 July that Tobruk was "painful like a boil, but it was not a cancer." See Moran, p. 284.
3. Brian Bond, ed., *Chief of Staff: The Diaries of Lieutenant General Sir Henry Pownall*, vol. 2 (London, 1974), pp. 61–62, 65, 66–67, 193.
4. "The Defence Works of Singapore," CHUR 4/255/106–9.
5. CHUR 4/255, fos. 118–24, 131.
6. *SWW* 4:37, 40–41, 43 and *SWWUS* 4:41–42, 46, 49; cf. CHUR 4/255/208–11.
7. *SWW* 4:38, 43, 855–59 and *SWWUS* 4:42–44, 49, 871–74.
8. Later amended to "Australasian Anxieties" because some material on New Zealand was included.
9. *SWW* 4:4, 7–8, 11 and *SWWUS* 4:4–5, 8, 12–13; cf. CHUR 4/253.
10. *SWW* 4:47–52 and *SWWUS* 4:54–59.
11. *SWW* 4:138 and *SWWUS* 4:157; cf. David Day, *The Great Betrayal: Britain, Australia and the Onset of the Pacific War, 1939–1942* (North Ryde, New South Wales, 1988), pp. 235–36, 241–42.
12. Quoting in sequence *SWW* 4:136–39, 143, 16 and *SWWUS* 4:155–58, 162–63, 18.
13. CHUR 4/261/198–231; cf. CHUR 4/256/3.
14. CHUR 4/253/208 ("reproach"); CHUR 4/261, fos. 121,131 (Brook); Leisching to Brook, 28 June 1950, CAB 21/2179.
15. Attlee to Menzies, 29 June 1950, and Menzies to Attlee, 18 July 1950, PREM 8/1321. Menzies lunched at Hyde Park Gate on 21 July (CHUR 2/616).
16. *SWW* 4:83, 118 and *SWWUS* 4:95, 133.
17. *SWW* 4:146–51 and *SWWUS* 4:166–71; cf. CHUR 4/261, fos. 39–51, 62.
18. *SWW* 4:165–66 and *SWWUS* 4:188.
19. CHUR 4/12, fos. 80, 130.
20. See drafts in CHUR 4/266.
21. Cf. CHUR 4/300C, fos. 492–93, 523.
22. CHUR 4/20B/366–67.
23. H. R. Trevor-Roper, ed., *Hitler's Table Talk, 1941–1944* (Oxford, 1988), pp. 573–74; cf. *SWW* 4:59 and *SWWUS* 4:67.
24. *SWW* 4:19, 30, 275 and *SWWUS* 4:21, 34, 308. Although Churchill may have wanted to give Auchinleck an ultimatum, the War Cabinet minute for 8 May 1942 states clearly: "The telegram should not give General Auchinleck a positive order, but should make it clear that the War Cabinet were prepared to assume full responsibility for the consequences if an attack took place and was not successful" (CAB 65/30/39, WM 59 [42] CA). Moreover, this was not a contest between the whole of Whitehall and one stiff-necked general: the Auk was backed by the full Middle East Defence Committee in Cairo, chaired by Richard Casey, which argued that the loss of Malta would not imperil North Africa, whereas the loss of Egypt would make Malta untenable. See also J. R. M. Butler, *Grand Strategy* (London, 1964), 3.2:459–61. This official history, pub-

lished in 1964, gives a more balanced view of the controversy without explicitly criticizing Churchill's account.

25. CHUR 4/269/102.

26. SWW 4:329, 378, 381 ("May"), 385 and SWWUS 4:369, 420–21, 423, 427; cf. CHUR 4/276/87.

27. CHUR 4/276, fos. 15, 67, 115, 123; cf. SWW 4:378 and SWWUS 4:420–21.

28. SWW 4:332, 343 and SWWUS 4:371, 383.

29. SWW 4:371–72 and SWWUS 4:413–14; cf. CHUR 4/276/126–29.

30. Bernard Fergusson, ed., The Business of War: The War Narrative of Major-General Sir John Kennedy (London, 1957), pp. 242–44.

31. Michael Carver, Tobruk (London, 1964), p. 21; for examples of WSC's terminology, see SWW 4:333, 374, 375 and SWWUS 4:372, 415, 417.

32. SWW 4:30–31 and SWWUS 4:34–35; CHUR 4/254, fos. 20, 31, 200–205. Auchinleck's dispatch "Operations in the Middle East from 1 November 1941 to 15 August 1942" was printed as a supplement to The London Gazette, 15 Jan. 1948, no 38177. A copy is in Churchill's files, sent by Pownall in Nov. 1948 (CHUR 4/254/195).

33. CHUR 4/297/379–93.

34. Cf. CHUR 4/297/123–31.

35. Auchinleck, "Operations in the Middle East," p. 309; cf. Lambert to Brook, 31 March 1950, CAB 21/2179. The Cabinet Secretary chose, however, to convey the War Office comments to Churchill in noncommittal form: "My own feeling was that Auchinleck's preoccupation with the northern front was brought out quite clearly in these Chapters. And his anxieties were proved by the event to have been excessive" (CHUR 4/254/81).

36. SWW 4:329 and SWWUS 4:368–69; cf. Jacob diary, 4 Aug. 1942, and the 1949–1950 correspondence in JACB 4/1 (CAC).

37. SWW 4:439, 444–45, 514–15 (emphasis added) and SWWUS 4:487–88, 494–95, 573–74.

38. The signals authorities picked up, for instance, on a telegram from Churchill to Auchinleck on 8 May 1942 warning that "the enemy himself may be planning to attack you early in June, and is trying to be ready by then." SIS wanted "presumably" inserted before "trying"; in the event, Churchill cut everything after the comma without indicating the omission. CHUR 4/269/100; cf. SWW 4:329 and SWWUS 4:369.

39. See Hinsley 2, chaps. 21–23.

40. CAB 65/31, WM 101 (42) 1-CA.

41. Alanbrooke, pp. 293–94.

42. CHUR 4/280/329; cf. SWW 4:413, SWWUS 4:457, and Alanbrooke, p. 294.

43. SWW 4:421 and SWWUS 4:467.

44. The phrase "at once impeccable but bleak" appears in Churchill's 1948 dictation. Deakin reversed the order of adjectives in the Feb. 1950 revision. See CHUR 4/278, fos. 26, 267.

45. CAB 65/31, WM 106 (42) 1 and WM 108 (42) 1, both CA. See also the original notes, much fuller, taken by Lawrence Burgis from Cabinet and Defence Committee meetings on 7 Aug. 1942 in BRGS 2/12 and 2/13 (CAC).

46. Cf. SWW 4:418–19 and SWWUS 4:462–63; CHUR 4/278/43.

47. SWW 4:465–66, 463 and SWWUS 4:518–20, 515.

48. Correlli Barnett, The Desert Generals, 2d ed. (London, 1983), pp. 300–301; Nigel Hamilton, Monty: The Field Marshal, 1944–1976 (London, 1986), pp. 890–97. For Brooke's insertion, see CHUR 4/280/329–30.

49. SWW 4:469, 526–27, 541 and SWWUS 4:523, 586–87, 602; cf. CHUR 4/284/128–30, and Francis de Guingand, *Operation Victory* (London, 1947), pp. 157–58.

50. There survives, however, an acute sentence in Churchill's telegram to Alexander on 23 September 1942, where he noted the magnitude of the enemy's defenses and suggested it was "the infantry who will have to clear the way for the tanks" and not the other way around. With his erratic but keen intuition, Churchill had put his finger on the weakness of Monty's initial plan for a tank-led breakthrough. SWW 4:528 and SWWUS 4:588; see also de Guingand, *Operation Victory*, chap. 8.

51. SWW 4:539–41 and SWWUS 4:602–3; cf. CHUR 4/284/18–21. At the fourth Alamein reunion in October 1949, Churchill declared: "Up till Alamein we survived. After Alamein we conquered." See Gilbert 8:492.

52. Figures from SWW 4:538–41 and SWWUS 4:601–3; Richard Overy, *Russia's War* (London, 1998), p. 185.

53. SWW 4:522–25, 637–38 and SWWUS 4:582–85, 712–13; cf. CHUR 4/283, fos. 49, 66–68, and CHUR 4/289, fos. 23–25, 38–39.

54. Reves's letters of 22 Aug. 1949 and [20?] July 1950 are in CHUR 4/12, fos. 129–37, 77–85. The former is published in *C-Reves*, pp. 300–304.

CHAPTER 20: SECOND FRONT: WHEN, WHERE, AND HOW?

1. SWW 4:698, 741 and SWWUS 4:780, 829.

2. CHUR 4/270/20. In this deleted material, he also observed that "all preparations for a speedy attack across the Channel in 1942, whether used or not, would be valid and stimulating to the main operation in 1943." See SWW 4:288–91 and SWWUS 4:322–25 for what he calls "my own view" on the Second Front issue, "which was persistent."

3. SWW 4:290 and SWWUS 4:324; cf. CHUR 4/270/20. By the time Ismay published his own memoirs in 1960, he felt that "it would have obviated future misunderstandings if the British had expressed their views more frankly" in April 1942. *The Memoirs of General the Lord Ismay* (London, 1960), p. 249.

4. SWW 4:290, 582–84 and SWWUS 4:324–25, 650–52; cf. CHUR 4/272/78.

5. SWW 4:316–18 and SWWUS 4:353–55.

6. SWW 4:345, 432 and SWWUS 4:385, 480; COS (42) 190 (0), PREM 3/333/2.

7. SWW 4:317, 783 and SWWUS 4:354, 887; cf. COS (42) 190 (0), para. 12.

8. SWW 4:289–90, 316 ("map") and SWWUS 4:323–25, 350. Cf. Tuvia Ben-Moshe, *Churchill: Strategy and History* (Boulder, Colo., 1992), chap. 7.

9. SWW 4:305, 430 and SWWUS 4:342, 478; cf. CHUR 4/271/76.

10. SWW 4:560, 564 and SWWUS 4:623, 628; cf. CHUR 4/285/41.

11. For the full text of these minutes, see CHUR 4/287, fos. 83, 97–99; cf. SWW 4:582, 587–91 and SWWUS 4:649, 655–58. On the intelligence, see Hinsley 2:464–67, 487–89. The Allies were similarly wrong-footed by Hitler's sudden decision in October 1943 to fight for Rome rather than concede most of Italy.

12. SWW 4:284, 288 and SWWUS 4:318, 322. Of the three Chiefs of Staff, Brooke and Pound felt the Germany First deployments agreed in Washington in December now required some amendment. Only Portal, Chief of the Air Staff, considered that the Washington agreement remained "in every respect a correct statement of the principles which should govern British-American strategy." See CAB 80/61, COS (42) 71 (0).

13. *SWW* 4:396–97 and *SWWUS* 4:439–41; cf. CHUR 4/277, fos. 7–8, 283–84. Churchill had already edited out of this telegram Dill's statement that both he and Admiral Sir Andrew Cunningham were sure the Joint Chiefs considered the Pacific the only alternative to an invasion of France.

14. *SWW* 4:584–85 and *SWWUS* 4:652–53; cf. Mark A. Stoler, *Allies and Adversaries: The Joint Chiefs of Staff, the Grand Alliance, and U.S. Strategy in World War II* (Chapel Hill, N.C., 2000), chap. 5.

15. CHUR 4/277/7.

16. *SWW* 4:176 and *SWWUS* 4:199; cf. Kelly on CHUR 4/263/81.

17. *SWW* 4:782 and *SWWUS* 4:886; CHUR 4/263, fos. 13–15, 25–27, 38. For the two letters, see *C-R* 1:648–50 and 2:44–45. The complicated story is disentangled in Kevin Smith, *Conflict over Convoys: Anglo-American Logistics Diplomacy in the Second World War* (Cambridge, 1996).

18. For "other measures," see *SWW* 4:114 and *SWWUS* 4:130; the drafts are in CHUR 4/259. For Allen's reliance on Morison and his concern that Churchill acknowledge this, see CHUR 4/259, fos. 97, 100, 103.

19. CHUR 4/18A/2–4; CHUR 4/300C/492–93.

20. CHUR 4/300C/492.

21. See Ismay papers, 2/3, esp. docs. 159, 161 and 228 (KCL).

22. *SWW* 4:165 (Wavell), 323 (Cologne) and *SWWUS* 4:187, 360–61; cf. *C-Reves*, p. 301.

23. Brian P. Farrell, *The Basis and Making of British Grand Strategy, 1940–1943: Was There a Plan?* 2 vols. (Lampeter, Wales, 1998), 1:381.

24. *SWW* 4:165 (Wavell), 495–97 (Trenchard), 783 (bombing) and *SWWUS* 4:187, 551–54, 887.

25. Removed from "Moscow: The First Meeting" when Deakin paraphrased the transcript into smooth narrative in April 1950. CHUR 4/279/245; cf. *SWW* 4:432 and *SWWUS* 4:480.

26. *SWW* 4:587, 634 ("shatter"), 741 (Rome) and *SWWUS* 4:654, 708, 828–29; cf. CHUR 4/287/107 ("paralyse").

27. *SWW* 4:687, 688, 692 and *SWWUS* 4:769, 770, 775. Pownall's Feb. 1950 draft is in CHUR 4/292/184–99.

28. The memo to Attlee is in PREM 3/499/9. It appears in the draft appendixes at, e.g., CHUR 4/297/190–92. On why it was deleted, see chapter 21, below. The "handmaid" quotation is from para. 15.

29. WSC to Attlee, 29 July 1942, para. 10, PREM 3/499/9.

30. *SWW* 4:781–84 and *SWWUS* 4:885–88, citing paras. 2 and 6. See generally David Reynolds, "Churchill the Appeaser? Between Hitler, Roosevelt and Stalin in World War II," in Michael Dockrill and Brian McKercher, eds., *Diplomacy and World Power: Studies in British Foreign Policy, 1890–1950* (Cambridge, 1996), esp. pp. 211–16.

31. Brian P. Farrell, "Symbol of Paradox: The Casablanca Conference, 1943," *Canadian Journal of History* 28 (1993): 35–37.

32. *SWW* 4:616–19 and *SWWUS* 4:688–91. See also Brook to WSC, 13 April 1950, CAB 21/3748; Ismay papers, 2/3/158/2a-b; and CHUR 4/300C/399 (Deakin). Reconstructing the chapter "The Casablanca Conference" is difficult because, most unusually, no file of drafts survives in WSC's papers.

33. *SWW* 4:613–16 and *SWWUS* 4:684–88. WSC's remarks in the Commons on 21 July and 17 Nov. 1949 are in *Speeches* 7:7826–31, 7888–90, but see also CHUR

5/26A/35–39 (which contains a fuller version) and CHUR 5/28A/244–50. A copy of Deakin's note of 17 Nov. 1949 is in CHUR 4/57/275–81.

CHAPTER 21: FIGHTING WITH ALLIES—AND COLLEAGUES

1. E.g., Alanbrooke, p. 680, 1 April 1945.
2. *SWW* 4:411, 426 and *SWWUS* 4:455–56, 473; Gilbert 7:217.
3. *SWW* 4:428–29, 437 and *SWWUS* 4:476–77, 485; cf. CHUR 4/279, fos. 157, 203; Cadogan, p. 471.
4. *SWW* 4:429–41 and *SWWUS* 4:476–91; Moran, chap. 7.
5. *SWW* 4:445–49 and *SWWUS* 4:495–99; A. H. Birse, *Memoirs of an Interpreter* (London, 1967), p. 103.
6. *SWW* 4:450 and *SWWUS* 4:501. In general, see Graham Ross, "Operation Bracelet: Churchill in Moscow, 1942," in D. N. Dilks, ed., *Retreat from Power: Studies in Britain's Foreign Policy of the Twentieth Century* (London, 1981), 1:101–19, and Martin H. Folly, *Churchill, Whitehall and the Soviet Union, 1940–1945* (London, 2000), chap. 4.
7. *SWW* 4:522 and *SWWUS* 4:582.
8. CHUR 4/291/228–36. On British handling of Katyn at the time, see P. M. H. Bell, *John Bull and the Bear: British Public Opinion, Foreign Policy and the Soviet Union, 1941–1945* (London, 1990), chap. 4.
9. *SWW* 4:678–81 and *SWWUS* 4:757–60; CHUR 4/291/113–48, quoting Deakin at fo. 137; also CHUR 4/300C/420. In fairness to Churchill, it should be noted that successive British governments, for diplomatic reasons, maintained the fiction of a "not proven" verdict until the Russians finally admitted Stalin's guilt in 1992. See text and documents in Foreign and Commonwealth Office Historians, *Katyn: British Reactions to the Katyn Massacre* (London, 2003).
10. François Kersaudy, *Churchill and de Gaulle* (London, 1981), p. 231.
11. *SWW* 4:565–80 and *SWWUS* 4:629–47.
12. *SWW* 4:563, 580 and *SWWUS* 4:628, 646–47; cf. CHUR 4/285, fos. 51, 116, 151–56.
13. *SWW* 4:579–80 and *SWWUS* 4:645–47; CHUR 4/286, fos. 64, 76; William D. Leahy, *I Was There* (New York, 1950), pp. 160, 171.
14. Leahy, *I Was There*, pp. 170–71; cf. Anthony Cave Brown, *The Secret Servant: The Life of Sir Stewart Menzies, Churchill's Spymaster* (London, 1988), pp. 447–53; David Stafford, *Churchill and Secret Service* (New York, 1997), pp. 249–52.
15. John Harvey, ed., *The War Diaries of Oliver Harvey, 1941–1945* (London, 1978), pp. 192–93. For the 10 Dec. 1942 speech, see CHUR 9/156.
16. *SWW* 4:609–11 and *SWWUS* 4:680–82; CHUR 4/300C/532.
17. *SWW* 4:716 and *SWWUS* 4:801; cf. CHUR 4/293/163–65 and Elisabeth Barker, *Churchill and Eden at War* (London, 1978), chap. 5.
18. *SWW* 4:716 and *SWWUS* 4:801–2; cf. CHUR 4/294, fos. 9, 61–64, and CHUR 4/300D/695. For the Foreign Office's opinion on the de Gaulle passages, see Passant to Brook, 27 June 1950, CAB 21/2179.
19. *SWW* 4:180, 478 and *SWWUS* 4:203, 533.
20. See *C-R* 1:344–46, 356–58, 360, and David Reynolds, *The Creation of the Anglo-American Alliance, 1937–1941: A Study in Competitive Co-operation* (London, 1981), pp. 269–80. Some of the relevant telegrams were drawn to WSC's attention in Sept. 1947, and he marked them for inclusion in the memoirs. See CHUR 4/401/57–61.

21. CHUR 4/290, fos. 207, 314; SWW 4:655–59 and SWWUS 4:731–34; cf. David Reynolds, *Rich Relations: The American Occupation of Britain, 1942–1945* (London, 1995), pp. 327, 343.

22. CHUR 4/292/3.

23. SWW 4:619, 730 and SWWUS 4:691, 817. For the Macmillan quote, see *The Sunday Telegraph*, 9 Feb. 1964, p. 4.

24. SWW 4:336–37, 341–42, 723 and SWWUS 4:374–75, 379–81, 809; CHUR 4/294/17; cf. Margaret Gowing, *Britain and Atomic Energy, 1939–1945* (London, 1964), p. 145n1. The internal Cabinet Office history of the bomb project was also unable to find any confirmatory material and relied on Churchill's memoirs. See John Ehrman, *The Atomic Bomb: An Account of British Policy in the Second World War* (Cabinet Office, 1953), p. 46, in CAB 101/45.

25. CHUR 4/19/319–20, 4/274/195.

26. Ismay papers, 2/3, docs. 200, 206, 207 (KCL); SWW 4:339–40 and SWWUS 4:377–79; cf. Martin J. Sherwin, *A World Destroyed: The Atomic Bomb and the Grand Alliance* (New York, 1977), p. 78.

27. SWW 4:504 and SWWUS 4:561–62. Both memos are in PREM 4/100/7. Churchill had used the "Jugged Hare" reference in 1923 in WC, 1:140–41, quoting a 1912 letter from his First Sea Lord, Admiral Fisher.

28. SWW 4:717–22 and SWWUS 4:802–6; cf. CHUR 4/294/10 on U.S. troops. The memo was printed for the Cabinet as WP (43) 233, CAB 66/37.

29. SWW 4:712–13, 717 and SWWUS 4:797, 802; cf. CHUR 4/293/169.

30. SWW 4:504 and SWWUS 4:562; WSC, *The End of the Beginning* (London, 1943), pp. 214–15. On the use for a time of "End of the Beginning" as a possible book title, see chapter 18, above.

31. SWW 4:185–90, 193–95 and SWWUS 4:208–14, 217–21; cf. PREM 4/48/9, fos. 743–45.

32. SWW 4:181–82, 196 and SWWUS 4:204–5, 221; cf. CHUR 4/264, fos. 1, 15, 183, 261.

33. SWW 4:660–61 and SWWUS 4:736–37.

34. SWW 4:53–54, 351–52 and SWWUS 60–61, 391–92.

35. Bridges to Brook, 5 Oct. 1949, CAB 21/3748.

36. In his July 1949 "Notes," Churchill was more candid, saying he "greatly regretted having weakened" to the press and public criticism in 1942. In retrospect, he writes, "I believe I was strong enough to spit in their faces. This was certainly not my Finest Hour." CHUR 4/256, fos. 2, 4.

37. Kevin Jefferys, *The Churchill Coalition and Wartime Politics, 1940–1945*, 2d ed. (Manchester, 1995), pp. 89–94, quoting Butler on p. 94.

38. SWW 4:184, 192 and SWWUS 4:208, 217. On the Cripps mission, see R. J. Moore, *Churchill, Cripps and India, 1939–1945* (Oxford, 1979), chaps. 3–5, quoting Attlee on p. 56.

39. SWW 4:497, 501, 502 and SWWUS 4:554, 558, 560.

40. CHUR 4/24A, fos. 35–38, 42, 66 (WSC) and CHUR 4/282/60–69; cf. SWW 4:497–503 and SWWUS 4:554–60.

41. CHUR 4/297B/163–64 and CHUR 4/297C, fos. 420 (Brook), 454–56.

42. Peter Clarke, *The Cripps Version: The Life of Sir Stafford Cripps, 1889–1952* (London, 2002), pp. 361–62.

43. CHUR 4/285/100.

44. *SWW* 4:861–62 and *SWWUS* 4:958–60; CHUR 4/297D/116–18; cf. ATLE 2/2/7–9 (CAC). See also Jefferys, *Churchill Coalition*, pp. 112–22.

45. *SWW* 4:78 and *SWWUS* 4:89.

46. *SWW* 4:78 ("compliance"), 80 ("resolved"), 498–99, 503 ("brooding") and *SWWUS* 4:89, 91, 555–56, 560.

47. *SWW* 4:493–94 and *SWWUS* 4:549–50; Clarke, *Cripps Version*, pt. 4, esp. pp. 365, 370. Churchill did not include in his published memoirs a draft passage, probably originating from Deakin, saying that in February 1942 "Goebbels in his diary records with relish the possibility of a combination between Sir Stafford Cripps and Mr Hore-Belisha [the embittered former Secretary of State for War and now a leading critic] to replace the administration of the war-mongering and incompetent Churchill." See CHUR 4/300/245.

48. R. A. Butler papers, G14/59; Harvey, ed., *War Diaries*, p. 165.

49. *SWW* 4:78 and *SWWUS* 4:89.

50. The letters and minutes of 4–8 March cited below are from PREM 3/119/6.

51. Pound to WSC, 7 March 1942, PREM 3/119/6, fos. 8–10.

52. WSC to Pound, 8 March, PREM 3/119/6, fos. 5–7.

53. Alanbrooke, p. 226; "The Naval Memoirs of Admiral J. H. Godfrey," TS. (1965) 5/2, pp. 308–12, GDFY 1/7 (CAC), quoting Cunningham to Roskill, 17 May 1956, on Pound's fears in spring 1942. Like Brooke, Admiral Godfrey concluded in retrospect that Pound's drowsiness was an early sign of the brain tumor that proved fatal in October 1943.

54. Brook overlooked a suggestive line in Churchill's reply asking Cripps not to "underrate the wisdom, knowledge, and precision of mind of the First Sea Lord." *SWW* 4:501 and *SWWUS* 4:558

55. After referring to "Dickie's" recent raid on St. Nazaire, he told FDR "for your personal and secret eye" about Mountbatten's promotion in rank and membership on the COS Committee. *SWW* 4:178 and *SWWUS* 4:202. For limited secondary accounts see Gilbert 7:71–72, and Stephen Roskill, *Churchill and the Admirals* (London, 1977), pp. 143 and 325, note 26. The fullest account is in Philip Ziegler, *Mountbatten: The Official Biography* (London, 1985), pp. 168–70.

56. *SWW* 4:234–38 and *SWWUS* 4:262–66.

57. WSC to 1st Lord and 1st Sea Lord, 26 July 1942, PREM 3/393/14, fo. 1035; WM 101 (42) 1 CA, CAB 65/31. The official naval historian, writing in 1956, noted the Cabinet minute and suggested that the account in *The Hinge of Fate* "seems therefore to show a lapse in the Prime Minister's memory." See S. W. Roskill, *The War at Sea, 1939–1945*, vol. 2 (London, 1956), p. 144.

58. CHUR 4/267, fos. 182, 206. Allen's recollections are quoted in David Irving, *The Destruction of Convoy PQ 17* (London, 1964), p. 127.

59. *SWW* 4:457–59 and *SWWUS* 4:509–11.

60. WSC memo, 20 March 1942, p. 4, in Ismay papers, 2/3/247; CHUR 4/280, fos. 292–95, 320. The original 1942 minutes are in PREM 3/256.

61. CHUR 4/25A/21–23.

62. Ismay papers, 2/3/258.

63. Ismay papers, 2/3/260.

64. CHUR 4/280/334–37.

65. Ismay papers, 2/3/261/1.

66. CHUR 4/17A/68; CHUR 4/280, fos. 9–18, 307–10, 334–37.
67. CHUR 4/280/158–59 (Ismay), and Brook to WSC, 29 July 1950, CAB 21/3748.
68. For the recent debate, see esp. Brian Loring Villa, *Unauthorized Action: Mountbatten and the Dieppe Raid* (Toronto, 1990); Peter J. Henshaw, "The British Chiefs of Staff Committee and the Preparation of the Dieppe Raid, March–August 1942: Did Mountbatten Really Evade the Committee's Authority?" *War in History* 1 (1994): 197–214; and Brian Loring Villa and Peter J. Henshaw, "The Dieppe Raid Debate," *Canadian Historical Review* 79 (1998): 304–15.

CHAPTER 22: "THE BEST OF WINNIE'S MEMOIRS"

1. *The Washington Post*, 26 Nov. 1950, copy in CHWL/PE Box 5, 80b.
2. *DT*, 10 Oct. 1950, pp. 1, 4; *NYT*, 10 Oct. 1950, pp. 1, 22, 30, 33.
3. *Life*, 23 Oct. 1950, p. 91, and 30 Oct., p. 89.
4. CHUR 4/14, fos. 168–70, 218–21; cf. Kelly to Nina Holton, 27 Sept. 1950, HM 318/1: Hinge, Gen. Corr.
5. *NYT*, *NYHT*, books sections, 26 Nov. 1950; *St. Louis Post-Dispatch*, 10 Dec. 1950. All in CHWL, box 5, PE/80b, which is also the source for the other American reviews cited below.
6. *The Washington Post*, 26 Nov. 1950; *The Nation*, 14 Dec. 1950; *Brooklyn Eagle*, 24 Dec. 1950; *The New Republic*, 25 Dec. 1950.
7. *The Saturday Review of Literature*, 25 Nov. 1950; *Chicago Tribune* and *The Washington Post*, 26 Nov. 1950; *The Milwaukee Journal*, 17 Dec. 1950.
8. *The Saturday Review of Literature*, 25 Nov. 1950; *NYT*, 27 Nov. 1950; *Los Angeles Times*, 10 Dec. 1950.
9. *The Washington Post* and Cleveland *Plain Dealer*, both 26 Nov. 1950.
10. *Atlantic Monthly*, Jan. 1951, pp. 71–73.
11. CHUR 4/24, fos. 413, 433, 458; *Evening Standard*, 5 July 1951.
12. *DT*, 3 Aug. 1951, p. 4; *Daily Mail*, 3 Aug. 1951, p. 2; *News Chronicle*, 31 Aug. 1951, p. 2. For the WMG campaign (a deliberate echo of "Balfour Must Go" in 1911), see Stuart Ball, ed., *Parliament and Politics in the Age of Churchill and Attlee: The Headlam Diaries, 1935–1951* (Cambridge, 1999), p. 623.
13. *The Manchester Guardian*, 3 Aug. 1951, p. 6.
14. *TLS*, 3 Aug. 1951, pp. 477–79; *The Times*, 3 Aug. 1951, p. 5. The *TLS* reviewer was again Alfred Ryan.
15. *The Listener*, 9 Aug. 1951, p. 235; cf. TS. 27 July 1951, in Liddell Hart papers, LH 10/1951/14 (KCL).
16. WLA, "This Yapping at Mr. Churchill," *The Yorkshire Post*, 14 Aug. 1951.
17. *New Statesman and Nation*, 4 Aug. 1951, p. 132.
18. *NYT*, 17 Oct. 1950, pp. 1, 33; Morison to Beck, 19 Oct. 1950, Samuel Eliot Morison papers, Harvard University Archives (Cambridge, Mass.), HUG(FP) 33.15, box 2.
19. CHUR 4/14/160–67 and CHUR 4/57/215.
20. Sydney *Sunday Telegraph*, 22 Oct. 1950, pp. 25–36; *The Herald*, 23 Oct. 1950 and 13 Nov. 1950, all in NAA A5954, 2054/2.
21. See papers in CHUR 4/253, esp. fos. 17–23; SWW 4:4 and SWWUS 4:4.
22. SWW 4:661 and SWWUS 4:736–37; *The Times*, 27 Sept. 1951, p. 3; CHUR 4/57/100–17 and CHUR 4/298/22–23 (Ismay and Kelly).
23. CHUR 4/57/4–5; SWW 4:659 and SWWUS 4:735.

24. CHUR 4/57, fos. 15–29, 118–21, 226–38, 271–73, 292–308, quoting WSC on 228.
25. *SWW* 4:416, 465 and *SWWUS* 4:461, 518; CHUR 4/58/5–8.
26. CHUR 4/58, fos. 3 (legal opinion), 84, 122–23.
27. Acheson to Brook, note, 16 June 1953, annex to CAB 21/2178 (PRO).
28. E.g., Pownall comments, 19 May 1953, CHUR 4/58/136–42, and Jacob to PM, 16 June 1953, CAB 21/2178 annex.
29. CHUR 4/58, fos. 142 (WSC) and 256 (Shawcross).
30. CHUR 4/58, fos. 159, 164–65 (Shawcross) and 294 (WSC).
31. CHUR 4/58/172. For Monty's efforts to solicit damning character references on O'Gowan, see Montgomery papers, BLM 57 (IWM).
32. Liddell Hart papers, LH 1/242, docs. 317–19.
33. *The Irish Press*, 2 July 1954, copy in CHUR 4/58/351. See also draft of 1 Feb. 1954 in CHUR 4/58/269. WSC's account of the July battle is in *SWW* 4:388–89 and *SWWUS* 4:431; cf. CHUR 4/276, fos. 48, 109, 168–70.
34. CHUR 4/58/275.
35. "Agreed Footnote," CHUR 4/58/313; cf. Lavinia Greacen, *Chink: A Biography* (London, 1989), p. 309.
36. Cf. Shawcross to Burrows, 14 April and 10 June 1954, in WCHL 8/94 (CAC).
37. *Irish Times*, 2 July 1954, and *The Times*, 3 July 1954, copies in CHUR 4/58, fos. 350, 346; also Shawcross to WSC, 3 July 1954, in CHUR 4/58/317.
38. A requirement that seems to have been circumvented on the grounds that the publishers brought out only new "impressions" and not new "editions."
39. *SWW* 4:541 and *SWWUS* 4:603; WSC to Shawcross, 7 Feb. 1954, CHUR 4/58/262.

V | CLOSING THE RING, 1943–1944, 1949–1952

CHAPTER 23: DEADLINES

1. The titles were again largely prompted by Emery Reves, who in Aug. 1951 urged Churchill to replace "The Supreme Adventure" with the more concrete "Teheran to Normandy." See *C-Reves*, pp. 323–24; CHUR 4/14A, fos. 109, 119, 123–24.
2. In the preface, he defended himself against the complaint that he failed in other volumes to print replies, pleading the modesty of his aim—"a contribution to history from the standpoint of the British Prime Minister and Minister of Defence"—and the limitations of space. See *SWW* 5:ix–x and *SWWUS* 5:vi.
3. Colville, p. 553.
4. WSC to Brook, 18 Aug. 1951, and Brook to WSC, 22 Aug. 1951, CAB 21/2180.
5. CHUR 4/326/36–54.
6. *Life*, 8 Oct. 1951, p. 110; *SWWUS* 5:82, 6:161; *SWW* 6:142. See also HM 318/1: Churchill-Laughlin misc. corr, 1951–3, and CHUR 4/14/47–57. Churchill's original version included a sentence about "Trouble about Hopkins and his new wife drunk in the White House, etc.," plus an explanation of the "variegated activities" that broke even his spirit—"dominating the President, comprehending the war, having a new marriage on blood transfusions." See CHUR 4/305/303.
7. CHUR 4/15/427 (Graebner).
8. Pownall to Ismay, 14 Jan. 1951, Ismay papers, 2/3/268 (KCL).
9. CHUR 4/301, fos. 144, 159; CHUR 4/25A/18 (to Syndicate); CHUR 4/24A/77 (to Brook).

10. CHUR 4/61/120–25, quoting Kelly on fo. 122; cf. SWW 3:585 and SWWUS 3:659.

11. CHUR 4/42/223; CHUR 4/41B/276; Gilbert 8:628, 630.

12. See CHUR 1/65/261–78, quoting from fo. 261. Some of the exchanges are printed in Gilbert 8:601–3.

13. CHUR 4/14A, fos. 117, 134. See also "Closing the Ring" files in HM 318/1 and 318/4. For Longwell's opinions, see CHUR 4/15/28–30.

14. CHUR 4/14A/113–17; also CHUR 4/342/281–82, CHUR 4/15/416–18.

15. Minahan to Laughlin, 24 July 1951, HM 318/4: Laughlin, 1951. This letter amended the figures Laughlin sent to WSC on 26 July 1951 (CHUR 4/14/113–16). The figure for Houghton Mifflin sales of volume 3 is less than that stated by Reves in July 1950 (see chapter 18, above), possibly because of returns from booksellers.

16. Flower to WSC, 7 June 1951, CHUR 4/24/458, as reproduced in the table in the text.

17. Reves to WSC, 2 Aug. 1951, in C-Reves, pp. 318–19.

18. Gilbert 8:628.

19. WSC to Graebner, n.d., CHUR 1/86: "Time & Life"; CHUR 4/13/46–47 (Camrose).

20. See CHUR 1/86: "Time & Life."

21. CHUR 4/342/354–57.

22. Dates of dispatch reconstructed from the cables in CHUR 4/14A/61–110. See also CHUR 4/331, 4/332.

23. CHUR 4/14A/62–63.

24. See Moran, pp. 365–66.

25. SWW 5:373, 389 and SWWUS 5:421, 440; cf. CHUR 4/325, fos. 92, 165, and 215 and CHUR 4/326/79. Moran's concern at the time about Churchill's heart is evident from comments he made in Dec. 1943 and March 1944. See Moran, chap. 18, esp. p. 176; Alanbrooke, p. 531.

26. Moran, p. 808. What follows draws on the biography by Richard Lovell, *Churchill's Doctor: A Biography of Lord Moran* (London, 1992); the introduction by his son John, the present Lord Moran, to an updated edition of the wartime "diaries" — Lord Moran, *Churchill at War, 1940–1945* (London, 2002), pp. xv–xxix; and those parts of the Moran papers (Wellcome Institute for the History of Medicine, London) that have been made available.

27. Lovell, *Churchill's Doctor*, p. 327. For contacts with publishers, see Moran papers, J 4/1.

28. Lovell, *Churchill's Doctor*, pp. 315–16. Moran's conviction that he was descended from the celebrated eighteenth-century essayist was an erroneous but revealing conceit.

CHAPTER 24: CHURCHILL AND
"THE MEDITERRANEAN STRATEGY"

1. SWW 5:226 and SWWUS 5:254; cf. CHUR 4/317/128.

2. Hanson W. Baldwin, *Great Mistakes of the War* (New York, 1950). WSC's annotations appear on pp. 31–44 of a copy of the book that he forwarded to Deakin on 3 April 1950. I am indebted to Sir William Deakin for showing this to me. See also WSC to Ismay, 17 June 1949, in which he dismisses claims that he favored "the large-scale invasion of the Balkans" as "absolutely without foundation" (Ismay papers, 2/3/160 [KCL]).

3. CHUR 4/303/173; Dwight D. Eisenhower, *Crusade in Europe* (Garden City, N.Y., 1948), p. 160; SWW 5:223 and SWWUS 5:251.

4. *SWW* 5:189 and *SWWUS* 5:213; cf. *C-R* 2:503 and Hinsley 3.1:103, 114–17, 173.
5. This last is described at length in *SWW* 4:623–37 and *SWWUS* 4:696–712.
6. *SWW* 5:584 and *SWWUS* 5:663; cf. Hinsley 3.1:43–46 and Noel Annan, *Changing Enemies: The Defeat and Regeneration of Germany* (London, 1995), pp. 66–67, 70–76, 84.
7. CHAR 20/104/22–23.
8. CHUR 4/336/309–10.
9. *SWW* 5:69–70, 75 and *SWWUS* 5:77, 84; cf. Michael Howard, *Grand Strategy*, vol. 4 (London, 1972), pp. 565–71. The evidence of Anglo-American arguments was readily to hand in Churchill's files, which contained a 200-page set of the British COS minutes for meetings en route to and from Quebec. See CHUR 4/306/315.
10. *SWW* 5:116 and *SWWUS* 5:130–31.
11. *SWW* 5:193, 199–200 and *SWWUS* 5:218, 224–25; cf. CHUR 4/313, fos. 5, 41.
12. Lambert to Brook, 27 March 1951, CAB 21/2180; CHUR 4/342/210; cf. CHUR 4/313, fos. 131, 139.
13. Alanbrooke, pp. 458–59.
14. PREM 3/344/1, fo. 20.
15. PREM 3/344/2, fos. 165–69.
16. CAB 79/66/151–54, COS 254 (43) 4.
17. *SWW* 5:254–55 and *SWWUS* 5:285–87. It was with reference to this telegram that Churchill originally drafted the three-point admonition to his readers, printed at the head of this chapter—see CHUR 4/317/128.
18. *SWW* 5:254–56, 276–79 and *SWWUS* 5:285–88, 310–14.
19. *SWW* 5:256, 276–79 and *SWWUS* 5:288, 310–14; CAB 79/66/152.
20. Cadogan, p. 571.
21. *SWW* 5:216–20, 257–58 and *SWWUS* 5:243–47, 289. The original is in PREM 3/344/2, fos. 151–56. Eisenhower's part 4 is printed in *The Papers of Dwight David Eisenhower: The War Years*, vol. 3 (Baltimore, 1970), p. 1529.
22. *SWW* 5:257–58 and *SWWUS* 5:289; PREM 3/344/2, fos. 143, 134–38, 148–49 and CHAR 20/122/44–47; comments on chap. 15 enclosed with Brook to WSC, 31 March 1951, CAB 21/2180.
23. See Henry L. Stimson, diary, 28–29 Oct. and 4 Nov. 1943 (Sterling Library, Yale Univ., New Haven, Conn.). Although American outrage was not conveyed directly to Churchill, British representatives in Washington were probably told. On 30 October, Churchill received a cable from Ambassador Halifax, who had seen FDR and Hopkins the previous day, telling Churchill that he and Dill (a confidant of Marshall) were both struck by "the misgivings entertained about your real intentions about 'Overlord.'" This telegram was printed for a January 1951 draft of "Advent of a Triple Meeting" (CHUR 4/318/112) but does not appear in the final version.
24. *SWW* 5:291 and *SWWUS* 5:329; WSC, note of 29 Nov. 1943, PREM 3/136/6, fo. 5. This was apparently dictated for the historical record. Churchill added by hand: "It is a necessary link in the story." The drafts are in the same file.
25. *SWW* 5:291–94 and *SWWUS* 5:329–33; cf. CHUR 4/319/248–50.
26. Henry L. Stimson and McGeorge Bundy, *On Active Service in Peace and War* (New York, 1948), chap. 17, quoting p. 448; William D. Leahy, *I Was There* (London, 1950), p. 247; *SWW* 5:303–6 and *SWWUS* 5:344–46.
27. *SWW* 5:367–69, 373 and *SWWUS* 5:415–17, 422; CHUR 4/317/129–30.
28. *SWW* 5:322, 370 and *SWWUS* 5:365, 418; Sherwood, pp. 802–3.

29. *SWW* 5:76, 267 and *SWWUS* 5:85, 300–301.

30. *SWW* 5:267–72, 296–300, 340, 369–70 and *SWWUS* 5:300–306, 335–40, 385, 418–19.

31. CHUR 4/201/157–61, 4/319/7.

32. PREM 3/336/1, fo. 137.

33. CHUR 4/313, fos. 42, 157. This paragraph, deleted in January 1951, echoes a similar comment made by WSC in Aug. 1946 when reading Field-Marshal "Jumbo" Wilson's dispatch on operations in the Middle East in 1943–1944: Eisenhower's attitude toward Rhodes "made me determined to have the Med[iterranea]n in British hands which I c[oul]d control" (CHAR 20/249/4). Churchill did briefly toy with the opposite point of view—"of course there is no doubt if we had kept Eisenhower in the Mediterranean we would have got far more from America than we did by placing the command under a British general"—but this was cut from a January 1951 typescript before it went to the printers. See CHUR 4/317/130.

34. See, for instance, the telegram he sent to Jumbo Wilson on 8 Feb. 1944 (not quoted in his memoirs): "While I do not wish to interfere with your direct communications to the Combined Chiefs of Staff, you are free if you wish to let me see privately beforehand what you propose to send. Such a message should come through 'C'"—the code name for Sir Stewart Menzies, head of the Secret Intelligence Service. Telegram T253/4, CHAR 20/156.

35. Ismay, note, n.d., CHUR 4/324/5; WSC, dictation, n.d., CHUR 4/342B/246–67; WSC note, 11 April 1950, CHUR 4/326/36–37; cf. *SWW* 5:370 and *SWWUS* 5:418–19.

36. *SWW* 5:374–76 and *SWWUS* 5:422–25; cf. PREM 3/336/1, fos. 81, 75, 68–69.

37. Brook to WSC, 16 April 1951, CAB 21/2180.

38. CHUR 4/306/312. For other criticism, also deleted, of the handling of the Italian collapse, see CHUR 4/304, fos. 174–75, 212, 379, 387.

39. *SWW* 5:370 and *SWWUS* 5:418. When asked by Robert Sherwood in August 1946 for comments on the issue of Overlord's commander, Churchill had been similarly tactful. He replied that when FDR indicated he could not spare Marshall, the appointment of Eisenhower "was most acceptable to His Majesty's Government and also to Mr. Churchill. Either of these great men was adequate to the task." Churchill added "most" in pen on the typescript. See CHUR 2/155/112.

40. CHUR 4/326/39.

41. My verdict is closer to that of Michael Howard, *The Mediterranean Strategy in the Second World War* (London, 1968), pp. 41–57, 71–73, than that of Tuvia Ben-Moshe, *Churchill: Strategy and History* (Boulder, Colo, 1992), pp. 245–56, 317–19, though I have benefited from both of these stimulating interpretations.

CHAPTER 25: THE TYRANNY OF OVERLORD

1. *SWW* 5:378–87, 424–26 and *SWWUS* 5:427–37, 479–81.

2. *SWW* 5:426–37 and *SWWUS* 5:481–94.

3. For the correspondence in February 1952, see CHUR 4/61/83–89. Chatting in August 1953, Churchill and Montgomery damned the inertia at Anzio as one of five "capital mistakes" committed by the Americans during the war. See Colville, p. 674.

4. Mark Clark, *Calculated Risk* (London, 1950), pp. 272–73, 291; Alexander's dispatch, "The Allied Armies in Italy from 3 September 1943, to 12 December 1944," supplement to *The London Gazette*, 12 June 1950, p. 2912; Carlo D'Este, *Fatal Decision:*

Anzio and the Battle for Rome (London, 1992), p. 405, quoting Penney. Subsequent scholarship, though critical of Lucas, has generally dismissed the idea that Rome could have been taken and held. The official British historian of the Mediterranean war wrote that "the operation, largely owing to Mr. Churchill's influence, was given quite an extraordinary degree of importance. It was fathered by wishful strategical thinking and was not made the subject of a searching tactical analysis." C. J. C. Molony, *The Mediterranean and the Middle East,* vol. 5 (London, 1973), p. 772. For similar judgments, see Hinsley 3.1:185.

5. Moran, p. 210; SWW 5:436–37 and *SWWUS* 5:493–94; cf. CHUR 4/326/42 (outline) and CHUR 4/327/136 (to Smuts).
6. SWW 5:126 and *SWWUS* 5:142; CHUR 4/309/133; cf. CHUR 4/308/155.
7. Moran, p. 191; CHUR 4/325/189.
8. SWW 5:393, 443, 514–15 and *SWWUS* 5:444, 500, 582–83; cf. CHUR 4/326/40.
9. SWW 5:521, 542–43 and *SWWUS* 5:590, 615. Churchill added the italics for additional emphasis in 1951. See also Dwight D. Eisenhower, *Crusade in Europe* (Garden City, N.Y., 1948), p. 245, and CHUR 4/335/57. It was Ismay, always attentive to Churchill's image, who suggested a direct riposte to Ike.
10. SWW 5:602, 608, 621 and *SWWUS* 5:689, 694, 706; cf. CHUR 4/336/660.
11. SWW 5:606 and *SWWUS* 5:692–93. Churchill revived the idea on 22 April 1944, in a minute he omitted from the appendix. See CHUR 4/336/67.
12. SWW 5:431, 543–44 and *SWWUS* 5:488, 615–16.
13. CHUR 4/336/106; Alanbrooke, p. 558.
14. Eisenhower, *Crusade,* p. 243; cf. PREM 3/160/7, fo. 479.
15. SWW 5:536, 557–58 and *SWWUS* 5:606–7, 631–32; cf. CHUR 4/335/9–10. See also Alanbrooke, p. 480 ("tyrant") and CHUR 4/328/9 (Pownall on Clark).
16. CHUR 4/336/530.
17. There is an allusion to Butler's Education White Paper in a minute in the appendix— SWW 5:598 and *SWWUS* 5:685.
18. There is a passing sneer to Smuts on 27 February about how the "chirrupings" of the "little folk" would be "stilled before long by the thunder of the cannonade." *SWW* 5:437 and *SWWUS* 5:494.
19. Kevin Jefferys, *The Churchill Coalition and Wartime Politics, 1940–1945* (Manchester, 1995), pp. 150, 158–59.
20. SWW 5:ix, 229–31, 540–41, 558 and *SWWUS* 5:v, 258–61, 612, 642; CHUR 4/25A/18, 4/342/110. Pownall's drafts, virtually unchanged by Churchill, are at CHUR 4/316/3–6 and 4/335/278–79.
21. Ismay papers, 2/3/237 (KCL); CHUR 4/25/14.
22. CHUR 4/333, fos. 144, 151–69; CHUR 4/329, fos. 2, 29, 103, 161; Garrod to Cherwell, 14 Jan. 1951, Cherwell papers (Nuffield College, Oxford), G550/28–29; cf. SWW 5:457, 462–64 and *SWWUS* 5:518, 524–26.
23. CHUR 4/329, fos. 9, 119, 193, 207 (Cherwell quotation); cf. Thomas Wilson, *Churchill and the Prof* (London, 1995), chap. 5; Richard Overy, *Why the Allies Won* (London, 1995), chap. 4; Bernhard Kroener et al., *Germany and the Second World War,* 5/2 (Oxford, 2003), pt. 2, chap. 4. On giving the Italians hell, see CHUR 4/304/376.
24. SWW 5:456, 458 and *SWWUS* 5:517, 519; cf. CHUR 4/329/126.
25. CHUR 4/314, esp. fos. 30–58, 72–89, 292–93.
26. R. V. Jones papers, RJVO B222 (CAC); cf. Hinsley 3.1:364–65.
27. SWW 5:208, 213 and *SWWUS* 5:234, 240; CHUR 4/314/294.

28. *SWW* 5:83, 144, 204, 563, 670 and *SWWUS* 5:93, 163, 230, 643, 748.

29. The agreement is printed in the British official history, Margaret Gowing, *Britain and Atomic Energy, 1939–1945* (London, 1964), appendix 4, and discussed in her chap. 5.

30. CHUR 4/306/196. A minute from Deakin to WSC, undated but probably early 1950, enclosed a copy of the agreement and explained how it was drafted. See Deakin papers (privately held): "WSC: drafts and correspondence, 1947–51."

31. See Simon Duke, *US Defence Bases in the United Kingdom: A Matter for Joint Decision?* (London, 1987), pp. 38–44, 62–69.

32. HC, 5th series, 482:1356; WSC to Truman, 12 Feb. 1951, and reply, 16 Feb. 1951, CHUR 2/28, fos. 132–33, 127–28.

33. WSC to Truman, telegram, 11 April 1951, CHUR 2/28/125. Behind the scenes, however, Norman Brook agreed to a request from the official historians of British wartime grand strategy to commission an internal study of the development and use of the bomb, initially to clarify its relationship to other strategic issues but with the possibility of publication left open. This may have been a response to Truman's intransigence. See Butler to Brook, 21 March 1951, and Brook to Rickett, 20 April 1951, CAB 140/61.

34. Sadly omitted was a telegram Churchill sent Evatt on 22 November 1943: "Am grieved to have to tell you that the platypus you kindly sent me died on the last few days of its journey to England. Its loss is a great disappointment to me. The Royal College of Surgeons is anxious to have the animal stuffed in the place of one they lost in the blitz and I have agreed to this, assuming you will have no objection." Bill Deakin drew attention to this telegram, with a couple of exclamation marks in the margin, but got no response. See CHUR 4/318/128.

35. CHUR 4/25/18.

36. *SWW* 5:64–65, 77, 79, 82–83 and *SWWUS* 5:69–70, 86, 89, 92–93; Michael Howard, *Grand Strategy*, vol. 4 (London, 1972), pp. 543, 577–78; CHUR 4/305/322.

37. *SWW* 5:362 and *SWWUS* 5:409.

38. *SWW* 5:78–79, 364–66 and *SWWUS* 5:88, 411–14.

39. Brian Bond, ed., *Chief of Staff: The Diaries of Lieutenant-General Sir Henry Pownall*, vol. 2 (London, 1974), pp. 116, 120–21, 135; CHUR 4/324, esp. fos. 24, 118–20, 126–33.

40. CHUR 4/331/98, fos. 122–58, and CHUR 4/332/98. For Mountbatten's pressure, see Ismay papers, 2/3/271.

41. *SWW* 5:504 and *SWWUS* 5:571; Ismay papers, 4/26/4/2b.

42. CHUR 4/332, esp. fos. 19, 76–81, 87. For the original minute, see CHUR 4/331/148.

43. CHUR 4/25/40–56; CHUR 4/342/70; CHUR 4/332/41. For the different endings, compare *SWW* 5:512–13 with *SWWUS* 5:580–81.

44. Alanbrooke, p. 515, cf. pp. 521–35.

45. *SWW* 5:106, 118, 145–46 and *SWWUS* 5:119, 133, 163–64; CHUR 4/310/101–2; Stephen Roskill, *Churchill and the Admirals* (London, 1977), pp. 236–37.

46. Alanbrooke, pp. 441–42.

47. I follow the account by Bryant published as an epilogue to David Fraser, *Alanbrooke* (London, 1983), pp. 540–41.

48. *SWW* 2:19–20, 233–34 and *SWWUS* 2:20–21, 265–66; *SWW* 3:555 and *SWWUS* 3:626.

49. *SWW* 4:413, cf. *SWWUS* 4:457; *SWW* 5:76 and *SWWUS* 5:85; cf. CHUR 4/306/210. A June 1950 draft did say that Brooke "was bitterly pained, but bore it all as a soldier

should," but this disappeared during chapter reorganizations in February 1951. See CHUR 4/319/7.

50. Alanbrooke, pp. xxi, 442; Fraser, *Alanbrooke*, p. 544.

CHAPTER 26: THE FUTURE OF EUROPE

1. The best critical account in English is Elena Agarossi, *A Nation Collapses: The Italian Surrender of September 1943* (Cambridge, 2000).
2. SWW 5:40, 48, 91, 141 and SWWUS 5:42, 51, 102, 158; cf. CHUR 4/312/187.
3. PREM 3/243/5, fos. 209, 221. The "played-out old man" was born in 1873, one year before Churchill!
4. CHUR 4/328, fos. 106, 114; SWW 5:455 and SWWUS 5:515.
5. SWW 5:445 and SWWUS 5:503. David W. Ellwood, *Italy, 1943–1945* (Leicester, 1985), chap. 4, provides a good account of this period as it concerns Anglo-American relations.
6. Deakin did insert into volume 6 a passing reference to Togliatti's return (SWW 6:102 and SWWUS 6:115), which might suggest the earlier omission was accidental. But the treatment of Italian politics in that volume is also very coy.
7. SWW 5:475–76 and SWWUS 5:538; cf. Llewellyn Woodward, *British Foreign Policy in the Second World War* (London, 1971), pp. 396–403.
8. CHUR 4/326/358. This chapter is the only one from *Closing the Ring* for which a separate file does not exist in the Churchill archives. I am grateful to Sir William Deakin for letting me see some relevant drafts.
9. CHUR 4/342/221–22.
10. I. S. Ivanovic, 4 Sept. 1951, notes, p. 2, Deakin papers: "Yugoslavia-WSC-FO. Drafts for book" (privately held).
11. CHUR 4/326/153–54. Similarly, the italicized deletions from a minute by the Chiefs of Staff on 6 June 1943 about the rival merits of the Cetniks and the Partisans, which cited "information available to the War Office *from most secret sources*" (CHAR 20/131/25). Final texts of both are in SWW 5:410–11 and SWWUS 5:463–64. See generally John Cripps, "Mihailovic or Tito? How the Codebreakers Helped Churchill to Choose," in Ralph Erskine and Michael Smith, eds., *Action This Day* (London, 2001), pp. 237–63.
12. SWW 5:162–63 and SWWUS 5:183–84; cf. François Kersaudy, *Churchill and de Gaulle* (London, 1981), pp. 296–97.
13. CHUR 4/311, fos. 20–22, 107–15 (Deakin's revisions) and Cherwell to WSC, 11 Jan. 1951, Cherwell papers, K69/21 (Nuffield College, Oxford); cf. Kersaudy, *Churchill and de Gaulle*, p. 292.
14. SWW 5:157–59 and SWWUS 5:177–79; PREM 3/181/8, fos. 30, 34–35. Eden printed extracts from his paper and diary in his own memoirs, couched as a complement to Churchill's account. See Lord Avon, *The Reckoning* (London, 1965), pp. 396–98. For the differences between the two men on France and other issues, see Elisabeth Barker, *Churchill and Eden at War* (London, 1978).
15. SWW 5:553–56 and SWWUS 5:626–30; cf. Kersaudy, *Churchill and de Gaulle*, pp. 345–47.
16. CHUR 4/326/48–49. On the typescript of his dictation WSC altered "beat up" to "scolded."

17. *SWW* 5:110–11 and *SWWUS* 5:124–25. For Law's speech and WSC's minute of 16 Feb. 1944 (not quoted in *Closing the Ring*), see PREM 4/27/10, fos. 1261–63. In a message to Attlee and Eden on 22 Sept. 1943, Churchill spoke of "the natural Anglo-American special relationship" (FO 954/22/197).

18. John Charmley, *Churchill: The End of Glory* (London, 1993), p. 541.

19. *SWW* 5:597 and *SWWUS* 5:684.

20. *SWW* 5:564–65, 585, 611–12 and *SWWUS* 5:644–45, 664, 697–99; for the 4 March 1944 cable, see *C-R* 3:17.

21. WSC to Eden, 5 Nov. 1942, PREM 4/27/1, fo. 48.

22. *SWW* 5:195 and *SWWUS* 5:220; cf. CHUR 4/313/5. For the unpublished minute, see CHUR 4/336/212.

23. Sherwood, pp. 733–34; cf. Elizabeth Kimball Maclean, "Joseph E. Davies and Soviet-American Relations, 1941–43," *DH* 4 (1980): 92, and *C-R* 2:283.

24. *SWW* 5:276–77, 320, 331 and *SWWUS* 5:311, 363, 375.

25. *SWW* 5:329–30 and *SWWUS* 5:373–74; cf. Elliott Roosevelt, *As He Saw It* (New York, 1946), pp. 186–91. *Life* checked Churchill's draft of this incident against other accounts (his original draft said Stalin proposed shooting 80,000 Germans), and Churchill grumpily made some revisions after Denis Kelly warned that "this needs care in case Elliott starts making a row." See CHUR 4/321, fos. 2, 108–9; CHUR 3/323/15–21; CHUR 4/329/54–55.

26. CHUR 4/301/187; cf. telegrams in CHAR 20/132.

27. CHUR 4/342, fos. 272–74, 276.

28. The original minutes are printed in CHAR 20/152. That of 16 Jan. 1944 appears in a draft version of the appendix. See CHUR 4/336, fos. 1, 4.

29. *SWW* 5:240 and *SWWUS* 5:270; Gilbert 7:664; cf. Martin H. Folly, *Churchill, Whitehall and the Soviet Union, 1940–1945* (London, 2000), pp. 105–15.

30. *SWW* 5:319–20, 348–51, 356–57 and *SWWUS* 5:361–62, 394–97, 403; cf. CHUR 4/323, fos. 86, 142, 144. Clark Kerr is quoted in Halifax diary, 18 Dec. 1943, Hickleton papers, A 7.8.19 (Borthwick Institute, York).

31. Gilbert 7:426; Charles Eade, ed., *Onwards to Victory* (London, 1944), pp. 134–35. Cf. Anita Prazmowska, "Churchill and Poland," in R. A. C. Parker, ed., *Winston Churchill: Studies in Statesmanship* (London, 1995), pp. 110–23.

32. *SWW* 5:530, 604 and *SWWUS* 5:600, 691; cf. CHUR 4/336/156 (Katyn).

33. *SWW* 6:63–64 and *SWWUS* 6:72–73.

CHAPTER 27: "ON THE DEFENSIVE"

1. WSC to Beaverbrook, 24 Oct. and 8 Nov. 1951, Beaverbrook papers, C89 (HLRO); Peter Catterall, ed., *The Macmillan Diaries: The Cabinet Years, 1950–1957* (London, 2003), p. 111, 27 Oct. 1951.

2. *NYT*, 5 Oct. 1951, pp. 1, 29, and 26 Oct. 1951, pp. 1, 18 ("revenge"); *DT*, 27 Oct. 1951, p. 4.

3. *Life*, 8 Oct. 1951, pp. 108–28; 22 Oct. 1951, pp. 86–110; 29 Oct. 1951, pp. 74–100.

4. Laughlin to Scherman, 20 June 1951, HM 318/4: Book of the Month, 1951; Evans to Olney, 24 Sept. 1951, HM 318/1: Closing the Ring, Overtakes; also CHUR 4/14A/62–64.

5. *Los Angeles Times*, 26 Nov. 1951, p. 26; *The New Republic*, 5 Nov. 1951, p. 3.

6. *Atlantic Monthly*, Dec. 1951, pp. 92, 94; *The Christian Science Monitor*, 29 Nov. 1951, p. 15; *NYHT*, 25 Nov. 1951, pp. 1, 22.

7. *The Washington Post*, 25 Nov. 1951, p. 6B; *The New Republic*, 24 Dec. 1951, pp. 18–19; *NYT*, 25 Nov. 1951, sec. 7, pp. 1, 50.

8. Sherwood draft, p. 1, 1 Nov. 1951, Sherwood papers (Houghton Library, Harvard Univ., Cambridge, Mass.), folder 2115; Sherwood to Marshall, 29 Oct. 1951, folder 1359, and reply, 30 Oct. 1951, folder 548.

9. Sherwood to Laughlin, 13 Nov. 1951, and Laughlin to Churchill, 23 Nov. 1951, HM 318/1: Churchill-Laughlin misc., 1951–3.

10. Moran, p. 380 (Atlantic); Evelyn Shuckburgh, *Descent to Suez: Diaries, 1951–56* (London, 1986), p. 32 ("Thank you"); Klaus Larres, *Churchill's Cold War: The Politics of Personal Diplomacy* (New Haven, 2002), p. 168 (Truman).

11. Anthony Seldon, *Churchill's Indian Summer: The Conservative Government, 1951–55* (London, 1981), pp. 28–38.

12. Simon Duke, *US Defence Bases in the United Kingdom: A Matter for Joint Decision?* (London, 1987), chap. 4, p. 80.

13. John W. Young, *Winston Churchill's Last Campaign: Britain and the Cold War, 1951–1955* (Oxford, 1996), pp. 78–81; Cherwell to WSC, 19 Feb. and 10 April 1952, Cherwell papers (Nuffield College, Oxford), J122, fos. 338–40, 242.

14. Cherwell to WSC, 27 and 29 Dec. 1952, and WSC to Cherwell, 1 May 1953, PREM 11/561, quoting fos. 70, 61, 40. See more generally Wayne Reynolds, *Australia's Bid for the Atomic Bomb* (Melbourne, 2000), chap. 6.

15. Gilbert 8:684–85.

16. See HM 318/1: Moran, 1952–64, quoting Laughlin to Brooks, 7 Aug. 1952; also Laughlin to Moran, 30 March 1965, Moran papers, L 23/46. For Laughlin's meeting with WSC, see CHUR 4/14, fos. 28, 34–35, 38.

17. HM 318/1: Moran, 1952–64, esp. Laughlin to Brooks, 7 Aug. 1952, and Moran to Laughlin, 16 Sept. 1952.

18. For Wood, see CHUR 1/65/253–60 and CHUR 4/25B/449.

19. CHUR 4/24B, fos. 467–68, 491–96; cf. Langworth, pp. 264, 268.

20. *The Yorkshire Post, News Chronicle, The Evening News, Western Mail*, all 3 Sept. 1952; *Sunday Times*, 7 Sept. 1952. A collection of British reviews may be found in CHWL/PE 30.

21. *Daily Mail* and *The Manchester Guardian*, 3 Sept. 1952; *TLS*, 5 Sept. 1952, p. 575; *Time and Tide*, 6 Sept. 1952; *The Observer*, 7 Sept. 1952. For Ryan's authorship of the *TLS* review, see the *TLS* Centenary Archive at http://www.tls.psmedia.com.

22. *Evening Standard*, 3 Sept. 1952; *Tribune*, 5 Sept. 1952; *The Illustrated London News*, 6 Sept. 1952; *Statesman and Nation*, 6 Sept. 1952, p. 268.

23. *The Times* and *DT*, both 3 Sept. 1952; Sir James Grigg to F. A. Grigg, 9 Sept. 1943, Grigg papers, PJGG 9/6/24 (CAC).

24. *TLS*, 5 Sept. 1952, p. 575; Sherwood to Laughlin, 13 Nov. 1951, HM 318/1: Churchill-Laughlin misc., 1951–3; *The Washington Post*, 25 Nov. 1951, p. 6B.

VI | TRIUMPH AND TRAGEDY, 1944–1945, 1950–1954

CHAPTER 28: A VERY DIPLOMATIC HISTORY

1. *SWW* 6:ix and *SWWUS* 6:v. The preface was drafted by Denis Kelly, but it reflected WSC's wishes. See draft of 26 July 1953, CHUR 4/343/171–72, and WSC to Kelly, 18 Sept. 1953, CHUR 4/63C/546.

2. What Kelly called the "Master Copy as it stood when Mr. Churchill took office" may be found in CHUR 4/382 and 4/383.

3. CHUR 4/41A/66.

4. Laughlin to Longwell, 15 April 1949, HM 318/1: Life; Longwell to WSC, 17 May 1949, CHUR 4/63C/729.

5. WSC, note, 16 May 1949, CHUR 4/63C/731.

6. WSC to Camrose, 3 April 1950, CHUR 4/13/42–44; Moir to Sturdee, 26 Oct. 1951, CHUR 1/7/188.

7. Contract dated 4 Nov. 1947, HM 318/1: Contract & Copyright; Laughlin to Reves, 8 Nov. 1950, HM 381/1: Reves.

8. Reves to WSC, 3 Nov. 1950, in C-Reves, pp. 311–14; cf. CHUR 4/63C/739–50, quoting WSC to Reves, 8 Nov. 1950, at fo. 747.

9. WSC to Reves, 24 May 1951, in C-Reves, p. 316; cf. CHUR 4/63C/754–66.

10. E. K. Thompson to Adler, 16 Feb. 1951, and Longwell to Heiskell, 23 March 1951, Time Inc. Archive (New York, N.Y.): WSC memoirs.

11. Longwell to Luce, 1 May 1951, and Longwell to Heiskell, 10 May 1951, Time Inc. Archive (New York, N.Y.): WSC memoirs.

12. CHUR 4/343/94.

13. WSC to CSC, 25 Dec. 1950, in Gilbert 8:580.

14. WSC minutes of 20 Sept. and 19 Oct. 1951, CHUR 4/25, fos. 38, 59. The October 1951 version is in CHUR 4/382 and 4/383.

15. Brook to Prime Minister, 16 Nov. 1951, and "Note for the Record," 28 Nov. 1951, CAB 21/2181.

16. WSC to Allen, 25 Oct. 1952, and reply, 28 Oct. 1952, CHUR 4/24, fos. 25 and 24. For similar correspondence with Deakin and Pownall, see CHUR 4/24/281–82 and CHUR 4/25/374–75.

17. The Memoirs of General the Lord Ismay (London, 1960), pp. 461–62; CHUR 4/392/468–71.

18. CHUR 4/25A/18.

19. See Kelly's marked-up copy of the record of the Churchill-Stalin dinner on 18 July 1945, CHUR 4/378A/60–61.

20. After Kelly had turned most of "The Polish Dispute" from documents into narrative, Churchill considered it "a great improvement" — "you have done it well." After reworking "The Battle of Leyte Gulf," Kelly wrote: "I earnestly hope you will have time to scrutinise this latest version. I have worked very hard on it." See WSC to Kelly, 16 Sept. 1952, CHUR 4/365/7; Kelly to WSC, 12 Jan. 1953, CHUR 4/353C/300.

21. CHUR 4/371/69.

22. Kelly to Prime Minster, 8 Aug. 1952, CHUR 4/392A/56.

23. CHUR 4/397E/48, p. 5.

24. WSC to Kelly, 2 Jan. 1953, CHUR 4/376/57.

25. John Bright-Holmes, ed., Like It Was: The Diaries of Malcolm Muggeridge (London, 1981), p. 409.

26. CHUR 4/63C, fos. 756–57.

27. This note said less than Reves wanted but more than Churchill had desired. His first draft stated that it was "not possible to make definite plans about publication till after the Presidential Election" and also that "Mr. Churchill cannot give any undertaking that he could complete or release the sixth volume while he holds present office." Camrose persuaded him to delete both points because they would endanger the finan-

cial package still being put together for volume 6. See WSC to Reves, 28 March 1952, CHUR 4/63C/786; cf. draft at fo. 781 and Camrose at fo. 793.

28. Longwell to WSC, 21 Jan. 1952, and Kelly to WSC, 16 Feb. 1952, CHUR 4/392/415–17.

29. The Prime Minister found time to read Wilmot's book. "It is on the whole very favourable to our point of view," he told Pownall on 3 Feb. 1952. See CHUR 4/25/360–61.

30. CHUR 4/63A/33–39, quoting WSC to Truman, 30 March 1953, and Truman to WSC, 14 April and 20 May 1953; cf. Hillman to Truman, 18 May 1953, Post-Presidential Papers, box 59 (HSTL). Churchill had, in fact, omitted from his letter much of the original draft by Norman Brook, explaining the thrust of book 2—see CHUR 4/63A/9–10.

31. Brook to WSC, 22 Dec. 1952, CHUR 4/385D/540–44.

32. WSC to Eisenhower, 9 April 1953, in Peter G. Boyle, ed., *The Churchill-Eisenhower Correspondence, 1953–1955* (Chapel Hill, N.C., 1990), p. 40. Brook's draft is in CHUR 4/63A/7–8.

33. Boyle, ed., *Churchill-Eisenhower Correspondence*, p. 42; cf. CHUR 4/392/619.

34. For details, see chapter 29, below. The main correspondence may be found in Walter Bedell Smith papers, box 21 (DDEL), and CHUR 2/217/40–74, quoting Brook to WSC, 22 July 1953, fos. 42–44.

35. Colville, pp. 665, 672.

36. Camrose to Laughlin, 29 April 1953, HM 318/4: Daily Telegraph.

37. SWW 6:400 and SWWUS 6:456; CHUR 4/367/158 and 4/370/209.

38. Gilbert 8:580–83; Denis Kelly, TS. memoirs (1985), chap. 5, pp. 23–24 (CAC). Kelly claims this happened in 1952 and says Churchill was working at the time on a chapter about the Anzio landing. Anzio appeared in volume 5, and Churchill visited Marrakech for Christmas 1947 and 1950—his next visit was not until 1959. Although Kelly got these details wrong—he was writing from memory more than thirty years later—there may be a kernel of truth in the story itself.

39. "Notes on Volume VI," p. 15, Ismay papers, 2/3/296 (KCL). Sir Martin Gilbert dates the original notes to December 1950 (Gilbert 7:1171 ff.), but elsewhere he says 1951 (p. 1169), and the text is missing from the file he cites, CHUR 4/362. Directives from WSC to Kelly imply a date of September 1951—CHUR 4/361/103–5.

40. SWW 6:186 and SWWUS 6:214, cf. CHUR 4/355/8. On Potsdam, see CHUR 4/380B/187.

41. Gilbert 8:659; *Speeches* 8:8296–97; John W. Young, *Winston Churchill's Last Campaign: Britain and the Cold War, 1951–1955* (Oxford, 1996), pp. 46–47. See also Jonathan Rosenberg, "Before the Bomb and After: Winston Churchill and the Use of Force," in John L. Gaddis et al., eds., *Cold War Statesmen Confront the Bomb: Nuclear Diplomacy Since 1945* (Oxford, 1999), pp. 171–93.

42. Colville, pp. 650, 654; Young, *Churchill's Last Campaign*, p. 130.

43. Klaus Larres, *Churchill's Cold War: The Politics of Personal Diplomacy* (New Haven, 2002), p. 181.

44. *Speeches* 8:8483–85.

45. Kelly's alternative had been more categorical: "the victory of the Grand Alliance failed to bring peace either to Europe or to Asia." See CHUR 4/343, fos. 89 (chapter titles) and 171–73 (preface). Smaller amendments reflect the same concerns. Churchill prints a telegram from Eden on 15 April 1945 about his forthcoming meeting with Molotov that begins, "It is stimulating to have a chance to get to grips. . . ." The rest of

the sentence actually reads "with the animal," but these words were cut by Churchill at the end of August 1953—Molotov was still the Soviet Foreign Minister. See *SWW* 6:422 and *SWWUS* 6:483; cf. CHUR 4/368/84.

46. CHUR 4/356, fos. 138, 154; CHUR 4/392/715. Eden said he recalled describing Bierut not as the Skunk but as the Stoat, which was "slightly less derogatory."

47. This followed a suggestion by the Queen (it was in a letter to her father) and correspondence with Brook and Kelly. See *SWW* 6:209 and *SWWUS* 6:239; cf. Gilbert 8:810 and CHUR 4/63A/26–32.

48. CHUR 4/370/209.

49. WSC to Eisenhower, 19 March 1953, in Boyle, ed., *Churchill-Eisenhower Correspondence*, p. 33; Brook to WSC, 23 March 1951, CAB 21/2181.

50. *SWW* 6:523 and *SWWUS* 6:602; cf. CHUR 4/376, fos. 76–78, 82, 102, quoting WSC, note, 13 Jan. 1953, at fo. 78.

51. Kelly, TS. memoirs, chap. 3, p. 24.

52. Longwell to WSC, 9 Dec. 1952, CHUR 4/15/2.

53. In August 1952, for instance, he borrowed £15,000 from Camrose, of which he repaid £10,000 in November. See CHUR 2/210/11B.

54. Camrose to Laughlin, telegram, 15 May 1952, in HM 318/4: Daily Telegraph.

55. The detailed story of the stroke is in Gilbert 8, chap. 45. The *DT* proof dated 3 July 1953 is in Violet Bonham Carter papers (Bodleian Library, Oxford), 329/15.

56. Gilbert 8:851.

57. CHUR 4/364/24; CHUR 4/367/180.

58. Moran, pp. 476–77.

59. CHUR 4/353, fos. 262 (quotation) and 412; Walter Graebner, *My Dear Mister Churchill* (London, 1965), p. 70; Graebner to Longwell, 4 Sept. 1953, Longwell papers/Churchill (Butler Library, Columbia Univ., New York, N.Y.), box 2: Graebner. For probable dating, see Moran, p. 484.

60. Laughlin to Sturdee, 20 Aug. 1953, CHUR 4/63/635–37; Laughlin to WSC, 21 Aug. 1953, CHUR 4/14/16–18.

CHAPTER 29: OVERLORD AND UNDERDOG

1. Colville, p. 564, entry for 23 Feb. 1945.

2. CHUR 4/343, fos. 64, 109.

3. WSC, note to Syndicate, 1 May 1951, Ismay papers, 2/3/276a (KCL).

4. *SWW* 6:12 and *SWWUS* 6:13.

5. CHUR 4/392/385 (Brook); CHUR 4/354/76 (Kelly); *SWW* 6:172 and *SWWUS* 6:197.

6. *SWW* 5:526 and *SWWUS* 5:595–96; *SWW* 6:9–10 and *SWWUS* 6:10–11.

7. Chester Wilmot, *The Struggle for Europe* (London, 1952), pp. 199–201; cf. CAB 21/3759, quotations from J. A. Drew to Guy Liddell, 3 Nov. 1952.

8. Wilmot, *Struggle*, esp. pp. v, 460, 464–65, 467–68. On the development of the historiography, see Carlo D'Este, *Decision in Normandy* (London, 1983), chap. 28, and G. E. Patrick Murray, *Eisenhower Versus Montgomery: The Continuing Debate* (London, 1996), chaps. 1–4.

9. Colville, p. 674.

10. *SWW* 6:33, 166–67 and *SWWUS* 6:36–37, 190–92; cf. CHUR 4/344/131 and CHUR 4/384B/192. See also Murray, *Eisenhower Versus Montgomery*, pp. 93–101.

11. *SWW* 6:175 and *SWWUS* 6:200; cf. CHUR 4/384B/189.

12. On the strategy and the breakout, see Martin Blumenson, *Breakout and Pursuit* (Washington, D.C., 1989), pp. 430–32.
13. See interview notes in Liddell Hart papers, 11/1944/39–40 (KCL).
14. Dwight D. Eisenhower, *Crusade in Europe* (Garden City, N.Y., 1948), p. 243; D'Este, *Decision*, p. 305; Omar Bradley, *A Soldier's Story* (New York, 1951), pp. 368–69.
15. SWW 6:171 and SWWUS 6:196. See also Tuvia Ben-Moshe, *Churchill: Strategy and History* (Boulder, Colo., 1992), pp. 301–3.
16. SWW 6:233 and SWWUS 6:266–67; cf. CHUR 4/357/23.
17. SWW 2:5–6 and SWWUS 2:5–6.
18. SWW 6:589, 590–91, 613 and SWWUS 6:685–86, 687, 709.
19. David French, *Raising Churchill's Army: The British Army and the War Against Germany, 1919–1945* (Oxford, 2000), pp. 243–46; Stephen Ashley Hart, *Montgomery and "Colossal Cracks": The 21st Army Group in Northwest Europe* (Westport, Conn., 2000), pp. 50–61.
20. CHUR 4/392, fos. 244, 587; CHUR 4/352/175.
21. Quoted in Richard N. Gardner, *Sterling-Dollar Diplomacy in Current Perspective* (New York, 1980), p. xiii.
22. WSC to Eisenhower, 31 Aug. 1944, CHUR 4/394E/27—marked for printing by WSC.
23. Eisenhower, *Crusade*, p. 356; SWW 6:239 and SWWUS 6:274–75.
24. SWW 6:245 and SWWUS 6:281–82. These quotations were already in Pownall's early drafts from 1951—see CHUR 4/358, fos. 201, 228.
25. *C-Reves*, pp. 332, 334; Daniel Longwell of *Life* actually wanted more rather than less on Burma. "Wasn't that really the unknown war?" he asked in November 1952. "It got very little recognition in this country." See CHUR 4/392/463.
26. CHUR 4/341/5–6.
27. SWW 6:538 and SWWUS 6:621; cf. CHUR 4/377/512.
28. SWW 6:196, 454 and SWWUS 6:225, 521; cf. drafts in CHUR 4/371.
29. Quotations from SWW 6:59, 659–60 and SWWUS 6:68, 719–20.
30. Copies in, e.g., CHUR 4/348/154–55.
31. Colville, p. 509.
32. CHUR 4/347, fos. 318, 336.
33. Bedell Smith to WSC, 14 July 1953, Walter Bedell Smith papers, box 21 (DDEL). The ensuing correspondence can be followed in this file, in CAB 21/2181, and also in CHUR 2/217/40–74.
34. Brook to WSC, 22 July 1953, CAB 21/2181.
35. The amendments are marked clearly by Kelly on the proofs of chapters 4 and 6 sent to Bedell Smith on 25 August 1953—Bedell Smith papers, box 21.
36. SWW 6:90 and SWWUS 6:100; cf. CHUR 4/349/31–32.
37. SWW 6:35 and SWWUS 6:39; cf. CHUR 4/392/571–72.
38. WSC to Jones, 19 Sept. 1953, R. V. Jones papers, RJVO B226 (CAC).
39. This account of chap. 3 is reconstructed from nearly five hundred pages in CHUR 4/346. The quotation about Cherwell is from SWW 6:44 and SWWUS 6:49.
40. SWW 6:48–49 and SWWUS 6:54–55.
41. SWW 6:32 and SWWUS 6:35; cf. CHUR 4/16/164 and CHUR 4/354/124.
42. *C-Reves*, pp. 333–35; CHUR 4/354, fos. 11, 17; SWW 6:175, 409–11 and SWWUS 6:200, 468–70.
43. CHUR 4/354/143; CHUR 4/357, fos. 7, 12–13. The original minute, M1144/4, may be found in PREM 4/30/8, fos. 488–90.

44. See M 1144/4, in PREM 4/30/8.
45. For 13 June and 15 Nov., see CHUR 4/354, fos. 126, 137. The 22 Oct. cable to FDR is edited on CHUR 4/356/161. Cf. SWW 6:211, 219 and SWWUS 6:242, 251. For warnings, see, e.g., CHUR 4/338/121.
46. SWW 6:25 and SWWUS 6:28; cf. CHUR 4/392, fos. 112, 114. For Colvin, see CHUR 4/390/230–49.
47. WSC, The Dawn of Liberation (London, 1945), p. 165.
48. See Patricia Meehan, The Unnecessary War: Whitehall and the German Resistance to Hitler (London, 1992), chaps. 9, 11; the WSC quotation is from p. 7. In the Commons on 21 July 1949, Churchill deliberately used the phrase "patriotic Germans" about the plotters, while saying he was "not at all sure" that "a new situation would have arisen" if the July 1944 plot had succeeded. Speeches 7:7827.
49. Hinsley 3.2:893–96; Peter Grose, Gentleman Spy: The Life of Allen Dulles (London, 1995), pp. 193–204.
50. SWW 6:597 and SWWUS 6:693. Cf. SWW 1:14 and SWWUS 1:17: "The wholesale massacre by systematised processes of six or seven millions of men, women and children in the German execution camps exceeds in horror the rough and ready butcheries of Genghis Khan, and in scale reduces them to pigmy proportions."
51. On the copy of "The Prime Minister's Personal Minutes, July 1944," CHUR 4/397E/47, pp. 9–10, the minutes of 8 and 11 July seem to have been marked up for the appendix and that of 7 July rejected.
52. Aryeh Wolpert (Haifa) to WSC, 24 Nov. 1954, and reply by Kelly, 4 Dec. 1954, CHUR 4/64/354–56.
53. Bernard Wasserstein, Britain and the Jews of Europe, 1939–1945 (Oxford, 1981), pp. 297 (quotation) and 307–20. For the controversy, see inter alia Richard Breitman, Official Secrets: What the Nazis Planned, What the British and Americans Knew (London, 1998); William D. Rubinstein, The Myth of Rescue: Why the Democracies Could Not Have Saved More Jews from the Nazis (London, pbk. ed., 1999).
54. SWW 6:138–39 and SWWUS 1:156–57; cf. CHUR 4/352/157–58, 174. For Aug. 1945 exchanges over Morgenthau's book Germany Is Our Problem, see CHUR 2/3/21–38. On 13 March 1946, an angry Morgenthau told Churchill in New York that he was tired of being "the whipping boy ever since Quebec." See Henry Morgenthau, Jr., papers, box 787: Churchill (FDRL).
55. See the discussion in David M. Glantz and Jonathan House, When Titans Clashed: How the Red Army Stopped Hitler (Lawrence, Kans., 1995), chaps. 13–14, and Steven J. Zaloga, Bagration 1944: The Destruction of Army Group Centre (Oxford, 1996).
56. Pownall's TS., "The Russian Advance," is in CHUR 4/392/93–98; cf. SWW 6:71–74. In the American edition, the map is unhelpfully placed in chap. 14—SWWUS 6:81–83, 207.
57. SWW 6:124 and SWWUS 6:141. "Men in the Kremlin" was WSC's own dictation— see CHUR 4/351/124.
58. See CHUR 4/348/116.
59. SWW 6:198 and SWWUS 6:227.
60. For the cut, see CHUR 4/356/16; cf. CHUR 4/63/536–37 on American reactions.
61. "Naughty document" was in the translator's notes of the meeting, before they were sanitized by the Cabinet Offices on the grounds that such language "would give the impression to historians that these very important discussions were conducted in a most unfitting manner." See CAB 120/158, quoting Ian Jacob, 26 Oct. 1944.

62. *SWW* 6:201–4 and *SWWUS* 6:231–35.

63. *SWW* 6:249–50 and *SWWUS* 6:285–86. Cf. this dictation in Nov. 1950: "my agreement with Stalin had accorded us the freedom to act in Greece and recognised it as our special task" (CHUR 4/359/409).

64. WSC to Eden, M1207/4, 11 Dec. 1944, in CHUR 4/381F/882, marked by Churchill in June 1951 for inclusion in the text. Note the presumptuous "we" about the percentages deal.

65. CHUR 4/381C/341; CHUR 4/369/438. In the margin of the latter, Pownall had noted that Churchill "may wish to modify some of the references to Tito in view of recent developments."

66. *SWW* 6:102 and *SWWUS* 6:115; cf. CHUR 4/349/330.

67. CHUR 4/349/226–33; CHUR 4/392, fos. 456, 460.

68. *SWW* 6:251–52 and *SWWUS* 6:288–89.

69. *SWW* 6:258, 270 and *SWWUS* 6:296, 311.

70. *SWW* 6:255, 266 and *SWWUS* 6:292–93, 305–6. Churchill had used this quote from Acheson in an essay for *Life* on 14 April 1947, welcoming the new Truman Doctrine on Greece and Turkey.

71. *SWW* 6:255, 616–17 and *SWWUS* 6:293, 712–13.

72. WSC to Eden, M1101/4, 10 Nov. 1944, in CHUR 4/381F/875.

73. *SWW* 6:208 and *SWWUS* 6:238; cf. WSC to War Cabinet, 17 Oct. 1944, CHAR 20/181, where the original read "dull care." Churchill was paraphrasing lines from the Victorian poet Charles Calverley, whose "Ode to Tobacco" includes a reference to "Black Care, at the horseman's back, perching."

CHAPTER 30: THE UNNECESSARY COLD WAR

1. Denis Kelly, TS. memoirs, ca. 1985, chap. 3, p. 22, Kelly papers (CAC); WSC notes, copy in Ismay papers, 2/3/296 (KCL); WSC to Kelly, 28 Sept. 1951, CHUR 4/361/103–5.

2. Alfred Grosser, *The Western Alliance: European-American Relations Since 1945*, trans. Michael Shaw (London, 1980), p. 40.

3. In the same spirit, Churchill cut his line about how "the Eagle suffers the little birds to sing." See CHUR 4/361/85–86 (Brook) and CHUR 4/362, fos. 267 (de Gaulle), 425 (Eagle).

4. Athan Theoharis, *The Yalta Myths: An Issue in U.S. Politics, 1945–1955* (Columbia, Mo., 1970), pp. 142–43; Edward R. Stettinius, Jr., *Roosevelt and the Russians: The Yalta Conference* (London, 1950), pp. 261, 285; Deakin to WSC, 17 Sept. 1949, CHUR 4/362/536.

5. See CHUR 4/390/224–27 and CHUR 4/63/645–47.

6. Sherwood, p. 867; Hanson W. Baldwin, *Great Mistakes of the War* (London, 1950), p. 72; Chester Wilmot, *The Struggle for Europe* (London, 1952), pp. 653–54.

7. *SWW* 6:341–42 and *SWWUS* 6:388–90; cf. CHUR 4/363/13 and M1025/4, 23 Oct. 1944, CHUR 4/381F/872. For a lengthy rebuttal of Churchill's claim that he simply went along with U.S. policy, see Forrest C. Pogue, *George C. Marshall, 1943–1945: Organizer of Victory* (New York, 1973), pp. 524–35.

8. Eden to WSC, 27 Jan. 1945, and WSC to Eden, 28 Jan. 1945, CAB 120/714.

9. *SWW* 6:319–20 and *SWWUS* 6:365–66; cf. the 30 June 1951 draft in CHUR 4/362/303–22.

10. SWW 6:321, 323, 336–37, 338 and SWWUS 6:368, 369, 385, 387; cf. CHUR 4/362/335.

11. SWW 6:312, 316 and SWWUS 6:358, 362–63. The "expansive" sentence was drafted by Kelly but approved by WSC—cf. CHUR 4/362/442.

12. As with earlier conferences, Churchill does not seem to have considered the fact that Stalin, through agents and bugging, had a good idea of British and American thinking. Cf. Christopher Andrew and Vasili Mitrokhin, *The Mitrokhin Archive: The KGB in Europe and the West* (London, 1999), pp. 175–76.

13. SWW 6:308 and SWWUS 6:353.

14. WSC's original comments are scribbled on the back of FO 371/40725, fo. 355. They are printed as minute M (Arg) 7/5 to Eden, 8 Feb. 1945, in CHUR 4/397F. In the official biography, the last sentence does not appear, changing Churchill's whole meaning—see Gilbert 7:1196.

15. Colville, pp. 562–63; Ben Pimlott, ed., *The Second World War Diary of Hugh Dalton* (London, 1986), p. 836; SWW 6:351 and SWWUS 6:400–401. For the amendment to the speech draft, see CHAR 9/206/126.

16. SWW 6:352 and SWWUS 6:401–2; cf. CHUR 4/362/339 and CHUR 4/390/222. See also Cranborne to WSC, 3 April 1945, PREM 4/31/7, fo. 588, and, on funding, WSC, minute M301/5 to Eden, 7 April 1945, in CHUR 4/397F.

17. SWW 6:369, 379 (pikestaff) and SWWUS 6:420, 432.

18. SWW 6:446 and SWWUS 6:511; WM 26 (45) 5 CA, CAB 65/51, fo. 93; Sargent to WSC, 2 May and 14 May 1945, PREM 3/396/14, quoting fos. 588, 585.

19. SWW 6:367–68, 399–400 and SWWUS 6:419, 455–56.

20. SWW 6:401–5 and SWWUS 6:457–63; CHUR 4/385/541–42 (Brook).

21. CHUR 4/367, fos. 55, 58; cf. SWW 6:409 and SWWUS 6:467.

22. Alanbrooke, p. 683, 12 April 1945; CHUR 2/142, fos. 39, 184; PREM 3/333/6, fos. 303–4, referring to minutes D106/5 and D118/5, 11 and 19 April 1945, which were the ones destroyed.

23. CHUR 4/392/704; cf. SWW 6:449 and SWWUS 6:515.

24. The passage was drafted by Denis Kelly, but Churchill read it closely. SWW 6:440–41 and SWWUS 6:504–5; cf. CHUR 4/370, fos. 131, 200 (Kelly quote) and CHUR 4/385/449.

25. WSC to Kelly, 20 Sept. 1952, CHUR 4/368/104; cf. notes of 16 and 17 Sept. in CHUR 4/392, fos. 647, 650.

26. Wood to WSC, 4 Feb. 1953, with Kelly annotation "I agree," CHUR 4/368/23–24; Kelly to Brook, 13 Feb. 1953, and WSC to Brook, 18 Feb. 1953, CAB 21/2181.

27. SWW 6:412, 417 and SWWUS 6:471, 478.

28. SWW 6:300 and SWWUS 6:344; "Notes," pp. 2, 3, 5, 7, in Ismay papers, 2/3/296; CHUR 4/368/72, cf. SWW 6:420 and SWWUS 6:481.

29. SWW 6:368, 374, 377, 394 and SWWUS 6:419, 426, 429, 448–49; CHUR 4/365/89.

30. See Kimball, p. 341. The Vietnam quote comes from Robert H. Ferrell, *The Dying President: Franklin D. Roosevelt, 1944–1945* (Columbia, Mo., 1998), p. 149.

31. SWW 6:394, 398 and SWWUS 6:448–49, 454; cf. CHUR 4/368/72 and C-R, 3:630.

32. E.g., SWW 6:447, 485, 489 and SWWUS 6:513–14, 556–57, 570.

33. Arnold A. Offner, *Another Such Victory: President Truman and the Cold War, 1945–53* (Stanford, Calif., 2002), pp. 30–34; cf. SWW 6:418–19, 429 and SWWUS 6:478–80, 492, and Washington tel. 2842, 23 April 1945, in CHAR 20/216/19–20. The memoirs of Truman's Chief of Staff, used elsewhere by the Syndicate, said that the President

spoke to Molotov "using blunt language unadorned by the polite verbiage of diplomacy"—William D. Leahy, *I Was There* (London, 1950), p. 412. See also *Cold War History* 4 (2004): 105–25.

34. *SWW* 6:441–43 and *SWWUS* 6:505–7; cf. CHUR 4/370, fos. 14 and 200, and Brook in CHUR 4/385D/543–44.

35. See CHUR 4/383, fos. 19, 86, 89, 95; also CHUR 4/370/170.

36. CHUR 4/370, fos. 200, 449; cf. Brook on CHUR 4/385D/544.

37. *SWW* 6:377, 383, 498–99 and *SWWUS* 6:429, 436, 573.

38. Clark Kerr, note of discussion on 18 May, PREM 3/396/12, fos. 363–65.

39. Colville to Eden, 20 May 1945, and WSC note, 22 May 1945, PREM 3/396/12, fos. 371–72; *SWW* 6:500–501 and *SWWUS* 6:575.

40. Even in 1998, when "discovered" in NA, the plan caused a sensation—e.g., *DT*, 1 Oct. 1998, pp. 1, 8–9—and the full text was printed in the Russian journal *Modern and Contemporary History*: O. A. Rzheshevsky, "Secretnye Voinye Plani u Cherchillia protin USSR v May 1945 g," *Novaia i noveishaia istoriia* (May 1999): 98–123.

41. Report by the Joint Planning Staff, "Operation 'Unthinkable,'" 22 May 1945, and COS to PM, 8 June 1945, CAB 120/691; Alanbrooke, p. 693, 24 May 1945.

42. PM to COS, 9 June, CAB 120/691. Churchill substituted "a purely hypothetical contingency" for the phrase in Jo Hollis's original draft: "a highly improbable event."

43. *SWW* 6:483–84 and *SWWUS* 6:554–56; cf. WSC to Truman, T899/5, 12 May 1945, CHUR 4/397F/57.

44. *SWW* 6:485–86 and *SWWUS* 6:556–58; Robert J. Donovan, *Conflict and Crisis: The Presidency of Harry S Truman, 1945–1948* (New York, 1977), p. 55; and generally the account in Melvyn P. Leffler, *A Preponderance of Power: National Security, the Truman Administration, and the Cold War* (Stanford, Calif., 1992), pp. 30–33.

45. Davies, TS. report, 12 June 1945, quoting pp. 2, 12–13, Joseph E. Davies papers, box 17 (LC).

46. *SWW* 6:501–5 and *SWWUS* 6:576–81. Churchill did not print his understated minute to Eden, in which he said of Davies, "I have not formed the best opinions of this man." WSC to Eden, M529/5, 28 May 1945, CHUR 4/397F/57.

47. *SWW* 6:434, 505–7 and *SWWUS* 6:498, 581–84; WSC to Mikolajczyk, T1195/5, 26 June 1945, CHUR 4/397F/58. Churchill sent this telegram at the request of the British Embassy in Moscow, which felt Mikolajczyk needed reassurance.

48. *SWW* 6:499, 523, 525, 528 and *SWWUS* 6:573–74, 602, 605, 609.

49. For Brook, see, e.g., CHUR 4/385C/271.

50. *SWW* 6:546–47 and *SWWUS* 6:631–32.

51. *SWW* 6:470–72 and *SWWUS* 6:540–42.

52. CHUR 4/372, fos. 36, 83–84.

53. Gilbert 7:1120n2 (quoting the papers marked missing from CHUR 4/390/228–29) and 1257–58. See WSC to COS, 28 March 1945, and the redraft (by Ismay, not Portal), which became the minute of 1 April, in PREM 3/12, fos. 22–25.

54. Max Hastings, *Bomber Command* (London, 1993 ed.), p. 344; *SWW* 6:471 and *SWWUS* 6:541; WSC to Air Ministry, 19 April 1945, PREM 3/12, fo. 3.

55. *SWW* 6:553 and *SWWUS* 6:639.

56. For earlier discussion, see chapters 21 and 25, above.

57. The TS. is in CHUR 4/390/212–19; for dating and background, see Cherwell papers, J 85/7–8 (Nuffield College, Oxford).

58. The letter was actually a draft by Lindemann (as Cherwell then was) which he planned

to send to the *DT* to discourage scare stories about a German bomb. Churchill asked the Secretary of State for Air whether he felt it should be printed, adding, "I expect Lindemann's view is right, i.e. that there is no immediate danger, although undoubtedly the human race is crawling nearer to the point when it will be able to destroy itself completely." See *SWW* 1:301–2 and *SWWUS* 1:386–87; cf. CHUR 4/83, fos. 13–14, 38–40 and CV 5/3:1586–87.

59. Both agreements are printed in full in the official history by Margaret Gowing, *Britain and Atomic Energy, 1939–1945* (London, 1964), pp. 439–40, 447, and discussed extensively in Martin J. Sherwin, *A World Destroyed: The Atomic Bomb and the Grand Alliance* (New York, 1977), pp. 85–89, 109–14. It was Churchill who changed the phrase "it should be used against the Japanese" to "it might, perhaps, after mature consideration, be used"—see draft in PREM 3/139/8A, fo. 308.

60. CHUR 4/352, fos. 126, 174, 191, 274; cf. Leahy, *I Was There*, p. 312.

61. Cherwell to WSC, 26 July 1945, PREM 3/139/9, fo. 640.

62. WSC to Cherwell, M662/4, 27 May 1944, PREM 3/139/11A, fo. 761.

63. Gowing, *Britain and Atomic Energy*, pp. 341–42; Sherwin, *World Destroyed*, p. 115; cf. PREM 3/139/9, fos. 660–61.

64. *SWW* 6:553 and *SWWUS* 6:639; WSC to Cherwell, 10 Jan. 1953, in Gilbert 8:794.

65. Pownall to Kelly, [Jan. 1953], CHUR 4/376/51; Cherwell memo, 28 Jan. 1953, CHUR 4/392/708–12; Kelly note, 21 Jan. 1953, CHUR 4/378/188.

66. *SWW* 6:552–57 and *SWWUS* 6:638–44.

67. CHUR 4/390C, fos. 372–73 (Cherwell), 397–99 (Kelly). In corroboration, Kelly cited a conversation with the official historian John Ehrman, who had written a secret, internal history of British policy on the bomb. But see John Ehrman, *The Atomic Bomb: An Account of British Policy in the Second World War* (Cabinet Office, 1953), pp. 267, 273–74, in CAB 101/45, which says that on 2 Aug. 1945 the Japanese Ambassador in Moscow was instructed to approach the Russians for mediation using the Potsdam Declaration as "the basis of study" regarding terms. Ehrman also notes that Stalin and Molotov did not return to Moscow until 6 August (the day the first bomb was dropped). Cf. Herbert Bix, "Japan's Delayed Surrender: A Reinterpretation," *DH* 19 (1995): 204–9.

68. CHUR 4/392/711–12.

69. *SWW* 6:579–80 and *SWWUS* 6:669–70; cf. CHUR 4/378, fos. 95–96; CHUR 4/390, fos. 338, 383, 399–400; CHUR 4/392, fos. 191–94. On Fuchs, see generally Ferenc Morton Szasz, *British Scientists and the Manhattan Project: The Los Alamos Years* (London, 1992), chap. 6.

70. David Holloway, *Stalin and the Bomb: The Soviet Union and Atomic Energy* (New Haven, 1994), esp. pp. 115–17, 129–30.

CHAPTER 31: "IT SEEMS INCREDIBLE"

1. Anthony Montague Browne, *Long Sunset* (London, 1996), p. 133.

2. Ibid.; Press Association Lobby Report, 15 Oct. 1953, CHUR 4/64/87–93; Laughlin to Thompson, 21 July 1954, HM 318/1: Nobel Prize. For CSC and Mary, see the dispatch from R. B. Stevens, British Ambassador in Stockholm, to Eden, NW 1051/53, 14 Dec. 1953, copy in CSCT 3/90/102 (CAC); also, Soames, pp. 439–40.

3. Copies of Siwertz's text are in CSCT 3/90A/142–45 and HM 318/1: Nobel Prize. See also Amos C. Miller, "Winston S. Churchill," in Walter E. Kidd, ed., *British Winners of the Nobel Literary Prize* (Norman, Okla., 1973), pp. 202–36.

4. WSC to Laughlin, 26 Dec. 1953, CHUR 2/343/11; WSC to CSC, 16 Oct. 1953, in Gilbert 8:901. For Siwertz's ending, see Stevens, dispatch, CSCT 3/90/102.

5. *DT*, 18 Dec. 1953, p. 6.

6. Longwell to Laughlin, 8 Sept. 1953, HM 318/1: Life, 1952–3; *Life*, 26 Oct. 1953, pp. 31, 81, 9 Nov. 1953, p. 71, and 16 Nov. 1953, p. 92 (FDR). Recalling in private WSC's comment about FDR, Longwell contrasted it with his first meeting with WSC, around 1935, when "he was violently against Roosevelt, or extremely sceptical of him." Longwell to Laughlin, 8 Sept. 1953, HM 318/1: Life, 1952–3.

7. Adler to Laughlin, 19 Aug. 1953, and Longwell to Laughlin, 6 Oct. 1953, HM 318/1: NYT, 1953; cf. Flower to Laughlin, 19 March 1948, HM 318/4: Cassell, 1947–51. For Camrose, see the correspondence in Longwell papers/Churchill: box 2, Camrose; also Graebner to Longwell, 14 Dec. 1949, in box 2: Graebner.

8. For Houghton Mifflin sales, see Smith to Moseley, memo, 4 Sept. 1953, HM 318/4: Churchill Memos, 1953 (also in table form in the text); for Cassell's, see the article by H. O. Ward in *Reynolds News*, 25 April 1954. For earlier discussion of profits, see chapters 9 and 28, above.

9. Longwell to Larsen, 16 Oct. 1953, Time Inc. papers (New York, N.Y.): WSC memoirs; Longwell to Beaverbrook, 13 Nov. 1953, Beaverbrook papers, C313 (HLRO).

10. New Orleans *Times-Picayune*, 29 Nov. 1953; AHR 59 (April 1954): 595; NYHT, 25 Nov. 1953, sec. 6, p. 22; *Saturday Review of Literature*, 28 Nov. 1953. Some American reviews are in CHUR 4/64/413–24.

11. *The Dallas Morning News*, 29 Nov. 1953, pt. 9, p. 8; *St. Louis Post-Dispatch* and *Saturday Review*, both 28 Nov. 1953; *The Nation*, 23 Jan. 1954, p. 76.

12. *Los Angeles Times*, 29 Nov. 1953, sec. 4, p. 6; *Atlantic Monthly*, July 1954, pp. 23–32.

13. Notes of 7 Dec. 1953 and 20 Jan. 1954 in Averell Harriman papers (LC), box 872; NYT, 29 Nov. 1953, sec. 7, pp. 1, 34; draft in Sherwood papers, folder 2143 (Houghton Library, Harvard Univ., Cambridge, Mass.).

14. NYHT, 30 Nov. 1953; SWW 6:348–49 and SWWUS 6:397–98.

15. Gilbert 8:896, 950, 964; Colville, p. 676.

16. WSC to Eisenhower, 1 April 1954, PREM 11/1074/190–91.

17. Woolton, diary, 6 April 1954 (Bodleian Library, Oxford); Moran, p. 566; and generally Gilbert 8:961–71.

18. *Speeches* 8:8604–5.

19. *Daily Herald*, 24 Nov. 1954; *Daily Mirror* and *The Times*, both 25 Nov. 1954. A large collection of press cuttings on the Woodford affair is in CSCT 8/32. See also Gilbert 8:1070–81. For a discussion of this issue, published before most of the documents became available, see Arthur L. Smith, Jr., *Churchill's German Army: Wartime Strategy and Cold War Politics, 1943–1947* (London, 1977).

20. *Daily Express*, 27 Nov. 1954 (Castle); *Speeches* 8:8609–20; Moran, p. 649.

21. The collected edition of WSC's addresses calls it a "brief speech" and quotes only the passages on foreign affairs (*Speeches* 8:8604–5), probably following the carefully expurgated version in WSC, *The Unwritten Alliance: Speeches 1953 to 1959*, ed. Randolph S. Churchill (London, 1961), pp. 196–97. For the full text and drafts, see CHUR 5/56A.

22. See CHUR 4/390/62–66 (for 1950) and CAB 21/3775 (for 1954).

23. Montgomery papers (IWM), BLM 162, esp. Monty to WSC, 6 Dec. 1954, and "The truth about the telegram," MS., June 1959.

24. Uri Bar-Noi, "The Soviet Union and Churchill's Appeal for High-Level Talks, 1953–1954: New Evidence from the Russian Archives," DS 9 (1998): 110–33; Roberts

to Kirkpatrick, 29 Jan. 1954, Avon papers (Birmingham Univ. Library), AP 20/15/155; USSR Ministry of Foreign Affairs, *Correspondence Between the Chairman of the Council of Ministers of the U.S.S.R. and the Presidents of the U.S.A. and the Prime Ministers of Great Britain During the Great Patriotic War of 1941–1945*, 2 vols. (Moscow, 1957), 1:5. On the 1948 debate, see chap. 10, above.

25. Unless specified, these and subsequent British reviews are all dated 26 April 1954 and may be found in CHWL/PE, box 5, file 80d. The review in *Reynolds News* appeared on 25 April.

26. Glasgow *Evening News*, 10 April 1954; *Sunday Times*, 25 April 1954. Leyte also featured in some Australian reviews but as a rare exception to Churchill's customary neglect of the Pacific War—e.g., Melbourne *Argus*, 5 June 1954, p. 10, under the headline "Low Rating for Our Diggers."

27. *Financial Times*, 24 April 1954; *The Observer*, 25 April 1954.

28. *New Statesman and Nation*, 24 April 1954.

29. *TLS*, 30 April 1954, pp. 273–74. For author, see the *TLS* Centennial Archive at http://www.tls.psmedia.com.

30. WSC to Flower, 12 May 1954, CHUR 4/24B/478; Desmond Flower, *Fellows in Foolscap: Memoirs of a Publisher* (London, 1991), pp. 301–2. For the calculations, see unsigned memo, n.d., in Cassell's file on vol. 6 (Littlehampton, Sussex), which is reproduced in my appendix, "Churchill's Six Volumes."

31. George W. Egerton, "The Lloyd George *War Memoirs*: A Study in the Politics of Memory," *JMH* 60 (1988): 85–86; Brian Bond, *The Unquiet Western Front: Britain's Role in Literature and History* (Cambridge, 2002), esp. pp. 46–48.

32. Denis Kelly, TS. memoirs (1985), chap. 3, p. 3 (CAC).

33. Correlli Barnett, *The Collapse of British Power* (London, 1972), pp. 588, 592; John Charmley, *Churchill: The End of Glory* (London, 1993), pp. 2, 559–61; Alan Clark, "A Reputation Ripe for Revision," *The Times*, 2 Jan. 1993, p. 12; John Charmley, "The Price of Glory," *TLS*, 13 May 1994, p. 8. For a critique, see David Reynolds, "Churchill the Appeaser? Between Hitler, Roosevelt and Stalin in World War II," in Michael Dockrill and Brian McKercher, eds., *Diplomacy and World Power: Studies in British Foreign Policy, 1890–1950* (Cambridge, 1996), pp. 197–220.

34. Richard Breitman, *Official Secrets: What the Nazis Planned, What the British and Americans Knew* (London, 1998), pp. 209, 227–28; Max Hastings, *Bomber Command* (London, 1993 ed.), pp. 343–44. See also Gerhard L. Weinberg, *Germany, Hitler, and World War II* (New York, 1995), pp. 292–93, and Tuvia Ben-Moshe, *Churchill: Strategy and History* (Boulder, Colo., 1992), pp. 328–33.

35. See Philip Williamson, *Stanley Baldwin: Conservative Leadership and National Values* (Cambridge, 1999), and David Dutton, *Neville Chamberlain* (London, 2001).

CHAPTER 32: LEAVING IT TO HISTORY, 1955–1965

1. Moran, p. 484; Maurice Ashley, *Churchill as Historian* (London, 1968), pp. 212–13.

2. After retiring in April 1955, WSC briefly contemplated another piece of autobiography to fill the gap between the end of *My Early Life* and the start of *WC*, roughly 1901 to 1911. See CHUR 4/42/11–12.

3. Kelly to WSC, 7 Sept. 1952, CHUR 4/25/110–13; Laughlin to WSC, 20 Sept. 1956, CHUR 4/469/89–91.

4. WSC, *The Second World War and an Epilogue on the Years 1945 to 1957* (London, 1959) [hereafter "SWW Abridged"]—the epilogue is on pp. 953–73. For the tax position, see CHUR 4/469/78–81.

5. On drafting, see CHUR 4/400, esp. fos. 268, 518–47, 588–92, 694–728; also Gilbert 8:1229–30, 1234–35. The essay was also sent unofficially to Norman Brook, who pronounced it "jolly good" on the basis of a quick read. Brook to Montague Browne, 1 June 1957, CAB 21/2182.

6. *SWW* Abridged, pp. 959–60 (Bevin, Marshall), 963–64 (bomb), 967 (India).

7. *SWW* Abridged, pp. 971–72; cf. CHUR 4/400/356–60 and Anthony Montague Browne, *Long Sunset* (London, 1996), p. 222.

8. CHUR 4/400, fos. 374 (Browne), 376–77 (Kelly); cf. *SWW* Abridged, p. 965.

9. CHUR 4/400/572–78; WSC to Eisenhower, 16 April 1956, CHUR 2/217/98–99.

10. *SWW* Abridged, p. 973. Marx "in his hovel" was Churchill's own addition—see CHUR 4/400/250.

11. Kelly to WSC, 24 April 1957, CHUR 4/469/60–61.

12. Kelly to Flower, 11 March 1958, and Flower to WSC, 25 March 1958, both in Cassell's papers: *SWW* Abridgement (Littlehampton, Sussex).

13. Kelly to WSC, 6 March 1958, CHUR 4/469/41; Flower to Brooks, 30 July 1958, Cassell's papers: *SWW* Abridgement.

14. Cassell's was naturally keen to have Dorman-Smith removed—see Flower's secretary to Kelly, 24 April 1957, Cassell's papers: *SWW* Abridgement.

15. The full Houghton Mifflin title is *Memoirs of the Second World War: An ABRIDGE-MENT of the Six Volumes of* The Second World War *with an EPILOGUE by the Author on the Postwar Years Written for This Volume* (Boston, 1959); see esp. pp. ii, iii, v. On Churchill's desire to keep his distance from the abridgement, see correspondence of August–December 1958 in Cassell's papers: *SWW* Abridgement; also CHUR 4/469/10–11.

16. See Cassell's papers: Life's Illustrated *SWW*.

17. CHUR 4/452, esp. fos. 74–91.

18. CHUR 4/452, fos. 134 (Prince Philip), 190 (title).

19. See scenario and Montague Browne to Peterson, 23 April 1960, in CHUR 4/452, fos. 15–28, 30–31.

20. CHUR 4/453, fos. 120 (Peterson), 143 (cognac).

21. CHUR 4/453, fos. 152–212, 241–49, 285, quoting from Peter Wright to Montague Browne, 14 Feb. 1961, at fo. 241.

22. Harry S Truman, *Memoirs*, vol. 1: *Year of Decisions* (Garden City, N.Y., 1955); Jean Lacouture, *De Gaulle: The Ruler, 1945–1970* (New York, 1991), pp. 155–58; *The Complete War Memoirs of Charles de Gaulle* (New York, 1998), p. 58.

23. Churchill and Eden did, however, manage to inspect the manuscript when it was submitted to the Cabinet Office, and they were able to remove some mildly critical comments about themselves. See CAB 21/4476 and generally the critique of G. M. Young, *Stanley Baldwin* (London, 1952), in Philip Williamson, "Baldwin's Reputation: Politics and History, 1937–1967," *HJ* 47(2004), 153–61.

24. Viscount Templewood, *Nine Troubled Years* (London, 1954), esp. pp. 112–13, 207, 426–27; cf. Templewood papers (Cambridge Univ. Library), XIX/10 and 11 and the book reviews in BR4, quoting *Sunday Express*, 3 Oct. 1954 (Owen), *The Manchester Guardian*, and *DT*, both 4 Oct. 1954.

25. This account is based on Aron papers, AP 33/1, esp. docs 61–108, 131–32 and AP 24/20, docs. 1–3, (Deakin) and AP 24/40 (Kelly); see also FO 370/1444B, esp. minute by Woodward, 1 July 1947.

26. AP 11/10/230, quoting Eden, minute, 22 Nov. 1954.

27. A Sailor's Odyssey: The Autobiography of Admiral of the Fleet Viscount Cunningham of Hyndhope (London, 1951), pp. 231–32 ("prodding"), 241 (Oran).

28. Ibid., pp. 647–48; cf. reviews in Cunningham papers, CUNN 4/1 (CAC), quoting Pawle in the Newcastle Journal, 28 March 1951.

29. WSC to Bridges, 17 July 1947, and minute of meeting of the Military Histories Committee, 19 Jan. 1951, both in CAB 103/422.

30. Roskill papers, ROSK 6/26 (CAC), quoting WSC to Allen, 11 Aug. 1953. For the double brandies, see Geoffrey Blake to Roskill, 5 Jan. 1954, ROSK 4/79.

31. CAB 103/534, quoting A. B. Acheson to Brook, 29 June 1955 (historians' discontent) and Brook to Acheson, 8 Aug. 1955 (on meeting with Churchill). For the guidelines, see also CAB 140/68.

32. John Ehrman, Grand Strategy, vol. 6 (London, 1956), pp. 324–25, 333, 335, 337; J. R. M. Butler, Grand Strategy, vol. 2 (London, 1957), p. 562; Daily Mail and Sunday Times, both 17 March 1957—copies in J. R. M. Butler papers (Trinity College, Cambridge), E3/6/2.

33. Butler, Grand Strategy, 2:562. For a similar judgment on WSC—equal to Chatham, greater than Lloyd George—see Ehrman, Grand Strategy, 6:334–35.

34. New Statesman and Nation, 6 April 1957, p. 450.

35. Alanbrooke's files about the book are still closed, but Bryant's jumbled papers at KCL provide a partial guide. This paragraph draws on "Memorandum on Mrs Long's Preliminary Research," 26 Feb. 1956, in Bryant papers, N36/1, quoting p. 5.

36. Arthur Bryant, The Turn of the Tide, 1939–1943: A Study Based on the Diaries and Autobiographical Notes of Field Marshal the Viscount Alanbrooke, KG, OM (London, 1957), pp. 16–17, 126 (Dunkirk), 31 ("Zoo"), and 38 ("greatest soldier").

37. Ibid., esp. pp. 29–31, also 671 ("concentric").

38. Ibid., pp. 23–25.

39. Ibid., pp. 201 ("intuition"), 337 ("pie" and "eagerness"), 501–7, 529–36, 626.

40. Ibid., pp. 190–94, 283 ("flinched"), 305, 723 ("difficult").

41. Norman Brook to Bryant, 18 Sept. 1956, Bryant papers, N36/1.

42. Bryant to Alanbrooke, 12 Oct. 1956, Bryant papers, N36/1.

43. Bryant, Turn of the Tide, p. 7; Gilbert 8:1232 (inscription). Clementine's words were recalled by Lady Soames at the International Churchill Society conference, Bermuda, 6 Nov. 2003.

44. Ismay to WSC, 26 Feb. 1957, Ismay papers, 4/1/18 (KCL); Gilbert 8:1233 (acknowledgment). Churchill's words to Alanbrooke echoed a comment in his essay on Haig in Great Contemporaries (London, 1941 ed.), p. 191, questioning the wisdom of a statesman or general keeping a diary.

45. Copies of letters to Bryant from Attlee, n.d., and G. M. Trevelyan, 22 March 1957, in Bryant papers, F7; Grigg to J. R. M. Butler, 14 March 1957, in J. R. M. Butler papers, E3/6/2.

46. Sunday Times, 17 Feb. 1957, p. 8; Sunday Express, 17 Feb. 1957, p. 8; Daily Mirror, 20 Feb. 1957, p. 4; Sunday Dispatch, 17 Feb. 1957, p. 6.

47. David Fraser, Alanbrooke (London, 1983), pp. 560–61.

48. Bernard Fergusson, ed., *The Business of War: The War Narrative of Major-General Sir John Kennedy* (London, 1957); cf. *Daily Mail*, 4 Nov. 1957. There is a large collection of reviews in J. N. Kennedy papers, 5/8 (KCL).

49. Arthur Bryant, *Triumph in the West, 1943–1946: Based on the Diaries and Autobiographical Notes of Field Marshal the Viscount Alanbrooke, KG, OM* (London, 1959), pp. 354, 362; cf. G. E. Patrick Murray, *Eisenhower Versus Montgomery: The Continuing Debate* (London, 1996), chaps. 5–6, and Nigel Hamilton, *Monty: The Field Marshal, 1944–1976*, paperback (London, 1987), pp. 883–902.

50. *The Observer*, 1 Nov. 1959 (Attlee); *Sunday Times*, 1 Nov. 1959 (Grigg).

51. See the discussion in John Ramsden, *Man of the Century: Winston Churchill and His Legend Since 1945* (London, 2002), chap. 3.

52. John Ramsden, "Refocusing 'The People's War': British War Films of the 1950s," *JCH* 33 (1998): 35–63 (for *The Eagle*, see p. 37). See more generally Angus Calder, *The Myth of the Blitz* (London, 1991), and Malcolm Smith, *Britain and 1940: History, Myth and Popular Memory* (London, 2000).

53. WSC memos of 11 April and 31 July 1946, CHUR 4/41, respectively fos. 130, 62; WSC to Randolph, telegram, 27 Feb. 1932, in Randolph S. Churchill, *Winston S. Churchill*, vol. 1 (London, 1966), p. xix.

54. Winston S. Churchill, *His Father's Son: The Life of Randolph Churchill* (London, 1996), pp. 316, 390–92.

55. This paragraph follows the candid and moving account in ibid., pp. 392–97.

56. Moran to Laughlin, 5 Feb. 1959, 5 Nov. 1960, HM 318/1: Moran; Moran to Laughlin, 12 June 1962, HM 318/1: Moran, Wylie file.

57. Moran to Laughlin, 12 Jan. 1961 [misdated 1960], HM 318/1: Moran. See also Richard Lovell, *Churchill's Doctor: A Biography of Lord Moran* (London, 1992), pp. 368–75.

58. Laughlin to Moran, 16 Jan. 1962, and Moran to Laughlin, 24 Jan. 1963, HM 318/1: Moran.

59. Soames, pp. 555–56.

60. See Violet Bonham Carter papers (Bodleian Library, Oxford), box 291, fos. 120–236, quoting Douglas Jerrold to VBC, 30 June and 30 Sept. 1955, fos. 120, 133.

61. Bonham Carter papers, box 291, fos. 52–55, and box 292, fos. 99–100, quoting James Holsaert to VBC, 2 July 1962 on fo. 99.

62. Coote to VBC, 6 Jan. 1964, Bonham Carter papers, box 291, fo. 73, and correspondence with Clementine, fos. 18–20; Jovanovich to VBC, 11 Sept. 1964, box 292, fo. 107.

PROLOGUE: JANUARY 1965

1. See Randolph S. Churchill, *Winston S. Churchill*, vol. 2 (London, 1967), pp. 697–705, quoting p. 705; Gilbert 4:208–11.

2. WSC, *Great Contemporaries* (London, 1941 ed.), p. 139. Note also his imagery in March 1916 when attacking A. J. Balfour for lethargy at the Admiralty: "You must continually drive the vast machine forward at its utmost speed. To lose momentum is not merely to stop, but to fall" (Gilbert 3:718).

3. SWW 6:583 and SWWUS 6:674. See the similar passage in volume 3 of WC, about his sense of letdown while waiting for Big Ben to strike eleven o'clock on the morning of

the Armistice in 1918. "The minutes passed. I was conscious of reaction rather than elation. The material purposes on which one's work had been centred, every process of thought on which one had lived, crumbled into nothing" (WC 3/2:541).

4. In March 1954, he told Rab Butler: "I feel like an aeroplane at the end of its flight, in the dusk, with the petrol running out, in search of a safe landing." *The Art of the Possible: The Memoirs of Lord Butler* (Harmondsworth, 1973), p. 175.

5. Mark Pottle, ed., *Daring to Hope: The Diaries and Letters of Violet Bonham Carter, 1946–1969* (London, 2000), p. 128, 6 Aug. 1953.

6. CAB 21/5978, esp. Lascelles to Brook, 5 Nov. 1953, and Sir George Bellow, notes on state funerals, 6 Dec. 1957; Anthony Montague Browne, *Long Sunset* (London, 1996), pp. 308–9. See also the historical summary of planning for the funeral in the Cabinet Office memo [Feb. 1965], PREM 13/204.

7. John Ramsden, *Man of the Century: Winston Churchill and His Legend Since 1945* (London, 2002), p. 15.

8. Alistair Horne, *Macmillan, 1957–1986* (London, 1989), p. 581. Macmillan went on to write six volumes of memoirs, each with a distinctly Churchillian title.

9. Montague Browne, *Long Sunset*, p. 317; private information; Soames, p. 521.

10. Gilbert 8:1339; Montague Browne to Ismay, 15 May 1962, Ismay papers, 2/1/48; Montague Browne, *Long Sunset*, pp. 302–3.

11. Gilbert 8:1354–55.

12. Moran, pp. 440–41 (black velvet); Pottle, ed., *Daring to Hope*, p. 230. See generally Paul Addison, "Destiny, History and Providence: The Religion of Winston Churchill," in Michael Bentley, ed., *Public and Private Doctrine: Essays in British History Presented to Maurice Cowling* (Cambridge, 1993), pp. 236–50.

13. *Othello*, act 2, scene 3; "The Union of the English-Speaking Peoples," in Michael Wolff, ed., *The Collected Essays of Sir Winston Churchill*, 4 vols. (Bristol, 1976), 4:438.

14. Washington *Sunday Star*, 29 Nov. 1964, p. C-3; A. J. P. Taylor et al., *Churchill: Four Faces and the Man* (London, 1969), p. 149.

15. Burke Trend, note on talk with Anthony Moir, 9 Feb. 1965, CAB 21/5847; Winston S. Churchill, *His Father's Son: The Life of Randolph Churchill* (London, 1996), pp. 462–63, 479–80, 497.

16. Violet Bonham Carter papers, box 290, fos. 145–49; Violet Bonham Carter, *Winston Churchill As I Knew Him* (London, 1965), pp. 15–16; cf. Pottle, ed., *Daring to Hope*, p. 298.

17. Moran, pp. 829–30; cf. Richard Lovell, *Churchill's Doctor: A Biography of Lord Moran* (London, 1992), chap. 23.

18. John Wheeler-Bennett, ed., *Action This Day: Working with Churchill* (London, 1968).

A NOTE ON MONEY

1. For figures and useful discussion, see the Economic History Resources website at http://www.eh.net.

2. See Guy Routh, *Occupation and Pay in Great Britain, 1906–79*, 2d ed. (London, 1980), pp. 60, 73, 76. For WSC's salary, see CHAR 20/10/2 and CHUR 1/7, fos. 217, 281. To set an example of austerity when he became Prime Minister in 1951, Churchill drew only £7,000 per year.

INDEX

ABOUT THE AUTHOR

DAVID REYNOLDS is professor of international history at Cambridge University, where he is also Fellow of Christ's College. He has held visiting appointments at Harvard and at Nihon University in Tokyo, and has lectured extensively all over the United States. He is the author of two prize-winning works on the United States and Britain during World War II—*The Creation of the Anglo-American Alliance: 1937–41* and *Rich Relations: The American Occupation of Britain, 1942–1945*. His other books include *An Ocean Apart: The Relationship Between Britain and America in the Twentieth Century* (with David Dimbleby), which accompanied the BBC/PBS TV series for which he was principal historical adviser, and an overview of twentieth-century British foreign policy entitled *Britannia Overruled: British Policy and World Power in the Twentieth Century*. His most recent volumes are *One World Divisible: A Global History Since 1945* and *From Munich to Pearl Harbor: Roosevelt's America and the Origins of the Second World War*. He lives in Cambridge, England, with his wife (an American architect) and son, but spends much of each summer in Cambridge, Massachusetts, and in the White Mountains of New Hampshire. *In Command of History* was awarded the 2004 Wolfson History Prize—one of Britain's most prestigious prizes for historical writing.

WINSTON
CHURCHILL

The
SECOND
WORLD
WAR

I

WINSTON
CHURCHILL

The
SECOND
WORLD
WAR

II

WINSTON
CHURCHILL

The
SECOND
WORLD
WAR

III